THE OXFORD HANDBOOK OF

MUSIC MAKING AND LEISURE

THE OXFORD HANDBOOK OF

MUSIC MAKING AND LEISURE

Edited by

ROGER MANTIE

and

GARETH DYLAN SMITH

OXFORD

UNIVERSITY PRESS

OXFORD
UNIVERSITY PRESS

Oxford University Press is a department of the University of Oxford. It furthers
the University's objective of excellence in research, scholarship, and education
by publishing worldwide. Oxford is a registered trade mark of Oxford University
Press in the UK and certain other countries.

Published in the United States of America by Oxford University Press
198 Madison Avenue, New York, NY 10016, United States of America.

© Oxford University Press 2017

Library of Congress Cataloging-in-Publication Data
Names: Mantie, Roger. | Smith, Gareth Dylan.
Title: The Oxford handbook of music making and leisure / edited by
Roger Mantie and Gareth Dylan Smith.
Description: New York, NY : Oxford University Press, [2017] |
Series: Oxford handbooks | Includes bibliographical references and index.
Identifiers: LCCN 2016010227| ISBN 9780190244705 (bound book : alk. paper) |
ISBN 9780190244736 (oxford handbooks online)
Subjects: LCSH: Music as recreation. | Music—Social aspects.
Classification: LCC ML3916 .O97 2016 | DDC 306.4/842—dc23
LC record available at http://lccn.loc.gov/2016010227

1 3 5 7 9 8 6 4 2
Printed by Sheridan Books, Inc., United States of America

CONTENTS

Contributors   ix

EDITORS' INTRODUCTION

1. Grasping the Jellyfish of Music Making and Leisure   3
   ROGER MANTIE AND GARETH DYLAN SMITH

PART I RELATIONSHIPS TO AND WITH MUSIC

2. Creating a Framework for Music Making and Leisure: Max Kaplan
   Leads the Way   13
   MARIE MCCARTHY

3. Well-Being and Music Leisure Activities through the
   Lifespan: A Psychological Perspective   31
   SUSAN HALLAM, ANDREA CREECH, AND MARIA VARVARIGOU

4. Aspiring to Music Making as Leisure through the Musical
   Futures Classroom   61
   ABIGAIL D'AMORE AND GARETH DYLAN SMITH

5. DIY Recreational Recording as Music Making   81
   ADAM PATRICK BELL

6. Contemplating Compilations: An Invitation to . . .   99
   JOSEPH PATE AND BRIAN KUMM

7. "While My Guitar Gently Weeps": Music Education
   and Guitar as Leisure   115
   DAVID LINES

8. Playing Music and Identity Development in Middle Adulthood:
   A Theoretical and Autoethnographic Account   131
   KEVIN RATHUNDE AND RUSSELL ISABELLA

9. (Un)popular Music Making and Eudaimonism   151
   GARETH DYLAN SMITH

PART II INVOLVEMENT AND MEANING

10. "The Violin in the Attic": Investigating the Long-Term Value
    of Lapsed Musical Participation   171
    STEPHANIE PITTS

11. Leisure-Time Music Activities from the Perspective of Musical
    Agency: The Breaking Down of a Dichotomy   187
    SIDSEL KARLSEN

12. The Musical Lives of Self-Confessed Nonmusicians   203
    JENNIE HENLEY

13. Popular Music Making and Young People: Leisure, Education,
    and Industry   223
    ZACK MOIR

14. "Perilous Blessing of Leisure": Music and Leisure in the
    United States, 1890–1945   241
    ANDREW KRIKUN

15. A Consumer Behavior-Influenced Multidisciplinary Transcendent
    Model of Motivation for Music Making   261
    VALERIE L. VACCARO

16. Developing a Cultural Theory of Music Making and Leisure:
    Baudrillard, the *Simulacra*, and Music Consumption   281
    KARL SPRACKLEN

17. Feeling Part of the Scene: Affective Experiences of Music
    Making Practices and Performances within Leeds's Extreme
    Metal Scene   297
    GABBY RICHES

18. Motivational and Social Network Dynamics of Ensemble Music
    Making: A Longitudinal Investigation of a Collegiate
    Marching Band   319
    SERENA WEREN, OLGA KORNIENKO, GARY W. HILL,
    AND CLAIRE YEE

PART III SCENES, SPACES, AND PLACES

19. Leisure Music Production: Its Spaces and Places   347
    ROBERT A. STEBBINS

20. Amateur and Professional Music Making at Dartington
    International Summer School   363
    HERMIONE RUCK KEENE AND LUCY GREEN

21. "What's Your Name, Where Are You From, and What Have You
    Had?": Utopian Memories of Leeds's Acid House Culture
    in Two Acts   385
    RONNIE RICHARDS

22. Red Light Jams: A Place Outside of All Others   405
    JOSEPH MICHAEL PIGNATO

23. The Beat of a Different Drummer: Music Making as
    Leisure Research   425
    BRETT LASHUA

24. "FX, Drugs, and Rock 'n' Roll": Engineering the Emotional
    Space of the Recording Studio   449
    JENNA WARD AND ALLAN WATSON

25. Music Making on YouTube   467
    CHRISTOPHER CAYARI

26. Italian Amateur Pop-Rock Musicians on Facebook: Mixed Methods
    and New Findings in Music Making Research   489
    ALBERTO TROBIA AND FABIO M. LO VERDE

PART IV ON THE DIVERSITY OF MUSIC MAKING AND LEISURE

27. Entering into an Indigenous Cypher: Indigenous Music-Dance
    Making Sings to Western Leisure   519
    KAREN FOX

28. Sonic Participatory Cultures within, through, and around
    Video Games   541
    JARED O'LEARY AND EVAN S. TOBIAS

29. "Singer's Music": Considering Sacred Harp Singing as Musical
    Leisure and Lived Harmony   565
    THOMAS MALONE

30. "DJ Hit That Button": Amateur Laptop Musicians in
    Contemporary Music and Society   585
    SHARA RAMBARRAN

31. Community Music Practice: Intervention through Facilitation 601
    GILLIAN HOWELL, LEE HIGGINS, AND BRYDIE-LEIGH BARTLEET

32. Leisure Grooves: An Open Letter to Charles Keil   619
    ROGER MANTIE

Index   639

Contributors

Brydie-Leigh Bartleet is an Associate Professor and Director of the Queensland Conservatorium Research Centre and Deputy Director (Research) at the Queensland Conservatorium Griffith University, Australia. She has worked on a range of national and international projects in community music, arts-based service learning with Australian First Peoples, intercultural community arts, and arts programs in prison. Many of these projects have been realized in partnership with a wide range of NGOs, arts and community organizations, and colleagues across Australia and the Asia Pacific. She has secured over a million dollars in research funding, and produced well over a 100 research outputs. In 2014 she was awarded the Australian University Teacher of the Year. She was the Co-chair of the International Society for Music Education's Community Music Activities Commission, Co-founder of the Asia Pacific Community Music Network, and serves on the Board of Australia's peak music advocacy body, Music Australia.

Adam Patrick Bell is an Assistant Professor of Music Education in the School of Creative and Performing Arts at the University of Calgary. He has published in the *Journal of Music, Technology and Education, Journal on the Art of Record Production, International Journal of Education and the Arts, Music Therapy Perspectives, British Journal of Music Education*, and *Action, Criticism, and Theory for Music Education*. Currently he is writing *Audio Autodidacts: A Multi-Track Story of DIY Music-Making, Home Recording, and Oblivious Learning* (Oxford University Press).

Christopher Cayari is an Assistant Professor of Music Education at Purdue University in West Lafayette, Indiana. He holds a PhD and MME in Music Education from the University of Illinois at Urbana-Champaign and a bachelor's degree in music education from Trinity Christian College in Palos Heights, Illinois. Christopher's research interests include mediated musical performance, YouTube, informal music learning, virtual communities, and online identity. He is an avid YouTube video creator. Christopher regularly publishes online performances, tutorials, and vlogs. He enjoys collaborating with his students to make user-generated content for YouTube.

Andrea Creech is Professor of Music in Community at the University of Laval, Canada. Following an international career in music performance and teaching, Andrea was awarded a PhD in Psychology in Education from the Institute of Education, University of London. Since then she has led extensive funded research and published widely on topics concerned with musical learning and participation across the lifespan. She is a Senior Fellow of the U.K. Higher Education Academy and Graduate Member of the British

Psychological Association. Andrea is coauthor of *Active Ageing with Music: Supporting Wellbeing in the Third and Fourth Ages* (2014) and coeditor of *Music Education in the 21st Century in the United Kingdom: Achievements, Analysis and Aspirations* (2010).

Abigail D'Amore is Chief Executive of Musical Futures, a global movement that transforms, engages, and inspires people through real-world learning methods. She has worked with Musical Futures since its inception as a Paul Hamlyn Foundation special initiative in 2004, initially as research officer with Professor Lucy Green; then as national coordinator supporting the rollout; later as project leader determining Musical Futures' strategic direction as an international grassroots movement; and manager of the transition of Musical Futures from a project to a nonprofit organization. She has consulted with various U.K.-based organizations and programs as an evaluator, project manager, writer, and editor. She has acted as a consultant for Musical Futures overseas, including delivering training, keynote presentations, and strategic support in Australia, Canada, and the United States.

Karen Fox is a Professor of Leisure Studies at the University of Alberta, Canada. Influenced by local urban Aboriginal hip-hop artists, Karen's research shifted to questions around Indigenous epistemologies as related to expressive arts and the connection to leisure. Attending to and grounding her scholarship in the voices and aspirations of Indigenous scholars and people, she continues to question and reimagine a Western leisure attentive to Indigenous stories and practices. She has published in *Leisure Studies, Musicultures, Issues in the North, Leisure/Loisir*, and *Leisure Sciences*. She and a colleague hold a grant from the Social Sciences and Humanities Research Council of Canada to understand how Kanaka 'Ōiwi responded to U.S. missionary leisure discourses as documented in Hawaiian-language newspapers. In her leisure, she is learning the ukulele and how to blend clowning and slam poetry.

Lucy Green is Professor of Music Education at University College London Institute of Education. Her research interests are in the sociology of music education, specializing in meaning, ideology, gender, popular music, informal learning, and new pedagogies. She is the author of six books and numerous shorter works, has given keynote speeches in countries across the world, and serves on the editorial boards of fourteen journals. Lucy created the "Informal Learning" pathway within the British project Musical Futures, and then took this work forward into instrumental tuition. Her current research, with Dr. David Baker, is on the lives and learning of visually impaired musicians.

Susan Hallam studied at the Royal Academy of Music before becoming Principal Second Violin in the BBC Midland Light Orchestra and Deputy Leader of Orchestra da Camera. Following further study she became an academic. She is currently Professor of Education and Music Psychology at University College London Institute of Education. Her research interests are learning and performance in music, issues relating to music education, and the wider impact of music on other skills. She has published extensively in relation to music psychology and music education, including *Instrumental Teaching: A Practical Guide to Better Teaching and Learning* (1998), *The Power of Music*

(2001, 2014), *Music Psychology in Education* (2005), and *Preparing for Success: A Practical Guide for Young Musicians* (with Helena Gaunt; 2012). She is also coeditor of *The Oxford Handbook of Music Psychology* (2009) and *Music Education in the 21st Century in the United Kingdom: Achievements, Analysis and Aspirations* (2010).

Jennie Henley is Area Leader in Music Education at the Royal College of Music, London. Her professional career has involved instrument teaching, ensemble directing and choir leading in different contexts within England. She has worked in schools with children of all ages, and has led an out-of-school music center providing musical activities for children up to the age of eighteen. She has taught many adults and directed adult ensembles. Her research interests include the development of musicianship of adults in different contexts, including music in criminal justice and the musical development of primary generalist teachers. In 2011, she joined the University College London Institute of Education as Programme Leader for the MA Music Education and Primary Music Subject Leader, before moving to the Royal College of Music in 2015.

Lee Higgins is the Director of the International Centre of Community Music based at York St John University, U.K. He has held previously positions at Boston University, the Liverpool Institute for Performing Arts, and the University of Limerick, Ireland. Lee has been a visiting professor at Ludwig Maximilian University, Munich, and Westminster Choir College, Princeton. He received his PhD from the Irish Academy of Music and Dance, and in 2016 became president of the International Society of Music Education. As a community musician he has worked across the education sector, as well as within health settings, prison and probation service, youth and community, and orchestra outreach. As a presenter and guest speaker, Lee has worked on four continents in university, school, and NGO settings. He is the senior editor for the *International Journal of Community Music* and author of *Community Music: In Theory and in Practice* (2012).

Gary W. Hill is Professor of Music and Director of Bands at Arizona State University. He is one of the most sought-after guest conductors and clinicians in the wind band field. Hill's current research agenda includes an exploration of biochemical reactions spawned by the musical process and work on a monograph concerning the future of instrumental music education.

Gillian Howell is a PhD candidate at Griffith University and lecturer in Community Music Leadership at Melbourne Polytechnic. Her research investigates community music in war-torn and post-conflict countries, among recently arrived refugees in Australia, and intercultural community music leadership. She has worked as a music leader and researcher in conflicted settings worldwide, and in 2016 was awarded a prestigious Endeavor Research Fellowship for research in Sri Lanka. Gillian is an award-winning musician and teaching artist, working with many of Australia's flagship ensembles and arts organizations. She was the founding creative director of the Melbourne Symphony Orchestra's Community Engagement Program, drawing the orchestra into challenging new collaborations and creating some of its most enduring learning and engagement programs. Gillian serves on several national and international music boards, including the Community Music Activity Commission of the International Society for Music Education, and Community Music Victoria.

Russell Isabella is an Associate Professor in the Department of Family and Consumer Studies at the University of Utah. Much of his research has focused on social and emotional development during infancy and childhood in the context of the developing family. Currently, with coauthor Kevin Rathunde, Isabella is studying the experience of pursuing passionate activities during middle adulthood and the effects of these pursuits on adjustments to identity throughout mid and later life. Additionally, Isabella and Rathunde currently are developing an arts-informed parent education program on the importance of play for children's development and lifelong learning.

Sidsel Karlsen is Professor of Music Education and General Education at Hedmark University of Applied Sciences in Norway as well as docent at the University of the Arts Helsinki, Sibelius Academy in Finland. She is educated as a music teacher and singer, and spent several years teaching and performing music in a variety of formal and informal contexts before deciding to pursue an academic career. Sidsel has published widely in Scandinavian and international research journals and is a frequent contributor to international anthologies and handbooks in sociology and music education, such as *Collaborative Learning in Higher Music Education* (2013) and *The Oxford Handbook of Social Justice in Music Education* (2015). Her research interests cover, among other things, multicultural music education, the interplay between formal and informal arenas for music learning, the many aspects of musical agency, and the social and cultural significance of music festivals.

Olga Kornienko is an Assistant Research Professor at the Institute for Interdisciplinary Salivary Bioscience Research and Department of Psychology at Arizona State University. Her interdisciplinary research focuses on how social networks shape development, health, and well-being across the lifespan. She has published in *Child Development, Social Neuroscience, Hormones and Behavior*, and other journals.

Andrew Krikun is Professor of Music at Bergen Community College in Paramus, New Jersey, where he teaches courses in songwriting, music history, and music business. His articles have appeared in the *International Journal of Community Music*, the *Journal of Popular Music Studies*, and the *Journal of Historical Research in Music Education*. In 2006, he was awarded a Teaching Excellence Award from the University of Texas's Community College Leadership program. As a singer-songwriter, Krikun maintains an active career as a performer, composer, and recording artist. His band, Andy and the Rattlesnakes, was a seminal force in the L.A. Punk/New Wave scene. A compilation CD of the band's recordings, *Last Summer to Dance*, was released in 2006 and the band is currently working on a new album. He has written music for theater and film, including the 1996 comedy *The Shot*, and continues to write, perform, and record for eclectic musical projects.

Brian Kumm is an Assistant Professor of Recreation Management at the University of Wisconsin–La Crosse. His research explores the intersections of daily life and artistic practices. Informed by developments in theories of affect, post-secular ethics, and post-humanist ontology, Brian's work approaches questions related to the expression, affirmation, augmentation, and intensification of life capacities within a Spinozan-Deleuzian conception of joy. Ultimately, his work attempts to engage micro-interventions within everyday encounters to engender living as an art form.

Brett Lashua is Senior Lecturer at Leeds Beckett University, U.K. His scholarship is concerned with ways that young people make sense of their lives through leisure and popular music, as well as how young people are "made sense of" through particular representational and narrative strategies. He is coeditor (with Stephen Wagg and Karl Spracklen) of *Sounds and the City: Popular Music, Place and Globalization* (2014).

David Lines is Associate Professor of Music Education at the University of Auckland, New Zealand. He is also Associate Dean, Academic of the Faculty of Creative Arts and Industries. David has many research interests in music education including music education philosophy, community music, early childhood and primary arts education and studio pedagogy. He plays piano in a jazz group and enjoys experimenting with improvisation. David has been a primary and secondary school teacher prior to his current career as a university teacher and researcher. He has a particular interest in exploring how music and the arts bring joy and richness to people's lives and stimulate ways of thinking, learning and expressions of self and community.

Fabio M. Lo Verde teaches Sociology and Sociology of Lifestyles and Consumption at the University of Palermo. From 2005 to 2010, he was Dean of the Social Sciences Department, and from 2005 to 2011 he coordinated the PhD program on Sociology, Territory, and Rural Development. His research interests focus on the transformations of lifestyles and consumption habits within Italian and European society, of the labor market and youth sociability, as well as of the new migrations in Italy. Recently, he has been working on leisure and amateur sport. Among his latest publications as author and editor are *Sociologia del tempo libero* (2009), *Consumare/investire il tempo libero: Forme e pratiche del leisure time nella postmodernità* (2012), *Mapping Leisure across Borders* (with Gianna Cappello and Ishwar Modi, 2013), *Sociologia dello sport e del tempo libero* (2014).

Thomas Malone is a composer, music educator, and researcher whose interest lies in pedagogies outside of the mainstream, including African and Caribbean drum and dance traditions, American rural and roots music, shape-note singing, and, more recently, the pedagogy and praxis of early hip-hop DJs. He received his undergraduate training at New England Conservatory, where he was a student of Richard Colwell, and completed his graduate work at Boston University with Anthony J. Palmer. Active as a teacher, clinician, and conductor, he has taught undergraduate and graduate music education at Boston University, Molloy College, and the University of Massachusetts at Lowell. He currently directs Choral and Classroom Music as well as Hip-Hop and Pop Music pedagogy programs at the Vassal Lane Upper School in Cambridge, Massachusetts.

Roger Mantie (PhD, University of Toronto; MM, Brandon University) is Associate Professor at Arizona State University. His teaching and scholarship are informed by his fourteen years as a school music educator. His work emphasizes connections between schooling and society, with a focus on lifelong engagement in and with music and the arts. A widely published author, he is coeditor of the *Oxford Handbook of Technology and Music Education* (2017).

Marie McCarthy is Professor of Music Education at the University of Michigan. Prior to this position, she was on the faculty of the University of Maryland from 1990 to 2006. Her research interests include the social and cultural foundations of music education history, the transmission of music process cross-culturally, and children's spirituality and arts education. She has published numerous articles and book chapters, and serves on the editorial boards of several journals. Her publications include two books, *Passing It On: The Transmission of Music in Irish Culture* (1999), and *Toward a Global Community: The International Society for Music Education, 1953–2003* (2004). She is editor of the *Journal of Historical Research in Music Education* and serves on the History Standing Committee of the International Society for Music Education.

Zack Moir is a Lecturer in Popular Music at Edinburgh Napier University and the University of the Highlands and Islands. He is also a Teaching Fellow/Research Assistant at the University of Edinburgh. His teaching includes courses in popular music composition, music literacy, music theory, music analysis, musicianship skills, and instrumental performance. Additionally, he was part of the team that wrote, produced, and delivered the highly successful online course entitled "The Fundamentals of Music Theory" (Coursera), which was designed to provide an introduction to music theory for those who have never studied music academically. Zack's research interests include popular music pedagogy, music in higher education, composition, and improvisation. He is one of the editors of *The Routledge Research Companion to Popular Music Education* (2016). In addition to teaching and research, Zack is an active composer and musician performing internationally in ensembles and as a soloist.

Jared O'Leary is a multiplicity whose research interests include interactive audio and learning; affinity, hybrid, and participatory music making and learning; skill acquisition and expertise; and critical discourse studies and discourse analysis. Visit JaredOLeary. com to stay up to date with his latest research.

Joseph Pate serves as an Assistant Professor of Outdoor Leadership at Young Harris College. Informed by his interests in music, connection, and meaning afforded through leisured spaces and experience, Joseph has engaged in research on music listening of those who report deeply significant, sought-after, and revered listening experiences. Joseph earned his doctorate in Recreation and Leisure Studies and a certificate in

Qualitative Inquiry at the University of Georgia, where he focused on the listening act as a site for reverie, reverberation, resonation, and voice. His ongoing scholarly interests include the phenomenology of leisured spaces and experiences, connection, meaning, and growth.

Joseph Michael Pignato is a composer, musician, and music education scholar. He currently serves as Associate Professor of Music at the State University of New York, Oneonta, where he teaches music industry and directs experimental music and improvised rock ensembles. As a musician, Pignato leads Bright Dog Red, an improvising quintet that fuses free improvisation, electronica, jazz, hip-hop, psychedelia, and noise music. Additionally, Pignato works under the moniker u.joe recording drum tracks for DJs and producers, including DJ M A N I K and producer Mr. Temmtation.

Stephanie Pitts is Professor of Music Education at the University of Sheffield, with research interests in musical participation, arts audiences, and lifelong learning. She is the author of *Valuing Musical Participation* (2005), *Chances and Choices: Exploring the Impact of Music Education* (2012), and, with Eric Clarke and Nicola Dibben, *Music and Mind in Everyday Life* (2010). She is currently working on several research projects relating to audience experience, including audiences for the contemporary arts, and an edited volume on these topics an edited volume on these topics, *Coughing and Clapping* (with Karen Burland), was published by Ashgate in 2014. *Coughing and Clapping* (edited with Karen Burland) was published by Ashgate in 2014.

Shara Rambarran is an Assistant Professor of Music and Cultural Studies at the Bader International Study Centre, Queen's University, Canada. Shara gained her PhD in Music at the University of Salford (U.K.). Her research and teaching interests include: musicology, postproduction, postmodernism, digital media, remixology, music industry, events management, education, and law (international property rights). She is an editor on the *Journal on the Art of Record Production*, and has written for *Popular Music, Popular Musicology, Popular Music and Society*, and *PopMatters*. Shara is the coeditor of *The Oxford Handbook of Music and Virtuality* (2016), and *The Routledge Research Companion to Popular Music Education* (2016).

Kevin Rathunde is a Professor in the Department of Family and Consumer Studies at the University of Utah. His research focuses on how intrinsically motivated experiences (e.g., flow) impact human development and learning, and how such experiences can be enhanced or disrupted by characteristics of individuals and contexts (e.g., family, school, and nature settings). Dr. Rathunde's latest research on leisure play and adult development draws on his past experience as a musician. Before receiving a PhD from the University of Chicago, he performed for over a decade in a pop-jazz-rock band and studied guitar improvisation at the Bloom School of Jazz and with noted educator and guitarist Frank Dawson.

Ronnie Richards is an Associate Lecturer in the Carnegie Faculty at Leeds Beckett University. His chapter in this volume is drawn from his current PhD research. His work serves to contextualize the leisure experiences of individuals who participated in the subculture of Acid House, situated in the U.K. during the late 1980s and early 1990s. His work is significant in terms of its scope to link individual leisure activities and national or global (subcultural) communities to social trends and longer historical trajectories, including assessments and critiques of postmodern leisure.

Gabby Riches is a PhD candidate in the Research Institute for Sport, Physical Activity and Leisure at Leeds Beckett University. Her doctoral research explores the role and significance moshpit practices play in the lives of female heavy metal fans in Leeds's extreme metal scene. Her research interests include the socio-spatial constructions of underground music spaces, subcultural performativity, affect, nonrepresentational theory, marginal leisures, and processes of embodiment.

Hermione Ruck Keene is currently researching a PhD in Sociology of Music with Lucy Green at the University College London Institute of Education. She is an Associate Lecturer at the University of Exeter, where she teaches on the Primary PGCE and MA Education–Creative Arts programs. Hermione continues to work extensively as a music educator. Her research interests include amateur musical participation, amateur and professional collaborations in music, singing and choirs, and lifelong musical learning.

Gareth Dylan Smith is an independent scholar based in London. He is at the forefront of research in popular music education, serving as editor for the *Journal of Popular Music Education* and *The Routeldge Research Companion to Popular Music Education* (2016), with numerous journal articles and book chapters published in the field. Gareth is a drummer and a long-time musical collaborator with other rockers, punks, theater musicians and songwriters, playing on various recordings and performing in bars, clubs, festivals, and theaters. His next commercial musical release will be a concept album entitled *Tinker Tailor Soldier Rock*. Following his cultural-psychological study of drum-kit players *I Drum, Therefore I Am: Being and Becoming a Drummer* (2013), his current research includes a phenomenological study of embodiment in drum-kit performance. His life in music, leisure and academia is comically chronicled at drdrumsblog.com.

Karl Spracklen's work on leisure uses history, philosophy, and sociology to understand the meaning and purpose of leisure: how free leisure choices are, and how much modern leisure is a product of constraints. He has published three key monographs on leisure theory: *The Meaning and Purpose of Leisure: Habermas and Leisure at the End of Modernity* (2009), *Constructing Leisure: Historical and Philosophical Debates* (2011), and *Whiteness and Leisure* (2013). Professor Spracklen has published widely on leisure in journals such as *Leisure Studies* and the *World Leisure Journal*. He is interested in subcultures, identities, spaces, and hegemonies of leisure—his research on tourism, folk music and morris, Goth, heavy metal, and sport is all underpinned by a concern with the problem of leisure. He is the Principal Editor of the journal *Metal Music Studies*. Professor Spracklen was the Chair of the Leisure Studies Association from 2009 to 2013. He remains actively involved in the work of the association. Professor Spracklen is the joint editor (with Karen Fox) of a book series for Palgrave Macmillan: *Leisure Studies in a Global Era*.

Robert A. Stebbins, FRSC, received his PhD from the University of Minnesota (1964). He has taught in the departments of sociology at the Memorial University of Newfoundland (1965–1973), University of Texas at Arlington (1973–1976), and the University of Calgary (1976–1999). Stebbins was elected Fellow of the Academy of Leisure Sciences (1996) and Fellow of the Royal Society of Canada (1999). His books include *Serious Leisure: A Perspective for Our Time* (2007), *Between Work and Leisure: The Common Ground of Two Separate Worlds* (2nd ed., 2014), *Careers in Serious Leisure: From Dabbler to Devotee in Search of Fulfillment* (2014), and *The Interrelationship of Leisure and Play* (2015).

Evan S. Tobias is Associate Professor of Music Education at Arizona State University, where his research interests include creative integration of digital media and technology, expanding beyond traditional music curricula, and integrating popular culture and music in music classrooms. Tobias heads the Consortium for Innovation and Transformation in Music Education at ASU and maintains a professional blog at http://evantobias.net.

Alberto Trobia is Associate Professor of Sociology and Social Research Methods at the University of Palermo. His main research interests are in the field of computational social sciences (with an emphasis on text analysis, network analysis, and agent-based simulation) and mixed methods. He is also interested in popular culture, mainly cinema (he participated in the *Lord of the Rings* Research Project) and popular music. Among his publications as author and editor are *La Ricerca Sociale Quali-Quantitativa* (2005); *Sociologia del Cinema Fantastico* (2008); *Social Network Analysis* (with Veronica Milia, 2011). He has also written some entries for *The Encyclopedia of Survey Research Methods* (2008).

Valerie L. Vaccaro is an Associate Professor of Marketing at Kean University. In 2001, she earned a PhD in Marketing from the Graduate Center of the City University of New York. Valerie has published her dissertation, journal articles, and conference papers on in-store music's influence on consumers. In the 1980s and 1990s, she was a music journalist who reviewed concerts and interviewed jazz, rock, and pop musicians. She was also a DJ and promotion director at her college radio station and worked for record companies in New York City. Valerie is a lifelong learner, music maker, and supporter of music education. Valerie believes that listening to and playing music is a gift that can contribute to people's well-being, health, and quality of life.

Maria Varvarigou is a Senior Lecturer in Music at Canterbury Christ Church University, a Senior Researcher at the Sidney de Haan Centre for Arts and Health, and a Visiting Research Associate at University College London, Institute of Education, University of London. Maria has been performing as solo singer, oboist, and chorister for many years. She has participated in several recordings of Greek traditional songs and has developed a great interest in performance practices of traditional music. Maria completed her PhD in 2009 as a scholar of the A. S. Onassis Foundation. Her special areas of interest include ear playing and performance practices of vernacular music, choral conducting education, effective teaching and learning in higher and professional education, music and well-being, and intergenerational music making. Maria is coauthor of *Active Ageing with Music: Supporting Wellbeing in the Third and Fourth Ages* (2014).

Jenna Ward is Senior Lecturer in Human Resources Management and Organisational Behaviour at Leicester Business School. Her research interests include qualitative, sociological appreciations of emotional labor and the development of arts-based methods in the field of management studies. Her research has been published in *Social Science and Medicine, Management Learning, Environment and Planning A*, and *Human Relations*. Her most recent publication, *The Dark Side of Emotional Labour* (2015), coauthored with Dr. Robert McMurray from Durham Business School, explores the often unspoken and hidden aspects of emotion work that the rest of society would rather ignore.

Allan Watson is Lecturer in Human Geography and member of the Centre for Research in Communication and Culture at Loughborough University. His research interests focus on the economic geography of the cultural and creative economy, and in particular on the global music industry. His research has been published in leading journals, including *Environment and Planning A, Global Networks*, and *Area*. Current research on the music industry is funded by Research Councils UK and the Royal Geographical Society. Allan is the author of *Cultural Production in and Beyond the Recording Studio* (2014).

Serena Weren is the Director of Bands and Assistant Professor of Music at Loyola University New Orleans. She earned her Doctor of Music Arts in wind band conducting from Arizona State University and also has degrees from Franklin and Marshall College, Temple University, and Arkansas State University. She was the Director of Bands at Middletown High School South and has served as a guest conductor and clinician for concert and marching bands nationally and internationally. Her current research interests include investigating the association of instrumental music making, social networks, and biomarkers to aid in understanding our social and physiological relationship to music making.

Claire Yee is a PhD student in Psychology at Arizona State University, where her research interests include investigating the biology of close relationships and the role of positive emotions in the formation and maintenance of relationships. Claire's research ultimately explores the tradeoffs of being in relationships across different contexts.

THE OXFORD HANDBOOK OF

MUSIC MAKING AND LEISURE

EDITORS' INTRODUCTION

CHAPTER 1

GRASPING THE JELLYFISH
OF MUSIC MAKING
AND LEISURE

ROGER MANTIE AND GARETH DYLAN SMITH

> Music educators, recording studios, publishers, promoters, and musi-
> cians' associations are only a small part of a social practice that is deeply
> rooted in the everyday life experiences of a broad mass of people.
>
> (George Lipsitz)

WHEN one considers the diversity of music making practices throughout the world, it
is clear that no single volume on music making and leisure could ever be exhaustive
or wholly inclusive. (A book could be written on the phenomenon of Elvis impersonators alone!) Even if one excludes musical practices and music makers falling outside
the amorphous boundaries of *leisure*, one is still left with a bewildering array of participatory forms, to say nothing of the various ways such experiences can be theorized and
understood. This is in no way to apologize for any shortcomings in, or to preclude criticisms of, the present volume. We are quite proud of how this first attempt at theorizing
music making and leisure has come together and the potential significance it holds for
informing the efforts of all those who care about *avocational* involvement with music
as an integral part of the human condition. Rather, we presage this handbook with the
disclaimer that, from inception through completion of the project, our aim has been to
reveal interdisciplinary intersections, commonalities, differences, and disjunctures in
scholarship related to what might be termed, nonpejoratively, "recreational music making"; the aim has never been to "speak" on behalf of all people who include music among
their many life interests.

The title of this handbook is intended to remind readers that, while music has had
and continues to fulfill many functions in human experience (Merriam 1964), leisure is,
oddly, often the most conspicuous *and* the most overlooked—at least among formally
trained musicians! Talking with laypeople about a book on music and leisure during the

production of this volume inevitably resulted in odd reactions, as if we, as academics, were guilty of investigating the blatantly obvious. *What next? A study to see if the sky is blue?* And yet, as with many everyday things, it is easy to gloss over the taken for granted. (Why is the sky blue?) While music has unquestionably played a major role in people's leisure for as long as we as a species have made musical sounds, academic interest in music making and leisure has been remarkably scant. Although leisure and recreation used to play a small part in American music education discourses in the first half of the twentieth century (see this volume, Kriķun, chapter 14, McCarthy, chapter 2), such interest has long since vanished.

No doubt to the dismay of those in Leisure Studies (sometimes Leisure *Sciences* in the U.S.), the word "leisure" has taken on undesirable connotations over the past fifty to sixty years. Although Max Weber's protestant work ethic portended our intensified, globalized, neoliberal-dominated world, where the obsession with "international competitiveness" apparently justifies the obliteration of any sense of community and "the good life" (or perhaps, in the eyes of those who proselytize human capital theory, work is synonymous with the good life?), one might hope that resistance through leisure might exist somewhere on the horizon. We, in fact, briefly toyed with trying to avoid the word "leisure" in the title of this handbook, but quickly concluded that to do so would be to further empower human capital discourses that denigrate the belief that people should entertain notions of personal enjoyment and fulfillment outside of "work." Thus, we offer the word "leisure" in the title as both a description of the volume's content and a political statement: *recreational music makers of the world unite!*

If it were but that simple. As Leo Hendry (1983) so wryly put it, "Attempts to define leisure have been compared with trying to grasp a jellyfish" (21). To paraphrase George Bernard Shaw, one person's leisure is another person's hell. It is easy to get caught up in the romanticization of leisure, as if music making of any kind is inherently good (and that work is inherently evil). Indeed, many of the chapters in this volume tend toward a more celebratory view of leisure. Others remind us of leisure's darker side. As one of the reviewers of this handbook observed, various dualities appear throughout the volume, such as excellence and inclusion, individual intention and social interaction, and process and product. None of these are mutually exclusive, but overlap with and within one another. Leisure is thus neither inherently good nor bad, but rather a facet of human experience filled with enormous potential. A better, richer understanding of music making *as* leisure, we believe, enhances the capacity of those with an interest in advancing human happiness and well-being.

As editors, we come from two different worlds: Roger was a school band director in Canada before pursuing doctoral studies in music education and a subsequent career in academia; Gareth is a drummer, partial to hard rock, with an intellectual bent that led him to doctoral studies with Lucy Green at the University College London Institute of Education.[1] What unites the two of us are shared beliefs and experiences relating to the importance of both music and leisure. While Roger spent many years teaching instrumental music in schools, this was done against the formative backdrop of experiences growing up around people (including his father, a very untrained, unpolished fiddle player) who chose to *make time for making music*. Such people, it seemed, did not aspire to so-called professional levels of performance, nor did they seem to regard their participation strictly as *learning*. Instead, the motivation and joy they exhibited appeared to derive from the social experience of music making, something done outside of or apart from their other commitments (work, family, etc.). In his youth, Gareth played snare drum in a Boys' Brigade marching band and clarinet in a local concert band, continuing with the "misery stick" through his first year of undergraduate studies before switching to drum set (on a Western classical music program) to align his formal studies more closely with his growing obsession with "rocking out." A sideline in bodhrán and guitar led to folk sessions and a lengthy relationship with London-based "psycho-ceilidh" (Celtic punk) band Neck. Parallel careers as an itinerant musician and peripatetic music (and driving) instructor led Gareth to the academy.

TAMING THE JELLYFISH

The challenges of any edited volume are numerous—an interdisciplinary, international volume even more so. Those from a given field may hold expectations that certain names or phenomena of interest are to be found in these pages. To this we can only offer that, within the constraints of a 250,000-word volume, many difficult choices needed to be made with respect to disciplinary field, topic of interest, country of origin, gender, and experience (aiming for a range of emerging to established scholars). While we feel we have achieved some semblance of balance among many "author variables," we make no pretense toward calling this any sort of comprehensive handbook; we consider this a first word, not a final one. Or perhaps more appropriately, we hope that this volume will be viewed as a logical extension that galvanizes the work of many progenitors. (The work of those associated with the Adult and Community Music Special Research Interest Group of the U.S. National Association for Music Education comes immediately to mind.) Throughout the following thirty-one chapters, one is reminded of the nuances and complexity of leisure and the variegated roles and meanings that music plays within it.

Although we began this project with a proposed outline, the final shape and structure of the handbook reflect the nature of the chapters. It is the contributing authors whom we have to thank for that which the book has become. We have situated chapters under headings that we feel help to frame, contextualize, and situate the insights that authors share. This being said, threads interweave through the chapters and sections of the book, bonding an eclectic collection of contributions around the subject of music making and leisure.

PART I: RELATIONSHIPS TO AND WITH MUSIC

The chapters in this section serve to illuminate various ways in which people *relate* to music. Relationships are personal, meaningful, and fulfilling. They are also challenging, frustrating, and complex. We have relationships with peers, co-workers, lovers, friends, children, and the state. We also nurture relationships with pets, cars, bicycles, buildings, and musical instruments. Relationships with some of these are mediated by relationships with others. For some people, making music is the activity or context through or in which everything else is understood. For others, music is a roughly equal part of the complex pattern of activities and relationships that comprise a life.

In the first three chapters, authors explore ways of construing and conceptualizing the contexts and characteristics of people's relationships with and to music. Marie McCarthy's retrospective (chapter 2) on Max Kaplan's scholarship sets the stage, demonstrating how this noted musician, sociologist, and leisure theorist, in many ways ahead of his time, construed intersections and interactions of music, education, and leisure in people's lives. The discussion then ranges from psychology, identity, selfhood, technology, music listening, and well-being (Hallam, Creech, and Varvarigou, chapter 3) to the international Musical Futures education initiative (D'Amore and Smith, chapter 4) that aims to harness the love that young people have for making music collaboratively and apply this effectively in schools. The broader brush-strokes of these opening contributions provide context for the next five chapters, which take a turn toward the personal, focusing especially on creative musicking.

Adam Patrick Bell (chapter 5) presents a furtive, first-hand account of compulsive musical collaboration in spaces typical of many popular music makers uncelebrated in mainstream literature and media. Pate and Kumm (chapter 6) present work on another kind of creativity—the construction and development of "mix tapes" and the mediation of relationships through them, even as media continue to evolve. The final three chapters in this section explore emotional and challenging personal connections to music making. David Lines (chapter 7) presents the first of two autoethnographic contributions revolving around relationships with the guitar; Lines moves from autoethnographic meditations as an instrumentalist through a Foucaultian analysis of power relations in contemporary music education contexts. Kevin Rathunde and Russ Isabella (chapter 8) then deliver a highly personal account of a return to music making after a long hiatus; their story is a journey of reconnection with music performance and ensuing negotiations of family, work, and identity. Gareth Dylan Smith (chapter 9) concludes the section with a conceptualization of music making through the Aristotelian and inherently Western concept of "eudaimonism."

PART II: INVOLVEMENT AND MEANING

Interactions with music always *mean* something. Authors in this section of the book explore meaning in two broad contexts: in the first instance related more or less directly to education and enculturation, in the second from diverse cultural and theoretical angles. The first four chapters look, from a range of perspectives, at music making's connections with music *learning*. Stephanie Pitts (chapter 10) explores life histories of lapsed music makers, asking people about their discontinuation with music and what might have encouraged them to maintain or reignite their involvement. At the other end of a spectrum of musical involvement, Zack Moir (chapter 13) describes an out-of-school music education initiative in Scotland that addresses youth music making at the intersection of industry, leisure, identity, and learning. Between them are two personal accounts of meaning in making music. Sidsel Karlsen (chapter 11) considers building repertoires of musical agency, combining literature from sociology (of music education) and personal responses to experiences in music throughout life. Jennie Henley (chapter 12) examines learning, identities, and "possible selves" among adult musicians and self-proclaimed "nonmusicians" via several examples of collaborative, participatory ensemble music making, including an autoethnographic perspective.

The next five chapters help to remind us that learning and education, though important, represent but one (albeit broad) dimension of music making and leisure. Andrew Krikun (chapter 14), for example, pans out to examine policy initiatives and dominant rationalities in the U.S. in the 1930s and 1940s, and the extent to which these currents encouraged music making as leisure and recreation. Two chapters, employing contrasting methodological approaches, explore *motivation* in music making. Valerie Vaccaro (chapter 15) presents a comparative literature review across music education, psychology, and consumer behavior in order to propose a new theory of motivation. Serena Weren and colleagues (chapter 18) use social network analysis and self-determination theory to examine motivation in a U.S. collegiate marching band. The setting of two chapters shifts to the city of Leeds and the phenomenon of "black" and/or "extreme" metal music. Karl Spracklen (chapter 16) and Gabby Riches (chapter 17) seek to uncover depths of meaning in leisure, exploring, respectively, agency and myth making through Baudrillardian and Habermasian lenses, and the formation and negotiation of spaces and identities from a feminist poststructural narrative perspective. The breadth of approaches in this section opens the door to a rich ethnographic and autoethnographic buffet in Part III.

PART III: SCENES, SPACES, AND PLACES

Location is central to every music making experience or activity. Often of equal or greater importance to music makers is the community within which music making is enabled, nurtured, challenged, and sustained. The chapters in this section focus on physical, social, geographical, and virtual scenes, spaces, and places as sites and subjects of practice and research. Methodologies include ethnographic, autoethnographic, qualitative, and mixed-method approaches to data gathering and analysis.

Robert Stebbins (chapter 19), whose "serious leisure perspective" has become a landmark in the study of music making (and other pursuits) *as leisure*, offers here a framework for viewing and understanding scenes, spaces, and places, including individual and collective manners of making music as leisure. In this section authors invoke and evoke the visceral, tangible sense of *being there*. Coauthors Hermione Ruck Keene and Lucy Green (chapter 20) examine eclectic accounts of the special amateur and professional music making community that has existed for decades at the Dartington Summer School in the U.K., while Ronnie Richards's remembered and fictional narratives (chapter 21) recall the vibrant, sometimes illegal Acid House party scene in the north of England in the late 1980s. Joseph Michael Pignato (chapter 22) evokes, through structured reminiscence, the *poietic* New Jersey basement space that was the backdrop to adolescence and the ontogeny of two lives in music. Brett Lashua (chapter 23) then takes drumming "to the city," as a participant musician-observer with various ensembles, exploring popular music rehearsal spaces and performance places in and around Liverpool. These chapters' theorized remembrances and responses give way to a group of empirical studies in physical and digital domains.

The next three chapters visit collective and community spaces, beginning with Jenna Ward and Allan Watson's discussion (chapter 24) of the emotional labor of producers and sound engineers in the complex professional and leisure environments of recording studios. Chris Cayari (chapter 25) surveys music making practices and the user-generated content phenomenon on YouTube, exploring this online environment as a platform for individual and collaborative performance, learning, and other professional and non-professional practices. Also in the virtual domain, sociologists Alberto Trobia and Fabio M. Lo Verde (chapter 26) present an analysis from mixed-methods research into social networks in music making and music learning communities among Italian amateur rock musicians. The increase of research on electronic- and digital-dependent musicking marks a noticeable shift toward conceptualizing the breadth and depth of leisure practices in these areas of new media.

PART IV: ON THE DIVERSITY OF MUSIC MAKING AND LEISURE

The contributions in this section are diverse in style, content, and approach, and share a sense of aliveness and contemporary relevance that, collectively, close a book that is keen to look to the future while it studies the present. The section opens with three descriptions of practice that serve to illustrate the incredible diversity that exists under the banner of music and leisure. First, Karen Fox (chapter 27) invites readers to consider holistic, embodied Indigenous music-dance making practices from Canadian Aboriginal hip-hop artists, and to embrace the ways that these and other hybridized practices play with (perceptions of) space-time. Next, Jared O'Leary and Evan Tobias (chapter 28) delve into the highly specialized "sonic participatory culture" of music composition and performance within games and gaming communities. The focus then shifts to the acoustic realm. Thomas Malone (chapter 29) transports us to the dynamic, embodied, somewhat timeless community phenomenon of Sacred Harp singing, which, while deeply meaningful in the lives of participants, is practiced but never performed.

The last three chapters in the section seek to problematize music as leisure. Shara Rambarran (chapter 30) examines the contested notion of performance in laptop music making, arguing for a consideration of the computer as a uniquely capable musical instrument. Next, Gillian Howell and colleagues (chapter 31), drawing on the U.K. tradition of "community music," present examples of music leadership as intervention and the facilitation of nonexpert participatory music making pursued for social and political ends. Finally, coeditor Roger Mantie (chapter 32) closes the section and the book with a critical homage to the work of sociomusicologist, activist, and "groovologist" Charles Keil, inviting readers to consider "all education as leisure education."

Back to the Future

Given the ubiquity of music in people's lives it feels in some ways odd to have produced a handbook on music making and leisure. We keep imagining what such a book might have looked like if published in 1916 rather than 2016. Would the idea of "music making and leisure" be so obvious as to be unthinkable? As evidenced, in part, in this handbook, we are at an historical moment when music and music making arguably mean more things than ever before. Traditional understandings of music making are increasingly challenged, as stable social hierarchies and simple dichotomies such as work/leisure and vocation/avocation have broken down. Our hope is that this handbook contributes to interdisciplinary, global conversations about music making as an intrinsic part of human existence. We hope that the frame of "music making and leisure" presents and permits possibilities, provocation, and other potentialities, both explicit and implied. If this book achieves anything, we hope it inspires readers to think differently and to encourage the same in others. Maybe, together, in our own small ways, we can help to effect positive change in the world.

Like other large-scale projects, this handbook represents the culmination of countless hours of work. It should go without saying that no project of this size and scope is the product of just two people. In addition to the contributing authors, and of course Norm Hirschy and the fabulous team at Oxford University Press, we wish to thank all those who have supported us, in their own special ways, in helping bring this volume to life. That list of people includes (but is certainly not limited to) Liz Burke, Susan Conkling, Gillian Glover, Lucy Green, Gavin Hammond, Lee Higgins, Mark Hunter, Charlie Keil, Angela Mantie, Clint Randles, Robert Stebbins, and Stephen Wheel.

Note

1. It seems like more than just a coincidence that Gareth is a drummer. Almost every band, it seems, needs a drummer (Allison Krauss/Union Station and Django Reinhardt's Quintette du Hot Club de France notwithstanding), leading to a condition where drummers, perhaps more than any other instrumentalist, are led into lives where the lines between work and

play, leisure and nonleisure, vocation and avocation, are blurred. It was not by design, but it has not escaped our notice that this handbook counts at least five drummers among its contributing authors. We say "at least" because, on one level, everyone is—or wants to be—a drummer!

REFERENCE CITED

Leo B. Hendry. 1983. *Growing Up and Going Out: Adolescents and Leisure* (Aberdeen: Aberdeen University Press, 1983).

PART I

RELATIONSHIPS TO AND WITH MUSIC

CHAPTER 2

....

CREATING A FRAMEWORK FOR MUSIC MAKING AND LEISURE

Max Kaplan Leads the Way

....

MARIE McCARTHY

INTRODUCTION

....

MUSIC making has been an integral part of leisure activity across time and culture. The pathways between music as an academic discipline and leisure studies, however, are curiously underdeveloped. Indeed, a primary goal of this book is to examine and theorize music making in the context of leisure. As the field of leisure studies developed in the mid-twentieth century, a lone scholar labored intensely to include music in the leisure revolution of that time. This individual was musician, sociologist, consultant, and scholar of leisure studies, Max Kaplan (1911–1998). His deeply sociological perspective, holistic vision of the function of music in society, and exceptional theoretical writings focused on the intersections of music, leisure, and education, and were timely in the context of a changing United States of America. However, the reception and implementation of his ideas were limited. This was due in part to conflicting values and beliefs about the function and form of music in education, a mid-century turn away from the social values of music education, and a turn toward the study of music as an academic discipline.

I approach Kaplan's ideas in retrospect, arguing that they are relevant and valuable in the context of contemporary discourse on music and leisure. The purpose of the chapter, then, is to revisit the writings of Max Kaplan and to identify ideas that may inform efforts to bring the worlds of leisure and music making together in academic discourse in the twenty-first century. In surveying selected works from his prolific body of writings, comprising 27 books and some 350 articles (Saxon 1998), it becomes evident that Kaplan was a scholar whose ideas were at the forefront of interdisciplinary thinking in music (and the arts in general), music education, sociology, and leisure studies. In his writings, he addressed scholars and practitioners whose work had potential to impact the quality of musical life in school, community, and the nation at large—recreation leaders, community musicians, music educators, scholars of leisure studies, and sociologists. There is little evidence to show that those he addressed heeded his words and labored like he did to integrate activities of music making and leisure studies.

A violinist and chamber musician, Kaplan graduated from Milwaukee State Teachers College in 1933. He became engaged in social work and community music projects in the 1930s and early 1940s, first in the Milwaukee area and later in Pueblo, Colorado, where he founded the music department at Pueblo College (Krikun 2010). He earned a master's degree in music at the University of Colorado, and master's and doctoral degrees in sociology at the University of Illinois, where he taught until 1957 (Saxon 1998). Robert Choate, Dean of the School of Fine and Applied Arts at Boston University, invited Kaplan to serve as Director of the Arts Center of Boston University. One of the first major projects of the center was the founding of the Greater Boston Youth Symphony Orchestra in the fall of 1958 (Kaplan 1966, 165).

Kaplan devoted much of his career to developing the field of leisure studies. In addition to several book contributions to the field, he founded and directed the Institute for Studies of Leisure at the University of South Florida and was a member of the Academy of Leisure and the World Leisure and Recreation Association. His work as consultant (e.g., Kaplan 1993) and lecturer extended to several European countries and to the Middle East (Kaplan 1998; Saxon 1998). Influenced by his interdisciplinary education and broad work experience in music and sociology, he reached out and made radical connections between disciplines involved in the cultivation of the arts in society (Kaplan 1966, 1990). He was a keen observer and critic of social institutions. Viewing the arts in society from an overarching vantage point allowed him to see connections with other social institutions and to identify commonalities and differences between their structures and functions. In sum, he used a systems theory approach to analyze the complex world of the arts from a sociological perspective (Kaplan 1966, 1990).

Beginning with his dissertation in 1951, "The Musician in America: A Study of His Social Roles. Introduction to a Sociology of Music," and ending with *One Life: The Free Academic* in 1998, a book that represented a summary of his ideas, Kaplan offers several constructs and propositions about the functions of music in personal and group development. His social philosophy of the arts is consistently articulated throughout his career, particularly in his books *Foundations and Frontiers of Music Education* (1966) and *The Arts: A Social Perspective* (1990). Some of his works have a practical dimension too, where he offers models for community music, public school music, and music in recreation centers (e.g., Kaplan 1952a, 1952b; Music Educators National Conference 1958; National Guild of Community Schools 1966). Kaplan was singular in his effort to develop a sociological framework that situated music within institutions of leisure and recreation.

In order to observe how Kaplan theorized the relationship between music making and leisure, I organize the chapter around the following topics: patterns of development in leisure and recreation, 1900–1960; changing conceptions of leisure and recreation in the mid-twentieth century; recreational music; community as fertile ground for observing leisure in action; school music in relation to music in leisure, music making in the context of leisure; and moving forward with Kaplan's vision.

PATTERNS OF DEVELOPMENT IN LEISURE AND RECREATION, 1900–1960

Kaplan (1955) provided a historical perspective on the recreation movement and identified five stages in its development in the twentieth century. The founding of the Playground Association of America in 1906 (later known as the Playground and Recreation Association of America [1911], National Recreation Association [1930], and National Recreation and Park Association [1965]), represented the beginning of an organizational framework for recreation and reflected the need for such a body at the national level. A second phase focused on the implementation of recreation programs during the First World War. During this time, neighborhood organizations and the War Camp Community Service expanded the definition of recreation in community. The search for a philosophy of recreation in the 1920s represented a third phase, reflecting increasing time for leisure, the impact of new technologies on work patterns, and expanded travel opportunities. The Depression in the 1930s prompted a new phase that stimulated federal public works programs, with almost every state in the nation developing a program of recreation. The Federal Music Project was founded in 1935 and subsumed by the Works Projects Administration (WPA) in 1939 as the WPA Music Program (see Krikun, this volume, chapter 14). Kaplan later observed that, "the Project, for the first time in American life, made music an integral part of the recreation philosophy.... Music now became a community possession" (1955, 4). Three categories of leaders for recreational music emerged: performing musicians, music educators (who taught music classes for the underprivileged, in congested city areas and in rural districts), and music leaders of community amateur groups (5).

The Second World War impacted the progress of the WPA and the Music Program was phased out. Finally, the postwar years marked "a highly significant searching for a reappraisal of the values and the directions of recreation" (Kaplan 1955, 6), in response to the recreation explosion among Americans. By the mid-1950s, Kaplan concluded that the recreation movement "is now accepted in all parts of the country as a public responsibility" (6). This public responsibility was extended to *all* people. The concept of leisure developed as a phenomenon of culture at large and was no longer limited to members of certain privileged social groups who had the time, resources, and social capital to avail themselves of recreational activities (Kaplan 1956a, 1960).

As the idea of leisure for all gained momentum and popularity, a "democracy of amateurism" (Kaplan 1954, 28) took root. The number of persons engaged in acting, painting, or making music increased dramatically (Kaplan 1956c, 47). The leading organization of music education in the United States, the Music Educators National Conference (MENC), set up a Commission on Music in the Community in 1954 to address new levels of musical activity in the community. Kaplan was deeply engaged in the commission's work, chairing the final report issued in 1958. The primary task of the commission, according to Kaplan, was "to awaken MENC and the whole musical world to the real possibility of a wider function and social integration of music and art in the changing society" (47). In his sociological view grounded in functionalism, he focused on the interconnectedness of institutions. Using the string quartet as a metaphor for the functions of institutions responsible for developing musical culture, Kaplan examined them from four perspectives: agencies of musical education, creation and production, dissemination or distribution, and consumption (Kaplan 1944, 1966, 1990).

He envisioned a central role for school music in the transition from the industrial society to what he called "the cultivated society," in which the arts would define the quality of life and patterns of leisure. His desire to connect school music with music in the community was evident in several publications (Kaplan 1956b, 1956c, 1963, 1966; Music Educators National Conference 1958), but the implementation of his vision to increase communication and influence between school and community music seems to have been limited. After his participation in the Tanglewood Symposium in 1967, there is evidence of a move away from music education, with leisure studies becoming his primary area of inquiry and publication (Kaplan 1975, 1978; Kaplan and Bosserman 1971). Even so, he continued to include the arts as an integral part of theories and models he developed, culminating in his book *The Arts: A Social Perspective* (1990).

Changing Conceptions of Leisure and Recreation in the Mid-Twentieth Century

As leisure activity became a reality in the lives of the masses in the mid-twentieth century, the theoretical study of leisure and its application to recreational practice gained momentum. The discipline of leisure studies became formalized by the mid-1970s. Much of Kaplan's scholarly career as a sociologist coincided with the rise of leisure studies, and one can trace both stable ideas and changing attitudes toward leisure through his writings. In his first book on the topic, *Leisure in America: A Social Inquiry* (1960), he set forth leisure as an ideal construct whose meanings combined an antithesis to work, a pleasant expectation and recollection, a minimum of social role obligations, a perception of freedom, a close relationship to values of the culture, and a range of activities from informal and inconsequential to weighty and important, often characterized by some element of play (Kaplan 1960, 22). By 1975, he had refined and somewhat expanded the meaning of leisure and offered the following definition:

> a relatively self-determined activity-experience that falls into one's economically free-time roles, that is seen as leisure by participants, that is psychologically pleasant in anticipation and recollection, that potentially covers the whole range of commitment and intensity, that contains characteristic norms and restraints, and that provides opportunities for recreation, personal growth, and service to others. (Kaplan 1975, 26)

The impact of leisure on personal growth and fulfillment was highlighted in this definition, as it was in his later book *Leisure: Perspectives on Education and Policy* (1978), in which he observed that leisure experiences had become "increasingly central and influential," providing "a potential source of life's meanings" (54). Furthermore, he envisioned a convergence and interaction of elements from work and leisure, thus moving away from the earlier definition of leisure as oppositional to and different from work. The differences that existed between work and leisure, he noted, resided more in the attitudes that surrounded them than in differences in the content of their activities. Now those attitudes were changing and the goal was to draw on the most productive qualities of work and leisure to benefit each other. He wrote:

> From work we have such potential elements as discipline, commitment, craft and skill, responsibility, and completion of a task; from leisure we have such elements as adventure, curiosity, play (in Huizinga's broad sense), and delight of discovery (in a childhood sense). . . . We are seeking a new formulation of leisure and work to enable a more successful transition into a new era of humanity. (Kaplan 1978, 43–44)

Kaplan viewed the arts as vitally important in this time of transition into "a new era of humanity." He engaged them as primary sources for nurturing the "cultivated society" he envisioned in response to the cultural, economic, and technological changes he witnessed around him. His placement of music at the center of leisure activity prompted him as early as 1956 to ask far-reaching questions about music's role and function in society:

> What are the functions of music and art in such a transitory period? What is the musician's role or his place in a philosophy of recreation? What new careers are now open to him, what old patterns are closed? How does he find new roots, in keeping with the times, yet not surrendering his standards and his own need for aesthetic affirmations and values? (Kaplan 1956b, 67)

As evident in some of these questions, the activity of music in recreation brought to the surface tensions, particularly in the roles of the music professional in the context of a world of amateurs and potential clashes of musical values. Kaplan addressed these tensions as part of the theory of recreational music he developed in the 1950s (1951, 1952c, 1955, 1960).

Recreational Music

Functions of Music

Early in his career, Kaplan (1952c, 1955) presented a philosophy of recreational music that included a set of principles and a model for building a music recreation program. In his first exploration of recreational music (1952c), he examined music through an analysis of its aesthetic and social functions. The function of music is aesthetic, he wrote, "when the music serves to relate its listeners and performers to materials, forms, sounds, or context inherent within the artistic creation" (Kaplan 1952c, 1). The social function of music is "that which serves to relate its hearers and performers to persons, ideas, cultural norms or patterns of behavior" (2). Although he identified the functions separately, he believed that both could be present in all music making in recreational or formal educational settings (2).

The social function of music was clearly dominant when he went on to identify five functions of recreational music: *a collective experience*, drawing its participants together and expressing their identity as a group; *a personal experience*, a means of escape or fantasy, or a way of reaching out to others; *a social symbol; a moral value*; or, *purely incidental or secondary* to an event, as in a parade or a game (Kaplan 1952c, 2). Again, Kaplan noted that in real situations, one function does not exist to the exclusion of others. He recommended a balance between personal, independent, isolated activity such as listening, and the common experiences of group participation and doing (67). What matters in recreational music, he emphasized, is *"what happens to the individual who partakes of it"* (Kaplan 1955, 68; emphasis in original).

The question of how music functions in leisure spanned Kaplan's career. Forty years later, in what was to be his final talk to music educators at their first sociology of music education conference in 1995, he again addressed the topic. Many functions were consistent with those identified in 1955 and some expanded the impact of music to more global dimensions: "a collective possession, a personal experience, a form of therapy, a moral and symbolic force, an incidental commodity, a forerunner of social change, and a link between the past, the present and scenarios for the future" (Kaplan 1997, 60). Throughout his career he struggled to reconcile the aesthetic and the social functions of music, a task that he saw at the crux of music making in leisure. In a sense, the binary of aesthetic-social represents one of the contradictions that surfaces in his writings between what he was enculturated to believe and value as a classical musician and what he came to know as he observed the social values of music play out in a variety of community settings—from chamber music to barbershop singing, harmonica playing to community bands and orchestras.

Principles of Recreational Music

Kaplan created principles and structures for the practice of recreational music. First, he wanted "the whole gamut of musical experience" to be available to participants so that there was "an enlargement of available styles, resources, tastes, audiences, and sounds" (Kaplan 1955, 11). His approach was people-centered. Recreational music begins with people and social contexts, and "it has no preferences in respect to the kinds of music or the functions they perform." Each kind of music, he wrote, "has a dignity given to it by the persons who need it or enjoy it" (11). An open-minded attitude and respect for music of all types, interests, and levels is thus developed. "Instead of asking the 'old question,' 'what is good music,' in the philosophy of recreation, we ask, 'what is music good for and for whom?'" (71).[1]

A third principle highlights the role of play in recreational music. Kaplan was influenced by Johan Huizinga's theory of the play element of culture (Huizinga 1949), and applied it to his theory of recreational music (Kaplan 1952c, 3–6). In these contexts, the music activity is voluntary. Prior ability is not always a requisite for participation, and repetition is integral to the experience. The activity is an end in itself (3). Play creates order, and order tends to be a thing of beauty, thus establishing an affinity of play to aesthetics. After the activity is over, the "play-community" tends to become permanent, thus becoming an "in-group." In practice, this can mean that the activity is colored with pleasure and fun, sessions are approached as experiences satisfying in themselves rather than as rehearsals for performance, participants can be joined in groups somewhat inconsistent with ordinary interaction patterns—for example, parents and children, young and old, persons of varying educational levels, and music can be integrated with other recreational activities, such as the dance, drama, pageants, and games (Kaplan 1955, 11).

A fourth principle of recreational music revolves around the social and musical roles of participants and leaders. There is a temporary suspension of everyday social roles to assume "prestige-less" roles—for example, an individual becomes a clarinet player and is no longer the town mayor. Therefore, interaction between individuals in recreational music is based on roles apart from routine work and social considerations (Kaplan 1952c, 4). Related to changes in the social roles of participants, Kaplan frequently addressed the role of the professional and the amateur in recreational music. He distinguished between them in terms of four elements or components of their social role: social circle, functions, status, and conception of the person. The professional is granted authority on the basis of recognized technical knowledge, he or she functions to uphold traditions, has a key status, and is expected to embody certain personal qualities. The amateur, on the other hand, is not held up as an authority and functions differently in relation to art, with more emphasis placed on "what art does to the amateur" than "what the amateur does to art." The amateur has no definite status as a musician and does not need to take on personal qualities assigned to the professional (Kaplan 1954, 26–27). At the same time, professional and amateur are not competitors, but, rather, "close allies," with interdependent roles (27). Both professional and amateur need to adjust their attitudes to music to align with the values and practices of the other in order to come into a relationship of "creative fellowship" (28).

Implementing Recreational Music Programs

The ideal music recreation program brings together persons from a variety of social backgrounds and origins. It is a basis for community participation, offering a variety of musical activities: singing, playing, listening, rhythmic movement, creating, and combined activities such as plays, festivals, folk dancing (Kaplan 1955, 13). It uses the full resources available to it in the home, neighborhood, ethnic and religious groups, school, community, and region. Activities vary across a spectrum from terminal to continuing, organized to spontaneous. Aligned with his view of music as a social process, recreational music can function as education, production, distribution, and consumption (14).

Although Kaplan put forth a comprehensive theory for recreational music in the 1950s, he continued to address the need for "a sound recreational philosophy" and an understanding of the relationships between recreation and the arts into the late 1970s (Kaplan 1978, 52). This may indicate that as social conditions and media change, philosophy needs to be updated to accommodate new or potential functions for the arts in leisure contexts. For example, "the electronic, cybernetic, post-industrial network of devices and applications" (Kaplan 1988, 13) affects how the arts function in society. The arts, he argued, must serve as "*a dynamic link between the humanistic and the technological*" (13; emphasis in original). Thus, educators in the arts must be "bolder than in the past" and integrate the affordances of technology with the humanistic potentials of the arts (Kaplan 1990, 232).

COMMUNITY AS FERTILE GROUND FOR OBSERVING LEISURE IN ACTION

Kaplan was active in establishing and maintaining community programs during the time he lived in Colorado. He conducted a survey of music in the town of Pueblo, using the four elements of musical life he identified—agencies of musical education, production, circulation or dissemination, and consumption (Kaplan 1944; Krikun 2010). Later, as a faculty member at the University of Illinois in the 1950s, he created music materials for recreation programs and their leaders under the auspices of the Music Extension program (Kaplan 1952a, 1952b, 1952c, 1955).

From his study and observations of recreational programs and musical life, he concluded that the community served as "a new frontier for the arts" (Kaplan 1956a, 37–46). A community, he observed, has within it some of the things needed to help along creative or expressive life, such as a library, a recreation department, a school; it has people who want to engage in leisure activities and to establish identity with those around them. The community can provide opportunities for many kinds of groups and institutions who need and use art, rather than the limited, traditional audiences. In the community, the arts can be a focal point around which human values can be built and a setting in which the art professional can mingle and work with the amateur (38–45).

The community has within it a variety of persons from different cultural traditions who can find common interests and understandings through participation in the arts. When music programs are developed in the community, all ages are served, all tastes in music are found, all ranges of skill may be expected, and varieties of personalities are found (Music Educators National Conference 1958, 11–12). Since resources may be limited in the community and equipment may be poor when compared to that in schools, Kaplan saw vital connections and mutual benefits from interactions between music in community and in school.

About the same time he was formulating ideas about music in recreation in the 1950s, he was active in the music education profession. He published articles in the *Music Educators Journal* (Kaplan 1954, 1956b, 1956c), and as described earlier, he chaired the MENC Commission on Music in the Community between 1954 and 1957. The final report of the commission (Music Educators National Conference 1958) identified a set of questions about music education in relation to the community. In the section about recreation departments, the report included questions that sought to build understanding of the relationship between music in school and recreation: What studies now exist within the MENC or other agencies on relationships between music teachers and public recreation agencies? What is a reasonable statement of objectives for music or procedures in its practice when a recreational context exists, as compared to an educational context? What are current trends of thought as to the place of music in recreation programs? Are teachers prepared to take on roles in recreational settings? How are practices in professional recreation agencies affected by changing leisure-time patterns in American life? Does this have relevance to school practice or to the future of the musician? (29).

Although the American music education profession, through its leading organization, MENC, addressed school-community relations in the work of this commission and later in the Tanglewood Symposium in 1967 (Choate and Kaplan 1967), no action plan was pursued and the commission's work did not result in the development of a model to connect music in school and in recreation. In retrospect, an opportunity to reimagine school music in the context of community was overlooked. Had the profession shifted its orientation to its role in the greater community, the shape of music education in the latter half of the twentieth century would likely have taken a different course. What remains is Kaplan's dynamic vision for a synergistic relationship between music in school and community via recreation settings.

School Music in Relation to Music in Leisure

Kaplan created sociological models that enabled a view of the intersections between social institutions and that suggested the relationship of leisure to other institutions

(Kaplan 1975, 26–33). When he looked across social institutions in his search for a theory of leisure and music, he identified the public school as having a primary responsibility in building a musically active society. He captured the essence of that responsibility when he addressed music educators in 1997, telling them that "every hour of music education is a potential contribution to the leisure destiny of your students for the rest of their lives" (59–60). Based on the strong and stable presence he observed in music in the schools, he reminded music educators that their work offered much toward nurturing a culture of amateur music making. He frequently acknowledged that the growth of community music ensembles was "a direct outgrowth of public school music" (Kaplan 1951, 428).

When he looked more broadly at the education of musical amateurs in society, he realized that there were several tensions and barriers arising from the culture of school music that worked against public education serving comprehensively the lifelong musical needs of all students. They included an elite music education philosophy, a narrow social role for the music (McCarthy 2000), a limited vision in music teacher education, lack of rapport between music education and the social sciences, and lack of relationship with other agencies responsible for the development of musical life. Of the three main roles of musical engagement that were popular in the mid-twentieth century—performers, teachers, or consumers—the consumer represented the larger body of the population and as such, "the attitudes implanted by the schools are enormously important to the leisure content of the future" (Kaplan 1960, 206).

Kaplan challenged music educators to evaluate their professional philosophy and to ask what role they were preparing their students to fill—amateur or professional. He urged them to somehow "extract the elite-orientation of *excellence* and apply it to the equalitarian ethos of *availability*" (Kaplan 1963, 35; emphasis in original). Herein lies another of the conundrums or contradictions underlying Kaplan's philosophy. He sought a cult of excellence, characteristic of school performance programs, to be transplanted to amateur music making in leisure programs. Performance standards were to be equal in all contexts of music making. Yet, this was in tension with some of the principles of recreational music making that he had advanced in earlier years—for example, the focus on process, with music making as an end in itself, and success measured by how music contributes to the life of the performer.

The role of the music teacher was central to Kaplan's vision for changing the relationship between school music and music in leisure. He recommended that, in addition to focusing on music in the school, the music teacher also contribute to the musical life of the community. Art, he wrote, moves "into and between various social structures and forms," so the music teacher, unlike teachers of other subjects, belongs to the whole community and must maintain close relations with all community resources and values, including recreation programs (Kaplan 1956b, 66; Music Educators National Conference 1958, 9). Expanding the role of the music teacher depended on change in teacher education. Kaplan believed that college faculty were not interested in educating amateur musicians (Kaplan 1951, 80). That value was not transmitted to music students during their teacher preparation programs. The situation could be improved, he believed, by "some vigorous shake-up" of the curriculum and by expanding student teaching practices to "far wider dimensions" than elementary and secondary schools (Kaplan 1963, 36). He projected that music educators would increasingly encounter the changing societal conditions that reveal the close tie between public school education and the rest of life where leisure activities reside. Addressing music educators at the 1988 Sesquicentennial of Music in American Schools, he identified social changes that teachers would encounter—a flexibility in lifestyles, a pluralism in social values, and a classlessness in the people they serve. He envisioned teachers working with students of all ages, in all stages of their lives, in patterns that departed from the familiar sequence of childhood, youth, adulthood, and retirement (Kaplan 1991, 7–8).

At a philosophical level, Kaplan pointed out the need for closer rapport between music education and the social sciences, arguing that music education could be informed by such connections at the school level. In addition to enriching research methodologies and intellectual perspectives, the connection would highlight the importance of relationships with other agencies responsible for the development of musical life and ultimately serve the cause of making music "a more significant element in American culture" (Music Educators National Conference 1958, 12). The core message Kaplan wanted to convey was that the artistic health of a nation is related to the interdependence of institutions that promote the arts, and that the social sciences can inform models of institutional cooperation and collaboration.

Music Making in
the Context of Leisure

As evident from Kaplan's writings, the institutions of music and leisure are part of a complex social system of beliefs, values, roles, and practices. The inclusion of music in leisure and recreation programs depends on a close network of communication with related groups and institutions, such as professional musicians, music educators, music therapists, leaders in lifelong learning, and social workers, among others. Several aspects of Kaplan's experience with and scholarship on leisure and recreational music contribute to our understanding of music making and leisure. First, he was a performing musician and a member of community orchestras and chamber groups. Second, he participated in several community projects and gained first-hand knowledge of the unique characteristics and challenges of music in leisure as compared to other settings, such as the public school or music school. Third, he used his sociological training to analyze institutions with music recreation programs and to advance models for locating them in the larger context of society. Finally, his experiences of consulting in several countries in Europe and the Middle East informed his views of the symbiotic relationship between political ideology, community structures, and the function and form of the arts, locally and nationally.

What insights can be gained from an examination of Kaplan's ideas for music in lei-sure presented in this chapter? I return to the chapter title, creating a framework for music making and leisure, and ask four questions based on contributions from Kaplan's body of writings: What are the functions of music in leisure? What principles can guide music recreation programs? In what ways does the concept of community serve to advance music making in leisure? What tensions, if any, are embedded in the notion of music as leisure?

What are the functions of music in leisure? Kaplan consistently included the aesthetic and social functions of music, acknowledging that all contexts of musical engagement can contain elements of both, "with blurred edges and forced distinctions" (1966, 54), and that one of the primary challenges of music making is to reconcile them. Since a philosophy of aesthetic education was the dominant paradigm in the discourse of school music for the greater part of his career, Kaplan did not have a like-minded group of scholars with whom he could advance ideas about reconciling the social and the aes-thetic. His identification in the 1950s of the functions of music in leisure—the collective and the personal, the therapeutic and the moral, the symbolic and the incidental—were developed well before music educators integrated social and sociological perspec-tives into their worldview (e.g., Froehlich 2007; Green 1988; Kelly 2008; McCarthy 2002; Rideout 1997). The "sociological turn" in music education expanded the profes-sion's foundational base, evident in theory and philosophy (Elliott and Silverman 2015; Froehlich 2015; Goble 2005; Jorgensen, 1997; Regelski, 2004), history (Cox 2002), psy-chology (MacDonald, Hargreaves, and Miell 2002; Madura Ward-Steinman 2011), and curriculum development (Philpott and Spruce 2012).

What principles can guide music recreation programs? Many of the principles that Kaplan identified in the 1950s are now valued in the broad context of music educa-tion—access to music making, a focus on the musical needs of individuals, use of diverse repertoire to reflect the diversity of musical cultures abroad, involvement of many generations in music activities, and a positive disposition toward the education of amateur musicians. One of the principles that Kaplan emphasized—that of fostering an atmosphere of play and playfulness in recreational music—is typically applied to the early music education of children. Given Kaplan's focus on this fundamental quality of human interaction, it would be beneficial to revisit this principle of music making with a view to deepening the experience of music making and improving dispositions toward music learning in a lifelong context.

In what ways does the concept of community serve to advance music making in lei-sure? Use of community as a core concept in recreational music has even more relevance today than in the mid-1950s. Community music has developed as a profession, with an academic and scholarly field of its own including the publication of the *International Journal of Community Music* since 2008 (e.g., Higgins 2012; Veblen et al. 2013; see Howell, Higgins, and Bartleet, this volume, chapter 31). It embraces a multitude of con-texts in theory and practice—for example, music in prison, church, school, or com-munity center. Scholars who study community music incorporate Lave and Wenger's use of communities of practice, among others (Lave and Wenger 1991; Wenger 1998).

Such study extends to music learning in online communities (Waldron 2011, 2013). The establishment of community music as a subdiscipline has served to bridge the worlds of music in school and community. However, in practice, Kaplan's vision for a closer rapport between music in community and in school has yet to be realized.

What tensions or challenges, if any, are embedded in the notion of music as leisure? In order to create a synergy between music in formal and in recreational settings, Kaplan thought it necessary to dissolve some boundaries that limited exchange. His ecological view of a vibrant musical society called for more continua than either/or, and more open and flexible views of the affordances of music in specific contexts. Specific dualisms that surface in his writings include: amateur versus professional social and musical roles; music in school versus recreation settings; and aesthetic versus social functions of music. Kaplan challenged the binary division of musicians into professional and amateur, arguing for a more fluid and interdependent relationship between them. The lines of professional and amateur are sometimes blurred today, as programs such as *The X Factor, American Idol*, and *Dancing with the Stars* showcase the technical and artistic talent of "amateur" performers (see this volume: Smith, chapter 9; Stebbins, chapter 19; and Lashua, chapter 23).

Just as Kaplan sought to break down the oppositional juxtaposition of work and leisure, and change the attitudes associated with each, his argument can be applied to the ways in which music educators perceive formal, informal, and nonformal music education. The priorities associated with formal music education—seriousness, discipline, order, and technical proficiency—can inform music making in informal and nonformal leisure settings. Similarly, the goals of informal music education—responsiveness to individual musical needs and preferences, the presence of personal meaning and fulfillment, the development of intergenerational settings, and the nurturance of elements of play—can serve to inform music making in formal settings.

Given that Kaplan advanced and advocated both social and aesthetic functions of music to the end of his career, if he were to read some contemporary literature in music education he would likely question the absence of aesthetic functions in musical experience. The social and the aesthetic are not mutually exclusive. A sociological approach, in his view, included the language of the aesthetic. In recent years, there has been a revival of interest in the use of the term "aesthetic" in relation to musical experience, moving away from the eighteenth-century interpretation of the word, instead connecting the aesthetic to everyday life experiences, including those of music making (Väkevä 2012).

Moving Forward with Kaplan's Vision

Max Kaplan was a scholar and musician who was of his time—trained as a classical musician and schooled in functionalist theory in sociology—but in many ways his ideas and outlook were ahead of their time. His contributions span the second half of the twentieth century, an era of radical social change and technological advancement, in which social hierarchies gave way to recognition of diverse human values. Sensitive and responsive to these changes, yet loyal to his own music education, Kaplan operated from multiple vantage points, viewing art as elite and at the same time of and for all people. He pointed the way toward reconciliation of the varying sociocultural values and meanings associated with music in human life. The period between 1950 and 2000 witnessed the unpacking of assumptions in music education about musical values and what constituted "good" music. A more inclusive and democratic philosophy of music and music education began to challenge the hierarchy implicit in the aesthetic viewpoint, something that was already evident in Kaplan's writings in the 1950s. Attitudes to leisure underwent a similar philosophical upheaval to embrace notions of artistic diversity that included all people, regardless of age, social class, or cultural background.

In what ways can the music and leisure professions engage and move forward with Kaplan's vision of the arts from a social perspective? First, the systems model that he created can serve as a basis for professionals in music and leisure studies to create a framework for connecting institutions that advance musical culture. This can occur at many levels, beginning with local community, which Kaplan viewed as a natural site for developing music programs in leisure settings. Using the idea of the annual survey of Best Communities for Music Education carried out by the NAMM (National Association of Music Merchants) Foundation, one might survey all stakeholders who are engaged in music performance, instruction, production, and dissemination in a community. The goal would be to create a network of cultural brokers who dialogue about the goals of their various institutions in the context of the community at large and who create strategies for improving access and opportunity for music making in its diverse forms across the lifespan.

Second, Kaplan urged professionals in leisure and music professions to cross the disciplinary lines and lay the groundwork for the kind of scholarship that is necessary to apply a theory of music making as it relates to leisure. He modeled such border crossing and stood on many platforms and synthesized perspectives from multiple disciplines. Leisure studies, he argued, demanded the kind of interdisciplinary efforts that he witnessed in the Tanglewood Symposium (Kaplan 1978). He sought to create two-way lines of communication between leisure studies and related disciplines; for example, he recommended that music education should include a theory of leisure in its overall philosophy. As the music education profession moves forward, this directive is of primary importance as a first step in creating a framework for music making and leisure and participating in dialogue with professionals in leisure studies.

A third way in which the professions can move forward with Kaplan's vision is by returning to the questions he posed in several of his writings (for example, Kaplan 1956b, 1958) as a starting point for developing programs that engage all those with interest in music making and leisure in a community—leisure specialists and program organizers, school music teachers, professional and community musicians, community leaders, music therapists, and social workers. In such cross-disciplinary conversations, a new language will emerge to establish mutual goals and situate leisure in an overall philosophy of music making that benefits all members of the community. In the process of developing "creative fellowship," as Kaplan called collaborative work between professionals and amateurs, a clearer view would emerge of the roles of various sociomusical institutions such as K–12 schools, colleges and universities, centers of performing arts, and other centers that include music as a component of leisure, therapy, or education.

Fourth, the breakdown of binaries that limited the scope of cross-disciplinary exchange was a theme woven throughout Kaplan's writings. He wanted to blur the lines between music as work and music as leisure, the function of the music professional versus the function of the amateur in leisure settings, and the social and the aesthetic affordances of music making. His ecological view of a vibrant musical society calls for more continua than either/or approaches to music, and more open and flexible views of the affordances of music in specific contexts. Recent trends in music education and community music indicate that this blurring of dualisms is taking place—in the work of scholars who advocate amateur music making and promote pedagogies of informal, vernacular, and popular music making in school settings (for example, Green 2002, 2008; Jaffurs 2004; Regelski 2007; Thibeault 2013; Woody and Lehmann 2010).

A fifth way forward with Kaplan is through "some vigorous shake-up" (Kaplan 1963, 36) in the music curriculum that prepares leaders and teachers for music making in schools and leisure settings. This has implications for the curriculum of community music or arts programs, performance, music education, and arts administration degree programs. Kaplan challenges music professionals to look out and beyond the confines of traditional music making in the academy and to imagine the communities their leaders and teachers will enter filled with diverse music makers, media-rich music events, intergenerational learning, and music serving a variety of functions in the lives of individuals and groups.

Max Kaplan's life's work indeed leads the way in creating a framework for music making in leisure. Let his vision guide those who work to develop theories and models for music making and leisure. As the professions listen to his call, revisit the questions he posed all those years ago, and implement his ideas in communities, the vision he generously labored to enact will be realized in a twenty-first-century world, serving to expand the scope and enrich the overall quality of music making in society.

NOTE

1. As early as the 1940s, Charles Seeger addressed the issue of what music is "good for": "While it is true that musical 'good' is inherent in music itself, it is equally true that it is found also in the function the music serves" (Seeger 1941, 18). Speaking at the National Institute for Music Education in Wartime in Chicago in 1942, Seeger encouraged teachers to approach and present music as "good for something" rather than solely as a good in itself; see McCarthy (1995). In the 1990s, beginning in the forum of the MayDay Group, Thomas Regelski addressed the functions and values of music in a way similar to Seeger and Kaplan, focusing on "what music is good for" rather than "what is good music"; see Regelski (2002).

REFERENCES CITED

Choate, Robert A., and Max Kaplan. 1967. "Music in American Society: Introduction to Issues." *Music Educators Journal* 53(8): 43–51.

Cox, Gordon. 2002. "Transforming Research in Music Education History." In *Second Handbook of Research on Music Teaching and Learning*, edited by Richard Colwell and Carol Richardson, 695–706. New York: Oxford University Press and MENC.

Elliott, David J., and Marissa Silverman. 2015. *Music Matters: A Philosophy of Music Education.* 2nd edition. New York: Oxford University Press.

Froehlich, Hildegard C. 2007. *Sociology for Music Teachers: Perspectives for Practice.* Upper Saddle River, NJ: Pearson Education.

Froehlich, Hildegard C. 2015. *A Social Theory for Music Education: Symbolic Interactionism in Music Learning and Teaching.* Lewiston, NY: Edwin Mellen.

Goble, Scott J. 2005. "On Musical and Educational Habit-Taking: Pragmatism, Sociology, and Music Education." *Action, Criticism, and Theory for Music Education* 4(1): 2–17. http://act. maydaygroup.org/articles/Goble4_1.pdf.

Green, Lucy. 1988. *Music on Deaf Ears: Musical Meaning, Ideology, and Education.* Manchester: Manchester University Press.

Green, Lucy. 2002. *How Popular Musicians Learn: A Way Ahead for Music Education.* Aldershot: Ashgate.

Green, Lucy. 2008. *Music, Informal Learning and the School: A New Classroom Pedagogy.* Aldershot: Ashgate.

Higgins, Lee. 2012. *Community Music: In Theory and in Practice.* New York: Oxford University Press.

Huizinga, Johan. 1949. *Homo Ludens: A Study of the Play-Element in Culture.* Translated by Richard F. C. Hull. London: Routledge and Kegan Paul.

Jaffurs, Sheri E. 2004. "The Impact of Informal Music Learning Practices in the Classroom, or How I Learned How to Teach from a Garage Band." *International Journal of Music Education* 22(3): 189–200.

Jorgensen, Estelle R. 1997. *In Search of Music Education.* Chicago: University of Illinois Press.

Kaplan, Max. 1944. *Music in the City: A Sociological Survey of Musical Facilities and Activities in Pueblo, Colorado.* Pueblo, CO: Self-published.

Kaplan, Max. 1951. "The Musician in America: A Study of His Social Roles. Introduction to a Sociology of Music." PhD dissertation, University of Illinois.

Kaplan, Max. 1952a. *The Harmonica Band: What Does it Offer?* Bulletin No. 32. Urbana: University of Illinois Music Extension.

Kaplan, Max. 1952b. *The Jug and Bottle "Orchestra": Its Construction and Use for Recreational Music.* Bulletin No. 31. Urbana: University of Illinois Music Extension.

Kaplan, Max. 1952c. *A Theory of Recreational Music, and, Current Practices in Recreational Music in the Community.* Bulletin No. 30. Urbana: University of Illinois Music Extension.

Kaplan, Max. 1954. "The Social Role of the Amateur." *Music Educators Journal* 40(4): 26–28.

Kaplan, Max. 1955. *Music in Recreation: Social Foundations and Practices.* Champaign, IL: Stipes.

Kaplan, Max. 1956a. *Art in a Changing America: Sociology 228.* Urbana: University of Illinois Press.

Kaplan, Max. 1956b. "Music, Community and Social Change." *Music Educators Journal* 43(1): 64, 66–67.

Kaplan, Max. 1956c. "Music, Community and Social Change." *Music Educators Journal* 43(2): 47–49.

Kaplan, Max. 1960. *Leisure in America: A Social Inquiry.* New York and London: John Wiley and Sons.

Kaplan, Max. 1963. "Music Education and National Goals." *Music Educators Journal* 49(5): 33–36.

Kaplan, Max. 1966. *Foundations and Frontiers of Music Education.* New York: Holt, Rinehart, and Winston.

Kaplan, Max. 1975. *Leisure: Theory and Policy.* New York: John Wiley and Sons.

Kaplan, Max. 1978. *Leisure: Perspectives on Education and Policy.* Washington, DC: National Education Association.

Kaplan, Max. 1988. "Society, Sociology, and Music Education." In *Music in the United States: Contemporary Issues,* edited by J. Terry Gates, 3–32. Tuscaloosa and London: University of Alabama Press.

Kaplan, Max. 1990. *The Arts: A Social Perspective.* Cranbury, NJ: Associated University Presses.

Kaplan, Max. 1991. "Music Education and American Culture." In *Music in American Schools, 1838–1988,* edited by Marie McCarthy and Bruce D. Wilson, 3–9. College Park: University of Maryland Press.

Kaplan, Max, ed. 1993. *Barbershopping: Musical and Social Harmony.* Cranbury, NJ: Associated University Presses.

Kaplan, Max. 1997. "Sociology and Music Education: Issues and Connections." In *On the Sociology of Music Education,* edited by Roger Rideout, 55–64. Norman: University of Oklahoma Press.

Kaplan, Max. 1998. *One Life: The Free Academic.* Cranbury, NJ: Associated University Presses.

Kaplan, Max, and Philip Bosserman, eds. 1971. *Technology, Human Values, and Leisure.* Nashville, TN, and New York: Abingdon Press.

Kelly, Steven N. 2008. *Teaching Music in American Society: A Social and Cultural Understanding of Music Education.* New York: Routledge.

Krikun, Andrew. 2010. "Community Music during the New Deal: The Contributions of Willem Van de Wall and Max Kaplan." *International Journal of Community Music* 3: 165–174.

Lave, Jean, and Étienne Wenger. 1991. *Situated Learning: Legitimate Peripheral Participation.* Cambridge: Cambridge University Press.

MacDonald, Raymond A. R., David J. Hargreaves, and Dorothy Miell, eds. 2002. *Musical Identities.* Oxford: Oxford University Press.

Madura Ward-Steinman, Patrice, ed., 2011. *Advances in Social-Psychology and Music Education Research.* Sempre Studies in the Psychology of Music. Farnham: Ashgate.

McCarthy, Marie. 1995. "On 'American Music for American Children': The Contribution of Charles L. Seeger." *Journal of Research in Music Education* 43(4): 270–287.

McCarthy, Marie. 2000. "Expanding the Foundations and Frontiers of Music Education: Max Kaplan's Perspective on the Social Roles of the Music Educator." In *On the Sociology of Music Education II,* edited by Roger R. Rideout and Stephen J. Paul, 142–152. Norman: University of Oklahoma Press.

McCarthy, Marie. 2002. "Introduction: Social and Cultural Contexts of Music Teaching and Learning." In *Second Handbook of Research on Music Teaching and Learning,* edited by Richard Colwell and Carol Richardson, 563–565. New York: Oxford University Press and Music Educators National Conference.

Music Educators National Conference. 1958. *Music Education in a Changing World: Part II of Report for Music in American Life Commission VIII, Music in the Community*. Max Kaplan, chairman. Washington, DC: Music Educators National Conference.

National Guild of Community Schools. 1966. *National Guild of Community Music Schools: Observations and Recommendations*. Englewood Cliffs, NJ: National Guild of Schools of the Arts.

Philpott, Chris, and Gary Spruce, eds. 2012. *Debates in Music Teaching*. New York: Routledge.

Regelski, Thomas A. 2002. "Musical Values and the Value of Music Education." *Philosophy of Music Education Review* 10(1): 49–55.

Regelski, Thomas A. 2004. "Social Theory, and Music and Music Education as Praxis." *Action, Criticism, and Theory for Music Education* 3(3): 2–42. http://act.maydaygroup.org/articles/Regelski3_3.pdf.

Regelski, Thomas A. 2007. "Amateuring in Music and Its Rivals." *Action, Criticism, and Theory for Music Education* (6)3: 22–50. http://act.maydaygroup.org/articles/Regelski6_3.pdf.

Rideout, Roger, ed. 1997. *On The Sociology of Music Education*. Norman: University of Oklahoma Press.

Saxon, Wolfgang. 1998. "Max Kaplan, 87, a Musician and Scholar in Art of Leisure." http://www.nytimes.com/1998/08/09/nyregion/max-kaplan-87-a-musician-and-scholar-in-art-of-leisure.html.

Seeger, Charles. 1941. "Inter-American Relations in the Field of Music: Some Basic Considerations." *Music Educators Journal* 27(5): 17–18, 64–65.

Thibeault, Matthew D. 2013. *The Participatory Field as an Alternative to Musical Specialization*. http://hdl.handle.net/2142/45872.

Väkevä, Lauri. 2012. "Philosophy of Music Education as Art of Life: A Deweyan View." In *The Oxford Handbook of Philosophy in Music Education*, edited by Wayne Bowman and Ana Lucia Frega, 86–110. New York: Oxford University Press.

Veblen, Kari K., Stephen J. Messenger, Marissa Silverman, and David J. Elliott, eds. 2013. *Community Music Today*. Lanham, MD: Rowman and Littlefield.

Waldron, Janice. 2011. "Locating Narratives in Postmodern Spaces: A Cyber Ethnographic Field Study of Informal Music Learning in Online Community." *Action, Criticism, and Theory for Music Education* 10(2): 32–60. http://act.maydaygroup.org/articles/Waldron10_2.pdf.

Waldron, Janice. 2013. "YouTube, Fanvids, Forums, Vlogs and Blogs: Informal Music Learning in a Convergent On- and Offline Music Community." *International Journal of Music Education* 31(1): 91–105.

Wenger, Étienne. 1998. *Communities of Practice: Learning, Meaning, and Identity*. Cambridge: Cambridge University Press.

Woody, Robert H., and Andreas C. Lehmann. 2010. "Student Musicians' Ear Playing Ability as a Function of Vernacular Music Experiences." *Journal of Research in Music Education* 58(2): 101–115.

CHAPTER 3

WELL-BEING AND MUSIC LEISURE ACTIVITIES THROUGH THE LIFESPAN

A Psychological Perspective

SUSAN HALLAM, ANDREA CREECH,
AND MARIA VARVARIGOU

INTRODUCTION

LISTENING to music is a highly valued leisure activity for many people (Rentfrow and Gosling 2003). Music is now available in a wide variety of formats, not only through radio and recordings, but also through smart phones and computers that can stream music on demand. These technologies have changed the way that people are able to interact with music (Nill and Geipel 2010), making music easily accessible at any time and in a wide variety of contexts (Heye and Lamont 2010; Juslin et al. 2008). Increasingly, individuals are able to control what, when, and how they listen to music. This has led to complex patterns of everyday music usage and storage, resulting in the highly personalized categorization of music (Greasley and Lamont 2006). Overall, digital music has enabled the development of greater interactivity between user, device, and music (Kibby 2009).

Alongside the increased availability of music for listening, there are also greater opportunities for actively making music. For example, many more people of all ages in the U.K. learn to play instruments or sing and participate in musical groups than was the case ten years ago, although the extent of and types of opportunity vary and participation may depend on financial resources, parental support, and other factors (e.g., ABRSM 2014). There is extensive evidence of the key role that music plays in people's lives (Lamont, Greasley, and Sloboda 2016). Music can generate feelings of well-being, can facilitate working through difficult emotions, and is frequently linked to spirituality (Hays and Minchiello 2005; Juslin and Sloboda 2010). It is widely used for exploring and regulating emotions and moods (Saarikallio 2011; Shifriss and Bodner 2014), and can be effective in inducing positive affective states (North, Hargreaves, and Hargreaves 2004) and also for coping with negative moods and emotions (Miranda and Claes 2009; Shifriss and Bodner 2014). The most common activity for mood regulation is listening to music (Saarikallio and Erkkilä 2007). Even adolescents who play an instrument report that the best activity for mood regulation is listening to music alone (Saarikallio 2006).

Music as it is engaged with in leisure time also contributes to how an individual defines themselves, that is, their identity (Hargreaves, Miell, and MacDonald 2002). It is seen to represent personality and is used in impression management and also to judge the characteristics of others (Krause and Hargreaves 2012). In the digital world this is achieved by controlling what music is shared with others and what is uploaded into personal collections (Voida, Grinter, and Ducheneaut 2006).

THE CONCEPT OF LEISURE

The concept of leisure is not new. As long ago as the fourth century BC, Aristotle acknowledged that engagement in music—by which he referred to an active and embodied experience of melody, drama, poetry, and dance—as leisure was an important element of the life of Athenian citizens. He conceived of such artistic experiences as noble uses of leisure time and essential in supporting the private happiness of citizens (Koeplin 2009; Solmsen 1964; Stamou 2002). In contrast, Plato saw music as a means for inculcating the citizen's moral character, what he called *ethos*, and he argued for its necessity in a citizen's education. Aristotle took an expanded view, considering music to fulfill four functions, including amusement, making the best use of free time, a moral function (*ethos*), and purgation, cleansing the soul. Music as amusement was seen as a "medicine for the ills of work" (Koeplin 2009, 120). Music as "employment of leisure" could contribute to practical wisdom. Solmsen (1964, 215) reminds us, however, that although Aristotle encouraged some practicing of music, he made it clear that "a person of liberal education should not aim at the degree of proficiency attained by professional musicians."

More recently, Kaplan (1960; see also McCarthy, this volume, chapter 2) noted that leisure has elements of play, pleasantness, and freedom of choice, and spans a range of activities from trivial to important, while Stebbins (2010) distinguished between casual leisure—which includes primarily social interactions and self-gratification behaviors which are "fun"—and serious leisure, which typically requires significant effort. According to Stebbins there are six distinguishing qualities of *serious leisure*: (1) the need to persevere with an activity, to stick "with it through thick and thin"; (2) finding a career in the serious leisure role; (3) significant personal effort "based on specially acquired knowledge, training, experience, or skill, and indeed, all four at a time"; (4) durable benefits, including self-development, self-expression, self-enrichment, developing "possible selves," social interaction, belonging, "lasting physical products of the activity"; (5) a unique ethos that stems from the social engagements and interactions among participants who pursue their free time interests; and (6) a person's strong identification with their chosen pursuit (Stebbins 2010, 20–21).

For Stebbins (1992, 5), serious leisure participants fall into three groups: *amateurs*, *hobbyists*, and *volunteers*. Amateurs are situated in a system of social relationships, which he describes as Professional-Amateur-Public (PAP) (10). Within this system, amateurs and professionals share similar expectations and rely on the general public to appreciate and support their activities. Hobbyists are similarly dedicated but there are no professional counterparts. Typically, their activities are undertaken alone. Stebbins also recognizes that some individuals participate in a leisure activity for a short time or to a limited degree; he calls these *dabblers* or *dilettantes*. Gates (1991) also identifies *recreationists*, who expend more time and effort than dabblers.

How do these various categories relate to the field of music? Amateur adult musicians are not motivated by financial rewards and the need to earn a living. While some engage with music for personal amusement, for others it constitutes a serious leisure activity, and many of the activities that they engage with are indistinguishable from those undertaken by professional musicians (Gates 1991). Music becomes a key element of their identity (Pitts 2005; Taylor 2010; Taylor and Hallam 2008), and they invest much time and energy in it (Finnegan 1997). The term *semiprofessional* has been coined to describe musicians whose skills are equivalent to those of full-time professionals and who carry out professional work but also have other employment (Musicians Union 2015). With many musicians now having portfolio careers, the distinction between professional and semiprofessional is likely to become even more blurred.

When individuals take up active music making for the first time their motivations may vary. Some children and young people may approach it as dabblers or dilettantes with no great commitment, which will influence the extent to which they practice, their musical development, and the benefits that they may derive from it. In contrast, others may be totally committed and see their musical future in terms of aspiring to amateur or professional status (Hallam et al. 2015). The terms *hobbyist* (Stebbins 1992) or *enthusiast* (Keown 2015) seem to best describe those whose focus is on listening and who have large collections of music, invest considerable time in learning about and adding to their collections, and ensuring that the equipment that they have is of high quality. Some may be committed concert or festival goers who typically will have higher levels of musical experience and rate music as more important in their lives than nonattenders. Some will be less committed listeners (recreationists), for whom music is important but not a major life focus.

Relatively little attention has been given to understanding the musical behaviors and responses of music enthusiasts and sound recording collectors (Keown 2015). They may actively participate in collecting sound recording albums to fulfill multiple motivational desires, including love of music, obsessive-compulsive behavior, accumulation and completism, selectivity and discrimination, and self-education and scholarship (Shuker 2004). Lacher and Mizerski (1994) propose three constructs to describe their behavior: *affective responses, experiential responses* (the ability to be "swept up" in the music), and the *need to reexperience the music*. Other influential factors include *perceived knowledge* (an illusion of knowing), *objective knowledge* (knowing based on data-supported information), *opinion leadership* (allowing other individuals' opinions to influence purchasing behaviors), and *enduring involvement* (the individual relates to a product in support of self-image). These are better predictors of motivation to purchase particular recordings than demographic variables such as age, social class, and marital status (Flynn, Eastman, and Newell 1995), although record collecting in general has been identified as a male characteristic (Straw 1997). Technological developments have led to further distinctions in terms of *technology users* and *technology consumers*, and different downloading profiles (*occasional downloaders, online listeners, explorer/pioneers, curious,* and *duplicators*) (Molteni and Ordanini 2003).

Related to the concept of enthusiasts is that of *fandom*, which has been conceptualized as a "psychological symptom of a presumed social dysfunction" (Jenson 1992, 9) and also as a logical consumer strategy focusing on pleasure and identity development in association with an identifiable capital (Stevens 2010). Fandom also is related to seeking out interpersonal relationships with other music "fans" (Duffett 2013). Whatever the musical activity, clearly the level of commitment and time spent engaging with music will impact on the benefits that can be derived from it (see Hallam 2015 for a review).

SUBJECTIVE WELL-BEING

The concept of subjective well-being refers to how people experience the quality of their lives, and includes both emotional reactions (moods and emotions) and cognitive evaluations of satisfaction with general and specific areas of life (Diener 1984; Diener et al. 1999).

A *needs satisfaction* approach refers to subjective well-being as reflecting the extent to which basic and universal human needs are met. Several researchers have proposed models of human psychological needs. Self-determination theory, for example, conceptualizes human basic needs as *competence, autonomy,* and *relatedness.* These must be satisfied in a sustained fashion in order for humans to function optimally as they strive for *effectiveness, connectedness,* and *coherence* (Deci and Ryan 2000). A variation on this is proposed by Steverink and Lindenberg (2006), who suggest a model that comprises *affection, behavioural confirmation,* and *status.* Affection is fulfilled when individuals feel liked, loved, trusted, accepted, and empathized with within relationships. Behavioral confirmation refers to the feeling of doing things well, contributing to a common goal, and playing a useful part in a functional group, while status is fulfilled when individuals are treated with respect and have skills or qualities that are recognized, and when they are independent and autonomous.

The relationship of subjective well-being to happiness is explored by Peterson, Park, and Seligman (2013). Three orientations are identified, including the *pursuit of pleasure, meaning* (becoming all that one can be), and *engagement* (the experience of losing oneself in deeply absorbing activity). The authors argue that the three orientations are distinct and individually related to life satisfaction, while also acknowledging that pleasure, meaning, and engagement may at times overlap (although not necessarily so). According to the authors, a "full life" may be one where all three orientations are met, although their own research has suggested that orientations to engagement and meaning are the strongest predictors of life satisfaction.

Subjective well-being can be measured through observation, self-report, or multi-item scales that focus on cognitive, emotional, and motivational attitudes toward life (Daatland 2005). There is debate as to whether the elements of well-being are stable across time and culture. Utilitarian perspectives presuppose that quality of life is universal, while the existential approach suggests that quality of life is self-determined, pluralistic, and diverse in nature; it is argued that the former approach does not take account of differences between social groups and societies (Allison, Locker, and Feine 1997; Hornquist 1990). Basic needs such as food, shelter, and warmth, as set out in Maslow's (1954) widely known model representing a "hierarchy of needs," are not contentious. However, other essential needs such as *autonomy* and *self-realization* are more difficult to define and to measure. Nevertheless, others have argued in favor of the idea that human needs "are universal and knowable, and the satisfiers necessary to meet them are dynamic and open ended" (Doyal and Gough 1991, 14). As well-being is only weakly related to demographic variables such as age, sex, marital status, and ethnicity (Andrews and Robinson 1991), there do seem to be at least some common characteristics which apply across different populations. The issue to be considered in this chapter is whether music as serious leisure or as a hobby can contribute to enhancing and maintaining well-being, potentially functioning as a vehicle through which basic needs such as those noted above may be met.

CAN MUSIC PROMOTE WELL-BEING?

The benefits of active engagement with music in relation to psychological well-being across the lifespan are increasingly well documented (Rickard and McFerran 2012). Positive associations between music engagement and health and well-being are evident in adolescents (e.g., Miranda and Gaudreau 2011), adults (Greasley and Lamont 2006; Saarikallio 2011), and the elderly (e.g. Creech et al. 2014b; Hallam et al. 2014; Hays and Minichiello 2005; Laukka 2007). Music is increasingly being recognized for its beneficial effects on physical health and well-being (e.g., Hanser 2010; MacDonald, Kreutz, and Mitchell 2012; Pelletier 2004). Some of these benefits are accrued through listening, others through active engagement with making music.

Listening to Music

An idealized view of musical listening is that it is a focused activity undertaken solely for the purpose of deepening understanding and appreciation of the music. In practice, most listening takes place alongside other activities, including those relating to travel, studying, and physical activity such as relaxation and taking exercise (Lamont, Greasley, and Sloboda 2016). Listening alongside these activities does not necessarily preclude listening with full attention (Herbert 2012), but it does raise the question of whether listening in this way constitutes a leisure activity. For the purposes of this chapter, where music is being used as a means of changing moods and emotions, listening will be considered as a leisure activity even when it might be accompanied by other activities.

There is an ever-increasing body of research demonstrating that music is used by many people to manage and regulate moods, emotions, and arousal levels, and to reminisce (e.g. DeNora 1999; Laiho 2004; Lamont, Greasley, and 2016; Saarikallio 2011; Schäfer et al. 2013). This research is compatible with Aristotle's conception of the use of music for purgation. Music can be used to maintain a positive mood, for revival, to create strong sensations, as a diversion, as discharge, for mental work, for solace, and for psyching up (Saarikallio 2011). Some people, for a range of reasons, choose to listen to sad music (Garrido and Schubert 2011; Tahlier, Miron, and Rauscher 2013; Van den Tol and Edwards 2014). Reminiscence is also a frequent function of self-chosen music listening, which is particularly prevalent in older adults (Hays and Minichiello 2005; Juslin and Laukka 2004), although it is also found in young people (Tolfree and Hallam, forthcoming). Box 3.1 provides an example of how young people in two age groups use music in their lives also taking account of gender differences.

Young people in the Western world spend a great deal of their time listening to music. There has been much less research globally, although this is a developing area. Miranda et al. (2015), focusing on cultural differences, argue that music can be meaningful in similar and different ways for adolescents living in diverse socio-cultural contexts, in which local and global cultures mix and hybridize (Larson, Wilson, and Richman 2009). Also taking a cross-cultural perspective, Boer and colleagues (Boer and Fischer 2012; Boer et al. 2012) argue that music functions can be organized along two axes—a *contemplation* or *affective* dimension (individual), and an *intrapersonal, interpersonal/social* dimension (collectivism). Adolescents in more collectivist societies use music to convey cultural identity more than those in individualistic societies. The research of Boer and colleagues in six countries (Germany, Kenya, Mexico, New Zealand, Philippines, and Turkey) revealed ten functions of music listening in late adolescence: *as background, focused listening, for venting, related to emotions, for dancing, related to friendship or family, politics, values,* and *cultural identity* (Boer et al. 2012). Research in seven countries revealed seven functions: *music in the background, memories through music, music as diversion, emotional experiences from music, self-regulation through music, music as a reflection of the self,* and *social bonding* (Boer and Fischer 2012). Overall, these functions are remarkably similar to those described by older listeners.

Box 3.1 Children and Adolescents' Use of Music

Tolfree and Hallam (forthcoming) interviewed thirty-eight children, divided into two age groups—nine to twelve and thirteen to seventeen—to establish the role of music in their everyday lives. Four main themes emerged from the data: emotions and moods, identity and friendship, playing an instrument, and homework. The largest category related to emotions and moods, and demonstrated how these young people used music to change moods, to relax, to reminisce, or for enjoyment. Almost all of the boys and the older girls used music to express anger. It provided a means of acceptable rebelliousness when they were angry with their parents or others in their family. Typically, they would go to their room and play music very loudly:

> If I had an argument with my mum or family I'd put on music to annoy then. . . . put it on really loud to let them know I'm annoyed. (Boy aged 16)

> It has the same effect as throwing something or stamping or screaming but slightly less destructive—a more sociable way of releasing my anger. (Girl aged 15)

Typically, they listened to music when angry rather than playing their instrument.

> If you're in a really bad mood you might feel tempted to chuck your instrument on the floor—I don't touch it when I'm in a bad mood. I wouldn't ever abuse it when I'm angry—I wouldn't bash a musical instrument. (Boy aged 10)

Relatively few used music to help them to reduce their anger. About half of the boys and a third of the girls listened to music to reinforce sadness:

> When you're sad it makes you think, "God, I've got this wrong and this wrong," but even though I know it'll make me feel sad if I'm unhappy, I'll get a depressing CD or some music that'll make me sad and listen to it (Boy aged 17)

Although none of the younger participants did so, about a third of the older boys and almost half of the older girls reported using music for reminiscence:

> Old pop music from when we were young . . . it's really happy music . . . . it brings out lots of memories for me . . . we remember all the things we did when we listened to that music . . . if it's music from when I was quite little it makes me feel really happy . . . remembering times when I was having a good time. (Girl aged 17)

Almost all of the participants reported using music to change their moods and to relax:

> It's really fun . . . it's really good . . . I use them (CDs) for pleasure . . . it really gives me a buzz . . . when I get up in the morning I normally am pretty grumpy and if I hear Courtney Pine playing downstairs I listen to it and cheer up because it sounds so satisfying. It's just music I'm into and it cheers me up. (Boy, aged 13)

Two-fifths of the younger boys and about half of the older boys reported using music to induce a positive mood. The proportions were lower for the girls (about a third for the younger girls and about a fifth for the older girls). About half of the younger boys used music for relaxation with smaller proportions for the other groups. The older boys were most likely to use music as a distraction from problems. The older girls and all of the boys were more likely than the younger girls to listen to music when bored. Listening when bored was more common than playing their instrument.

(continued)

Box 3.1 Continued

Very few of the young people reported learning to play an instrument to be with their friends, although the older boys and girls reported listening to music with friends. Having a sense of achievement from playing an instrument was reported by all age groups, although it was most prevalent among the younger boys and the older girls, who also expressed taking pride in playing well more frequently than the other groups:

> I get a lot out of playing the drums . . . if it doesn't sound good I'll make it better . . . try to make it ten times better. (Boy aged 12)

> If I play a piece that I'm good at, that sounds really good, then it cheers me up . . . it makes me feel quite proud, playing music that I'm good at. (Girl aged 17)

All age groups reported frustration when they did not achieve. This was mentioned least by the older boys:

> When the trombone was cold . . . playing a piece you'd play a wrong note . . . that made me frustrated . . . it doesn't sound right. (Boy, aged 12)

> It can make me feel frustrated if I haven't played for a long time . . . if I can't remember how to do a certain thing that'll annoy me. (Girl aged 16)

The older boys indicated that music aided concentration when they were doing homework. They were the only group to mention this. The younger boys and the older girls indicated that music hindered concentration. The boys were also most likely to identify when music was helpful to homework tasks or not and the kind of music:

> For general homework, I'd have classical . . . I wouldn't have pop because I'd be tempted to listen to the pop and not do any homework . . . it's more brain catching . . . I can switch off more to classical music. When I read I don't usually have music . . . it takes your brain away from the reading. (Boy aged 10)

Hays and Minichiello (2005) carried out interviews with fifty-two older Australians exploring the role of music in their lives. These interviewees reported being involved with music for much of the time, listening, making music, or volunteering, for instance working in community radio as broadcasters and programmers, in music administration and concert development, or teaching. When they chose to listen, perform, or compose music, it became an expression of their individuality and a way of defining themselves. Listening to particular music led to the recall of events and experiences in their lives along with the emotions associated with those experiences. Music provided ways for them to maintain positive self-esteem, to feel competent and independent, avoid feelings of isolation or loneliness, to be distracted from health problems, to feel uplifted physically and psychologically, and feel rejuvenated. They used music as an accompaniment to their daily activities and reported feeling "more competent" and motivated. When faced with challenging tasks, music provided distraction but also support. Music reduced anxiety, stress levels, and increased the threshold for pain endurance. The participants indicated that they felt more "whole," more "in tune," and more "competent" when they engaged with music. Some spoke of music providing them with a sense of "inner happiness," "inner contentment," and "inner peace." Music had a therapeutic value and had the potential to make them feel more positive about life. They spoke of using music to make them feel more cheerful, more hopeful, more contented, and more relaxed and peaceful. They talked of being moved to tears and listening to music for the sheer joy and beauty of the experience. Music was reported to be able to calm, excite, thrill, and entertain in ways not easily accessible through other means. For some, it was an addiction. It enabled them to escape reality and stimulate the imagination, the sense of beauty connecting them with feelings of spirituality. For some, this was closely associated with a particular religious perspective, while for others it was understood as a personal feeling of being in the world. Overall, there were many perceived benefits, all of which, in different ways, contributed to self-assessed well-being.

Not all the effects of listening to music are positive. Adolescents may use music as a distraction and to avoid thinking about problems (Saarikallio and Erkkilä 2007). This can have a negative impact on their psychological adjustment (Hutchinson, Baldwin, and Oh 2006). Listening to music that explores negative themes—for instance distress, suicide, or death—can increase depressive symptoms and suicidal thoughts, but at the same time it could be argued that people with suicidal tendencies or depression might be drawn to particular kinds of music (Martin, Clarke, and Pearce 1993; Scheel and Westefeld 1999). These negative outcomes can be exacerbated through interactions with like-minded peers through music subcultures.

Two of the functions of music for adolescents are identity formation and communication of those identities. Musical preferences are used for self-identifying as members of specific peer groups and musical subcultures (Miranda and Claes 2009; North and Hargreaves 2008; Rentfrow and Gosling 2006), creating social identities and membership of an in-group (Bakagiannis and Tarrant 2006; Hargreaves, North, and Tarrant 2006; Rentfrow, McDonald, and Oldmeadow 2009), including the family unit (Morgan, MacDonald, and Pitts 2014). Adolescents who belong to minority ethnic groups often use music as a means of developing their ethnic identity and resilience (Buffam 2011; Lundström 2009; Schweigman et al. 2011; Travis and Bowman 2012). However, Karlsen (2013) stressed that the issue of identity and "homeland" music listening among immigrant adolescents, especially within a school context, is complex and delicate, as some might choose not to be associated with their homeland music as a means of protecting their "right to self-definition" (170) and to thwart cultural exclusion. Adolescents also use music preferences to acquire valid and reliable information about others (Rentfrow and Gosling 2006). Young people tend to make friends with those with similar musical tastes (Lewis, Gonzalez, and Kaufman 2012; Selfhout et al. 2009).

There are differences in the extent to which listeners are aware of how music affects them. More engaged listeners are acutely aware of how music can change as well as fit their moods (Greasley and Lamont 2011). Lamont and Webb (2010) describe "squirrel" listeners who seem better able to access and implement musical mood regulation strategies, choosing music to fit any given situation and their own physical, psychological, and social needs. This has been described as lay therapeutic practice by Batt-Rawden and DeNora (2005). Saarikallio (2011) found that older people were more aware of how music fits particular moods and situations, and women are more likely to use music to regulate emotions and moods than men (Sloboda 1999).

The extent to which people are able to control the type of music they are listening to is crucial in terms of its benefits (Krause, North, and Hewitt 2015). This is particularly important when music is being used to reduce anxiety or pain (Bernatzky et al. 2012; Mitchell and MacDonald 2012). When individuals are exposed to music that they do not like in contexts where they have no control, they may remove themselves from the situation. If that is not possible the music can cause extreme distress.

Attending Live Musical Events

Those who attend live music performances tend to have a higher level of musical experience and rate music as more important in their lives than nonattenders (Pitts and Burland 2013). Attending a live music event suggests a greater level of commitment than listening to recorded music. The main motives for attending live events include hearing a particular artist or style, learning about new music, affirming or challenging existing musical tastes, and personal and social reasons, such as engaging in social interaction and being part of a community (Pitts and Burland 2013; Pitts and Spencer 2008).

Strong experiences of music most commonly occur in live settings (Gabrielsson [2008] 2011; Lamont 2011). Experiences are enhanced if the performers appear to be enjoying the experience and if they interact with the audience (Brand et al. 2012; Pitts and Burland 2013; Pitts and Spencer 2008; Radbourne, Glow, and Johanson 2013). Physical proximity between performers and audience can support this (Brand et al. 2012). The quality of the experience is also influenced by audience membership. Interactions between audience members and between the audience and performers transform the experience from a passive to an active one (Dobson and Sloboda 2014). New technology has enabled members of particular fan communities to upload set lists and photos to online forums and also use Twitter, which helps nonattending fans to feel involved (Bennett 2012).

Music festivals offer unique opportunities for engagement with music. The excitement of physical proximity to the performers, social interaction with other attendees, and the music itself contribute to the experience (Oakes 2003; Paleo and Wijnberg 2006; Pitts 2005). Engagement with music in a festival context can contribute to the creation of a sense of community, providing opportunities to engage in social activities (Frith 1996; Gibson and Connell 2005). It also contributes to the development of identity (Karlsen and Brändström 2008; Matheson 2005), although there can be negative outcomes and risks relating to the use of alcohol or drugs, overcrowding, mob behavior, and other public health issues (Earl et al. 2004).

Packer and Ballantyne (2010) established that a sense of connection between participants and a separation from everyday life distinguished festivals from other musical experiences, providing a sense of disconnection that prompted festival attendees to reflect on their lives and their understanding of themselves. They reported benefits in terms of enhanced interpersonal relationships, a greater sense of belonging, being valued, a deeper understanding of self and emotions, enhanced self-perceptions, confidence, mastery, purpose in life, a greater sense of agency, better strategies for coping with stress, a sense of making a contribution, and being more hopeful. These benefits reflect those reported by those engaged in making music.

Actively Making Music

Music constitutes a serious leisure activity for some amateur musicians, sharing many characteristics with the work of professional musicians, while for others it is merely a hobby engaged with for personal amusement (Gates 1991). Reported reasons for participation in active music making include a love of music, the desire to develop skills and respond to challenge and opportunities to meet with like-minded others. Musical activities also provide pleasure, relaxation, and an opportunity for self-expression (Cooper 2001; Taylor and Hallam 2008).

Taylor (2010) argues that amateur musicians seek affirmation, validation, and verification of their musical selves as part of a community of practice in a similar manner to their professional counterparts. However, for amateurs this is less well defined and they strive to attain a group affiliation based on a cultural ideal of musical competence. In Taylor's research this came in part through participating in a master class as part of broader music club activities. Rewarding membership of a community of practice can also develop through group lessons (Wristen 2006), where mastering new repertoire in the company of others can facilitate the enhancement of self-confidence (Coffman and Adamek 2001).

Pitts (2005) also found that musical participation is a potential source of confirmation and confidence, providing opportunities to demonstrate existing skills and acquire new ones. Music can give a structure to life and offers opportunities to perform with others, develop friendships, engage in social interaction, get relief from family and work pressures, and provide spiritual fulfillment and pleasure. It can also promote prosocial behavior, leading to feelings of belonging, social adjustment, trust, and co-operation (Anshel and Kipper 1988; Odena 2010). Box 3.2 sets out the example of an intergenerational community opera project, where an "unexpected magic" experienced in the intergenerational music making was reported by participants, aged fourteen to eighty.

A wide range of benefits has been established for singing. In a study of young people who were members of a university choir, Clift and Hancox (2001) identified six dimensions associated with the benefits of singing: *well-being and relaxation, benefits for breathing and posture, social benefits, spiritual benefits, emotional benefits*, and *benefits for heart and immune system*. Reviews of the research have identified benefits in terms of: physical relaxation and release of physical tension; emotional release and reduction of feelings of stress; a sense of happiness, positive mood, joy, elation, and feeling high; a sense of greater personal, emotional, and physical well-being; an increased sense of arousal and energy; stimulation of cognitive capacities—attention, concentration, memory, and learning; an increased sense of self-confidence and self-esteem; a sense of therapeutic benefit in relation to longstanding psychological and social problems; a

Box 3.2 Intergenerational Community Music Making: The Unexpected Magic

IMAGO was a community opera commissioned in the U.K. by Glyndebourne Opera Education Department in partnership with Scottish Opera. The opera premiered at Glyndebourne in March 2013, following a rehearsal period of five months. The project aimed to provide an inspirational experience for participants and audiences, to provide intergenerational musical experiences, to engage people from diverse backgrounds, and to nurture the talent and skills of community and professional singers and instrumentalists.

A cornerstone of the project was the juxtaposition of three choruses: Youth, Adult and Elders. This intergenerational chorus, drawn from the local community, worked alongside professional singers and amateur soloists. In the orchestra, young musicians from the community were mentored by professionals and sat side by side with them in the orchestra pit. The project took place in the extraordinary context of Glyndebourne Opera House, a center of international artistic excellence set in the heart of rural East Sussex, in the U.K. Glyndebourne's full professional resources, including the education and creative teams, the technical and stage management team, as well as box office and marketing and communications teams, supported the project.

An evaluation of the project used mixed methods in order to capture a rich picture of personal, social, and musical processes and outcomes experienced by participants. The evaluation involved contributions from community participants, amateur soloists, professional soloists, the creative team, the Glyndebourne education team, and audience members.

IMAGO was found to provide a rich context where personal and social well-being was nurtured. A strong sense of "belongingness" and social cohesion evolved through working as a team toward a shared goal. Equally, individuals took control of their own learning, taking personal responsibility with regard to the commitment, and investing considerable time and resources in learning their individual parts. The whole project, while challenging at times and certainly demanding on a number of levels, was also a highly pleasurable one; participants in all sectors of the IMAGO company reported high levels of enjoyment, fun, and pleasure. Finally, the project offered a context where participants, community, and professionals alike were supported in developing to their full personal and artistic potential. Some exceeded their own expectations, and all achieved remarkable things (Creech 2014).

> Coming in and singing this funky music, which is contemporary and relevant . . . the different strands about the use of technology and internet and gaming . . . seem very relevant, not only to the older generations, but to the young people. It's so wonderful to be involved in the community. . . . All ages . . . everybody loves singing it. Very special. (IMAGO participants)

sense of exercising systems of the body through the physical exertion involved, especially the lungs; a sense of disciplining the skeletal-muscular system through the adoption of good posture; and being engaged in a valued, meaningful, worthwhile activity that gives a sense of purpose and motivation (e.g., Clift 2012; Clift et al 2008; Stacey, Brittain, and Kerr 2002).

People from a range of different backgrounds can experience benefits to their emotional and physical well-being from making music, developing an increased sense of self-worth, enhanced social skills, and wider social networks (Judd and Pooley 2014). Bailey and Davidson (2002, 2003, 2005) found benefits for homeless and marginalized individuals. People with chronic mental health problems, physical disabilities, and intellectual disabilities have also been found to benefit in terms of *personal impact* (positive emotions, emotional regulation, spiritual experience, self-perception, finding a voice), *social impact* (connectedness within the choir, connection with audience, social functioning), and *functional outcomes* (health benefits, employment capacity, and routine) (Dingle et al. 2012).

Older people engaged in music making have been found to experience fewer health issues, fewer falls, fewer doctor's visits, and less use of medication than control groups (Cohen et al. 2006, 2007), and experience overall improvements in quality of life (Hillman 2002). They also have lower mortality rates (Bygren et al. 1996). Furthermore, there is evidence that the immune system can be enhanced after singing (Beck et al. 2006; Kreutz et al. 2004; Kuhn 2002), although studies on the impact of lung function are mixed (see Clift 2012).

For older people, participation in a wide range of musical activities provides a source of enhanced social cohesion, enjoyment, personal development, and empowerment, supporting group identity, collaborative learning, friendship, social support, a sense of belonging, enhanced subjective well-being, and access to new social roles and relationships (Allison 2008; Coffman 2002; Coffman and Adamek 2001; Langston 2011; Langston and Barrett 2008; Lehmberg and Fung 2010; Sixsmith and Gibson 2007; Southcott 2009; Wood 2010). Music making contributes to psychological well-being, alleviating loneliness and supporting older people in coping with the challenges of aging, providing opportunities for progression and enjoyment, and adding meaning to life (Forssen 2007; Hays and Minichiello 2005; Lehmberg and Fung 2010; Saarikallio 2011). It can provide a sense of contentment, satisfaction, and peace (Hays and Minichiello 2005), reduce anxiety and depression, foster positive moods and emotions, and reduce the decline in subjective well-being often found in older people (Lally 2009; Morrison and Clift 2012; Sandgren 2009). Box 3.3 sets out a detailed example of a recent study— the Music for Life Project.

To be classed as "leisure," an activity must be voluntary. For children and young people this excludes musical activity undertaken as part of the school curriculum. However, there is evidence that active music making in school time can have beneficial effects on social cohesion, team working, feelings of social inclusion, co-operation, empathy, and psychological well-being, promoting confidence and enhanced self-esteem (for a review see Hallam 2015).

Classifying young musicians as amateurs, hobbyists, dabblers, dilettantes, or recreationists is problematic, as their status may change over time as their skills develop. Hallam et al. (2015) found that as musical expertise developed in those participating in extracurricular instrumental or vocal lessons, music became an integral part of their identity. This impacted on the extent to which they reported wanting to become a professional musician or be engaged in music making throughout their lifespan. As the level of commitment increased, the need for support and social affirmation tended to

Box 3.3 The Music for Life Project

The Music for Life Project aimed to explore the ways in which participating in creative music making could enhance the lives of older people through its influence on their social, emotional, and cognitive well-being, while also examining the specific process through which any such impact occurred (Creech et al. 2014b). Three case study sites in the U.K. acted as partners in the initial research: The Sage, Gateshead; Westminster Adult Education Service; and the Connect program at the Guildhall School of Music and Drama. The Sage, Gateshead, offered an extensive program of choirs and instrumental groups facilitated by community musicians. The Music Department of the Westminster Adult Education Service was a more formal adult learning context, offering choirs, music appreciation classes, and keyboard classes, while the Guildhall Connect program offered creative intergenerational music workshops within sheltered housing centers. Overall, the musical activities engaged with included singing in small and large groups, rock groups, and classes for guitar, ukulele, steel pans, percussion, recorder, music appreciation, and keyboard. A control group was made up of individuals attending language classes (four groups), art and craft classes, (five groups), yoga, social support (two groups), a book group, and a social club.

The research was undertaken using a variety of methods including:

- Questionnaires for participants, music ($n = 398$) and nonmusic ($n = 102$), at the beginning of the research including the CASP-12 measure of quality of life and the Basic Psychological Needs Scale (Deci and Ryan 2010);
- Questionnaires for music participants at the end of the nine-month period ($n = 143$);
- Individual interviews with music participants ($n = 30$);
- Focus group interviews with music participants (fifteen focus group interviews);
- Videos and observations of music sessions (forty-five videos, notes made of twenty-five sessions);
- Videos and observations of musical performances (three); and
- Interviews with music facilitators (twelve).

Statistical analyses showed significant differences with regard to scores on the CASP-12 and Psychological Needs measures between those participating in the musical and nonmusical groups, with consistently more positive responses from the musical groups (Hallam et al. 2014). Factor analyses using the items from the CASP-12 and the Basic Psychological Needs Scale to assess the extent of conceptual overlap between the two measures produced three factors: *purpose* (having a positive outlook on life), *lack of autonomy and control*, and *social affirmation* (positive social relationships, competence, and a sense of recognized accomplishment). Comparisons of those engaged in music making with those participating in other activities revealed statistically significant differences on all three factors, with the music groups having more positive responses. Comparisons of those in the third (fifty to seventy-five) and fourth (over seventy-five) age in the music groups revealed no differences in relation to factors relating to autonomy/control or social affirmation, although there was a deterioration in relation to sense of purpose, suggesting that the benefits of music participation supported the prevention of decline (Hallam et al. 2014).

Individual and focus group interviews with participants and facilitators revealed a range of perceived benefits of active musical engagement, including those related to

(continued)

Box 3.3 Continued

social activity, cognition, emotional and mental health, and physical health (Hallam et al. 2012b; Varvarigou, Hallam, et al. 2012). Social benefits included a sense of belonging and a sense of playing a valued and vital role within a community. Participants also noted that being a member of a musical group helped to provide a routine and structure to their daily lives, providing motivation for leaving the house and for engaging in daily individual practice. The activities were also perceived as being fun and were recognized as a vehicle for respite for carers. Cognitive benefits included improved concentration, memory, and meeting new challenges. The activities generated a sense of achievement, particularly when rehearsals culminated in musical performances, and the participants appreciated engaging in new activities. Participants also felt that they were making progress. Progression, building on previous experiences, and new learning played key roles in underpinning these benefits. Health benefits included a renewed sense of vitality and rejuvenation and improved mobility. Emotional and mental health benefits were noted by participants, including reduction in stress and alleviation of depression.

Overall, when questioned on what was special about music as opposed to other activities, the creative and expressive qualities of music were mentioned. One participant wrote a song that was well received by his group and led him to plan to continue his creative activities (Varvarigou et al. 2013). For some, music was a vehicle for redefining their identity or rediscovering a lost "possible self" (Creech et al. 2014a). Through music making, participants developed, or in some cases rekindled, strong musical identities. This was bolstered by a sense of being part of a community of musicians, performing with their professional musician facilitators, and through many hours making music and practicing.

Opportunities for performance played a major role in the perceived benefits, constituting a means of receiving position affirmation from others. For many participants, performances offered an important opportunity to "be a musician," sharing the results of their hard work with friends and relatives. Performances were opportunities for positive feedback and contributed significantly to a strong musical self-concept, although it was important that participants perceived their contribution to be valued and meaningful.

The older people from the sheltered-housing community engaged in intergenerational activities with children from local primary schools (Varvarigou, Creech, et al. 2012). This energized them, was enjoyable, and gave them an opportunity to relate to the younger generation. The intergenerational activity was an opportunity for different generations to socialize, show respect for each other, and enjoy each other's company.

decrease. At the same time, the role of music in their social lives, enjoyment of performance, and belief in their own competence increased.

Research on the benefits of playing an instrument and participating in extracurricular music groups has shown impact in terms of self-confidence and self-esteem (see Hallam 2015 for a review). However, there is mixed evidence regarding the impact of active engagement with music on self-beliefs, as this depends on whether the feedback received from others is positive. If this is not the case, then no enhancement will occur. If feedback is critical then there could be a negative impact. Students in higher education reflecting on previous and current extracurricular group music making activities have also reported benefits in terms of pride, developing a strong sense of belonging, gaining popularity and making friends with "like-minded" people, and the enhancement of social skills (Kokotsaki and Hallam 2007, 2011).

El Sistema programs and those inspired by El Sistema, some of which are extra-curricular, prioritize the psychological and physical well-being of their students. Evaluations of individual programs report strengthening children's sense of individual and group identity, of children taking pride in their accomplishments, of an enhancement in determination and persistence, and of children being better able to cope with anger and express their emotions more effectively. Children reportedly value their participation as a social activity, a way to enjoy music with others, strengthened friendships with peers, working in teams, and acquiring musical skills (Creech et al. 2016). Box 3.4 sets out a summary of findings from research concerned with participation in music programs inspired by the El Sistema philosophy, suggesting that learning and participation in these musical contexts contributed to enhanced personal and social well-being.

Box 3.4 Social, Emotional, and Cognitive Well-Being Experienced within El Sistema–Inspired Contexts

Instrumental and vocal programs inspired by El Sistema are founded on the fundamental principle that social development may be achieved through music education that is founded on inclusive ensemble work and high aspirations. The key tenets of such programs are that they should be accessible to all and should offer "immersion" in music, with daily participation in ensembles. Intensive ensemble activities are seen as a rich opportunity for nurturing positive citizenship skills, including "respect, equality, sharing, cohesion, team work, and, above all, the enhancement of listening as a major constituent of understanding and cooperation" (Majno 2012, 58).

In 2013, a review of research and evaluation relating to Sistema-inspired programs around the world was undertaken, and subsequently revised in 2016 (Creech et al. 2016). Eighty-five research and evaluation papers, representing forty-four Sistema or Sistema-inspired programs in nineteen countries, were reviewed in the original version. An additional thirty-three peer-reviewed research papers were reviewed in the revised version. There was strong support among the papers reviewed for the notion that participation in El Sistema and Sistema-inspired programs supported social, emotional, and cognitive well-being. Nearly all of the studies reviewed, representing programs in diverse cultural contexts, reported some aspect of positive personal development among children who participated in Sistema-inspired programs. Personal development was conceptualized in broad terms, with at least thirty-two different constructs mentioned:

---

1. Attention
2. Autonomy
3. Commitment
4. Concentration

5. Confidence/self-efficacy
6. Coping
7. Determination
8. Discipline

(continued)

Box 3.3 Continued

9. Effort	21. Perseverance
10. Emotional well-being;	22. Personhood
11. Engagement with learning	23. Positive attitudes toward school
12. Expression	24. Pride
13. Focus	25. Raised aspirations
14. Happiness	26. Resilience
15. Health	27. Responsibility
16. Life satisfaction	28. Self-concept
17. Listening skills	29. Self-esteem
18. Motivation	30. Self-regulation
19. Obedience	31. Time-management
20. Optimism	32. Well-being

Among these, discipline, positive attitudes toward school, concentration, and raised aspirations were the most frequently cited positive outcomes. Participation was found to strengthen children's sense of positive individual and group identity, and contributed to raised aspirations. Some reports noted that individual children had grown in confidence, developed better social listening skills, and had become generally more settled at school, attributing these positive changes to participation in the program.

Many studies included indicators of social skills. As with personal development, the overarching notion of "social skills" was represented with several constructs:

1. Co-operation	9. Prosocial behavior
2. Belongingness	10. Relationships
3. Collaborative learning	11. Social advancement
4. Communication	12. Social networking
5. Community spirit	13. Solidarity
6. Group integration	14. Teamwork
7. Helping others	15. Interaction
8. Group identity	16. Taking turns

Very often, the findings relating to social skills were based upon parent and teacher perceptions of change, captured via rating scales or qualitative data. One of the most often-cited outcomes was "teamwork."

The characteristics of the El Sistema programs that were perceived as being important in supporting positive social, emotional, and cognitive outcomes included:

- Opportunities for developing new skills and performing,
- Acquiring cultural capital,
- Interpersonal bonds and solidarity in pursuing shared goals,
- Intensity and frequency of contact,
- Mutual respect,
- Recognition and rewards for excellence.

Overall, the study corroborates a body of research that demonstrates the wider social, emotional, and cognitive benefits of participation in music making (Hallam 2015).

How Does Music Promote Well-Being?

The impact of music on psychological well-being and subsequently good health is largely, though not exclusively, through the emotions and changes in arousal it evokes. Music can reduce stress and increase relaxation (Fukui and Yamashita 2003; Kreutz et al. 2004), although the outcomes depend on the nature of the music (Brownley, McMurray, and Hackney 1995; Gerra et al. 1998). The most comprehensive attempt to outline the mechanisms that may underpin music's impact on the emotions is the BRECVEMA framework (Juslin and Västfjäll 2008; Juslin et al. 2010). This framework features eight mechanisms (as well as appraisal):

(1) *Brain stem reflex*: a hard-wired attention response to simple acoustic features such as extreme or increasing loudness or speed (Simons 1996);

(2) *Rhythmic entrainment*: a gradual adjustment of an internal body rhythm (e.g., heart rate) toward an external rhythm in the music (Harrer and Harrer 1977);

(3) *Evaluative conditioning*: a regular pairing of a piece of music and other positive or negative stimuli leading to a conditioned association (Blair and Shimp 1992);

(4) *Contagion*: an internal "mimicry" of the perceived voice-like emotional expression of the music (Juslin 2001);

(5) *Visual imagery*: inner images of an emotional character conjured up by the listener through a metaphorical mapping of the musical structure (Osborne 1980);

(6) *Episodic memory*: a conscious recollection of a particular event from the listener's past, triggered by the music (Baumgartner 1992);

(7) *Musical expectancy*: a reaction to the gradual unfolding of the musical structure and its expected or unexpected continuation (Meyer 1956); and

(8) *Aesthetic judgment*: a subjective evaluation of the aesthetic value of the music based on an individual set of weighted criteria (Juslin forthcoming).

Music can engender intense emotional experiences, linking in some cases with pleasure and more specifically with meaning and engagement, as outlined by Peterson, Park, and Seligman (2013) as the three orientations for the achievement of a "full life." Strong experiences of music (Gabrielsson and Lindström Wik 2003) generally occur when listening to music rather than performing (Gabrielsson 2010, [2008] 2011). They have been identified as having seven components: *overall general characteristics, physical reactions and behaviors, perception, cognition, feelings or emotions, existential and transcendental aspects,* and *personal and social aspects*. Sensations of joy, happiness, rapture, euphoria, calm, and peace tend to dominate such experiences.

Strong and intense musical experiences are of high significance and can have long-term effects, with lives becoming more fulfilling, spiritual, and harmonious (Schäfer et al. 2014). Gabrielsson and Lindström (1995) argue that music is not only very powerful but can reach people in a unique way. They suggest that strong emotional experiences with music enable insights into alternative ways of being. Long-term effects may be derived through *valuable memory of the experience* (experience is a resource that can be used as a means for self-therapy), *increased interest in music* (inspiration, motivation, and insights into the value of music), and *personal and social consequences* (self-realization, insights into what life and existence mean, and into the value of relationships) (Gabrielsson [2008] 2011). Most strong experiences of music occur in adolescence and early adulthood (Gabrielsson and Lindström Wik 2003), and have the potential to increase the well-being of young listeners (Lamont 2011) and young musicians (Lamont 2012).

Emotion regulation (processes by which individuals reduce, maintain, or intensify emotions) may act to mediate the relationship between musical engagement and well-being (Chin and Rickard 2014). Engaging with music for the purposes of cognitive and emotional regulation seems to enhance well-being through cognitive reappraisal. However, if music listening, music making, and social engagement are coupled with a tendency to regulate emotions and thoughts by expressive suppression, negative outcomes may occur. High levels of active music engagement and music listening are associated with greater use of cognitive reappraisal. This may be because music provides a safe platform for exploring and expressing emotions, both positive and negative (Huron 2006).

Music may also contribute to well-being through its role in supporting the formation and maintenance of identity. This is particularly important during adolescence (Tarrant, North, and Hargreaves 2001). Young people use music to explore, express, and develop their identities (Miranda and Claes 2009; North and Hargreaves 2008) and to communicate their personal values, ambitions, beliefs, and perceptions of the world and themselves (Rentfrow and Gosling 2006). Individuals who express preferences for specific musical genres tend to be more socially attracted toward other individuals or communities who value and share the musical preferences (Boer et al. 2011), nowadays not only in face-to-face interactions but also through Internet message boards, video conferencing, and social media (Perkins 2012).

Music may also support well-being through the way that it supports social cohesion. The survival value of music is perceived as lying in synchronizing the mood of many individuals, who can then collectively take action to strengthen their means of protection and defend themselves from attack (Dowling and Harwood 1986). Moving together rhythmically seems to reinforce this process (Hove and Risen 2009; Trainor 2014). Group music making involves strong elements of sociability, and the links between music and social bonding (Cross 2009; Hagen and Bryant 2003) and music and emotion (Juslin and Sloboda 2001) may contribute to explaining why group music making enhances perceived well-being. A sense of belonging has been found to be an important outcome of participation in group musical activities. Social networks developed through music making have been found to support group identity, collaborative learning, friendship, social support, and a strong feeling of belonging among group members (Faulkner and Davidson 2004; Coffman 2002; Creech et al. 2013; Lehmberg and Fung 2010).

CONCLUSIONS

Music constitutes a leisure activity for a great many people, either through listening or making music. For some, singing or playing constitutes a "serious" leisure activity, while for others it is recreational. Similarly, listening for some is a hobby to which they devote considerable time and energy, while for others it constitutes casual engagement. Despite these differences in forms and levels of engagement, music can have a considerable impact on well-being. Well-being can be enhanced through listening while undertaking other tasks or through deliberately using music to change moods and emotions. However, music can cause distress when it is not to the liking of a listener and s/he has no control over it. Music can also play a role in the development and maintenance of identity through the kind of music listened to. This is particularly important in adolescence, but not exclusively so. Attending concerts or festivals requires a greater level of interest but leads to similar benefits, in terms of well-being, as actively making music.

Making music usually requires greater levels of commitment than listening. In addition to the benefits that accrue from listening to music in relation to the impact on moods and emotions, there are additional benefits in terms of the development of social networks, a sense of belonging, pride in progress made, and performance achievements, with a subsequent impact on self-concept, cognitive, and health benefits. Of course, these will be realized only if the experience is positive. This relies on the quality of teaching and facilitation of the activities. This has implications for the training of those facilitating musical activities.

Changes in technology have already impacted on the ways in which music can be beneficial to well-being. Social networking means that individuals engaging in musical and related social interactions do not have to be in the same physical space. Young people who are familiar with and confident in using new technologies are making ever-increasing use of a range of networking and other systems in relation to musical interactions. It remains to be seen if, in the long term, this is sustained, and if it subsequently has an impact on the way that music can enhance well-being.

REFERENCES CITED

Allison, Paul J., David Locker, and Jocelyne S. Feine. 1997. "Quality of Life: A Dynamic Construct." *Social Science and Medicine* 45(2): 221–230.

Allison, Theresa A. 2008. "Songwriting and Transcending Institutional Boundaries in the Nursing Home". In *The Oxford Handbook of Medical Ethnomusicology*, edited by Benjamin D. Koen, 218–45. New York: Oxford University Press.

Andrews, Frank M., and John P. Robinson. 1991. "Measures of Subjective Well-Being." In *Measures of Personality and Social Psychological Attitudes*, edited by John P. Robinson, Phillip R. Shaver, and Lawrence S. Wrightsman, 61–114. San Diego, CA: Academic.

Anshel, Anat, and David A. Kipper. 1988. "The Influence of Group Singing on Trust and Cooperation." *Journal of Music Therapy* 25: 145–155.

Associated Board of the Royal Schools of Music (ABRSM). 2014. *Making Music: Teaching, Learning and Playing in the UK.* London: ABRSM.

Bailey, Betty A., and Jane W. Davidson. 2002. "Adaptive Characteristics of Group Singing: Perceptions from Members of a Choir for Homeless Men." *Musicae Scientiae* 6: 221–256.

Bailey, Betty A., and Jane W. Davidson. 2003. "Amateur Group Singing as a Therapeutic Agent." *Nordic Journal of Music Therapy* 12: 18–32.

Bailey, Betty A., and Jane W. Davidson. 2005. "Effects of Group Singing and Performance for Marginalized and Middle-Class Singers." *Psychology of Music* 33: 269–303.

Bakagiannis, Sotirios, and Mark Tarrant. 2006. "Can Music Bring People Together? Effects of Shared Musical Preference on Intergroup Bias in Adolescence." *Scandinavian Journal of Psychology* 47: 129–136.

Batt-Rawden, Kari, and Tia DeNora. 2005. "Music and Informal Learning in Everyday Life." *Music Education Research* 7: 289–304.

Baumgartner, Hans. 1992. "Remembrance of Things Past: Music, Autobiographical Memory, and Emotion." *Advances in Consumer Research* 19: 613–620.

Beck, Robert J., Terry L. Gottfried, David, J. Hall, Caitlin A. Cisler, and Kenneth W. Bozeman. 2006. "Supporting the Health of College Solo Singers: The Relationship of Positive Emotions and Stress to Changes in Salivary IgA and Cortisol during Singing." *Journal of Learning through the Arts: A Research Journal on Arts Integration in Schools and Communities* 2: 19.

Bennett, Lucy. 2012. "Patterns of Listening through Social Media: Online Fan Engagement with the Live Music Experience." *Social Semiotics* 22: 545–557.

Bernatzky, Gunter, Simon Strickner, Michaela Presch, Franz Wendtner, and Werner Kullich. 2012. "Music as Non-Pharmacological Pain Management in Clinics." In *Music, Health and Wellbeing*, edited by Raymond A. R. MacDonald, Gunter Kreutz, and Laura Mitchell, 257–275. Oxford: Oxford University Press.

Blair, M. Elizabeth, and Terence A. Shimp. 1992. "Consequences of an Unpleasant Experience with Music: A Second-Order Negative Conditioning Perspective." *Journal of Advertising* 21: 35–43.

Boer, Diana, Ronald Fischer, Micha Strack, Michael H. Bond, Eva Lo, and Jason Lam. 2011. "How Shared Preferences in Music Create Bonds between People: Values as the Missing Link." *Personality and Social Psychology Bulletin* 37: 1159–1171.

Boer, Diana, and Ronald Fischer. 2012. "Towards a Holistic Model of Functions of Music Listening across Cultures: A Culturally Decentred Qualitative Approach." *Psychology of Music* 40: 179–200.

Boer, Diana, Ronald Fischer, Hasan Gürkan Tekman, Amina Abubakar, Jane Njenga, and Markus Zenger. 2012. "Young People's Topography of Musical Functions: Personal, Social and Cultural Experiences with Music across Genders and Six Societies." *International Journal of Psychology* 47: 355–369.

Brand, Gail, John A. Sloboda, Ben Saul, and Martin Hathaway. 2012. "The Reciprocal Relationship between Jazz Musicians and Audiences in Live Performances: A Pilot Qualitative Study." *Psychology of Music* 40: 635–651.

Brownley, Kimberley A., Robert G. McMurray, and Anthony C. Hackney. 1995. "Effects of Music on Physiological and Affective Response to Graded Treadmill Exercise in Trained and Untrained Runners." *International Journal of Psychophysiological Research* 19: 93–201.

Buffam, Bonar. 2011. "Can't Hold Us Back! Hip-hop and the Racial Motility of Aboriginal Bodies in Urban Spaces." *Social Identities* 17: 337–350.

Bygren, L. A., B. B. Konlaan, and W. E. Johnasson. 1996. "Attendance at Cultural Events, Reading Books or Periodicals, and Making Music or Singing in a Choir as Determinants for Survival: Swedish Interview Survey of Living Conditions." *British Medical Journal* 313(7072): 1577–1580.

Chin, Tan Chyuan, and Nikki S. Rickard. 2014. "Emotion Regulation Strategy Mediates both Positive and Negative Relationships between Music Uses and Well-Being." *Psychology of Music* 42: 692–713.

Clift, Stephen M. 2012. "Singing, Wellbeing and Health." In *Music, Health and Wellbeing*, edited by Raymond A. R. MacDonald, Gunter Kreutz, and Laura Mitchell, 111–124. Oxford: Oxford University Press.

Clift, Stephen, M., and Grenville Hancox. 2001. "The Perceived Benefits of Singing: Findings from Preliminary Surveys of a University College Choral Society." *Journal of the Royal Society for the Promotion of Health* 121: 248–256.

Clift, Stephen M., Grenville Hancox, Rosalia Staricoff, and Christine Whitmore. 2008. *Singing and Health: A Systematic Mapping and Review of Non-Clinical Research*. Canterbury: Sidney de Haan Research Centre for Arts and Health, Canterbury Christ Church University.

Coffman, Don D. 2002. "Music and Quality of Life in Older Adults." *Psychomusicology: A Journal of Research in Music Cognition* 18: 76–88.

Coffman, Don D., and Mary S. Adamek. 2001. "Perceived Social Support of New Horizons Band Participants." *Contributions to Music Education* 28: 27–40.

Cohen, Gene D., Susan Perlstein, Jeff Chapline, Jeanne Kelly, Kimberley M. Firth, and Samuel Simmens. 2006. "The Impact of Professionally Conducted Cultural Programs on the Physical Health, Mental Health, and Social Functioning of Older Adults." *The Gerontologist* 46: 726–734.

Cohen, Gene D., Susan Perlstein, Jeff Chapline, Jeanne Kelly, Kimberley M. Firth and Samuel Simmens. 2007. "The Impact of Professionally Conducted Cultural Programs on the Physical Health, Mental Health and Social Functioning of Older Adults: 2-Year Results." *Journal of Ageing, Humanities and the Arts* 1: 5–22.

Cooper, Thelma L. 2001. "Adults' Perceptions of Piano Study: Achievements and Experiences." *Journal of Research in Music Education* 49: 156–168.

Creech, Andrea. 2014. "Ageing in a Digital World: Developing Possible Selves in an Intergenerational Community Opera." Paper presented at the 31st ISME World Conference of Music Education, International Society for Music Education, Porto Alegre, Brazil, July 21–25.

Creech, Andrea, Patricia González-Moreno, Lisa Lorenzino, and Grace Waitman. 2016. "El Sistema and Sistema-Inspired Programmes: A Literature Review." London: Institute of Education, for Sistema Global. http://sistemaglobal.org/litreview/ 2013.

Creech, Andrea, Susan Hallam, Maria Varvarigou, Helena Gaunt, Hilary McQueen, and Anita Pincas. 2014a. "The Role of Musical Possible Selves in Supporting Subjective Well-Being in Later Life." *Music Education Research* 16: 32–49.

Creech, Andrea, Susan Hallam, Maria Varvarigou, and Hilary McQueen. 2014b. *Active Ageing with Music: Supporting Wellbeing in the Third and Fourth Ages*. London: Institute of Education Press.

Cross, Ian. 2009. "The Evolutionary Nature of Musical Meaning." *Musicae Scientae* 13(2 supplement): 143–159.

Daatland, Svein O. 2005. "Quality of Life and Ageing" In *The Cambridge Handbook of Age and Ageing*, edited by Malcolm L. Johnson, Vern L. Bengtson, Peter G. Coleman, and Thomas B. L. Kirkwood, 371–377. New York: Cambridge University Press.

Deci, Edward L., and Richard M. Ryan. 2000. "The 'What' and 'Why' of Goal Pursuits: Human Needs and the Self-Determination of Behavior." *Psychological Inquiry* 11: 227–268.

DeNora, Tia. 1999. "Music as a Technology of the Self." *Poetics* 27: 31–56.

Diener, Ed. 1984. "Subjective Well-Being." *Psychological Bulletin* 95: 542–575.

Diener, Ed, Eunkook M. Suh, Richard E. Lucas, and Heidi L. Smith. 1999. "Subjective Well-Being: Three Decades of Progress." *Psychological Bulletin* 125: 276–302.

Dingle, Genevieve A., Christopher Brander, Julie Ballantyne, and Felicity A Baker. 2012. "To Be Heard: The Social and Mental Health Benefits of Choir Singing for Disadvantaged Adults." *Psychology of Music* 41: 405–421.

Dobson, Melissa, and John A. Sloboda. 2014. "Staying Behind: Explorations in Post-Performance Musician-Audience Dialogue." In *Coughing and Clapping: Investigating Audience Experience*, edited by Karen Burland and Stephanie Pitts, 159–173. Aldershot: Ashgate.

Dowling, W. Jay, and Dane L. Harwood. 1986. *Music Cognition*. New York: Academic.

Doyal, Len, and Ian Gough. 1991. *A Theory of Human Need*. Hong Kong: Macmillan.

Duffett, Mark. 2013. *Understanding Fandom: An Introduction to the Study of Media Fan Culture*. New York: Bloomsbury.

Earl, Cameron, Elizabeth Parker, Andrew Tatrai, and Mike Capra. 2004. "Influences on Crowd Behaviour at Outdoor Music Festivals." *Environmental Health* 4: 55–62.

Faulkner, Robert, and Jane W. Davidson. 2004. "Men's Vocal Behaviour and the Construction of Self." *Musicae Scientiae* 8: 231–255.

Finnegan, Ruth. 1989. *The Hidden Musicians: Music-Making in an English Town*. Cambridge: Cambridge University Press.

Finnegan, Ruth. 1997. "Music, Performance and Enactment." In *Consumption and Everyday Life*, edited by Hugh Mackay, 113–158. London: Sage/Open University.

Flynn, Leisa. R., Jacquline Eastman, and Stephen J. Newell. 1995. "An Exploratory Study of the Application of Neural Networks to Marketing: Predicting Rock Music Shopping Behavior." *Journal of Marketing Theory and Practice* 3: 75–85.

Forssen, Annika S. K. 2007. "Humour, Beauty, and Culture as Personal Health Resources: Experiences of Elderly Swedish Women." *Scandinavian Journal of Public Health* 35: 228–234.

Frith, Simon. 1996. *Performing Rites: On the Value of Popular Music*. Oxford: Oxford University Press.

Fukui, Hajime, and Masako Yamashita. 2003. "The Effects of Music and Visual Stress on Testosterone and Cortisol in Men and Women." *Neuroendocrinology Letters* 24: 173–80.

Gabrielsson, Alf. 2010. "Strong Experiences with Music." In *Handbook of Music and Emotion: Theory, Research, Applications*, edited by Patrik N. Juslin and John A. Sloboda, 547–574. Oxford: Oxford University Press.

Gabrielsson, Alf. (2008) 2011. *Strong Experiences with Music: Music Is Much More than Just Music*. Oxford: Oxford University Press.

Gabrielsson, Alf, and Siv Lindström. 1995. "Can Strong Experiences of Music Have Therapeutic Implications?" In *Music and the Mind Machine: The Psychophysiology and Psychopathology of the Sense of Music*, edited by Reinhard Steinberg, 195–202. Berlin: Springer.

Gabrielsson, Alf, and Siv Lindström Wik. 2003. "Strong Experiences Related to Music: A Descriptive System" *Musicae Scientiae* 7: 157–217.

Garrido, Sandra, and Emery Schubert. 2011. "Individual Differences in the Enjoyment of Negative Emotion in Music: A Literature Review and Experiment." *Music Perception* 28: 279–296.

Gates, J. Terry. 1991. "Music Participation: Theory, Research, and Policy." *Bulletin of the Council for Research in Music Education* 109: 1–35.

Gerra, G., A. Zaimovic, D. Franchini, M. Palladino, G. Giucastro, N. Reali, D. Maestri, R. Caccavari, R. Delsignore, and F. Brambilla. 1998. "Neuroendocrine Responses of Healthy Volunteers to 'Techno–Music': Relationships with Personality Trait and Emotional State." *International Journal of Psychophysiology* 28(1): 99–111.

Gibson, Chris, and John Connell. 2005. *Music and Tourism: On the Road Again*. Cleveland, OH: Channel View.

Greasley, Alinka E., and Alexandra Lamont. 2006. "Music Preference in Adulthood: Why Do We Like the Music We Do?" In *Proceedings of the 9th International Conference on Music Perception and Cognition*, edited by Mario Baroni, Anna Rita Adessi, Roberto Caterina, and Marco Costa, 960–966. Bologna: University of Bologna Press.

Greasley, Alinka E., and Alexandra Lamont. 2011. "Exploring Engagement with Music in Everyday Life Using Experience Sampling Methodology." *Musicae Scientiae* 15: 45–71.

Hagen, Edward, and Gregory Bryant. 2003. "Music and Dance as a Coalition Signalling System." *Human Nature* 14: 21–51.

Hallam, Susan. 2015. *The Power of Music: A Research Synthesis of the Impact of Actively Making Music on the Intellectual, Social and Personal Development of Children and Young People*. London: International Music Education Research Centre (iMerc), University College London Institute of Education.

Hallam, Susan, Andrea Creech, Maria Varvarigou, Teresa Gomes, Ioulia Papageorgi, Jennifer Lanipekun, and Tiija Rinta. 2015. "Changes in Motivation as Expertise Develops: Relationships with Musical Aspirations." Paper presented at the ESCOM conference Royal Northern College of Music, Manchester, August 17–22.

Hallam, Susan, Andrea Creech, Maria Varvarigou, Hilary McQueen, and Helena Gaunt. 2012. "Perceived Benefits of Active Engagement with Making Music in Community Settings." *International Journal of Community Music* 5: 155–174.

Hallam, Susan, Andrea Creech, Maria Varvarigou, Hilary McQueen, and Helena Gaunt. 2014. "Does Active Engagement in Community Music Promote Enhanced Quality of Life in Older People?" *Arts and Health: An International Journal for Research, Policy and Practice* 6: 101–116.

Hanser, Suzanne B. 2010. "Music, Health, and Well-Being." In *Handbook of Music and Emotion: Theory, Research, Applications*, edited by Patrik N. Juslin and John A. Sloboda, 849–878. Oxford: Oxford University Press.

Hargreaves, David J., Dorothy Miell, and Raymond A. R. MacDonald. 2002. "What Are Musical Identities, and Why Are They Important?" In *Musical Identities*, edited by Raymond A. R. MacDonald, David J. Hargreaves, and Dorothy Miell, 1–20. Oxford: Oxford University Press.

Hargreaves, David J., Adrian C. North, and Mark Tarrant. 2006. "Musical Preference and Taste in Childhood and Adolescence." In *The Child as Musician: A Handbook of Musical Development*, edited by Gary E. McPherson, 135–154. Oxford: Oxford University Press.

Harrer, G., and H. Harrer. 1977. "Music, Emotion, and Autonomic Function." In *Music and the Brain: Studies in the Neurology of Music*, edited by MacDonald Critchley and R. A. Henson, 202–216. London: William Heinemann.

Hays, Terrence, and Victor Minichiello. 2005. "The Contribution of Music to Quality of Life in Older People: An Australian Qualitative Study." *Ageing and Society* 25: 261–278.

Herbert, Ruth. 2012. "Musical and Non-Musical Involvement in Daily Life: The Case of Absorption." *Musicae Scientiae* 16: 41–66.

Heye, Andreas, and Alexandra Lamont. 2010. "Mobile Listening Situations in Everyday Life: The Use of MP3 Players while Travelling." *Musicae Scientiae* 14: 95–120.

Hillman, Sue. 2002. "Participatory Singing for Older People: A Perception of Benefit." *Health Education* 102: 163–171.

Hornquist, Jan Olof. 1990. "Quality of Life: Concept and Assessment." *Scandinavian Journal of Public Health* 18: 69–79.

Hove, Michael J., and Jane L. Risen. 2009. "It's all in the Timing: Interpersonal Synchrony Increases Affiliation." *Social Cognition* 27: 949–960.

Huron, David. 2006. *Sweet Anticipation: Music and the Psychology of Expectation.* Cambridge, MA: MIT Press.

Hutchinson, Susan L., Cheryl K. Baldwin, and Sae-Sook Oh. 2006. "Adolescent Coping: Exploring Adolescents' Leisure-Based Responses to Stress." *Leisure Sciences* 28: 115–131.

Jenson, Joli. 1992. "Fandom as Pathology: The Consequences of Characterization." In *The Adoring Audience: Fan Culture and Popular Media*, edited by Lisa A. Lewis, 9–29. New York: Routledge.

Judd, Marianne, and Julie A. Pooley. 2014. "The Psychological Benefits of Participating in Group Singing for Members of the General Public." *Psychology of Music* 42: 269–283.

Juslin, Patrik N. 2001. "Communicating Emotion in Music Performance: A Review and a Theoretical Framework." In *Music and Emotion: Theory and Research*, edited by Patrik N. Juslin and John A. Sloboda, 309–337. Oxford: Oxford University Press.

Juslin, Patrik N. 2013. "From Everyday Emotions to Aesthetic Emotions: Toward a Unified Theory of Musical Emotions." *Physics of Life Reviews* 10: 235–266.

Juslin, Patrik N., Laszlo Harmat, and Tuomas Eerola. 2014. "What Makes Music Emotionally Significant? Exploring the Underlying Mechanisms." *Psychology of Music* 42: 599–623.

Juslin, Patrik N., and Petri Laukka. 2004. "Expression, Perception and Induction of Musical Emotions: A Review and a Questionnaire Study of Everyday Listening." *Journal of New Music Research* 33: 217–238.

Juslin, Patrik N., Simon Liljeström, Daniel Västfjäll, Goncalo Barradas, and Ana Silva. 2008. "An Experience Sampling Study of Emotional Reactions to Music: Listener, Music, and Situation." *Emotion* 8: 668–683.

Juslin, Patrik N., Simon Liljeström, Daniel Västfjäll, and Lars-Olov Lundqvist. 2010. "How Does Music Evoke Emotions? Exploring the Underlying Mechanisms." In *Handbook of Music and Emotion: Theory, Research, Applications*, edited by Patrik N. Juslin and John A. Sloboda, 605–642. Oxford: Oxford University Press.

Juslin, Patrik N., and John A. Sloboda. 2001. *Music and Emotion.* New York: Oxford University Press.

Juslin, Patrik N., and John A. Sloboda, eds. 2010. *Handbook of Music and Emotion: Theory, Research, Applications.* Oxford: Oxford University Press.

Juslin, Patrik N., and Daniel Västfjäll. 2008. "Emotional Responses to Music: The Need to Consider Underlying Mechanisms." *Behavioral and Brain Sciences* 31: 559–575.

Kaplan, Max. 1960. *Leisure in America: A Social Inquiry.* New York and London: John Wiley and Sons.

Karlsen, Sidsel. 2013. "Immigrant Students and the 'Homeland Music': Meanings, Negotiations and Implications." *Research Studies in Music Education* 35: 161–177.

Karlsen, Sidsel, and Sture Brändström. 2008. "Exploring the Music Festival as a Music Educational Project." *International Journal of Music Education* 26: 363–373.

Keown, Daniel J. 2015. "A Descriptive Analysis of Film Music Enthusiasts' Purchasing and Consumption Behaviours of Soundtrack Albums: An Exploratory Study." *Psychology of Music* 1–15. doi: 10.1177/0305735615575418.

Kibby, Marjorie. 2009. "Collect Yourself: Negotiating Personal Archives." *Information, Communication, and Society* 12: 428–443.

Koeplin, Aimee. 2009. "The *Telos* of Citizen Life: Music and Philosophy in Aristotle's Ideal." *Polis: The Journal of the Greek Political Thought* 26: 116–132.

Kokotsaki, Dimitra, and Susan Hallam. 2007. "Higher Education Music Students' Perceptions of the Benefits of Participative Music Making." *Music Education Research* 9: 93–109.

Kokotsaki, Dimitra, and Susan Hallam. 2011. "The Perceived Benefits of Participative Music Making for Non-Music University Students: A Comparison with Music Students." *Music Education Research* 13: 149–172.

Krause, Amanda E., and David J. Hargreaves. 2012. "MyTunes: Digital Music Library Users and Their Self-Images." *Psychology of Music* 41: 531–544.

Krause, Amanda E., Adrian C. North, and Lauren Y. Hewitt. 2015. "Music-Listening in Everyday Life: Devices and Choice." *Psychology of Music* 43: 155–170.

Kreutz, Gunter, Stephan Bongard, Sonja Rohrmann, Volker Hodapp, and Dorothee Grebe. 2004. "Effects of Choir Singing or Listening on Secretory Immunoglobulin A, Cortisol and Emotional State." *Journal of Behavioural Medicine* 27: 623–634.

Kuhn, Dawn. 2002. "The Effects of Active and Passive Participation in Musical Activity on the Immune System as Measured by Salivary Immunoglobulin A (SIgA)." *Journal of Music Therapy* 39: 30–39.

Lally, Elaine. 2009. "The Power to Heal Us with a Smile and a Song: Senior Well-Being, Music-Based Participatory Arts and the Value of Qualitative Evidence." *Journal of Arts and Communities* 1: 25–44.

Lacher, Kathleen T., and Richard Mizerski. 1994. "An Exploratory Study of the Responses and Relationships Involved in the Evaluation of, and in the Intention to Purchase New Rock Music." *Journal of Consumer Research* 21: 366–380.

Laiho, Suvi. 2004. "The Psychological Functions of Music in Adolescence." *Nordic Journal of Music Therapy* 13(1): 49–65.

Lamont, Alexandra. 2011. "University Students' Strong Experiences of Music: Pleasure, Engagement, and Meaning." *Musicae Scientiae* 15: 229–249.

Lamont, Alexandra. 2012. "Emotion, Engagement and Meaning in Strong Experiences of Music Performance." *Psychology of Music* 40: 574–594.

Lamont, Alexandra, Alinka Greasley, and John A. Sloboda. 2016. "Choosing to Hear Music: Motivation, Process and Effect." In *The Oxford Handbook of Music Psychology*, edited by Susan Hallam, Ian Cross, and Michael Thaut, 711–724. 2nd ed. Oxford: Oxford University Press.

Lamont, Alexandra, and Rebecca Webb. 2010. "Short- and Long-Term Musical Preferences: What Makes a Favourite Piece of Music?" *Psychology of Music* 38: 222–241.

Langston, Thomas W. 2011. "It Is a Life Support Isn't It? Social Capital in a Community Choir." *International Journal of Community Music* 4: 163–184.

Langston, Thomas W., and Margaret S. Barrett. 2008. "Capitalizing on Community Music: A Case Study of the Manifestation of Social Capital in a Community Choir." *Research Studies in Music Education* 30: 118–138.

Larson, Reed W., Suzanne Wilson, and Aimee Rickman. 2009. "Globalization, Societal Change, and Adolescence across the World." In *Handbook of Adolescent Psychology*, vol. 2: *Contextual Influences on Adolescent Development*, edited by Richard M. Lerner and Laurence Steinberg, 590–622. 3rd ed. Hoboken, NJ: Wiley.

Laukka, Petri. 2007. "Uses of Music and Psychological Well-Being among the Elderly." *Journal of Happiness Studies* 8: 215–241.

Lehmberg, Lisa J., and C. Victor Fung. 2010. "Benefits of Music Participation for Senior Citizens: A Review of the Literature." *Music Education Research International* 4: 19–30.

Lewis, Kevin, Marco Gonzalez, and Jason Kaufman. 2012. "Social Selection and Peer Influence in an Online Social Network." *Proceedings of the National Academy of Sciences* 109: 68–72.

Lundström, Catrin. 2009. "'People Take for Granted that You Know How to Dance Salsa and Merengue': Transnational Diasporas, Visual Discourses and Racialized Knowledge in Sweden's Contemporary Latin Music Boom." *Social Identities* 15: 707–723.

MacDonald, Raymond A. R., Gunter Kreutz, and Laura Mitchell, eds. 2012. *Music, Health and Wellbeing*. New York: Oxford University Press.

Majno, Maria. 2012. "From the Model of El Sistema in Venezuela to Current Applications." *Annals of the New York Academy of Sciences, the Neurosciences and Music IV: Learning and Memory* (1252).

Martin, Graham, Michael Clarke, and Colby Pearce. 1993. "Adolescent Suicide: Music Preference as an Indicator of Vulnerability." *Journal of the American Child and Adolescent Psychiatry* 32: 530–535.

Maslow, Abraham H. 1954. *Motivation and Personality*. New York: Harper and Row.

Matheson, Catherine M. 2005. "Festivity and Sociability: A Study of a Celtic Music Festival." *Tourism Culture and Communication* 5: 149–163.

Meyer, Leonard B. 1956. *Emotion and Meaning in Music*. Chicago: Chicago University Press.

Miranda, Dave, Camille Blais-Rochette, KaroleVaugon, K, Muna Osman, and Melisa Arias-Valenzuela. 2015. "Towards a Cultural-Developmental Psychology of Music in Adolescence." *Psychology of Music* 43: 197–218.

Miranda, Dave, and Michel Claes. 2009. "Music Listening, Coping, Peer Affiliation and Depression in Adolescence." *Psychology of Music* 37: 215–233.

Miranda, Dave, and Patrick Gaudreau. 2011. "Music Listening and Emotional Well-Being in Adolescence: A Person and Variable-Oriented Study." *European Review of Applied Psychology* 61: 1–11.

Mitchell, Laura A., and Raymond A. R. MacDonald. 2012. "Music and Pain: Evidence from Experimental Perspectives." In *Music, Health and Wellbeing*, edited by Raymond A. R. MacDonald, Gunter Kreutz, and Laura Mitchell, 230–238. Oxford: Oxford University Press.

Molteni, Luca, and Andrea Ordanini. 2003. "Consumption Patterns, Digital Technology and Music Downloading." *Long Range Planning* 36: 389–406.

Morgan, Jill P., Raymond A. R. MacDonald, and Stephanie Pitts. 2014. "'Caught between a Scream and a Hug': Women's Perspectives on Music Listening and Interaction with Teenagers in the Family Unit." *Psychology of Music*, January 29. doi: 10.1177/0305735613517411.

Morrison, Ian, and Stephen Clift. 2012. *Singing and Mental Health*. Canterbury: Canterbury Christ Church University.

Musicians Union. 2015. "Advice about Your Career: Interview with Martin Taylor." *Musicians Union*. http://www.musiciansunion.org.uk/Home/Advice/Your-Career.

Nill, A. Alexander, and Andreas Geipel. 2010. "Sharing and Owning of Musical Works: Copyright Protection from a Societal Perspective." *Journal of Macromarketing* 30: 33–49.

North, Adrian C., and David J. Hargreaves. 2008. *The Social and Applied Psychology of Music.* Oxford: Oxford University Press.

North, Adrian C., David J. Hargreaves, and Jon J. Hargreaves. 2004. "Uses of Music in Everyday Life." *Music Perception* 22: 41–77.

Oakes, Steve. 2003. "Demographic and Sponsorship Considerations for Jazz and Classical Music Festivals." *Service Industries Journal* 23: 165–178.

Odena, Oscar. 2010. "Practitioners' Views on Cross-Community Music Education Projects in Northern Ireland: Alienation, Socio-Economic Factors and Educational Potential." *British Educational Research Journal* 36: 83–105.

Osborne, John W. 1980. "The Mapping of Thoughts, Emotions, Sensations, and Images as Responses to Music." *Journal of Mental Imagery* 5: 133–136.

Packer, Jan, and Julie Ballantyne. 2010. "The Impact of Music Festival Attendance on Young People's Psychological and Social Well-Being." *Psychology of Music* 39: 164–181.

Paleo, Ivan Orosa, and Nachoem M. Wijnberg. 2006. "Classification of Popular Music Festivals: A Typology of Festivals and an Inquiry into Their Role in the Construction of Music Genres." *International Journal of Arts Management* 8: 50–81.

Pelletier, Cori L. 2004. "The Effect of Music on Decreasing Arousal Due to Stress: A Meta-analysis." *Journal of Music Therapy* 41: 192–214.

Perkins, Alicia. 2012. "How Devoted Are You? An Examination of Online Music Fan Behaviour." *Annals of Leisure Research* 15: 354–365.

Peterson, Christopher, Nansook Park, and Martin E. P. Seligman. 2013. "Orientations to Happiness and Life Satisfaction: The Full Life versus the Empty Life." In *The Exploration of Happiness: Present and Future Perspectives*, edited by Antonella Delle Fave, 161–173. Dordrecht: Springer Science and Business Media.

Pitts, Stephanie. 2005. *Valuing Musical Participation.* Aldershot: Ashgate.

Pitts, Stephanie E., and Karen Burland. 2013. "Listening to Live Jazz: An Individual or Social Act?" *Arts Marketing: An International Journal* 3: 7–20.

Pitts, Stephanie E., and Christopher P. Spencer. 2008. "Loyalty and Longevity in Audience Listening: Investigating Experiences of Attendance at a Chamber Music Festival." *Music and Letters* 89: 227–238.

Radbourne, Jennifer, Hilary Glow, and Katya Johanson. 2013. *The Audience Experience: A Critical Analysis of Audiences in the Performing Arts.* Chicago: University of Chicago Press.

Rentfrow, Peter J., and Samuel D. Gosling. 2003. "The Do Re Mi's of Everyday Life: The Structure and Personality Correlates of Music Preferences." *Journal of Personality and Social Psychology* 84: 1236–1256.

Rentfrow, Peter J., and Samuel D. Gosling. 2006. "Message in a Ballad: The Role of Music Preferences in Interpersonal Perception." *Psychological Science* 17: 236–242.

Rentfrow, Peter J., Jennifer A. McDonald, and Julian A. Oldmeadow. 2009. "You Are What You Listen to: Young People's Stereotypes about Music Fans." *Group Processes and Intergroup Relations* 12: 329–344.

Rickard, Nikki S., and Katrina McFerran. 2012. *Lifelong Engagement with Music: Benefits for Mental Health and Wellbeing.* New York: Nova Science.

Saarikallio, Suvi. 2006. "Differences in Adolescents' Use of Music in Mood Regulation." In *Proceedings of the 9th International Conference on Music Perception and Cognition*, edited by Mario Baroni, Anna Rita Addessi, Roberto Caterina, and Marco Costa, 953–958. Bologna: Alma Mater Studiorum, University of Bologna.

Saarikallio, Suvi. 2011. "Music as Emotional Self-Regulation throughout Adulthood." *Psychology of Music* 39: 307–327.

Saarikallio, Suvi, and Jaakko Erkkilä. 2007. "The Role of Music in Adolescents' Mood Regulation." *Psychology of Music* 35: 88–109.

Sandgren, Maria. 2009. "Evidence of Strong Immediate Well-Being Effects of Choral Singing— With More Enjoyment for Women than for Men." Paper presented at the 7th Triennial Conference of European Society for the Cognitive Sciences of Music (ESCOM), Jyväskylä, Finland. August 12–16.

Schäfer, Thomas, Peter Sedlmeier, Christine Städtler, and David Huron. 2013. "The Psychological Functions of Music Listening." *Frontiers in Psychology* 4: 1–33.

Schäfer, Thomas, Mario Smukalla, and Sarah-Ann Oelker. 2014. "How Music Changes Our Lives: A Qualitative Study of the Long Term Effects of Intense Musical Experiences." *Psychology of Music* 42: 525–544.

Scheel, Karen R., and John S. Westefeld. 1999. "Heavy Metal Music and Adolescent Suicidality: An Empirical Investigation." *Adolescence* 34: 253–273.

Schweigman, Kurt, Claradian Soto, Serena Wright, S., and Jennifer B. Unger. 2011. "The Relevance of Cultural Activities in Ethnic Identity among California Native American Youth." *Journal of Psychoactive Drugs* 43: 343–348.

Selfhout, Maarten H. W., Susan J. T. Branje, Tom F. M. ter Bogt, and Wim H. J. Meeus. 2009. "The Role of Music Preferences in Early Adolescents' Friendship Formation and Stability." *Journal of Adolescence* 32: 95–107.

Shifriss, Roni, and Ehud Bodner. 2014. "When You're Down and Troubled: Views on the Regulatory Power of Music." *Psychology of Music* July 2, 2014. doi: 10.1177/0305735614540360.

Shuker, Roy. 2004. "Beyond the 'High Fidelity' Stereotype: Defining the (Contemporary) Record Collector." *Popular Music* 23: 311–330.

Simons, Ronald C. 1996. *Boo! Culture, Experience, and the Startle Reflex.* Oxford: Oxford University Press.

Sixsmith, Andrew, and Grant Gibson. 2007. "Music and the Well-Being of People with Dementia." *Ageing and Society* 27: 127–145.

Sloboda, John A. 1999. "Everyday Uses of Music Listening: A Preliminary Study." In *Music, Mind and Science,* edited by Suk Won Yi, 354–369. Seoul: Western Music Institute.

Solmsen, Friedrich. 1964. "Leisure and Play in Aristotle's Ideal state." *Rheinisches Museum fur Philologie* 107: 193–220.

Southcott, Jane E. 2009. "And as I Go, I Love to Sing: The Happy Wanderers, Music and Positive Aging." *International Journal of Community Music* 2: 143–156.

Stacey, Rosie, Katie Brittain, and Sandra Kerr. 2002. "Singing for Health: An Exploration of the Issues." *Health Education* 102: 156–162.

Stamou, Lelouda. 2002. "Plato and Aristotle on Music and Music Education: Lessons from Ancient Greece." *International Journal of Music Education* 39: 3–16.

Stebbins, Robert A. 1992. *Amateurs, Professionals, and Serious Leisure.* Montreal. QC: McGill-Queen's University Press.

Stebbins, Robert A. 2010. "Addiction to Leisure Activities: Is It Possible?" *LSA Newsletter* 86: 19–22.

Stevens, Carolyn S. 2010. "You Are What You Buy: Postmodern Consumption and Fandom of Japanese Popular Culture." *Japanese Studies* 30: 199–214.

Steverink, Nardi, and Siegwart Lindenberg. 2006. "Which Social Needs Are Important for Subjective Well-Being? What Happens to Them with Aging?" *Psychology and Aging* 21: 281–290.

Straw, Will. 1997. "Sizing up Record Collections: Gender and Connoisseurship in Rock Music Culture." In *Sexing the Groove: Popular Music and Gender,* edited by Sheila Whiteley, 3–16. New York: Routledge.

Tahlier, Michelle, Anca M. Miron, and Frances H. Rauscher. 2013. "Music Choice as Sadness Regulation Strategy in Resolved versus Unresolved Sad Events." *Psychology of Music* 41: 729–748.

Tarrant, Mark, Adrian C. North, and David J. Hargreaves. 2001. "Social Categorisation, Self-Esteem, and the Musical Preferences of Male Adolescents." *Journal of Social Psychology* 141: 565–581.

Taylor, Angela. 2010. "Participation in a Master Class: Experiences of Older Amateur Pianists" *Music Education Research* 12: 199–218.

Taylor, Angela, and Susan Hallam. 2008. "Understanding What It Means for Older Students to Learn Basic Musical Skills on a Keyboard Instrument." *Music Education Research* 10: 285–306.

Tolfree, Elinor, and Susan Hallam. Forthcoming. "Young People's Uses of and Responses to Music in their Everyday Lives." *Research Studies in Music Education*.

Trainor, Laurel J. 2014. "The Importance of Rhythm and Interpersonal Synchrony in Social Development." Paper presented at the conference The Neurosciences and Music—V: Cognitive Stimulation and Rehabilitation, Grand Théâtre / Palais des Ducs, Dijon, May 29–June 1.

Travis, Raphael, and Scott W. Bowman. 2012. "Ethnic Identity, Self-Esteem and Variability in Perceptions of Rap Music's Empowering and Risky Influences." *Journal of Youth Studies* 15: 455–478.

Van den Tol, Annemieke J. M., and Jane Edwards. 2014. "Listening to Sad Music in Adverse Situations: Music Selection Strategies, Self-Regulatory Goals, Listening Effect, and Mood-Enhancement." *Psychology of Music* 43: 473–494.

Varvarigou, Maria, Andrea Creech, Susan Hallam, and Hilary McQueen. 2012. "Bringing Different Generations together in Music-Making: An Intergenerational Music Project in East London." *International Journal of Community Music* 4: 207–220.

Varvarigou, Maria, Andrea Creech, Susan Hallam, and Hilary McQueen. 2013. "Different Ways of Experiencing Music-Making in Later Life: Creative Music Sessions for Older Learners in East London." *Research Studies in Music Education* 15: 103–118.

Varvarigou, Maria, Susan Hallam, Andrea Creech, and Hilary McQueen. 2012. "Benefits Experienced by Older People Who Participated in Group Music-Making Activities." *Journal of Applied Arts and Health* 3: 183–198.

Voida, Amy, Rebecca E. Grinter, and Nicholas Ducheneaut. 2006. "Social Practices around iTunes." In *Consuming Music Together: Social and Collaborative Aspects of Music Consumption Technologies*, edited by Kenton O'Hara and Barry Brown, 57–84. Netherlands: Springer.

Wood, Abigail. 2010. "Singing Diplomats: The Hidden Life of a Russian-Speaking Choir in Jerusalem." *Ethnomusicology Forum* 19: 165–190.

Wristen, Brenda. 2006. "Demographics and Motivation of Adult Group Piano Students." *Music Education Research* 8: 387–406.

CHAPTER 4

ASPIRING TO MUSIC MAKING AS LEISURE THROUGH THE MUSICAL FUTURES CLASSROOM

ABIGAIL D'AMORE AND GARETH DYLAN SMITH

ROGER MANTIE (2015, 169), writing about an American context, observes that "In the first half of the 20th century the learning and teaching of music was connected with an appreciation of leisure and recreation, aspects viewed as central to 'the good life' and the 'art of living.'" He goes on to note, however, that "leisure and recreation do not currently register as the proper concerns of music educators" (170). In this chapter we argue, similarly, that making music for purposes of leisure is not valued highly within the formal construct of many English secondary school music classrooms. While we acknowledge that this is a concern in other territories (Kratus 2007; Music Learning Profiles Project forthcoming), we concentrate on England for the purposes of this chapter.

The focus of our discussion is Musical Futures (MF),[1] an organization "with a charitable purpose to transform, engage and inspire people through making music that is meaningful to them" (Musical Futures 2015). MF provides resources to schools and school teachers, including training in music pedagogy, continued professional development, and a range of tools for use in the music classroom. We explore the impact that the informal making and learning of music can have on teenagers' social, personal, and emotional development and how bringing leisure-oriented musicking practices into schools can help to improve students' overall perceptions of and attitudes toward school in general, and their identities and agency into the future (Wright 2010). We also discuss the transformative effect MF can have on teachers who implement its strategies and we explore conflicts that can arise from bringing informal "real-world" learning approaches into the classroom.

Drawing on empirical data gathered from two studies on MF take-up and long-term impact with teachers and students, we present evidence from one school as an example of how an MF pedagogical approach has provided a positive influence. We further outline how a global community of practice is developing around MF as part of an international movement to improve the provision of music education in schools—what Randles (2015a, 195) refers to as a dynamic "change movement." Thus, we propose that educators, parents, students, and other stakeholders conspire to construe, construct, create, and curate liminal music education spaces (Smith and Shafighian 2014) through MF pedagogy, aspiring to music making as leisure in and beyond school music provision.

MUSIC, IDENTITY, AND LEARNING

Music forms an intrinsic part of the lives of the majority of teenagers in the societies of developed nations. They live music (Bennett 2006; DeNora 2000, 2006; Frith 1981; Green 2002; Smith 2013), whether through creating, producing, making, consuming, or, increasingly, combinations of these activities, in physical spaces and online (see this volume, O'Leary and Tobias, chapter 28; Moir, chapter 13). Hendry highlights how "leisure is a central concern in young people's lives" (1983, 26); the type of leisure that we focus on in this chapter is explained by Hendry as "*positive*—leisure offers the chance of finding self-identity, the opportunity to build meaningful and fulfilling life styles. It includes activities which involve wide social interaction" (24). Teenagers engage with music in their leisure time in multifarious ways, from learning and perfecting music in groups to using digital technologies for music creation, production, publishing, and listening. As the boundaries between music consumption and production continue to merge and blur (Jenkins 2006; Partti 2012; Tobias 2015; Waldron 2009), it is perhaps more helpful to think of time spent actively engaging with music. Whether they acknowledge themselves as "musicians" or "being musical" or not, 84 percent of young people under the age of twenty-five cite music as an important part of their lives (Warwick Commission 2015).

Lucy Green's groundbreaking research into how popular musicians learn (2002) describes the ways in which young musicians create music in their leisure time via collaborating with friends, learning "their" music, and directing their own musical learning and progress. As Baker (2013, 291) emphasizes, "outside the dominion of curricular, schools and colleges, a great deal of music-making and learning, in childhood and into adulthood, occurs most successfully." Green (2008, 42) describes these ways of making and learning music as involving some "natural" elements, that is, elements that are shared by youngsters without their having been taught them or having necessarily observed them happening in practice—a notion supported in earlier research by Stålhammar (2003). Smith (2013), in a study involving drummers, explains how young musicians engage in making music: "without the intention of learning per se, they did it as part of their building on being drummers, as part of the active realization" of identities as drummers. Bamberger (1978, 173) writes of "intuitive musical knowing" in ways that resonate with the practices of teenage music maker-learners, an idea to which Campbell

(1998, 48) responds, observing that "intuitive learning is part of becoming enculturated, and this learning proceeds informally through children's immersion within and exploration of a culture." As Green (2002, 22) explains, "the concept of enculturation refers to the acquisition of musical skills and knowledge by immersion in the everyday music and musical practices of one's social context."

The centrality of music listening, and of music making as highly meaningful leisure activities in the lives and social contexts of teenagers is highlighted in Green's (2002) assertion that "identity . . . is intrinsically and unavoidably connected to particular ways of learning." This notion is affirmed by Smith's observation that learning is "part of the narrative process of identity construction and construal" (2013, 16), what Wenger describes as "how learning changes who we are and creates personal histories of becoming" (1998, 5). Whatever and however students are learning music and learning about music in their own time, they are thus developing as individual musical agents in their socio-cultural contexts. We believe that this identity realization through leisure-like music making is worth aspiring to in the musical classroom too.

There remains, however, a disconnect between this rich world of creating, producing, consuming, enjoying, and "living" music and the music making environment of many school music classrooms (Allsup 2010, 220). Thus, "one can . . . easily identify myriad musics that exist *outside* of the official knowledge among many music educators" (Music Learning Profiles Project forthcoming). Beyond the formal construct of the school, music is not perceived by teenagers as a "subject." Yet the music classroom is not always a place where students' "outside" culture(s) connect with activity and learning inside schools (Music Learning Profiles Project forthcoming; Randles 2015b; Wright 2010).

In England, music education is statutory for all students in secondary or high school between the ages of eleven and fourteen (Department for Education 2013). This provides an excellent opportunity to engage, motivate, and support teenagers with a set of rich musical experiences that relate to their own concepts of music and musical culture. This opportunity embraces a moral obligation for music educators to place students at the heart of approaches to curating music learning experiences in the classroom:

> The main curricular question facing "school music" educators is whether it is "the music" that is to be served—that is, perpetuated for its own sake—or whether music (in the sense of a conceptual category that includes many musics) and, hence, music education exist to serve the various social needs that bring both into existence in the first place. (Regelski 2009, 78)

The social needs to which Regelski alludes include the realization of overlapping contextual identities (Smith 2013, 15) of young people in music, and in other areas of their lives such as various roles adopted in classrooms, on the playground, at home, and so on. Music educators need to be aware of young people's identity realization—how they are who they are, and how they become who they will be—in order to serve well those in their care. As Smith (2013, 53) states, "it is indeed vital for teachers to maintain an awareness of the impact of their influence not only upon students' learning but also upon their identities." Beyond this awareness, Jorgensen (2006, 38) underlines the imperative for teachers "to come to their own versions of how they believe they should intervene in the identity construction of young and old alike, because whatever they do, they will be having an impact on the students in their charge."

It is in this context that Baker (2013, 292) observes that "in recent years, there has been a proliferation of attention to popular music . . . and 'informal learning' in music education." Yet, a 2012 report by England's schools regulatory body, the Office for Standards in Education, Children's Services and Skills (Ofsted), outlined that "too much provision" of music in secondary schools was "inadequate or barely satisfactory," and that music teaching "continued to be dominated by the spoken or written word rather than musical sounds." Music has a low uptake as an examination subject beyond the statutory requirement—a national average of 7 percent (Gill 2012)—a further indication of the low value placed on music as a school subject by students.

Why should this be the case? We know that music forms a critical part of teenagers' lives. There is plentiful research documenting the wider benefits of learning and creating music, including the potential to increase the overall health, well-being, social, personal, and intellectual development of a child (Hallam 2010; Hallam, Creech, and Varvarigou this volume, chapter 3; MacDonald, Kreutz, and Mitchell 2012). Research indicates that one of the key reasons for poor levels of engagement with music is that there is often very little music making happening in school classrooms (Zeserson 2014). Perhaps, as with a recent study conducted in the U.S., "secondary school music instruction [w]as a main reason [English secondary school students] stopped seeing themselves as musicians" (Salvador 2015, 222). Like other initiatives developing on the fringes of music education's cultural hegemony, MF aims "to help nurture genuine engagement with music learning in all of its marvelous abundance" (Music Learning Profiles Project forthcoming).

Following Wright (2012), scholars explain that:

> There is a tangible and increasing yearning in the music education community for a reflexive refreshment and re-invigoration of the profession from scholars and practitioners, to bring meaningful music experiences to all young people through the powerful means of the education system—not "just" so that people enjoy better *musical* lives, but so that, overall, people's lives, self-esteem and happiness might improve. (Music Learning Profiles Project forthcoming)

Consistent with this belief, MF recognizes "the continued importance of opening up what we conceive to be 'music education'" (Green 2011, 19). The work of MF exists as part of:

> Recent moves . . . in which educators are respecting and incorporating the informal music-making and music-learning practices that take place outside the school or other formal education institutions, and are developing new teaching methods that aim to reflect such practices, as well as the values and identities that go along with them. (Green 2011, 18)

Similarly, Randles and Smith find that "student musical creativity, coupled with the explosion of computer-based music technology, and the saturation of popular music in the lives of students globally . . . presents the greatest potential for growth in school music programs in England and the US" (2012, 184). Thus, Smith and Durrant (2006, 54) suggest, "the obligation on music teachers . . . is to accommodate the learning needs of all their students. . . and make adjustments in practice accordingly." It is worth underlining here that the authors do not suggest that MF offers a panacea for all perceived ills of school music, or that it is in any way guaranteed to meet the music making or learning needs of all children in schools. We acknowledge, however, what Dewey (1997, 38) considers teachers' ethical obligations, believing that "the mature person, to put it in moral terms, has no right to withhold from the young on given occasions whatever capacity for sympathetic understanding his [or her] own experience has given him [or her]." MF offers one approach to embracing this ideal.

MUSICAL FUTURES:
PROCESS VERSUS PRODUCT

MF is a learning system that deeply values people creating and making music, first and foremost *for the sake of making music*, supporting the individual and social imperatives and contexts of music making discussed above. Established in 2003[2] to address issues surrounding student disengagement and disenfranchisement with music in formal settings, MF is now used by thousands of teachers in schools in the U.K. and internationally.

Pedagogically, MF incorporates learning practices from the "real world" of musical learning outside of formal educational institutions, combining these methods with students' own musical interests and passions to create compelling approaches for classroom music learning. These are:

- An informal learning model, developed by Lucy Green at the University College London Institute of Education (Green 2008, 2014);
- Classroom workshopping, developed in partnership with Guildhall Connect, Guildhall School of Music and Drama, London: teaching and learning strategies for large-group composing, improvising, and performing, where students provide the musical material and teachers facilitate its development, drawn from successful techniques of community music practitioners;
- Find Your Voice:[3] a process for students to explore using their voices and mobile technologies to create and make music.

For many young musicians, the creation of music informally, outside of school is an extensive and time-consuming leisure pursuit, in which context they have considerable control over how, when, and if they perform (and what constitutes "performance") or whether they participate in music making purely for its own sake, without the need to perform. A key tenet of MF is that it emphasizes the process of making music in a safe, nurturing environment. While performance (whether, for instance, being filmed, performing to peers, or performing to a broader audience) is encouraged at intervals, to increase student confidence and aspiration and to support mandatory assessment requirements, it is the creative and identity-building process of making music—of becoming a musician—that is the primary focus.

Within a whole-school context, music is often viewed as a "showcase," where musicals and public performances by choirs, bands, and orchestras take precedence over the statutory delivery of the curriculum (Zeserson 2014). MF challenges this by encouraging music teachers and schools to make the classroom a place where high-quality music learning takes place, and where the development of a range of musicalities (composing, listening, performing, improvising) are supported and nurtured. With the pedagogical focus on the process, enabled and empowered students are the product.

LEISURE IN THE MUSIC CLASSROOM

In this section we focus on one aspect of MF—the informal learning model—to illustrate how bringing small-group, student-led, collaborative music learning into a classroom context resonates with meaningful activities undertaken as leisure. Hendry (1983, 166) categorizes young people's leisure in terms of three activity types: (1) organized (i.e., adult-led) activities, (2) casual activities (i.e. socializing with friends, often lacking adult supervision), and (3) commercial activities (attending gigs, pubs, clubs, cinemas, etc.). The informal learning model takes a "casual leisure" activity (with boundaries blurring with "commercial leisure") and places it in a setting that is "organized." It is based on five guiding principles, which are directly drawn from the ways popular musicians learn outside the classroom: learning music that learners choose for themselves and with which they identify; learning in friendship groups; learning aurally; acknowledging that the learning process is not always linear; and integrating listening, performing, composing, and improvising (Green 2008, 10).

Voice, Choice, and Collaboration in the Classroom

An implicit aspect of the informal learning model is that student voice and choice are intrinsic. Students are autonomous, self-directed, and make regular conscious and unconscious choices regarding elements, including what music they learn, who they learn with, which combination of instruments or voices and/or technologies they use, how and when they access expert support, and how and when they access resources (e.g., notation, guitar tab, lyrics, tutorial videos from YouTube). A survey of 691 teachers and 1079 students in MF schools indicated that giving students this level of autonomy over their learning led to enhanced musical skills, increased motivation, self-esteem and confidence, greater focus, improved behavior, better concentration, greater demonstration of leadership, and improved small group skills (Hallam et al. 2008).

Working collaboratively in a self-directed manner can also lead to the acquisition of transferable skills that are valuable elsewhere in the school. Hallam, Creech, and McQueen (2011) reported that one-third of students agreed that working in groups in MF lessons helped them in other school subjects; nonmusic teaching staff noted improvements in concentration, team work, organizational skills, and independent learning skills. One-half of students agreed that MF supported them to feel more positive about school in general. Engaging in this style of learning often also results in an increased continuity between school music, extracurricular musical activities and out-of-school music activities (Hallam et al. 2008). After implementing MF, teachers reported an average increase of 42 percent in the take-up of optional music at age fourteen (Hallam et al. 2008) as against the national average of 7 percent cited above. Over one-third of students felt that in MF lessons, including those from the Classroom Workshopping strand, they were able to draw on music activities and interests from outside school (Hallam, Creech, and McQueen 2011)—aspiring to, and learning from, music making as leisure.

Impact on Staff-Student Relationships

A critical factor for the success of bringing informal learning into the classroom is the role adopted by the teacher. One of the major differences between in-school and (most) out-of-school musical learning is that there is an adult supervising, guiding, or facilitating the overall process in the classroom. Therefore, to be successful with utilizing an MF approach, a teacher needs to establish an environment of mutual trust and respect, where students feel their musical interests are valued and they can have control over their learning styles. Teachers are advised to set a task going, and then enter into a period of standing back, observing students working, before diagnosing need, guiding, and modeling in order to help students achieve the objectives they set for themselves (D'Amore 2009; Green 2008).

This mode of working is not prescriptive, and effective practice is often dependent on individual teacher style and approach, plus a reliance on experienced intuitive decision making. If support and guidance are offered too quickly, or too forcefully, students' sense of ownership can deteriorate, resulting in disengagement with the process. If students are left for too long without any input, and are unsure of how to progress with a musical, technical, or collaborative issue they can stray off task and behavior can decline (Hallam, Creech, and McQueen 2011, 56). Effective teachers offer help via musical modeling, and leave students to internalize and process their advice, under supervision (Green 2008, 30–38; 2014, 84–98). Teachers recognize that they are not the experts of every musical style and genre, but that they can help to craft and enable musical collaborations and performances. As Randles (2012, 44) observes, "these types of teachers transcend tradition for the sake of their students' futures." They place emphasis on the expertise of students within the room, or older students within the school, and encourage peer-to-peer learning as an integral part of the process (Green 2008, 119–149).

In the intensive study by Hallam, Creech, and McQueen (2011) of seven schools across a three-year period, researchers captured qualitative data on teacher-student relationships in MF lessons:

> The kids learn from each other. One will come out of one group and say, can you help me with the drums? And then that kid comes out of their group and helps them with the drums and then goes back into their group. I love that. It's having the freedom and they know they can come out of their rooms to help other people and they know who to ask as well. (Head of Music)

> I get feedback about how it's good and then how I can improve. It's more helpful than just saying it's good. Teachers quite often go yes, that's OK and then just carry on. (Year 10, boy)

These quotes exemplify aspects of the informal learning approach explained by Green's (2002, 2008) and Randles's (2012) notion of music teachers as producers—a role that Smith and Shafighian (2014, 263) describe as "the nurturing and curating of liminal spaces—musical and physical—by teachers who are comfortable to adopt the role of producer."

Informal Learning Enabling the Teacher as Musician

When students are learning in a self-directed, informal way in the classroom, research indicates a positive impact not only on student-teacher relationships, but on teachers' own sense of identity as musicians (Hallam, Creech, and McQueen 2011; Hallam et al. 2008). As Randles (2015a, 195) puts it, "we as teachers grow personally and collectively by going through the processes of enacting change." The demands on teachers are varied, and can present new challenges, for example: playing by ear; demonstrating and modeling musical skills and techniques on instruments and in musical genres with which they may be unfamiliar; singing or vocalizing in a range of styles (including beatboxing); being prepared to learn alongside the students; supporting and coaching students through developing creative ideas and refining musical performances; using technology (including mobile technology) as part of creative and performance processes.

The perceived demands faced by teachers are rarely to do with embracing the above, but concern a fear of losing control (Hallam, Creech, and McQueen 2011). However, for many teachers this eventually becomes a more "musical" and engaging way of teaching; as these teachers reported in Hallam, Creech, and McQueen (2011, 73):

> I get a lot of professional satisfaction from it. You go through this sort of, you know, week 3 or 4, where you wonder what are they doing and then there are suddenly moments, amazing moments, those special moments in music education certainly

where suddenly you hear someone sing for the first time and you think wow isn't that amazing. And they enjoy performing, they're not frightened to perform mostly. And they'll be here at lunchtimes practising for it when they've got to play. To have a whole class on task, working and wanting to perform is amazing. (Music teacher)

A number of teachers reported that MF helped them to become more effective, confident teachers, generally increasing their enjoyment in teaching music and raising awareness of the music with which students engage outside of school (Hallam, Creech, and McQueen 2011, 75), for example:

It's contributed to making us focus on learning in the department. What is musical learning? How do they learn? How do they learn best? We've redone all our schemes of work in response to that. We've looked at assessing work and the fact that it can be perfectly adequately assessed. We've looked at collating data as evidence that things are going well. Attainment is higher. (Head of Music)

Using MF in the classroom thus represents a departure from traditional, "transmission-style" formal teaching methodologies employed in classrooms (Jorgensen 1997, 24), and toward the more "natural" model of learning discussed above (Green 2008, 42), that celebrates students' learning as part of the enculturation in music that they experience outside of the classroom (Smith 2013, 34). It may be helpful to conceive of the music learning environment in terms of the construct of "pedagogic authority" proposed by Bourdieu and Passeron (1977, 10). Smith (2013, 35) explains this notion as "the question of whence learners choose to seek or accept instruction, information and understanding—to whom does one ascribe the wisdom and right to impart that which one is willing to consider valuable and desirable knowledge?" The informal learning approach relinquishes teachers of some traditionally presumed pedagogic authority, ascribing it instead to the music, the students, and (as far as is possible given the culture in individual music classrooms and the education system within which they operate) to the cultures within which these musics and music learning practices exist beyond formal education contexts. When teachers learn through this process, they too are ascribing pedagogic authority to musics and cultures (instead of wielding it themselves), and also ascribing pedagogic authority to the informal learning process.

MUSICAL FUTURES AS
A GROWING MOVEMENT

MF was piloted in sixty schools across England during 2004–2006. It is now being used by approximately 1,500 teachers in the U.K., and by at least 500 teachers in other countries, with organized programs running in Australia (Jeanneret et al. 2011), Canada

(Wright et al. 2012), Singapore (Chua and Ho 2016), and Brazil (Narita 2015), where university departments are embedding the practices into initial teacher education.[4]

Due to all materials being freely and widely available, it is difficult to track the exact reach of MF; therefore, these numbers are based on a variety of unpublished internal surveys completed by MF and other anecdotal data, emails, and personal experience and observation. The nature of the global spread of MF indicates that the philosophy and associated pedagogy for connecting in- and out-of-school learning, placing emphasis on music as a leisure activity within schools, and valuing students' own musical interests as the starting point, resonate with and have impact on teachers and students that transcends the educational context.

CHALLENGES FACING MUSICAL FUTURES INITIATIVES IN SCHOOLS

Despite the demonstrable benefits to students and teachers, a dichotomy exists between the evident success and impact of informal learning, and the challenges and barriers that can be presented by the organizational systems and processes of many schools. Hallam, Creech, and McQueen (2011) and Hallam et al. (2008) identified the main challenges stated by teachers as accommodation issues, resource implications (lack of instruments or finances to purchase equipment), the difficulty of managing with only one staff member, and scheduling. While such challenges are not specific to MF, the informal learning approach in particular can demand a rethink of managing statutory music provision in a department.

Space, Time, and Resources

It can be challenging to replicate within a school situation the varied contexts in which young people make music outside of school. We should like to highlight that we are aware of the complexities of the debates surrounding notions of authenticity in the music classroom, especially those pertaining to popular music practices and culture (e.g. Green 2002; Lilliestam 1995; Söderman 2013). As Parkinson and Smith note:

> A range of ideological and aesthetic values are encoded in the tastes, practices, and genre affiliations of musically diverse student cohorts. Some of these values may sit in contradiction to those inhering in curricula and pedagogy designed to accommodate popular music as a holistic genre, rather than a vast and internally disparate field. (2015, 95)

Musical Futures' pedagogical approach, however, is primarily concerned with curating meaningful, valuable experiences in the music classroom, rather than with faithful replication of particular genre-specific practices or adherence to popular (sub)cultural ideologies (Kallio, Westerlund, and Partti 2015); we will not, therefore, be venturing further in this chapter into the epistemological minefield of authenticity in the music classroom.

Teachers embracing an MF pedagogical approach should always be sensitive to the habitus (Bourdieu 1984) of each of the students in their care, embracing the MF vision of "a future where everybody benefits from the value of making music" (Musical Futures 2015). The worth resides in the engagement, in the doing, in what Christopher Small (1998) identified as the centrality of "musicking." MF's pedagogy thus aligns with a worldwide community of music teachers and music education advocates, who "believe that lived experiences of music . . . are a vital part of the life of all people" (International Society for Music Education 2015).

Students need a space to be able to work independently in small groups, where they can hear each other and listen closely to the music they are trying to replicate and create. In some school music departments only one classroom is available. Many teachers have negotiated additional space, or have experimented with workstations where students work on electronic instruments and headphones are connected to a central hub (e.g., Williams and Randles 2016), with varying degrees of success. Music lesson lengths within busy timetables can be as short as thirty-five minutes once per week, or can be longer, for instance if placed in rotation with other arts subjects on a school timetable. Yet outside of school, students are able to dedicate hours of their time to informal music making. A common outcome of embedding informal learning practices in a school is the numbers of students wanting to continue to work before and after lessons, during break times, and after school (Green and Walmsley 2006).

While the informal learning approach can be implemented using basic instruments and equipment (Green and Walmsley 2006), there are evident improvements in student motivation when they are able to use instruments and technologies that they see as more "authentic" and relevant to the musical styles and genres about which they are passionate. Many teachers have found effective approaches to distributing instruments, for example by putting students in charge of managing the rotation of groups around spaces and particular pieces of equipment, such as drum kits. Other successful ventures have included organizing fundraising events such as student-run gigs, or having students put proposals and bids to head teachers in order to secure more funding for equipment.

Staffing

Thousands of music teachers use MF in the classroom single-handedly, but many teachers report that while it is a highly enjoyable and motivating approach to facilitating music learning in the classroom, it can be an intense drain on energy, leading to "burn-out" (Hallam, Creech, and McQueen 2011, 57). Some teachers have overcome this by drawing on specialist support they have available in their music departments—for example, peripatetic instrumental teachers—by team-teaching classes, and occasionally by engaging older students in the school to support with specific practical tasks and activities.

Perceived Risks to Teachers

Green identifies that while informal learning practices can introduce constructive ways for music teachers to understand and approach their work, they can generate conflicts with broader curricular requirements, as well as with their existing views of how music "should" be taught. Teachers typically experience a dip after three weeks of engagement (Green 2008, 2014; Green and Walmsley 2006), when learning seems chaotic and sporadic, and teachers feel there is little progress occurring. However, Green clearly identifies the "haphazard learning process" of popular musicians, where "getting worse before getting better" is a common element, as key to informal learning processes. Hallam, Creech, and McQueen (2011, 75) quotes a music teacher who grew in confidence through applying an MF approach over time:

> The first time I did Musical Futures it was a little bit more stressful because you get less control, it's the whole control freak thing. I think being a teacher you generally are a control freak and handing it over to the students is quite frightening at first. When you get used to it, you still set the boundaries, the students get used to it, they know what they're doing a bit more. (Music Teacher)

Assessment forms a central part of the informal learning process (Green 2002; Lebler 2007), but unlike traditional assessment models, it is a subtle, peer-to-peer assessment against "their own past and projected performances" (Green 2002, 209), often with reference to the music of students' peers and of the models that they are copying. In cases where they are supported by their senior leadership teams, teachers have been encouraged to be creative and innovative with assessment methods, for example making use of audio and film to create digital portfolios of students' work.

All of this indicates the necessity for senior management and leadership teams in schools to give full support to the implementation of informal learning approaches in music classrooms, as it is likely to have an impact on school resources as well as introducing a possibly new culture into the school that some staff, walking past or into the music department while informal learning is in action, may need to (learn to) understand in order to appreciate. Zeserson (2014) argues that it is the responsibility of U.K. music education sector organizations to generate better understanding among senior leaders of how music can transform their overall school environments in order to avoid the dual risk of constraining good practice and encouraging bad practice. To this end, a commission called INSPIRE Music,[5] comprising members from across the music education sector, has been established in the U.K. The commission aims to address issues of advocacy and promote and support the sharing of emerging, effective, and innovative practice.

MUSICAL FUTURES IN PRACTICE: GREENFIELD COMMUNITY COLLEGE, SUNNYDALE CAMPUS, COUNTY DURHAM

Following the attendance at an MF training session in 2007, Head of Music Allison Brown and Head of Music Technology Ursula Massingham have used MF across their entire music department. Both were interviewed for this chapter, along with one of their students.

Impact on Students

Allison and Ursula inherited a department where music had a history of staff absence, which in turn led to students having little respect for the department. Behavior was poor and required continual support from senior managers. The two music staff chose to adopt MF in their context with the hope that the learning approaches would engage, motivate, and inspire their students:

> We have few behavior issues now . . . I'm shocked when I see students' bad behavior for other teachers, when we don't see that in music at all. Eight years down the line music regularly is cited as the most popular subject by students, even surpassing physical education. (Ursula Massingham)

As well as improvements in behavior and motivation, achievement has dramatically improved. The average percentage of students receiving A–C grades in music[6] prior to MF taking place was 33 percent. Following implementation of MF this has increased to a consistent average of 84 percent.

Chloe (aged fifteen), who took music as an optional examination subject following using MF approaches from age eleven to fourteen, reflected on her experience:

> I'm a singer, but I learnt to play piano by listening to YouTube clips and teaching myself how to play it. What we did in class gave me the courage to do that. We might be loud, but there is always more productive work going on than messing about. You want your work to be good! Everyone comes together when it's fun and productive.

The nature of small group work enabled Allison and Ursula to get to know their students and to understand more about individuals' often diverse and challenging learning needs. Ursula stated:

> In a [traditional] classroom situation some of our kids are impossible. In a small group you can allow them be themselves without feeling any loss of control as a

teacher. They have more freedom to express themselves. You get to know them as learners more.

Connecting In and Out of School Music Activities

Through small group work Allison and Ursula have been able to identify students who have active musical lives outside of school, but who had not previously demonstrated their musicality in school:

> You don't always realize what music means to some students . . . but then they post music online, write about things, articulately express themselves. You realize then just how important music is to them, and the impact it has on their voices within school. (Allison Brown)

This serves to illustrate how, by integrating informal approaches, some of the boundaries between how students experience music as a leisure activity in their own lives and how they approach it in their school-based time, are significantly narrowed.

In Summary

As discussed above, MF is a learning system that can be both challenging and exciting to integrate into a school environment. It requires teachers to reflect and reevaluate their individual and departmental approaches to music teaching and organization, for instance by reframing "teaching" as "learning" activities (e.g., Bamberger 1978; Green 2002; Stålhammar 2003). The approach has proven popular, although it is not statutory, and even when its implementation holds multiple challenges. The impact on students is demonstrable in diverse international contexts; however, many approaches to teaching and learning music have positive impacts on students. One possible reason is that MF has united teachers and practitioners through a shared belief, a set of values and principles that approaching music in this way, in schools, is a highly effective way of enabling music learning to happen. Moreover, it connects teachers and students with the reasons why and the ways in which they (would) make music in the first place—those identified by Green (2008) and Stålhammar (2003) as "natural." As such, MF offers one powerful and convincing answer to Regelski's question, that we quoted, above—"whether it is the music that is to be served—that is, perpetuated for its own sake—or whether music . . . and, hence, music education exist to serve the various social needs that bring both into existence in the first place" (2009, 78).

Spurred on by the spread of social media sites Twitter, Facebook, and Instagram, MF has been driven by the grassroots—teachers and students—and developed as an international movement and "community of practice." Wenger (1998) defines communities of practice as groups of people who have a shared domain of interest, a commitment to learning from each other, and a community—joint activities, discussions, and building of relationships. Crucially, communities of practice, once established, are not static, but vital and dynamic. As Wenger (1998, 7) explains, "for *individuals*, it means that learning is an issue of engaging in and contributing to the practices of their communities. For *communities*, it means that learning is an issue of refining their practice and ensuring new generations of members." Understanding the international MF community in these terms captures the relentless need (and desire) in the community for teachers and practices to evolve in real time, in response to the needs of individual students, particular school environments, and broader cultural evolution.

Conclusions

In this chapter we have explored the Musical Futures pedagogical model and approach, focusing on its alignment with the (re)emerging attention being paid to music making and leisure. The joint frame of an MF approach and the aspiration to leisure has clear implications for considering adolescents' identity and learning realization, for the continued professional development of teachers, and for the democratization of classroom spaces, where issues of power and pedagogic authority are raised, challenged, and negotiated. One of the most exciting aspects of MF is that it focuses on the process(es) in and of music learning. Of course MF is not alone in urging and affording this emphasis, but it is exciting to see how returning to a "natural" means of music making (Green 2008, 42) and nurturing this in an institutionalized learning space can engage, encourage, and grow young and older musicians.

There is surely also much to critique about MF, and the authors welcome insights from such criticism as valuable and necessary feedback for the development of a still-emergent paradigm. There is certainly a need for ongoing study—action research, interview studies, and the gathering and analysis of quantitative data—to monitor the application and implications of MF as it spreads as a concept, a construct, and a learning model. We hope, nonetheless, that the emphasis in the chapter on what we see as the positive effects of an MF approach in music classrooms, schools, and communities (of practice) will provoke discussion among colleagues and peers, and, ideally, lead to improvements in the musical experiences and lives of young people.

After Mantie (2015, 179), we aspire "to resurrect leisure and recreation" as valid and worthwhile means and ends, in and for music education in English secondary schools and beyond. To bring about such change in understanding the value of making music will require some cultural change in our society around what is perceived as "successful" or "good" music. Recognition of process *as* product is a feature of some musical cultures (see Malone, this volume, chapter 29), but rarely, if ever, is it sufficient in the current educational climate, where excellence and measurable outcomes are the name of the game. As Mantie urges music education professionals to remember, "Appreciating music is fine; doing music, however, holds greater potential for realizing more of music's goodness as a healthy and worthy use of leisure time" (179). Where better to learn and embed this understanding—this aspiration—than at school?

NOTES

1. www.musicalfutures.org.
2. MF was established, funded, and managed by the Paul Hamlyn Foundation (www.phf.org. uk), a U.K.-based independent grant-making foundation
3. Developed in partnership with The Sage Gateshead.
4. See www.musicalfuturesaustralia.org and http://musicalfuturescanada.org.
5. See the Paul Hamlyn Foundation (www.phf.org.uk) for more information on INSPIRE Music.
6. The post-14, nonstatutory graded examination GCSE system grades students from A to E, with C constituting a pass, and A* representing the highest grade attainable.

REFERENCES CITED

Allsup, Randall. 2010. "Choosing Music Literature." In *Critical Issues in Music Education: Contemporary Theory and Practice*, edited by Harold F. Abeles and Lori A. Custodero, 215–235. New York: Oxford University Press.

Baker, David. 2013. "Music, Informal Learning and the Instrumental Lesson Teacher and Student Evaluations of the Ear Playing Project (EPP)." In *Developing the Musician: Contemporary Perspectives on Teaching and Learning*, edited by Mary Stakelum, 291–310. Farnham: Ashgate.

Bamberger, Jeanne. 1978. "Intuitive and Formal Musical Knowing: parable of Cognitive Dissonance." In *The Arts, Cognition and Basic Skills*, edited by Stanley S. Madeja, 173–106. St. Louis, LA: Cemrel.

Bennett, Andy. 2006. "Subcultures of Neotribes. Rethinking the Relationship between Youth, Style and Musical Taste." In *The Popular Music Studies Reader*, edited by Andy Bennett, Barry Shank, and Jason Toynbee, 106–113. London: Routledge.

Bourdieu, Pierre. 1984. *Distinction: A Social Critique of the Judgement of Taste*. Translated by Richard Nice. Cambridge, MA: Harvard University Press.

Bourdieu, Pierre, and Jean-Claude Passeron.1977. *Reproduction in Education, Society and Culture*. Translated by Richard Nice. London: Sage.

Campbell, Patricia Shehan. 1998. "The Musical Futures of Children." *Research Studies in Music Education* 11: 42–51.

Chua, Siew-Ling, and Hui-Ping Ho. 2016. "Towards 21st-Century Music Teaching-Learning: Reflections on Student-Centric Pedagogic Practices Involving Popular Music in Singapore." In *The Routledge Research Companion to Popular Music Education*, edited by Gareth Dylan Smith, Matt Brennan, Zack Moir, Shara Rambarran, and Phil Kirkman. Farnham: Routledge.

D'Amore, Abigail, ed. 2009. *Musical Futures: An Approach to Teaching and Learning*. London: Paul Hamlyn Foundation.

DeNora, Tia. 2000. *Music in Everyday Life*. Cambridge: Cambridge University Press.

DeNora, Tia. 2006. "Music and Self-Identity." In *The Popular Music Studies Reader*, edited by Andy Bennett, Barry Shank, and Jason Toynbee, 141–147. London: Routledge.

Dewey, John. 1997. *Experience and Education*. New York: Touchstone.

Department for Education. 2013. *Statutory National Curriculum in England: Secondary Curriculum*. London: Department for Education.

Frith, Simon. 1981. *Sound Effects: Youth, Leisure and the Politics of Rock 'n' Roll*. New York: Pantheon.

Gill, Tim. 2012. *Uptake of GCSE Subjects 2011*. Cambridge: Cambridge Assessment.

Green, Lucy. 2002. *How Popular Musicians Learn: A Way Ahead for Music Education*. Aldershot: Ashgate.

Green, Lucy. 2008. *Music, Informal Learning and the School: A New Classroom Pedagogy*. Aldershot: Ashgate.

Green, Lucy. 2011. "Introduction." In *Learning, Teaching, and Musical Identity: Voices across Cultures*, edited by Lucy Green, 1–19. Bloomington: Indiana University Press.

Green, Lucy. 2014. *Hear, Listen, Play: How to Free your Students' Aural, Improvisation and Performance Skills*. Oxford: Oxford University Press.

Green, Lucy, and Abigail Walmsley. 2006. *Classroom Resources for Informal Learning*. London: Paul Hamlyn Foundation.

Hallam, Susan. 2010. "The Power of Music: Its Impact on the Intellectual, Social and Personal Development of Children and Young People." *International Journal of Music Education* 28: 269–289.

Hallam, Susan, Andrea Creech, and Hilary McQueen. 2011. *Musical Futures: A Case Study Investigation*. London: Institute of Education, University of London.

Hallam, Susan, Andrea Creech, Clare Sandford, Tiija Rinta, Katherine Shave, and Hilary McQueen. 2008. *Survey of Musical Futures: A Report from the Institute of Education University of London for the Paul Hamlyn Foundation*. London: Institute of Education, University of London.

Hendry, Leo B. 1983. *Growing Up and Going Out: Adolescents and Leisure*. Aberdeen: Aberdeen University Press.

International Society for Music Education. 2015. http://www.isme.org.

Jeanneret, Neryl, Rebecca McLennan, and Jennifer Stevens-Ballenger. 2011. "Musical Futures: An Australian Perspective Findings From A Victorian Pilot Study." Retrieved from www.musicalfuturesaustralia.org/uploads/1/2/0/1/12012511/musical_futures_an_australian_perspective.pdf.

Jenkins, Henry. 2006. *Convergence Culture: Where Old and New Media Collide*. New York: New York University Press.

Jorgensen, Estelle R. 1997. *In Search of Music Education*. Chicago: University of Illinois Press.

Jorgensen, Estelle R. 2006. "Toward a Social Theory of Musical Identities." In *Music and Human Beings: Music and Identity*, edited by Börje Stålhammar, 27–54. Örebro: Universitetsbiblioteket.

Kallio, Alexis, Heidi Westerlund, and Heidi Partti. 2014. "The Quest for Authenticity in the Music Classroom: Sinking or Swimming?" *Nordic Research in Music Education Yearbook* 14: 1–26.

Kratus, John. 2007. "Music Education at the Tipping Point." *Music Educators Journal* 94(2): 42–48.

Lebler, Don. 2007. "Student as Master? Reflections on a Learning Innovation in Popular Music Pedagogy." *Music Education Research* 10(2): 193–213.

Lilliestam, Lars. 1995. *Gehormusik: Blues, Rock och Muntlig Tradering*. Göteborg: Akademiforlaget Corona.

MacDonald, Raymond A. R., Gunter Kreutz, and Laura Mitchell, eds. 2012. *Music, Health and Wellbeing*. New York: Oxford University Press.

Mantie, Roger. 2015. "Liminal or Lifelong: Leisure, Recreation, and the Future of Music Education." In *Music Education: Navigating the Future*, edited by Clint Randles, 167–182. New York: Routledge.

Music Learning Profiles Project. Forthcoming. "Let's Take This Outside: Flash Study Analysis and the Music Learning Profiles Project." *Action, Criticism, and Theory for Music Education*.

Musical Futures. 2015. "Who We Are." https://www.musicalfutures.org/who-we-are.

Narita, Flávia Motoyama. 2015. "Informal Learning in Action: The Domains of Music Teaching and Their Pedagogic Modes." *Music Education Research* 1–13.

Office for Standards in Education (Ofsted). 2012. *Music in Schools: Wider Still, and Wider*. Report No. 110158. London: Ofsted. https://www.gov.uk/government/uploads/system/uploads/attachment_data/file/413347/Music_in_schools_wider_still__and_wider.pdf.

Parkinson, Tom and Gareth Dylan Smith. 2015. "Towards an Epistemology of Authenticity in Higher Popular Music Education." *Action, Criticism, and Theory for Music Education* 14(1): 93–127.

Partti, Heidi. 2012. *Learning from Cosmopolitan Digital Musicians: Identity, Musicianship, and Changing Values in (In)formal Music Communities*. Helsinki: Sibelius Academy.

Randles, Clint. 2012. "Music Teacher as Writer and Producer." *Journal of Aesthetic Education* 46(3): 35–52.

Randles, Clint. 2015a. "A Quest for the Perfect Tone: Luthiering, Pedal Boards, and Curriculum Expansion." *Journal of Music, Technology and Education* 8(2): 183–197.

Randles, Clint. 2015b. "A Theory of Change in Music Education." In *Music Education: Navigating the Future*, edited by Clint Randles, 323–339. New York, Routledge.

Randles, Clint, and Gareth Dylan Smith. 2012. "A First Comparison of Pre-Service Music Teachers' Identities as Creative Musicians in the United States and England." *Research Studies in Music Education* 34: 173–187.

Regelski, Thomas A. 2009. "Curriculum Reform: Reclaiming 'Music' as Social Praxis." *Action, Criticism and Theory for Music Education* 8(1): 66–84.

Salvador, Karen. 2015. "Identity and Transformation: (Re)claiming an Inner Musician." In *Music Education: Navigating the Future*, edited by Clint Randles, 214–232. New York: Routledge.

Small, Christopher. 1998. *Musicking: The Meanings of Performing and Listening*. Middletown, CT: Wesleyan University Press.

Smith, Gareth Dylan. 2013. *I Drum, Therefore I Am: Being and Becoming a Drummer*. Farnham: Ashgate.

Smith, Gareth Dylan and Colin Durrant. 2006. "Mind Styles and Paradiddles—Beyond the Bell Curve: Towards an Understanding of Learning Preferences, and Implications for Instrumental Teachers." *Research Studies in Music Education* 26: 51–62.

Smith, Gareth Dylan, and Atar Shafighian. 2014. "Creative Space and the 'Silent Power of Traditions' in Popular Music Performance Programmes." In *Developing Creativities in Higher Music Education: International Perspectives and Practices*, edited by Pamela Burnard, 256–267. London: Routledge.

Söderman, Johan. 2013. "The Formation of Hip-Hop Academicus: How American Scholars Talk about the Academisation of Hip-Hop." *British Journal of Music Education* 30(3): 369–381.

Stålhammar, Börje. 2003. "Music Teaching and Young People's Own Musical Experience." *Music Education Research* 5(1): 61–68.

Tobias, Evan S. 2015. "Inter/Trans/Multi/Cross/New Media(ting): Navigating an Emerging Landscape of Digital Media for Music Education." In *Music Education: Navigating the Future*, edited by Clint Randles, 91–121. New York: Routledge.

Waldron, Janice. 2009. "Exploring a Virtual Music Community of Practice: Informal Music Learning on the Internet." *Journal of Music, Technology and Education* 2(23): 97–112.

Warwick Commission. 2015. "Enriching Britain: Culture, Creativity and Growth." *Warwick: The Warwick Commission Report on the Future of Cultural Value*. Available at: http://www2.warwick.ac.uk/research/warwickcommission/futureculture/finalreport/warwick_commission_report_2015.pdf.

Wenger, Étienne. 1998. *Communities of Practice: Learning, Meaning, and Identity*. Cambridge: Cambridge University Press.

Williams, David A., and Clint Randles. 2016. "Navigating the Space Between Spaces." In *The Routledge Research Companion to Popular Music Education*, edited by Gareth Dylan Smith, Matt Brennan, Zack Moir, Shara Rambarran, and Phil Kirkman. Farnham: Routledge.

Wright, Ruth. 2010. "Democracy, Social Exclusion and Music Education: Possibilities for Change." In *Sociology and Music Education*, edited by Ruth Wright, 263–282. Farnham: Ashgate.

Wright, Ruth. 2012. "Art for art's Sake, Music for Whose Sake? Democracy, Social Stratification, Social Exclusion and Music Education." Paper presented at the Institute of Contemporary Music Performance "Rock and Roles" Conference, London, July 23–24.

Wright, Ruth, Carol Beynon, Betty Anne Younker, V. Meredith, Jennifer Hutchison, and Leslie Linton. 2012. "Tuning into the Future: Informal Learning and Music Education." http://ir.lib.uwo.ca/cgi/viewcontent.cgi?article=1056&context=researchday.

Zeserson, K. 2014. *Inspiring Music for All: Next Steps in Innovation, Improvement and Integration*. London: Paul Hamlyn Foundation.

CHAPTER 5

DIY RECREATIONAL RECORDING AS MUSIC MAKING

ADAM PATRICK BELL

> CLICK-click-click-click, CLICK-click-click-click, CLICK-click-click-click, CLICK-click-click-click . . . *And so we meet again, it's just us now: metronome, music, me. So far, so good. I think I'm in the pocket with this track; this ought to be the take. Wait . . . I swear the metronome's clicks are slowing down. What the . . . ?*

ABRUPTLY the music stops blaring through my headphones and I snap out of my trance of concentration. Arching out of my slouch over the snare drum to sit up straight, I look up to see my bandmate, Martín, giving me a hand signal that I have never seen before but I intuitively and correctly interpret as, "You messed up. Start over." "Sorry," I say, to which Martín responds ever so nonchalantly, "Nah, it's cool, we'll do another one." That was Take 1.

DIY RECREATIONAL RECORDING

I am a drummer, and I play in a recreational band with two other New York transplants; I am from Canada, and Martín is from Mexico, which leaves Jonathan as the lone American in our continental trio. We started playing together when we were graduate students at New York University, each of us studying a different discipline under the umbrella of music (education, composition, and film scoring, respectively). While we have all since graduated from our studies and lead increasingly busy lives as we take on greater personal and professional responsibilities, we continue to meet once or twice a week to make music by recording. We have not played a gig yet, but we do have an album.

In this chapter I present a portrait of DIY (do-it-yourself) recreational recording as it exists currently, using the example of my band's music making processes. I also examine the evolution of DIY recording from its genesis to its current iteration to illustrate how present practices have been informed and influenced by past practices. While DIY recording may not always be recreational by nature, in the context of this chapter I focus specifically on DIY recording as a leisurely pursuit. Spencer (2008) states, "The 'do-it-yourself' approach to music making is all about producing your own music using whatever resources are available to you" (187), encapsulating the ethos of DIY: self-sufficiency. Interspersing autoethnographic excerpts with an analysis of select primary and secondary historical documents on recording, this chapter charts the development of DIY recreational recording as a process-based music making practice tethered to the tenets of ease of access and ease of use.

The Pop-Up Studio

I have yet to play a single note, and already I am sweating as if I had spent the morning running laps of Central Park. It's July, and New York is in the midst of a heatwave; as expected, the rehearsal room we rented for $22 an hour is not air-conditioned. Up on the eighteenth floor of a building on West 36th Street, just around the corner from Madison Square Garden, the venerated venue for sports and other entertainment where Billy Joel always seems to be playing, my bandmates and I convert this rental jam space into a temporary recording studio. As New Yorkers, we're accustomed to "pop-up stores," a practice where retailers lease a storefront temporarily, especially for seasonal merchandise like Halloween costumes. For us, this is prime recording season, and we mimic this mercantile model to make our own pop-up studio. We pooled our collective technological resources, such as a laptop, audio interface, and microphones, and decided that we would record our songs piecemeal in two-hour increments. When one walks through the hallways of a rehearsal facility in a multicultural hub such as New York City, the mélange of musics is aurally apparent as hip-hop and heavy metal blaring from different directions bang on your ear drums in simultaneity. Knowing that bands tend not to practice early in the morning, we chose the earliest—which conveniently correlated with the cheapest—timeslot, employing the logic that this would be our best chance to make recordings with reduced extraneous noise from the adjacent practice rooms.

Drummers don't often have the luxury of playing their own drums at shows and practices (in New York, at least), because most of us don't have space to store our kits in our shoebox-sized apartments. As a result, we're somewhat nomadic, roaming from kit to kit as we go from gig to gig. For my band, this practice has extended to the recording realm. Each time we record, it's in a new room, and I have to acclimate to a new drum kit. It's like drum kit roulette; you're not certain what you're going to get and just hope for the best. I bring my own cymbals, but everything else is rented and characteristically worn and weathered from being pounded on day in and day out by other drifting drummers like me.

From my experiences in professional recording studio ecosystems, it is typical for the first day of recording to be devoted to a painstaking process of arriving at a desired drum sound through a combination of tuning and damping the drums, careful microphone choice and placement, and routing these sounds through a chain of various signal processors such as gates, compressors, limiters, and equalizers. But for a band on a budget like ours, the adage "good enough for rock and roll" governs our minimalistic method and we just plug the microphones into the computer's external audio interface and proceed with a swift sound check. We only have two hours to set up, record, and tear down before Jonathan heads off to work at the bookstore in Grand Central station, so we scurry to get set.

Short on proper microphone stands, we use electrical tape to clumsily mount some microphones on guitar stands and then proceed to position them around the drum kit: Shure SM57s over and under the snare, Sennheiser 421s on the rack and floor toms, AKG D112 on the kick, AKG 414s hanging above the left and right cymbals, and a Neumann TLM 103 at an arbitrary distance of "away from the kit" to capture the room's ambience. In the sound recording world, there are no rules, per se, but there are well-established conventions, and most of the aforementioned microphone and drum pairings are industry standards. I can't precisely place where I acquired this knowledge, but I know this pooled source is supplied by the flow of several informational tributaries: reading articles and web forums, watching rock docs (documentaries), talking to other musicians, and observing recording practices in others' studios. Like almost all of my gear, I acquired these microphones second-hand, slowly over time as I could afford them. These microphones, combined with a computer, audio interface, recording software, and three pairs of keen ears are all we need to make a recording that, to most listeners, will sound on par with everything else distributed on the various audio avenues online.

Some of my peers who work in more professional studios would be sorely disappointed if they saw how we set up the room, as it demonstrates a complete disregard and irreverence for cable management. Cords are haphazardly strewn in knots and nests requiring ninja-like agility to navigate the room without being snared by an XLR cable and crashing into a cymbal. I pull my wallet out of my back pocket and lay it onto the skin of the snare drum to serve as a damper to eliminate its ringing overtones. A few more tweaks here and there on the kit to position each drum and cymbal to achieve an ergonomical feng shui and I am content in my drum kingdom, seated at the throne and ready to kick out some jams. Martín instructs me to hit each drum a few times to set levels, ensuring that the recording won't clip (distort), and with that we're ready to record.

"Wait, what song is this?" I ask.
"It's the first one, the instrumental," Martín replies.
Jonathan pipes in, "You said you had some ideas for it you could try out."
"Right . . . play it for me and I'll try out some things."

I have heard this song before, but I have never played it. We prerecorded a string quartet and then added an assortment of electronic ambient sounds to this performance; the song has a beginning, an end, and a loosely defined "gradual build" section, but that's the extent of direction I have to follow. The purposeful omission of a predefined plan certainly has its drawbacks: for starters, I only have ideas about what I will play, and I have only "heard" these ideas in my head. I assume I'll be able to execute these ideas, but I won't actually know until we start recording. This raises the rather obvious question, "Why don't you rehearse first?" The response is that the recording is the rehearsal and vice versa; they are symbiotic at this stage of songwriting. Since I'm improvising my part, at the very least we want to be able to listen back to each take and distil the best bits. More optimistically, I hope I can enter a one-take-wonder fugue state and the first take will be all that's needed. This happens very rarely, however, as I have a tendency to get excited and rush ahead of the metronome. (Go ahead. Lob one of those stock jokes at me about the drummer's inability to keep time. It's warranted in my case.) Jonathan and Martín are either too kind or too invested in the task at hand to joke around at my expense. I find myself extra motivated by their earnestness and I feel as though I owe it to these two guys to deliver my best. "There is no time like the present," I tell myself. I peel off my shoes and socks so that I can get a good feel for the hi-hat and bass drum pedals and then give Martín the nod to start recording. I love this moment—the brief silence before the recording starts—it's a difficult phenomenon to describe as time seems to move both fast and slow while a jolt of adrenaline-induced nervous excitement courses through my veins. This is my idea of fun. CLICK-click-click-click, CLICK-click-click-click . . . Take 1 ensues.

Starting with Recording

Starting with recording may seem like an odd strategy for a band, given that traditionally recording has often been framed as a culminating activity. In the conventional recording studio model, characteristic of the first half of the twentieth century, artists laboriously rehearsed until they were deemed ready to record, meaning that they were primed and prepared to commit their very best performances to the recording medium; the recording was the finishing line. Until the mid-point of the twentieth century, recording, with few exceptions, entailed the musicians performing their pieces from start to finish repeatedly until an acceptable take was "captured." This mentality led to positioning the perfect or ideal recording as a destination that was seemingly always a daunting distance away, like the mirage of an oasis beyond the horizon. Chanan (1995) explains how this approach to recording put considerable pressure on the recording musicians: "By making a performance repeatable, it gives an authority that is entirely foreign to its nature—or was, until it began to affect the art of interpretation. . . . A new kind of performer is needed, the virtuoso of the repeated take" (18). Despite the fact that the recording technologies of (roughly) the second half of the twentieth century more easily afforded a bit-by-bit approach to recording, the perfect-take mentality still looms large in the recording studio. This is especially true of music traditions that preexisted recording (i.e., prior to 1877), which have a tendency to regard recording not as a process, but as a product, a *record* of an event. With a few notable exceptions, until the late 1940s the modus operandi of the music recording industry was to proffer the illusion that a recording was simply a pristine reproduction of a real-time musical performance, but as Sterne (2003) rightly reasons, "Making sounds for the machines was always different than performing for a live audience" (235). The "live" ideal adhered to the tenet that recording was unobtrusive—like a fly on a wall it would eavesdrop on the performance without being detected. In turn, this led to major recording companies seeking out studio spaces that mimicked the flattering acoustics of performing spaces but did away with its patrons, whose momentary coughs, fidgets, and whispers would tarnish the recording (Simons 2004). In "Learning to live with recording," Tomes captures a chamber musician's perspective of the adverse effects of being under the scrutiny of the microphone, regarding recording as a rather restrictive experience:

> In short, the process of recording has a way of isolating each person in a bell jar of self-consciousness. Instead of having a wide and free perspective, your world shrinks to the little pinpoint of light which is yourself. Instead of focusing outward on what signals you can give out and what you can add to the whole performance, you focus instead on reliability and on the surface perfection of your own part. This is closing down instead of opening up, and needless to say it's against the essential spirit of chamber music, as well as the spirit of communication. (Tomes 2009, 11)

In contrast to Tomes, we *live to learn with recording*. When my band embarks on the recording process we embrace "errors" by encouraging each other to take chances. For us, the recording act is serious but not sacred. We strive to make every take *the* take, but recognize that there is always another take waiting for us should we want to *take* it. After all, little to nothing is riding on our recording sessions. We're not employing anyone to record us; we take turns as the audio engineer, which in our case entails little more than pressing the space bar on the laptop to start and stop the recording of each take. Any deadlines we might have for finishing a recording are arbitrary and self-imposed. We're not accountable to a record label or an external stakeholder of any sort. No one in our band is banking on recordings paying the rent and putting food on the table. The measly fractions of a cent we receive for each stream on Spotify do not cover the cost of a pizza slice, let alone an hour at a rehearsal space. We're holed up together in this windowless sweatbox with the unified goal of making music. To us, recording is not a thing, it's a thing we do.

TAKE 4

. . . CLICK-click-click-click, CLICK-click-cli *(abrupt stop). Four tries. That's how many times it took me to get this particular part right. Actually, my third attempt may have been better, but I was hitting the snare so rowdily that the take was too distorted, or so I was told. I didn't listen back to what I had played, I just took Martín's word for it that the take was unusable. He apologized, acknowledging it was a good take and explained that we couldn't use it because we didn't get the mic levels right. Rather than eulogize the take that could have been, I found myself miming his typical response to my previous apologies for botched takes: "Nah, it's cool, we'll do another one." On the fourth try I was able to execute many of the rhythmic ideas I had enaudiated (the sound parallel to envisioned) and incorporated successions of rim shots following Martín's suggestion, "bah-bah-b-bah!" I also included some spur-of-the-moment improvised rhythmic variations like "bah-bah-b-bah! bah!" No verbal affirmation was needed from Jonathan or Martín to indicate their approval for this take because as soon as I glanced upwards after the final snare hit I could glean as much from their assured facial expressions. In those brief moments after the take, nobody said anything initially because we wanted to let those last notes ring out without our voices marring them in the recording. We waited patiently as the shimmer of the cymbals decayed with the metronome persistently clicking in our headphones.*

This is representative of how we "wrote" most of our songs. We reacted to our previous actions. We played and improvised with our previously recorded selves, a reflexive process that hinged on our willingness to experiment. There was a collective understanding among the group that we were all taking turns on this sonic sketchpad and that recording as music making is a process. Recording was not our end goal; it was our beginning toward a goal. Instead of gigging live shows until we felt we were good enough to record, we recorded until we felt we were good enough to gig live shows. We had become a cover band of our recorded selves. We listened to our recordings and tried to remember how we made them. Our goal was not to replicate the recording, but to create an ever-evolving performance that we deemed better than the previous version. We subscribed to the recording-as-commodity paradigm too, but our motivation for committing a song to a fixed form for the purposes of digital distribution was to share more than to sell; to financially break even would be considered a smashing success. Whatever version ended up being distributed was simply a version. Inevitably we rerecorded and rerecorded, making versions of versions.

DAWN OF THE DAW

Our entire recording process hinged on the affordances of the digital audio workstation (DAW), a generic categorization for music making software. The first DAWs were essentially just digital audio editors that had the capacity to record (although initially tape remained the recording medium of choice in studios because DAWs were slow and expensive), but as computing power has increased exponentially, most modern DAWs now have the capacity to serve as a multitrack audio recorder, MIDI sequencer, notation program, mixing console, and meta software instrument. Like the recording technologies that preceded the DAW (i.e., cylinders, discs, wire, tape, MIDI, DAT, ADAT, etc.), it has often been touted as the catalyst of democratic change in the recording industry: "The shift to software-enabled recording has significantly reduced the cost of entry-level equipment, which has improved the quality and capacity of home recording" (Leyshon 2009, 1325). For the DIY-er, a more affordable recording technology that promises to deliver "improved" quality is enticing, and DAW developers, such as Evan Brooks, the cocreator of Pro Tools (first released in 1991), reinforced this rhetoric:

> You can't play this game as a professional unless you're able to produce material that was of high enough quality, sonically, to be able to be played on the air. At that time, the only way to do that was in a professional recording studio. What we did was remove the barrier. (quoted in Milner 2009, 298)

Brooks suggests that, prior to the advent of Pro Tools, a divide existed in recording practices; the benchmark of a "professional" recording was whether or not it could be played on the radio. For many DIY recreational recorders the allure of the DAW is not so much the promise of so-called professional recording capability; it is ease of access and use. Having access to a music making experience by engaging with a DAW on a computer, tablet, or smartphone presents the opportunity to be an active participant in the creation of new music: "Whereas passive listeners to the phonograph were once content to bring the concert hall into their homes, and might engage in music as amateur players, now the strong desire to feel part of the music, coupled with the exchange of mouse manipulating skills for traditional motor skills, creates a new practice of productive consumption" (Barrett 2009, 102). Is Barrett's notion of "productive consumption" a uniquely digitally dependent practice, one that was ushered in by the dawn of the DAW? Could my band have existed in a different decade? Was our engagement with DIY recreational recording part of a recent phenomenon, a recording revolution of sorts? An examination of ease of access to and ease of use of recording technologies helps to contextualize current practices of DIY recreational recording.

DIY Recording Pre-1945: Recording as Fun

Initially, the phonograph's inventor, Thomas Edison, did not envision music recording as its primary purpose: "As the final design began to take shape, it was clear that Edison had office dictation in mind rather than entertainment or the other applications he had suggested in the 1870s" (Morton 2004, 18). Listing potential uses of the phonograph, Edison (1878) included recording music among other activities such as dictation, books, educational purposes, family records, toys, clocks, and advertising:

The phonograph will undoubtedly be liberally devoted to music. A song sung on the phonograph is reproduced with marvellous accuracy and power. Thus a friend may in a morning-call sing us a song which shall delight an evening company, etc. As a musical teacher it will be used to enable one to master a new air, the child to form its first songs, or to sing him to sleep. (quoted in Taylor, Katz, and Grajeda 2012, 35)

Despite the fact the earliest phonographs produced were equipped to record, low public demand for this feature in the late nineteenth and early twentieth centuries pushed the phonograph and its competing devices toward being used solely for sound reproduction. Morton (2000) details that, up until approximately 1900, the phonograph could both record and reproduce, and that the manufacturers "expected their customers to make their own recordings" (14). Katz (2004) asserts that the ability to self-record continued into the early 1900s: "Home recording was widely popular, discussed at length in the phonograph journals and even promoted by the industry" (69). Schmidt Horning relates society's heightened interest in recording at this time to the rise of recreational pursuits:

> Amateur publications and societies became increasingly popular, especially in sports, art, and engineering where amateur activity—doing something for pleasure rather than for financial gain—proliferated. The phonograph, then, came at the historical moment when its use as a recreational and creative tool could fill a sociocultural need. (Schmidt Horning 2013, 58)

One such example of DIY recreational recording during this era is presented in *How We Gave a Phonograph Party*, distributed by the National Phonography Company in 1899 (as cited in Taylor, Katz, and Grajeda 2012). The portrayal of this particular party details how the invitations sent out to guests requested they bring their instruments or voices. For example, "To Beverly Dunlap's we added a line 'Bring your Cornet,'" and "In each of the other notes, we wrote the mystifying words, 'Please bring your voice.'" (48). Complete with phonograph-shaped ginger snaps, the phonograph party is depicted as a fun-filled evening, with anecdotes such as: "The most effective records we made during the entire evening were two chorus records. All stood close together in a bunch about three feet from the horn and sang 'Marching through Georgia' and it came out fine. Our success lead us to try another 'Onward Christian Soldiers' and it was every bit as good" (51).

Based on these accounts it seemed that DIY recording was off to a formidable start in the twentieth century, but with Emile Berliner's disc-based gramophone design supplanting Edison's cylinder-based phonograph system—due to the fact that it was easier to mass-produce discs than cylinders—came a major conceptual shift. The inability to record on discs

> introduced a structural and social division between making a recording and listening to it. With Edison's design, access to one assumed access to the other as well; sound recording was something people could *do*. With Berliner's design, a wedge

was driven between production and consumption; sound recording was something people could listen *to*. (Suisman 2009, 5; emphasis in original)

As a result of this conceptual shift, "Recordings would be made solely by manufacturers, not by consumers" (Morton 2004, 32). The act of recording was no longer participatory, it was proprietary. In the ensuing years it was still possible to make a DIY recording, but it was considerably more difficult: "Although these 'instantaneous' disc recording systems were widely used in commercial applications and in schools, they were far too complex for the amateur" (Millard 2002, 158). Schmitt Horning (2013, 61) details that in the early 1930s one of the owners of Presto Recording Corporation published "how to" guides for avid hobbyists such as *Home Recording and All About It* (1932), claiming, "The home recordist can achieve results that will be almost on par with commercially-pressed records." To most people, however, disc-based recording was unwieldy, and "It was not until tape recorders became available in the 1950s that home recording became popular again" (Katz 2004, 70).

In the brief period of the phonograph's infancy before the disc usurped the cylinder, recording provided a means for people to make music in the recreational sphere. The experience of recording provided a surrogate audience as people gathered round and performed to the phonograph as if it had the ability to listen. Although the role of "recordist" existed in professional recording studios, in domestic life the people operating the recording equipment were the same people performing for it. Recording in this context was a self-sufficient process that was intended to be fun. DIY recreational recording is as old as the phonograph.

DIY Recording Post-1945: Sticking to the Tape Mentality

> The more recent home tape recorders have been ingeniously designed to make recording as simple as possible. A number of machines are push-button operated, still others have greatly simplified control mechanisms. Well on its way toward becoming America's new pastime hobby, home tape recording is as simple as clicking a camera shutter for ever-increasing thousands of American sound enthusiasts. No matter how inexperienced or inept the tape-recorder owner may be, the chances are overwhelming that he will come up with acceptable sound on his tapes. (Westcott and Dubbe 1965, 23)

Upon the arrival of audiotape in the United States following World War II, when it was first retrieved from Nazi Germany, tape recording was promoted to the public as an easy-to-do hobby. Publications from the proceeding decades including consumer magazines such as *Tape Recording* (1953–1969), and recreation-oriented books such as *Family Fun in Tape Recording* (Ahlers 1965) and *Tape Recording for the Hobbyist* (Zuckerman

1967) covered a wide range of activities related to recording, with music being one of the many possibilities. For example, making sound effects, recording community events such as weddings or church services, and getting guests to recite tongue twisters into a microphone at parties were all part of a larger culture of DIY recreational recording. Meanwhile, outside of home life, DIY recording studios began to surface, made possible by the proliferation of reel-to-reel tape recorders. Millard suggests, "This was an accessible technology which permitted more people to enter the professional recording industry. Studies of the origins of rock 'n' roll have stressed that this technology empowered the small record studio owners who now had the means to compete with the larger corporate studios on the same technological footing" (2002, 158). Most DIY studios had little in the way of state-of-the-art recording technology, lacking the requisite capital to purchase high-end (usually German) microphones and custom-built recording consoles. Instead, they repurposed ramshackle radio equipment and more affordable American-made microphones (Cogan and Clark 2003), and set up their studios:

> in all manner of unlikely spaces—storefronts, garages, and shacks, as well as radio stations and proper, if spartan, studios. Cosimo Matassa's J&M studio in New Orleans, the site of innumerable historic recordings, including those of Fats Domino and Little Richard, was set up in a room adjacent to his family's appliance store. Sam Philips' Memphis Recording Service was a storefront. Bill Putnam's original Universal Recording was in an upstairs room in the Chicago Civic Opera House. Many records were recorded on location in a YMCA, church, VFW hall, or house, almost anyplace with roof and walls. (Zak 2010, 80)

In comparison to the professional recording practices of the period, the "anyplace with roof and walls" approach of the DIY-ers was a radically different world, and it was precisely this deviation from the standard that redefined recording practices: "These studios did not have the facilities or equipment to make strides in high-fidelity recording, but they could use what they had to achieve something more important for rock and roll: a new sound" (Morton 2000, 42). Guitarist and technology-tinkerer Les Paul spearheaded this "new sound." His DIY recordings of him and his wife, Mary Ford, from the early 1950s featured an impressive display of tape-based overdubbing and other tape trickery. Paul and Ford recorded in their kitchen and other rooms in their home to attain different effects:

> I would have Mary sing a certain part while standing in the hallway, and other parts in different rooms to give each track its own sound. . . . We had the bathroom, which produced an echo-like sound, and once I determined exactly where to position Mary and the mic, the hallway was a great place for natural reverb. (Paul and Cochran 2008, 250)

The tape techniques that Paul popularized in the late 1940s and early 1950s were adopted within recreational recording culture and are referenced frequently in "how to" guides of the era. For example, Westcott and Dubbe (1965) provide a succinct explanation of the rather complicated process of overdubbing, coined as "sound-on-sound" by Paul: "Sound-on-sound recording is a monophonic function which allows the performer to accompany himself over and over on a single tape to create a composite recording with almost endless variations" (210). In *ABC's of Tape Recording*, Crowhurst (1968) explains: "You can use a tape recorder to produce your own multiple recordings. You can make like a one-man orchestra or choir (as Les Paul and Mary Ford did so wonderfully a few years ago)" (71). Further, Zuckerman relates how one could adopt Paul's tape-based "speed trick" to imitate the high-pitched novelty singing of the Chipmunks or, in the following example, feign violin virtuosity:

> The speed trick can make a mediocre instrumentalist sound like the greatest musician of the ages. Have a violinist play one octave down from normal pitch, and at about three-quarters regular tempo. Record this at 3¾ ips, then play back at 7½ ips.[1] The fingering will sound so fantastic that, compared to it Paganini would have been a piker [*sic*]. (Zuckerman 1967, 48)

By the mid-1960s, recording practices, especially for emerging styles such as rock and roll, embraced the creative capacities afforded by tape. The process of overdubbing in "unreal time" with tape became entrenched as a defining characteristic of recording practice: "Tape and the editing process made possible the creation of an entirely studio-based music whose sole mode of existence was as a recording" (Clarke 2007, 54). Recording was no longer pitted as a process of "capturing" but as "creating" and evolved to emulate the studio-as-instrument approach made famous by Paul. Musician and producer Brian Eno reflected, "You could make a piece over an extended period of time. . . . It started being a process that you could engage in over months, even years" (Crane and Baccigaluppi 2011, 40). DIY recreational recording guides from this period such as *Creative Tape Recording* positioned editing as an integral part of the recording process:

> Most commercial gramophone records are made in this way, not only lengthy sections being interposed and changed, but even short passages of a few bars. So the recordist should not feel he is cheating in some way, but that he is using every means available, in this case his editing skill, to get as flawless a performance as possible on tape. (Capel 1972, 128)

Editing, however, was not as simple as "clicking a camera shutter," a comparison that Westcott and Dubbe (1965) had made regarding the ease of tape recording just years earlier. Rather, as Zuckerman (1967) asserted, "When you get into editing, you pass the thin boundary that distinguishes tape recording as a mere pastime from a serious hobby" (73). Tape recording was now becoming an increasingly technical and less accessible pursuit. On one hand, the more evolved and involved discipline of editing likely alienated the happy-go-lucky recreational recorder who was just as content to record party gags as music, but on the other hand it also gave self-recording musicians new compositional tools.

The concept of editing as integral to the recording process constituted a seminal change in both professional and recreational recording practices. Certainly, recording technologies have changed dramatically since the heyday of Les Paul's tape exploits, but the foundational concept that recordings entail a process of creative construction at the hands of the person wielding the technology perseveres to the present day. For the DIY recreational recorder, this development constituted a figurative fork in the road with added possibilities beyond simply pressing a button to record came the necessity for more training. The DIY-er wanting to edit multiple takes together had to learn how to splice tape using a razor blade and special adhesive tape. If DIY-ers wanted to sing with themselves like Mary Ford had, they had to master the technique of overdubbing. Most books about tape recording aimed at DIY-ers from the 1960s and 1970s contained chapters steeped in more technical topics to cater to this crowd, including but not limited to the mechanical principles of tape recording, editing techniques, machine maintenance, acoustics, and microphone selection and placement (Capel 1972; Crawford 1974; Crowhurst 1968; LeBel 1963; Salm 1969; Westcott and Dubbe 1965; Zuckerman 1967). This more technical and less accessible path of DIY recording continued along the same trajectory throughout the remainder of the twentieth century, and in many regards still persists presently in the digital domain. It was around this time in the late 1960s and early 1970s that the DIY trailhead diverged into two distinct paths, the Lo-Fi (low-fidelity) movement, which continued to value ease of access and ease of use over quality, and the Hi-Fi (high-fidelity) movement, which remained self-sufficient, but often compromised ease of access and ease of use in its pursuit to rival the quality of professional studios.

Parting Paths:
DIY Hi-Fi versus DIY Lo-Fi

In the 1970s, the practice of "home recording" gained popularity as multitrack reel-to-reel tape recorders became more affordable (Alberts 2003). Instead of simply having a portable tape recorder that one could pull out of the closet to record a few friends singing at a party, the home studio involved cordoning off a part of one's humble abode and designating it for music production. While these studios were DIY in that they were self-sufficient, they resembled scaled-down versions of professional studios, with separate spaces for the musicians and the engineers to carry out their respective roles. Home studio enthusiasts built sound isolation booths and installed sound treatment materials ranging from egg cartons to specialized absorbers and reflectors in their basements and bedrooms in an effort to wrangle ideal acoustics. Separate control rooms were constructed to house the expanding fleets of gear they captained, such as the one described by Milano:

> Monstrous metallic panels, strewn with blinking LED eyes, gleam in the darkness. An imposing bank of gadgetry towers darkly in the corner, dripping with wires

and cables. . . . Could this be a top-secret air-defense installation? The bridge of a nuclear-powered submarine? The hidden headquarters of a telephone company bent on world domination? Nothing so dramatic. It used to be your living room. (1988, 1)

With the arrival of MIDI in the early 1980s, which enabled the sequencing of electronic instruments, especially keyboards and drum machines, the complexity of home studios continued to increase. Out of necessity, DIY instructional resources from this period, such as *The Home Recording Handbook* (Everard 1985) and *Multi-Track Recording for Musicians* (Hurtig 1988), covered considerably more ground than their "how to" counterparts from previous decades. The cutting-edge DIY home studio user not only had to be adept with analog multitrack tape recording, but now also had to delve into digital sequencing with MIDI. To support the communities of these increasingly sophisticated studios, trade magazines surfaced that addressed relevant issues with "how to" articles such as *Mix* (1977–present), *Sound on Sound* (1985–present), *Electronic Musician* (1985–present), *EQ* (1993–2011), and *Tape Op* (1996–present).

In contrast to the DIY Hi-Fi movement, the DIY Lo-Fi movement prided itself on the fact that the more sophisticated reel-to-reel recorders and MIDI sequencers could be bypassed, and that home renovation was not necessary to participate in the self-sufficient recording process. Pivotal to the DIY Lo-Fi movement was the making of "demo" (demonstration) recordings on cassette tapes using a home stereo or a "four-track" recorder such as the TASCAM Portastudio—the first of its kind, released in 1979, that soon had many imitators. Much like the DAW technology that succeeded them, cassette four-tracks provided an all-in-one approach by incorporating both the mixer and the recording mechanism in a single unit. Ease of use was almost assured because most music listeners were already familiar with how to operate a cassette player: "Musicians could finally record, overdub, EQ, bounce, and mix down multiple tracks all from the foot of their beds" (Alberts 2003, 31). Makers of these recorders provided sufficient information in their thin but informative product manuals for users to commence recording almost immediately, but in time, a body of literature in support of demo recording culture emerged with more exhaustive "how to" books such as *Recording Demo Tapes at Home* (Bartlett 1989), *Using Your Portable Studio* (McIan 1996), and *Making the Ultimate Demo* (Robair 2000). The DIY recordings disseminating from cassette studios tended to circulate in regional music scenes such as punk (Boulware and Tudor 2009; Spencer 2008), hardcore (Azerrad 2001), indie (Oakes 2009), and hip-hop (Chang 2005), and were critical in helping emerging artists establish fan bases. Since cassettes were easy to reproduce using home stereos, a pre-Internet network of grassroots music distribution was spun that subverted the recording industry. Central to demo culture was the mentality that quality was willingly compromised in exchange for convenience: "In the world of home recording, the cassette had become good enough to record commercially and cheap enough to become an attractive alternative to the top-of-the-line home recorders. To the musician, the portability and lower price of the tape cassette more than made up for any deficiencies in fidelity" (Millard 2002, 162).

CONVERGENCE

DIY recreational recording in its current state has inherited traits from both the DIY Hi-Fi and the DIY Lo-Fi movements, marking out a new path that seeks the best of both worlds. The all-digital DIY-er demands ease of access and use, but also expects greater functionality and fidelity. The traditional means of self-sufficient learning continue to prosper with many of the aforementioned trade magazines still in circulation and an ever-expanding body of "how to" books being published that feature catchy titles such as *Home Recording for Musicians for Dummies* (Strong 2014) and *Home Recording 101: Creating Your Own Affordable Home Recording Studio (D.I.Y. Music)* (Helson 2014). YouTube tutorials cater to the DIY-er too, most notably Pensado's Place, hosted by Grammy-winning mixer Dave Pensado, a veteran of the recording industry, whose videos have garnered more than 6.7 million views and whose weekly show has over 100,000 subscribers. Even more impressive is the Pensado-endorsed The Recording Revolution, hosted by amateur-turned-authority on recording Graham Cochrane, who has over 170,000 subscribers and more than 12.4 million views. The short tutorials hosted on these and similar YouTube channels endorse a "how to" approach to recording and provide a community hub for subscribers to dialogue with each other or pose questions to the channel host on best practices for recording. Similarly, a slew of forums such as homerecording.com and gearslutz.com constitute major meeting points online for the DIY music making community to post questions, solve problems, and sell or swap equipment with each other. Taken together, DIY recreational recording enthusiasts of the twenty-first century have access to a community that has expanded and evolved for over a century, guided by the ideals of ease of access and ease of use in the interest of self-sufficiency.

KEEP RECORDING TO KEEP MAKING MUSIC

My band is just one of countless numbers on the planet that have benefited from over a hundred years of evolving DIY recreational recording practices. Recording is so engrained in our concept of music that it is easy for us to take it for granted. Any member of our band could join another band that does not subsist on recording and fit in just fine. We are all competent players and have gigged steadily with other "weekend warrior"–type acts. But our North American trio seems to thrive on recording and has a tendency not to get together unless we have something to record. Like the first generation of DIY recreational recorders, we've had recording parties because it's the easiest way to convince a gang of people to sing on our recordings. We eat, drink, sing, and record. Sometimes we cling to the rawness of cassette demo culture too, by setting up and recording as quickly as possible to see what stems from the spontaneity of the moment. What vocal melodies will Jonathan find within himself? What bass lines will

Martín stumble upon? What rhythms will I pound out? Most importantly, how will these three elements sound together? By recording we will not forget; we can concentrate on playing, and then revisit our improvised jams later to listen for the parts that we want to develop further.

Admittedly, there have been times when the recording process seemed to cross the threshold from overstimulating to underwhelming—such as the days when our band huddles around a laptop for hours on end while we mix and tamper with the timbres of our original recordings in search of new sounds in the vein of Les Paul—but never has recording felt like a chore. Even the more tedious sessions where nothing seems to happen have their moments of richness. For example, during a mixing session, I started to improvise along to one of our songs on Martín's ukulele and one of the riffs I played caught Jonathan's attention: "That sounds good," he said: "You should record it." So we did. At other times, minuscule movements in the right direction such as slightly shifting the sound of the attack of the beater on the skin of the bass drum such that it could be more easily discerned from Martín's throbbing bass line seem like major accomplishments. It used to frustrate me that we never seemed to finish a recording. Just when it seemed that we had reached an end, one of us would utter a reservation (I've earned the nickname "Picky Adam"), and by the next day we had disassembled and reassembled our tracks to create an entirely new sonic species. I have come to appreciate the fact that we're never quite done recording, because it means we always have something to do. If we didn't record, what else would we do? Recording is how we make music. If we stop recording, we stop making music. Someone else can't make *our* music for us, and if recording is music making, then *we* must record. This is the very core of DIY recreational recording: keep recording to keep making music.

"Hey Martín, I've got another idea. We recording?" *CLICK-click-click-click* . . .

NOTE

1. "ips" is an abbreviation for inches per second, the measurement of tape speed.

REFERENCES CITED

Ahlers, Arvel W. 1965. *Family Fun in Tape Recording*. New York: Popular Library.

Alberts, Randy. 2003. *Tascam: 30 Years of Recording Evolution*. Milwaukee, WI: Hal Leonard.

Azerrad, Michael. 2001. *Our Band Could Be Your Life: Scenes from the American Indie Underground, 1981–1991*. New York and Boston: Little, Brown.

Barrett, James. 2009. "Producing Performance." In *Recorded Music: Performance, Culture, and Technology*, edited by Amanda Bayley, 89–106. New York: Cambridge University Press.

Bartlett, Bruce. 1989. *Recording Demo Tapes at Home*. Indianapolis, IN: Howard W. Sams.

Boulware, Jack, and Silke Tudor. 2009. *Gimme Something Better: The Profound, Progressive, and Occasionally Pointless History of Bay Area Punk from Dead Kennedys to Green Day*. New York: Penguin.

Capel, Vivian. 1972. *Creative Tape Recording*. London: Fountain.

Chanan, Michael. 1995. *Repeated Takes: A Short History of Recording and its Effects on Music*. London: Verso.

Chang, Jeff. 2005. *Can't Stop Won't Stop: A History of the Hip-Hop Generation*. New York: Picador.

Clarke, Eric F. 2007. "The Impact of Recording on Listening." *Twentieth-Century Music* 4: 47–70.

Cogan, Jim, and William Clark. 2003. *Temples of Sound: Inside the Great Recording Studios*. San Francisco: Chronicle.

Crane, Larry, and John Baccigaluppi. 2011. "Brian Eno: Hampered by Intellectual Considerations." *Tape Op* 85: 38–47.

Crawford, Doug. 1974. *Tape Recording from A to Z*. London: Kaye and Ward.

Crow, Bill. 2006. "Musical Creativity and the New Technology. *Music Education Research* 8: 121–130.

Crowhurst, Norman H. 1968. *ABC's of Tape Recording*. 2nd ed. Indianapolis, IN: Howard W. Sams.

Everard, Chris. 1985. *The Home Recording Handbook*. New York: Amsco.

Helson, Rake. 2014. *Home Recording 101: Creating Your Own Affordable Home Recording Studio*. Rake Helson. [Kindle edition]

Hurtig, Brent. 1988. *Multi-Track Recording for Musicians*. Cupertino, CA: GPI.

Katz, Mark. 2004. *Capturing Sound: How Technology Has Changed Music*. Berkeley: University of California Press.

LeBel, Clarence Joseph. 1963. *How to Make Good Tape Recordings*. New York: Audio Devices.

Leyshon, Andrew. 2009. "The Software Slump? Digital Music, the Democratization of Technology, and the Decline of the Recording Studio Sector within the Musical Economy." *Environment and Planning A* 41: 1309–1331.

McIan, Peter. 1996. *Using Your Portable Studio*. New York: Amsco.

Milano, Dominic. 1988. *Multi-Track Recording: A Technical and Creative Guide for the Musician and Home Recorder*. Cupertino, CA: GPI.

Millard, André. 2002. "Tape Recording and Music Making." In *Music and Technology in the Twentieth Century*, edited by Hans-Joachim Braun, 158–167, Baltimore, MD: Johns Hopkins University Press.

Milner, Greg. 2009. *Perfecting Sound Forever: An Aural History of Recorded Music*. New York: Faber and Faber.

Morton, David L. 2000. *Off the Record: The Technology and Culture of Sound Recording in America*. New Brunswick, NJ: Rutgers University Press.

Morton, David L. 2004. *Sound Recording: The Life Story of a Technology*. Baltimore, MD: Johns Hopkins University Press.

Oakes, Kaya. 2009. *Slanted and Enchanted: The Evolution of Indie Culture*. New York: Henry Holt.

Paul, Les, and Michael Cochran. 2008. *Les Paul: In His Own Words*. York, PA: Gemstone.

Robair, Gino. 2000. *Making the Ultimate Demo*. Emeryville, CA: EM Books.

Salm, Walter G. 1969. *Tape Recording for Fun and Profit*. Blue Ridge Summit, PA: Tab Books.

Schmidt Horning, Susan. 2013. *Chasing Sound: Technology, Culture and the Art of Studio Recording from Edison to the LP*. Baltimore, MD: Johns Hopkins University Press.

Simons, David. 2004. *Studio Stories: How the Great New York Records Were Made*. San Francisco, CA: Backbeat.

Spencer, Amy. 2008. *DIY: The Rise of Lo-Fi Culture*. London: Marion Boyars.

Sterne, Jonathan. 2003. *The Audible Past: Cultural Origins of Sound Reproduction*. Durham, NC: Duke University Press.

Strong, Jeff. 2014. *Home Recording for Musicians for Dummies*. 5th ed. Hoboken, NJ: Wiley.

Suisman, David. 2009. *Selling Sounds: The Commercial Revolution in American Music*. Cambridge, MA: Harvard University Press.

Taylor, Timothy D., Mark Katz, and Tony Grajeda, eds. 2012. *Music, Sound, and Technology in America: A Documentary History of Early Phonograph, Cinema, and Radio*. Durham, NC, and London: Duke University Press.

Tomes, Susan. 2009. "Learning to Live with Recording." In *The Cambridge Companion to Recorded Music*, edited by Nicholas Cook, Eric Clarke, Daniel Leech-Wilkinson, and John Rink, 10–12. Cambridge: Cambridge University Press.

Westcott, Charles G., and Richard F. Dubbe. 1965. *Tape Recorders: How They Work*. 2nd ed. Indianapolis, IN: Howard W. Sams.

Zak, Albin J. 2010. *I Don't Sound Like Nobody: Remaking Music in 1950s America*. Ann Arbor: University of Michigan Press.

Zuckerman, Art. 1967. *Tape Recording for the Hobbyist*. 2nd ed. Indianapolis, IN: Howard W. Sams.

CHAPTER 6

···

CONTEMPLATING COMPILATIONS

An Invitation to . . .

···

JOSEPH PATE AND BRIAN KUMM

STEEP IN THE SAUCE

···

It makes its own sauce.

Zappa (1979)

IT's interesting to consider moments in my life[1] where words such as Zappa's, spoken just loud enough to be caught by a microphone in a recording studio but not necessarily intended as part of a song, can hold profound significance in their unexpected and playful inclusion in a track. I wonder if that was Phillip's intention when he included the song "Joe's Garage" on a compilation CD he recently sent me as a Christmas gift. Holding the CD in my hand on a bright Christmas morning, after the frenzy of activity with wife and children had settled down, a glint of sunlight reflected off of its surface and triggered a memory of something he had shared in an interview several years prior when I was first conducting research on the phenomenon of music listening. That was simply, "When you're looking at music, don't get blinded to what's most important about it. Like my wife would say, 'music is best when listened to, not dissected.' It's a gift to be shared and what's shared is a surplus of the generosity that music gives to us all." This generosity is something sensual, something in excess of any individual song, as if the individual songs were making their own sauce. Of course, Phillip was a musician, an artist through and through, and he seldom said anything to me that didn't involve multiple layers of meaning, continually reminding me that "What makes a good song great is that you can never really pin it down to what it's really all about." As I listened to the compilation CD, I found myself, as many times before, steeping and stewing in a sauce, in a complex mix of sensations that cannot be pinned to a precise meaning, but that profoundly affected my senses, my habits of attention and inattention, my learned responses, tropisms, hopes, dreams, and desires (Massumi 2012).

In that listening moment I unfolded the little note that Phillip had crammed into the CD case. "Have a saucey [*sic*] Christmas, you Vixen," Phillip had scrawled in black sharpie, the only words accompanying this mix. As I thought about the many times in my own life when I had created compilation CDs, mix tapes, MP3 playlists, and so on, I wondered what had prompted this gift to arrive so unexpectedly during this holiday season. In my own experiences, I labored for hours over carefully crafting a compilation of songs to memorialize significant moments—the birth of my children, profound friendships, intense moments of love and passion, the writing of my dissertation, and even more recently when contemplating what might happen when I'm dying, or to be played at my funeral. In my way of thinking, the gift of a compilation, *the gift of music*, in its "generous sensuality," as Phillip put it, is not unlike the residue of feelings that linger once various intense moments have passed.[2] With each track or cut we include, the compilations themselves become works of art. We create, out of small fragments, slices of memories of life events, a compound of the feelings they involve. A compilation is not so much a memorial as it is an invitation, something to be shared.

This chapter, thus, stands as an invitation. We invite you to consider music's sensuality, its "sauce," the pleasure of listening, the moments intensified, the meanings carried, and how affirmation is in the act of sharing. This chapter is our attempt to share some of these qualities of music compilations with you, the reader, whom we assume (rightly or wrongly) to have shared music with a lover, a friend, a child, another. Within this chapter we contend that the act of crafting music compilations, of sharing and gifting in its sauciness, is an art. We discuss this art not by examining, or looking at, but rather by looking along (Lewis 1970) processes of resonation, repercussion, and reverberation (Bachelard [1958] 1994). Ultimately, we contend this art enacts Pieper's ([1948] 1998) conceptualization of leisure as an orientation to, and celebration of, wonder within a poetic space of connection (Bachelard [1958] 1994).

THE ART OF COMPILATIONS

There is an *art* to the creation of a good compilation[3] of music. It is a subtle art, focused on the craft of self-expression as a gesture toward connection to one's self, others, and the larger world. The making of compilations, at its core, is an act of celebration: A celebration of music's ability to *speak to* and thus to *speak for*. And for individuals who engage in this creative endeavor, the ability of music to *speak to* and thus *speak for* may expand capacities for self-expression. Creating compilations can afford opportunities for a sonic collection of connection: connection to self, connection to meaningful experiences, connection to others, and thus a connection to the world writ large. We posit music compilations as a mode of communicating, as well as constructing, deeply felt connections, significant resonances, and multiple meanings emergent from accessing others' words and music to reverberate and speak forth through celebration and as an orientation toward the wonderful (Pieper [1948] 1998).

Like many others, we (the authors) have engaged in the creation of numerous compilations throughout our lives. When this began in earnest, the various compilations that were created "spoke to" us in variegated and diverse ways, striking multiple "chords" deep inside, hauntingly echoing in the marrowed depths of our beings (Pate and Johnson 2013). These internally resonating words and melodies often whispered and hummed, invoking subtle aural backdrops as we respectively navigated through, and attempted to make sense of, the world. Accessing these songs and making intentional structural decisions as to their sequential order and arrangement within a compilation facilitated multiple spaces for self-expression. These spaces for self-reflection and self-expression opened leisured moments, moments of affirmation and enchantment (Pieper [1948] 1998), what we identify, following Bachelard ([1958] 1994), as poetic spaces of connection: expansive, expressive, connected.

Originally, the creation of many of these compilations was solely personal, only for behind-closed-doors listening, serving as a reminder and comforter as we struggled with the complexity and confusion of the varied and diverse emotions we experienced in our lives.[4] Soon, however, this act evolved into the creation of compilations for others, specifically dear friends and romantic interests. Compilations served as media to communicate and express deeply felt and significant emotions and experiences with another. Tracks were purposefully chosen, each selection contributing an essential part to the grander, gestalted whole, achieving an overarching message or theme. Furthering the creative aspects of these endeavors, compilations were often accompanied with artwork in the form of covers and/or liner notes (for examples of such additional creative undertakings, the use of collages, pictures, and drawings as liner notes and cover art, see Pate 2012). Gifted, these compilations were able to be accessed, digested, felt, and experienced over and over again, in public or in private, loudly, softly, superficially, as an auditory backdrop or "atmosphere-ing" experience, or deeply and purposefully as the listener engaged with the music, lyrics, feelings, and expressions of the songs. For us, as well as for many of those to whom we have spoken, compilations are, at their core, gifts. They serve as extensions of one soul to another, in the hope of communicating, extending, connecting, and sharing certain thoughts, ideas, feelings, emotions, and experiences, sometimes arousing inherent, delineated, or even self-created meanings through varied modes of listening (Green [1988] 2008).

The sharing of any creative endeavor, like the crafting and gifting of musical compilations, results in exposure. There is a vulnerability and fragility associated with forwarding any artistic act or artifact for the consumption and critique of another. Further, there is a delicacy to this creative undertaking. Here one takes the words, expressions, emotions, and feelings of musicians and songwriters to assist in individual expressions of life, feelings, and understandings. The entire endeavor is based upon an interpretive act, gleaning and/or creating meaning in its slippery, ephemeral, and delicate manifestations so as to express and share. Like all artistic undertakings, these are risk-filled actions as soon as they meet the experiences and interpretations of another.

Arguably, the technological advent of cassettes expanded capacities to create music compilations through the medium of mix tapes. Mix tapes, which, according to Sheffield (2007), represented a principal undertaking of the "MTV generation," made possible the grafting of lyrics, music, and song from aurally diverse artists for the intention of sharing and gifting through playful rearrangement of source music. Sheffield mused, in *Love Is a Mix Tape: Life and Loss One Song at a Time*, that there were all kinds of mix tapes, noting "there is always a reason to make one" (17). He cited the following examples: the Party tape; the I Want You tape; the You Like Music, I Like Music, I Can Tell We're Going to Be Friends tape; the Road Trip tape; the You Broke My Heart and Made Me Cry and Here Are Twenty or Thirty Songs About It tape; the No Hard Feelings, Babe, tape; the Walking Tape; and so on. Sheffield felt when one was making a mix tape, one was making history: leveraging, appropriating, and creatively crafting "all your ill-gotten loot into something new . . . [stealing] moments from all over the musical cosmos, and [splicing] them into a whole new groove" (23). Through the crafting of mix tapes, self-expression through the art of others is actualized.

As already noted, those who partake in this undertaking exert intentional thought and effort into the crafting of a compilation. Nick Hornby noted in *High Fidelity* (1995), "[M]aking a tape is like writing a letter—there's a lot of erasing and rethinking and starting again. A good compilation tape is hard to do. You've got to kick off with a corker, to hold the attention. Then . . . up it a notch, or cool it a notch . . . oh, there are loads of rules" (88–89). For many, these kinds of compilation rules are internally driven and monitored as songs are started and stopped, listened to again and again, resulting in the ordering and reordering of the overall symphonic and melodic synchronicity of the piece.

So popular is this undertaking that there are numerous platforms available to participate in this creative act, combining advances in technology with this elemental need for self-expression. Examples include playlist platforms through Spotify, Facebook, Shazzam, Pandora, and the website Stayed Up All Night (http://suan.fm/about), which affords users the space to access different styles and brands of virtual tapes to create playlists, tape covers, and liner notes and then send these to others.[5] These resources are not meant just for those who self-identify as artists, but also those who are lovers of music yet lack the skills, abilities, or desire to create their own songs.

Music compilations have also been the focus of scholarly work, investigating not only personal meanings but also the social functions of sharing music in shaping communities, and the object of the mix tape as a cultural artifact, an archive or repository of larger cultural practices (Ball 2011; Drew 2005; Lashua 2013; Moore 2005). Further, the first author took up Parry and Johnson's (2006) call for leisure scholars to conduct research that utilized creative analytic practices (CAP) through an extended study of individuals who experienced deeply meaningful and significant lived experiences through music listening (Pate 2012). As he (the first author) contemplated ways to create a concordant structure, format, and presentation of that larger study, he mused over how best to represent the complexities of connection one may experience through music listening by way of crafting an elucidatory text illuminating findings. Ultimately, he resolved to produce a polyvocal phenomenology through the crafting of an accompanying musical compilation in addition to the written text, thus resisting producing a traditional text discursively constructed of merely empirical or theoretical observations and accounts. Influenced by Ihde's (2007) caution leveled against dominant and traditional knowledge[6] dissemination accessed through sight alone, he desired a format which would access multiple senses and purposefully engage the *reader-as-listener* experientially and aurally. By structuring this work as a compilation and accessing music as an accompaniment to his participant's words, the first author attempted to share and gift explicit and implicit emotions, feelings, ideas, and thoughts by creating a complementary aural and emotive experience. Here, his intent was to be playfully expressive by communicating deeply meaningful and significantly felt experiences woven throughout each piece of the grander whole. Thus, this work humbly sought an empathetic reading *and* listening, most poignantly demonstrated through the invitation for readers-as-listeners to engage with the associated compilation and liner notes, further demonstrating the beauty of gifting music to help create, inform, illuminate, as well as share these lived experiences.

For this discussion, we draw not only from our own experiences making compilations, but we are informed equally by the first author's previous research, the experiences of the participants of that study, and the practices of making compilations that were shared along that journey. Many of these participants within the study spoke of their own involvement in the crafting of musical compilations and mix tapes, noting the intentional, deeply personal, fragile, and artistic qualities of this undertaking. For example, Zoë shared:

> For me it's huge—If I'm going to make a collection of music for someone, I'm going to be intentional about it. I'm not just going to randomly pull stuff, especially with something like this. I put thought into it and it's a part of me, it's a piece of who I am— each song has impacted me in some way. It might sound weird, but it's almost like every time I share it with someone else, I'm giving them a part of myself. I'm exposing myself a little bit more; I'm letting them have that insight into another layer of who I am. There's that trust and also that vulnerability at the same time—like are they going to think this is lame or are they going to be like that was just "ok?" It's a sharing of a part of your soul with someone else, especially with pieces that have resonated with you in a deep way, in a lasting way.

Another participant, Naomi, spoke of the narrative qualities of creating a compilation:

> I think that's why we make mixes: you want to tell a story, you know. You want to evoke emotion. So you're thinking, I'm going to put this song first and this song second, then I'm going to put this one in because it'll do this or that. It's like you're kind of writing your own little story.

A third participant, Aimee, remembered all of the time and energy that went into the selection of the songs and the crafting of the mix tape's accompanying case and liner notes:

> I remember making this first one. If you open it up, on the spine of it, it's a piece of old wrapping paper. It's like this little craft project, the care that was put into it. The cover,

I did on the reverse of that wrapping paper and then I glued it on. It's just really very sweet to me that I put this together with such care and attention. It's really sweet, and it's this great little gift when we were in high school. I mean, what did we have? We didn't really have very much, you know, but I think this probably took me like 5 hours to put it together and figure out which songs I wanted to go where. It's a whole flood of memories.

What these participants' quotes immediately reveal are three levels upon which the *art* of this art of compilation takes place. First, there is an immediate recognition of the fragility and vulnerability of this art to criticism. We interpret this fragility and vulnerability to relate not only to questions of whether or not a compilation as a work of art can endure criticism, but also in terms of its personal relevance and material composition over time.[7] Second, there is a recognition of the inventiveness of this art, including inventing one's own story to communicate, invoke, or otherwise transmit something of emotional value that gives that story significance, meaning, and relevance. Third, there is an artistic practice of bringing together other elements, exterior to the sonic material of the compilation (e.g., liner notes, decorative cases, and/or labels), that construct around it a sensual package, a presentation making it worthy to be given as a gift. Doubtless there are other ways in which the artfulness of this activity may manifest itself. These identified here connect to three levels of a process—of resonance, repercussions, and reverberations (Bachelard [1958] 1994)—that we believe is inherent to the experience of crafting, as well the gifting and receiving of a compilation.

A POETIC SPACE OF CONNECTION

A compilation neither begins nor ends with the individual making this compilation; it simply passes through the person who compiles. It starts outside, in an extensive world, broad, full of people, sounds, activities, events, and experiences. It's only when the extensive world is contracted into an intensive force that a quality of that extensive world registers on a personal level, becoming sensible, comprehensible, understandable, meaningful. On the other end, these contractions produce dilations whereby the gift of a compilation reenters the extensive, shared as it is within our social networks.

Drawing upon Bachelard ([1958] 1994), we can give names to each of these phases: the extensive may be considered as *resonation*, or a pool of resonance in which we find our social lives; the intensive, or contraction of the extensive toward the personal, can be thought of as *repercussion*; and the dilations that move the personal back toward the social in the gifting of a compilation can be called *reverberations*. Thus, the advent of a compilation is really a passage through the personal to rearrive at the social. We acknowledge the risk of oversimplifying Bachelard's ([1958] 1994) intended use of these concepts; framing these concepts as processual does not fully engage the sense one gathers from Bachelard—that they are three facets of one and the same thing, something like a triptych. Yet, we found a processual treatment of this triptych helpful for understanding the experiences of creating compilations. For example, when Zoë said, "I'm just looking for sounds that click, that hit those strings inside of me. . . . All of a sudden it grabs me. Whether it's a lyric or a line or an emotion or a melody, all of a sudden, it's like striking that chord that you were looking [for]," what she was talking about was a resonance, an immediate visceral connection to music that then could become a resource for going deeper in exploring some kind of personal significance for her, thus informing the compilations she was making for others.

Resonance, according to Bachelard ([1958] 1994), involves the initial hearing and the visceral connections that arise from listening; repercussions then follow to "invite us to give greater depth to our own existence" (xxii). Or, to use Aimee's words, repercussions are moments when a song "infiltrates different parts of my being. I can feel it in my heart and maybe in my brain. It captures me. That connection really becomes personal, because it's like they're talking to me." Another participant, Ron, described it this way:

> You ever been distressed and somebody just understands? It's that comfort where you're so exhausted that you don't want to talk anymore, but you don't have to because somebody goes, "I get it." It's like that. It's a completion. . . . At least I'm not the only one that knows what I'm feeling. There's something about that I am not the only one who has ever felt this. He felt it too, and made it through it.

Whereas repercussions give a greater depth to one's existence, reverberations, according to Bachelard ([1958] 1994), "bring about a change of being" (xxii). Speaking about Paul Simon's song "Graceland" (1986), Phillip described this change of being as: "Graceland. Grace. Land. It takes me there. Totally transformed, where I don't feel disconnected anymore. I feel part of something bigger than me, part of something that validates the core of who I am and I've got to share that with somebody." Taking these three facets of this experience together, following Bachelard ([1958] 1994, xxii), we can summarize with an aphorism every music lover knows well: I was "possessed" by the song.

We consider the act of "possession" to be generative of a liminal, poetic space of connection—the connection to others is apparent at every phase of our processual treatment of Bachelard ([1958] 1994): in resonance, a visceral connection with a piece of music; in repercussions, a deepening of personal experience through the connections made with the expressions of artists' experiences in song; and in reverberations, a connection to one's self that engenders sharing it with another. It is within this poetic space of connection that we see the potential for the *art* of compilations to arise. It is in these spaces where the ineffable, the ephemeral, and the elusive are accessed and expressed. Feelings, emotions, sensations, and meanings are given voice and find purchase in the resonations and reverberations of one to another. For Bachelard, in resonance we hear or are spoken to; in reverberation we speak it—it is our own.

Through Bachelard's ([1958] 1994) phenomenology, or what has been conceptualized as an "aesthetic rethinking of ontology which foregrounds creativity and affect" (Bhatti et al. 2009, 65), we understand lived experiences that arise from the arts which reveal moments of resonance and reverberation, resisting the use of traditional reductionist scientific methods based in deterministic causality for understanding aesthetic experiences. Bhatti et al. suggested this understanding affords new avenues to describe these experiences as ontological, in terms related to sound waves, sonority, vibration, echoes, and motion. These deeply felt and meaningful aesthetic moments move beyond a mere sentimental, surface, or superficial enjoyment or appreciation of the activity (repercussions). These experiences are ontological, affecting the very being of the individuals involved. We liken resonation and repercussions to music's capacity to *speak to*, and reverberation to the capacity to appropriate music to *speak for*.

Once an aesthetic experience is felt and embodied via being *spoken to* (resonation and repercussions), reverberations (potential to *speak for*) are animated through the creation of a change in being within the experiencer. Through resonation, repercussion, and engagement with an aesthetic experience, the felt, embodied meaning and understanding takes hold, rooting and finding purchase within us, speaking to us and ultimately becoming our own. In "becoming our own," things internally begin to shift, change, and find reverberating expression, now understood through and by the aesthetic experience and its deeply felt and significant meaning. It is at this point that one begins creating anew through continual engagement with and the leveraging of the work, or its aesthetic particularities in an appropriative manner where the source music not only *speaks to*, but also *speaks for* the person making the compilation. Through this existential and creative act, expressions are sounded forth as reverberating inflections of the initial intensities of visceral resonations and the deepening significance of repercussions. As an aesthetic experience, any such expression affords opportunities for subsequent felt resonations, repercussions, and reverberations within the self and relationally with others.

A CELEBRATION OF APPROPRIATION

What is it to use music to *speak for* in this way? The word "appropriation" is not an inappropriate descriptor of this *speaking for* through the creation and gifting of a compilation. Indeed, appropriation is at work at each of the three levels we previously described as the " 'art' of the art of compilations"—through its fragility and vulnerability to endure criticism and/or time, its inherent inventiveness to narrate emotive and meaningful life experiences, and its extrasonorous packaging and presentation. The word "appropriation" carries negative connotations within everyday, academic, and artistic discourses, where "original" work is revered and celebrated. Yet, as Miller (2004, 2008) noted, what is not talked about within these discourses is how difficult and laborious appropriation is. Moreover, there is something appropriative about any creative or inventive activity.

The artistic work of deejays (DJs), for example, may be considered an appropriative art par excellence. Not unlike Sheffield's description of creating a mix tape, deejays also "steal moments from all over the musical cosmos and splice them into a whole new groove" (2007, 23). Technological advances from the mid-twentieth through the first decade of the twenty-first centuries have made possible the proliferation of source material for these appropriative and creative arts. Regardless of the source, the creative work of a deejay is to *decontextualize* the material from its "original" context, intentions, and functions, to *recontextualize* it as a remixed, playful, and sometimes subversive mode of music. When "spliced into a whole new groove," the material performs new functions, takes on new qualities, and is experienced in new and different ways.

One deejay who has written both scholarly and creative texts on this art, Paul D'Shonne Miller (2004), a.k.a. DJ Spooky, That Subliminal Kid, referenced Goethe as another example of an appropriative artist. In fact, he grounded his defense of the generative and creative act of appropriation in Goethe's own words:

> What would remain to me if this art of appropriation were derogatory to genius? Every one of my writings has been furnished to me by a thousand different persons, a thousand things: wise and foolish have brought me, without suspecting it, the offering of their thoughts, faculties and experience. My work is an aggregation of beings taken from the whole of nature. (Goethe, cited in Miller 2004, 75)

This is not unlike Naomi's explanation that she used mix tapes to "write her own story." She labored over the order of songs, fretting over their interaction to convey a narration of the emotional and meaningful moments of her life, although other artists furnished the source material. Again, the critical operation of the artist, whether literary or mix tape,[8] is to decontextualize found sources, sounds, and then to recontextualize[9] them to convey a different story.

This is not to say that all acts of appropriation are affirmative. Some indeed may be hurtful, but there is, nonetheless, something creative in such acts. Our purpose in introducing this idea is to point to a process of appropriative creativity, not necessarily to judge its end results.[10] It is in this creativity that we find the potential for art in music compilations. It is critical to bear in mind that it is not just the act of taking material from another source—decontextualization—but also the recontextualition, the laborious work of intentionally recomposing these slices into a new groove. Thus, the creative work of compilations lies not just in the sourcing of material for inclusion, but the intentional, purposeful, and even playful engagement with that material to recast it in a new mix.

To reiterate, we see this act of appropriation, both a decontextualization and recontextualization of source material, occurring on the three levels we mentioned above. First, we take the lyrics, melodies, rhythms, and tempi of others and recast them to speak for us. This happens on both a metaphorical and a literal level. Bachelard's ([1958] 1994) concepts of resonation, repercussion, and reverberation afford a way to understand the phenomenological experience of *speaking to* so as to *speak for* (metaphorical), which is manifest in the literal appropriation of songs to narrate one's own story, a reverberative act born of visceral and repercussive encounters with music. Second, any such recasting or remixing of source material in a compilation to narrate one's intended story is inherently vulnerable to criticism, misinterpretation, or even disinterest, as Zoë shared. One hazards a risk in mixing one's own story—that not only might its intentions potentially be lost on another but also the physical product is subject to decompose over time (e.g., scratches on a CD's surface, a magnetic tape losing its traction from extended play, an MP3 playlist becoming lost in the shuffle, or the liner notes and case art fading from extended exposure to sunlight). Arguably, it is this fragility and vulnerability that lend each compilation some of its value, sometimes engendering a carefully crafted case for its preservation. As Aimee indicated, these cases are an additional appropriative and artistic endeavor. By incorporating various types of paper, images, and clippings from magazines, drawings, and photographs, as well as textual representations of track listings and liner notes, these cases can become veritable compositions in their own right, incorporating visuals to enhance the sonorous listening experience (for examples, see Pate 2012).[11]

Again, we acknowledge not all appropriation is affirmative. For example, there are contentious debates regarding intellectual copyright. Moreover, we wish to acknowledge the necessity of being sensitive to a history of cultural appropriation, that certain groups or populations may deem certain recontextualizations of music as defamatory or derogatory. However, we simply wish to emphasize its creative potential and highlight that this is not a frivolous undertaking, but one that often comes with a high level of investment, intention, and care. In the case of creating musical compilations, we see this as an affirmative, even celebratory act taking place in poetic spaces of connection. Arguably, this entire undertaking can be thought of as leisure insofar as it also generates a space of enchantment, affirmation, and an orientation toward wonder (Bachelard [1958] 1994; Bhatti et al. 2009; Pieper [1948] 1998).

A Celebration of Affirmation: Enchantment as Leisure

There are numerous moments that surround the creation and gifting of a compilation. There are moments when a song first takes hold of you, speaks to you, and registers in your Rolodex of emotions and experiences. There is the moment of deciding to make a compilation, feeling the surge of energy as you think about the story you want to tell, the person for whom it is intended, and the creative germ of its composition. There are moments of gifting, handing over this piece of you for someone to partake in, the butterflies, the nerves, the pride, and the hope that it will be well received and appreciated. There are moments of receiving a compilation, unwrapping it, hitting "play," and settling in for a sonic, spiritual, visceral, and embodied journey. And there are multiple moments of embodied resonance and connection. We contend that these moments may be viewed as experiences of enchantment (Bachelard [1958] 1994; Bhatti et al. 2009). Enchantment, here, is to be understood as "encounters that temporarily transform our connection with the social/natural world" (Bhatti et al. 2009, 63), and such that are "pro-voked by a surprise, by an encounter with something that one did not expect ... an energizing feeling of fullness or plentitude" (Bennett as quoted in Bhatti et al. 2009, 63). These enchanting encounters meet at the intersection of felt resonation or repercussion and the associated reverberation, "which become for a moment the centre of the entire universe, the evidence of a cosmic situation" in which subjective particularities and per-ceived universalities combine (Bachelard as quoted in Bhatti et al. 2009, 66).

To be enchanted is to be struck, surprised by an uncommon encounter with some-thing that is perhaps ordinary, or understood as ordinary, but that becomes uncanny in a moment where it is seen in a new light, encountered as if it were the first time, or heard with a fresh set of ears. When making a compilation a surge of creative energy, of desire to compose a mix, may come as a surprise. The visceral responses experienced when listening to a song, perhaps heard a thousand times but striking your ears differently as if heard for the first time, may be equally surprising. Moreover, one may be surprised that a song can deepen and enhance one's own existence. What is important in these moments is the extraordinary encounter, not the object of the encounter.[12]

Forgoing debates regarding what constitutes an extraordinary object over one of banality, our interest in enchantment is related to how Pieper described leisure as an "orientation toward the 'wonderful'" ([1948] 1998, 69). For Pieper, the "wonderful" was quite simply the capacity to be enchanted, to be struck, astonished, or amazed by an uncommon encounter with the ordinary. In short, it is the orientation and capacity to experience everything in a new light. This orientation toward the wonderful, this capac-ity to be struck, surprised, or astonished in encounters, was grounded in celebration. Although Pieper intended celebration to be thought in specific ways connected to the cultic, he also posed this concept as a fundamental act of affirmation. The festival, or cultic celebration, was considered an affirmation of the world, one's varied connections with that world, as well as the means to "live out and fulfill one's inclusion in the world, in an extraordinary manner, different from the everyday" (33–34). Indeed this was, in Pieper's conceptualization of leisure, the highest form of affirmation, to which belong "peace, intensity of life, and contemplation all at once" (33). Yet, the experience of peace and contemplation in this affirmative leisure was not the same as an absence of activity, quiet, or inner peace; rather, Pieper likened this intensity and stillness to "the conversa-tion of lovers," which involved "a celebratory, approving, lingering gaze of the inner eye on the reality of creation" (33). This "reality of creation" undoubtedly involves intimate connections, visceral responses, and enchanting moments where the everyday is expe-rienced with a similar affection to the conversation of lovers. With a music compilation, the creator and listener encounter songs heard numerous times, but each strikes a chord that is tender and intimate, often going deeper into one's existence and reverberating outward. The poetic, or even potentially *poietic* space of connection we described in relation to music compilations now takes on additional qualities of leisure as affirma-tion. And as Pieper wrote, "leisure lives on affirmation" (33).

If indeed "leisure lives on affirmation," we take this as a celebration, wonderment, and striking resonation and reverberation of existence. That Pieper connected this conception of leisure to the cultic—imbued with various connotations related to ritual, mystery, and rites—is not surprising when we consider the multitude of ritualistic practices involved with music compilations. Not only does the activity draw us into uncanny relations with others, in the sharing and receiving of tapes, CDs, and so on, but the creation of compilations draws us into mysterious processes where emotions, events, and materials take on new significance. In creating a music compilation, one is taking Pieper at his word—one lives out one's relationships in a manner different from the ordinary, and though the individual tracks one selects for inclusion may be well known, they become recast in a new light. One is affirming and celebrating the intensive moments when life events contract to take on the sensuous and sonic meanings carried in a song. Finally, one is caught in the act of creation, enchanted in composing a mix of songs that invites, engenders, and solicits connections that are affirmative at their core.

THE INVITATION

> I don't believe people are looking for the meaning of life
> as much as they are looking for the experience of being alive.
>
> (Joseph Campbell)

When I think about Phillip's recent gift to me (the first author), a short compilation of tracks intended to help me to have a "saucey" Christmas, I am struck by the music's capacity to make me feel alive. I don't know what Zappa meant when he said, "It makes its own sauce," but for me it doesn't really matter. The way I hear this phrase, subtly spoken as the music begins, reminds me of a feeling, of being caught up in a mix of different songs, rhythms, melodies, tempi, that seems not dissimilar to the different ingredients that go into making a meal. It's something about the mix that makes its own sauce that makes me feel alive, that nourishes me in ways similar to a Christmas dinner. Sure, I can get by without the sauce. Existentially my needs and ends may be met by the bare necessities of life, but the sauce makes it so much sweeter, or more savory if your tastes prefer it, adding nuanced sensations to the experience of eating. In no way does this diminish the gift Phillip gave me as something extra, nonessential; rather, it becomes crucial to how I understand what art does, what leisure does, and what music does in the lives of so many.[13]

Again, this chapter stands as an invitation. Each section heading followed as "an invitation to . . ." "steep in the sauce," "the art of compilations," "a poetic space of connection," "a celebration of appropriation," and "a celebration of enchantment, leisure, and affirmation." Through this chapter the crafting of compilations was explored as an act, art, and expression of music making. Music becomes repositioned and repurposed as found/sound objects that pass through Bachelard's ([1958] 1994) triptych of resonance, repercussion, and reverberations, a process of music *speaking to* so as to *speak for* deeply personal and significantly meaningful experiences of individuals. Ultimately, we were interested in addressing the question, "What is it that gives rise to someone's motivation to partake in this personally meaningful, vulnerable, and artistic endeavor?" Through the lens of Pieperian conceptions of leisure as celebration and an orientation toward the wonderful and an act of affirmation (Pieper [1948] 1998), the creation and crafting of compilations afford poetic spaces for connection, enchantment, felt-aliveness, or what van Manen charged as an "incantative, evocative speaking, a primal telling, wherein [the] aim [is] to involve the voice in an original singing of the world" (1990, 13).

Now we extend one last invitation: listen to some music, steep in it, and if you feel so inclined, remix, recast, and share what you love, what strikes you, what connects you with someone else. But do this only if you are willing to accept the risk of opening yourself up to criticism, of having your gift become damaged, getting lost in the shuffle, or becoming irrelevant over time, *and* only if you are willing to "put yourself out there."

Notes

1. The story shared here, to introduce the topic of this chapter as the idea of music compilations as art, is written as the experience of the first author.
2. The significant moments the first author describes in the previous sentences are certainly intense; however, these are just examples, and doubtless individuals experience felt residues of various intense moments that linger long after the moments are passed.
3. Compilations can be created in many different media: audiocassette tapes (mix tapes), MP3 files on CDs, playlists. Please read "compilations" broadly and interchangeably.
4. Several scholars (e.g., Baker 2001; Campbell, Connell, and Beegle 2007; Lincoln 2005) exploring the relationship between music and identity development noted that music was an integral component with regard to acceptance, inclusion, separation, distinction, and independence with family, immediate social circles, and the larger, evolving world. Thus, music has more often than not been associated with the critical identity formation stage of adolescence (Erikson 1976). However, it is important to note the participants from the study from which this chapter was developed were all adults, and this practice still carried, in spite of their status as adults, deep, personal, and significant meanings (Pate 2012).
5. Note that of the examples we listed only the last (Stayed Up All Night) provides a virtual facsimile of the analog task of creatively packaging a playlist (e.g., creating liner notes, decorating a tape, etc.). One may wonder what might be lost in these digital formats. Certainly there are sensual elements, tactile, olfactory, and visual, that have become altered in a digital format. One may argue that they have become more singular in their modality whereas they were previously multimodal, incorporating a wider spectrum of senses and media. Our intention in referencing these various formats is simply to draw attention to the ways in which creating a music compilation has proliferated with the advent of various digital technologies.
6. Ihde referenced the scientific revolution's privileging of vision through the discovery and use of optics and instruments, usurping the original, more foundational ways of knowing through multiple senses. He asserted that this ultimately led to the construction of truth, knowledge, and meaning within "essentially a *silent* world" (2007, 6).
7. Although compilations such as ones that we are describing are often gifted in a particular moment, they are also listened to over and over, as we described earlier in the chapter. This repetitive listening may diminish sound quality, the listening experience, as well as the physical medium through which the compilation was shared (e.g., the magnetic tape of the cassette may wear out, lose its traction, become unspooled; the CD may become scratched; and playlists may be taken down from websites or lost in a vast library of music; etc.).

8. We are not equating every mix tape to a work of art, just as we would not equate every piece of writing to literature. We are, however, arguing that the degree to which either writing or compiling music reaches a category of "art" involves the artistic operation, at some level, of decontextualizing and recontextualizing source material to produce something new or different.

9. For a philosophical exposition of artistic practices that operate in this way, see Deleuze and Guattari ([1980] 2011; [1991] 1994). Note that Deleuze and Guattari use the terms "deterritorialize" and "reterritorialize." Although these philosophers' work have very specific political implications, we draw inspiration for our way of thinking about mix tapes from their broader discussions of art-making processes.

10. Certainly there are contentious legal, moral, and ethical concerns regarding acts of appropriation. Not only do some acts of appropriation cause harm and damage to others, but within this discussion of music there are concerns related to intellectual property rights. We simply want to acknowledge these concerns.

11. Historically, album art was an integral dimension to the listening experience. As the first author, I vividly remember sitting in front of my stereo, donning large, bulky, overreaching head phones as I opened up and scoured through Derek and the Dominos' (1970) album *Layla and Other Assorted Love Songs*. Fixating on the haphazardly strewn rock and roll paraphernalia among dominos and sound recording material, I read over and over the liner notes and stories accompanying the album and its creation. These elements are not only visual enhancements to the aural experience, but equally involve tactile, olfactory, and other sensuous qualities.

12. Much of the phenomenological or explanatory framework applied to creating compilations also describes the songwriting process. For thoughtful exploration of the songwriting process as one of appropriating and reworking social and personal narratives for a positive outcome, please see Kumm (2013) and Kumm and Johnson (2014).

13. Like the anecdote that serves as the opening to this chapter, this short reflective note was written in the voice of the first author of his experience.

REFERENCES CITED

Bachelard, Gaston. (1958) 1994. *The Poetics of Space*. Translated by Maria Jolas. Boston: Beacon.
Baker, Sarah. 2001. "'Rock on, Baby!': Pre-teen Girls and Popular music." *Journal of Media and Cultural Studies* 15(3): 359–371.
Ball, Jared A. 2011. "I Mix What I Like! In Defense and Appreciation of the Rap Music Mixtape as 'National' and 'Dissident' Communication." *International Journal of Communication* 5: 278–297.
Bhatti, Mark, Andrew Church, Amanda Claremont, and Paul Stenner. 2009. "'I Love Being in the Garden': Enchanting Encounters in Everyday Life." *Social and Cultural Geography* 10(1): 61–76. doi: 10.1080/14649360802553202.
Campbell, Patricia Shehan, Claire Connell, and Amy Beegle. 2007. "Adolescents' Expressed Meanings of Music in and out of School." *Journal of Research in Music Education* 55(3): 220–236.
Deleuze, Gilles, and Félix Guattari. (1980) 2011. *A Thousand Plateaus: Capitalism and Schizophrenia*. Translated by Brian Massumi. Minneapolis: University of Minnesota Press.

Deleuze, Gilles, and Félix Guattari. (1991) 1994. *What is Philosophy?* Translated by Hugh Tomlinson and Graham Burchell. New York: Columbia University Press.

Derek and the Dominos. 1970. *Layla and Other Assorted Love Songs.* Atco Records SD 2-704. LP.

Drew, Rob. 2005. "Mixed Blessings: The Commercial Mix and the Future of Music Aggregation." *Popular Music and Society* 28(4): 533–551.

Erikson, Erik Homburger. 1976. "The Life Cycle." *International Encyclopedia of the Social Science,* edited by David L. Stills and Robert K. Merton, vol. 9, 286–292. New York: Macmillan.

Green, Lucy. (1988) 2008. *Music on Deaf Ears: Musical Meaning, Ideology, and Education.* Bury St. Edmunds: Abramis Academic.

Ihde, Don. 2007. *Listening and Voice: Phenomenologies of Sound.* 2nd ed. Albany: State University of New York Press.

Kumm, Brian E. 2013. "Finding Healing through Songwriting: A Song for Nicolette." *International Journal of Community Music* 6(2): 205–217.

Kumm, Brian E., and Corey W. Johnson. 2014. "Becoming-Shaman, Becoming-Sherpa, Becoming-Healer: Leisure as Becoming." *Leisure/Loisir: Journal of the Canadian Association for Leisure Studies* 38(2): 103–118.

Lashua, Brett D. 2013. "Community Music and Urban Leisure: The Liverpool One Project." *International Journal of Community Music* 6(2): 235–251.

Lewis, C. S. 1970. "Meditation in a Toolshed." In *God in the Dock: Essays on Theology and Ethics,* 212–215. Grand Rapids, MI: Eerdmans.

Lincoln, Sian. (2005). "Feeling the Noise: Teenagers Bedrooms and Music." *Leisure Studies* 24(4): 399–414.

Massumi, Brian. 2012. "Floating the Social: An Electronic Art of Noise." In *Reverberations: The Philosophy, Aesthetics, and Politics of Noise,* edited by M. Goddard, and B. Halligan, and P. Hegarty, 40–57. New York: Continuum International Publishing Group.

Miller, Paul D. 2004. *Rhythm Science.* Cambridge, MA: MIT Press.

Miller, Paul D., ed. 2008. *Sound Unbound: Sampling Digital Music and Culture.* Cambridge, MA: MIT Press.

Moore, Thurston. 2005. *Mix Tape: The Art of Cassette Culture.* New York: Universe.

Parry, Diana C., and Corey W. Johnson. 2006. "Contextualizing Leisure Research to Encompass Complexity in Lived Leisure Experience: The Need for Creative Analytic Practice." *Leisure Sciences* 29: 119–130.

Pate, Joseph A. 2012. "A Space for Connection: A Phenomenological Inquiry on Music Listening as Leisure." PhD dissertation, University of Georgia.

Pate, Joseph A., and Corey W. Johnson. 2013. "Sympathetic Chords: Reverberating Connection through the Lived Leisure Experiences of Music Listening." *International Journal of Community Music* 6(2): 189–203. doi: 10.1386/ijcm.6.2.189_1.

Pieper, Josef. (1948) 1988. *Leisure: The Basis of Culture.* South Bend, IN: St. Augustine's.

Sheffield, Rob. 2007. *Love Is a Mix Tape: Life and Loss One Song at a Time.* New York: Three Rivers.

Simon, Paul. 1986. "Graceland." On *Graceland.* Warner Bros. Records 1-25447. LP.

Stayed Up All Night. 2015. http://suan.fm/about.

van Manen, Max. 1990. *Researching Lived Experience: Human Science for an Action Sensitive Pedagogy.* Albany: State University of New York Press.

Zappa, Frank. 1979. "Joe's Garage." From *Joe's Garage Act I.* Zappa Records SRZ-1-1603. LP.

CHAPTER 7

···

"WHILE MY GUITAR GENTLY WEEPS"

Music Education and Guitar as Leisure

···

DAVID LINES

O Guitar which I had in my youth
Weep with me now as I cry
For indeed I am weeping
Let your strings strum out strongly
Together we shall summon the mountain breeze
Which shall come to strengthen our songs
And carry them out to every village
That there they be heard loud and clear

Literary Review (1998)

INTRODUCTION

···

THE BEATLES' 1968 *White Album* featured George Harrison's "While My Guitar Gently Weeps." In an explanation of the song's lyrics, Harrison wrote that it depicted his interest in Eastern concepts of relativity—by chance he had picked up a book at random, read the text "gently weeps," laid down the book, and began writing the song (Beatles 2000, 306). By the time "While My Guitar Gently Weeps" was released, "Beatlemania" had gripped much of the Western world and brought with it a surge in the popularity of guitar bands (Ryan and Peterson 2001).

As the Beatles became known around the globe through concerts, recordings, and marketing media, local guitarists took the Beatles' sound and made it their own in casual, personal, and semiprofessional guitar leisure contexts. Bennett and Dawe (2001, 2) note that "the guitar exist[ed] in cultural space nuanced by the convergence of both local and global [glocal] forces." This was reflected in the way in which recordings of guitar-based popular music groups and radio and television broadcasts merged with personal guitar interests and desires; as an instrument of personal use the guitar traveled well, having a certain flexibility and mobility that made it an enjoyable musical companion. The guitar was also very versatile; it could fit in well with many different kinds of music environments, genres, and styles. And while the electric guitar brought with it a vibrant and contemporary sound through electronic manipulation, the acoustic guitar encouraged more personal use in everyday recreation. Through these cultural spaces the guitar became more than an instrument of commercial culture—it also became a source of personal emotion, strength, and empowerment to many, as the poem at the start of this chapter attests. Because of this, the guitar has had an impact on our everyday views of music, leisure, and pedagogy. Indeed, through its potential for emotional connection and social transformation, the guitar has challenged normative views of music practice and meaning (Waksman 1999).

I have a personal connection to this "world of guitar." I took "serious" lessons on classical piano from the age of nine and started on the guitar, in an informal fashion, at the age of twelve. Now, as a music education teacher and researcher at a university, I look back with some insight at how I came to develop my guitar knowledge and practice—how my casual guitar beginnings began to fuse with more serious, career-minded music interests over time. For me, an interesting point is that I initially studied piano and guitar in very different ways—a duality that has given me insight into diverse ways of thinking about music and leisure. Further, my research in educational philosophy has opened up a range of conceptual frameworks that highlight how "leisure guitar culture," while not currently part of the dominant educational discourse, may nevertheless become part of the solution to its difficulties.

Put simply, I see the guitar as a "crossroads instrument" in music education. On the one hand it is a popular leisure instrument—many people play guitar for personal enjoyment and as a way to participate in their favorite songs. In this sense, the guitar is part of the daily life of its players and listeners, a focus of meaning, pleasure, desire, and cultural identity and expression. On the other hand, guitar has also become part of the more intensive business of music education. Guitar groups and rock bands are now common in schools and universities, sometimes as extracurricular groups, other times connected with classroom music programs. Jazz guitar, a popular instrument in jazz schools, rivals the piano in terms of its capacity to come to terms with complex harmonic relationships, melodic solos, rhythmic intensity, and improvisation. Further, as a minority instrument among piano, voice, and orchestral instruments, classical guitar still has a presence in classical music programs, although there is often a degree of separation between classical guitar and mainstream orchestral instrumentation.

The guitar, then, is an interesting example of both leisure and schooling. Sometimes it is seen as an instrument of leisure, sometimes as one associated primarily with learning and the school. As such, the guitar tells us how people with an interest in music think about the relationship between music education and leisure, often, I will argue, in ways that are problematic. In this chapter, I explore the place of the guitar within leisure and music education. My interest here is theoretical, in that I am looking at using the guitar to discover better ways to theorize and think about leisure and music education than are currently taken for granted and normalized in society and in education. I seek to draw out the value of the guitar as a leisure instrument and to problematize the educational discourses that fail to recognize that value. It is hoped that the insights from this inquiry will affect the way people think not only about guitar as a musical instrument but also about music as a leisure pursuit in education in general. I continue in a somewhat unorthodox (but in my view appropriate) manner with a series of personal meditations on leisure guitar initially using an autoethnographic approach.

Autoethnography is an approach to research and writing that is both evocative and analytical, one that affords a place where the self can be integrated into leisure research (Anderson and Austin 2012) and into music education research (Bartleet 2010; Gouzouasis 2011). Indeed, autoethnography borrows from the autobiographer's practice of writing about epiphanies—"remembered moments perceived to have significantly impacted the trajectory of a person's life" (Ellis, Adams, and Bochner 2011, 3). My own epiphanies presented here are memories of the more "intense situations" (3) and reflections of guitar that I now pick out and meditate on as an older (I hope, wiser) music education teacher and researcher. In particular, these experiences account in part for what Anderson and Austin describe as the "body, emotion, and knowledge in action," (2012, 137) aspects of autoethnographic memory that challenge normative conceptions of knowledge, or knowledge premised on a prescribed set of understandings. In this sense, my autoethnographic writing is an act of subjectification (Foucault 1982a, 1982b), a reinscription of a personal voice in response to a critical awareness of musical discourse. The meditations thus evoke something of the indescribable but not to be ignored aspects of knowledge that emerge from "events" rather than from "things" (Biesta 2013, 22); in other words, of situational, process knowledge.

Following the autoethnographic leisure guitar meditations and discussion I move to the field of education, where I problematize the notion of leisure (as symbolized by guitar) within a prevailing educational discourse of musical "mastery" and "learning." I use the work of Foucault (1977, 1982a, 1982b, 1986, 1991) to tease out the features of music education discourses that I suggest are counterproductive to the kind of meaningful music making that we find in leisure guitar. While the idea of "learning" has become disciplined in neoliberal music education, I call for more diverse ways of embracing musical subjectivity in music education. These alternative ways of thinking suggest that leisure and education should not be as separate in music as many would presume.

AUTOETHNOGRAPHIC MEDITATIONS

What follows is a series of six meditations based on my own guitar epiphanies, reflections, and theoretical understandings of a selection of guitar-as-leisure experiences. They aim to show my embodied feelings and interpretations of leisure guitar culture. The six meditations have been thematically arranged according to the strings of the guitar and conceptually arranged as: tacit experiences, closeness to music, community spaces, cultivating curiosity, caring for a sound, and taking responsibility.

Low E String. Tacit Experiences: The Unstated Nature of My Leisure Guitar

Having my guitar with me in my teenage years was like having a form of personal expression close by, ready at hand. It meant I could pick it up whenever I wanted to and play—engage in musical play—and work my way around notes and riffs that were musically pleasing and accessible. Through this, I progressed on guitar quite rapidly in and around my other activities like schoolwork and sport. Guitar play happened not in a planned or purposeful way, but in a tacit or unthought way; it happened out of personal desire and casual intention. This process was not "learning" in the educational sense of the term. Rather, I remember guitar play more as "working-with" (Lines 2005) guitar—as a process of living with the instrument, engaging with its sounds and it being an expression of my will to live. My guitar was portable and usually tucked away in some convenient corner of the living room, ready to be picked up and "noodled" with. People came around to our house and chatted with our family in weekends, and during these visits I would often pick up the guitar and create a musical atmosphere—as long as nobody minded. This was not a performance as such but more like the creation of a mood or a prompting of musical play behind the social chatter. You could say it was an exploration of tacit and relational knowledge, a playing with hints, questions, calls, prompts, responses, analogies, contrasts, and repetition in the moment with others and with my immediate environment.

A String. Closeness to Music: Playing Guitar Was an Activity that Brought Me Nearer to Music

Through guitar play, I developed a fondness for the different kinds of sounds I could make. The sounds could be a twang, a gentle pluck, a strike of the wood, a ringing strum, or a padded tone—a whole variety of possibilities that the guitar afforded. The sounds could be both beautiful or ugly . . . it didn't matter. Ugly, harsh sounds disrupted nice, beautiful tones; striated sounds contrasted with smooth sounds—the different sounds made a geography out of the music, a geography that I self-designed. The closeness I felt to the guitar and its sound was a body-felt kind of closeness. It involved holding the guitar, its shape and the tension of the strings. It involved the sweeping rhythms of my arms in strumming and the delicacies of faster picking—which became automatic once they were mastered. There was also a closeness in my awareness of the movement of chords and improvised melodies, of the physical shapes and of knowing and recognizing the melodic or harmonic movements those shapes symbolized. It was a kind of knowing that was instinctive, an instinct of melodic shape or interval that brought forth an affect. In improvised jams—with other friends, guitarists—the body became part of the rhythmic movement of the ensemble, a process of interaction, negotiation, response, and figuration. The prize was not a "musical outcome"; rather, it was the intensity of the experience, the kind of togetherness found in collective music making.

D String. Community Spaces: Recollection of a Guitar Party as a First-Year University Student

It was just an ordinary party in many respects, except myself and a fellow student—Jo, a Māori bloke from Hawke's Bay, New Zealand/Aotearoa—had guitars and we were happy to use them. Jo, more confident than me in singing, launched into a series of songs, ones that everyone seemed to know well, and the whole room joined in with the two of us furiously strumming on our guitars. The room was full, twenty people or so who had not known each other at all in the weeks prior to this event (for they were from all over the country and had come together in a university hostel), but somehow the guitars, the singing, and the songs forged a bond of common interest and celebration in us. Songs that everyone knew—that were reimagined—through the two guitars and the enthusiasm of the crowd. We strummed through each song and the party of students enthusiastically sang—led by Jo's distinctive Māori voice. It was strange that the group had known each other for only a few weeks yet there was a shared musical memory that allowed us to celebrate. With guitar in hand I responded to a call to bring the group together. In this sense the guitar and songs built an "imagined community" (Anderson 1991) in the shared space of the cultural memory of youth in this hostel room and it was my duty, as guitarist, to assist in the shaping of this community. This space also opened up boundaries of difference, for the members of the group came from the different farms, towns, and urban areas of New Zealand—all walks of life—together in one place.

G String. Cultivating Curiosity: Tracing My Interest in Music

It was playing guitar by ear from the age of twelve that cultivated a sense of musical curiosity in me. I was already a "musician" of sorts, for I learnt piano—the old-fashioned way, by notation. But for some reason I picked up the guitar by ear, except for the odd bit of chord recognition and reading. It seemed to be the natural way to learn guitar, picking it up by means of personal desire and with a curiosity for what I could hear. The curiosity came from listening to guitar music—mainly rock and jazz, but also folk guitar music. Being formally trained in music—the schooled piano experience—certainly helped my overall understanding of music, but on guitar I listened to recordings and figured out parts by ear. This occupied my leisure time—and I spent hours doing it. It was practice in both senses of the word. I identified acoustic guitar solos that I liked and copied them as best I could (through repetition), playing along with the recording in celebration of each new achievement. With each new listening came a sense of curiosity about what the guitarist was doing on the recording, and how the part could be played. In addition to solo lines I picked out bass parts, riffs, strumming rhythms, and chords. I was always interested in finding exotic chords, different ways to play standard chord shapes that made them new and fresh. The directness of learning through listening enabled me to pick up not only notes and chords but also style—the way a particular guitarist played. This curiosity was not planned or intentional, at least not in any structured sense, it was never comprehended as "learning" or "education"; rather, it was a spontaneous desire and interest in guitar and guitar music. Practice was akin to desire.

B String. Caring for a Sound: How the Guitar Emulated Certain Sounds

The sound of my generation, as expressed in recorded media, was dominated by the electric guitar, which through my listening I came to think of as a kind of pinnacle of musical possibility and strength. A guitar sound formed the style of many of the bands I listened to: Beatles, Pink Floyd, Dire Straits, Steely Dan, Fleetwood Mac, and America, to name a few. Each band had a particular sound, a definable sound that also emulated and connected with a certain musical style, a way of living, and an attitude to go with it. The sound reflected a sonic culture; it represented something of which I could be a part, and with which I could live, along with others around me. I recall the first time I heard Steely Dan, a refined, musical, jazz-influenced band, and this impressed on me the possibilities of what kind of guitarist I could become—that is, someone who could play sophisticated melodic lines within carefully orchestrated arrangements. I never really listened to song lyrics, which I note is different from the experience of many of my peers. What lasted musically to me was the sound, and the disposition and attitude that went with it. This translated into a care for the sound, and also care for a potential that the music represented.

High E String. Taking Responsibility: The Beach Sing-along

A group of us were staying at the beach. It was nighttime and the natural thing to do was to walk down the beach together in the stillness of the night, find a spot, and sit down. The softness of the sand squeaked under our bare feet while the backdrop of the ocean waves became part of our shared being. Large pieces of driftwood became convenient seats and someone made a fire in the center. I kept an old nylon-string guitar for the beach, and I started off with a song I knew would spark some kind of enthusiasm in the circle. I had a mate who didn't care what people thought of his singing—and he belted out the first song with gusto. His enthusiasm was infectious and gradually the whole group joined in to the backdrop of the guitar and waves behind. Guitar events like these—playing on the beach, parties, youth clubs, sing-alongs, and playful jamming—all seemed to meet a cultural call. These events were not solo acts but events that threw me into casual connections—with people, places, things, buildings, communities. This is what Biesta (2013, 23) calls "the possibility of the event of subjectivity, [that] has to do with the situations in which we are called, in which we are singled out, in which we take responsibility for our responsibility." I became more aware of the value I had as a guitarist to act in ways that led to things that were cared about and enjoyed. With this awareness came the willingness to take the risk and engage in the "responsibility" that was there to be taken. It was an enjoyable and meaningful risk.

DISCUSSION

The meditations above emphasize the tacit, tactile, aural, desiring, exploratory, and ethical dimensions of leisure guitar culture, elements that stand out to me as critical features of my early guitar experiences. Put differently, the leisure guitar themes that emerge from my autoethnographic writing bring out the intimacy and closeness of playing a musical instrument and the social connectedness that comes from playing music meaningfully and responsibly in a living music culture. These aspects made leisure guitar a vibrant and pleasurable embodied experience for me—an experience of the body.

Music making can be a vibrant and meaningful personal experience. In this respect the guitar became a very personal and close instrument, an extension of my daily life (DeNora 2000; Green 2008) that had a physical connection with my body and a social connection with others. It also became a focus of freedom, a place where I could explore and journey into territories of personal choice and interest, a singular but mobile kernel of discovery that enabled extensions into new connections, new sonic and cultural places of meaning and new openings of interest and knowledge.

The tacit and close nature of guitar leisure in the meditations emphasizes the place and space of the body in music. The notion of "the body" is a recurring theme in leisure studies, prevalent not only in the arts but also in recreational sport, dance, and the growing fitness industries (Boyd 2014; Hubbard 2013). In music education there is a small but growing literature on the body and its relation to the music learning experience. Bowman (2010, 4) suggests that the bodily experience is "the basis for perception of such essentially musical qualities as rhythm, groove, movement, gesture, tension and release, and all manner of so-called expressive qualities." Similarly, playing music by ear, as in the way I learned guitar, is a tacit form of music making that establishes a close body-aural relationship with music (Lilliestam 1996). These understandings imply there is a greater connection between the body and taken-for-granted concepts of music than are commonly realized. In this sense, the personal and tactile experience of leisure guitar culture opened me up to a *more connected* sense of musical gesture and a bodily awareness of the expressive qualities of music.

A similar expression of musical embodiment can be seen in the emerging literature on music education and gender. Björck's (2011) study of gendered discourses in music describes the engagement of the body in performative expressions of gendered space in popular music education. She maintains there is a need for girls and women to "claim space" and that spaces can be sustained through both outward (e.g., performative or stage) and inward (musical expression) body orientations. The act of claiming space heightens one's awareness of the gendered physicality and situational sense of the body in the act of music making. This amounts to a movement of subjectification through the productive act of repositioning taken-for-granted performances of gender on stage. The act of raising one's body awareness in music is this way brings one closer to the tacit, tactile, and performative experience of the body in music events. This is what Shusterman, drawing from Foucault, suggests in his book *Body Consciousness*, as he advocates for a "critical, disciplined care of the self that involves self knowledge and self cultivation" (2008, 15) through a philosophy of the body. In this respect, Foucault's (1986) concept of the "care of the self" can facilitate a better understanding of the active creativity that comes with the self-aware actions of desiring, relational, musical bodies.

Extending from my personal, bodily connection with music and guitar was the connection with the social world, which brought with it an ethical connection with the people and events that emerged from the various worlds of leisure guitar. While the social guitar events like the university guitar party cultivated a sense of togetherness and community, they also fostered a sense of ethical responsibility and care for the friends involved in each shared leisure experience. Social and ethical learning also arose from my guitar listening that was mediated by music recording technologies. In these cases I could still adopt a stance toward a sound that I liked without actually meeting the recording artists themselves, and the recordings allowed me to follow certain traces of interest and the cultural attitudes toward which those areas of interest pointed.

I now turn the discussion to matters of music education. While the experiences of leisure guitar culture above unpack a whole range of immanent and musical expressions of life, I argue that these expressions are not always appropriated or valued in educational settings. The "weeping guitar" is a symbol of a lack of embodied meaning in music education; there is a need to unravel the contexts and discourses that continue to deny music-as-leisure freedoms. I draw on Foucault to assist me in the unraveling of music education discourses that fail to affirm the value of the leisure guitar experience, and by extension, other similar life-enriching musical experiences.

FOUCAULT AND MUSIC EDUCATION

While leisure music occupies a space of liberty in the sense that musical subjects (music students and learners) work with music through personal desire, interest, impulse, and ethical action, schooled music education systematizes and disciplines teaching and learning structures behind seemingly neutral liberal notions of freedom and autonomy (Mantie and Tucker 2012). While music for leisure is often positioned as a casual pastime, it can nevertheless be a vehicle for meaningful music engagement, as my own personal guitar meditations attest. Although school music education practices are presumably designed to make music education more efficient and effective through good teaching, the discourses of schooling can have a reverse effect—they can limit and narrow a musical subject's vision and concept of self through ascetic pedagogical practices. In what follows, I use Foucault to build an argument that suggests ways in which a musical subject can resist and creatively reinscribe the practice of liberty in music learning in places and spaces where educational (and other) discourses limit and subjugate opportunities for meaningful musical experiences.

Michel Foucault is well known for his examination of power as it is played out between individuals and within institutions. He sees power primarily in terms of relations—as actions of force that impact upon other actions. His book *Discipline and Punish* (Foucault 1977) is concerned with the body as an object of disciplinary technologies of power. His writing also touches on the area of schooling for children, of the "art of distributions," "partitioning" (classrooms), "ordered activities" (lessons), and other ways in which the schooled child becomes a mechanism for training, and a "pedagogical machine" (system of learning and assessment) (Foucault 1977, 141, 143, 154, 172). By means of these types of practice and the operation of power, subjects are coerced into certain courses of action in different ways. Children thus partake in schooling procedures and their bodies yield to actions of power. The exercise of power does not necessarily have to be violent in its coercion (although it may be). To quote Foucault (1982a, 789):

> [Power] is a total structure of actions brought to bear upon possible actions; it incites, it induces, it seduces, it makes easier or more difficult; in the extreme it constrains or forbids absolutely; it is nevertheless always a way of acting upon an acting subject or acting subjects by virtue of their acting or being capable of action. A set of actions upon other actions.

Where a significant power relation is evident a power block is formed and the manifestation of power is repeated and reinforced time and time again, the power relation can be said to be dominating. Such power endures over time through the repetition of practices and the active compliance of subjects. Foucault maintains that this is not done through a center of control, but by means of repetitions and reinforcements of different relations in different events. Despite his ideas on power, Foucault tends to foreground the productive nature of power. He has an interest in the possibilities of resistance and the particular conditions that support human subjects acting in ways that explore freedoms beyond the immediate obvious restraints of common practice, habit, and institutional policy structures.

A key aspect of leisure guitar culture, as reflected in my meditations and themes, is the way the guitar tacitly "adds" to a given situation, be it the friendly chat of visitors, the university party, or the beach sing-along. In this sense, leisure guitar culture can be seen as a vehicle of what Foucault would call "productive power"; it becomes a catalyst for something more concerned with mobilizing curiosity, the transformation of one's ethical self, the emergence of a sense of community of the party, and the pleasure and intensity of the sharing of the moment together on the beach. When this productive and "free" element of power is absent from pedagogy there is a danger in that our bodies may yield to a systematized or nonmeaningful series of ordered activities without the means to find a musical connection. Problems thus occur when the "pedagogical machine" becomes the means by which music learning is entered.

Foucault used the term "governmentality" (1991, 103) to mean the art of government, a concept that led to his analyses of mentalities of rule that governed modern liberal politics (state reason). Foucault extended his notion of governmentality to the notions of the "government of oneself," the "government of others," and the "government of children" (Besley and Peters 2007, 137). He was interested in *how* a subject comes to be governed in a certain way, that is, he inquired into the practices that determine *how* a subject can submit to or play with rules concerning their own actions, and interface with the actions of others. These ideas are linked to the Socratic dialogues, the care of the self, knowledge of the self, and the way in which one might act ethically in relation to this knowledge.

For Foucault, the concept of governmentality makes it possible to bring out the *ethos*— or practice of freedom—of the self and its relationship with others. In this sense, his ideas help illuminate the notion of pedagogy in music in this discussion. The musical actions and practices of freedom, such as those articulated in this chapter, go to the heart of the pedagogical nature and significance of leisure culture. Music pedagogy is a matter of ethical self-constitution and intention in music practices. In order to develop its potential we need to gain the facility to discern and act in musical contexts and in ways that relate to our musical selves, as was found in my own experience of leisure guitar culture.

In my leisure guitar meditations, my connection with guitar was a kind of "government of oneself," to use Foucault's language. There was a certain freedom and intentionality in the way I chose to submit to each guitar moment and with the guitar enter into a place of musical expression. Importantly, I *chose* to employ the guitar as a tactile and embodied means of expression, often quite tacitly, and as an integral aspect of my daily life. It is these choices that are in danger of being nullified in the context of systematic music education.

THE SELF AND THE POLITICS OF LEARNING

The government and management of the contemporary school occur in a particular global and economic context unique to this moment of time, at least in postindustrial Western countries. Peters discusses the emergence of a "new prudentialism" (2005, 123) in contemporary education that rests on the concept of the entrepreneurial self that "responsibilizes" (122) him- or herself to make decisions and choices that will insure against risk. He finds that the new economically focused educational discourses of these times represent a move away from a welfare-based, liberal education model (and in music away from music as leisure) to a citizen-consumer model of the self, where individuals "calculate the risks and invest in themselves at various points of the life cycle" (123). This new model and way of thinking in education cut to the core of who we are and become in an explicit fashion—the individual self becomes a key player in an underlying philosophy of consumerism. Risk avoidance of this kind stands in contrast to the more open liberty or practice of freedom embodied by leisure guitar culture.

The combined discourses of risk avoidance, prudentialism, and consumerism have profoundly impacted on the provision and focus of music education in schools. Schooled music education (in its various forms of private and public education) adopts certain characteristics that work to fashion the schooled musical subject. One discursive process is the systematic classification of music knowledge and the subsequent distribution of musical subjects (bodies) within a filtered stratification of music fields. In this system we have increasingly specialized music fields that filter and distribute students, not only physically, but conceptually through systems of thinking and processing of genres and levels, such as classical, jazz, popular music, rock, composition, performance, musicology, instrumental band, singing, early childhood, primary school, secondary school, music technology, and so on. While these disciplinary classifications are demarcated at the university level, they are also present through contextualized forms of curriculum and pedagogy at the earlier stages of education. Increased specialization of this kind leads to certain forms of asceticism, of narrow definitions of curriculum knowledge, listening, analyzing, quasi-scientific fragmentation of music "elements," and the distribution of bodies in specific, normalized music settings and contexts.

Another discursive feature commonly found in systemized, schooled music education is the objectification of the musical subject through machine-like conceptions and actions based on normalized educational language. For instance, whereas talk of "aims" suggests broader philosophical contemplation, objective terms like "outcomes" and "competencies" suggest more production-line discourse about education that assumes music learning is preconditioned, prearranged, and systematically demonstrated through "objective" performance drills, where "skills" are imitated and assessed. Within this system the musical subject (student) is expected to be docile, that is, conform to a normalized set of expectations and dutifully perform them without resistance and without the semblance of a creative voice. Learning, here, is reduced to a production-line system where the student participates in a performative output for accreditation.

Biesta (2013) problematizes the political construction of the notion of "learning" in this way. He suggests that the concept of learning is normalized in education in a process where the subject becomes submissive to the demands of learning. The discourse of what he terms "learnification" (62) has developed from a "new language of learning" (63) in the context of the politics of neoliberalism. This is associated with individualistic and neutral (without content) meanings of learning that contrast markedly with those associated with the open, holistic term "education"—which, ironically, has a closer meaning to the experiences of leisure guitar culture. The new, narrowed idea of learning can be seen in current taken-for-granted expressions of the now common phrase "life-long learning," which assumes that individuals have to work toward "learning" (the nature of which is decided for them) all their life. This is not about autonomy or agency, or about people being able to decide and act on their own learning. *Learning* has thus become a very stratified concept, one that is separated into various categories (formal learning, informal learning, nonformal learning, lifelong learning, learning community, etc.), an empty word, and devoid of meaning. It is also seen as a very necessary, natural, and neutral concept that the individual must submit to—something that has power over us rather than something we should have power over (60).

The implications of this in music education are significant. Biesta's critique of the politics of learning opens up a debate in music about whether music learning should be something that occurs through neutral action with little awareness of the cultural implications of learning, such as learning a piece of music without appreciating its cultural relevance, or learning a musical technique or method without comprehending its connection with musical, personal, or social meaning and development. A good example of this is in music performance studies where music students learn notes efficiently, purely for an assessment, or obediently subject themselves to repetitive instrumental practice to the degree that they cause personal physical and psychological injury to themselves. These kinds of circumstances begin to separate music learning from the potential meaningful contexts of music in daily life and of the willing social connections and moments of creative curiosity that arise when a student actively engages in meaningful music learning, as happened to me with my guitar.

The master-apprentice discourse is also customary in music education, particularly in more private music teaching settings and in more elite, performance-based music institutions (Davidson and Jordan 2007; Gaunt 2010). The main problematic issues in this discourse tend to be in the area of professional ethics and in the controlling and managing of students' fields of learning and engagement. Master-apprentice learning in music works well where there is more freedom in these two areas, where the student's personal, cultural, and musical background is honored, expressed, and reimagined, and where there is openness to creativity and difference through engagement and dialogue with alternative forms of musical expression. However, the master-apprentice discourse, at least in Western European and colonial contexts, has also been characterized by excessive teacher control, a narrowing of limits for the student, and an increasingly ascetic approach in association with docile and imitative constructions of the musical subject. Discipline in this context enforces nonidleness and through constant imitation and repetition an increasingly narrow view of creative freedom (Nielsen 2006; Tait 1992).

Conclusion

How can music teachers ensure that they do not succumb to the disabling discourses of neoliberalism, mastery, and narrow conceptions of learning? How can music students move from situations where they are treated as docile bodies in music learning production lines or mastery contexts to places of creative freedom, expression, and meaning? Teachers need to be aware of the ways youth of today construct themselves in terms of a response to their other—namely in response to what they see in the world through global media and consumer society. This can be problematic in music education systems that cling on to institutionalized forms of musical subjectivity. While students continue to be disciplined and compliant to production learning and the mastery paradigm, they may feel increasingly defensive of their minority position in a broader, commodified music culture that glorifies mass docile listening and media-based performativity. The danger here is that rather than construct themselves as active, participatory musicians in the context of their daily music cultures, they will revert to nihilistic positions of subjectivity as a result of ascetic, disciplined study that has no meaning beyond the sphere of its own study culture.

I maintain that an "enactive" (Van der Schyff 2015) position of subjectivity can be realized in music education and that the experience of leisure guitar culture, as an example of an emergent space of learning, can be a source of inspiration for pedagogical practice. In other words, the experience of music as leisure should and must inform our experience of music education and the ongoing process of subjectification and managing of strategies of power. As Olssen suggests:

> Practices of the self, Foucault's later interest, are operated by individuals themselves who have the agency to utilize strategies of power to manage and affect their constitution as subjects through a recognition of the possible subject positions available, and through resistance, to change history. (Olssen 2006, 33)

Pedagogical action can thus be taken in music education to ensure that students have opportunities to work with their subjective positions in music and, if necessary, exercise resistance to schooling discourses that negatively impact on open and creative subject positions.

A key theme emerging from this discussion is the importance of a tacit pedagogy of the body and the enhancement of body awareness. We can be mindful of Foucault's critique of the "docile body" in schooling and the way in which in some circumstances in music education our body experience can be subservient and neutral. Shusterman (2008, 215) writes that "we must develop greater sensitivity to the body's environmental conditions, relations, and ambient energies." Awareness of the body in all its dimensions (skin, touch, gesture, hearing, listening, rhythm) is critical for the mobilization of desire, instinct, and impulse in music. This means understanding how music is involved in expressions of power in different ways—ways that are emotive, gendered, physical, sounded, and tacit. Training in the body can involve not just method and imitation, but also reflection and dialogue (Powell 2010) so as to encourage open-mindedness to the process of embodied music learning. Musicians, music listeners, and music educators engage in "the sensualization of power" (Siisiäinen 2013, 67), in discovering how power is formed through body-sense and desire, and is constituted through specific musical actions and pedagogies. Further, Lamb cautions that "It is not possible to be embodied with neutrality" (2010, 48), and that music and the body are already laden with gendered difference. In this sense, body-mindfulness also involves becoming more responsive to the subjectification of the body through expressions of power through critical awareness.

A related area that emerges from this discussion is the need for a critical philosophy of music education that further takes into account both the subtleties of the musical experience and the dangers expressed by Foucault and others of debilitating discourses affecting the educational process. Such a philosophy can be drawn from the experiences of leisure guitar culture and other forms of personal and social desire. In this respect I have attempted to model a process of reflection and critical inquiry by capturing an autoethnographic reading of leisure guitar culture and then positioning it alongside concerns about schooling and music education through a critical educational philosophy. The process of reflection, as embodied through autoethnography, can be a way of critically entering a creative space of subjectification through the exploration of limits, hybridity, and crossover thinking. This can open up the possibilities of resistance to disabling discourses and creative pedagogies for a reconstituted music education. The trope of the weeping guitar introduced in the poetry at the start of this chapter laments the loss of the creative inner voice, the process of critical subjectification in music education. The loss of the desiring, truth-telling musical subject is a concern in contemporary music education; however, there is hope that a critical pedagogy can work to raise awareness of the subject's position through embodied action. As the opening poem suggests, we can strengthen our songs and carry them to another village. This chapter has moved from a personal inquiry into leisure guitar culture into a critical exploration of music education discourses through a Foucaultian lens. It has shown that music leisure culture and music education do not need to be seen as distinct and separate entities but can be envisaged together as synchronic forms of musical action.[1]

NOTE

1. Many thanks to Dylan van der Schyff and anonymous reviewers and editors for their extremely helpful comments on this paper.

REFERENCES CITED

Anderson, Benedict. 1991. *Imagined Communities: Reflections on the Origin and Spread of Nationalism*. New York: Verso.

Anderson, Leon, and Mathew Austin. 2012. "Auto-Ethnography in Leisure Studies." *Leisure Studies* 31(2): 131–146.

Bartleet, Brydie-Leigh. 2010. "Behind the Baton: Exploring Autoethnographic Writing in a Musical Context." *Journal of Contemporary Ethnography* 38(6): 713–733.

Beatles. 2000. *The Beatles Anthology*. San Francisco: Chronicle Books.

Bennett, Andy, and Kevin Dawe. 2001. *Guitar Cultures*. New York: Berg.

Besley, Tina, and Michael A. Peters. 2007. *Subjectivity and Truth: Foucault, Education and the Culture of the Self*. New York: Peter Lang.

Biesta, Gert. 2013. *The Beautiful Risk of Education*. Boulder, CO: Paradigm.

Björck, Cecilia. 2011. *Claiming Space: Discourses on Gender, Popular Music, and Social Change*. Gothenburg: ArtMonitor, University of Gothenburg Press. https://gupea.ub.gu.se/bitstream/2077/24290/1/gupea_2077_24290_1.pdf.

Bowman, Wayne. 2010. "Living Philosophy, Knowing Bodies, Embodied Knowledge." *Action, Criticism, and Theory for Music Education* 9, no. 1: 1–8. Accessed May 5, 2015.http://act.maydaygroup.org/articles/Bowman9_1.pdf.

Boyd, Jade. 2014. "'I Got to Dance Right?' Representation/Sensation on the Gendered Dance Floor." *Leisure Studies* 33(5): 491–507.

Davidson, Jane W., and Nicole Jordan. 2007. "'Private Teaching, Private Learning': An Exploration of Music Instrument Learning in the Private Studio, Junior and Senior Conservatories." In *International Handbook of Research in Arts Education*, edited by Liora Bresler, 729–754. New York: Springer.

DeNora, Tia. 2000. *Music in Everyday Life*. Cambridge: Cambridge University Press.

Ellis, Carolyn, Tony Adams, and Arthur Bochner. 2011. "Autoethnography: An Overview." *Forum: Qualitative Social Research* 121: article 10.

Foucault, Michel. 1977. *Discipline and Punish: The Birth of the Prison*. Translated by Alan Sheridan. New York: Pantheon.

Foucault, Michel. 1982a. "The Subject and Power." *Critical Inquiry* 8(4): 777–795.

Foucault, Michel. 1982b. "The Subject and Power." In *Michel Foucault: Beyond Structuralism and Hermeneutics*, 2nd ed., edited by Hubert L. Dreyfus and Paul Rabinow, 208–216. Chicago: University of Chicago Press.

Foucault, Michel. 1986. *The History of Sexuality*. Vol. 3, *The Care of the Self*. Translated by Robert Hurley. New York: Random House.

Foucault, Michel. 1991. "Governmentality." In *The Foucault Effect: Studies in Governmentality, with Two Lectures by and an Interview with Michel Foucault*, edited by Graham Burchell, Colin Gordon, and Peter Miller, 87–104. Chicago: University of Chicago Press.

Gaunt, Helena. 2010. "One-to-one Tuition in a Conservatoire: The Perceptions of Instrumental and Vocal Teachers." *Psychology of Music* 38(2): 178–208.

Gouzouasis, Peter. 2011. "Toccata on Becoming Arts Based Teacher Researchers." In *Pedagogy in a New Tonality: Teacher Inquiries on Creative Tactics, Strategies, Graphics Organizers and Visual Journals in the K–12 Classroom*, edited by Peter Gouzouasis, ix–xv. Rotterdam: Sense.

Green, Lucy. 2008. *Music, Informal Learning and the School: A New Classroom Pedagogy*. Aldershot: Ashgate.

Hubbard, Philip. 2013. "Carnage! Coming to a Town near You? Nightlife, Uncivilized Behavior and the Carnivalesque Body." *Leisure Studies* 32(3): 265–282.

Lamb, Roberta. 2010. "Mind the Gap!" *Action, Criticism and Theory for Music Education* 9(1): 44–53. http://act.maydaygroup.org/articles/Lamb9_1.pdf.

Lilliestam, Lars. 1996. "On Playing by Ear." *Popular Music* 15(2): 195–216.

Lines, David. 2005. "'Working-With' Music: A Heideggerian Perspective of Music Education." *Educational Philosophy and Theory* 37(1): 65–75.

Literary Review. 1998. "Idir." 41(2): 294.

Mantie, Roger, and Lynn Tucker. 2012. "Pluralism, the Right, and the Good in Choirs, Orchestras, and Bands." *International Journal of Music Education* 30(3): 260–271.

Nielsen, Klaus. 2006. "Apprenticeship at the Academy of Music." *International Journal of Education and the Arts* 7(4). http://www.ijea.org/v7n4/v7n4.pdf.

Olssen, Mark. 2006. *Michel Foucault: Materialism and Education.* London: Paradigm.

Peters, Michael. 2005. "The New Prudentialism in Education: Actuarial Rationality and the Entrepreneurial Self." *Educational Theory* 55(2): 123–127.

Powell, Kimberly. 2010. "Somaesthetic Training, Aesthetics, Ethics and the Politics of Difference in Richard Shusterman's *Body Consciousness*." *Action, Criticism, and Theory for Music Education* 9(1): 75–91. http://act.maydaygroup.org/articles/Powell9_1.pdf.

Ryan, John, and Richard Peterson. 2001. "The Guitar as Artifact and Icon: Identity Formation in the Babyboom Generation." In *Guitar Cultures*, edited by Andy Bennett and Kevin Dawe, 89–116. New York: Berg.

Shusterman, Richard. 2008. *Body Consciousness: A Philosophy of Mindfulness and Somaesthetics.* New York: Cambridge University Press.

Siisiäinen, Lauri, 2013. *Foucault and the Politics of Hearing.* New York: Routledge.

Tait, Malcolm. 1992. "Teaching Strategies and Styles." In *Handbook of Research on Music Teaching and Learning: A Project of the Music Educators National Conference*, edited by Richard Colwell, 525–534. New York: Schirmer.

Van der Schyff, Dylan. 2015. "Music as a Manifestation of Life: Exploring Enactivism and the 'Eastern Perspective' for Music Education." *Frontiers in Psychology* 6(345). http://dx.doi.org/10.3389/fpsyg.2015.00345.

Waksman, Steve. 1999. *Instruments of Desire: The Electric Guitar and the Shaping of Musical Experience.* Cambridge, MA: Harvard University Press.

CHAPTER 8

PLAYING MUSIC AND IDENTITY DEVELOPMENT IN MIDDLE ADULTHOOD

A Theoretical and Autoethnographic Account

KEVIN RATHUNDE AND RUSSELL ISABELLA

IDENTITY tells us who we are and how others view us (Erikson 1968). It provides meaning and direction in life by helping to clarify our unique role in the world. A central question in the present volume on music and leisure is: How does recreational music making become meaningful for people? This chapter engages the question by exploring how playing music affects identity development in middle adulthood. More specifically, the chapter explores the question of music and identity from two contrasting perspectives, one conceptual and one more descriptive and experiential. The conceptual framework is based on a review of identity theories and other process models of growth, as well as on insights from an ongoing study of leisure play and identity development in middle adulthood (Rathunde and Isabella forthcoming). These conceptual ideas are brought to life in the second half of the chapter by an experience-based autoethnography emerging from the first author's recreational music making. These two parts of the chapter, though very different in content and tone, inform each other and attempt to shed light on how playing music in middle adulthood can enhance both identity development and quality of life.

TAILORING IDENTITY THROUGH LEISURE PLAY: A CONCEPTUAL FRAMEWORK

Several theories on human development highlight the promise of identity growth in midlife (see Lachman 2004 for a review); however, they are seldom clear about *how* to take advantage of this window of opportunity before aging and declining health start to close it. The approach here suggests that *tailoring identity through leisure play* (i.e., an intrinsically motivated and deeply enjoyable activity) is an excellent way to stimulate identity development (see also Csikszentmihalyi 1996; Huizinga 1955; Kleiber 1999; Stebbins 1982).

The perspective here on identity development relies heavily on the analogy of tailoring a handcrafted suit to represent the process. Erikson's (1950, 50) classic definition of identity as "the *style of one's individuality* ... that ... coincides with the sameness and continuity of one's *meaning for significant others* in the immediate community" inspired the selection of this analogy. Identity can be thought of as a style of individuality that we wear like a suit of clothes; the suit represents and expresses the self *and* it conveys meaning about the person to others. To the extent that what we see in a mirror coincides with what is mirrored by the reactions of significant others in our immediate community (i.e., the meaning for those others), there is a healthy continuity of identity. This analogy is useful for communicating the process of identity change in midlife because it works well for describing the small or large changes that can be made. Tailoring can mean making minor adjustments to improve a fit in an environment; or it can indicate the creation of an entirely new outfit that fundamentally alters one's style of individuality along with the perceptions of others.

Erikson (1968) cited identity development as the primary task of adolescence, while also acknowledging that there are lifelong issues of personal identity. Adolescents are viewed as being able to explore their interests and forge an identity with the help of a moratorium granted by parental and societal protection. This moratorium provides them with a sheltered space to play, explore, and learn about themselves and the world. Recent societal trends of young adults postponing typical adult commitments related to marriage, parenthood, and career (Arnett et al. 2011) have in many cases delayed the establishment of identity and extended the moratorium into the early years of adulthood. Even so, the identity, or style of individuality, formed at this time of life is not likely to maintain a good fit as we grow older. As one's life circumstances change, so should the ensemble of goals, values, and beliefs that needs to be stitched together. Just as a young person might purchase suits from a department store before learning to be more discriminating, the choices that start defining a young person's self and future path are often heavily influenced by off-the-rack identities. Through the accumulation of experience, however, and if all goes well in terms of fortunate life circumstances that offer opportunities for growth, a more tailor-made and handcrafted identity can be fashioned.

Midlife can be an opportune time for such tailoring. Developmentalists have historically associated this stage of life with a turn toward new priorities, increased introspection, and more attention to neglected aspects of the self after many years prioritizing family and/or career concerns (Jung 1955; Lachman 2004; Levinson 1978; Neugarten 1968). Midlife, therefore, can offer new opportunities to engage leisure activities that help one age more successfully (Brown, McGuire, and Voelkl 2008; Vaillant 2002). The autoethnography presented in the second half of the chapter illustrates these dynamics and suggests how playing music can set in motion positive identity change.

The Identity Tailoring Process: Measurement, Design, Pattern Making, and Alteration

A coherent identity is the result of a learning and creative process that produces knowledge about the self and its role in the world. The tailoring model is elaborated next by focusing on this process and briefly examining models of design, experiential learning, and creativity. All of these models suggest a similar, multistep procedure that characterizes the growth of knowledge in ways that are thought to be relevant to understanding how music making can affect identity development. Specifically, each model focuses on exploring novel information, having an idea, finding a way to apply the idea in the world, and bringing closure by actively problem solving.

When creating a new suit, tailors go through (more or less) the same process. First, measurements are taken to ascertain an individual's unique characteristics and posture. Next, these measurements are integrated in an overall design. A third step moves the abstract design to concrete application as patterns are cut in fabric and tested as prototypes by draping them on a facsimile of the body (e.g., a mannequin). A last step involves making final alterations on the selected patterns to complete the suit and refine the fit. In terms of identity, the perspective here is that leisure play activities like making music can tailor identity when these activities lead us to explore new facets of the self (measurement), discover how these attributes can be combined in a new self-conception (design), search for ways to bring this imagined self into existence (create patterns), and finally, select a course of action and make the necessary adjustments to complete the process and realize a change in identity (alterations).

These four steps of tailoring, not surprisingly, match up closely to leading models of design. For example, the British Design Council in 2005 (Norman 2013; Onarheim and Friis-Olivarius 2013) articulated a "double-diamond" model with four stages: discover, define, develop, and deliver. In the discover phase, designers use divergent thinking to expand the scope of the problem and examine all sides of it. Then they converge upon a single way to define the problem at hand. Next, in a second phase of divergence, designers develop possible ways to solve the identified design problem. Finally, convergent thinking is used again to deliver a final solution (see Figure 8.1, from Onarheim and Friis-Olivarius 2013). The human-centered design (HCD) model, another approach frequently used by design firms, suggests similar steps of observation, idea generation, prototyping, and then testing (Norman 2013).

These design models do a good job portraying how any learning or creative process unfolds. Norman (2013, 219) makes a similar argument: "Design thinking is not an exclusive property of designers—all great innovators have practiced this, even if unknowingly, regardless of whether they were artists or poets, writers or scientists, engineers or business people." Examining two well-established perspectives on

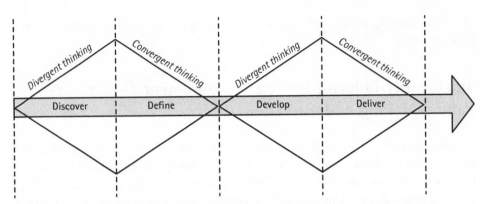

FIGURE 8.1 The double-diamond design model. (Based on Onarheim and Friis-Olivarius 2005.)

learning and creativity would seem to support this view. Kolb's (1984) framework on experiential learning and Wallas's (1926) classic model of creativity have both been widely discussed and incorporated in numerous studies looking at knowledge creation.

Experiential learning has a long history in social and educational sciences that can be traced back to Dewey, Lewin, and Piaget, all of whom influenced Kolb's (1984) theory. Kolb thought that learning was set in motion by two inescapable, dialectical tensions: the movement between concrete experience and abstract conceptualization, and the interaction between person and environment. When Kolb crossed these two dialectics and considered individual learning styles (Kolb, Boyatzis, and Mainemelis 2001), it resulted in his familiar fourfold scheme: (1) concrete experience started a divergent process that generated new information; (2) reflective observation grasped the meaning of the new information; (3) abstract conceptualization generalized what was learned to new situations; and (4) active experimentation tested generalizations and applied them. Kolb thought one could enter this process at different points, but traversing the entire cycle optimized learning.

Taking a similar approach to understanding the creative process, Wallas (1926) offered a framework that, with recent modification (Csikszentmihalyi 1996; Hansen, Lumpkin, and Hills 2011), proposes a five-stage model of *preparation, incubation, insight, evaluation,* and *elaboration.* Preparation is an immersive, information-gathering phase that Wallas described as consciously accumulating information in multiple directions. Incubation is a phase more characteristic of a creativity model than a learning model, in that it describes a time when the mind rests, focuses on other things, and subconsciously mulls over the information gathered in the first phase. Insight occurs when disparate elements come together in the realization of a new idea. The final two phases of evaluation and elaboration check whether the new idea is viable in the real world. Evaluation draws out the consequences of an idea and explores ways to test it. Finally, elaboration is the hard work put into refining an idea, resolving any remaining problems, and communicating it well (Csikszentmihalyi 1996; Hansen, Lumpkin, and Hills 2011).

Table 8.1 Similarities in Process across Tailoring, Design, Learning,
and Creativity Models

Tailoring model	Measurement	Design	Pattern-making	Alterations
Design models	Discover	Define	Develop	Deliver
	Observation	Idea	Prototype	Test
Learning model	Experience	Reflect	Conceptualize	Experiment
Creativity model	Preparation	Incubation/ Insight	Evaluation	Elaboration

The sequential phases described in the experiential learning and creativity models share strong similarities; both, in turn, resemble the tailoring and design process discussed earlier. The claim here is not that each framework depicts an identical process, but that emphasizing the similarities sheds light on how identity development may proceed, and how music making can set the process in motion. Table 8.1 organizes the comparisons and similarities between the models. As the table shows, there is a common movement from a divergent information-gathering phase to a convergent idea-generation phase that synthesizes information. Then all of the models reverse direction, so to speak, and focus more on the environment. A common theme in the third phase is a new divergent process, but this time one directed toward exploring ways to implement and test an idea. Finally, each model concludes the cycle with another convergent phase that makes adjustments and moves the process toward clarity and resolution.[1]

The Tailoring Process and Theories of Identity Development

How do these observations about the fourfold process of tailoring identity mesh with prominent theories on identity development? This section draws on the contemporary views of Marcia (1980) and Berzonsky (1990), as well as the classic approaches of Erikson (1968) and symbolic interaction theory (Cooley 1902; Mead 1934), in order to further articulate the tailoring model.

Marcia (1980) operationalized Erikson's ideas about identity using the notions of exploration and commitment. The former involves a search for new information about choices and values that are relevant to forming an identity; commitment is the sorting through of this information and the selection among alternatives to arrive at a coherent set of goals and values (i.e., an identity). Marcia further suggested that the ideal identity outcome or status—referred to as an "identity achievement"—occurred when a commitment was made after first exploring a variety of options. An identity status that resulted from exploration without commitment (i.e., moratorium), commitment without exploration (i.e., foreclosure), or a lack of both (i.e., diffusion), was seen as potentially damaging to psychological health. Marcia's perspective focuses on relatively stable

identity statuses that emerged from exploration and commitment; other identity theorists like Berzonsky (1990) focus less on stable outcomes and more on the style used to
form identity. Nevertheless, the same dynamic of exploring alternatives before selec-
tively making a commitment is emphasized as the optimal choice. Berzonsky referred
to this combination as an informational style and associated it with the potential for
identity growth and revision. Using an informational style, therefore, would lead one to
Marcia's status of identity achievement (Schwartz 2001).

In addition to the interplay between exploration and commitment, the interrelationship between self and other plays a fundamental role in classic theories of identity.
Erikson integrated psychological and socio-cultural considerations in his definition to
counter an overemphasis on mental forces in other conceptions. In other words, a person's identity provided a sense of meaning both internally for the self and externally for
others. Schwartz (2001, 9) notes that most post-Eriksonian theories carry forward this
link between the personal and the social: "Ego identity . . . represents a coherent picture
that one shows both to oneself and to the outside world. . . . The more complete and consistent that mosaic is, the closer to ego identity synthesis one is." To have a healthy identity at any age, it is not enough to have a strong sense of internal meaning; this meaning
must be shared with others.

Conceptions of identity informed by symbolic interaction theory also emphasize its
development in collaboration with social interaction. Part of one's identity is shaped
through personal experience and self-reflection; these subjective operations have an
undeniably important impact on our perceptions of the world. However, this private
sense of meaning is not the endpoint of the process; a person's identity is also validated and further shaped through social interaction. This is the meaning of the well-
known concepts of *looking-glass self* and *taking the role of the other* (Cooley 1902; Mead
1934): a person monitors others' reactions to their own actions to see if they are acceptable and consistent with their perceived identity (Turner 2013). The imaginative and
sometimes idealized view of one's own identity, in fact, needs "role support" through
social feedback to help legitimize it. When there is a perceived discrepancy between
one's self-generated view and the feedback received, it can prompt a range of responses,
from selective perception of cues, to withdrawal from social interaction, to the outright
rejection of an "audience" and abrupt switching of identity (McCall and Simmons 1978;
Turner 2013).

Toward a More Complete Model: Self-Differentiation, Social Integration, and Flow

A more complete tailoring model can now be specified by integrating these theoretical views on identity with the earlier observations about the process of identity change
(see Figure 8.2). The first two phases of tailoring—measurement and design—represent
exploration and commitment in relation to a self-differentiation process. Measurement
is analogous to discovering what attributes best suit the individual, whereas the design

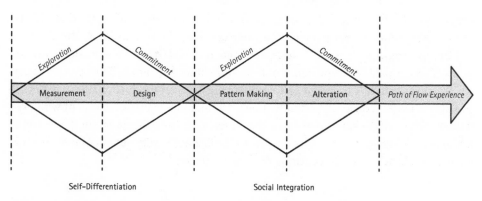

FIGURE 8.2 The tailoring model of identity development.

phase represents the imaginative thinking and self-reflection needed to select and combine the most essential attributes in a cohesive view of the self. These contrasting divergent and convergent movements presumably reflect the need to maintain unity-in-variety and optimize arousal and experience (Rathunde and Csikszentmihalyi 2006). In the narrative on leisure music making in the second half of the chapter, the measurement phase will describe the new challenges and musical experiences that broadened the self. The design phase will relate the personal insights and decisions that were made as a result of reflecting on these experiences and integrating them. These first two phases of tailoring identity are important because they result in changes in self-conceptions that affect one's future plans. However, these self-differentiating steps are incomplete because they are not yet actualized in a social role. In other words, one has been measured for a new suit and the design has been completed, but the suit exists only in imagination.

The next two actions of tailoring—pattern making and alteration—represent a movement toward social integration as a new design is enacted in a social environment. Social integration connects one to others and gives a sense of belonging to a larger group and being recognized by it. It requires a new divergent-convergent cycle of exploration and commitment, but this time in an outward, other-directed process as an "individual constructs an identity out of socially possible faces and voices" (Adams and Marshall 1996, 431). In the upcoming autoethnography about music, pattern making will illustrate the efforts made to find ways to play music for others and share some of the newfound sense of meaning; the alteration phase will describe the actions taken to develop a specific opportunity to connect with others.

Finally, the perspective here is that engaging *leisure play* activities is one of the best ways to set the entire tailoring process in motion. Such activities are characterized by freedom of choice and intrinsic motivation (i.e., motivation that comes from doing an activity, not the external rewards associated with it), and these two qualities are known to enhance many types of learning (Deci and Ryan 1985; Dewey 1913; Renninger, Hidi, and Krapp 1992). Furthermore, these qualities are conducive to triggering flow experiences (Csikszentmihalyi 1996), unusually intense "optimal" states that dissolve self-consciousness, fuse a person with their chosen activity, and boost the attention available for engaging it. Alan Waterman's (1990, 1993) extensive work on identity development recognized the importance of flow for healthy outcomes: "Experiences of personal expressiveness, from feelings accompanying intrinsic motivation, through flow, to peak experiences, constitute a sign that one is acting in a manner consistent with one's daimon [true self]" (Waterman 1990, 56). In terms of the conceptual model in Figure 8.2, experiencing flow in the tailoring process indicates identity outcomes that are more likely to feel handcrafted and custom-made to fit the self.[2]

Playing Music and Identity Development: An Autoethnographic Account

The second part of the chapter presents an experience-based autoethnography emerging from the first author's recreational music making. This narrative is intended to add detail and evocative description to the conceptual infrastructure just presented. The use of autoethnography has been growing in the social sciences for several decades, especially in the fields of sociology, anthropology, communication, and education (Jones, Adams, and Ellis 2013). The method combines autobiography with ethnography, or observations pertaining to personal and socio-cultural meaning. A primary strength of the approach is that a researcher is not artificially removed from the study of some phenomenon in order to maintain the appearance of objectivity. Autoethnography, instead, makes the subjectivity of an author a vehicle for critical reflection and assumes that in some research endeavors more harm is done to understanding a phenomenon when authors provide decontextualized accounts and conceal their own voice and perspective (Dupuis 1999; Ellis and Bochner 2000). For this reason, and because the authors' own leisure interests (i.e., music and photography, respectively) have proven to be informative in the ongoing study of leisure play and identity development (Rathunde and Isabella forthcoming), an autoethnographic account is included in this chapter.

The narrative here condenses and represents a three-year timespan (age fifty-three to fifty-six). It begins with a brief personal history in order to set the stage for a more in-depth account of how leisure music making affected identity development; it ends with thoughts about ongoing identity tailoring. The account draws on extensive notes accumulated over the relevant years and is presented in a first-person voice, as is customary with autoethnography. This sudden change in the content and tone of the chapter sheds a different kind of light on the notion of tailoring identity, one that is meant to inform the conceptual framework from the inside out.

Some Background: Music and Identity in Adolescence and Early Adulthood

Playing music as a middle-aged adult is a reconnection to my past that included eight years of on-and-off music lessons and practice as a child and young adolescent, and approximately twelve years as a professional musician (from ages seventeen to twenty-nine). In terms of the identity I forged in late adolescence and early adulthood, I thought of myself—and was recognized by others—as a musician. This identity was developed across years of experience in each of the four stages described by the tailoring identity model: playfully exploring the guitar and songwriting; envisioning desired goals and outcomes; investigating various opportunities to perform in public; and working hard to bring a few of them to fruition. Primary among those fully developed opportunities was a pop-rock band that survived over a decade and provided hundreds of chances to perform across the United States and occasionally in Canada. The band was also fortunate to have several opportunities to perform as an opening act for successful and well-known musicians (e.g., Bryan Adams, Survivor, the Ramones) and record in state-of-the-art studios (e.g., Sound City in Los Angeles) with noted producers (e.g., David Foster). When my two beautiful daughters were born and I decided to go to graduate school, my guitars were, for the most part, put back in their cases. Being a working musician became a thing of the past.

One aspect of being a musician, however, accompanied me to graduate school: my fascination with the intense experiences I often had while improvising, performing, practicing, or writing music. I discovered an appropriate name for these experiences when I was seventeen and performing one night in a rundown club in a suburb of Chicago. At the time, I was attending Loyola University of Chicago during the day and reading Abraham Maslow's *Toward a Psychology of Being* in the evening in order to prepare for a Philosophy of Psychology course. I would try to read on breaks between sets in a storeroom that doubled as a "dressing room" for the band. The book described transcendent, peak experiences that Maslow thought occurred while doing intrinsically motivating and self-actualizing activities. I immediately realized that occasionally, especially while improvising, I was having such intense experiences. In fact, some of them were so memorable that I documented them on small pieces of paper that I would place behind an electronic access panel on the back of my Les Paul guitar.

For the next twelve years, as things progressed professionally in music, I began avidly reading about these "optimal" experiences and why researchers thought they were linked to learning and creativity. Eventually, I applied to graduate school at the University of Chicago so I could study flow experiences with Mihaly Csikszentmihalyi, the person doing the best contemporary research on optimal experience. Being accepted to Chicago and having the opportunity to study flow in graduate school made me feel as though I was carrying forward my identity as a musician, at least in an indirect way.

Measurement: New Musical Challenges

For a period lasting about twenty years, as I finished my PhD and began working as a professor at the University of Utah, my direct involvement playing music was minimal. This pattern of putting valued interests on hold, unfortunately, is an all-too-familiar one. Research on the life course shows that the adult years often proceed at a hectic pace and are filled with extrinsic pressures. Family and career concerns take center stage and can force the passions of youth to the background, no matter how well loved and important they were at the time. My identity as a musician started slowly disappearing and only surfaced occasionally through stories and memories shared with close friends. My identity as a professor, on the other hand, began to grow as the years in Utah accumulated. When I was promoted to full professor in 2010, an event that closely followed my two daughters moving out of the family home to live independently, I began to think about the role music had played in my life. I wanted to rediscover this source of inspiration for my academic work and renew this fundamental, but fading part of my identity. These goals became part of an ongoing conversation in my family. When my wife and sister-in-law bought a guitar for me as a promotion gift, the journey back to music began, and so did the opportunity to tailor a new identity that included being a musician.

The first step in any learning or creative process, including identity development, is the exploration of new challenges that extend the reach of the self. Music, again, provided a huge array of such challenges to explore. The central one was to find a way to make music again in an entirely new context. In the absence of bandmates who created a rhythm section and sang lead vocals, I put the focus on writing instrumental music as a solo musician. An equally difficult challenge was learning a new style of playing the guitar. Instead of using a plectrum or guitar "pick" to strum or strike individual notes, there are advantages on a guitar for combining harmony and melody in a solo performance by using a fingerstyle technique. My experience and training on the guitar, which included studying as a young adult with some esteemed jazz musicians and teachers (e.g., the late Frank Dawson of Columbia College and the Chicago Jazz Ensemble and David Bloom at the Bloom School of Jazz), never included plucking the strings with my fingers.

In addition to these main challenges, there were many other obstacles that stood in the way of getting started. Did my seventies-era Mesa Boogie amplifier still work, or did the tubes and capacitors need to be replaced? The guitar I received as a gift was in good shape, but how were the neck and intonation on my vintage Epiphone Casino guitar that had been sitting in its case for over a decade? Given the new interest in fingerpicking, where were the best music stores if I wanted to add a steel- and nylon-string acoustic guitar? The challenge of becoming a solo musician also would be aided by embracing new technologies that made it easier to use a computer for creating professional-sounding backing tracks for accompaniment. This "solution," however, brought with it the additional complications of learning about MIDI (Musical Instrument Digital Interface) keyboards, MIDI controllers, audio interfaces, recording software, studio monitors, and too many other things to mention here. On top of all this, there was the never-ending problem of finding time to engage all of these challenges within the constraints of my continuing family and career obligations. Although much more could be said here about the matter of finding time, it is worth noting that I was extraordinarily fortunate to have family members who were entirely supportive of this path back to music. Furthermore, I had the good fortune of having a flexible work schedule, stable finances, and good health, all of which put me in a privileged position to take on these many challenges.

Mentioning the many musical and nonmusical challenges faced in this leisure play activity is useful for several reasons. The most obvious one is that it illustrates how a measurement phase of tailoring identity can set a vigorous change process in motion that modifies the "size" and dimensions of individuality. These challenges also illustrate that leisure play need not be something that is frivolous or easy to accomplish. The challenges were formidable and lacking in any extrinsic rewards for pursuing them. The lack of extrinsic rewards is perhaps the most important point about this exploratory phase of identity development. Without the intrinsic enjoyment I experienced while doing these complex and varied tasks, it would have been impossible to summon the patience, perseverance, and attention needed to take them all on. I already understood the importance of intrinsic motivation from years of research on motivation and education. Nevertheless, this felt experience reaffirmed my understanding in ways that were more convincing than significant research findings.

When I could find the time, my primary leisure play focus was on writing music and learning to fingerpick. During the times when I did not have the guitar in my hand, I embraced the various equipment-related challenges (e.g., exploring relevant technical information on the Internet, learning to use recording software, and so on). Immersed in these many new directions, I was learning a great deal about music, my abilities, and my limitations.

Design: Beautiful and Blue

As things progressed and a few songs started to take shape, I started having insights about the importance of having music back in my life. In the language of the tailoring model, reflecting on the many new experiences began pulling me into the design phase of identity development, where I could start to see a way forward that felt meaningful. I was not yet thinking about any public or social role related to music; in fact, I still sought a great deal of privacy as I worked on things in the relative seclusion of a basement "studio." However, I was beginning to get glimpses of what Waterman (1990) would describe as a path of self-actualization connected to my daimon or authentic self.

One of the strongest moments of revelation occurred well over a year after diving into the pile of new challenges. Although it is difficult to recall the time sequence with which these insights unfolded, I started to see a common theme running through much of what I was experiencing. For example, the first instrumental song I wrote (unnamed at the time) brought to mind one of the songs I had written as a young adult playing in the pop-rock band. That song, called "Looking Back," had a decidedly melancholy feeling associated with it, both lyrically (e.g., "it seems I can't help looking back") and musically. The new instrumental song, as well as the first few others I had written, all had a similar bittersweet aesthetic. As I thought more about this particular connection, I saw others that started to reveal a pattern. For example, the guitarists I enjoyed most as a young musician (e.g., Carlos Santana, John McLaughlin, Al Di Meola) often used minor scales (e.g., Phrygian mode) in emotional ballads or in Spanish-inspired guitar compositions. What appealed to me was how the music made me feel. There clearly was an element of melancholy and sadness, but also a joyful and uplifting quality. This quote from an article on aesthetics (Brady and Haapala 2003, section 3) says it well: "Melancholy is an emotion with various shades: a shade of longing; a shade of sadness; and a shade of feeling uplifted."

As I thought and read more about this emotional state, there was little doubt that it was more than just an aesthetic preference; it connected to something that was deeply embedded in my personality. A melancholy temperament has historically been associated with introversion, contemplation, solitude, a love of nature, and other attributes that seem to fit me (Cain 2013). Perhaps the best description of this state of mind that I have come across is the Japanese aesthetic concept of *mono no aware*, or finding beauty in an awareness of the impermanent and fleeting nature of things (Minor 1968). Describing this experience in Japanese art, Anesaki (1932, 53) comments: "In such moments . . . joy mingles with a kind of agreeable melancholy." I felt this agreeable melancholy often while playing music again, and realized that music was the primary source of this feeling in my youth as well. Here was an undeniable music-identity connection that set in motion a flow-like cascade of insights related to many other aspects of my life. The color blue, my favorite color and the color of the guitar that was given to me as a gift, became a symbol of this feeling. I made the decision to incorporate it into various song titles (e.g., "Elevation Blue," "Blue-Collar Hearts") and eventually thought of all of the music I was creating in terms of the broad theme "beautiful and blue."

It may not be surprising that my taste in music or aesthetic sensibilities would be similar as I aged from a young adult to a middle-aged adult. But this view dismisses the importance I attributed to recognizing and accepting these aspects of self. These insights, directly linked to playing music again, gave me the sense of moving toward a style of individuality that was more handcrafted and tailored, and less ready-made or off-the-rack. More importantly, it led to this realization: music was a primary pathway toward this beautiful-and-blue experience that was deeply rooted in my identity and the way I experienced life. Therefore, I had to keep playing music. Leaving it behind as a young man perhaps could not have been avoided given the circumstances at the time; that decision could not be changed. Looking forward, however, these personal insights were at the heart of my motivation to keep playing music and find a way to share it with others again.

Pattern Making: The Fundraiser

The phases of measurement and design represent self-differentiation. However, the framework on tailoring identity suggests this is only half of the learning/creative process; identity is also created between self and others (Erikson 1968; McCall and Simmons 1978; Mead 1934; Schwartz 2001). Just as a child full of playful enthusiasm says "watch me" to her parents, a social-integration phase that includes being watched and connecting with others adds an essential element to identity tailoring. The phase of pattern making signals the start of such social integration. Pattern making for a tailor is a divergent process of exploring what colors, fabrics, textures, shapes, and so on are best suited for realizing a design. For me, pattern making meant trying to find a way to connect music to the interpersonal world I inhabited.

The strong insights about melancholy and *mono no aware* increased my desire and readiness to play music for others and hopefully evoke a similar feeling in them. A natural place to start was with family members and friends. Even though they represent a relatively small community and audience, family and friends are primary social mirrors for our sense of self (Mead 1934). My first opportunity to play for others occurred one holiday season when I performed three songs for my wife and daughters. Shortly after that, I performed the same songs for a few close friends. These were important and rewarding first steps of social integration and becoming a musician (again) in the eyes of others. However, perhaps because I had been a musician in the past, or since I set the challenge level so high in these new music activities, playing for friends and family did not fully express the design for music I had in mind. I continued to think about a range of options to perform for others, but many of them did not seem feasible given my academic career and the eclectic music I was creating.

One opportunity that was appealing turned up unexpectedly while talking with my wife. For several years she had considered the possibility of holding a fundraiser for the Movement Disorders Clinic at the University of Utah. We discussed finally organizing a fundraiser and having me provide the music for the evening. This opportunity fit the design I had imagined. It would have a thoughtful audience that was more likely to appreciate melancholy instrumental music, and an audience that would permit me the artistic freedom that other musicians might not have when hired to entertain at an event. Performing at a fundraiser seemed to be an ideal challenge for social integration. However, it was also an opportunity that exceeded my level of preparation and would require a great deal of work. Like a tailor who cuts patterns to model on a mannequin, I needed to assemble the pieces needed to build the fundraiser we had started calling *Beautiful and Blue*.

The primary challenge of this next step in the identity process was writing at least an hour of music for the event. Creating the music would also require generating backing tracks for songs that needed more than solo guitar. This would take time, so we pushed the event a year into the future. It was also necessary to consider many other aspects of the performance and presentation. I decided to work on video backgrounds that would accompany the music and make the overall performance more interesting. Most of the videos consisted of interesting shapes and colors, much like screensavers or music visualizers that were easily created and synced to the music. A few of them, however, included content that fit the beautiful and blue theme of the fundraiser (e.g., melancholic paintings by Friedrich, Munch, and Picasso). Preparations had to be made in terms of searching for a sound system, projection system, lighting system, and most importantly, computing technology and software that could coordinate all of the music, video, lighting, and guitar-sound transitions that would be used in the performance. Finally, I made a website and invitation using words and images that I hoped would give attendees some idea about what to expect from the evening.

Alterations: Notes, Lists, and Practice

The last phase of tailoring identity is one of making final adjustments and alterations that move the process toward resolution and a "good fit." The importance of the fundraiser being part of an intrinsically motivated and freely chosen process cannot be overestimated here. All of the last-minute details of the performance that needed attention could, in another context, be seen as tedious and burdensome. However, this was not the case. The motivation to get ready for the fundraiser and perform for a larger audience made these final alterations as enjoyable as they were intense. Many accounts of optimal, "aha" moments in a creative process tend to focus on the moments when an idea or design comes to mind (Csikszentmihalyi 1996), not the moments when loose ends are being tied together. However, it is accurate to say that I had as many flow and peak experiences associated with this public part of the process as I did during the private phase of insight.

Describing some of the details of this last phase of tailoring identity would seem to confirm it as the most mundane, but it would be a mistake to view it that way. I needed to make detailed notes about song order, lighting transitions, arrangement of the equipment on the stage, even where to hang a guitar cord when trying to make a fast switch to another guitar. To make these notes required taking over the living room in my home for a month, so I would have the necessary space to test things using the same equipment that would be used during the fundraiser. The living room became the place to practice, over and over, both the music and the sequence of button pressing and footswitch stepping that would choreograph the entire performance. Perhaps the best single example to represent this stage of alterations was a three-ring binder put together a week before the performance. In it were lists describing what to bring to the fundraiser, where to pack everything and in what cases, the settings on equipment that might need to be reset after being moved, various backup strategies that could be used in case of an equipment failure, and on and on.

Finally the night of the fundraiser arrived and everything could not have gone more smoothly. The weather was nice. The venue was ideal. We raised money for a good cause and encountered only a few small glitches. I enjoyed the performance, and through the

FIGURE 8.3 Kevin Rathunde the night of the fundraiser. (Photo by Russ Isabella.)

feedback received from a much larger social mirror (i.e., about 100 people), was certain that others enjoyed the night as well. I had anticipated that when this event was over I might feel like a musician again, and for the first time in twenty-plus years, I did. This feeling was solidified the following day when I received a group of photographs from the coauthor of this chapter who was exercising his passion for photography by taking photos of the event. Seeing the event objectified through the lens of a camera reinforced the feeling of being a performing musician. Several of the photos, including the one in Figure 8.3, have become valued reminders of the event and the journey back to music.

Epilogue: In Search of a Professor-Musician Fit

In the identity literature, the notion of M-A-M-A cycles refers to the idea that identity growth often moves forward through moratorium (i.e., new explorations), then achievement (i.e., new commitments), then moratorium again, then achievement again, and so on, in a perpetual cycle (Stephen, Fraser, and Marcia 1992). In other words, achieving some expansion of identity is not a once-and-for-all, static outcome. A change in identity bridges the self to others in new ways and opens up new possibilities for growth that did not exist before the change.

A few weeks after the fundraiser, I framed one of the photos from the event and hung it on a wall in my office at the University of Utah. That action indicated a new question that was already on my mind: Now that music was again a part of my life and identity, how might it feed back into my academic work? It did at one time when I started graduate school; how might it now, twenty-five years later? In one sense, music had already influenced my work through the decision a few years earlier to study how play activities in midlife can affect identity development. That decision, however, could easily have been made in the absence of music, given the previous work I had done on flow experience and lifelong learning. I was interested in finding a more direct professor-musician link; and this interest set in motion a brand new cycle of tailoring identity. Without describing the phases of this new cycle in detail, it is worth noting that approximately a year and a half after the fundraiser, one result of continuing identity development is this chapter on playing music. This chapter, and the autoethnography within it, reflects my growing interest in arts-informed research (Coles and Knowles 2008) and finding additional ways to combine music with my academic work. These career developments were set in motion by the identity changes resulting from playing music.

Conclusions

Identity provides a bridge to others and is an essential source of meaning in life. Its first formulation in adolescence or early adulthood, however, occurs when life experience and self-knowledge are just starting to accumulate. As a person learns more about the kinds of activities and experiences that resonate with their sense of self, they are in a much better position to modify their identity in ways that better represent their character and values. In other words, they are better able to tailor an identity that feels made-to-order and less constricting. Next, some final thoughts are added on the importance of lifelong identity growth and the tremendous potential of leisure play activities to stimulate it.

Leisure play activities have enormous potential to help people tailor their identities and improve their quality of life. The intrinsically motivated character of these activities helps to focus and strengthen attention, which in turn improves learning and creativity (Rathunde and Csikszentmihalyi 2006). Doing an enjoyable and deeply engaging activity generates an inexhaustible source of energy that propels the entire tailoring process. From start to finish, through the divergent and convergent movements of self-differentiation and social integration, the experiential rewards of a passionate leisure interest create momentum that keeps one focused on finding challenges, having insights, searching for real-world opportunities to connect, and working hard to realize a new style of individuality. The many hours of intense engagement also provide optimal conditions for triggering flow and peak experiences that momentarily boost energy even higher. As Waterman (1990) notes, these occasional episodes that suspend time and fuse a person with their activity are experienced as confirmations of the activity's self-actualizing potential.

An equally important reason why leisure play activities are ideal for tailoring identity is the free choice involved. Kleiber (1999, xvi) suggests the same: "To the extent that we are in an age where structural determinants of behavior and personality such as religion, occupation, nationality, and regional identification have lost much of their determining hold, leisure becomes especially relevant to development as it is individually constructed." If one is fortunate enough to have a stable life structure that provides some moratorium from the extrinsic pressures of life, one is better able to choose a leisure activity one wants to do and the time at which to do it. The narrative in the chapter told one such story about how playing music resulted in identity growth. However, many different leisure activities besides music play a similar role and can result in equally idiosyncratic stories of growth and discovery (see Rathunde and Isabella forthcoming). While a specific path of identity development is unique to each person and cannot be predicted in advance, one of the best ways to tailor a meaningful identity may be similar for everyone who is lucky enough to have some social support and leisure time available—choosing to do something you really love to do.

Notes

1. The alteration of divergent and convergent phases in these various models is consistent with the need for optimal arousal and the way the human mind appears to process information (see Rathunde and Csikszentmihalyi 2006, for a more in-depth discussion).
2. The tailoring model is proposed here as a heuristic guide to understanding the multifaceted process of identity development. In other words, the sequential nature of the model generally captures the way identity growth unfolds; however, it is recognized that the process is less straightforward and more intricate in the lives of real people. For example, formulating an idea after a period of information gathering generally captures the appropriate sequence of events; however, having an idea sometimes sets in motion the need for more information gathering before that idea fully takes shape. Similarly, implementing an idea can take place only after an idea is formed; however, successful implementation sometimes requires a new cycle of information gathering and tweaking an idea before it can be successfully applied. Finally, identity development is an ongoing, complex process comprising many cycles of tailoring. Therefore, the phases of measurement, design, pattern making, and alterations will look different *depending upon the timeframe one selects.*

References Cited

Adams, Gerald R., and Sheila K. Marshall. 1996. "A Developmental Social Psychology of Identity: Understanding the Person-in-Context." *Journal of Adolescence* 19: 429–442.

Anesaki, Masaharu. 1932. *Art, Life, and Nature in Japan.* Boston: Marshall Jones.

Arnett, Jeffrey Jensen, Marion Kloep, Leo B. Hendry, and Jennifer L. Tanner. 2011. *Debating Emerging Adulthood: Stage or Process?* New York: Oxford University Press.

Berzonsky, Michael D. 1990. "Self-Construction over the Lifespan: A Process Perspective on Identity Formation." In *Advances in Personal Construct Psychology*, vol. 1, edited by Robert A. Neimeyer and Greg J. Neimeyer, 155–186. Greenwich, CT: JAI.

Brady, Emily, and Arto Haapala. 2003. "Melancholy as an Aesthetic Emotion." *Contemporary Aesthetics* 1. www.contempaesthetics.org/newvolume/pages/article.php?articleID=214.

Brown, Carroll A., Francis A. McGuire, and Judith Voelkl. 2008. "The Link between Successful Aging and Serious Leisure." *International Journal of Aging and Human Development* 66: 73–95.

Cain, Susan. 2013. *Quiet: The Power of Introverts in a World that Can't Stop Talking*. New York: Crown.

Cole, Ardra L., and J. Gary Knowles. 2008. "Arts-Informed Research." In *Handbook of the Arts in Qualitative Research*, edited by J. Gary Knowles and Ardra L. Cole, 55–70. Thousand Oaks, CA: Sage.

Cooley, Charles H. 1902. *Human Nature and the Social Order*. New York: Scribners.

Csikszentmihalyi, Mihaly. 1996. *Creativity: Flow and the Psychology of Discovery and Invention*. New York: HarperCollins.

Deci, Edward L., and Richard M. Ryan. 1985. *Intrinsic Motivation and Self-Determination in Human Behavior*. New York: Plenum.

Dewey, John. 1913. *Interest and Effort in Education*. Cambridge, MA: Riverside.

Dupuis, Sherry L. 1999. "Naked Truths: Towards a Reflexive Methodology in Leisure Research." *Leisure Sciences* 21: 43–64.

Ellis, Carolyn, and Arthur P. Bochner. 2000. "Autoethnography, Personal Narrative, Reflexivity: Researcher as Subject." In *Handbook of Qualitative Research*, 2nd edition, edited by Norman K. Denzin and Yvonna S. Lincoln, 733–768. Thousand Oaks, CA: Sage.

Erikson, Erik H. 1950. *Childhood and Society*. New York: Norton.

Erikson, Erik H. 1968. *Identity: Youth and Crisis*. New York: Norton.

Hansen, David J., G. Thomas Lumpkin, and Gerald E. Hills. 2011. "A Multidimensional Examination of a Creativity-Based Opportunity Recognition Model." *International Journal of Entrepreneurial Behaviour and Research* 17: 515–533.

Holman Jones, Stacy, Tony E. Adams, and Carolyn Ellis. 2013. *Handbook of Autoethnography*. Walnut Creek, CA: Left Coast.

Huizinga, Johan. 1955. *Homo Ludens: A Study of the Play-Element in Culture*. Translated by Richard F. C. Hull. Boston: Beacon.

Jung, Carl Gustav. 1955. *Modern Man in Search of a Soul*. New York: Harcourt.

Kleiber, Douglas. 1999. *Leisure Experience and Human Development*. Boulder, CO: Westview.

Kolb, David. A. 1984. *Experiential Learning: Experience as the Source of Learning and Development*. Englewood Cliffs, NJ: Prentice Hall.

Kolb. David. A., Richard E. Boyatzis, and Charalampos Mainemelis. 2001. "Experiential Learning Theory: Previous Research and New Directions." In *Perspectives on Cognitive, Learning, and Thinking Styles*, edited by Robert J. Sternberg and Li-Fang Zhang, 227–247. Mahwah, NJ: Lawrence Erlbaum.

Lachman, Margie E. 2004. "Development in Midlife." *Annual Review of Psychology* 55: 305–331.

Levinson, Daniel J. 1978. *The Seasons of a Man's Life*. New York: Knopf.

Marcia, James E. 1980. "Identity in Adolescence." In *Handbook of Adolescent Psychology*, edited by Joseph Adelson, 159–187. New York: Wiley.

Maslow, Abraham H. 1968. *Toward a Psychology of Being*. New York: D. Van Nostrand.

McCall, George J., and Jerry L. Simmons. 1978. *Identities and Interactions*. New York: Free Press.

Mead, George H. 1934. *Mind, Self, and Society*. Chicago: University of Chicago Press.

Minor, Earl. 1968. *An Introduction to Japanese Court Poetry*. Stanford, CA: Stanford University Press.

Neugarten, Bernice L. 1968. "Adult Personality: Toward a Psychology of the Life Cycle." In *Middle Age and Aging: A Reader in Social Psychology,* edited by Bernice L. Neugarten, 137–147. Chicago: University of Chicago Press.

Norman, Don. 2013. *The Design of Everyday Things*. Revised and expanded edition. New York: Basic Books.

Onarheim, Balder, and Morton Friis-Olivarius. 2005. "Design Council." *A Study of the Design Process-The Double Diamond*. http://www.designcouncil.org.uk/sites/default/files/asset/document/ElevenLessons_Design_Council%20(2).pdf.

Onarheim, Balder, and Morton Friis-Olivarius. 2013. "Applying the Neuroscience of Creativity to Creativity Training." *Frontiers in Human Neuroscience* 7. doi: 10.3389/fnhum.2013.00656.

Rathunde, Kevin. 1992. "Serious Play: Interest and Adolescent Talent Development." In *Interesse, Lernen, Leistung*, edited by Andreas Krapp and Manfred Prenzel, 137–164. Münster: Aschendorff.

Rathunde, Kevin. 2013. "Experiential Wisdom and Lifelong Learning." In *Positive Psychology: Advances in Understanding Adult Motivation*, edited by Jan D. Sinnott, 269–290. New York: Springer.

Rathunde, Kevin, and Mihaly Csikszentmihalyi. 2006. "The Developing Person: An Experiential Perspective." In *Handbook of Child Psychology*, Vol. 1, *Theoretical Models of Human Development*, 6th edition, edited by Richard M. Lerner and William Damon, 465–515. New York: Wiley.

Rathunde, Kevin, and Russell Isabella. Forthcoming. "Play, Flow, and Tailoring Identity in Middle Adulthood." In *Identity Flexibility during Adulthood*, edited by Jan Sinnott. New York: Springer.

Renninger, K. Ann, Susan Hidi, and Andreas Krapp, eds. 1992. *The Role of Interest in Learning and Development*. Hillsdale, NJ: Lawrence Erlbaum.

Schwartz, Seth J. 2001. "The Evolution of Eriksonian and Neo-Eriksonian Identity Theory and Research: A Review and Integration." *Identity: An International Journal of Theory and Research* 1: 7–58.

Stebbins, Robert A. 1982. "Serious Leisure: A Conceptual Statement." *Pacific Sociological Review* 25: 251–272.

Stephen, Joanne, Eugene Fraser, and James E. Marcia, 1992. "Moratorium-Achievement (Mama) Cycles in Lifespan Identity Development: Value Orientations and Reasoning System Correlates." *Journal of Adolescence* 15: 283–300.

Turner, Jonathan H. 2013. *Contemporary Sociological Theory*. Newburry Park, CA: Sage.

Vaillant, George E. 2002. *Aging Well*. Boston: Little Brown.

Wallas, Graham. 1926. *The Art of Thought*. New York: Harcourt Brace.

Waterman, Alan S. 1990. "Personal Expressiveness: Philosophical and Psychological Foundations." *Journal of Mind and Behavior* 11: 47–74.

Waterman, Alan S. 1993. "Two Conceptions of Happiness: Contrasts of Personal Expressiveness (Eudaimonia) and Hedonic Enjoyment." *Journal of Personality and Social Psychology* 64: 678–691.

White, Robert W. 1959. "Motivation Reconsidered: The Concept of Competence." *Psychological Review* 66: 297–333.

CHAPTER 9

....

(UN)POPULAR MUSIC
MAKING AND EUDAIMONISM

....

GARETH DYLAN SMITH

INTRODUCTION: A EUDAIMONIC LIFE

....

FOR as long as I can remember I have found fulfillment through every aspect of being
a drummer. I like loading car or the van; I like driving—I like every part of driving:
the freedom, the autonomy and responsibility, the feel of the car, the loud music, the
silence, the time to think; I like the setting up in a new space: the sound check—I *love* the
sound check,[1] getting to hear my drums in a new space in front of new people, and to run
through a song; I love the gig—playing the drums with people I like, creating feelings we
share and making timeless moments; Voegelin (2010, 64) refers to a "sonic now . . . an
expansion of experience in timespace." After a performance I enjoy packing the drums
away, knowing the whole kit's in the car, driving home again, getting back late, sneaking
into the house, carrying all the drums in without waking my wife or child (formerly my
housemates, and sometimes waking them all anyway). In between gigs, I like downloading, checking, setting up, and triggering samples in my sound module and loading backing tracks onto my iPad; I like learning songs, grooves, new styles; I especially love to
practice, alone. I love the whole thing. Drumming is my sanctuary. I have to make time
for making music.

Being a drummer is central to who I am—it has guided my decisions to live in particular places, to study certain topics, and to use my time and resources in specific ways.
I play drums in a range of contexts—some for money, mostly not for money, and (crucially) only in situations that interest and/or excite me. I have crafted a life in drumming,
teaching, and academia that affords me opportunities for fulfillment. My entire social
network comprises either family members, or people I have met through drumming,
or an activity that enables me to keep drumming. In 2009, I bought a t-shirt bearing the
slogan "I drum, therefore I am." Since then I have published a doctoral dissertation, a
book, and a series of magazine articles under that title, and my business cards also make

the claim. Drumming (playing drum kit) is so central to my being (Smith 2013a, xiii–xiv) that my website's homepage carries the following original haiku:

> I am a drummer
> Drumming is when I am me
> Then is who I am

Researching lives in drumming and being a drummer led me to the concept of eudaimonism (Smith 2013a, 57). This helped to describe and to understand how central my drummer identity is to me, and how important such identity realization (17) was to many of the drummers in my study.

In this chapter I explore the music making of my peers—all "(un)popular" musicians inasmuch as their music, "although in similar styles, and using virtually all of the same gestures as more commercially successful artists [playing popular styles] is, by contrast (if we take traditional indicators like album sales and fame as the yardsticks of success), wholly *un*popular" (Smith 2013b, 33). As Kirschner notes, regarding the culture of rock music making, there is "a huge amateur and quasi-professional realm supported by a well developed production and distribution infrastructure," and "[e]ven though most popular music consumption revolves around major label star acts, there are far more bands, venues, record labels, support personnel, etc., that exist at the low end of the spectrum" (1998, 250). As Kirschner is keen to emphasize, I too would highlight that "low" in this sense refers to the visibility and celebrity of bands in comparison to that of star acts, and does not reflect the craft or quality of music produced. The present chapter is not intended to focus on me, but I have intentionally included my voice. In doing so, as Goodall (1991, 116) observes, "the ontological status of autobiography reveals a text as the site of individual identity," so I cannot, and thus nor would I seek to, hide my authorial bias and perspective. Moreover, I would contend, in accordance with the tradition of writing about integrity to oneself—indeed, with integrity about *one's self*—that writing this chapter "is my destiny" (Norton 1976, xiii) and is a product of my eudaimonic life.

Happiness, Fulfillment, and the Daimon

> There are isolated individuals in whom the intuition of their own unique potential worth has in some measure proved formative. For them the world's din has not stilled the inner voice, and they are quietly and decisively living their lives according to their own inner imperative.
>
> (Norton 1976, xiii)

The ongoing fulfillment of the search for meaning has been called such things as "self-actualization" (Maslow [1968] 2014) and "individuation" (Jung 1933, 26). I have called it "identity realization" (Smith 2013a). In my study of drummers, I describe (57–61) how drummers often live eudaimonic lives that are both highly challenging and highly rewarding. Numerous participants in that study reported that they "love" drumming and being drummers, and that it was of great importance to them. For these drummers, "identity realization" is meant in its passive and active senses—understanding who one is, and also acting upon that understanding: being, becoming, actively realizing an identity in the world, akin to what Hegel ([1807] 1910, 417) describes as a person "realizing his [or her] individuality." Passive and active identity realizations exist symbiotically; the two "are mutually dependent. Each is an inevitable and necessary, although insufficient, condition for the other" (Smith 2013a, 19). Acting on one's passive identity realization—what Laing (1960) and Giddens (1991) both call "ontological security"—in the unending process of active identity realization, is described by Bauman as, "the incessant and non-linear *activity* of self-constitution that makes the identity of the agent" (1992, 193). Norton (1976, 8) observes that truthfully pursuing one's daimon, or "eudaimonistic 'integrity' exhibits a marked kinship to the 'identity' that contemporary men and women are said to be searching for" (and that, as the accounts below show, they are living out).

Waterman (1993, 678) writes about two conceptions of happiness, distinguishing "(a) eudaimonia (feelings of personal expressiveness) [from] (b) hedonic enjoyment" (679). Similarly, Ryan, Huta, and Deci (2008) write about "approaches to wellness" in terms of the hedonic and eudaimonic; for them, "the hedonic approach defines wellbeing as happiness" (139), whereas "the concept of eudaimonia [is] generally defined as living a complete life, or the realization of valued human potentials" (140). Dierendonck and Mohan (2006, 232) affirm, "Hedonic well-being [is] more related to feeling relaxed, happy, and without problems, whereas eudaimonic well-being [is] related to feeling challenged and to activities that offer the opportunity for personal growth and development." As the findings and discussion below demonstrate, following one's daimon can prove to be challenging emotionally, logistically, socially, and ethically; while it may at times lead to happiness, it also leads to conflict, guilt, and obsession.[2]

The happiness/fulfillment distinction is an important one, for, while the hedonic is concerned primarily with pleasure (Ryan, Huta, and Deci 2008, 140), eudaimonism deals with how people "live in accordance with the *daimon* or 'true self'" (Waterman 1992, 58). Norton similarly identifies eudaimonism as "a feeling and a condition . . . It signals that the present activity of the individual is in harmony with the daimon that is [her or] his true self" (Norton 1976, 5). Eudaimonism is an ideal, a philosophy, a way of life; I have chosen it as a framework for this study because it seems to capture, encapsulate, describe, and vindicate the approach I have taken and continue to take to my life, and that many colleagues and friends in music seem to take to theirs. Eudaimonic philosophy is founded on the principle that a person's "search for meaning is the primary motivation in [their] life. . . . This meaning is unique and specific in that it must and can be fulfilled by [her or him] alone; only then does it achieve a significance which will satisfy [her or his] own *will* to meaning" (Frankel 1959, 121). Frankel goes on to assert that a person indeed has a responsibility to her or himself to live in this way.

Seeking fulfillment over happiness or pleasure invites challenge and friction. Frankel argues that this is indeed necessary to lead a fulfilling, eudaimonic life. He argues:

> I consider it a dangerous misconception of mental hygiene to assume that what man [sic] needs in the first place is equilibrium or, as it is termed in biology, "homeostasis," i.e. a tensionless state. What man actually needs is not a tensionless state but rather the striving and struggling for a worthwhile goal, a freely chosen task. What he needs is not the discharge of tension at any cost, but the call of a potential meaning waiting to be fulfilled by him. What man needs is . . . the existential dynamics in a polar field of tension where one pole is represented by a meaning that is to be fulfilled and the other pole by the man who has to fulfill it. (Frankel 1959, 127)

Eudaimonism, then, is about fulfillment, not endless happiness per se. As Frankel further urges us to consider, "Ultimately, man [sic] should not ask what the meaning of life is, but rather he must recognize that it is *he* who is asked. In a word, each man is questioned by life; and he can only answer to life by *answering for* his own life; to life he can only respond by being responsible" (Frankel 1959, 131, emphasis in original). Taking control of one's own fulfillment and destiny in this way is similar to Jung's notion of "bringing into reality of the whole human being—that is, individuation" (Jung 1933, 26); this in turn shares much in common with what Norton, borrowing from Maslow ([1968] 2014), calls "self-actualization," to describe the ongoing process of living according to "the ethics of eudaimonism" (1976, 15).

I would emphasize here, by way of an ethical and intellectual disclaimer, that eudaimonism arguably presupposes a world of opportunity in which individual freedom and privilege are reified and presumed. This is a concern to which I return, below, critiquing eudaimonism as a privileged paradigm. For the most part, however, this chapter explores eudaimonism as a framework for understanding musicians' practices and perspectives. I propose that eudaimonism may be a valuable lens through which to view the lives of music makers, because it draws attention to aspects central to lives lived in music that may remain unseen and unexamined through other approaches.

Eudaimonism, Flow, Play, and Careers

Norton identifies eudaimonism's closeness with Csikszentmihalyi's (1991) construct of "flow," and differentiates the concepts, insofar as flow explains obtaining and maintaining (arguably hedonic) optimal or peak experiences for shorter periods, whereas eudaimonism is about being true to oneself, which may in turn lead to a frequent or even largely constant sense of flow. "Flow" generally refers and is applied to things that one does in life, rather than to the living of an entire life or way of life—this is eudaimonism's domain. As Waterman (1992, 57) notes, eudaimonism is about "the strength of a person's investments in particular identity elements and the centrality of that identity to the manner in which he or she chooses to live." So while the notion of a near-constant sense of flow may seem improbable, I suggest that my own recent experiences qualify as such:

for the past thirteen months I have barely rested; I have consistently worked sixteen- to twenty-hour days, six or seven days a week, writing papers, editing books, touring the U.K. with bands, traveling internationally for conferences, teaching a heavy load, taking on a significant administrative workload, and managing responsibilities as a husband and father. And I have never, ever felt as fulfilled. It's like I feel a permanent "runners' high," while on my rare days off I feel strange, adrift, and without purpose. I am constantly exhausted, irritable, emotional, and impatient, which has impacted friendships and family life, and is not sustainable long term. But I also feel challenged, capable, and empowered. For me, this is flow meeting eudaimonism. As the discussion below indicates, I may not alone in pursuing such a life.

Another construct that intersects with eudaimonism is "leisure play," discussed in Rathunde and Isabella's chapter (this volume, chapter 8) and in Rathunde and Isabella (forthcoming). Leisure play is related to Gadamer's remarks on "play," whereby, "The player himself knows that play is only play and that it exists in a world determined by the seriousness of purposes. But he does not know this in such a way that, as a player, he actually intends this relation to seriousness. Play fulfills its purpose only if the player loses himself in play" (Gadamer 2004, 107). While Gadamer wrote about games, what he described can be seen as an analog for musicians' lives, wherein they are utterly committed to making music—to play. I have previously tried to explain this from my own perspective as a drummer, playing the drums: "going in to the music, I am happy to descend, contented to be enveloped by it entirely. Being *in* a song, or *in* a piece of music is like a total immersion of my self—emotionally, mentally, physically" (Smith 2013a, 185). Making music has always been like this to me—in the act of drumming in a band, and in living my life as a maker of music. I enjoy it, I am compelled to do it, and I take it very seriously—it fulfills me. As Huizinga (1976, 51) notes, "The need for [play] is only urgent to the extent that the enjoyment of it makes a need." "Enjoyment" of "play," however, is complicated in a eudaimonic life, where it extends to the rich, multidimensional experiences of fulfillment, becoming dissociated from its more normative hedonic implications.

My previous research with drummers indicated that many seem to live eudaimonically. For instance, I found that 93 percent of the drummers responding to Likert-type questions on a survey reported that they "love" being drummers, complemented by responses from interview participants typically reporting similar feelings about playing the instrument and being musicians (Smith 2013a, 58). These responses were also tempered with more nuanced descriptions of the experience of life as a musician; for instance, Sean Lee, while loving his life as a drummer and collaborative musician, also found that "Sometimes I hate it . . . yeah, sometimes it does my fucking head in . . . sometimes it gets really frustrating when you can't, when you're trying to get something and it's not working." I have previously noted the "unbridled enthusiasm for playing their instrument that unites drummers, despite inherent hassles in playing [the drums]." (Smith 2013a, 57).

Drummer, bandleader, composer, and producer Bill Bruford (2009, 347) describes how "musicians go a long way, literally, in search of that most intense of feelings" that can derive only from doing that which is pursuit of the daimon—making music. He also describes "the crippling self-absorption, the shameful navel-gazing, the sleep-deprivation, the recurrent self-loathing, the debilitating jetlag, the endless soundchecks, the relentless self-promotion . . . the patient dovetailing of domestic and professional . . . the never being there, the haggle at check-in, the pushing and shoving" (337–338) that accompany and are the yin to the yang of the epic highs of a musical life. Gill and Pratt (2008, 14) identify similar traits in the lives of cultural workers who experience "long hours and bulimic patterns of working; the collapse or erasure of the boundaries between work and play; poor pay . . . passionate attachment to the work and to the identity of creative laborer; an attitudinal mindset that is a blend of bohemianism and entrepreneurialism" in working lives that combine "desire, sociality, pleasure, and fulfilment" with "fatigue, exhaustion, frustration, anxiety, and the "individualized shame" from having the self completely bound up with one's work. Teague and Smith's (2015) study of work-life balance among popular musicians discusses in similar terms the entrepreneurial nature of participants' lives, characterized by complexity and intensity. Weber (2004) observes that for at least 200 years musicians have worked in the sorts of ways described by Teague and Smith; his findings are corroborated and expanded by writers including Cottrell (2004), Bennett (2008, 2013), Gaunt and Papageorgi (2010), Hallam and Gaunt (2012), Partti (2012), and Hewison (2014). Highlighting some of the difficulties in distinguishing "life" from meaningful "work," Bennett (2008, 8) also uses discusses "protean careers," which are "defined as careers in which multiple roles are undertaken . . . protean careerists self-manage their careers and adapt their practice as necessary to meet personal and professional needs." In a eudaimonic life, the personal and professional merge.

METHOD

I undertook a small-scale empirical study, in which I conducted interviews with eleven musicians based in the U.K., selected through a process of convenience sampling (Robson 2011, 275). I knew all of the participants prior to undertaking the study. As a drummer, I had performed or played music with most of the participants, except for four whom I knew as a former teacher during their undergraduate studies in popular music performance. One participant I met through acquaintance with her husband, with whom I am a frequent musical collaborator. I knew all of the musicians as active in (broadly) popular music, as well as in other styles and traditions.

Musicians such as those who took part in this study form the majority population of musicians in stable, developed Western capitalist "democracies" (see e.g., Bennett 2008; Cottrell 2004; Smith 2013a, 2013b), in that they are the (un)popular musicians (Smith 2013b, 33) mentioned in the title and introduction of this chapter. Kirschner refers to a "continuum of success" (1998, 257), observing that there are "many little worlds of popular music," into a handful of which some insight is hopefully provided below. Participants ranged in age from twenty-two to forty-seven, the sample comprising six males and five females. Ethnically, the sample was nondiverse, with participants being white and British. Nine of the participants were English; two were Welsh. Six lived in London, where I reside. One lived in York (210 miles north of London), one lived in Milton Keynes (55 miles north of London), another lived in Hertfordshire (30 miles north of London), and two others lived just outside of Cardiff, Wales (150 miles west of London). The musicians all played instruments, and several also sang as a significant part of their music making activity. Two of the participants performed principally as singers. All wrote music, either collaboratively or in groups. None of the participants was a celebrity, or a full-time performer or composer. Participants were all selected on the grounds that they appeared to be committed and dedicated to making music in ways that seemed to me to be eudaimonic and that fit each of the criteria for Stebbins's notion of "serious leisure" (2014, 9), discussed further below.

All interviews were conducted using Internet video call technology; in one instance the video failed to work, so the call remained voice-only. Interviews lasted between 11′44″ and 27′50″, with most being between fourteen and sixteen minutes in duration; while brief, I felt that these interviews were sufficiently long and deep to provide meaningful answers and usable data, since I knew the participants, thus a rapport, openness, and conversational ease preexisted or were immediately established in each case. Interviews were semistructured, comprising six questions and usually some brief discussion around answers. The questions were:

- What does the term "making music" mean for you?
- How important to you is making music?
- To what extent is your music making a leisure activity?
- To what extent do you think of your music making in terms of words such as "professional," "semiprofessional," "amateur," or "hobbyist"?
- In what ways is it important or unimportant to categorize one's music making in these sorts of ways?
- What do you do when you're not making music?

The calls were audio recorded using a digital sound recorder. I listened to the recordings to code the data according to themes I found recurring in the interviews. While my intention was to code these as faithfully as possible to the participants' meanings and intentions, my interest in eudaimonism will doubtless have guided my interpretation. Indeed, I invite readers to engage in what Smith, Flowers, and Larkin (2009, 41) identify as "a third hermeneutic level [for] the imagined reader . . . trying to make sense of the researcher making sense of the participant making sense of X!" The presentation of findings has been shared with each interview participant, amended where necessary, and met with their approval. Accordingly, participants are all referred to by their real names.

FINDINGS

In this section I have included responses from all of the participants, under the headings of "motivation," "making music," "making time," and "is it leisure?" I attempt to contextualize the findings with reference to theoretical frameworks in eudaimonism and leisure.

Motivation

Every participant reported a need to make music. As Gillian explained, "Things that are truly important to you, you're duty-bound to participate in them." Hannah described making music as "mission critical." Amy said "I have to do it," and Steve appeared to speak for several of the participants when he said music "defines me." Similarly, Ben remarked that music was "as important as breathing, absolutely intrinsic to everything." While all the participants expressed a need to make music, some were keen to emphasize how unexceptional they felt in this regard—a banality expressed by Ben in opposition to the awe or amazement with which nonmusician acquaintances seemed to regard him simply for making albums and occasionally touring the country with his band. For Ben, "music is something I've always done . . . it's mundane . . . it's just what I do—it is literally what I do: I can't imagine life without it." Typical comments from others were: "it's instinctive to me" (Alex G), "I just do what I do" (Hannah), and "people in our situation just do, we just do make music without really thinking about it, we just do" (Alex B).

Reasons that participants gave for needing to make music were varied. Participants mostly spoke of an inner drive or intrinsic motivation to make music—a eudaimonic need, being true to themselves. As Hannah explained, "It's part of who I am, and I'm not happy when I'm not doing it." Several participants reported that responding to the call to music serviced an emotional or psychological need. Charlotte said that music helped her to process emotions that might otherwise have "gnawed at me, driven me insane," and Gavin said that it was through making music that "I feel less mad."[3] Perhaps similarly, Alex G said, "It scratches an itch—I feel happier when I'm doing it, more complete." For Alex B, making music "makes me feel satisfied; I feel frustrated when I'm not doing it." Amy described the diverse personal emotional needs met by music making, which for her served as "a way of expressing myself, an escapism, a way of getting out anger or frustration, or just chillin' out." According to Hannah, "It's like off-loading something."

John, however, seemed to regard music as an external force or agent that enjoined him to engage with it, describing a "compulsion" wherein "you don't pick it—it picks you." John also described feelings of guilt when not making music, compounded by further feelings of guilt for being distracted from his day-job by thinking about making music. He also reported that, despite making music as often as possible, "it's not fun . . . rarely have I found it to be that." John's experience helps to articulate some of the complexity that can exist in a eudaimonic life, and that differentiates eudaimonic well-being and fulfillment from seeking merely hedonic pleasure.

Making Music

A strong emerging theme was that many of the participants thought of their music making in two ways—a solo, creative mode of writing or playing (or singing) music and a collaborative mode of performing or performing-and-writing. For some, one mode often outweighed the other in its importance, while for the others the two were more equal. For several of the interviewees, "making music" meant engagement in a creative act—either alone or with others—whereas performing was considered as other than (or less than) "making" music. Hannah described this as the difference between "making music" and merely "doing music." For Charlotte, composing and performing both amounted to making music, since "you're just putting a little bit of you out there . . . you're giving yourself to everybody else in the form of music." Charlotte thought of "doing music" as teaching people to sing; when teaching songwriting, however, this could sometimes amount to "making" music. However it was construed by individual participants, *making music* was where the *daimon*—truth to self—was found.

For Steve and Gavin, originating new music was paramount; Steve described making music as "writing, composing, and recording . . . taking those ideas, and playing and recording them . . . not even performing them really." Similarly, for John, making music meant "writing, recording, trying to capture the sound in your head." This sense of the urge to bring ideas to life was echoed by Gillian, for whom "the main thing it means for me is collaboration . . . being creative with somebody else." Gillian described how, having for years expressed her creativity through the solo act of painting, working with others to make music was "an epiphany." For Alex G, making music was an "interactive creative process," a sentiment echoed by Alex B. The immediacy of responding to a music making impulse was important when writing alone or together—the exciting real-time element of "getting in a room with other people, looking for a spark, taking whatever inspires you, and running with it," as Ben described it; for Hannah, this was "something that happens spontaneously." To Amy, this responsiveness was equally important, although less about realizing or harnessing new ideas. For her, making music included "singing 'round the house, banging on the piano," and taking part in a jazz band and choir. Adele, like Amy, was "not very creative" in her making music, but similarly expressed a need for making music on her own terms, with a need to "keep it fun."

Making Time

All of the participants work outside of their making music in order to earn a living, or—in one case—to raise a family. Most have family obligations in addition to work, and all—were it not for the musicking compulsion described above—would doubtless find life logistically easier without making music. Ben summarized a feeling among most of the participants when he said, "Outside of relationships with people, life is the stuff that you do to have the money to do what you wanna do, which is music." This sentiment was not shared by Adele, who was "trying to move away" from music, following a higher-education experience that made music occupy more of her life than she subsequently desired. The centrality of making music in the lives of participants, though, was universal. Some participants were able to "make music" at almost any time of the day or night—such as Amy, who enjoyed singing around the house, in the shower, and with a choir in lunchtimes at work—whereas for others, for whom making music was an inherently collaborative activity, they needed to be in the company of others, often in a dedicated rehearsal or performance space, so that making music required creating and curating time aside from other activities.

Gillian spoke for all when she admitted, "It's something that I don't think I can get away from any more; if you love making music you have to fit it in there somehow"—one has to be true to one's daimon. "Fitting it in" manifested itself in ways such as carrying a note pad at all times (for Hannah, Gillian, Steve, and Charlotte) for jotting lyrics, melodies, riffs, other song ideas, and track listings for future album and EP releases. Gavin's mind was so occupied with his music that he confessed, "There is no time when I'm not creating." Similarly, Steve said, "I go to bed thinking about music, wake up thinking about it," and he was always working on music in the car on the way to work, in the shower, between the guitar lessons he teaches at a school, and when keeping fit. Steve's and Gavin's are perhaps the closest accounts from the interviewees in terms of matching my own constant immersion in my work and devotion to my daimon; indeed, as musical collaborators and friends we frequently empathize in this regard.

Some participants spoke about a need to keep (the compulsion for) music in check, and not to (let themselves) let it take over. Gavin confessed, "My girlfriend thinks it's more important to me than her. Perhaps she's right." John was "trying not to let [making music] be the only thing," realizing that he must not do it "at expense of everything else," since one "can't create in a vacuum." Adele was keen, too, to keep her music making on her terms. Feeling some pressure from peers, she was keen to ensure that music did not become "a career," because the "professional side" of music "freaks me out," and people "take it too seriously." For Alex G, it was essential to make time for music around his obligations to his family and a demanding full-time job in academia. Gavin reported making music to be a solace, a place and time of "nurturing and guidance and comfort." For Gillian, despite the complications on "the logistical side of it all, once you get [to the collaborative writing or rehearsal space], then the leisure begins, then it becomes fun."

Is It Leisure?

As well as asking participants to what extent they considered their music making to be a leisure activity, I invited them to position their music making on a hypothetical continuum from "professional" to "hobbyist"—notwithstanding what such a reductive and simplistic spectrum implies; in every case we discussed the inherent inadequacies of such terminology, and produced richer data from the discussion provoked. Participants each seemed to position themselves on this hypothetical continuum with some awkwardness, mixed with confidence more about where they did *not* see themselves fitting than where they did. The eudaimonic lives of the musicians in this study can be viewed as at the intersection of Stebbins's constructs of "serious leisure" and "devotee work." While serious leisure is "experienced in free time," in devotee work "the sense of achievement is high and the core activity endowed with such intense appeal that the line between this work and leisure is virtually erased" (Stebbins 2014, 4).

Although none of the participants made music full-time or earned a living wage from it, some were keen to distance themselves from the notion of music making as a hobby. For Steve, "it's not a hobby, it's an obsession; it's a drive." Gillian replied that she "hate[s] that word for music," saying she was "not as flippant with it as having it be a hobby." Hobbies were largely considered to be of a lower order of importance—for Steve baking cakes, and for Charlotte playing football, at which she confessed to being "not very good." Adele, however, was keen "to do [music] now for fun. I can choose to play [drums] when I wish, to do it as a hobby."

Overall, participants were happy to bifurcate conceptions of music making as professional or not-professional—the latter thus being construed as leisure, although with some caveats. John conceded that music making for him, while hard work, was leisure "in the sense that it's not a profession," and Ben said music making for him was "very much a leisure activity . . . [although] that might make it seem less important . . . I take it pretty seriously." Participants were keen to stress the seriousness of music making, some describing this in terms of professionalism or a professional attitude, without anyone identifying as "a professional." Steve, for example, stated, "My conduct is professional," and Ben explained that "you have to have a professional attitude—getting back from gigs at 4.30 a.m., loading tons of gear into the studio, then going home, getting up for work the next day, and doing it over and over again, for its own sake . . . you have to be extremely professional." Hannah, while acknowledging a high degree of "professionalism" in her music making, said "I always aim to be as *un*professional as possible," avoiding "going in there with the musical equivalent of a briefcase" like it's "a bloody corporate job." Gavin, too, was keen to distance himself from notions of the "professional" that he found distasteful, saying "there's something toxic about pursuing a career or money in music," but at the same time feeling a deep sense of accomplishment in producing music audio and video products that stood up alongside "anything produced by an independent label in the U.K.," and which "people assume are professionally produced."

Steve rejected the leisure paradigm, saying that to him it was unimportant to categorize his music making in such terms, saying instead that that "it's personal," and that the meaning of it was also personal. Gillian, too, felt unable to describe her music making in these terms, explaining, "it's not leisure and it's not my job—it's something I feel I must engage in to express myself as a human being." Alex G said, "I do it in the time that I would use for leisure." Alex B, meanwhile, said that making music is "both a hobby and an income stream—you need the work, because it's your job, and you also love doing it," thereby reducing the time for what he considered "leisurely activity." Thus, a very strong sense emerged that participants' music making served primarily, and even only, their own ends, their own needs. As Hannah put it, "it's to do with following my own internal direction, and I'm not terribly concerned with any external measurement of what that is." Ben looked slightly more outwardly, finding that "the only recognition, the only feedback you want is from the other four musicians in the room and from the music itself."

The music making of these musicians meets all of the six "distinguishing qualities" that Stebbins outlines as defining "serious leisure." These are: (1) the need to persevere, (2) finding a career[4] in the serious leisure role, (3) significant personal effort in the specialist domain, (4) durable benefits, (5) a unique ethos derived from the particular social world that is the locus of the agents' eudaimonic orientation, and (6) a person's identification with their chosen pursuits (Stebbins 2014, 9). As such, these musicians can be seen to engage in what Stebbins has termed "fulfillment careers" (although "career" was a term that, when it was used by interviewees, referred only to traditional, paid-employment careers). I submit, therefore, that *eudaimonism* is potentially a more helpful and applicable term for understanding the lives and life choices of musicians: it's about being true to oneself.

Discussion: Problematizing Eudaimonism

The recurring, and indeed overwhelming sense from participants that they aimed not necessarily to please anyone else, but rather to fulfill their own personal sense of purpose, is to be expected of lives lived (however inadvertently) according to eudaimonic ethics. As Ryan, Huta, and Deci underline, "[w]e cannot deem a person eudaimonic except insofar as we attribute his or her seeking of excellence and virtues to the person's own volition" (2008, 145). This is not to say that musicians in touch with their daimons have an inflated sense of self-worth; each person, rather, judges him- or herself on their own terms. The interviewees gave me an impression not of having a sense of their own particular greatness, but of possessing a strong sense of how inherently worthwhile all of their music making was *to them*. Affirming this view, Norton observes, "The individual who is confident of his own worth does not feel threatened by the worthiness of others" (1976, 11). As Hannah, Steve, and Ben articulated, they required little or no outside recognition for their music making.

As I mentioned above, there is arguably an ideologically liberal and, indeed, neoliberal stance inherent in a eudaimonic lifestyle and philosophy, wherein, according to Norton (1976, 8), "living one's own truth constitutes integrity, the consummate virtue." Scholars writing about eudaimonism do not propose that individuals' daimons should be pursued at the expense of others, or of others' daimons, but neither do they, on the whole, rule this out. Della Fave et al. highlight an emphasis "apparently uniformly spreading in Western societies," on individual needs over those of communities, and they point out that this "contradicts Aristotle's definition of eudaimonia as the fulfillment of one's deepest nature in harmony with the collective welfare" (2011, 204). Eudaimonic philosophy and its proponents therefore raise important ethical questions.

While the musicians whose lives are discussed in this chapter do not benefit hugely in relative economic terms in their resident country of the United Kingdom, on a global scale all pursue individualistic ends as though their individual fulfillment is the presumed inalienable right of one pursuing or living according to his or her daimon. There is an irony, perhaps, in that through pursuing noncommercial and nonmainstream success on "their own" terms, musicians in fact exemplify the "market discipline [that] now regulates all aspects of social life, and the regressive economic rationality that drives it [and] sacrifices the public good, public values and social responsibility to a tawdry consumerist dream" (Giroux 2014, 185)—a dream in which consumption is of the ideal fulfilling lifestyle to which we feel an unassailable sense of entitlement. Ernst Bloch (cited in Rabinach 1977) suggests that, unlike Stebbins's "fulfillment career," what these musicians exemplify is actually "the swindle of fulfillment." They are caught up in a neoliberal ideological vortex composed of "individual freedom, creativity, and hedonism" (Hewison 2014, 4)—notwithstanding the semantic separation discussed above between hedonism and eudaimonism, where the former is concerned more with gratification, and the latter with fulfillment.

Is it, as Orwell (1945, 51–52) predicted, that "some animals" (those born to relative privilege in wealthy Western or Northern hemispheric developed nation-states with opportunities to live the fulfilled life of their abundant choice) "are more equal than others" (those born without privilege and thus unable to pursue the idealized life imagined by powerful ancient Greek males and perpetuated in contemporary, neoliberal, individualistic societies that masquerade as "democracies")? There is a tension, in that musicians living eudaimonically appear, on the one hand, to be pursuing just the kind of individualistic ends reified by the neoliberal ideology that has for decades pervaded contemporary Western societies to the point of invisible normativity, whereas, on the other hand, everything for which this system stands and which it embodies (pursuit of financial gain, individualism, commercial success, and recognition) is anathema to them.

Eudaimonism also embodies and promotes an overtly masculine stance, with its overtones of privilege, and thus imperial, colonial, and postcolonial violence and power (McClintock 1995, 235–236) in its assumption of the possibility of a fulfilling career, remunerated or unpaid. Although the focus of this study was on musicians "beneath" the echelon of fame and fortune in popular music, eudaimonism arguably shares ideological fundamentals with the mainstream music industry, where Kirschner (1998, 252) observes that "Conditions of production are a constellation of forces that also include powerful ideological and mythmaking machines acting on positions of gender, race, and class." Bourdieu (2001, 54) refers to this shared "historical unconscious" as "masculine domination"—a pervasive, androcentric worldview, "not linked to a biological or psychological nature," but a socio-historical construction—one that finds writers on eudaimonism bypassing reference to women in their writing in further application of masculine domination's "symbolic violence" (35). Eudaimonism can be viewed, then, as a double-sided coin, promising simultaneously acceptance into an exclusive ideological system and freedom from that dehumanizing structure. Welten explains:

> Humanity has become an object. The criteria for having a "meaningful" life are not constituted by existential values, Aristotelian purposes, modelled after the virtues of our vocations, a striving after happiness, but they are valuated on the market place. In our times, we do not speak of labourers or even personnel, but of "Human Resources" that have to be managed, like tools. In a society like ours, we recognise this "in-humanisation", and we try to escape it. We "use" work, not to produce, but to regain our humanity. (Welten 2012, 23)

Eudaimonic lives, then, may offer the opportunity for emancipation from the neoliberal system that they also support, and in which they may be both an ill and a perfect fit. However, an *ethical approach* to eudaimonic living requires that individuals seeking to understand and curate their niche(s) in society do so with an awareness of others and of the opportunities that such an ethics affords or prohibits to all, however "invisible" (Gould 2007) or "worthless" those people may be contrived—or "brutally stigmatized"—to appear, on account of (for instance) their gender, class, or ethnicity (McKenzie 2015).

CONCLUSIONS

I propose that eudaimonism, while not unproblematic, is a useful theoretical counterpart to other, more commonplace ways of viewing the work and play of musicians. As is beginning to be increasingly appreciated in academic circles (e.g., Smith 2013b), there is value in looking at the lives of popular musicians who make music that maybe is not all that popular, that is, lives of workaday musicians like those featured in this chapter, who are "just" pursuing fulfillment. One arena in which it is perhaps especially important, even urgent, to understand the eudaimonic momentum behind some people's (obsession with, addiction to, and) pursuit of making (un)popular music is in the burgeoning higher popular music education (HPME) sector. Teague and Smith (2015) argue:

> The disparity between, on the one hand, the complex and diverse lives managed and negotiated by the participants, and, on the other hand, the "adherence to a tacit and under-interrogated epistemology of 'success' in [and beyond] higher music education" (Smith 2013b, 27) based on conflation of "musician" with "high-profile, full-time performer" supports Bennett's (2008, 82) assertion that there is widespread, endemic "lack of understanding about the roles in which musicians engage" [and, moreover, the reasons for that engagement].

Similarly, Parkinson and Smith describe challenges in reconciling various "authentici-ties"—musical, personal, employment, pedagogical, etc.—and how these intersect with ideas and experience in industry and the marketplace(s) for graduates and musicians. A lifetime of fulfilling but unpaid "leisure" seems an arguably inadequate reason to pay to study for three years at a higher education institution,[5] "thus program teams are obliged to subscribe, outwardly at least, to a conception of educational value traceable to a dom-inant neoliberal meta-policy that totemizes global competition" (Parkinson and Smith 2015, 105). Further exploration around music making, eudaimonism, and leisure may thus be salient for scholars, educators, and students in the area of HPME.

There is a way to go before the terms "eudaimonism" and "serious leisure" have any currency beyond the rarified world of the academy. In everyday parlance, the notion of leisure, serious or otherwise, tends to imply fun, which, while certainly not absent from the lives and music making discussed in this chapter, is clearly insufficient to account for their breadth, depth, and complexity. Discussion of music making in terms such as "devotee work" or "leisure" (Stebbins 2014) could incur derision or bafflement from spouses, partners, and friends of music makers whose lives are utterly absorbed in a pastime that appears to be anything but leisurely or "work." There is little to no research connecting scholarship on eudaimonism with music making as it is described in this chapter, and I propose that there are considerable insights to be gained from further such research. Despite, and indeed precisely because of, the importance of music mak-ing—its eudaimonic meaning—in musicians' lives, it is important that scholars, and ideally wider society, find ways to explore, understand, and capitalize on this. We need to get to grips with what music actually means to and for people who live their lives under its spell. Furthermore, inasmuch as perhaps we might all wish to live eudai-monic lives, it may be interesting to explore the ways in and extent to which this is pos-sible through music.

Notes

1. See Lashua and Cohen (2010) for a rich ethnographic account of participating in sound checks as an aspect of the life of a musician.
2. I understand "obsession" in a colloquial sense rather than a scientific one in this chap-ter. Whereas in psychology the term refers to "intrusive, repetitive thoughts, images, or impulses that are unacceptable and/or unwanted and give rise to subjective resistance (Rachman and Hodgson 1980, 251), I use it to mean an overwhelming desire, perceived as a need, and not generally undesired.
3. In British English, this refers to what speakers of (e.g.) North American English might more commonly refer to as "crazy," as opposed to "angry."
4. By "career," Stebbins is referring to his concept of the "leisure career framework," includ-ing the fulfillment career discussed later in the chapter. See Stebbins (2012, 2014) for fuller exploration of this type of experience and activity that exists at an intersection of work and leisure.
5. For discussion of the value of higher popular music education, see Parkinson (2014), Parkinson and Smith (2015), and Smith (2016).

References Cited

Bauman, Zigmunt. 1992. *Intimations of Postmodernity*. London: Routledge.

Bennett, Dawn E. 2008. *Understanding the Classical Music Profession: The Past, the Present and Strategies for the Future*. Aldershot: Ashgate.

Bennett, Dawn E. 2013. "The Role of Career Creativities in Developing Identity and Becoming Expert Selves." In *Developing Creativities in Higher Music Education: International Perspectives and Practices*, edited by Pamela Burnard, 234–244. London: Routledge.

Bourdieu, Pierre. 2001. *Masculine Domination*. Translated by Richard Nice. Cambridge: Polity.

Bruford, Bill. 2009. *The Autobiography: Yes, King Crimson, Earthworks, and More*. London: Jawbone.

Cottrell, Stephen. 2004. *Professional Music-Making in London: Ethnography and Experience*. Farnham: Ashgate.

Csikszentmihalyi, Mihalyi. 1991. *Flow: The Psychology of Optimal Experience*. New York: Harper and Row.

Della Fave, Antonella, Ingrid Brdar, Teresa Freire, Dianne Vella-Brodrick, and Marié P. Wissing. 2011. "The Eudaimonic and Hedonic Components of Happiness: Qualitative and Quantitative Findings." *Social Indicators Research* 100: 185–207.

Dierendonck, Dirk van, and Krishna Mohan. 2006. "Some Thoughts on Spirituality and Eudaimonic Well-Being." *Mental Health, Religion and Culture* 9(3): 227–238.

Frankel, Viktor E. 1959. *Man's Search for Meaning*. New York: Washington Square Press.

Gadamer, Hans-Georg. 2004. *Truth and Method*. Translation by Joel Weinsheimer and Donald G. Marshall. London: Bloomsbury.

Gaunt, Helena, and Ioulia Papageorgi. 2010. "Music in Universities and Conservatoires." In *Music Education in the 21st Century in the United Kingdom: Achievements, Analysis and Aspirations*, edited by Susan Hallam and Andrea Creech, 260–278. London: Institute of Education.

Gill, Rosalind, and Andy C. Pratt. 2008. "In the Social Factory? Immaterial Labour, Precariousness and Cultural Work." *Theory, Culture and Society* 25(7–8): 1–30.

Goodall, H. Lloyd. 1991. *Living in the Rock 'n' Roll Mystery: Reading Context, Self, and Others as Clues*. Carbondale: Southern Illinois University Press.

Giddens, Anthony. 1991. *Modernity and Self-Identity: Self and Society in the Late Modern Age*. Oxford: Blackwell.

Gould, Elizabeth. 2007. "Legible Bodies in Music Education: Becoming-Matter." *Action, Criticism, and Theory for Music Education* 6(4): 201–223.

Giroux, Henry A. 2014. *The Violence of Organized Forgetting: Thinking beyond America's Disimagination Machine*. San Fancisco: City Lights.

Hallam, Susan, and Helena Gaunt. 2012. *Preparing for Success: A Practical Guide for Young Musicians*. London: Institute of Education, University of London.

Hegel, Georg W. F. (1807) 1910. *Phenomenology of Mind*. London: George Allen and Unwin.

Hewison, Robert. 2014. *Cultural Capital: The Rise and Fall of Creative Britain*. London: Verso.

Huizinga, Johan. 1976. "Nature and Significance of Play as a Cultural Phenomenon." In *Ritual, Play, and Performance: Readings in the Social Sciences/Theatre*, edited by Richard Schechner and Mady Schuman, 46–66. New York: Seabury.

Jung, Carl Gustav. 1933. *Modern Man in Search of a Soul*. Oxford: Routledge.

Kirschner, Tony. 1998. "Studying Rock: Towards a Materialist Ethnography." In *Mapping the Beat: Popular Music and Contemporary Theory*, edited by Thomas Swiss, John Sloop, and Andrew Herman, 247–268. Oxford: Blackwell.

Laing, Ronald D. 1960. *The Divided Self*. Harmondsworth: Penguin.

Lashua, Brett D., and Sara Cohen. 2010. "Liverpool Musicscapes: Music Performance, Movement, and the Built Urban Environment." In *Mobile Methodologies*, edited by Benjamin Fincham, Mark McGuiness, and Leslie Murray, 71–84. Basingstoke: Palgrave Macmillan.

Maslow, Abraham H. (1968) 2014. *Toward a Psychology of Being*. Bensenville, IL: Lushena.

McClintock, Anne. 1995. *Imperial Leather: Race, Gender and Sexuality in the Colonial Contest*. New York: Routledge.

McKenzie, Lisa. 2015. "The Estate We're In: How Working Class People Became the 'Problem'". *The Guardian*, January 22. http://www.theguardian.com/society/2015/jan/21/estate-working-class-problem-st-anns-nottingham?CMP=fb_gu.

Norton, David L. 1976. *Personal Destinies: A Philosophy of Ethical Individualism*. Princeton, NJ: Princeton University Press.

Orwell, George. 1945. *Animal Farm*. London, Victor Gollancz.

Parkinson, Tom. 2014. "Values in Higher Popular Music Education." PhD dissertation, University of Reading.

Parkinson, Tom, and Gareth Dylan Smith. 2015. "Towards an Epistemology of Authenticity in Higher Popular Music Education." *Action, Criticism, and Theory for Music Education* 14(1): 93–127.

Partti, Heidi. 2012. *Learning from Cosmopolitan Digital Musicians: Identity. Musicianship, and Changing Values in (In)formal Music Communities*. Helsinki: Sibelius Academy.

Rabinach, Anson. 1977. "Unclaimed Heritage: Ernst Bloch's *Heritage of Our Times* and the Theory of Fascism." *New German Critique* 11: 5–21.

Rachman, Stanley J., and Ray J. Hodgson. 1980. *Obsessions and Compulsions*. Englewood Cliffs, NJ: Prentice-Hall.

Rathunde, Kevin, and Russell Isabella. Forthcoming. "Play, Flow, and Tailoring Identity in Middle Adulthood." In *Identity Flexibility during Adulthood*, edited by Jan Sinnott. New York: Springer.

Robson, Colin. 2011. *Real World Research*. 3rd ed. Chichester: John Wiley and Sons.

Ryan, Richard M., Veronika Huta, and Edward L. Deci. 2008. "Living Well: A Self-Determination Theory Perspective on Eudaimonia." *Journal of Happiness Studies* 9: 139–170.

Smith, Gareth Dylan. 2013a. *I Drum, Therefore I Am: Being and Becoming a Drummer*. Farnham: Ashgate.

Smith, Gareth Dylan. 2013b. "Seeking 'Success' in Popular Music." *Music Education Research International* 6: 26–37.

Smith, Gareth Dylan. 2016. "Neoliberalism and Symbolic Violence in Higher Music Education." In *Giving Voice to Democracy in Music Education: Diversity and Social Justice*, edited by Lisa C. DeLorenzo. New York: Routledge.

Smith, Jonathan A., Paul Flowers, and Michael Larkin. 2009. *Interpretative Phenomenological Analysis: Theory, Method and Research*. London: Sage.

Stebbins, Robert A. 2012. *The Idea of Leisure: First Principles*. New Brunswick, NJ: Transaction.

Stebbins, Robert A. 2014. *Careers in Serious Leisure: From Dabbler to Devotee in Search of Fulfillment*. New York: Palgrave Macmillan.

Teague, Adele, and Gareth Dylan Smith. 2015. "Portfolio Careers and Work-Life Balance among Musicians: An Initial Study into Implications for Higher Music Education." *British Journal of Music Education* 32(2): 177–193.

Voegelin, Salomé. 2010. *Listening to Noise and Silence: Towards a Philosophy of Sound Art*. New York: Continuum.

Waterman, Alan S. 1992. "Identity as an Aspect of Optimal Psychological Functioning." In *Adolescent Identity Formation: Advances in Adolescent Development*, edited by Gerald R. Adams, Thomas P. Gullotta, and Raymond Montemayor, 50–72. London: Sage.

Waterman, Alan S. 1993. "Two Conceptions of Happiness: Contrasts of Personal Expressiveness (Eudaimonia) and Hedonic Enjoyment." *Journal of Personality and Social Psychology* 64: 678–691.

Weber, William, ed. 2004. *The Musician as Entrepreneur, 1700–1904: Managers, charlatans, and idealists*. Bloomington, IN: Indiana University Press.

Welten, Ruud. 2012. "Work and Leisure in a Consumer Society." *Studia Universitatis Babes-Bolyai-Philosophia* 57(2): 21–33.

PART II

INVOLVEMENT AND MEANING

"THE VIOLIN IN THE ATTIC"

Investigating the Long-Term Value
of Lapsed Musical Participation

STEPHANIE PITTS

INTRODUCTION: LESSONS FROM
LAPSED LEARNERS

THE motivations and experiences of adults who participate in music making have attracted increasing research attention in recent years (Pitts 2005), but less is known about the far greater number who have "given up" playing an instrument or lapsed in their participation (Lamont 2011). While it may seem perverse to look for evidence of the value of music education within the experiences of people who have ceased to learn, this proportion of the population has a lot to tell music educators about the lasting effects of their teaching. These lapsed or liminal participants also demonstrate some of the ways in which an understanding of music and music making pervades society, shaping citizens' decisions about how and whether to support the arts, who the arts are for, and what they contribute to the world.

In *Touching Eternity* (Barone 2001), a thought-provoking account of the effects of one teacher's career in arts education, the visual art teacher Donald Forrister is portrayed through interviews with his current and former students at a high school in North Carolina. The study was commissioned after Forrister had been awarded an "outstanding teacher" prize, and is full of appreciative tributes from students who had subsequently forged creative careers or maintained an active love of art into adulthood. They recall the skills and confidence that Forrister's teaching gave them, and his willingness to spend hours outside lessons encouraging them in their artistic endeavors and talking with them as they faced the identity challenges of adolescence. But the most powerful narrative of the book is one of doubt—about the students whose potential Forrister missed or crushed, the dependence on his approval felt by some of those who were within his selective circle, and the disappointment for Forrister that, in adulthood, few of his students continued to engage in art: "the artistic publicizing of secret places was rarely practiced in busy adult lives" (141). Forrister's story—and those of his students—illustrates how the lifelong impact of a teacher can be profound, but far from predictable. Moreover, these unpredictable but strong outcomes are very rarely acknowledged in research or policy, where the immediate, measurable effects of teaching hold prominence (Southgate and Roscigno 2009). Much is lost in this short-term view of how and why arts education can shape young people's lives and attitudes, not least in an understanding of the contribution of lifelong music making to leisure and well-being.

While predicting the impact of learning in the arts is fraught with difficulties, much can be learned from taking a retrospective, life history approach to understand the place that music learning holds in people's lives. This retrospection is itself full of complexities, communicating as much about the ways in which people construct their musical stories as about the facts of their musical education and experience (Holt 1978; Pitts 2012). However, these stories themselves, and the interpretations that individuals bring to the musical access and attitudes that they encountered in childhood, offer insights into the place of music in education and in society more widely. Learning an instrument, for example, can shape experiences of childhood and adolescence and lay foundations for the musical skills and cultural attitudes that a young player takes into adulthood. Parents, siblings, and wider family members can all present role models for musical encounters—and not only when they are active players, but just as much in their selection of repertoire to listen to (or not), and the place and priority of music in their daily routines.

Past studies of musical life trajectories have tended to focus on exceptional achievement in instrumental learning, documenting the practice regimes of those students who achieve mastery or professional success, and noting the influence of their teachers (Howe and Sloboda 1991). First teachers, typically nurturing and encouraging, have been shown in these high-achieving cases to give way to the greater challenge and technical prowess of a performer role model—with the latter approach persisting into conservatoire training, where the "master-apprentice" teaching style remains the dominant model (Lebler, Burt-Perkins, and Carey 2009). Useful though this insight has been for demonstrating that musical accomplishment is a matter of sustained effort more than arbitrary "genius" (Sloboda, Davidson, and Howe 1994), the focus on expert instrumental skills defines the goals of musical success rather narrowly, and so the recent growth in studies of "ordinary" musical lives is a welcome contribution to music education research. This chapter will draw on some of these (e.g., McPherson, Davidson, and Faulkner 2012; Smilde 2009) in a discussion of formative musical experiences, as well as analyzing empirical evidence from my own life history research with musically active adults (Pitts 2012).

Another approach to understanding the long-term effects of musical learning is to consider the participation and consumption of music in adulthood and, in particular, how the motivations of those who currently engage in musical activities might differ from the recollected experiences of those who no longer participate. In other words, what does music contribute to adult life—and how might this contribution be better supported, during or beyond education? The benefits of musical participation are relatively well documented, and case studies have repeatedly shown how membership of a musical ensemble can provide well-being, social support, and a creative outlet for groups as diverse as homeless men in Canada (Bailey and Davidson 2002), elderly citizens in Australia (Southcott 2009) and England (Creech et al. 2014), professionals in mid-career and retirement (Pitts 2005), university students in England (Kokotsaki and Hallam 2011) and disaffected high school students in the United States (Mahoney 2000) and England (Finney et al. 2005). Much less is known about why people, including those who have experienced these benefits, cease participation in music, most notably on leaving school, when organized activities and resources for music come to an end (Mantie and Tucker 2008), but sometimes later in adulthood, when other work and life priorities become obstacles to participation. By examining motivations to cease or continue playing an instrument beyond school, this chapter explores how musical participation looks "from the outside" and how those who no longer actively engage with music articulate the benefits—and costs—of music learning. The empirical data for this discussion come from a recent study with current and former amateur musicians in England (Pitts 2014; Pitts, Robinson, and Goh 2015) that sheds new light on the relationship between social, musical, and personal goals in amateur musical participation.

After considering the implications that the reported formative and lifelong experiences of musical engagement have for current music education aims and practices, the chapter concludes with the suggestion that the value of musical learning needs to be recognized in the broadest terms, as affecting the cultural responsiveness and responsibilities of future generations, whether or not they are active participants themselves.

FORMATIVE EXPERIENCES
OF MUSIC LEARNING

If young children, when they were first given a musical instrument, were told about the thousands of hours of practice needed to achieve expert performance (Ericsson, Krampe, and Tesch-Romer 1993), along with the potential injuries they might incur (Burkholder and Brandfonbrener 2004) and the risks to self-esteem and well-being in pursuing advanced study (Williamon and Thompson 2006) or a musical career (Kenny, Driscoll, and Ackermann 2014), it seems likely that the uptake for instrumental lessons would be even lower than the estimated 14 percent of students currently having extracurricular music tuition in English schools (Ofsted 2012). Instead, children's instrument choice is motivated by the sound and appearance of the instrument—and, more pragmatically, its availability and fit to their family's lifestyle—and by the opportunities the instrument brings to be in the school band, join with friends in rehearsals, and enjoy the excitement and applause of performing (McPherson, Davidson, and Faulkner 2012). After some months or years of more or less enthusiastic practice and participation, commitment to playing is put at risk by the transition to high school, increased demands of homework, and pressure to conform to peer-accepted teenage activities (Lamont et al. 2003). The young players who survive these challenges are likely to be those who have strong parental support (McPherson 2009), including encouragement or supervision of practice (Hallam and Creech 2010) and opportunities within or beyond school to make music with like-minded adolescents and supportive teachers (Pitts 2007), through which they can experience the satisfaction of musical belonging and develop a secure musical identity.

The development of skills and competence is the most obvious and measurable outcome of the first years of instrumental learning, but also of lasting impact is the formation of attitudes toward music making and self-identity as a musician. Expectations of instrumental learning can be self-fulfilling: parents who consider making music to be a "normal" thing to do—most often because they have learned an instrument themselves—are most likely to encourage their children in this activity (Pitts 2012). Similarly, children who have high ambitions for their own playing will tend to succeed above those who expect to cease playing after primary school (McPherson 2005). The sense of musical success is often fragile (O'Neill and Sloboda 1997), and young players are reliant to varying degrees on the reinforcement of their musical identity through encouragement from teachers, parents and peers, as well as from the affirmation of audiences, exam results, and a demonstrable increase in ability as a performer. Participants in my musical life history study (Pitts 2012) could often identify the individual, even the specific moment, that had helped them to realize that they had musical potential and ability—a musical "possible self" (MacIntyre, Schnare, and Doucette 2012). Others regretted that this moment had never come, or that their response to parental encouragement of practice had not been more diligent, so limiting their capacity for music making in adult life. Either way, the extent to which people identify themselves with music—and are willing to call themselves musicians—is strongly shaped by the opportunities and experiences of adolescence. This personal identification then has far-reaching social consequences for their own future support of the arts in their families and communities.

One group of young players more likely to avoid this motivational dependence on teachers and parents is emerging popular musicians, whose learning is often self-directed and peer-supported (Green 2002), encompassing the private musical lives of self-taught drummers, guitarists, bassists, other nonorchestral instrumentalists, and the collective learning of singers and band members who develop their skills through the process of writing and playing music together. Lucy Green, whose work in this area has been influential on understanding ways of teaching both classroom and instrumental music (Green 2008), offers the hypothesis that "young musicians who acquire their skills and knowledge more through informal learning practices than through formal education may be more likely to continue playing music, alone or with others, for enjoyment in later life" (56). Green's proposal is that the higher level of self-motivation involved in learning without a teacher could be more readily sustainable into adulthood, and she suggests that longitudinal research is needed to test the hypothesis. There were relatively few popular musicians in my life history cohort to provide this longitudinal testing, but the few who did contribute had contrasting stories that leave the debate unresolved for the moment. Some individuals who strongly identified themselves as popular musicians had succeeded in building professional careers as performers and/or teachers (see also Robinson 2012), but others who had tried to bring their informally acquired skills to organized amateur music making, such as singing in a choir, were frustrated by gaps in their learning, related to technique or sight-reading (Pitts 2012, 169). An alternative hypothesis would be that it is the level of self-concept as a musician that differs in these examples—and that self-taught and formally taught musicians acquire that self-concept from different sources: the former through intrinsic motivation, peer approval, and success in performance, the latter through these routes also, but with teacher approval and external recognition (such as exam results) playing an additional and potentially dominant role. There are plenty of studies to show that lack of self-belief in musical skills is an inhibiting factor to making progress and forming a secure musical identity (e.g., McPherson and McCormick 2006), and indeed the group of Italian, self-taught musicians included in my life history study showed low recognition of their skills, dismissing their guitar playing and songwriting abilities as being inferior to the performing expertise of their conservatoire-educated peers (Pitts 2012, 78). Young people's confidence in their own musical learning, and the extent to which this is validated by both peers and teachers, has a strong effect in placing music more or less prominently within their emerging adolescent identities.

From another perspective, the high dropout rate from the strongly teacher-directed American wind band system (Mantie and Dorfman 2014; Mantie and Tucker 2008) provides some evidence that music making that is heavily dependent on institutional structures and resources can be hard to replicate in adult life—either for practical reasons, or because of the psychological barriers of associating musical participation with a past phase of life. One of the "lapsed" musicians I interviewed in the U.K. explained how memories of school music had inhibited his adult participation in exactly this way: "for me, classical music is very tainted by childhood—by school and adolescence. [I'm] ambivalent because I don't just unproblematically dislike it, but there is always a bit of that about it for me." While this example is counteracted by many respondents recalling inspiring performances during their school years, the sense of musical attitudes being shaped in and by school is apparent, and illustrates the risk of school-leavers being ill equipped to find or invent opportunities for continuing their playing in adulthood. Musicians of all kinds can find themselves insufficiently adaptable or receptive to the amateur or community music scene beyond school, and without a secure foundation of musical skills and confidence, will easily become one of the many adults with "a violin in the attic."

MOTIVATIONS TO CONTINUE OR CEASE PARTICIPATION IN ADULTHOOD

Another perspective on the long-term effects of musical participation in adolescence can be sought from those who remain actively involved in adulthood, and in the past few decades there have been a number of case studies depicting the musical lives of individuals, performing groups, and whole communities (e.g., Dabback 2008; Finnegan [1989] 2007; Pitts 2005). From this empirical evidence, the benefits of musical participation are often argued in relation to well-being, health, and social connection, and several recent reports have urged arts organizations to do more to promote these aspects of their work: "publicly-funded cultural organizations around the country are currently responsible for a very considerable quotient of public value in the realms of social capital and health and wellbeing [. . . but] much of this important aspect of cultural value is currently hidden" (Vella-Burrows et al. 2014, 50). These outcomes of arts engagement are certainly important, but they tend not to be the primary motivations of those people who belong to amateur orchestras, bands, and choirs, who join instead for the pleasures of rediscovering and developing skills, being among like-minded people, and making music together (Pitts 2014). There are dangers in portraying the side-effects of musical participation as its primary function, just as the "transferable skills" argument, while compelling (see Hallam 2015), can be damaging to music education by shifting emphasis away from musical activity toward its associated cognitive and emotional benefits.

A comparison of the motivations of those who are currently playing in amateur orchestras with those who have lapsed illustrates the fine line between continued musical engagement and ceasing to play. Players in our U.K.-based study reported the effects of significant life transitions on their inclination and ability to pursue musical activities, with leaving home, changing jobs, starting relationships, having children, and encountering ill-health, stress, or retirement all influencing the decision to join or leave ensembles (Pitts, Robinson, and Goh 2015). The main difference between continuing and lapsed players was not in these external circumstances, but in the extent to which musical participation was seen to enhance, rather than conflict with, other life demands. While one player would find rehearsals "physically demanding, a bit demoralizing," another would see them as a necessary escape: "it's fantastic, once a week, to switch [the work-related] part of my brain off [and] just focus on making music." Often a practical reason for ceasing playing—time, energy, health—masked a more deep-seated crisis of confidence or identity, manifest in musical experience but strongly connected to other aspects of life. One player described how after a personal tragedy in her life she experienced a kind of musical breakdown: "I think with music, you know that whole saying of "losing your mojo," where your confidence goes down, so your ability goes down, that kind of happened to me" (see Pitts 2014). The challenging aspects of musical participation—reported to include finding time to practice, feeling "judged" by other players, lacking confidence, and struggling to keep up in rehearsals—create a vulnerability in participants that accounts in part for the emotional effects, both positive and negative, of belonging to an ensemble. Where players feel supported and valued in their ensemble, their playing is a counterbalance to pressures of bereavement, ill-health, or anxiety; where these experiences are combined with a sense of insecurity as an ensemble member, withdrawing from musical participation can seem a necessary coping strategy.

Those players in our study who had joined an ensemble primarily for social reasons had sometimes been disappointed: "one of the reasons was to meet people, but I don't know, maybe musicians are quite shy in general because they express themselves through their music. I never found it very easy in the social—like, in the breaks and things." Breaking into a new musical scene had sometimes proved difficult too, either because established players already knew each other, or because standards in the ensemble provided too much or insufficient challenge. Nonetheless, the sense of friendship, like-mindedness, and pursuit of a common creative goal through collective music making was important to continuing players, and those who were most contented in their ensemble membership had thought carefully about their "fit" to the group, both musically and socially, and changed ensembles to find a better fit as needed. Friendship was described as an important aspect of musical participation by many continuing respondents, just as it was in the recollections of adults looking back at their adolescent music making (Pitts 2012). However, as in previous studies with audiences (Pitts and Burland 2013), these friendships appeared to be strongly embedded in the shared activity, operating within rehearsals but more rarely spreading into other areas of life. In a study of musical leisure activities in Milton Keynes, U.K., Ruth Finnegan ([1989] 2007) noted differences between musical genres in the extent to which musical friendships generated wider social support networks, finding that both country and western enthusiasts and brass banders were more likely than classical musicians to share other aspects of life beyond music, perhaps because of the strong family links that were also a part of those worlds (99).

A strong source of motivation for continuing players was the sense of recreating enjoyable musical experiences from adolescence, with those players who had experienced high levels of musical satisfaction, friendship, and belonging in their school ensembles feeling destined to seek out these activities later in life. One formerly professional player described how his gradual return to the amateur scene had brought some of the pleasure he had first experienced as a student: "I think I found what I missed as a young person again—as a student, maybe—you could take risks and it didn't matter, to try different things." Other positive memories of school music were linked to particularly memorable performances, unexpected or resounding successes, or inspirational teachers—but the converse was also true, when music in school had been compulsory or dull, and participation rather more unwilling. While my research has not so far been extensive enough to demonstrate a direct correlation between enriching school experiences and the tendency to continue playing into adulthood, there was certainly a trend in that direction, which is supported by previous work with adult singers (Turton and Durrant 2002), "non-musicians" (Gavin 2001), and American college students (Mantie and Dorfman 2014). Helen Gavin also urges caution against predicting musical futures from early experiences, quoting a professional flutist who says "'[My parents] bought me a flute when I asked, so I suppose that set me off to where I am today, but they also bought me a bike, and I'm not in the Tour de France" (Gavin 2001, 57). Positive experiences of music in childhood are undoubtedly one ingredient in lifelong musical engagement, but need to be supported by lasting intrinsic motivation and a determination to find time for music among the competing demands of adult life.

LASTING EFFECTS OF MUSIC LEARNING

The many obstacles to acquiring and maintaining a secure musical identity outlined in this chapter help to explain the low proportion of the adult population actively engaged in making music: the annual *Taking Part* survey run by Arts Council England estimates that under 10 percent of adults would rank playing a musical instrument as their main leisure activity, compared to the 79 percent who rank listening to music most highly (DCMS 2012, 31). The ubiquity of music as a soundtrack to daily life has been much commented upon in recent years (Bull 2005; Clarke, Dibben, and Pitts 2010; DeNora 2000), and yet few adults would see this lifelong informal engagement with music as a direct continuation of their school music education. However, understanding the full range of musical behaviors in adulthood as being at least in part a response to formative experiences can be enlightening for music educators and arts promoters alike. Even when the opportunity to make music has been set aside after school, adults' levels of open-mindedness to the arts, their support for their own children's musical education, and their understanding of the value of leisure and creativity, will have been affected to some degree by the musical contexts in which they grew up. The "hidden curriculum" of music education—those implicit messages sent through the status of music in a school, and the music teacher's choice of repertoire and activities—can create a sense of whether music is readily accessible to all, throughout the lifespan, or is solely the preserve of privileged child prodigies (Wright and Froehlich 2012). This implicit knowledge will translate into attitudes to learning an instrument in adulthood, for example, affecting the extent to which the absence of past success in this area remains a lasting regret or something that can be remedied at any stage of life.

Some of the frequent classical music concert-goers in my life history studies have reflected on how their attempts at learning an instrument in childhood, while leading to limited technical prowess, had nonetheless shaped their future listening: "if the organist [who taught me] had found a way to make my eyes and hands work together at the piano, then I might have benefited from more player-side appreciation of my listening. . . . But I'm a very contented audience member and listener" (Pitts 2012, 150). Others endorsed this with reference to their longer engagement in instrumental lessons and school orchestras: "I think the experience you get playing music, as a musician, is quite different from if you tried to approach it just as someone who listens to it: I don't know if it's richer or something in some way, but it's a lived experience." The "player-side appreciation" referred to by these respondents is also evident in studies of adolescent musical role models, where playing an instrument has been shown to increase the range of available role models beyond the pop stars prominent in the media, and to raise awareness that building a musical career requires effort and ability as much as luck (Ivaldi 2013; Ivaldi and O'Neill 2008).

Sharing listening preferences with parents, siblings, and friends, or acquiring the concert-going habit as a family could also have lasting effects, even though these practices have changed across generations with the increase in portable listening technology and the decline in classical concert attendance (Kolb 2001). As adolescents form and display their own musical tastes, these contribute to friendships and wider social behaviors (Tarrant, North, and Hargreaves 2002) and have an impact in the home, either positively, through the exchanging of new musical knowledge with family members, or negatively, through disputes about the quantity and volume of music listening emanating from behind the closed bedroom doors of teenage offspring (Morgan, MacDonald, and Pitts 2014). These strong teenage preferences and recollections of family listening habits will be further developed through young adulthood and beyond (Lamont and Webb 2010), so building musical tastes and memories that will have lasting self-regulating and therapeutic effects for each individual (Batt-Rawden and DeNora 2005; Saarikallio 2011).

The shaping of musical expertise and attitudes in childhood has a further effect beyond the individual, through the numerous instances in which these experiences are eventually passed on to others through parenting, teaching, and other acts of sharing skills and understanding. Many of the respondents referred to in this chapter spoke of the connections between their own music making and that of their children, sometimes noting how their musical participation declined during early years of childcare, but was revived when their offspring started learning instruments themselves. One amateur oboist, now reluctantly retired from playing, described how his own practice regime— "half an hour in the morning and another twenty minutes at night, much to [the family's] annoyance"—was intended as a model for his eldest son: "there's two ways, you can bully [them] or you can demonstrate." Similar examples are to be found in the *New Horizons* movement in the U.S.A., which has seen many older adults return to ensemble playing and articulate the benefits of these experiences for their health, well-being, and quality of life (Coffman and Levy 1997; Dabback 2008). Other adults in my study had forged careers as music teachers, often quite accidentally, as their confidence and enjoyment in music had drawn them into acquiring piano pupils or helping with music activities at their local schools, so "recycling the benefits" of their own musical education (Pitts 2012, 137). Since confidence for teaching music has been repeatedly observed to be lacking in generalist teachers (e.g., Hennessy 2000; Wiggins and Wiggins 2008), this lasting effect of musical learning should not be undervalued—and indeed, the role of past musical experience in the attitudes of those underconfident teachers deserves further exploration (see Biasutti 2010).

Beyond the readily visible effects of playing, teaching, or supporting music into adulthood, it is interesting to speculate on how public decisions are affected by the hidden musical backgrounds of cultural and educational policy makers. Politicians, in the U.K. at least, tend to be reticent in declaring their aesthetic interests, and indeed in recent times of financial recession have been outspoken about the alleged career advantages of encouraging children into sciences rather than arts subjects (Paton 2014). Wayne Bowman has observed that "where our most influential decision and policy makers have had no musical experience—or worse still, where experience in mediocre programmes has 'turned them off' rather than 'on' to musical experience—we can reasonably expect to reap only what we have permitted to be sown" (Bowman 2001, 14). Expecting all future politicians and policy makers to be musically proficient is clearly too bold an aim for music education, but we might hope that general education would make the majority of the population musically and culturally aware, sufficient to respect, if not actively engage in, the rich possibilities of musical leisure activities.

Looking Forward, Looking Back

In conclusion to this chapter, it is worth considering how the empirical evidence presented here can contribute to practice and debate in music education and music as leisure: namely, whether the foundations for lifelong valuing of musical participation could be laid more securely in formative education, and the routes back into musical engagement made more accessible in adulthood. The past century has seen an accumulation of claims made for music education (Pitts 2000), from its role as a civilizing force on adolescents (Cox 2002), to its capacity to improve school engagement and team work (Mahoney 2000), not to mention its benefits for brain function, disciplined learning, and other transferable skills (Hallam 2015). Such passionate advocacy for music education is understandable, since it is a subject that has always had to fight for curriculum time and resources, but there are dangers in claiming too much, and in attributing these benefits too widely. Not all school children have a positive or meaningful experience of music education, and while it is right to focus on how this might be improved through more widespread inspiring teaching, it is also valid to accept that full engagement in musical learning requires a commitment and motivation that will not be universal in the adolescent population (Lamont and Maton 2010). Schools should therefore be places of opportunity and possibility in the arts, but perhaps not of compulsion and obligation, since the life history evidence suggests that this can be counterproductive in obscuring the musical engagement that young people bring from their home and peer relationships.

One factor in securing a long-term positive impact for music education appears to lie in achieving coherence between school music and lifelong musical engagement, by equipping young people during their formative years with skills, open-mindedness, and enthusiasm that will be of lasting musical and personal value. This effect was most readily observed in older generations of life history respondents—those who sang in the school choir, listened to classical music on the newly acquired gramophone in the home, and grew up to attend concerts and sing with an amateur choral society (Pitts 2012, 40). Those specific connections depended on narrowly defined boundaries for musical engagement, and operated less reliably in the younger generations, as music education has become (rightly) more diverse in its genres and activities, and access to live and recorded music has become ever richer and more plentiful. Other educational disciplines—most notably information technology—are well acquainted with the notion of "future-proofing" their teaching, such that students acquire flexible learning skills that will be of lasting use, rather than focusing entirely on current information that will become obsolete. In music teaching, Julie Ballantyne and Don Lebler suggest that this can be achieved through "a multiplicity of music types and pedagogical approaches" (2013, 218), so as to offer young people a variety of routes into musical engagement and the resources and motivation to continue to seek out their own such routes in the years after school.

Further challenges lie outside music education, in the sustaining and developing of opportunities for meaningful musical participation in adulthood. Continuing with the choral singing example, the problem of an aging membership is well known to the directors of amateur choirs, with a survey carried out in U.K., Australia, and Germany showing that the traditional large choral society is in decline, with a largely middle-aged or retired membership, many of whom have been involved in singing for several decades (Clift et al. 2008). In the United States, Cindy Bell offers examples of "the gradual erosion of a once glistening choral society to a barely functioning non-select group of singers" (2008, 236), with difficulties arising not so much from the reduced personnel of the choir, but on their insistence on maintaining their "core" repertoire and failing to adjust the performance expectations of the choir: "a choral group of thirty non-auditioned singers cannot sustain a Mozart *Requiem*" (236). Bell argues that with changing membership should come changing purpose—not necessarily a decline in performance standards, but an adjustment to the skills that new generations bring to the choir, with the democratic hope of including and developing all who wish to participate. Some successful examples of this approach are reported both anecdotally, on the many community choir websites online, and in the research literature, which includes studies of intergenerational choirs (Conway and Hodgman 2008) and the growing numbers of "cambiata" choirs that aim to support boys in continuing to sing during and after puberty (Ashley 2013). Caroline Bithell describes the recent growth in community choirs as "one of the most intriguing and potentially momentous developments in the world of amateur, voluntary, participatory arts in the United Kingdom" (2014, 13) and offers many examples of how collective singing can mobilize communities and empower individuals.

The example of choral singing illustrates how collaborative music making can evolve to meet the needs and interests of younger participants—and perhaps we should therefore remain optimistic that the collective impulse to make music together will ensure that people (should they wish to) will always find ways to make music that are appropriate to them and the society in which they live. To take this for granted, however, would almost certainly be a mistake: opportunities can be taken only if they are readily available, and these new practices have grown up not by chance, but through the efforts of committed individuals who have identified social and expressive needs in their communities that can be fulfilled through music. Music education holds a large part of the responsibility both for training future musical leaders, and for enthusing future potential participants, listeners, and advocates for the arts. Politicians, meanwhile, could do much more to support and promote arts engagement in education and society, rather than viewing these as luxurious benefits to be funded only in prosperous times. Economizing on the arts is a sure route to an impoverished society, lacking in the fulfillment and community engagement that an aesthetically rich life can provide. Viewing the music curriculum and wider school arts provision through this lens of lifelong engagement—noting the benefits of lapsed involvement as well as ongoing participation—is one way to make music "part of the art world" (Becker 1982), and to ensure that the value of music in the lives of adult participants, whatever form this takes, is intentionally rooted in their formative experiences of musical learning.

REFERENCES CITED

Ashley, Martin R. 2013. "Broken Voices or a Broken Curriculum? The Impact of Research on UK School Choral Practice With Boys." *British Journal of Music Education* 30(3): 311–327.

Bailey, Betty A., and Jane W. Davidson. 2002. "Adaptive Characteristics of Group Singing: Perceptions from Members of a Choir for Homeless Men." *Musicae Scientiae* 6: 221–256.

Ballantyne, Julie, and Don Lebler. 2013. "Learning Instruments Informally: A Collaborative Project across Disciplines in Popular Music and Education." In *Collaborative Learning in Higher Music Education*, edited by Helena Gaunt and Heidi Westurland, 212–218. Farnham: Ashgate.

Barone, Tom. 2001. *Touching Eternity: The Enduring Outcomes of Teaching*. New York: Teachers College Press.

Batt-Rawden, Kari, and Tia DeNora. 2005. "Music and Informal Learning in Everyday Life." *Music Education Research* 7: 289–304.

Becker, Howard S. 1982. *Art Worlds*. Berkeley: University of California Press.

Bell, Cindy L. 2008. "Toward a Definition of a Community Choir." *International Journal of Community Music* 1(2): 229–241.

Biasutti, Michele. 2010. "Investigating Trainee Music Teachers' Beliefs on Musical Abilities and Learning: A Quantitative Study." *Music Education Research* 12(1): 47–69.

Bithell, Caroline. 2014. *A Different Voice, a Different Song: Reclaiming Community through the Natural Voice and World Song*. New York: Oxford University Press.

Bowman, Wayne. 2001. "Music Education and Post-Secondary Music Studies in Canada." *Arts Education Policy Review* 103(2): 9–17.

Bull, Michael. 2005. "No Dead Air! The iPod and the Culture of Mobile Listening." *Leisure Studies* 24(4): 343–355.

Burkholder, Kristen R., and Alice G. Brandfonbrener. 2004. "Performance-Related Injuries Among Student Musicians at a Specialty Clinic." *Medical Problems of Performing Artists* 19(3): 116–122.

Clarke, Eric F., Nicola Dibben, and Stephanie E. Pitts. 2010. *Music and Mind in Everyday Life*. Oxford: Oxford University Press.

Clift, Stephen, Grenville Hancox, Ian Morrison, Bärbel Hess, Don Stewart, and Gunter Kreutz. 2008. *Choral Singing, Wellbeing and Health: Summary of Findings from a Cross-National Survey*. Canterbury: Sidney De Haan Research Centre for Arts and Health, Canterbury

Christ Church University. https://www.canterbury.ac.uk/health-and-wellbeing/sidney-de-haan-research-centre/documents/choral-singing-summary-report.pdf.

Coffman, Don D., and Katherine M. Levy. 1997. "Senior Adult Bands: Music's New Horizon." *Music Educators Journal* 84(3): 17–22.

Conway, Colleen, and Thomas M. Hodgman. 2008. "College and Community Choir Member Experiences in a Collaborative Intergenerational Performance Project." *Journal of Research in Music Education* 56: 220–237.

Cox, Gordon. 2002. *Living Music in Schools, 1923–1999*. Aldershot: Ashgate.

Creech, Andrea, Susan Hallam, Maria Varvarigou, and Hilary McQueen. 2014. *Active Ageing with Music: Supporting Wellbeing in the Third and Fourth Ages*. London: Institute of Education Press.

Dabback, William M. 2008. "Identity Formation through Participation in the Rochester New Horizons Band Programme." *International Journal of Community Music* 1(2): 267–286.

Department for Culture, Media and Sport (DCMS). 2012. *Taking Part 2011–12: Annual Adult and Child Release*. London: DCMS. https://www.gov.uk/government/publications/taking-part-the-national-survey-of-culture-leisure-and-sport-adult-and-child-report-2011-12.

DeNora, Tia. 2000. *Music in Everyday Life*. Cambridge: Cambridge University Press.

Ericsson, K. Anders, Ralf Krampe, and Clemens Tesch-Romer. 1993. "The Role of Deliberate Practice in the Acquisition of Expert Performance." *Psychological Review* 100: 363–406.

Finnegan, Ruth. (1989) 2007. *The Hidden Musicians: Music-Making in an English Town*. 2nd ed. Middletown, CT: Wesleyan University Press.

Finney, John, Richard Hickman, Morag Morrison, Bill Nicholl, and Jean Rudduck. 2005. *Rebuilding Engagement through the Arts*. Cambridge: Pearson.

Gavin, Helen. 2001. "Reconstructed Musical Memories and Adult Expertise." *Music Education Research* 3 (1): 51–61.

Green, Lucy. 2002. *How Popular Musicians Learn: A Way Ahead for Music Education*. Aldershot: Ashgate.

Green, Lucy. 2008. *Music, Informal Learning and the School: A New Classroom Pedagogy*. Aldershot: Ashgate.

Hallam, Susan. 2015. *The Power of Music: A Research Synthesis of the Impact of Actively Making Music on the Intellectual, Social and Personal Development of Children and Young People*. London: International Music Education Research Centre (iMerc), University College London Institute of Education.

Hallam, Susan, and Andrea Creech. 2010. "Learning to Play an Instrument." In *Music Education in the 21st Century in the United Kingdom: Achievements, Analysis and Aspirations*, edited by Susan Hallam, and Andrea Creech, 85–104. London: Institute of Education.

Hennessy, Sarah. 2000. "Overcoming the Red-Feeling: The Development of Confidence to Teach Music in Primary School amongst Student Teachers." *British Journal of Music Education* 17(2): 183–196.

Holt, John. 1978. *Never Too Late: My Musical Life Story*. New York: Merloyd Lawrence.

Howe, Michael J. A., and John A. Sloboda. 1991. "Young Musicians' Accounts of Significant Influences in their Early Lives: 2. Teachers, Practising and Performance." *British Journal of Music Education* 8(1): 53–63.

Ivaldi, Antonia. 2013. "Specialist Young Musicians' Role Models: Whom Do They Admire and Why?" *Music Education Research* 15(2): 180–195.

Ivaldi, Antonia, and Susan A. O'Neill. 2008. "Adolescents' Musical Role Models: Whom Do They Admire and Why?" *Psychology of Music* 36(4): 395–415.

Kenny, Diana, Tim Driscoll, and Bronwen Ackermann. 2014. "Psychological Well-Being in Professional Orchestral Musicians in Australia: A Descriptive Population Study." *Psychology of Music* 42(2): 210–232.

Kokotsaki, Dimitra, and Susan Hallam. 2011. "The Perceived Benefits of Participative Music Making for Non-Music University Students: A Comparison with Music Students." *Music Education Research* 13: 149–172.

Kolb, Bonita M. 2001. "The Decline of the Subscriber Base: A Study of the Philharmonia Orchestra Audience." *Market Research* 3(2): 51–59.

Lamont, Alexandra. 2011. "The Beat Goes On: Music Education, Identity and Lifelong Learning." *Music Education Research* 13(4): 369–388.

Lamont, Alexandra, David J. Hargreaves, Nigel A. Marshall, and Mark Tarrant. 2003. "Young People's Music In and Out of School." *British Journal of Music Education* 20(3): 229–241.

Lamont, Alexandra, and Karl Maton. 2010. "Unpopular Music: Beliefs and Behaviours towards Music in Education." In *Sociology and Music Education*, edited by Ruth Wright, 63–80. Aldershot: Ashgate.

Lamont, Alexandra, and Rebecca Webb. 2010. "Short- and Long-Term Musical Preferences: What Makes a Favourite Piece of Music?" *Psychology of Music* 38: 222–241.

Lebler, Don, Rosie Burt-Perkins, and Gemma Carey. 2009. "What the Students Bring: Examining the Attributes of Commencing Conservatoire Students." *International Journal of Music Education* 27(3): 232–249.

MacIntyre, Peter, Ben Schnare, and Jesslyn Doucette. 2012. "Possible Selves as a Source of Motivation for Musicians." *Psychology of Music* 40(1): 94–111.

Mahoney, Joseph L. 2000. "School Extracurricular Activity Participation as a Moderator in the Development of Antisocial Patterns." *Child Development* 71(2): 502–516.

Mantie, Roger, and Lynn Tucker. 2008. "Closing the Gap: Does Music-Making Have to Stop upon Graduation?" *International Journal of Community Music* 1(2): 217–227.

Mantie, Roger, and Jay Dorfman. 2014. "Music Participation and Nonparticipation of Nonmajors on College Campuses." *Bulletin of the Council for Research in Music Education* 200(1): 41–62.

McPherson, Gary E. 2005. "From Child to Musician: Skill Development During the Beginning Stages of Learning an Instrument." *Psychology of Music* 33(1): 5–35.

McPherson, Gary E. 2009. "The Role of Parents in Children's Musical Development." *Psychology of Music* 37(1): 91–110.

McPherson, Gary E., Jane W. Davidson, and Robert Faulkner. 2012. *Music in Our Lives: Rethinking Musical Ability, Development and Identity*. New York: Oxford University Press.

McPherson, Gary E., and John McCormick. 2006. "Self-Efficacy and Music Performance." *Psychology of Music* 34(3): 322–336.

Morgan, Jill P., Raymond A. MacDonald, and Stephanie E. Pitts. 2014. "'Caught between a Scream and a Hug': Women's Perspectives on Music Listening and Interaction with Teenagers in the Family Unit." *Psychology of Music*, January 29. doi: 0305735613517411.

Office for Standards in Education (Ofsted). 2012. *Music in Schools: Wider Still, and Wider*. London: Ofsted. http://www.ofsted.gov.uk/resources/music-schools-wider-still-and-wider.

O'Neill, Susan A., and John A. Sloboda. 1997. "The Effects of Failure on Children's Ability to Perform a Musical Test." *Psychology of Music* 25(1): 18–34.

Paton, Graeme. 2014. "Pupils 'Held Back' by Overemphasis on Arts." *Daily Telegraph*, November 10. http://www.telegraph.co.uk/education/educationnews/11221081/Nicky-Morgan-pupils-held-back-by-overemphasis-on-arts.html.

Pitts, Stephanie E. 2000. *A Century of Change in Music Education: Historical Perspectives on Contemporary Practice in British Secondary School Music.* Aldershot: Ashgate.

Pitts, Stephanie E. 2005. *Valuing Musical Participation.* Aldershot: Ashgate.

Pitts, Stephanie E. 2007. "Anything Goes: A Case Study of Extra-Curricular Musical Participation in an English Secondary School." *Music Education Research* 9(1): 145–165.

Pitts, Stephanie E. 2012. *Chances and Choices: Exploring the Impact of Music Education.* New York: Oxford University Press.

Pitts, Stephanie E. 2014. "Dropping in and Dropping out: Understanding Cultural Value from the Perspectives of Lapsed or Partial Arts Participants." Draft report, University of Sheffield. http://www.sparc.dept.shef.ac.uk/research/.

Pitts, Stephanie E., and Karen Burland. 2013. "Listening to Live Jazz: An Individual or Social Act?" *Arts Marketing* 3(1): 7–20.

Pitts, Stephanie E., Katharine Robinson, and Kunshan Goh. 2015. "Not Playing Any More: A Qualitative Investigation of Why Amateur Musicians Cease or Continue Membership of Performing Ensembles." *International Journal of Community Music* 8(2): 129–147.

Robinson, Tim. 2012. "Popular Musicians and Instrumental Teachers: The Influence of Informal Learning on Teaching Strategies." *British Journal of Music Education* 29(3): 359–370.

Saarikallio, Suvi. 2011. "Music as Emotional Self-Regulation throughout Adulthood." *Psychology of Music* 39: 307–327.

Sloboda, John A., Jane W. Davidson, and Michael J. A. Howe. 1994. "Is Everyone Musical?" *The Psychologist* 7(8): 287–309.

Smilde, Rineke. 2009. *Musicians as Lifelong Learners: Discovery through Biography.* Delft: Eburon.

Southcott, Jane E. 2009. "And As I Go, I Love to Sing: The Happy Wanderers, Music and Positive Aging." *International Journal of Community Music* 2: 143–156.

Southgate, Darby E., and Vincent J. Roscigno. 2009. "The Impact of Music on Childhood and Adolescent Achievement." *Social Science Quarterly* 90(1): 4–21.

Tarrant, Mark, Adrian C. North, and David J. Hargreaves. 2002. "Youth Identity and Music." In *Musical Identities*, edited by Raymond A. R. MacDonald, David J. Hargreaves, and Dorothy Miell, 134–150. Oxford: Oxford University Press.

Turton, Angela, and Colin Durrant. 2002. "A Study of Adults' Attitudes, Perceptions and Reflections on their Singing Experience in Secondary School: Some Implications for Music Education." *British Journal of Music Education* 19(1): 33–50.

Wiggins, Robert A., and Jackie Wiggins. 2008. "Primary Music Education in the Absence of Specialists." *International Journal of Education and the Arts* 9(12). http://ijea.org/v9n12/index.html.

Williamon, Aaron, and Sam Thompson. 2006. "Awareness and Incidence of Health Problems among Conservatoire Students." *Psychology of Music* 34(4): 411–430.

Wright, Ruth, and Hildegard Froehlich. 2012. "Basil Bernstein's Theory of the Pedagogic Device and Formal Music Schooling: Putting the Theory into Practice." *Theory into Practice* 51(3): 212–220.

Vella-Burrows, Trish, Nick Ewbank, Stephanie Mills, Matt Shipton, Stephen Clift, and Fred Gray. 2014. *Cultural Value and Social Capital: Investigating Social Capital, Health and Wellbeing Impacts in Three Coastal Towns Undergoing Culture-Led Regeneration.* Folkestone: Sidney De Haan Research Centre for Arts and Health. http://www.nickewbank.co.uk/downloads/Cultural-value-report.pdf.

CHAPTER 11

....

LEISURE-TIME MUSIC ACTIVITIES FROM THE PERSPECTIVE OF MUSICAL AGENCY

The Breaking Down of a Dichotomy

....

SIDSEL KARLSEN

LEISURE-TIME music activities have been investigated by music scholars from many angles and for quite some time, but have not always been denoted explicitly as such. Rather, researchers have shown an interest in amateur musicians' musical engagements (Finnegan [1989] 2007), the functions music serves in individuals' everyday lives (DeNora 2000; Sloboda, O'Neill, and Ivaldi 2001), or the musical learning, upbringing, and education of children and adolescents that happen outside of formal schooling (Green 2002; Partti and Karlsen 2010; Söderman and Folkestad 2004), without necessarily making specific connections to the field of leisure studies. Still, what these phenomena of investigation have in common is that they mostly take place in the participants' free time. As such, they can be understood and defined precisely as leisure-time activities. A similar understanding of what constitutes leisure-time music activities is employed for the purpose of this chapter; it is music-related pursuits that are undertaken in a person's free time, mostly, but not always completely, detached from the workplace or from formal educational contexts. Conceiving of the music activities described in this chapter through key concepts borrowed from leisure studies, they can be framed through the notions of, for example, identity, pleasure, escape, social class, and cultural capital (Harris 2005). However, since my academic home ground is that of the sociology of music education, I have chosen another overarching conceptual point of departure, one which also accommodates the above concepts in various ways, namely that of *musical agency*.

That is, I explore how individuals' and groups of people's recreational practices involving music can be seen as means for expanding their capacities for acting in the world. The exploration works through both theoretical and experiential accounts. First, I draw on a wide range of literature taken from general sociology (Barnes 2000; Giddens 1984; Martin and Dennis 2010a) and music sociology (DeNora 2000, 2005; Small 1998), as well as the sociology of music education (Karlsen 2011b; Karlsen and Westerlund 2010) in order to explicate and elaborate on the notion of agency as it is broadly understood within the realm of sociology, as well as on the more field-specific concept of musical agency. Second, I explore a variety of music-related agency modes through narrating some of my own experiences, acquired during the past forty years, of participating in, leading, and observing leisure-time music activities—as a music-loving child and teenager, as a music educator, and as a researcher in the field of music education. Third, based on my theoretical as well as my autoethnographically inspired accounts, I set out to dissolve what I believe to be a somewhat artificial dichotomy, namely the seemingly binary opposition between recreational music production and music consumption. It is not uncommon in the scholarly literature on musical development and music education to distinguish between "the musician" (the producer) and "the listener" (the consumer) or between "musicianship" and "listenership"[1] (see, e.g., Elliott 1995; North and Hargreaves 2008), and, for example, Finnegan's ([1989] 2007) work, referred to above, concentrates mainly on the production side of leisure-time music engagement—the actual making of music. However, I argue, from the point of view of musical agency, that the two poles of production and consumption can be more usefully understood as rich, complementary, and inseparably intertwined venues for the constitution of agency, and, on a related note, also for the production and construction of, among other things, taste (Bennett et al. 2009; Bourdieu 1984; Hennion 2007) and music-related learning trajectories (Dahlberg 2013; Dreier 1999; Wenger 1998).

THE QUESTION OF HUMAN AGENCY FROM A SOCIOLOGICAL POINT OF VIEW

The relationship between structure and agency has been central to sociological debates for many decades, and it is a phenomenon with which several highly acknowledged sociologists, such as Habermas (1985), Bourdieu (1984), Giddens (1984), and Foucault (1982), have struggled to provide an all-convincing account. Their task has been, simply put, to find a link between social structures on the macro level of society and acting human beings on the micro level, and to reach a decision on to what extent "occurrences and processes on the micro-level determine macro phenomena" (Guneriussen 1999, 277–278, my translation) or vice versa. That there seems to be no universal answer to this particular question has led sociologists to come up with very different solutions and theories. Some emphasize very strongly the structural forces' hold on the human agent and their predetermination of the individual's capacity to act, while others focus on the freedom that individuals have when it comes to changing and cocreating their social realities, as well as the need to see human beings as knowledgeable actors who know how to move efficiently within the institutional frames of society. Recently, contributors to the ongoing debate (see Martin and Dennis 2010a) have even claimed that the whole structure-versus-agency discussion is, in fact, invalid, because it is practically impossible to demonstrate the existence of social structures (Martin and Dennis 2010b, 5–9) and hence study them. Instead, they propose that "[t]he proper focus of sociological attention . . . is the human world of everyday experience, a world which is neither 'macro' nor 'micro' and cannot be captured analytically by the dualism of 'structure' and 'agency' (or by attempts to 'link' them)" (15).

While not denying altogether the existence of structuring social forces, the view of human agency as conveyed in this chapter, and which forms the point of departure for outlining that of *musical* agency, has in common with the ideas expressed above that the domain of everyday experience constitutes the foremost ground for exploring how individuals execute, negotiate, and expand their capacity for acting in the social world. Combining the perspectives of British sociologists Giddens (1984) and Barnes (2000), it has been possible to establish an understanding of agency that takes into account both individuals' power to act independently and freely and their capacity to transcend individualism.[2]

In Giddens's view, macro structures are not fixed or determining entities. Rather, they carry affordances for action and are things we all produce and reproduce as we live our everyday lives and consciously repeat, change, or adjust our patterns of behavior—a continuous process that Giddens has framed as the "concept of *routinization*" (1984, 60; emphasis in original). In this chapter, music is seen as a medium or structure through which such processes of routinization may take place. As DeNora puts it, music may function as a technology of the self, and individuals draw on its affordances to "regulate, elaborate, and substantiate themselves as social agents" (2000, 47). While Giddens is first and foremost occupied with the individual agent's capacity for action, the main focus of Barnes's (2000) theories is how we, as groups of people, are able to transcend individualism and coordinate our behavior so that we can act *together*, in a state of collective agency. He reminds us that "human beings are independent social agents, who profoundly affect each other as they interact" (64), and what it takes for us to engage in successful interaction is, among other things, that others perceive us as responsible agents, a social status which can be achieved "through accountability and susceptibility" (Karlsen and Westerlund 2010, 231). *Accountability* is needed in order to coordinate understandings and have a shared sense of where we have been and where we are going, action-wise. Moreover, *susceptibility* is required so that we can coordinate our actions and reach a "coherent ordering around collectively agreed goals" (Barnes 2000, 74). Everyone engaging in real-time musical interplay would recognize these two premises as crucial traits of any person who wants to make music successfully as part of an ensemble.

MUSICAL AGENCY: FOCUSING THE LENS

Building from the broader view of individual and collective agency explicated above, I later constructed a more fine-grained understanding and lens of *musical* agency (see Karlsen 2011b), based on the works of DeNora (2000), Batt-Rawden and DeNora (2005), and Small (1998). These particular works were chosen mainly because they contain critical and sociologically informed analyses of the wide variety of actions that humans perform in and through music, and they also align well with the individual and collective dimensions drawn from the writings of Giddens (1984) and Barnes (2000). In addition to creating the musical agency lens as a theoretical and philosophical endeavor, I employed and tested it as a methodological tool as part of a larger empirical research project (see Karlsen 2012, 2013, 2014b).

The musical agency lens comprises eleven aspects. Six of these are categorized as belonging to the individual dimension. That is, they denote the music-related practices and actions that are mainly used for negotiating and extending one's own room for action; namely, using music for: self-regulation, the shaping of self-identity, self-protection, matters of being, as a medium for thinking, and for developing music-related skills. The remaining five aspects are categorized as belonging to the collective dimension, and encompass practices and actions that allow for experiences and negotiations of shared and collaborative forms of agency; that is, using music for: regulating and structuring social encounters, coordinating bodily action, affirming and exploring collective identity, the purpose of "knowing the world," and establishing a basis for collaborative musical action. Without going into details on all of the eleven facets of the lens (for a more detailed account, see Karlsen 2011b), I choose here to elaborate on the ones I later use as points of departure for exploring my own leisure-time experiences of music. They are borrowed from both the individual and the collective dimensions of the lens, and encompass the following five aspects: *shaping self-identity, self-regulation, self-protection, affirming and exploring collective identity*, and *coordinating bodily action*.

Using music as a part of shaping *self-identity* is well documented in the literature (see, e.g., MacDonald, Hargreaves, and Miell 2002; Ruud 2013) and points to two interrelated phenomena, namely the habits that humans have of constructing, reinforcing, and repairing the "thread of self-identity" (DeNora 2000, 62) through "inner" modes, such as reconnecting with the self, performing biographical work, and narrating their lives via music, as well as through "outer" modes, using the delineated meanings of music (Green 1999) to construct "badges" in order to signal who they are or wish to become to the surrounding world.

When individuals use music for *self-regulation*, the practices in which they engage go beyond the mere identity-related work, and focus on bringing together various facets of the psychological and physical self through three interrelated practices, namely emotional work,[3] memory work, and the work of regulating bodily comportment. The emotional and mood work (DeNora 2000) is something we all engage in when, for example, we listen to a piece of music known to have the effect of bringing us into a particular emotional state. Likewise, we use music for working through moods, for enhancing emotions, and also for recalling how we felt at particular points in our lives. Memory work represents an extension of the latter aspect, and concerns the practice of remembering relationships, events, or a particular time through consciously engaging with music specific to the phenomenon a person needs or wants to recall. The work of regulating bodily comportment, on the other hand, covers the ways we use music for shifting energy levels, recalibrating our energy, enhancing strength, endurance, and coordination, and achieving a feeling of embodied security. In DeNora's (2000) understanding, music "affords materials—structures, patterns, parameters and meanings—that bodies may appropriate or latch on to" (99), and these properties are what I attend to when I, for example, use music to calm myself down before I go to sleep.

Somewhat related to the self-regulation mode is the aspect of using music for *self-protection*. In a world where we are constantly exposed to myriad visual and, not least, audial forms of expression, we sometimes attend to music as a way of creating a "sonic bubble"—a calmer and less confusing private space. This applies, for example, to train commuters during the rush hours, as well as to students trying to create environments "that afford concentration" (DeNora 2000, 58) in the midst of a chaotic and noisy classroom.

While the three aspects above all belong to the individual-dimension side of the musical agency lens, the next two are classified as belonging to the collective dimension. Just as music can be employed for shaping various features of the self, it can also be used for *affirming and exploring collective identity*. This particular function of music is also widely acknowledged in the literature (see, e.g., Frith 1996; Merriam 1964) and is quite powerfully expressed by Small (1998), who reminds us that music is used for confirming a unity among individuals already existing, for exploring a community that might come into existence, and "as an act of celebration (to rejoice in the knowledge of an identity not only possessed but also shared with others)" (95). The collective identity function of music might have inner and outer modes, just as with the aspect of shaping self-identity explained above. While the inner modes are related to groups of people who gain an understanding of themselves as communities "*through* cultural activity" (Frith 1996, 111; emphasis in original), the cultural or musical event can also be used in outer modes, for example by groups employing a music festival for municipality "branding," in other words for presenting their community to the outside world (Karlsen 2007, 199).

The second collective dimension examined here is that of using music for *coordinating bodily action*. While Barnes (2000) is interested in the collective ordering of bodies, for example in military activities, he neglects to mention how music often plays a crucial role in providing key information about the details of such movements. DeNora (2000), however, investigates this phenomenon through ethnographic research in aerobics sessions and is able to show how music, in these and similar situations, becomes an important "device for collective ordering" (109). For anyone who has ever participated in music-based gym classes or, for that matter, watched the carefully choreographed performances of a North American marching band, the power that music possesses when it comes to coordinating joint bodily efforts is evident.

PERSONAL EXPERIENCES OF LEISURE-TIME MUSIC ACTIVITIES: RECALLED AND EXPLAINED

In this section, the five musical agency dimensions previously discussed are used as starting points for understanding and classifying some of the leisure-time music activities that I have participated in throughout my life. I will oscillate between describing modes and experiences of production—the actual making of music—and consumption, since both dimensions have been prevalent in my musical life and seem inseparable from the point of view of my personal music-related development. However, before I delve into specific experiences and memories, I give a brief account of my musical upbringing and education in order to give readers some background information to support their understanding.

My mother enrolled me in musical kindergarten when I was two-and-a-half years old. I learned to sing, play the recorder, read staff notation (in fact, I cannot remember a time in my life when I did not know how to read music), and to have fun with and enjoy music. At eight I started playing the piano, and at thirteen I joined a youth choir in the local church. From the age of sixteen, my musical education became part of my general education and vice versa. In upper secondary school I specialized in music with piano as my main instrument. Then I went on to a music academy for a bachelor's degree as a specialist music teacher and a voice teacher (having changed my main instrument to voice). My master's degree was in vocal performance and early romantic opera performance practice, topped off a few years later with a PhD in music education. All along I worked as a freelance singer, choir conductor, and voice teacher, including spending a few years working to produce a large, annual church music festival in the Norwegian capital, Oslo.

The music-related practices that I have participated in form an intricate weft in and out of my own and other people's professional and leisure time. Furthermore, as explained above, they have always oscillated effortlessly between modes of production and consumption, which is why the stories below encompass both "sides." Often, but not always, my chosen practices have also contained rich possibilities for the enhancement of my own and of others' musical agency.

Leisure-Time, Music, and Self-Identity: Becoming and Being a Musician

From very early on I had a self-conception of being musically gifted—not talented to the extreme, perhaps, but definitely with an understanding that making music was something I wanted to do, something I was good at, and something that was a big part of *me*, of my self-identity. One may of course say that this was due to the early training I received, but I could have had that without developing this intense relationship between my self and the music through the various leisure-time music activities in which I participated. My parents bought a piano when I was eight, and I remember jumping up and down in front of the hallway mirror for what must have been about an hour. I had never ever experienced such joy in my life, and from then on I believe I started to think of myself as someone who would, one day, become a professional *musician*—a magical word to me. Despite the advice of teachers and parents (why would a clever girl like me want to waste my chances of becoming a lawyer or a medical doctor?), I steered toward educational opportunities as well as out-of-school activities that allowed me to practice and develop my musicianship and to take up the subject position of "a young musician" (O'Neill 2002, 79), becoming more of what I already was. At the same time, listening to other people playing or singing, whether in concerts or in recordings, represented, and still represents, additional ways to explore and express myself through music.

For many years I spent hours and hours listening to other singers—how they performed certain kinds of repertoire, the quality of their timbre, and how they went about using their technique. The North American mezzo-soprano Frederica von Stade was an absolute favorite, as her voice type was close to mine. After I decided to pursue an academic career and stop regular singing, I was unable to listen to a particular recording of hers for a long time; it was simply too painful. Nowadays, slowly reconnecting with my voice, I can also reconnect with my "singer self" through listening to von Stade's interpretations of Mozart and Rossini arias—the repertoire I once wanted to perform on stage. In addition to this introspectively directed listening mode, I, as most people, wear my music listening as a badge toward the outer world, too. From wanting to present myself as something of a highbrow classical music snob (Peterson and Kern 1996) as a student, I now admit to listening to a broader variety of music, fashionably aiming to occupy the subject position of a cultural and musical omnivore (Dyndahl et al. 2014).

The Self-Regulation of Practicing and Listening: Emotional Outlet, Meditation, and Remembrance

To me, practicing the piano or singing has always constituted a technology for self-regulation when it comes to both processing emotions and to regulating bodily comportment. As a young girl I went to the piano with my joys and sorrows and played them out in solitude. A crisis occurred when, one day, I had to stop playing because I developed tendinitis in my lower arms and hands. From a twenty-five-year distance, I can see that the inflammation probably was connected to other life-changing events; more than ever I needed musical practice to process emotional turmoil and grief. Unable to make music, however, I sank into a deep depression, which I overcame by becoming a singer. The emotional outlet and self-regulation were transferred from sitting in front of a keyboard to exercising my vocal cords, not to mention the entire body, as is necessary for singers of all types in order to support the tone and maintain healthy voice habits. Later on, as a newly educated mezzo-soprano, this bodily regulation became, in itself, one of the main reasons I engaged in a particular musical practice. Looking for some kind of vocal community as an addition to my solo-singing practices, I joined a women's group performing Gregorian chant. While I was, at the time, a professional singer, this group became one of my favorite leisure-time activities. The work was barely paid and I engaged in it, as I now recall, for reasons that had to do with the bodily and mental states of being that the music afforded me. While my ordinary classical music singing required much bodily strength and expression, Gregorian chant was performed with less vocal power and a minimum of outwardly directed gestures. This music and its related practices allowed me to reach another bodily mode than the loud and hectic everyday one, and to recalibrate my energy (DeNora 2000) through a kind of musical meditation.

My music listening has, in a way similar to my music making, always been a site for various self-regulatory strategies—the emotional work, the regulation of my body and, not least, memory work of different kinds. Listening to a particular recording of Shostakovich's chamber symphony can take me right back to a lonely walk one rainy day when I was nineteen years old. I can remember exactly where I walked, what the smell was in that particular place, and also the immense sadness I felt after the break-up of what was my first "real" love affair. On a happier note, I can put on ABBA's "Mamma Mia" and recall myself as a preschooler, probably around the age of six, singing along with the tune at the top of my lungs and inventing mock-English lyrics, using the end of my jumping rope as a microphone and quarrelling with my best friend about who was going to be the lead singer. Such music-related memory work helps me reconnect to "who [I was] at a certain time" (DeNora 2000, 65), and it is similarly one way to process memories and emotions and come to terms with who I am now and how I came to be this way.

Leisure-Time Self-Protection: A Musical Room of My Own

While practicing has always afforded me an emotional outlet, I can see now that it has often also allowed me to protect myself and to mentally withdraw from noisy or demanding situations. Although I am quite sociable, I have learned through the years that I am mainly an introvert. This means not only that I prefer my own company, but also that I need solitude in order to "recharge my batteries." Too much social activity and I am simply overloaded and exhausted. Since much of a classical singer's or a pianist's work consists of solitary practicing, this has always presented a welcome, and socially acceptable opportunity to absent myself from whatever went on in my everyday life. Sometimes I have also used music listening for similar purposes. Surrounded by chatty co-passengers on long-haul flights, I put in the ear buds of my smart phone and I am then immediately provided with a much-needed musical and private sonic bubble, without having to worry about whether or not my neighbors perceive me as being unfriendly or rude. That I am not alone in using technologically mediated sound for such purposes is shown, for example, by the work of Bull (2010) and Skånland (2011), who describe their study participants' use of MP3 players respectively as a way to create "a personalized sound world" (Bull 2010, 55) and as a resource that allows the listener "to cope successfully with everyday stressors" (Skånland 2011, 15). Furthermore, looking to leisure studies in general, self-protection and self-restoration often seem to be actions and effects sought by individuals when engaging in leisure-time activities (Kleiber, Hutchinson, and Williams 2002). Hence, solitary music practicing and listening have been *my* ways of seeking similar effects and experiences during my free time.

Exploring and Affirming Collective Identity as Audience Member and Conductor

One of my absolutely most memorable experiences of exploring and affirming collective identity through a music-related event came when I took part in an outdoor festival concert in the role of a participant-observer researcher (Karlsen 2011a, 2014a). Although I visited the event principally because it was a part of the festival that constituted the "case" of my doctoral study, I was drawn into the concert in a way that left deep imprints, emotionally and with regard to my experience of belonging to the local community in which I then lived. The band playing on that occasion consisted of musicians from the area. Their popularity had peaked about a decade earlier, although many still cherished their folk-rock music. This was the band's revival concert and it became a three-hour-long celebration of local and collective identity tied to the area, namely the town of Piteå in North Bothnia, Sweden. The identity affirmation took place mainly through the song lyrics, which mostly addressed local ways of thinking and doing and showed disdain for any viewpoints coming from the capital area. Local narratives were delivered through small talks in between the songs as well; however, the strongest collective-identity output for me, and I believe for many of the other participants as well, came through the strong emotions evoked by the combination of the lyrics and music, and the fact that we all experienced this together, "in concert" (Becker 2001, 152), in a way that allowed us to feel "as individual[s] within a community" (151), even if we were not necessarily locally born and raised.

A related experience occurred when I conducted a choral concert some years prior to the festival event. For some time, the amateur vocal ensemble that I then led cooperated with a group of musicians consisting of Bosnians who had fled to Norway during the Balkan war and Norwegians who wanted to play music from that region of southern Europe. By merging and coarranging Norwegian and Bosnian folk music, we built up a shared repertoire with which we toured southeastern Norway. Our concerts were most often crowded with Bosnian refugees and asylum seekers, who used these opportunities to listen to the songs and *sevdalinke*[4] of their native country and, I believe, to celebrate their collective identity as Bosnians. On one occasion we were just about to finish the well-known *sevdalinka* "Kad ja podjoh na Bembasu" when a man in the audience leapt to his feet, grabbed the microphone, and continued to sing all the remaining verses with tears streaming down his face. The musicians joined in, and somehow we all became part of his sorrowful longing for the country he had been forced to leave and of the Bosnian diaspora identity that was explored, affirmed, and celebrated right there and then.

Musical Coordination of Bodily Action: Choir Conducting and Spinning Classes

Working as a choir conductor for about fifteen years, I came to pay close attention to the musical ordering of bodies, or, rather, to how my own body could be used to generate the ordering of others' bodies so that they—the singers—could produce the desired musical output, which would in turn spur a seamless regeneration of this process until the piece of music performed had concluded. Studying choir conductors' communication with their singers, Jurström (2009) analyzes the various semiotic "repertoires of action" (107) that the conductors have at hand, and how they implement these repertoires through resources such as gestures, eye contact, bodily movement, speech, singing, and piano playing. She also shows how these resources are often combined, for example by the conductor simultaneously playing the tenors' part on the piano with the right hand and singing the part of the altos, while making gestures with the left hand to indicate the phrasing of the piece of music and using one foot to highlight the beat. Some of the available resources can be fully utilized only if the conductor is placed in front of the choir, and they are effective only insofar as the singers are able to "read" them. For professional singers, the skills and knowledge needed to read the conductor—and, vice versa, for the conductor to read her singers—will have been explicitly taught as part of their education. For amateur singers, however, this process of learning can more accurately be described as one of implicit and long-term socialization, learning how to react appropriately to the conductor's signs and repertoires of action through participating in the community of practice constituted by the choir, and using peers and old-timers as role models (Balsnes 2009, 157–158). Hence, working mainly with inexperienced amateur singers, I found that I could not rely too much on the singers' ability to read my conventional conductor's hand and arm gestures. Rather, the best way of leading came through starting the music as a "proper" conductor, then joining the choir as a fellow singer, letting the ongoing music order *my* body in concert with everyone else's. For this arrangement to be musically efficient, we all had to act as mutually responsible agents during the interaction, similarly ordering our actions "around collectively agreed goals" (Barnes 2000, 74)—namely, producing the music.

A similar bodily coordination is produced every time I join a gym class in which the music constitutes the rhythmic and energetic driving force. Unlike with the choir, I do not make the music myself and neither do I care much for the types of music played. For example, I am not a big fan of deadmau5's house music, which is played during some of my spinning classes.[5] However, I acknowledge that it *works*—sometimes to astonishing ends—to create a soundtrack toward which we can all appear to be "mutually oriented, co-ordinated, entrained and aligned" (DeNora 2000, 109), as well as sweating and exhausted. As such, the bodily ordering capacities of the house music can be tremendously strong if I allow them to affect me, even if this style is not of my personal preference.

DISSOLVING THE DICHOTOMY: PRODUCTION AND CONSUMPTION AS TWO SIDES OF THE SAME COIN

Through relating my own experiences with music, outlined above, I have aimed to show that, from the perspective of musical agency, the division between recreational music production, on the one hand, and leisure-time music consumption, on the other, makes a somewhat artificial binary opposition that does not necessarily exist in individuals' musical life-worlds. Rather, the two modes of engaging with music represent two sides of the same coin, that is, a variety of modes of *doing* music or of letting music into individual or social *doings*—specific repertories of action for enhancing, exploring, and expanding one's abilities to be and act in the world. However, these repertoires can be activated only to the extent that we *allow* the music to become a structuring property of our actions. There is nothing automatic about these processes. DeNora (2005) describes it thus: "[M]usic is a medium to which agents may turn as they engage in their routine, full-time sense-making procedures in real-time daily life. Music structures action, but only reflexively, in so far as it is acted upon, i.e., recognized as a condition of action by participants" (134). Reconnecting to the theories of Giddens (1984), it takes a knowledgeable and conscious actor to execute one's musical agency, and a person's engagement with music—even through so-called passive or distracted listening (Green 2008)—is always a doing, a willed music-related act with specific and intended purposes.

In addition to being a "musical agency act" in itself, each single "doing" is included in chains of actions which, when taken together, constitute larger, more or less coherent behavioral patterns over time. Some of these patterns will be commonly recognized as musical preference or taste, and will thus represent larger units of actions that individuals employ for navigating the social landscape and for producing and reproducing social structures, a process captured by Giddens (1984) through the aforementioned concept of routinization. Looking beyond the binary production/consumption duality in my stories above, and also further on from the musical doing as something happening right here and now, or there and then, it is possible to read the text from the point of view of music-related actions being inseparably intertwined with the acquisition and expression of musical taste, as well as with the coproduction of social class (see Bennett et al. 2009; Bourdieu 1984; Dyndahl et al. 2014; Peterson and Kern 1996). An attentive reader will have noticed distinct taste patterns along the way: my training as a musician took place within the paradigm of classical music, and it is there that many of my performance and listening preferences resided and still reside. Yet, I listen to various kinds of popular music as well—more now than I did as a student, I must admit—and I have a certain inclination toward hybrid musics, among other things expressed by my engagement with various folk musics. Combined with the classical music familiarity, these traits might make me appear omnivorous, to a certain extent. In addition, the reader will note that I have not been able to escape the temptation of expressing my distaste;[6] house music is clearly not one of my favorite styles.

According to Hennion (2007), expressions of cultural taste can no longer "be explained . . . by hidden social causes" (98). Rather, by analyzing taste we come to understand how "we make ourselves become sensitized, to things, to ourselves, to situations and to moments" (98), much in the manner that I have aimed to describe above. Still, from a different sociological angle, Hennion's position may appear as slightly innocent with respect to the social structures reproduced by individuals through rehearsing their patterns of cultural preference. For example, following the Bourdieu-inspired analyses of cultural and musical taste patterns in contemporary Britain (Bennett et al. 2009) and the town of Aalborg in Denmark (Faber et al. 2012)—contexts that are not too different, culturally speaking, from the Norwegian one in which I live my everyday life—my familiarity with and preference for classical music, along with certain "omnivorous tendencies" (Bennett et al. 2009, 93), represent forms of cultural capital commonly associated with the middle class and which function as a specific kind of asset with which I can navigate socially and professionally.

Yet another structural reading of my stories is possible. If placed diachronically, the recalled events could be understood as episodes along one learning trajectory, or perhaps several trajectories (Dreier 1999; Wenger 1998)—personal paths of learning experiences that have allowed me to participate in particular social contexts in certain ways. Looking back, my early musical kindergarten experiences launched me on a lifelong trajectory toward increasing participation in systems and institutions of higher music education. However, as Dahlberg (2013) reminds us, for musicians' (and music academics'), personal learning trajectories to be meaningful and productive, they need to go beyond those offered by the institutions, and stretch into other arenas as well—professional, semiprofessional, and those dominated by amateurs' leisure-time music activities.[7] Moreover, the trajectories will weave seamlessly between modes of production and consumption, since it is the entirety of musical engagement that provides the ground for an individual's musical agency. This is not something exclusive to those who wish to become professional musicians. Rather, it is one of the main characteristics of the building of any kind of musical agency repertoire, regardless of the social status of the individual agent.

Notes

1. This is of course hardly done without emphasizing that the latter constitutes an important and indispensable part of successful execution of the former.
2. For a broader account of this particular understanding of agency than the format of this chapter allows for, see Karlsen and Westerlund (2010), the article in which it was first articulated.
3. It is important to note that the concept of "emotional work," as utilized in this chapter, is a very different construct from that of "emotional labor," referred to in Ward and Watson (this volume, chapter 24). While the former denotes individuals' inwardly directed emotional experiences and regulations, the latter is outwardly directed and concerns individuals working to produce a proper state of mind in others.
4. A *sevdalinka* is a particular type of vocal folk music and "one of the strongest Bosnian cultural symbols" (Bujic and Petrović n.d.). The songs are characterized by rather slow tempi as well as elaborate and melismatic melodic lines; they are emotionally charged and most often sung with much passion and fervor.
5. Spinning is a form of indoor gym class performed on stationary bikes, and with music constituting an important part of the program.
6. According to Bourdieu (1984), taste is first and foremost expressed as distaste; it is "asserted purely negatively, by the refusal of other tastes" (56).
7. It is also important to remember that these arenas or domains are not necessarily easily identified or separated. See for example Finnegan ([1989] 2007) on the intertwinement of amateur and professional musicians' practices and worlds.

References Cited

Balsnes, Anne. 2009. "Å lære i kor: Belcanto som praksisfellesskap" [Learning in choir: Belcanto as a community of practice.] PhD dissertation, Norwegian Academy of Music.

Barnes, Barry. 2000. *Understanding Agency: Social Theory and Responsible Action.* London: Sage.

Batt-Rawden, Kari, and Tia DeNora. 2005. "Music and Informal Learning in Everyday Life." *Music Education Research* 7(3): 289–304.

Becker, Judith. 2001. "Anthropological Perspectives on Music and Emotion." In *Music and Emotion: Theory and Research*, edited by Patrik N. Juslin, and John A. Sloboda, 135–160. Oxford: Oxford University Press.

Bennett, Tony, Mike Savage, Elizabeth Silva, Alan Warde, Modesto Gayo-Cal, and David Wright. 2009. *Culture, Class, Distinction.* London: Routledge.

Bourdieu, Pierre. 1984. *Distinction: A Social Critique of the Judgement of Taste.* Translated by Richard Nice. Cambridge, MA: Harvard University Press.

Bujic, Bojan, and Ankica Petrović. n.d. "Bosnia-Hercegovina." *Grove Music Online. Oxford Music Online.* http://www.oxfordmusiconline.com/subscriber/article/grove/music/40881.

Bull, Michael. 2010. "iPod: a Personalized Soundworld for Its Consumers." *Comunicar* 34(17): 55–63.

Dahlberg, Magnus. 2013. "Learning Across Contexts: Music Performance Students' Construction of Learning Trajectories." PhD dissertation, Norwegian Academy of Music.

DeNora, Tia. 2000. *Music in Everyday Life.* Cambridge: Cambridge University Press.

DeNora, Tia. 2005. *After Adorno: Rethinking Music Sociology.* Cambridge: Cambridge University Press.

Dreier, Ole. 1999. "Læring som ændring af personlig deltagelse i sociale kontekster" [Learning as transformation of personal participation in social contexts.] In *Mesterlære: Læring som social praksis*, edited by Klaus Nielsen, and Steinar Kvale, 76–99. Copenhagen: Hans Reitzels Forlag.

Dyndahl, Petter, Sidsel Karlsen, Siw G. Nielsen, and Odd Skårberg. 2014. "Cultural Omnivorousness and Musical Gentrification: An Outline of a Sociological Framework and its Applications for Music Education Research." *Action, Criticism, and Theory for Music Education* 13(1): 40–69.

Elliott, David J. 1995. *Music Matters: A New Philosophy of Music Education.* New York: Oxford University Press.

Faber, Stine T., Annick Prieur, Lennart Rosenlund, and Jakob Skjøtt-Larsen. 2012. *Det skjulte klassesamfund* [The hidden class society.] Aarhus: Aarhus Universitetsforlag.

Finnegan, Ruth. (1989) 2007. *The Hidden Musicians: Music-Making in an English Town.* 2nd ed. Middletown, CT: Wesleyan University Press.

Foucault, Michel. 1982. "The Subject and Power." *Critical Inquiry* 8(4): 777–795.

Frith, Simon. 1996. "Music and Identity." In *Questions of Cultural Identity*, edited by Stuart Hall and Paul du Gay, 108–127. London: Sage.

Giddens, Anthony. 1984. *The Constitution of Society.* Berkeley: University of California Press.

Green, Lucy. 1999. "Research in the Sociology of Music Education: Some Introductory Concepts." *Music Education Research* 1(2): 159–170.

Green, Lucy. 2002. *How Popular Musicians Learn: A Way Ahead for Music Education.* Aldershot: Ashgate.

Green, Lucy. 2008. *Music, Informal Learning and the School: A New Classroom Pedagogy.* Aldershot: Ashgate.

Guneriussen, Willy. 1999. *Aktør, handling og struktur: Grunnlagsproblemer i samfunnsvitenskapene* [Agent, action and structure: Foundational problems in the social sciences.] Oslo: Tano Aschehoug.

Habermas, Jürgen. 1985. *The Theory of Communicative Action.* Vol. 2, *Lifeworld and System: A Critique of Functionalist Reason.* Translated by Thomas McCarthy. Boston: Beacon.

Harris, David E. 2005. *Key Concepts in Leisure Studies.* London: Sage.

Hennion, Antoine. 2007. "Those Things That Hold Us Together: Taste and Sociology." *Cultural Sociology* 1: 97–114.

Jurström, Ragnhild S. 2009. "Att ge form åt musikaliska gestaltningar: En socialsemiotisk studie av körledares multimodala kommunikation i kör" [Shaping musical configurations: A social semiotic study of choir conductors' multimodal communication with choirs.] PhD dissertation, University of Gothenburg.

Karlsen, Sidsel. 2007. "The Music Festival as an Arena for Learning: Festspel i Pite Älvdal and Matters of Identity." PhD dissertation, Luleå University of Technology.

Karlsen, Sidsel. 2011a. "Music Festivals in the Lapland Region: Constructing Identities Through Musical Events." In *Learning, Teaching, and Musical Identity: Voices across Cultures*, edited by Lucy Green, 184–196. Bloomington: Indiana University Press.

Karlsen, Sidsel. 2011b. "Using Musical Agency as a Lens: Researching Music Education from the Angle of Experience." *Research Studies in Music Education* 33(2): 107–121.

Karlsen, Sidsel. 2012. "Multiple Repertoires of Ways of Being and Acting in Music: Immigrant Students' Musical Agency as an Impetus for Democracy." *Music Education Research* 14(2): 131–148.

Karlsen, Sidsel. 2013. "Immigrant Students and the 'Homeland Music': Meanings, Negotiations and Implications." *Research Studies in Music Education* 35: 161–177.

Karlsen, Sidsel. 2014a. "Context, Cohesion and Community: Characteristics of Festival Audience Members' Strong Experiences with Music." In *Coughing and Clapping: Investigating Audience Experiences*, edited by Karen Burland and Stephanie Pitts, 115–126. Farnham: Ashgate.

Karlsen, Sidsel. 2014b. "Exploring Democracy: Nordic Music Teachers' Approaches to the Development of Immigrant Students' Musical Agency." *International Journal of Music Education* 32(4): 422–436.

Karlsen, Sidsel, and Heidi Westerlund. 2010. "Immigrant Students' Development of Musical Agency: Exploring Democracy in Music Education." *British Journal of Music Education* 27(3): 225–239.

Kleiber, Douglas A., Susan L. Hutchinson, and Richard Williams. 2002. "Leisure as a Resource in Transcending Negative Life Events: Self-Protection, Self-Restoration, and Personal Transformation." *Leisure Sciences* 24(2): 219–235.

MacDonald, Raymond A. R., David J. Hargreaves, and Dorothy Miell, eds. 2002. *Musical Identities.* Oxford: Oxford University Press.

Martin, Peter J., and Alex Dennis, eds. 2010a. *Human Agents and Social Structures.* Manchester: Manchester University Press.

Martin, Peter J., and Alex Dennis. 2010b. "Introduction: The Opposition of Structure and Agency." In *Human Agents and Social Structures*, edited by Peter J. Martin and Alex Dennis, 3–16. Manchester: Manchester University Press.

Merriam, Alan P. 1964. *The Anthropology of Music.* Evanston, IL: Northwestern University Press.

North, Adrian, and David Hargreaves. 2008. *The Social and Applied Psychology of Music.* Oxford: Oxford University Press.

O'Neill, Susan, A. 2002. "The Self-Identity of Young Musicians." In *Musical Identities*, edited by Raymond A. R. MacDonald, David J. Hargreaves, and Dorothy Miell, 79–96. Oxford: Oxford University Press.

Partti, Heidi, and Sidsel Karlsen. 2010. "Reconceptualising Musical Learning: New Media, Identity and Community in Music Education." *Music Education Research* 12(4): 369–382.

Peterson, Richard A., and Roger M. Kern. 1996. "Changing Highbrow Taste: From Snob to Omnivore." *American Sociological Review* 61(5): 900–907.

Ruud, Even. 2013. *Musikk og identitet* [Music and identity.] 2nd ed. Oslo: Universitetsforlaget.

Skånland, Marie S. 2011. "Use of MP3 Players as a Coping Resource." *Music and Arts in Action* 3(2): 15–33.

Sloboda, John A., Susan A. O'Neill, and Antonia Ivaldi. 2001. "Functions of Music in Everyday Life: An Exploratory Study Using the Experience Sampling Method." *Musicae Scientiae* 5(1): 9–32.

Small, Christopher. 1998. *Musicking: The Meanings of Performing and Listening.* Middletown, CT: Wesleyan University Press.

Söderman, Johan, and Göran Folkestad. 2004. "How Hip-Hop Musicians Learn: Strategies in Informal Creative Music Making." *Music Education Research* 6(3): 313–326.

Wenger, Étienne. 1998. *Communities of Practice: Learning, Meaning, and Identity.* Cambridge: Cambridge University Press.

CHAPTER 12

....

THE MUSICAL LIVES
OF SELF-CONFESSED
NONMUSICIANS

....

JENNIE HENLEY

PENNY is a secondary school teacher who has taught science for nearly thirty years. John runs a software company. Pat is a retired secondary teacher and Andrew works in a hospital.[1] These people all describe themselves as "not musical," yet they learn an instrument through a process of immersing themselves in active music making and performance within an ensemble. They are self-confessed "nonmusicians," yet they lead rich musical lives.

MUSICAL OPPORTUNITIES IN ADULTHOOD

....

In seeking to understand what conservatoire students can gain from working within a U.K. community-based music project for adults (Rhythm for Life), Perkins, Aufegger, and Williamon (2015) acknowledge that the population of older adults participating in musical learning activities is growing. As with other music projects for older adults (Creech et al. 2013, for example), the Rhythm for Life project involved music making in community-based groups. However, learning an instrument as an adult within a community-based group is not a new phenomenon. There have been adult learning opportunities in well-developed organizations such as the East London Late Starters Orchestra (ELLSO) in the U.K. and the New Horizons International Music Association (NHIMA) in the U.S.A. for over thirty years or so. ELLSO started as a result of a program in the London borough of Tower Hamlets in the early 1980s for children to learn string instruments in large groups (Nelson 1985). The parents of the children wanted to learn too, and ELLSO was born (http://www.ellso.org). The NHIMA offers a wide variety of programs of music making for adults who have had no previous music learning experience or who last participated in music learning in school. The association also offers a professional network for providers of adult music opportunities, which helps to raise the international profile of adult music making (http://www.newhorizonsmusic. org).

The NHIMA is built on the philosophy that anyone and everyone can participate in music making activities. For many people, however, the last time they were able to access music making was at elementary school. In the U.K., school music has not necessarily been the biggest or only influence in adults' childhood musical lives. Pitts (2012) found that different generations of adults in the U.K. were more likely to have had strong musical influences at home and outside of school than others, and this to some extent fueled their musical activity in adulthood. Statistical information regarding the take up of school music qualifications in the U.K. suggests that there is a population of adults who participated in secondary school music to the age of sixteen, yet did not want to continue their musical studies at a higher level. A 2012 U.K. government report noted that 7 percent of the school population in England took the GCSE Music qualification at sixteen, and 1 percent of the school population in England took the A-level Music qualification at eighteen (Ofsted 2012).

In considering the needs of older music learners, Dabback and Smith (2012) highlight programs that focus on music mastery as being common within opportunities provided for adults. However, music mastery might not necessarily be the aim of the adult or the reason why they have chosen music making as a leisure activity. If a person did not want to study music mastery at school, why might it be assumed that they want to study music mastery as an adult? Perkins, Aufegger, and Williamon (2015) found that working with adults helped young tutors to realize that "learning music is not always about mastering how to read notation or to achieve technical perfection; rather learning music can . . . be about being able to make and enjoy music making" (86). The change of focus from mastery to enjoyment was a significant shift in thinking for the young tutors. Furthermore, they came to appreciate that focusing on making and enjoying music rather than technical mastery does not mean adults are not motivated in their learning or that the potential for learning and achievement is reduced; it merely changes the perspective of what achievement is.

There is a wealth of research demonstrating the impact of music making on the social and mental well-being of adults. From neurobiological effects of music making (Altenmüller and Schlaug 2012), the rehabilitative potential of music making activities (Henley 2015a; LaGasse and Thaut 2012), interdisciplinary understandings of musical flourishing (Ansdell and DeNora 2012), and the impact of music making for aging adults (Creech et al. 2013), research is bringing together new understandings of the relationship between music making and *being*.

Many, although by no means all, beginner adult musical learning opportunities are housed within continuing education programs. There has been little research into the ways adult music learning may be distinct from that of younger learners (Myers 2012). What, precisely, does it mean to *be* a continuing learner, for example? Many models of musical development show that musicianship involves continual development. In their exploration of the process of learning to play an instrument, Hallam and Bautista (2012) outline the theory of Developing Expertise. A person develops their expertise with continued exposure to musical opportunities, progressively building skills, knowledge, and understanding. Yet, adults who have played for some years in an ensemble often appear to "stand still" in their learning and not progress beyond a certain place in their playing. The process of developing expertise requires a reconceptualization as the learner progresses. Interestingly, this reconceptualization needs to be generated by the learner; the learner needs to have a concept of why and what they are learning in order to continue to develop their expertise. This would suggest that crucial to an adult's successful continuation in a music making activity is a sense of objective, and that the object will determine what expertise is being developed.

A Socio-Cultural Activity

My own experience of adult learning and music making comes from working within an adult learning program in England offered by a local authority music service. The program began in 2002, starting with a wind band and string orchestra. Within five years, the program expanded to offer a variety of progressive ensembles from beginner and intermediate to advanced, with wind bands, string orchestras, jazz bands, and an orchestra. Each group performed at an annual showcase event, and each year the performances showed a progression in terms of the cohesion of the ensembles and the repertoire performed. Moreover, the number of adults joining the ensembles increased each year and retention was high. An initial internal evaluation of the program suggested that the adults involved enjoyed this way of learning and interacting with music making, and the music service deemed the program a success.

Working first as a tutor and then musical director within this program, I was interested in why so many adults chose to learn within an ensemble and why it appeared to be a successful way of learning for them. To explore these questions I conducted an in-depth investigation of how adults learn within ensemble contexts (Henley 2009). Using a qualitative methodology involving case-study and autoethnographic research, the aim of the study was to investigate the ways that adults constructed meaning in their music making. The study comprised six groups from across England designed as "learning ensembles," offering instrument tuition within and as part of the ensemble. A learning ensemble was understood to be an ensemble where the development of the instrument technique needed to play the music is incorporated into the activity of the ensemble, rather than an ensemble that assumes a level of instrument technique has already been acquired, or that it is being developed outside and separate to the ensemble. Rehearsals were observed and learners and tutors were interviewed, firstly in groups and then individually. The autoethnographic strand involved joining a learning ensemble from a musical tradition different from my own experience in order to investigate my learning processes. Data were collected over a four-year period via a research diary. This also enabled the creation and development of shared understandings in line with the social constructionist perspective taken in the research (Schwandt 2000).

The ensembles were a mixture of wind bands, orchestras, and gamelans, and the research aimed to explore the learning processes in depth, the role of performance in learning, and how musical identity developed and was used in learning. Acknowledging that music ensembles are embedded in socio-cultural practice, Cultural Historical Activity Theory (CHAT) underpinned the research. Building on Vygotsky's theories of the relationship between individuals and their physical and social environment, CHAT has been developed by Engeström (1999) as a way of viewing socio-cultural activity. Activity is understood and analyzed through the activity system, providing a map of the different ways that an individual interacts with various different tools that mediate their actions (known as *mediating artifacts*) to reach a goal (an *object*). Tools, or mediating artifacts, are understood to be the physical entities and cognitive structures and systems that a person develops and uses in order to achieve an object. For example, tonic *sol-fa* is a cognitive tool that is used to internalize the structures of the Western tonal system (Rainbow and Dickinson 2010). *Sol-fa* may be learned using hand signals, symbols, or memorized pitch relations. For a person who has learned *sol-fa*, the activity of singing may be mediated through the use of these hand signals, symbols, or memorized pitch relations; it is through using these tools that the person is able to learn a new song, therefore the tools mediate the learning.

CHAT acknowledges that the individual is not separated from the social world, and the interactions between the individual and their objective, mediated by physical and cognitive tools, also interact with the *community*, the *rules* of the community and the *division of labor* within that community. The community within which the learning takes place, the rules of that community, and the way the labor is divided will have direct impacts on the tools used for learning. If you are learning within a school that uses a particular methodology—Suzuki, for example—then that will impact on the cognitive tools that you develop and the way that you use them (Barrett 1995). In short, CHAT brings together the psychological and sociological aspects of learning in order to understand learning processes (see Henley 2015b for a detailed exploration of CHAT).

When CHAT is applied to learning within an ensemble, the different resources that learners draw on in their learning can be seen. The type of ensemble might predict what cognitive tools are developed, such as notations, aural skills, tonal systems, and so on, and how the physical tools are used; for example, different flute embouchures might be used in different types of ensembles to produce different sounds. The rules of the ensemble might or might not support peer learning within it; it may be acceptable to speak to a fellow player and ask them about a hand position or performance style, or it may not be acceptable to talk at all during the rehearsal. The structure of the ensemble might allow the labor to be explicitly divided between players so that there is an opportunity for different people to engage in the music at different levels, or players might be expected to practice outside of the ensemble to ensure that they can play the part given to them. Moreover, moving into different communities with new rules and a change of division of labor in, for example, a performance or a different ensemble may enable people to reconceptualize their learning in order to develop their expertise (Henley 2008).

Applying CHAT to the activities of the adult ensembles studied within the research outlined in this chapter revealed many "nonmusical" reasons for engaging in musical activity, and inspiring stories emerged of how adults had overcome illness, bereavement, stress, and even marital problems through immersion in musical activity (Henley 2009). The research gave an insight into the ways in which the adults used nonmusical identities to motivate them in developing musicianship, but also how they used music to develop and maintain nonmusical identities. Furthermore, it was found that adults move between musical and nonmusical identities many times in their learning. When a shift in identity occurred, the adult was able to change their objective and therefore utilize a different set of resources. The reasons for doing so were understood using the concept of *possible selves*.

Possible Selves

Hallam (1998) highlights *Self Concept* as a motivational factor in learning an instrument; within this she includes *ideal self, desired possible self,* and *feared possible self.* The theory of Possible Selves has been used to understand the different ways that people engage in music, such as the impact of music making on older adults' well-being (Creech et al. 2014) and boys singing (Freer 2010). The idea of the possible self was put forward by Markus and Nurius (1987). They describe possible selves as representations of "individuals' ideas of what they might become, what they would like to become and what they are afraid of becoming" (170). Within any activity, people construct a whole repertoire of possible selves that are "the cognitive manifestations of enduring goals, aspirations, motives, fears, and threats" (158). An image of the different possible selves that could occur as the result of an activity is the driving force of the activity: "the crucial element of a goal is the representation of the individual himself or herself approaching and realizing the goal" (Markus and Ruvolo 1989, 211). In order to reach what they desire, a person will construct a self-image of who they want to be, and it is the fulfilment of this self-image that drives the person to achieve. The more elaborate the picture, the greater chance there is of success, and a person may be able to actually feel what it is like to be their future possible self at different points during the execution of the action that takes them towards it: "By imagining a possible self, one may anticipate and actually experience part of the affect, positive or negative, associated with the end state" (230). The important point to note is that possible selves can be positive or negative. Furthermore, it has been argued that it is the balance of positive possible selves and feared possible selves that affords the greatest opportunity to succeed (Oyserman and Markus 1990).

When a positive possible self is balanced against a feared possible self a *road map* for the activity is constructed (Oyserman et al. 2004). This balancing can be explained using the example of preparing for a graded music examination. Some countries place a great emphasis on a level of musicianship being certified through a graded examination system. The graded examination system in the U.K. provides a framework for assessing performance through a progressive series of grades (1 being the lowest, 8 being the highest).[2] Assessments are made based on a combination of criteria relating to technical control and musical communication, and the grades provide a benchmark for ensemble auditions and entry to school, college, and university programs. This being the case, there are certain social meanings attached to achieving a particular grade. Being a grade 8 flautist means that a particular standard of playing has been achieved, but also this is often a requirement for an undergraduate music program or to join many youth and adult ensembles. A student may construct an imaginary picture of what it is like to pass a grade 8 flute examination and be a "grade 8" flutist: how they would feel, what it would mean to them, how others may view them once they have achieved this level and where it may take them in the future. This is a positive possible self. On the other hand, the student may fail that grade 8 exam. Another picture is constructed of the self as a failure. The person may be able to feel how they would react on failing the exam, how others may react to them, and what their self would be like as someone who has not achieved the level that they want.

The key to whether individuals succeed in their pursuit of a goal depends on whether they can balance the two possible selves and use the negative possibility to drive them on toward the positive outcome. If the negative possibility is too strong, then it may overtake the positive one and become a reality: "I can't do it; therefore I won't do it." If the positive possibility is too strong then it may lead to over-confidence and perhaps a lack of preparation. When the two are suitably balanced, the greatest success can be expected. The implication of possible selves to an adult learning in an ensemble is that having a view as to what a musician is alongside an idea of how and whether it is achievable is key to motivating musical engagement. Therefore, before exploring the musical lives of the adults in the study in relation to their possible selves, it is important to explore their concept of what it is to "be" a musician.

MUSICAL IDENTITIES

When the adults in my study were asked whether they would consider themselves to be a musician, the most common response was, "no way I'm a musician" or "I'm a potential musician." John, Pat, Penny, and Andrew all give reasons for this.

John
Well I think a musician is able to play their instrument with a reasonable degree of competence. I mean, I view my son as a musician because I think he can play with a reasonable degree of competence, he has a certain amount of musicality as well. I think those two elements are necessary, both the ability to operate the instrument and a sort of a feeling for what you're playing. I think I have a feeling for what I'm playing, but it's the operation of the instrument that's the problem!

Pat
I think the actual word "musician" almost implies somebody for whom music is their profession, someone who plays in an orchestra for money. When you talk about somebody being a musician, that's what it conjures up in my head. And when people

talk to me about music I say, "oh I dabble in music" or "music's my hobby," so I don't describe myself as a musician although I suppose technically I am, because I sing as well. In the choral society where I sing, the standard's pretty high and we perform with professionals, both players and soloists, so in that sense I might say I'm an amateur musician technically.

Penny

Well. If you stick the word "amateur" in front of it, then it does make a world of difference doesn't it? I'm all too aware of the limitations to my talent and ability in that direction. I've got some God-given musical ability, I think I have because I learnt to sing and taught myself and at best it's a reasonable voice and a good enough ear in order to learn. But I haven't got perfect pitch by even close. But compared with my son I mean, I'm pathetic. He has such a good ear and such a good feel for it, a natural feel and natural ability. You know, children that I've worked with, that I see in the school are really, really able musicians. They've got a level of talent beyond what I've got. So it does put it all into scale.

Andrew

You get bores at concerts that have never touched an instrument in their lives; they know everything and they're unconscious incompetents. Then you get people like me that are struggling and we're conscious incompetents. And then the next wonderful step up must be conscious competence and then you get unconscious competence; that must be wonderful.

In describing their views of what being a musician is, John, Pat, Penny, and Andrew are making comparisons between themselves and people who they perceive as musicians. These role models are either children or well-known professionals who have reached an extremely high standard. It is not uncommon for music students to think that they are not musicians. Pitts (2013) explored the musical identity of music students during the transition from the last year of secondary school to the first year of an undergraduate degree program. She found insecurity regarding self-perception as a musician. In the group of first year undergraduates she studied there emerged:

Close connections between demonstrable achievement and musical identity. . . . Suggesting that to be a "musician" involves not just ability and experience, but must also incorporate a degree of recognition from others and a strong sense of self-identification with the values and skills attributed to this label. (Pitts 2013, 6)

Applying this to adult music makers who have a clear idea of who their musical role models are, unless the adults can self-identify with the values and skills of their role models, and others recognize it, they will never feel that they are musicians.

Defining the term musician is complex, and there are different ideas of what a musician is. Initiatives such as the *Every Child a Musician* (ECaM)[3] program provided by a London borough aim to bring musical experiences to every child living in the local area through learning an instrument within a group environment. The use of the term *musician* here seems to imply that anyone who engages in musical experiences is a musician. The growing body of research in the field of music psychology suggesting that every person is musical adds weight to the definition of *musician through activity* (Hargreaves, MacDonald, and Miell 2012; Lamont 2011; McPherson and Williamon 2006; Welch 2005), as do philosophical understandings of the way we engage in the practice of music and develop musical knowledge (Elliott 1991). But, as Pat describes above, the term musician can also mean somebody for whom music making is a profession. The view of *musician through profession* might appear to be clearly defined, but professional musicianship is multifaceted. There is a lively debate surrounding music teacher identities, for example, and the tensions that exist between teacher-identities and musician-identities (Mark 1998; Pellegrino 2009; Russell 2012; Triantafyllaki 2010; Watson 2010). With professional musicians participating in a myriad of musical activities as part of portfolio careers, and new opportunities arising as musicians become more entrepreneurial in their professional lives, the practice of a musician is becoming more diverse (Bennett 2013). Furthermore, the affordances that digital technologies bring to the development of musicianship and musical practice blur the boundaries even further, with musicians moving between different professional and practice domains as their careers develop (Partti 2014).

It would then be a simplification to suggest that a dichotomy exists between *musician through profession* and *musician through activity*. This is particularly apparent when the term amateur is introduced. Elkington and Stebbins (2014) illustrate the complexities of categorizing amateur leisure pursuits, outlining the distinctions between serious leisure pursuits, project-based leisure pursuits, and casual leisure pursuits. Furthermore, my own experience of performing in amateur orchestras consists of auditioning, being "tried out," and gaining a place in a competitive environment playing with other musicians who also carry out some form of professional music work such as teaching, directing other amateur ensembles, or paid performance work. Just as the term professional musician has certain connotations in some social contexts, so does the term amateur musician.

According to Hargreaves, MacDonald, and Miell (2012, 133), "The concept of 'being a musician,' and the development of our musical identities, are influenced by nonmusical factors within the immediate and wider social environment, in particular by the ways in which we relate to people around us." Therefore, in order to understand why people who make music do not necessarily categorize themselves as musicians, it is useful to consider musical activity in relation to the different musical and nonmusical possible selves that are constructed and traveled toward in the development of musicianship.

BEING A MUSICIAN

Mills (2007) explains that being an instrument teacher enables teachers to develop and deepen their own "musical knowledge and ideas" (11). Through personal engagement with music, teachers are able to teach musically by exemplifying certain "aspects of being a musician" in their teaching. These are:

- Creating, interpreting, and responding to music;
- Joining in performances that everyone feels proud of;
- Feeling "musical";
- Being moved by music.

She argues that these aspects should be present in any musical learning; therefore, they provide a useful framework within which to discuss the musical lives of adults who learn within an ensemble.

Creating, Interpreting, and Responding to Music

As previously discussed, a *learning ensemble* is understood to be a group that has been specifically designed in order for students to learn how to play their instruments simultaneously with learning how to play in an ensemble. As their note range extends, so does the complexity of both the music that they play and how it fits with the other ensemble instruments. They may start off playing simple beginner exercises and eventually move on to play full band or orchestral arrangements. The emphasis is on the students learning together while creating an ensemble sound.

Pat is a retired teacher and she has been learning to play the horn for seven years. When we first met she told me, "I've no musical background really except a daughter who plays." At first she took some individual lessons, but kept her horn playing quiet until someone she worked with "found out about my big secret, which I never used to tell anybody, and she said, 'Why don't you join [the ensemble]? It's just what you need.' And it is just what I need; it's great."

As it turns out, Pat has a whole lifetime of musical experience: "I've sung since I was 10. Not on my own; in a choir." Not only this, her husband plays guitar and her daughter "who plays" is a professional viola player. Therefore, for most of Pat's life she has been surrounded by music making. As a member of a choir Pat has sung with soloists and orchestras, and her experience of what a musician is consists of seeing highly trained individuals perform to a very high standard. When I asked Pat how she would feel if her group was taken away from her, she said,

> Devastated. If it was taken away I'd have to try and find something else to join. I mean, now I'm retired, if I hadn't found the horn, life would not be nearly so interesting. If you like, it's made my retirement. I wish I'd started it earlier, but then as things were, I mean when you're working, full-time teacher and all the rest of it, you don't have an awful lot of time.

Discussions with Pat revealed that her musical life is about social music making, about giving a purpose to her retirement. Her possible self may be a person for whom music is in their life, but she knows that reaching a very high standard of musical achievement takes a lifetime, whereas she has only just begun; therefore, the possible self of a "musician" is not likely from where she stands.

John is a software developer and his ensemble provided the opportunity to learn to play the trombone and make meaningful music when more traditional ways of learning would not have provided that:

> It's the instant gratification thing, isn't it? Within what is only a few weeks you're able to play something as a band, which is absolutely amazing. . . . And it sounded like music. You just can't believe it is possible because you know traditional sort of learning where you spend endless hours doing boring, mundane things . . . that turn you off even faster when you're an adult than if you're a child.

The notion that learning individually is not as musically fulfilling was a common theme amongst the adults. Janet was learning the cello and she echoed this:

> The fundamental thing . . . is that it's placed in the context of an orchestra from the first day. . . I think that is what makes the early stages of individuals' instrument learning very, very difficult, is the fact that you are doing these very basic, very rudimentary things in a vacuum. In this context, by the end of their first four hours, people who've never picked up a violin before . . . are doing something and it's making musical sense.

Lave and Wenger (1991, 35) write, "[L]earning is an integral part of generative social practice in the lived-in world." The idea that a person learns through the situation that they are in, and that the learning is a fundamental ingredient of the social world that they are a part of, is the essence of Lave and Wenger's concept of *legitimate peripheral participation*. As a person participates, their learning expands and develops. The more experience the learner has of the group, the greater their development. The learner belongs to a community of practice, traveling along different "trajectories," each holding a valid learning experience that is unique to the particular community of practice of which they are a part (Wenger 1998). In relation to adult learning ensembles, the key factor to learning is the practice of the community. If the learner has no desire to participate in social music making, then being part of a community of practice where the practice is that of learning an instrument on an individual basis may suffice. However, if the learner wishes to be part of a musical experience with others and join an ensemble, performing music in a social context, then they can only do so by being part of the practice of the social creation of music.

Many of the adults in this study purposefully sought out more music making activities as they moved deeper into their community. John explained his reasons for joining a second ensemble: "I joined the second group because I felt that . . . I wanted some more different music to play. . . . Just playing more really. I wanted to play more." Andrew explained that participation in a summer school with the person he sat next to in his orchestra "brought us closer together musically, and that should have a beneficial effect on Thursday nights." Yet, when talking about his desire to join a traditional Irish group, he revealed his fear of disrupting the music because of his perceived level of ability. This fear prevented him from joining in.

Unlike an "amateur" ensemble in the U.K. sense, as outlined previously, the emphasis of the ensembles discussed here is on participation and making music through learning together. Although the emphasis is not on perfection of performance, public perform- ing has a significant role to play in the learning process. The performance is a catalyst for the fusing of learning and practice; learning and the social creation of music are bound together in the performance as the learner applies their learning to their practice in a different context. Thus the performance provides both a source of knowledge to the learner in that something new is achieved within the performance, and a demonstration of knowledge that affirms their learning (Elliott 1991). However, it is fear of failure in performance that often prevents an adult like Andrew from participating.

Performing Music

In terms of possible selves, a performance can be a positive experience, giving a sense of achievement and realizing a positive possible self, or it can be a negative experience, having the effect of realizing a negative possible self. The benefit of performing within an ensemble is that the performance is shared between participants; if a performance does not go to plan for an individual, the collective achievement often outweighs per- sonal dissatisfaction with one's own performance. "What is painful at the individual level becomes a source of pride at the group level—a badge of distinction rather than a mark of shame" (Brewer 2000, 58). Through performance, the adult learner might get a glimpse of a negative possible self, but because it is in the context of an ensemble perfor- mance, they can still get a sense of achievement through the performance. It provides an opportunity for them to balance their possible selves.

In addition to two other ensembles, John joined the ensemble that I directed midway through the year. After each rehearsal he would tell me how he did not know where he was, how he was completely lost and how he was sorry and how he would try to be bet- ter next week. After his first performance with the group he said, "Although I couldn't play any of my notes, I knew that everything around me was working." He was dissat- isfied with his own performance, but he was fully engaged in the performance of the group, and to him the experience was "electrifying." This performance consisted of both his feared possible self—that of not being able to play a note—and his desired possible self—that of being a trombonist in a performing concert band. The fusion of his two possible selves in that one performance inspired him to practice and gave him confi- dence as a band member. As a result, he progressed from being an isolated trombonist to being able to integrate his part into the ensemble as well as playing solo sections with confidence.

Taking pride in a group performance, even when one's own performance was not bril- liant, is something that I have discovered myself as an adult learner. I joined a Javanese gamelan so as to experience learning in an ensemble as an adult and investigate my own learning processes, keeping a research diary of my experiences. This extract was written a couple of weeks before a big performance.

> I am so annoyed I can't play "Sumyar." I was just totally lost, couldn't remember the *sekaran* and couldn't get the *imbal*. I couldn't even get the basic bit right. I was rubbish. I just gave up in the middle and felt like crying. [The tutor] came over and explained some things to me and then we tried it again and it was a bit better but I was still rubbish. I just think the whole piece would be better if I didn't play it. I was really looking forward to [the performance] but I'm not now, not at all.

Here my feared possible self was acutely realized. Despite this, I did go on and do the performance and this was my diary extract afterwards:

> That was brilliant. Everyone was on a real high after the gig. That bit that I couldn't do. . . . I just smiled and kept hitting the thing! I turned round to [another student] at one point and said "Are we at that 2 yet," and she just turned round, smiling, and said "I don't know." We were both totally lost. I felt good about it. It was a good performance; I totally enjoyed it.

Regardless of wanting to give up a few weeks before the performance, I performed and even though my individual technical performance was not brilliant, it made me feel good. Without that performance I may well have given up after the bad rehearsal.

Other adults spoke of difficult performances. Marie explained her first performance on the oboe with her orchestra: "I was shaking and I thought, 'I don't want to do this; I want to go home.' I was tempted to just run and then I heard them say 'oh, where is [Marie]?' and I thought . . . 'I've got to do it' and I did. It wasn't very good but at least it broke the ice." Marie was able to overcome this, but some adults are not. For Mills (2007), motivation is crucial in being able to continue to engage in music making. She explains her belief that there is no such thing as a "nonmusician," and that the "degree to which one feels able, and the degree to which one *is* able . . . depends on the encouragement and support that has been received" (15). Marie described the approach of the conductor of her ensemble in relation to performance:

> You can make the most appalling noise and the appalling mess up and she will not say anything. It's as if she's playing . . . at the Albert Hall. I mean like [name] . . . plays violin, it's chronically out of tune and yet everybody loves [name]. It's a dreadful noise, she knows it and [the conductor acts] as if it's perfect and I think that's marvelous to be able to do that. She just inspires us.

Echoing the Rhythm for Life project (Perkins, Aufegger, and Williamon 2015), when interviewed, the conductor revealed that the purpose of performance for her orchestra is not so the performers can demonstrate technical perfection and music mastery;

rather, it is to provide an opportunity that enables the performers to engage in the music so as to feel musical without fear of technical imperfection.

Feeling Musical

Andrew likes to achieve and excels in all he does. Outside of work he used to run. He ran competitively for thirty years and, although modest about it, reached a fairly high level. However, after an injury he needed to find something else to occupy the space that running previously had, and so he started to play the violin. Talking about his learning, he told me, "I don't think it's really self-improvement, it's perhaps self-fulfillment. It's all about pushing yourself." Andrew is very self-driven. So why is he learning through a learning ensemble where some might argue that he would not learn as effectively as he would through intense private tuition? He said, "I'm sure that if I hadn't come here or something like it, I'd have just been . . . [pauses] . . . it's a bit like learning to touch type, you know, just going through the motions, whereas music is a much more rounded thing and there's a lot more to it than just putting fingers in the right place." Through playing in his ensemble, Andrew began to understand that he needed to "feel" the music: "I'm beginning to feel at [my group] that at least I'm understanding and feeling. It's definitely a feeling thing rather than a thinking thing. I think I can feel how the different sections bounce off each other."

As a regular concertgoer and having seen many professional orchestras and soloists, this is where Andrew's possible self was: "If I've ever had two fantasies in my life that were serious, one was winning the Olympic 800 meters and one was playing a concerto in front of a great orchestra. That's part of it. Part of it is knowing that it's worth doing." Andrew wanted to play with an orchestra and therefore the only way to really feel orchestral music, as he described above, was to learn within an orchestra:

> [My group] is played with others, full stop. You've got to watch your own music, you've got to watch the conductor, or at least be conscious of the conductor, you've got to be conscious of what's going on within the other violins in terms of tuning and playing, you've got to be conscious of what's going on for example in the violas or cellos especially, and then in the wider orchestra. And to be involved in one of the major symphonies must be until you get used to it, perhaps you never do, must be quite an experience really.

The way that learning within an ensemble increases feelings of being musical was touched on in a conversation with a group of adults who learn within a string orchestra:

> It's really improved my listening, which I hadn't really realized, I was in a shop with somebody and heard a tune that was playing and a couple of weeks later . . . I could remember it.
> Right. [*in agreement*]

And I think I would never have been able to do that before. And when I hear things
on the radio I can work out complicated rhythms a lot better.
You can isolate different strands.
Yes, isolating strands better. And that's something which has just happened.
. . . It's the difference between being musical and being a musician [*agreement from
others*], because I would say I think I'm musical but in no way I'm a musician.

According to Mills (2007, 15), "feeling that we can do music contributes to our ability to
do it." She goes on to suggest that when we are able to pay attention to music, we are able
to understand the evocative power of music and enable ourselves to be moved by it.

Being Moved by Music

When I am in the gamelan, I am surrounded by the most beautiful musical sound. The
sounds of the different instruments lock together to produce something that no instrument on its own could. I smile when I have reached the end of a cycle and I hear the gong,
or I am playing *imbal* and it is working and I know that we are playing as one. There is
a spiritual experience in connecting with each other in a nonverbal way, knowing that
although you do not know anyone particularly, you are as one; and it is the music bringing you together. The more I experience this, the more I let myself go with it. The more
I feel the music, the more I am moved by it. It is difficult to ensure that all participants
in music making are moved by the music that they are making, but Mills suggests that
tutors can "help to establish conditions where this can occur" (2007, 16).

Penny has had breast cancer. She fought the illness for five years and has now made a
full recovery. When I asked her why she joined her learning ensemble she said:

I'm not far off retirement. I suppose you've had a long working life and I studied a lot
to become a teacher and I'm academically qualified in sciences and so on, I got to the
stage, well I for one had breast cancer anyway, so you really do start to evaluate your
life, you don't know how long you're going to be fit and active for do you? Or how
long you're going to live. I mean, it's a depressing thought but it's true.

Penny had reached a point in her life when she decided that she needed to do more than
work, and so she took up the clarinet within an ensemble. The social nature of the
ensemble was an important aspect in her motivation to join:

I felt that all of my social interaction was with other teachers, as a teacher I didn't
have much social life outside of school anyway because of evenings being tied up and
everything. I thought "I want to meet other human beings who are not teachers." In
fact there is an awful lot of teachers in that band, so I haven't quite achieved it! But
it was definitely, you know, I want to widen my social circle, again, and that's a good
thing for people because if you're not going to always be at work, if you are forced
to stop work for some reason or you retire then you don't want to suddenly go from

having a life where you're with people all day to having a life of sitting at home having no friends and no-one to mix with and no hobbies.

It was an opportunity to participate in an activity that took Penny out of a stressful working life and enabled her to meet a new group of people and to relax:

> My job, you know what secondary school teaching's like, it is so stressful and your confidence is constantly undermined and, much as I love kids, in many ways it's now so hard to teach them because of all the other things that go on in schools, that I think I've become in some ways quite disillusioned with education. I do my best still or I'd get out. I consider I do as good a job as I can and I try hard to fulfil my obligation to the children, but it is quite depressing really working in a school. And learning, actually going out on Saturdays and doing something else it's given me something else to think about, talk about, something else to relax with. I love gardening, for instance, but you can't do that all the year because this time of year it's miserable, isn't it? And dark and cold and you can't relax out in the garden but you can get your clarinet out at midnight if you feel like it.

This suggests that, for Penny, music takes her out of a depressing working life, gives her a new social circle, and it has given her life new meaning after having serious health problems. Also, the development of her musical skill through the group has enabled her to surround herself in her own music making whenever she likes, wherever she likes; getting her clarinet out at midnight if she so wishes. In her words, it has "brightened up [her] life."

What is interesting with Penny and many others in a similar position is that the music is not necessarily the objective of the activity. For Penny, the music is the tool that she is using to relieve stress; it is the *mediating artifact* in her objective to move away from her feared possible self and toward a positive possible self. Penny's story highlights the idea of fluid objectives through shifting identities. On reflecting on her playing she related how sometimes she feels able to describe herself as an "amateur musician" and at other times she describes her playing as "pathetic really." Depending on her context, she changes her objectives through a change of identity: an amateur clarinetist, someone who "dabbles in music," someone who is using music for stress relief, and someone who does not want to be lonely when she retires. This in turn helps her to overcome frustrations, cope with difficult performances, and to motivate her to continue in her music making.

FLUID OBJECTIVES AND SHIFTING IDENTITIES

Julie explained why she joined her string orchestra: "One of the reasons why I wanted to take up an instrument was that I honestly thought that it would be good for my brain . . .

and I was told like if you do different things, creatively, you can work different parts [of your brain]." Julie's objective at the time of joining was clear. By exercising her brain through playing the violin she was producing music, but her desired objective was to use a new mental process. Therefore music was *mediating* the learning rather than being the *object* of learning; it was the tool by which she aimed to fulfill her goal, not the goal itself.

She explained that her objective changed over time and her goal became to make music with others. As her musicianship developed and she moved further into her community of practice, her objective changed and the tools that she used to reach her objective were her new mental processes. The mediating artifacts became the object and the object became the mediating artifact. Nardi (1996, 75) writes, "[A]ctivity theory recognises that changing conditions can realign the constituents of an activity." The changing condition of becoming more embedded in the ensemble caused the emphasis of learning to shift from learning an instrument in order to work her brain to making music in an orchestra. In other words, as the music shifted from mediating artifact to object she also reconceptualized her learning. In Hallam and Bautista's (2012) terms, this reconceptualization allowed her to continue to develop her expertise in violin playing.

This exchange between mediating artifact and object moving from nonmusical objectives to musical objectives is common (Henley et al. 2012); however, the exchange also happens the other way. Many instances were found in this study where the music shifted from the goal of learning to the tool of learning, usually at times of deep frustration. The participants talked openly about how frustrated they have been with themselves when learning their particular instrument and how they felt when they had done something "wrong" in front of the group. For some, the group provided a safety net within which to do this, as Andrew explained:

> I've been tolerated cheerfully [laughter] and that's important for somebody in my position. . . . I'd already tried another small orchestra thing and it didn't work at all, in fact I rather resented the fact that I was told that people that didn't stick it didn't have any gumption. I felt that at my age and my time of life and after all I'd done, I didn't need some formidable woman who'd never done music in her life telling me about gumption. So I was very relieved to find somewhere that I could at least get started.

When I started learning in my gamelan, the object was to experience learning an instrument within a group as an adult for the purpose of the autoethnographic strand of my research study. The music was a *mediating artifact* through which I strove to fulfill the *object* of autoethnographic research. However, as I moved more deeply into my community of practice, my objective changed: "On a Tuesday night I leave the kids, the husband, the house, the work, the routine behind and I envelop myself in pure music. I relax. I enjoy it, something just for me." Over a four-year period, I observed a progression in my possible selves moving from researcher to gamelan musician, but my research diary shows that when I was experiencing deep frustration in my own learning, I changed my objective. When things were going well, I was able to identify myself as a gamelan musician and use a positive possible self to continue; I can be an amazing gamelan player and this is what I need to do to get there. When I was too close to a feared possible self, I changed my identity, which changed the positive possible self that I was moving toward; it did not matter if I was terrible at playing gamelan—I was a researcher and in order to complete my doctorate I needed to continue playing gamelan. By identifying as a nonmusician in that context, I was able to continue with my musical learning.

DOES IT MATTER IF YOU ARE OR IF YOU ARE NOT A "MUSICIAN"?

Music has the ability to touch lives. No other reason to participate is needed than enjoyment, yet music can have a life-changing effect on a person who participates in it. This is music at its best. There are many complex reasons why adult musical learners do not class themselves as musicians, but maybe the key to understanding and conceptualizing adult music making lies in an understanding and respect for the reasons why adults want to make music but do not necessarily want to be a "musician." Janet explained, "I mean [music is] certainly a huge part of my life, in a way that it wasn't before. I think people are wary of using [the term musician] because it sounds quite pretentious in a way." She went on to say that "if a musician means being somebody who sees music as a vital part of their life and who really does have an urge to play as well as possible then I suppose I already am." It does not seem important to Janet whether she is or is not a musician; what is important is that everyone was participating: "We do what we can. That's the important thing and everyone does absolutely as well as they can."

In seeking to acknowledge and respond to the growing ways that people make music and broaden understandings of what it is to be a musician, understandings of why people lead rich musical lives but do not wish to classify themselves as musicians are also necessary. As the students in the Rhythm for Life project found, if you are going to enter a profession where it is expected that you will work in engaging different people in music making in different social contexts, it is important to understand the diverse reasons why people make music (Perkins, Aufegger, and Williamon 2015). Moreover, it is important to understand that musicianship is multidimensional, fluid, and relational. The research outlined above describes ways that people moved between different musician and nonmusician identities in order to motivate them in their music making. It would be interesting to see how far this is reflected in different kinds of music making. Fundamentally, if we want a truly diverse understanding of what it is to be a musician, we need to listen to and celebrate the music making of the growing number of adults who make music for leisure.

NOTES

1. All names have been changed for the purposes of anonymity.
2. Graded music examinations are offered by U.K.-based international examination boards as part of a suite of qualifications in arts subjects such as Music, Speech and Drama, and Dance. Examination boards offering music performance qualifications include ABRSM (www.abrsm.org), Trinity College London (www.trinitycollege.com), London College of Music (www.uwl.ac.uk/academic-schools/music/lcm-exams), and Rock School (https://www.rslawards.com/music/graded-music-exam). Examinations are offered in different genres, including jazz and pop, and also include ensemble performance. The highest level of examinations includes teaching diplomas as well as performance diplomas that are at a level equivalent to study at a conservatoire. According to the ABRSM website, they assess more than 630,000 candidates in ninety-three different countries each year.
3. "Every Child Matters," *Newham London*, http://www.newham.gov.uk/Pages/ServiceChild/Every-child-matters.aspx#NewhamsEveryChildaMusiciannbspnbsp.

REFERENCES CITED

Altenmüller, Eckart, and Gottfried Schlaug. 2012. "Music, Brain, and Health: Exploring Biological Foundations of Music's Health Effects." In *Music, Health, and Wellbeing*, edited by Raymond A. R. MacDonald, Gunter Kreutz, and Laura Mitchell, 12–24. New York: Oxford University Press.

Ansdell, Gary, and Tia DeNora. 2012. "Musical Flourishing: Community Music Therapy, Controversy, and the Cultivation of Wellbeing." In *Music, Health and Wellbeing*, edited by Raymond A. R. MacDonald, Gunter Kreutz, and Laura Mitchell, 97–113. New York: Oxford University Press.

Barrett, Carolyn M. 1995. *The Magic of Matsumoto: The Suzuki Method of Education*. Berlin: ETC Publications.

Bennett, Dawn E. 2013. *Understanding the Classical Music Profession: The Past, the Present and Strategies for the Future*. Aldershot: Ashgate.

Brewer, Marilynn B. 2000. "The Social Self: On Being the Same and Different at the Same Time" in *Motivational Science: Social and Personality Perspectives*, edited by E. Tory Higgins and Arie W. Kruglanski, 50–59. Philadelphia, PA: Psychology Press.

Creech, Andrea, Susan Hallam, Maria Varvarigou, Helena Gaunt, Hilary McQueen, and Anita Pincas. 2014. "The Role of Musical Possible Selves in Supporting Subjective Well-Being in Later Life." *Music Education Research* 16: 32–49.

Creech, Andrea, Susan Hallam, Maria Varvarigou, Hilary McQueen, and Helena Gaunt. 2013. "Active Music Making: A Route to Enhanced Subjective Well-Being among Older People." *Perspectives in Public Health* 133(1): 36–43.

Dabback, William M., and David D. Smith. 2012. "Elders and Music: Empowering Learning, Valuing Life Experience, and Considering the Needs of Aging Adult Learners." In *The Oxford Handbook of Music Education*, vol. 2, edited by Gary E. McPherson and Graham F. Welch, 229–242. New York: Oxford University Press.

Elkington, Sam, and Robert A. Stebbins. 2014. *The Serious Leisure Perspective: An Introduction*. Abingdon: Routledge.

Elliott, David. 1991. "Music as Knowledge." In *Philosopher, Teacher, Musician*, edited by Estelle R. Jorgensen, 21–40. Urbana: University of Illinois Press.

Engeström, Yrjö. 1999. "Activity Theory and Individual and Social Transformation." In *Perspectives on Activity Theory*, edited by Yrjö Engeström, Reijo Miettinen, and Raija-Leena Punamäki, 19–38. Cambridge: Cambridge University Press.

Freer, Patrick K. 2010. "Two Decades of Research on Possible Selves and the 'Missing Males' Problem in Choral Music." *International Journal of Music Education* 28(1): 17–30. doi: 10.1177/0255761409351341.

Hallam, Susan. 1998. *Instrumental Teaching: A Practical Guide to Better Teaching and Learning.* Oxford: Heinemann Educational.

Hallam, Susan, and Alfredo Bautista. 2012. "Processes of Instrumental Learning: The Development of Musical Expertise." In *The Oxford Handbook of Music Education*, vol. 1, edited by Gary E. McPherson and Graham F. Welch, 658–76. New York: Oxford University Press.

Hargreaves, Andrew J., Raymond MacDonald, and Dorothy Miell. 2012. "Musical Identities Mediate Musical Development." In *The Oxford Handbook of Music Education*, vol. 1, edited by Gary E. McPherson and Graham F. Welch, 125–42. New York: Oxford University Press.

Henley, Jennie. 2008. "Learn as You Play; Gloucestershire's Ensembles from Scratch." *NAME Magazine* 31–35.

Henley, Jennie. 2009. "The Learning Ensemble: Musical Learning through Participation." PhD dissertation, Birmingham City University.

Henley, Jennie. 2015a. "Musical Learning and Desistance from Crime: The Case of a 'Good Vibrations' Javanese Gamelan Project with Young Offenders." *Music Education Research* 17 (1): 103–20. doi:10.1080/14613808.2014.933791.

Henley, Jennie. 2015b. "Prisons and Primary Schools: Using CHAT to Analyse the Relationship between Developing Identity, Developing Musicianship and Transformative Processes." *British Journal of Music Education* 32(2): 1–19. doi: 10.1017/S0265051715000133.

Henley, Jennie, Laura S. Caulfield, David Wilson, and Dean J. Wilkinson. 2012. "Good Vibrations: Positive Change through Social Music-Making." *Music Education Research* 14(4): 499–520. doi: 10.1080/14613808.2012.714765.

LaGasse, A. Blythe, and Michael H. Thaut. 2012. "Music and Rehabilitation: Neurological Approaches." In *Music, Health, and Wellbeing*, edited by Raymond A. R. MacDonald, Gunter Kreutz, and Laura Mitchell, 153–63. New York: Oxford University Press.

Lamont, Alexandra. 2011. "The Beat Goes on: Music Education, Identity and Lifelong Learning." *Music Education Research* 13(4): 369–388.

Lave, Jean, and Étienne Wenger. 1991. *Situated Learning: Legitimate Peripheral Participation.* Cambridge: Cambridge University Press.

Mark, Desmond. 1998. "The Music Teacher's Dilemma: Musician or Teacher? / Das Dilemma Des Musiklehrers: Musiker Oder Lehrer?" *International Journal of Music Education* 32(1): 3–23. doi:10.1177/025576149803200102.

Markus, Hazel, and Paula Nurius. 1987. "Possible Selves: The Interface between Motivation and the Self-Concept." In *Self and Identity: Psychosocial Perspectives*, edited by Krysia Yardley and Terry Honess, 157–172. Oxford: John Wiley and Sons.

Markus, Hazel, and Ann Ruvolo. 1989. "Possible Selves: Personalized Representations of Goals." In *Goal Concepts in Personality and Social Psychology*, edited by Lawrence A. Pervin, 211–231. Hillside, NJ: Lawrence Erlbaum.

McPherson, Gary E., and Aaron Williamon. 2006. "Giftedness and Talent." In *The Child as Musician: A Handbook of Musical Development*, edited by Gary E. McPherson, 239–256. New York: Oxford University Press.

Mills, Janet. 2007. *Instrumental Teaching.* Oxford: Oxford University Press.

Myers, David E. 2012. "Commentary: Adult Learning in a Lifespan Context." In *The Oxford Handbook of Music Education*, vol. 2, edited by Gary E. McPherson and Graham F. Welch, 223–28. New York: Oxford University Press.

Nardi, Bonnie A. 1996. "Studying Context: A Comparison of Activity Theory, Situated Action Models, and Distributed Cognition." In *Context and Consciousness: Activity Theory and Human-Computer Interaction*, edited by Bonnie A. Nardi, 69–102. Cambridge, MA: MIT Press.

Nelson, Sheila M. 1985. "The Tower Hamlets Project." *British Journal of Music Education* 2(1): 69–93. doi: 10.1017/S0265051700004617.

Office for Standards in Education (Ofsted). 2012. *Music in Schools: Wider Still, and Wider*. Report No. 110158. London: Ofsted. https://www.gov.uk/government/uploads/system/uploads/attachment_data/file/413347/Music_in_schools_wider_still__and_wider.pdf.

Oyserman, Daphna, Deborah Bybee, Kathy Terry, and Tamera Hart-Johnson. 2004. "Possible Selves as Roadmaps." *Journal of Research in Personality* 38(2): 130–149. doi: 10.1016/S0092-6566(03)00057-6.

Oyserman, Daphna, and Hazel Markus. 1990. "Possible Selves in Balance: Implications for Delinquency." *Journal of Social Issues* 46(2): 141–157.

Partti, Heidi. 2014. "Cosmopolitan Musicianship under Construction: Digital Musicians Illuminating Emerging Values in Music Education." *International Journal of Music Education* 32(1): 3–18. doi: 10.1177/0255761411433727.

Pellegrino, Kristen. 2009. "Connections between Performer and Teacher Identities in Music Teachers: Setting an Agenda for Research." *Journal of Music Teacher Education* 19(1): 39–55.

Perkins, Rosie, Lisa Aufegger, and Aaron Williamon. 2015. "Learning through Teaching: Exploring What Conservatoire Students Learn from Teaching Beginner Older Adults." *International Journal of Music Education* 33(1): 80–90. doi: 10.1177/0255761414531544.

Pitts, Stephanie E. 2012. *Chances and Choices: Exploring the Impact of Music Education*. New York: Oxford University Press.

Rainbow, Bernarr, and Peter Dickinson. 2010. *Bernarr Rainbow on Music: Memoirs and Selected Writings*. Woodbridge: Boydell and Brewer.

Russell, Joshua A. 2012. "The Occupational Identity of In-Service Secondary Music Educators Formative Interpersonal Interactions and Activities." *Journal of Research in Music Education* 60(2): 145–165. doi: 10.1177/0022429412445208.

Schwandt, Thomas A. 2000. "Three Epistemological Stances for Qualitative Inquiry." *Handbook of Qualitative Research* 2: 189–213.

Triantafyllaki, Angeliki. 2010. "'Workplace Landscapes' and the Construction of Performance Teachers' Identity: The Case of Advanced Music Training Institutions in Greece." *British Journal of Music Education* 27(2): 185–201. doi: 10.1017/S0265051710000082.

Watson, Amanda. 2010. "Musicians as Instrumental Music Teachers: Issues from an Australian Perspective." *International Journal of Music Education* 28(2): 193–203. doi: 10.1177/0255761410362939.

Welch, Graham F. 2005. "We Are Musical." *International Journal of Music Education* 23(2): 117–120.

Wenger, Étienne. 1998. *Communities of Practice: Learning, Meaning, and Identity*. Cambridge: Cambridge University Press.

Wertsch, James V. 2007. "Mediation." In *The Cambridge Companion to Vygotsky*, edited by Harry Daniels, Michael Cole, and James V. Wertsch, 178–192. Cambridge: Cambridge University Press.

CHAPTER 13

....

POPULAR MUSIC MAKING
AND YOUNG PEOPLE

Leisure, Education, and Industry

....

ZACK MOIR

INTRODUCTION

....

IT is safe to assume that those reading this volume will have an understanding of, or interest in finding out, what is meant by the term "leisure." That said, it would be useful to discuss this briefly by way of eliminating any ambiguity with regard to the way in which it is used in this chapter. Clearly the term is one that is used differently depending on context and can relate to the ways in which people categorize their time (i.e., leisure time versus work time) or their activities (i.e., leisure pursuits versus employment or other obligations). Although it may be the case that leisure is generally understood as "free time," this is perhaps overly simplistic, as the very notion of *free* time is intrinsically linked to work and other obligations.

As Frith explains, "leisure is a particularly complex organization of free time, related to the organization of work itself" (1981, 249). Drawing on the work of historians of leisure, Frith goes on to suggest that the emergence of the concept of leisure is closely linked to the development of industrial capitalism. As industrial production developed and work became closely linked to factories and specific machinery, workers were increasingly subject to the social organization of the factory. Progressively, the notion of leisure was no longer associated with occasional communal events such as carnivals or festivals, but, rather, with the idea of "non-work" (250); that is, the daily or weekly time in which one is not engaged in paid employment. This conception of leisure is useful in considering the organization and categorization of one's time in relation to work; however, this is not simply to say that "nonwork" is synonymous with leisure. While not engaged in the activities we are employed to do, we may also be required to perform tasks that would be difficult to define as "leisure." For example, when someone returns home from work they may have to clean their house or wash their car; although such activities will take place in nonwork or "free" time (e.g., evenings or weekends), we would be unlikely to describe them as *leisure*.

As Stebbins (2014a, n.p.) suggests, "One can examine life's ordinary activities according to three domains: work, nonwork obligation, and leisure." The example above of cleaning the house or washing the car during free (i.e., nonwork) time would be classed as nonwork obligation—that is to say, an activity (likely disagreeable) that one has to do out with work. Leisure is thus defined by Stebbins as "Un-coerced, contextually framed activity engaged in during free time, which people want to do and, using their abilities and resources, actually do in either a satisfying or a fulfilling way (or both)." Work in this case refers to the activities one is employed to do in order to gain an income. However, for the purposes of this chapter, given that the focus is on young people, use of the term "work" (and by extension, nonwork) will also refer to courses or programs of compulsory and postcompulsory education. As Roberts (1997, 150) notes when discussing trends in work, education, and leisure, "young people's time that has become surplus to productive requirements has mostly been absorbed by other forms of work. . . . [I]n education . . . this work is typically unpaid, but it is still work." When using the term *leisure*, I do so in reference to Stebbins's conception of the term as outlined above. I believe it serves as a helpful and thought-provoking framework with which one might understand the leisure music activity of young people. Additionally, it brings to light an interesting issue relating to the blurred line between activities that one might class as leisure on one hand and, on the other, activities, practices, and behaviors that may be seen as crucial in the development of the careers of burgeoning music professionals—particularly those involved in popular music.

This chapter considers some issues relating to the nature of music making as leisure among young people and highlights relationships with education and industry. In exploring these interrelated areas, I draw on my practical experience of teaching popular music in further- and higher-education institutions and of running youth music projects.[1] One particular project that will serve as a source of information for this chapter is a youth music initiative that affords young musicians, aged up to twenty-five years, an opportunity to work with music industry mentors, including professional musicians, composers, and audio engineers, over a six-month period in order to write, record, produce, publicize, and sell their own music. This project is based in Edinburgh, U.K., and involves participants from all over Scotland.[2] Throughout the chapter I present qualitative data gathered from interviews with eight young people (aged sixteen to eighteen) who recently participated in this project in order to highlight the interconnected nature of leisure, education, and industry, and their impact on the musical activity of young people. Individual semistructured interviews were conducted with each of these musicians; interview topics covered related to four main areas: music education, music performance, the music industry, and musical creativity. All names are pseudonyms to preserve the anonymity of the interviewees.

POPULAR MUSIC AS LEISURE

For a great many people, music has become so embedded in everyday life that it is an almost ubiquitous phenomenon that permeates all areas of their social and cultural lives, intentionally or otherwise (see, e.g., DeNora 2000). Popular music is frequently used in shops, bars, cafés, and restaurants to create an atmosphere or ambience that suits or enhances the mood and style of the establishment; it is used in advertising on television, radio, and, increasingly, on the Internet; it is used in television and cinema soundtracks; it is played at sporting events and is often also "piped" into other large public spaces, such as train stations and airports. One might go as far as to suggest that popular music is *expected* in such environments. As Bennett suggests, it seems to have become "part of the urban soundscape" (2005, 333). In this sense we might say that, due to its ubiquity, popular music has become something of a sonic backdrop to many areas of our life and particularly those activities that we might class as leisure.

The aforementioned are examples of the ways in which people may experience popular music in environments in which they have little (if any) control over the music to which they are exposed. Clearly, however, engagement with music is not in every case simply a passive phenomenon, and for many people, listening to and engaging with popular music extends far beyond what may be described as a leisure pursuit or as a "sonic backdrop," such that it is an integral part of their life and conception of self. One issue that is particularly important is the idea that music in general, but arguably popular music in particular (especially among young people), can serve as a tool with which a listener can construct or manipulate an environment designed to reinforce and project their personal values or perceived self-image. Although people use music in a multitude of different ways, Frith (1987) suggests that there are four main functions of popular music: to create a form of self-definition, to create a way to manage and balance private and public emotional life, to shape and construct popular memory thus organizing one's private sense of time, and to provide a feeling of ownership or possession in a musical sense. DeNora (2000, 62) suggests that music can serve as a way in which people regulate themselves as aesthetic agents in their everyday lives. Although this is in reference to the consumptive uses of music, these functions are no less applicable when considering other ways in which people engage with music—for example, through performance.

Many scholars have written extensively about the value of popular music, its place within society, and the importance it has in people's lives (see, e.g., Frith 1987, 1996, 2001; Green 1988; MacDonald, Hargreaves and Meill 2002; Negus 1996; Shuker 2007). Generally speaking, however, the majority of this literature pertains to passive engagement with popular music or music as "passive entertainment" (Stebbins 2013, 144), that is, people engaging "passively" or in an "inactive" way. As Mantie notes, "it seems self-evident that a good many people do find leisure in music and music-making" (2013, 135); however, music making, when considered as leisure, is a cultural and social phenomenon that seems to enjoy interesting and complex relationships with education, industry, and commerce—particularly so when we consider people involved in making *popular music* as leisure.

MUSIC EDUCATION *AS* LEISURE

Although music is a part of the school curriculum in many countries around the world, it is also the case that a great many people engage in forms of music education as cocurricular activity, extracurricular activity or, indeed, as a leisure pursuit. Examples may include students receiving instrumental lessons in school, playing in school bands, orchestras, or ensembles, attending summer schools, and so on. However, there is an interesting distinction to be made between those activities that would be considered as cocurricular or extracurricular and those that we may be more likely to define as *leisure* pursuits.

The Associated Board of the Royal Schools of Music (ABRSM) recently published research that provides interesting and encouraging insight into the teaching, learning, and playing of musical instruments in the U.K. The key finding of this work is an increase, in recent years, in the number of children and adults learning a musical instrument and making music. Among the findings, it is reported that 40 percent of the children surveyed are "making music outside of school: for fun, with friends, at festivals and in other ways" (ABRSM 2014, 4). While it is undoubtedly true that many people engaged in formal cocurricular or extracurricular music instruction in schools and other educational institutions will find their activity "fun" (4) or "fulfilling" (Stebbins 2014b), it is likely that they will be organized and facilitated by adults and probably also linked to specific educational or social goals. As such, they can be described as "structured activities" (Fletcher, Nickerson, Wright 2003, 642) and their structured and organized nature may be said to detract from the autonomy of the participants. In pursuing such activities, students are likely to encounter external pressure from people in positions of authority (e.g., teachers and parents) to practice or attend group rehearsals, for example—something that is very different from the type of pressure exerted by peers or, indeed, their own conscience. This chapter is concerned with the autodidacticism and self-directed forms of music education in which young people engage voluntarily in their "free" time.

MUSICAL EXPLORATIONS

It is not uncommon for children (and many adults for that matter) to experiment with instruments. Think, for example, of a child pushing the keys of a piano or strumming the strings of a guitar. These people are undoubtedly finding some sort of pleasure in the activity. This sort of *dabbling* may be considered as a type of play; that is, disinterested activity (i.e., there is no long-term goal) "engaged in for its own sake, for curiosity, for hedonic experience" (Stebbins 2013, 147). Green (2002, 22) also provides the example of people experimenting with playing some notes on instruments and of children "bang-ing" objects rhythmically, but frames such activity not as disinterested play but as the beginnings of musical exploration. She states that for those who progress beyond this phase of musical enculturation, there is often a "fork in the road" (22)—one path lead-ing to formal "Western" music education, and the other to continued and increasingly sophisticated explorations of sound.

Green's "fork in the road" analogy hints at the duality of educational experiences of many young popular musicians. It must be stressed that these paths are not mutually exclusive (Green 2002, 59) and, more and more frequently, people find that their musi-cal activity and education may incorporate aspects of both formal, structured "tradi-tional" music education (i.e., the grade system in the U.K. and playing in school training orchestras, etc.) and exploratory, experimental ventures into informal music learning. Folkestad (2006, 135) suggests that we should not think about the issue of formal and informal education as a dichotomy, but rather as "the two poles of a continuum" and states that both the formal and the informal aspects of learning (to varying degrees) interact in "most learning situations" (135). Similarly, Smith refers to "hybridized learn-ing" (2013a, 26–32), stating, "Some learning involves teaching, while other learning does not. It is all part of enculturation" (52).

From a personal perspective, this accurately describes my experience of music educa-tion, particularly during my secondary school years, and it is clearly the case for many of the young musicians with whom I work (regardless of educational context). However, the reality for many of my students and project participants is that the structured or for-mal aspect of their music education is often dissatisfying, unengaging, and perceived as irrelevant to the music that they are interested in and want to play. For example, a recent participant in the aforementioned youth music project noted the following when dis-cussing his school-based music education:

> I only get a certain type of music education there [school], you know, like learning why Baroque music sounds different to Romantic music—not much use to me, really. I learn most from just putting on the songs that I like and trying to play along— I sometimes get the tab too and work it out from there but . . . I don't know . . . that feels like I'm *actually learning* music.[3] (John, seventeen-year-old guitarist)

Jill, who received formal school-based music instruction in vocals, bass, guitar, and drum kit, made a similar comment in relation to the difference between in-school music lessons and her independent self-directed music education:

> I watch loads of "tuts" [tutorials] on YouTube. Sometimes they're teaching you how to play chords or how to strum, or something, but some teach you to play songs and you're meant to play along . . . that's more fun than the boring stuff we do in school! (Jill, eighteen-year-old multi-instrumentalist)

These quotes are typical of conversations I have with young people who are primar-ily interested in learning about and making popular music. They both make a clear distinction between school music education and the (self-directed) learning that they are engaged in while not in school. Also, they highlight the fact that some approaches to music education are viewed by individual learners as more useful, relevant, or interesting than others, based on their prior experience and aesthetic motivations. It is important to note that an apparent dissatisfaction with school-based music education in the U.K. has encouraged these young people to *voluntarily* engage in self-directed, autonomous learning in their nonwork time. These excerpts provide examples of pupils who, to use Green's analogy of the fork in the road, seem to follow both paths and could be described as bimusical. This is to say that both of the pupils receive formal music lessons in school, but each felt that the more valuable "lessons" and educational experiences came in the form of their more experimental, self-directed, exploratory pursuits.

I argue that young people pursuing popular music on their own time are engaging in music education *as* leisure. To refer again to Stebbins's definition (above) we can say that the activities described by these interviewees fit his concept of leisure perfectly, in that they are "uncoerced," take place in free-time, and are satisfying or fulfilling for the participants, who do not view this activity as an obligation.

How then, does the concept of music education *as* leisure (i.e., people engaging in educational processes and practices *as* leisure pursuits) affect our understanding of such activity or practice? Does this, to borrow a phrase from Mantie's discussion of the rhetoric surrounding lifelong learning and recreational pursuits, change the role of people "from doers into learners" (2012, 225)? If so, does this have an influence on the goals, motivations, and social relations of the participants, and does it impact on the ways in which they conceive of themselves (i.e., as learners, rather than participants)?

Although in some contexts it may be the case that engaging in education *as* leisure may turn "doers into learners" (Mantie 2012, 225), it would seem that the interview extracts above do not necessarily reflect this. I believe that they are actually indicative of people seeking to gain knowledge and experience, and developing skills for fun or pleasure, often with the idea that these skills will be useful to them in their leisure-time music making activities, such as writing music or playing in bands. They are, in this sense, simultaneously doers and learners. In other words, these young people are engaging in self-directed learning (*as* leisure) but are doing so in order to *become* participants. By learning about popular music and developing the skills and knowledge required to play certain techniques or styles, they are preparing themselves to be able to participate in a way that will "provide the sociability, personal pleasure, challenge and fulfillment usually associated with other leisure activities" (Blackshaw 2010, 126), and thus we might describe their activities as "leisure education."

LEARNING TO PLAY AND PLAYING TO LEARN

Both of the interviewees above mentioned "playing along" with music. Although unlikely to surprise anyone with a background in popular music, it is important to highlight because it is (in my opinion) one of the first and most fundamental steps in the development of vital aural skills, music theory, improvisation, and composition techniques required to be a successful popular music practitioner.[4] As Green notes, "the overriding learning practice for the beginner popular musician . . . is to copy recordings by ear" (2002, 60). This is, I believe, important for a number of reasons, chief among which is that it allows young instrumentalists to experiment with sound production and techniques by way of exploring their instrument and its role in the given music. In this sense, the playing along or copying process is a key stage in which popular musicians develop their technical and aural understanding of the music they choose to work with. Paul referenced this, but also touched on the idea of developing an aural understanding of key and harmony through "playing along":

> [I]t's kinda cool, actually, because if you decide that you're gonna learn a new song then you just put it on your iPod, or whatever, and I get my bass and figure out the starting note. Then you can just kinda work out the scale or the shape they're using and get it from there . . . and usually play the riff . . . or maybe even just the chord bass notes to start with.[5] (Paul, seventeen-year-old bassist)

When asked about the process of writing music, Steve gave a particularly insightful answer:

> I suppose that when I want to write something for the band I just put on loads of songs and play along for ages—something usually comes out. So, if I want to write a heavy song I'll put on tonnes of heavy songs and, kind of, copy what they're doing—if I can work it out. Then I change it a bit or just try to make something up that kinda sounds close. (Steve, sixteen-year-old guitarist)

It is interesting to note the importance placed on being able to "sound a bit like" something (a song or a band, etc.) and how, in this sense, we may view imitation as the basis for composition and improvisation. The early stages of self-directed, creative music education and development seem to be consciously based on the works of others (Green 2002). Therefore, we can also say that the process of playing along and copying is useful in musical enculturation and the development of stylistic or aesthetic awareness. In purposefully copying the works of others, young musicians learn a great deal about the sounds or styles and techniques that are appropriate to their musical environment and, just as Steve alluded to, this can lead to the adaptation and development of musical ideas as a basis of composition.

Although this type of learning and development does occur individually, it can often be an approach taken by groups of players or whole bands by way of writing material or simply as a way to begin playing together as a leisure activity. Alex alluded to the idea of *jamming* (Green 2002, 43) as a process of group composition:

> [S]ometimes we all like a song and we'll say that we are going to write something that sounds a wee bit like it . . . by just, kinda, playing. Like, the drummer might start

playing something and we, sort of, layer other things on top that *fits* with it—if that makes sense? (Alex, eighteen-year-old guitarist and singer)

Observe here the idea that the musicians involved in this activity will "layer" other things that "fit" on top of other musical ideas. This, again, highlights the importance of listening and engaging with the compositional process by considering how one's individual musical contribution may adhere to the (perhaps tacitly) agreed aesthetic of the music that is being created and how this relates to the material that is being copied.

For most of the young people I encounter in my work as an educator, such self-directed "leisure education" (Blackshaw 2010, 126) activities have been (and continue to be) important aspects of their (informal) music education. Consequently, imitation is one of the main processes by which they have learned and developed and continue to explore the musical worlds in which they are working. By its nature, such a self-directed approach can be haphazard and the music that the young people engage with is usually restricted to bands, acts, and composers that they already enjoy, respect, and in some ways identify with (this is often also evidenced in their appearance and behavior). As such, their aural understanding is often limited to the styles of music that fit with their aesthetic and creative values. Although this is not problematic in and of itself, it may be suggested that this process could lead to a situation in which young players struggle with playing, appreciating, and identifying with other types of music. This leads to a very specific type of musical enculturation occurring: "idiomatic enculturation," perhaps. If so, it is interesting to consider how we, as educators and mentors, may be able to relate to and build on this if, or when musicians who have trained and developed in this way decide to study popular music in further or higher education.

THE PROFESSIONALIZATION OF MUSICAL LEISURE ACTIVITY: "WORK" AS LEISURE

In this section I consider a paradox that seems to exist in relation to the music making of young people involved in activities that may be considered as "leisure" (according to Stebbins's definition, above), such as playing in bands, making demo recordings, playing gigs, attending "open mic nights" (Behr 2012), and so on. Such activities are typically undertaken in the young people's spare time, that is, when they are not in school, college or university, or working, for example.

It is interesting to observe how some activities associated with music making seem to mark it as different from many other leisure pursuits. Let us consider a young person who engages in mountain biking as a leisure activity. In order to participate, she or he needs access to a bike, safety equipment, food and drinks, and may require transport to take her to the place that she will ride, and so on. If someone's chosen leisure pursuit is watching sport, they may require tickets for sporting events or TV subscriptions to allow them to see the action. They may feel more involved in the activity if they show their support by purchasing and wearing a favorite team's replica kit or other merchandise. The point is that many leisure pursuits can be expensive. This is no less the case for those young people who choose to form and play in bands; paying for rehearsal space, buying and maintaining instruments and traveling and gigging, for instance, can all be expensive elements of this activity. However, two important (interrelated) aspects of *making* popular music as a leisure activity (particularly in bands) come to mind that seem to separate it from other pursuits (such as those noted above) that may be classed as *hobbies*. First is the notion of income generation—specifically, the recognition that there is a potential for bands to make money, even if a very small amount, from making music and "behaving" as a band.[6] Second is the idea of drawing on one's skills and expertise in *making* something—craft.

We can view this in terms of Stebbins's classification of *casual* versus *serious* leisure. Casual leisure is mainly superficial and "consumptive and involves largely non-productive activities" (Blackshaw 2010, 41) such as watching sport, playing computer games, or going to the pub. Serious leisure, however, is a type of leisure pursuit that is "'craftsman-like' and built on the idea of the entitlement to enjoy the products of one's own labour" (41). Stebbins (1982) suggests that serious leisure activities involve perseverance through stages of achievement and the development of specialized skills and knowledge. Additionally, participants involved in serious leisure activities have a tendency to "identify strongly" (257) with their pursuits and will talk about themselves proudly and enthusiastically in terms of the activity. Clearly, then, the *making* of popular music can undoubtedly be classed as a *serious* leisure activity and may (as with photography, sculpture or filmmaking, for example) be distinguished from hobbies in that it is an activity based on creating or making and craftsmanship (see Smith, this volume, chapter 9).

Although "it is characteristic of serious leisure that its practitioners are not dependent on whatever remuneration they derive from it" (Stebbins 1982, 225), the potential for income generation seems to be valued by young musicians engaged in making popular music as leisure in two key ways. First, as a way to subsidize the aforementioned activities (rehearsal room fees, studio time, instruments, transport, etc.) that facilitate and perpetuate the activity. If bands are able to generate some income from performing or from selling recordings of their music then this can go toward funding their musical activity and other related practices such as the creation and distribution of saleable products. Second, if bands have CDs and merchandise such as t-shirts, badges to sell, a website, and (even better) music available on services such as iTunes and Amazon, and so on, this will give them a sense of credibility and "worth" among their peers and anyone interested in their music. This projects an image of success and professional behavior for the benefit of their peers, rivals, potential customers, bookers, and representatives from other areas of the music industry. As Tom (a seventeen-year-old drummer) noted, "[I]t's cool that my songs will be on iTunes—people who see it on there will think "wow, that's really pro[fessional].'"

Why, then, is it important for young bands and musicians to present a professional image and develop such a reputation when making music as a leisure activity? Surely presenting oneself as professional is something that is more comfortably aligned with conceptions of work, not leisure, which we may regard as the "happy, carefree refuge from our earnest pursuit of money and social standing" (Stebbins 1982, 255). As Kirschner suggests, "Every upwardly mobile band seeks to be more successful" (1998, 254); if this is true, we may postulate that appearing professional is linked to ideas of success. In the case of young musicians and bands, playing their music live and gaining an audience is often one of the most appealing aspects of this leisure activity. This is sometimes seen as a signifier of a difference between those players or bands who stay in their bedrooms or in school practice rooms and do not actively try to improve or engage in this activity publicly (thus reaching out to wider networks) and those who strive to develop and gain an audience. In order to get noticed by the industry gatekeepers (Hirsch 1972) who have the power to offer opportunities for your music to be heard by audiences it is important to present yourself to promoters and venues in a way that inspires confidence in your ability to perform and to interest audiences (and thus attract custom to venues). As John stated:

> I don't really see the point of rehearsing and trying to write songs and stuff to just waste it by never playing them to anyone. That's why I'm so mad about trying to get a recording finished—then we can use it to try to get gigs . . . and girls [laughter]! (John)

Additionally, we must consider the importance of personal identity as a motivation for engagement in this type of activity. One's taste in popular music can be seen as a badge of distinction, that is, a form of self-definition or to project a particular image of self to the world (Frith 1987; North and Hargreaves, 2008). As Cook states, "Deciding on what music to listen to is a significant part of deciding and announcing to people . . . who you *are*" (1998, 5; emphasis in original). This is no less the case for those young people who choose to *make* popular music as a leisure activity. Not only is it important for such people to be able to display their musical tastes and influences in order to develop a social image (North, Hargreaves, and O'Neill 2000) and to shape and regulate their peer groups (Miranda and Claes 2009), it is important to project a sense of *musicianness*. One way that this can be achieved is by mimicking the professional activities and outputs of well-known or famous bands and musicians, such as having a website, selling band merchandise, or posting music videos. Given that there can be considerable cost implications in developing such promotional materials, many young people choose to create their own. In most cases, engaging the services of creative professionals to develop and produce these materials is prohibitively expensive; thus, many young musicians decide to embrace the wide range of technologies available (and affordable) to them to produce materials that will help with the promotion of their music. Young people in this situation may be able to get a hold of a digital camera and some photo-editing software or use online website builders, for example, and will learn some of the skills that they need "on the job," as it were, often also via free online tutorials.

My uncle used to be into photography so he gave me a loan of one of his cameras. It was a good one and I figured out that it took videos too—so we managed to take some band "pics" and even made a wee video. They're probably shit but at least we can put them on Facebook and show people we're doing stuff. (Tom)

In recent years, the use of social media has become an important aspect of the way in which musicians develop a band or musician identity and communicate with and market to their audiences (Boyd and Ellison 2007; Weaver and Morrison 2008). Since the early 2000s, it may be said that a band web presence has become a commercial necessity (Dubber 2012).[7] Social networking sites allow bands and musicians to "distribute, and promote their own music" (Sargent 2009, 470). Research participants frequently noted that the main way they could engage with people who may be interested in their music, or with the music industry in general, was via social media (particularly Facebook and Twitter) and other self-promotion channels, including Bandcamp, SoundCloud, or personal websites and blogs.[8] Participants noted that they use Facebook, Twitter, and YouTube to post audiovisual materials of themselves performing, and information about themselves and their activities, including upcoming gigs or photos of rehearsals. The audiovisual materials posted were always self-created and typically showed music performed in their houses (usually their own bedrooms) or rehearsal spaces. The material was usually captured with devices such as mobile phone cameras, PC webcams, or hand-held video recorders and, as such, did not require expensive equipment or involve the services of other media professionals. When asked why they engaged in this type of activity, participants gave somewhat varied answers. Jill referred directly to creating an online presence and presenting an image of herself as an "artist":

[P]utting stuff online makes it look like you are actually doing something . . . people anywhere in the world can see me playing in the videos and follow what I'm doing on Facebook or Twitter. . . . It makes it look like you're a *proper* artist or something.

John also referred to building an online presence but was motivated by the belief that, by posting this type of content, there is more of a chance that he might be "discovered" by industry representatives:

[L]oads of people were discovered because they uploaded videos of themselves to YouTube—just look at [Justin] Bieber [laughter]—I mean, not the music, but he is very famous now and he started on YouTube.

In making popular music as a leisure pursuit, young people often also develop many creativities and skills not directly linked to instrumental technique or musicianship but that they view as hugely important in allowing them to participate with this level of music making and to feel engaged in the wider "music industry." In this sense, making popular music as leisure is, at least for the participants discussed in this chapter, about far more than simply *making* (i.e., creating or crafting) popular music.

The "Music Industry"

The musicians described in this chapter are, according to Stebbins's (1982) subcategorization of serious leisure participants, amateurs. They are drawn to a certain leisure pursuit because of its strong appeal. However, in contrast to other leisure participants (e.g., hobbyists), they desire to improve and develop themselves so they do not remain "players" or "dabblers." For these young people, the leisure pursuit of making popular music, and the associated nonmusical activities (e.g., self-promotion, selling music and merchandise, building websites, making music videos) becomes an "avocation" (258), and the desire to persevere, ameliorate, and succeed is "motivated by seriousness and commitment" (258). There is no contradiction in amateurs mimicking the behavior of professionals. As Drew suggests, "Amateurs share many professional attributes, if at less intensive levels" (1997, 449). There are many relationships between professionals and amateurs that suggest we should not conceive of these terms as a distinction, but rather, points on a "continuum" (Kirschner 1998, 252). In fact, it is almost inevitable that professionals in this area will begin their careers as amateurs, and it can be difficult to determine when the change in status occurs. As Frith notes, "In popular music, the distinction between professional and amateur is hard to draw and easy to confuse" (Frith 2001, 26). That said, it is important to highlight the phenomenon of young people (particularly those in full-time education) voluntarily using their free time to engage in activities that are generally undertaken as part of the employment obligations of professionals in the creative industries.

As has been noted, this phenomenon is particularly prevalent in young musicians who are involved in popular music. One proposed explanation could be that this is a result of the inextricable links between popular music and commerce. To copy or mimic professional bands or popular musicians in their behavior and output is to mimic some of the workings of the music industry, and many young amateur musicians choose to engage with it in this way as part of their leisure activity. As such, interviewees were questioned on their conceptions of the music industry and their perceived access to it as contributors and practitioners. Most of the interviewees stated they believe that the music industry is in a period of transition from an environment dominated by major recording, publishing, and promotion companies, to a more democratic sector in which people are afforded greater access as contributors.

> [T]he industry is, kind of, changing—you know? . . . [S]o people can do things for themselves without relying on big companies or spending a fortune of their own money on demos and stuff. (Jill)

Similarly, John observed:

> I didn't realize that you could just contact newspapers or radio stations to tell them about your music—I thought they had to find you . . . mind you, I don't exactly know how they would do that.

Both of these comments draw attention to the perceived agency of young musicians and the fact they believe that they have potential access to and operate within certain areas of the music industry. Also, both mention the idea of doing things for themselves with regard to producing and promoting their own music. This does not necessarily mean that amateur musicians engaging in making popular music as a serious leisure pursuit will suddenly "storm the charts," nor is it suggested that the major players in the recording industry are now obsolete due to the increased potential for DIY recording, dissemination, and promotion. This simply suggests that these amateur musicians feel empowered to engage in (albeit the lower levels of) the music industry.

Jones asserts, "Making music is an activity that occupies musicians; selling music *goods is an activity that occupies music businesses*" (2012, 2; emphasis added). Although, at least superficially, this is true, it is problematic when considering the commercial activity of many professional musicians who do not have careers that map neatly onto the traditional model of the "music industries" and amateur musicians alike.[9] There is an inherent lack of employment in the music industries that results in a "majority of musicians relying on self-employment for a large proportion, if not all, of their income" (Coulson 2010, 255). Coulson suggests that such individuals might be "'accidental entrepreneurs' since most of them did not set out to start a business" (251). It is true, particularly in the case of those musicians who have been described in this chapter, that both the "making" *and* the "selling" (along with the promoting and distributing, for example) are activities that also occupy amateur musicians. In this sense, individuals or small groups involved in making music and engaging in associated activities (see above) can act as musicians *and* music businesses simultaneously.

> [I]t's brilliant—now we have some music on iTunes we can sell it and make some money . . . [laughter] well, in theory! You know what I mean, though . . . *we've* done it all—writing, playing, selling, and all that crap—so anything we do make goes to *us*. (Paul)

All of the interviewees felt encouraged by changes in the business of music and believed that this, coupled with the ease of dissemination and promotion afforded by the Internet, might lead to a situation in which young people can be involved in the music industry at some level. Clearly these participants are not referring to the upper echelons of the international music industry; however, this type of entrepreneurial behavior is the norm for many self-employed professionals and does constitute an important sector of the local music industry. Smith poses an excellent question: "In our commercialized, media-rich world, have we become enculturated to equate 'musician' with 'celebrity performer'?" (Smith 2013b, 30). I believe that, for many people, this is the case. As Smith goes on to note, "Musicians of the future are coming from a substantially changed cultural understanding of what it means to be a musician." The point is that amateurs are able to sell their music in the same places (e.g., iTunes or Amazon), post content to the same networks, and receive attention from the same publications as professionals. Although this may not be an entirely new phenomenon, the ease of production and dissemination afforded by digital technology has surely made this easier and quicker.[10] It is fair to suggest that, while many people in this situation are unlikely to receive the same revenues as "signed" professionals, this does not negate that they are choosing to engage with the music industry in this practical way as leisure, and often at their own expense.

CONCLUDING REMARKS

This chapter has considered links between the music making of young people as leisure, music education, and the "music industry." It has described ways in which some young people choose to spend their "free" time engaging in what may be described as "leisure education" (Blackshaw 2009, 125) in order to develop skills and knowledge of areas of music which they believe to be unaddressed by school curricula. It has also considered the ways in which some young people choose to spend their so-called "nonwork" time engaging in activities that mimic the employment of professional musicians and other creative industry professionals. In essence, this chapter has considered the ways in which young people choose to engage in education and "work" *as leisure*—something that many would consider to be contradictory. As Frith states:

> [S]ince at least the 1920s, youthful styles and situations have been held up as general models for adult play.... Youth cultures, similarly, have been explained as leisure cultures, and the meaning of leisure itself has been taken for granted—leisure is "free time" and young people have more of it than anyone else. (1981, 249)

What is particularly interesting in the context of the discussion set forth in this chapter is the apparent contradiction between commonsense definitions and conceptions of leisure, such as Frith's above, and the activities and behaviors of many young people who are engaging in making popular music as a leisure activity. The connections between youth and leisure that Frith refers to are particularly salient in the context of the current discussion. If leisure is free time and young people "have more of it than anyone else," then we may consider that *electing* to work or to study during this time negates the concept of leisure—*particularly* for young people. Conceiving of the type of pursuit(s) discussed in this chapter as part of what Stebbins defines as a "Fulfilment Career" (see, e.g., Stebbins 2014b), however, reframes many activities that may be considered as work or study as "persevering along the four dimensions of effort, skill, knowledge, and experience" (53) that lead to development and fulfillment.

This chapter has provided examples of young people spending their nonwork time engaging in activities such as promoting themselves as "professional," trying to sell and promote the music they make and merchandise that they design and produce by way of generating income (even if negligible amounts), often by mimicking the work of professionals. Is it the case that such activities are merely obligations that have to be dealt with in order to be free to pursue the chosen leisure activity of making and playing popular music? This is doubtful, as the remuneration is unlikely to be sufficient to either fund the activity entirely or to free the participants from the burden of employment or nonwork obligations that preclude greater involvement in musical activities. Engaging in what could be described as *micro-enterprise* seems to be valued as an important and meaningful aspect of the leisure pursuit. This is potentially related to the "craftsman-like" (Blackshaw 2010, 41) nature of such activity when viewed as a serious leisure pursuit, in that a central aspect of the pursuit is the making or crafting of something (in this case pop music).

Perhaps this leisure dimension is a function of the inescapable link between popular music and commerce. In a culture in which popular music, advertising, social media, and television are so prevalent and interconnected, it may not be surprising that young people either want to, or feel pressure to, create, market, and disseminate *products* (whether physical or intellectual) and cultivate an image of professionalism and success. In conceiving of such people as amateurs (Stebbins 1982), involved as part of a Professional-Amateur-Public framework (Stebbins 1980), we can go some way toward reconciling the supposed work *as* leisure paradox, as it is expected that amateurs will fulfill similar roles to professionals and at times also "serve" the same publics.

How should we view youth popular music activities in light of music and leisure? How might we understand the leisure pursuit of making popular music? Does it necessarily involve playing, writing, and producing music? Does the leisure pursuit include the making, marketing, and selling of *products*? In other words, at what point do the types of activities described above stop being classed as leisure and start to become the early stages of a business or even a profession? Is this even an appropriate distinction to make? For the research participants discussed in this chapter, making popular music as a leisure activity involves a great deal more than just playing instruments. This may be because popular music and industry seem to be natural bedfellows, or perhaps because, for the young people I spoke with, such activity offers something of a developmental path or focus in what might otherwise be considered a haphazard or idiosyncratic learning process.

More work in this area is required in order to fully understand the relationships between this leisure pursuit, industry, and education. More detailed knowledge of the reasons why and the ways in which young people choose to engage in the types of self-directed developmental activities described in this chapter will provide deeper understandings of this phenomenon and may highlight areas in which schools, colleges, universities and nonformal youth music projects, for example, can provide support for those young people who are interested in this area of music making. One particularly interesting area for further study will be the impact on the field of popular music education and the development of popular music pedagogies, particularly when considering popular music and the role of popular musicians in formal education settings.[11] If making popular music is about more than simply creating sonic artifacts and potentially encompasses many associated activities and disciplines, then understanding this ecology may be instructive in the design and development of meaningful, relevant and inspiring popular music curricula at the secondary and further or higher education levels.

NOTES

1. In the context of the U.K., further education (FE) is a description of the education that occurs in addition to that received at secondary school (referred to as "Continuing Education" in the U.S.A., for example). This includes any level above compulsory secondary education and may refer to vocational training or foundation degrees undertaken as preparation for university study. Higher education (HE) primarily describes learning that takes place at universities and other institutions that offer academic degrees and professional qualifications. Although this distinction is, for some, linked to pedagogic approaches and inevitably results in value judgments, such debates are not of relevance to this chapter. For the purposes of this chapter, suffice it to say that such references are to study undertaken beyond secondary education.

2. The project, supported by Creative Scotland's Youth Music Initiative, comprises three stages: (1) a *pre-production* phase, in which the bands work with the project mentors in order to develop their ideas and create original material; (2) a *recording/mixing* phase, in which the musicians are given access to a number of leading commercial recording studios in Scotland and a professional audio engineer to record, mix, and master their music; and (3) a *publicity/release* phase, in which bands (guided by their mentors and other music industry professionals) release and publicize their recordings, ultimately selling them on CD and through iTunes and other digital outlets.

3. "Tab" is an abbreviation of tablature, a form of musical notation that indicates finger position on an instrument, rather than pitch. Often, when using the term "tab" young musicians are referring to a combination of this type of notation and chord or lyric sheets, essentially, some form of (nonstandard) notation that provides them with information relating to how to play the music. This is often only usable if the player has an aural knowledge of the music.

4. Clearly, the process of copying and creating pastiches of existing material is not exclusive to popular music. For example, composition students often spend time, in their early training, learning about compositional style through copying existing works or styles.

5. Regarding the use of the word "shape": it is not uncommon for guitarists or bassists (particularly those with little music theory knowledge) to conceive of scales and chords in terms of the shapes that the positions of the notes create on their fretboards.

6. The youth music project described in this chapter includes some workshops on making money from music. These sessions have a specific focus on intellectual property rights, collection agencies, and marketing.

7. Myspace, for example, was originally a social music site designed to allow independent musicians to communicate and share media with their fans.

8. I am aware that, at the time of publication, musicians are also using social media services such as Snapchat and Instagram to share "promotional" content.

9. For the purposes of this chapter, the term "music industries" may be taken to mean the tripartite classification of (1) recording, (2) music publishing, and (3) live performance.

10. Interesting parallels can be drawn with the DIY ideals of the punk movement in the 1970s, in which antiestablishment attitudes saw an increase in home recording, independent record labels, independent concert promotion, and fanzines, for example. In the case of the participants described in this chapter, digital technology and online communication have possibly made this easier and more efficient.

11. On the subject of popular music education, see, for example, Smith et al. (2016).

REFERENCES CITED

Associated Board of the Royal Schools of Music (ABRSM). 2014. *Making Music: Teaching, Learning and Playing in the UK*. London: ABRSM.

Behr, Adam. 2012. "The Real 'Crossroads' of Live Music: The Conventions of Performance at Open Mic Nights in Edinburgh." *Social Semiotics* 22(5): 559–573.

Bennett, Andy. 2005. "Editorial: Popular Music and Leisure." *Leisure Studies* 24(4): 333–342.

Blackshaw, Tony. 2009. "Leisure Education." In *The SAGE Dictionary of Leisure Studies*, edited by Tony Blackshaw and Garry Crawford. New York: SAGE.

Blackshaw, Tony. 2010. *Leisure*. New York: Routledge.

Boyd, Danah, and Nicole B. Ellison. 2007. "Social Network Sites: Definition, History, and Scholarship." *Journal of Computer-Mediated Communication* 13(1): 210–230.

Cook, Nicholas. 1998. *Music: A Very Short Introduction*. Oxford: Oxford University Press.

Coulson, Susan. 2012. "Collaborating in a Competitive World: Musicians' Working Lives and Understandings of Entrepreneurship." *Work, Employment and Society* 26: 246–261.

DeNora, Tia. 2000. *Music in Everyday Life*. Cambridge: Cambridge University Press.

Drew, Robert S. 1997. "Embracing the Role of the Amateur: How Karaoke Bar Patrons Become Regular Performers." *Journal of Contemporary Ethnography* 25(4): 449–468.

Dubber, Andrew. 2012. *Music in the Digital Age: Making Sense of the Commerce and Culture of Popular Music*. Bristol: Bristol City University.

Fletcher, Anne C., Pamela Nickerson, and Kristie L. Wright. 2003. "Structured Leisure Activities in Middle Childhood: Links to Well-Being." *Journal of Community Psychology* 31(6): 641–659.

Folkestad, Göran. 2006. "Formal and Informal Learning Situations or Practices vs Formal and Informal Ways of Learning." *British Journal of Music Education* 23(2): 135–145.

Frith, Simon. 1981. *Sound Effects: Youth, Leisure, and the Politics of Rock 'n' Roll*. New York: Pantheon.

Frith, Simon. 1987. "Towards an Aesthetic in Popular Music". In *Popular Music: Music and Identity*, edited by Simon Frith. New York: Routledge.

Frith, Simon. 1996. *Performing Rites: On the Value of Popular Music*. Oxford: Oxford University Press.

Frith, Simon. 2001. "The Popular Music Industry". In *The Cambridge Companion to Pop and Rock*, edited by Simon Frith, Simon, Will Straw, and John Street, 26–52. Cambridge: Cambridge University Press.

Green, Lucy. 1988. *Music on Deaf Ears: Musical Meaning, Ideology, and Education*. Manchester: Manchester University Press.

Green, Lucy. 2002. *How Popular Musicians Learn: A Way Ahead for Music Education*. Aldershot: Ashgate.

Hirsch, Paul M. 1972. "Processing Fads and Fashions: An Organization-Set Analysis of Cultural Industry Systems." *American Journal of Sociology* 77: 639–659.

Jones, Michael, L. 2012. *The Music Industries: From Conception to Consumption*. Basingstoke: Palgrave Macmillan.

Kirschner, Tony. 1998. "Studying Rock: Towards a Materialist Ethnography." In *Mapping the Beat: Popular Music and Contemporary Theory*, edited by Thomas Swiss, John Sloop, and Andrew Herman, 247–268. Oxford: Blackwell.

MacDonald, Raymond A. R., David J. Hargreaves, and Dorothy Miell, eds. 2002. *Musical Identities*. Oxford: Oxford University Press.

Mantie, Roger. 2012. "Learners or Participants? The Pros and Cons of 'Lifelong Learning.'" *International Journal of Community Music* 5(3): 217–235.

Mantie, Roger. 2013. "Music and/as Leisure: Old Wine in New Bottles?" *International Journal of Community Music* 6(2): 135–139.

Miranda, Dave, and Michel Claes. 2009. "Music Listening, Coping, Peer Affiliation and Depression in Adolescence." *Psychology of Music* 37: 215–233.

Negus, Keith. 1996. *Popular Music in Theory: an Introduction.* Cambridge: Polity.

North, Adrian C., and David J. Hargreaves. 2008. *The Social and Applied Psychology of Music.* Oxford: Oxford University Press.

North, Adrian C., David J. Hargreaves, and Susan A. O'Neill. 2000. "The Importance of Music to Adolescents." *British Journal of Educational Psychology* 70: 255–272.

Roberts, Ken. 1997. "Work and Leisure in Young People's Lives." In *Work, Leisure and Well-Being*, edited by John T. Haworth, 145–164. London: Routledge.

Sargent, Carey. 2009. "Local Musicians Building Global Audiences" *Information, Communication and Society* 12(4): 469–487.

Shuker, Roy. 2007. *Understanding Popular Music Culture.* New York: Routledge.

Smith, Gareth Dylan. 2013a. *I Drum Therefore I Am: Being and Becoming a Drummer.* Farnham: Ashgate.

Smith, Gareth Dylan. 2013b. "Seeking 'Success' in Popular Music." *Music Education Research International* 6: 26–37.

Smith, Gareth Dylan, Matt Brennan, Zack Moir, Shara Rambarran, and Phil Kirkman, eds. 2016. *The Routledge Research Companion to Popular Music Education.* Farnham: Routledge.

Stebbins, Robert A. 1980. "'Amateur' and 'Hobbyist' as Concepts for the Study of Leisure Problems." *Social Problems* 27(4): 413–417.

Stebbins, Robert A. 1982. "Serious Leisure: A Conceptual Statement." *Pacific Sociological Review* 25: 251–272.

Stebbins, Robert A., 2013. "From Dabbler to Serious Amateur Musician and Beyond: Clarifying a Crucial Step." *International Journal of Community Music* 6(2): 141–152.

Stebbins, Robert A. 2014a. "Leisure." In *Encyclopædia Britannica Online.* http://www.britannica.com/EBchecked/topic/335512/leisure.

Stebbins, Robert A. 2014b. *Careers in Serious Leisure: From Dabbler to Devotee in Search of Fulfillment.* New York: Palgrave Macmillan.

Weaver, Alfred C., and Benjamin B. Morrison. 2008. "Social Networking." *Computer* 41(2): 97–100.

CHAPTER 14

"PERILOUS BLESSING OF LEISURE"

Music and Leisure in the United States, 1890–1945

ANDREW KRIKUN

IN a famous scene from Meredith Willson's *The Music Man* (1950), the impostor-bandmaster Harold Hill admonished the community of the fictional town, River City, Iowa, in 1912: "Either you're closing your eyes to a situation that you don't wish to acknowledge or you are not aware of the caliber of disaster indicated by the presence of a pool table in your community."[1] In the number "Ya Got Trouble," he warns the crowd about the afterschool activities of the young citizens of River City:

> One fine night they leave the pool-hall headin' for the dance at the Arm'ry.
> Libertine men and scarlet women and ragtime,
> shameless music that'll drag your son and your daughter
> to the arms of a jungle animal instinct mass-ster-i-a!
> Friends, the idle brain is the devil's playground, trouble!

Hill concluded his sermon, "Gotta figger out a way to keep the young ones moral after school." He eventually convinced the upstanding citizens of River City that the solution for all their "trouble" would be the formation of a marching band.

Since the late nineteenth century, a number of American institutions, representing education, government, business, and nonprofit organizations, have put forward initiatives to encourage music making as a worthwhile leisure-time activity, an alternative to the unhealthy leisure of "pool parlors, social clubs, dance halls, crapshooting, prize fighting, pleasure parks, corner-store activities and street-corner loafing" (Rosenstein 1917, 75). This chapter provides an overview of the rationales, efforts, and results of public and private initiatives promoted by musicians, educators, government officials, businessmen, and other advocates to encourage active music making as a positive leisure activity in the United States during the first half of the twentieth century. Although some advocates recommended all forms of music making as worthwhile, many advocates strove to encourage the performance of "good music," in other words, music making following the practices of the Western European art music tradition.

MUSIC AND LEISURE IN THE
NINETEENTH CENTURY

As the United States entered the nineteenth century, the fledgling nation struggled to create a common culture. In his book *High-Minded and Low-Down*, music historian Nicholas Tawa (2000) described the breadth and ubiquity of musical activities encompassing all classes and ethnicities of Americans during the antebellum period (1781–1860):

> A traveler could journey anywhere, from eastern city to wagon train to California settlement, and find music encouraged and practiced whenever possible.... Little by little, the musical usages in the newly settled lands acknowledged, by force of circumstances, a dependence and trust in cultural equity for all. By midcentury the young American democracy, too, had articulated shared concepts of cultural beliefs and sentiments, in harmony with its principles of political and social equality for all. (Tawa 2000, 291)

It was also during this period that music education began to gain influence on the everyday musical practices of the American citizenry. In the *American Musical Landscape*, music historian Richard Crawford credited music educator Lowell Mason[2] with expanding the role of music education beyond the purpose of the refinement of church music. According to Crawford, "Mason's transforming insight was to recognize psalmody as part of a larger world of music, one of many worthwhile kinds of American music-making" (1993, 54).

> Music-making, his insight taught him, was not only an indispensable way to enter a state of grace in worship. It was also a pleasurable human activity: a wholesome, enjoyable way to spend leisure time, and a gratifying social pastime. And a society growing more urban and middle class was beginning to find the accessibility of musical experience a more urgent matter than the devotional concerns of an earlier age. Teaching, Mason perceived, could be the key to accessibility. (54–55)

In addition to the expansion of music education, the music instrument and music publishing businesses began to flourish, providing the necessary tools for both the music educator and all varieties of the amateur musician. According to Tawa:

> [P]ianos and melodeons by the thousands entered American parlors during the antebellum years. Failing these, there were violins, flutes, and guitars. As the years

went by and demand increased, native manufacture of instruments grew tremendously and the price of instruments dropped significantly. Their acquisition became all the more easy. For the penniless, homemade banjos, reed pipes, fiddles, and percussion instruments answered. (2000, 293)

Following the American Civil War (1861–1865), the popularity of professional wind bands, such as those led by Patrick S. Gilmore and the U.S. Marine Band led by John Philip Sousa, inspired both amateur and professional bands across the nation. According to Crawford, "a vast network of amateur groups, that like church choirs, were part of many Americans' musical experience, as both performers and listeners. Nourished by the spread of music teaching, the growth of the music instrument business, and the appetite for music at local functions, the amateur band provided amusement for people in towns and villages" (2001, 455). Hazen and Hazen (1987, 43–60) described a wide variety of amateur bands active in the nineteenth century, including town bands, industrial bands, institutional bands, lodge bands, ethnic and national bands, women's bands, and children's bands.

THE PROGRESSIVE ERA (1890–1920)

By the turn of the twentieth century, the rapid development of Tin Pan Alley and the rise of ragtime in the 1890s had transformed American musical culture.[3] Music publishers printed millions of copies of sheet music favorites, such as "After the Ball" by songwriter Charles K. Harris and "Maple Leaf Rag" by ragtime pianist-composer Scott Joplin, mainly for the vast market of amateur musicians. Several technological innovations introduced during this era, including the phonograph and the pianola (player piano), also impacted the nature of music making and music listening. In his article "The Menace of Mechanical Music," composer and bandmaster John Philip Sousa feared that the recent proliferation of the phonograph and the pianola would have deleterious effects on the practice of amateur music making: "Under such conditions the tide of amateurism cannot but recede, until there will be left only the mechanical device and the professional executant" (Sousa 1906, 281). Sousa painted a picture of a country rife with amateur music making, aided by the guidance of a legion of music teachers.

There are more pianos, violins, guitars, mandolins, and banjos among the working classes of America than in all the rest of the world, and the presence of these instruments in the homes has given employment to enormous numbers of teachers who have patiently taught the children and inculcated a love for music throughout the various communities. (Sousa 1906, 280)

First introduced in 1896 at Tony Pastor's Café in New York by pianist Ben Harney, ragtime soon became a national craze. "Within weeks after Harney's appearance at Pastor's, ragtime became a fad. Performers (mostly white) were playing, dancing, and singing this new music supposedly in the style of the southern Negroes" (Waldo 1976, 28). Concurrent with the ragtime fad, Americans yearned to play the music for themselves, and soon music publishers and entrepreneurial music teachers were seeking ways to profit. According to Jasen and Tichenor:

> As ragtime became part of the pop music scene, publishers had their own composers write easy-to-play rags for the amateur pianist. Ragtime was now big business, with schools like Axel Christensen's which advertised "Ragtime Taught in Ten Lessons." The large firms not only employed staff composers to turn it out, but bought rags from outsiders. The demand was so great that everyone had an opportunity to be published—amateur and professional alike. (1978, 134–135)

Ragtime composer and pianist Alex Christensen succeeded in establishing and franchising a network of music schools using his instructional method to teach ragtime and popular music. Establishing the first Christensen School of Popular Music in Chicago in 1903, Christensen soon opened four branch schools in Chicago; by 1918, there were branch schools in over twenty-five cities. He published a series of books and a magazine, *The Ragtime Review* (1914–1918), containing instructional material for both amateur and professional pianists. Even though both amateur and professional musicians clamored to master ragtime, most music educators trained in the European art music tradition refused to accept the genre as worthy of serious musical study. When Christensen moved his teaching studio to the Fine Arts Building in Chicago, the traditional piano teachers scoffed and tried to evict him from the building. "Christensen had demeaned their profession by his advertising, they said, and he was committing the unpardonable sin of teaching ragtime. When the landlord refused to remove Christensen, the teachers tried harassment, standing in the hallway during his lessons, chanting the junk man's cry, 'Any rags? Bones? Old iron?' " (Jasen and Jones 2000, 125).

The bourgeoning of the musical instrument manufacturing industry led to promotional efforts to spur sales by encouraging active music making. Piano sales grew from 171,138 in 1900 to a range of 220,000 to 365,000 during the 1910s and early 1920s (Litterst and Malambri 1999, 9–10). There was also a growing demand for more affordable and portable stringed instruments such as the banjo, guitar, violin, double bass, mandolin, and ukulele; wind instruments used in town bands such as the clarinet, cornet, and trombone; and pocket-sized instruments such as the harmonica and kazoo.

Charles Milton Tremaine (1870–1963) had worked for several piano dealers between 1889 and 1916, including a stint as vice president of the profitable Aeolian Piano Company, manufacturers of the pianola from 1898 to 1909. In 1909, he took over ownership of his father's company, Tremaine Piano Co., which went well until the company declared bankruptcy in early 1916. Later that year, Tremaine founded the National Bureau for the Advancement of Music with the cooperation of the National Piano Manufacturers Association and the Music Industries Chamber of Commerce. Active from 1916 until its dissolution in 1942, the bureau influenced the development of American musical culture, promoting community music, music in the home, music in industry, and public school music in a series of publications and events. Although his work contributed to musical instrument sales, Tremaine "insisted that he be allowed to serve all of music, not just the interests represented by those providing financial support" (Koch 1990, 269–270). As the director of the National Bureau for the Advancement of Music, Tremaine organized several nationwide activities in the late 1910s and throughout the 1920s, including music memory contests,[4] state and national school band and orchestra contests, music weeks, and industrial music.[5] The bureau, under Tremaine's able leadership, also published a series of books on a range of subjects, including music therapy, community music, and college music programs.

Concurrent with the growth of the popular music industry was the establishment of major cultural institutions in major centers of commerce, such as Boston, New York, Philadelphia, Baltimore, and Chicago, usually funded and supported by the local self-styled "aristocracy." The founding of music conservatories, university schools of music, and nonprofit institutions supported the furtherance of the values of Western European art music, creating a cultural hierarchy between the "highbrow" music of the upper classes and the "lowbrow" music of the middle and lower classes.[6] The development of this cultural hierarchy resulted in initiatives undertaken by professional educational organizations to promote a particular type of leisure music making rooted in the practices of the art music tradition. A number of educational and community-based organizations were founded during this period to help fund and promote active music making (as well as music listening and concert attendance) as a leisure activity, including the National Federation of Music Clubs (1898) and the Music Division of the National Federation of Settlements (1911). Other professional and trade organizations were instrumental in endorsing amateur music making as a leisure activity, such as the Music Teachers National Association (1876), the Department of Music of the National Education Association (1883), the National Association of Piano Dealers of America (1901)—which changed its name to the National Association of Music Merchants (NAMM) in 1919—the Music Supervisors National Conference (1907), and the National Recreation Association (1906).

During the Progressive Era, the women's club movement resulted in hundreds of organizations formed by women to create educational opportunities for women and to help alleviate some of the most pressing social problems of the time (Croly 1898; Gere 1977). "Wherever the public health, beauty or morality may be benefitted, there the Women's Club is quick to find its opportunity. . . . Women have the leisure, at least all the leisure there is, and they may wisely use it to look about them and discover the ugly, the unwholesome and the unlovely," one description explained (Ward 1906, 15). Women's clubs raised money to build local libraries, establish settlement houses, and promote literature and music.

At the Chicago World's Columbian Exposition in 1893, Rose Fay Thomas (1852–1929), the wife of Theodore Thomas, the conductor of the Chicago Symphony, arranged for amateur women's music clubs across the country to take part in the World's Fair Congress of Musicians. Thomas was given the title of Honorary President of the National Federation of Music Clubs (NFMC), which was officially launched in 1898 in

New York City. One of the primary goals of the organization was to promote and support American composers and performers. "Singing contests" were held between music club choruses, later to be expanded to festivals and choral competitions at state conventions. In 1905, the NFMC charter was amended to include men and men's music clubs. During the next decade, state music club federations were formed. By 1935, the membership of the NFMC had grown to 500,000 members (Ottaway 1935).

The community music movement as it arose from the Settlement movement[7] provided another impetus for amateur music making during the Progressive Era. Some of the first sites to include community music education were the late nineteenth-century settlement houses, beginning with the Hull House in Chicago in 1892. One purpose of the settlement house was to offer educational and recreational opportunities to immigrants living in impoverished and overcrowded urban communities. Johan Grolle of the Settlement Music School in Philadelphia emphasized the importance of amateur music making for all citizens including adult workers:

> Music is a valuable recreational factor because it employs a high form of self-expression; it brings various groups and families together; it makes racial cleavages less visible; it opens new avenues of thought, and it gives the wage-earner something to look forward to after the day's grind. (Rosenstein 1917, 75–76)

By the mid-1920s, there were 143 community music schools in forty-one cities, the majority of these being departments of settlement houses (Schenck 1926, 27).

An important component of community music during this period was the organization of community singing. Frank Damrosch (1859–1937), born in Breslau, Germany, was the son of the violinist, conductor, and composer Leopold Damrosch. The Damrosch family immigrated to the United States in 1871, when Leopold was appointed conductor of the German opera in New York. In 1892, Frank Damrosch founded the People's Singing Classes in New York, to offer affordable lessons to the community. In 1894, he established the People's Choral Union, "whose purpose shall be the cultivation of the love of music among the working people" (Stebbins and Stebbins 1945, 171). Damrosch insisted that the governance of the organization would be shared by its primarily working-class membership of 500. The People's Singing Classes continued to flourish and an outdoor concert in Central Park during the summer of 1896 drew over 50,000 people (178). Damrosch later founded the Institute for Musical Art in 1905, which merged with the Juilliard Graduate School to form the Juilliard School of Music in 1926. Damrosch served as the dean of the Juilliard School until 1933.

An early leader of the community music movement was music educator Peter Dykema (1873–1951). Dykema was the director of the music program at the Ethical Culture School in New York from 1901 to 1913, before becoming a professor of music at the University of Wisconsin and, later, chair of the music education department at Columbia University Teachers College. Dykema was also the founding editor of the *Music Supervisors Journal* in 1914 and was president of the Music Supervisors National

Conference from 1916 to 1917. With a strong background as a vocalist and choral director, Dykema was one of the main promoters of the "community singing" movement. According to Dykema, "community music is socialized music; music, to use Lincoln's phrase, for the people, of the people, and by the people" (1916, 218). In 1913, he was selected by the Music Supervisors National Conference (MSNC) as the committee chair to select twelve songs for group singing. The first pamphlet, published by C. C. Birchard, contained eighteen songs, including patriotic songs such as "America" and "The Star-Spangled Banner," popular songs such as "My Old Kentucky Home" and "Swanee River," folk songs such as "O How Lovely Is The Evening," and hymns such as "Come Thou Almighty King" (Mark and Gary 2007, 285n1).

The patriotic fervor stirred up in the United States before and during World War I provided a boost to the community singing movement, and Dykema remained a tireless supporter of community singing. In 1917, the committee published an expanded songbook, *55 Songs and Choruses*, declaring that "there has been such a remarkable development of group or community singing that the original eighteen songs are no longer adequate" (Dykema et al. 1917, Introductory Note). The songbook came out weeks before the United States declared war on Germany in April. Community singing played an important role during World War I, both in the military and in the factories, with the assistance of trained song leaders. In movie theatres, audiences would sing along to the projected words of patriotic and traditional songs (Mark and Gary 2007, 272–273). After the war, community singing continued to be a popular pastime activity. "There was a great deal of singing during the war, and with peace came a temporary reaction from what had been, in the public mind, a purely war-time activity," Dykema explained. "That reaction subsided and Community Singing has been resumed with fresh interest and vigor" (Dykema et al. 1923, Preface).

THE JAZZ AGE (1920–1929)

One of the programs that took shape during World War I and escalated in the 1920s was the establishment of National Music Week.[8] As director of the National Bureau for the Advancement of Music, Tremaine had begun preparations for a Music Week in New York in 1917 but was unprepared to complete the project. In 1919, several cities, including Boise, Idaho, Dallas, Texas, Sharon, Pennsylvania, and St. Louis, Missouri, presented civic events dedicated to music. The first Music Week took place in New York City during the week of February 1–7, 1920, including "thousands of clubs, schools, churches, musical societies, industrial plants, settlements, theaters, motion-picture houses, and other institutions" (Tremaine 1925, 22). In 1923, the National Music Week Committee was formed to organize the annual events of National Music Week, beginning each year on the first Sunday in May. The committee was chaired by Otto Kahn, a banker and patron of the arts, with Tremaine serving as secretary and Kenneth S. Clark as assistant secretary. The president of the United States, Calvin Coolidge, agreed to chair the Honorary Committee (38–39). Seven hundred and eighty American cities celebrated the first National Music Week, increasing to 2,012 cities in 1928 (Zanzig 1932, 9).

In 1925, sociologists Robert and Helen Lynd conducted ethnographic fieldwork in Muncie, a small city in Indiana that they anonymized as "Middletown." Clark Wissler (1929, v), the Curator of Anthropology for the American Museum of Natural History commented, "No one had ever subjected an American community to such scrutiny." To the Lynds, Middletown represented a typical American small city. Using archival data from 1890 as the baseline for their study, the authors contrasted the cultural landscape of Middletown in the mid-1920s with similar activities in the previous generation. The Lynds found that more children from both working-class and business-class families were taking music lessons than in 1890, and they attributed this trend to "the muscularity injected into the music by jazz, the diffusion of instruments other than the piano, and the social and sometimes financial accompaniments of knowing how to 'play'" (Lynd and Lynd 1929, 243). Working-class boys, they claimed, were motivated to play the musical instruments favored in dance orchestras.

> The energetic jazz aggregation of four or five boys, featuring the easily learned saxophone, presents a new and relatively distinguished occupation by which sons of working class parents are seeking in some cases to escape from the industrial level. The city has several of these small groups seeking engagements playing for dances. (244)

The Lynds noted decreased adult participation in community music making in 1925 in comparison to 1890: "Music for adults has almost ceased to be a matter of spontaneous, active participation and has become largely a passive matter of listening to others. The popular singing societies of the nineties have disappeared, with one working class exception" (Lynd and Lynd 1929, 245). The authors concluded, "when great artists or dance orchestras are in the cabinet in the corner of one's living room or 'on the air,' the ability to 'play a little' may be in increasingly less demand" (247).

Community music advocates looked to Europe's governmental support of the arts for rationales to encourage similar funding in the U.S. at the national, state, county, and municipal levels. In 1924, it was reported that 310 cities in the U.S. were each contributing an annual average of over $5,700 for musical activities. The National Recreation Congress that year adopted a resolution proposed by Peter Dykema, "that the various municipal governments should, in the expansion of their recreation programs, give increasing attention to the question of municipal appropriation which shall aid in meeting the city's growing needs in the providing of such activities as open-air band concerts, a community orchestra, municipal organ recitals, a civic auditorium, community singing, civic opera or other musical advantages which may be needed to enrich that city's life" (Clark 1925, 16).

The city of Baltimore was the first to have a municipal department of music, with the Baltimore Symphony Orchestra being the first city-sponsored orchestra. In 1917, Mayor James Preston asserted, "That the people of Baltimore and all other American Cities are entitled to municipal Symphony Orchestras, Municipal opera, Municipal organizations

which provide for individual aesthetic development, just as they are entitled to municipal service in education, sanitation, and public safety" (Human 1917, 29). During the
next two decades, the city sponsored a municipal band, a community orchestra, community singing, community dancing, and a separate band, orchestra, and chorus for the
African American population (Disharoon 1980).

The industrial city of Flint, Michigan, was another to sponsor community music
activities. The population of Flint had exploded during the 1910s with the development
of the automobile industry. By 1917, more than 14,000 workers were employed in the
Buick, Dort, and Chevrolet plants and ancillary industries. The Flint Community Music
Association was created in 1917, funded by the Board of Education, the Manufacturer's
Association, and the Board of Commerce (Spurgeon 1994, 30). The first leader of the
organization, George Oscar Bowen, organized Sunday afternoon community sings,
with attendance sometimes reaching 1,000 participants (32). The Association also organized noontime factory sings at the automobile plants, which "often included as many
as one thousand men and women on their noon break." These sings became so popular
that factory choruses began competing against each other (33). According to Spurgeon,
"The CMA watched over Flint's music for years. When its protective influence disappeared, so did much of Flint's music" (42).

In 1921, Iowa became the first state to pass a law authorizing municipal band funding. The law enabled Iowan cities with a population below 40,000 people to levy a tax
for the support of municipal bands (Clark 1925, 44–47). The Iowa Band Law was soon
followed by similar laws passed in Illinois, Indiana, Kansas, Maryland, Massachusetts,
Michigan, Minnesota, Mississippi, Montana, Nebraska, New York, Ohio, Pennsylvania,
Texas, Utah, Vermont, and Wisconsin (Clark 1925, 44–61).

In addition to public initiatives, private industries sponsored music making as a recreational activity for their workers. According to Tremaine, recreational music benefited both the profitability of business and the well-being of the workers:

> When conclusive testimony as to the practical value of music in industry is given by
> successful business men in a wide variety of industries, music acquires the status of
> an economic asset entitled to the serious consideration of all business men. When
> William Green, president of the American Federation of Labor, makes the state-
> ment that "music is a friend of labor, for it lightens the task by refreshing the nerves
> and spirit of the worker and makes work pleasanter as well as profitable," this makes
> music in industry of direct interest to every labor leader and to the great body of
> workingmen. (Tremaine 1929, v)

In a national survey of 679 companies, Clark (1929, 204–212) found that there were 911
active musical groups: 182 orchestras, 176 choruses, and 133 plants with community singing. He estimated that approximately 50,000 workers participated in musical activities
at their workplaces. The survey included an assortment of companies such as railroads
(115), department stores (89), steel manufacturers (27), miscellaneous manufacturers
(107), electric companies (38), textile companies (30), and oil refineries (21). There were

an assortment of instrumental groups including ukulele clubs (15), harmonica bands (10), drum corps (6), mandolin clubs (4), and saxophone quartets (2). Vocal ensembles included choruses: mixed (76), men's (68) and women's (34); quartets: men's (30), mixed (5), colored (4), and women's (3); and Christmas carolers (11). Miscellaneous musical activities included operettas (21), minstrel shows (12), and musical shows (9).

Augustus Delafield Zanzig, director of music for the Brookline public school system, was chosen by the Playground and Recreation Association to direct a nationwide study of community music. Zanzig began his survey in October 1928. Zanzig emphasized the importance of the quest for musical excellence for the true amateur musician: "Leisure may mean merely freedom from outer compulsion, merely 'time off'; but for the amateur it means for something, freedom for inner, lasting propulsions and the happiness rather than mere pleasure that these can bring" (1930, 29). Zanzig envisioned a time when cities and towns across the nation would have "at least one good civic chorus, a symphony orchestra and a band, and a company of amateurs presenting a good light opera now and then; and not only these, but also string quartettes and other small groups of men and women, young and old, from the shops, mills, offices, and professions, singing or playing excellent music as well as they can as a means of recreation" (29). According to Zanzig, the attainment of these objectives would necessitate the employment of recreational leaders who would possess a combination of professional musicianship, recreational leadership abilities, and pedagogical experience (33).

In the Foreword to Zanzig's *Music in American Life* (1932), composer and Columbia University professor Daniel Gregory Mason attested to the timeliness of Zanzig's survey and decried American musical culture dominated by the mass media and the professionalization of musical performance:

> Such a survey was greatly needed because our American musical culture has always been too passive, too dependent on specialized professionalism, too without roots in the every-day life and feelings of our people, and has of late become so unbalanced in this way that one sometimes wonders whether it can survive at all. In 1929, for example, America purchased only 92,000 pianos—or 238,000 less than it had purchased in 1909—while it spent 890 million dollars on the passive and vicarious delights of radio. How can such steadily diminishing individual initiative in the production of music be compensated? Obviously only through the means Mr. Zanzig studies: through amateur groups—in schools, colleges, settlements, playgrounds, art museums, summer camps, public libraries, and above all in homes. Only through the activities of such groups can music, atrophied and mummified as it tends to be by exclusive professionalism, remain a living art among us. (Zanzig 1932, v)

Zanzig looked back on the musical developments of the 1920s and wondered if there were still resources for the advancement of community music during the Great Depression. "But the whole outer structure of our prosperity has crashed beneath us like Sinbad's ship, and no one will venture to say, when, if ever, it can be recovered. What is the use of proposing musical developments now? Should not all the labor and money asked for them rather go to physical relief of the unemployed?" (Zanzig 1932, 543).

Presaging the rationale for the ambitious federal programs introduced by the Roosevelt administration in 1935, Zanzig asked:

> What would be the effect if such a chorus as the Bethlehem Bach Choir or any other good sort in every city could attract many of the unemployed to its ranks now, when rehearsals could be held in the day time and frequently.... Group instruction in singing and playing might also be offered, and orchestras, bands and smaller playing or singing groups be formed—all without charge, and instruments loaned. (1932, 544)

The Great Depression (1930–1940)

Although musical instrument and record sales plummeted in the years following the stock market crash of 1929, amateur music making and leisure activities continued to grow during the years of the Great Depression. According to Snyder:

> For leisure enjoyment, enforced or otherwise, there were radio programs to listen to and movies to attend. There were parks and playgrounds, family picnics, neighborhood parties, amateur sports, and games. For those with dancing feet there were "big bands." There was church on Sunday for the faithful. And with changing times ordinary folk were beginning to sing again because there was something to sing about. True, there were war clouds in Europe but America was at peace. (1993, 14)

Sunderman stated that, "in 1933 at least 15,000,000 people in America could play some musical instrument." He further stated that of these, 9,000,000 could play the piano and 2,000,000 more were studying the violin (1971, 270).[9] Clarke (1935) observed, "As a nation, we have recently—almost suddenly it seems—become aware that music belongs somewhere in our lives. Immense energy, both professional and voluntary, and private and public money, are being lavished on musical undertakings" (v–vi).

In a study prepared for the National Recreation Association, Eugene Lies hoped that participation in school music activities would lead to greater adult community music participation:

> One next thinks of the great possibilities for enrichment of community life from the successive waves of graduates who come out of school possessed of this musical training. If they could somehow be marshaled into permanent organizations for continuance of their singing and playing, what a great asset they would be in American life. (Lies 1933, 28)

Audre Stong (1897–1976) joined the music faculty at Pasadena Junior College in southern California in 1929 and took over the leadership of the college marching band, known as the Bulldog Band (Krikun 2014, 141–143). For his master's thesis at the University of

Southern California School of Education, "The Relation of Music as Taught in Junior College to Certain Leisure-Time Activities of Students" (1934), he studied a cohort of 232 students taking eight classes at Pasadena Junior College. Stong investigated the relationship between enrollment in junior college music instruction and participation in various leisure activities, such as going to movies and concerts, listening to radio programs, reading books, newspapers, and magazines, as well as extracurricular musical activities. He also investigated the difference in the selection of leisure activities between students who chose active participation in music (band, orchestra, glee club) and students who engaged in passive music listening classes such as music appreciation. Stong pointedly warned of the dangers of spending leisure time on immoral activities:

> A very large proportion of the inmates of America's famous prison, Sing-Sing, are there because of a misuse of leisure. Records show that 98 per cent never belonged to a boys' club. Time spent with trashy magazines, listening to worthless broadcasts, dancing in a vile atmosphere, and most dangerous of all, attending moving pictures, turns precious new-found leisure into one of the gravest perils of modern civilization. Radios and moving pictures are among the richest of present-day blessings but by perversion they may really be changed into organized agencies for crimes against society. (Stong 1934, 13)

Stong concluded, "the study of music in the upper level of the secondary school[10] does tend to raise the selection of certain leisure-time activities of the students" (1934, 85). He also concluded that "studying music in active class work does more to improve the selection of musical activities than does the studying of music in passive appreciation classes" (85). He recommended, "Music should be taken from its elite, purely cultural place in the school curriculum and made a practical, usable subject for everyone" (86), and, "Every student should take music courses in the upper level of secondary education, and these courses should be classes in participation. Where students do not play instruments they should enter choral, a cappella, or glee club classes" (86–87).

During the height of the Great Depression, the federal government intervened to create economic opportunities for artists and arts educators. As an initiative of Franklin D. Roosevelt's New Deal to combat mass unemployment, the government-funded Federal Music Project of the Works Projects Administration (1935–1939) employed thousands of musicians and music educators across the nation. The director of the Federal Music Project, Nikolai Sokoloff, formerly the conductor of the Cleveland Orchestra, reported that, nine months into the project, 15,000 musicians and music teachers had been employed by the government (1937, 7). The project had three objectives: "first, in the presentation of the finest music, foreign and American, at little or no cost to the public; second, in the conducting of instructional classes in singing, instrumental playing, and music appreciation; third, in research aimed at broadening knowledge about music in America" (Tawa 1984, 108). Although the program was national in scope, projects were woven into local music cultures, with the result that "interest in music—making it, learning about it, and hearing it—grew tremendously" (109). With impending war in Europe, and faced with the objections of conservative politicians and music businesses who felt threatened by the low-cost alternatives of the Federal Music Project, the Roosevelt administration terminated the program in August 1939. In its brief existence, the Federal Music Project had provided music instruction to 15 million people and presented over 200,000 performances to 150 million people (118).

Willem van de Wall[11] (1887–1953) was one of the founders of music therapy in the United States following World War I. Throughout his career, van de Wall studied the role of music as a positive influence in various institutions, including hospitals and prisons. In *Music in Institutions* (1936), he declared, "[J]azz music should be considered a constructive musical activity for institutions." He believed that popular music would have a healthy impact on the prisoners: "To play, sing, dance, and listen to jazz often means to an inmate that he is keeping up with the times" (179–180). Van de Wall further suggested that popular music be accepted as a legitimate leisure-time activity:

> Many parents and teachers of music in the United States have observed that, in spite of their efforts to teach a knowledge of the traditional art music, children will turn to popular music in their leisure time. This trend must not be belittled. It indicates that there is something in that music which expresses and satisfies what lives in the hearts of the people. (1938, 3)

In *Music of the People* (1938), van de Wall described various community music projects, sponsored by city, county, and state governments and universities. Van de Wall surveyed community music in a variety of settings: urban, suburban, and rural. He noted a particular need for music in rural communities: "the need in rural areas for the inspiration that the arts offer is fully as great as in the cities, especially during the winter months when farm folk have many leisure hours" (van de Wall 1938, 16). Echoing Zanzig's call a decade earlier for recreational leaders, van de Wall suggested training professional musicians for community music leadership: "The time has come when vocational music institutions, like the Curtis, the Juilliard, and the Eastman schools and the various conservatories of music, large and small, must give attention to the problem of training music leaders equipped not only as artists but also as personalities and community workers ready to meet the cultural needs of the community" (24).

WORLD WAR II (1941–1945)

The prelude to and the entrance of the United States into World War II in December 1941 brought about significant changes for the role of music in society. Federal funding for the arts was discontinued and available resources were redirected to the war effort. According to Tawa (1984): "No longer would musicians need employment. If not in music, there would be plenty of work available elsewhere for all who needed it" (118). As the nation focused on the war effort, music educators had to justify the importance of music, often highlighting the social role of music instead of aesthetic enrichment. Sociologist and music educator Max Kaplan (1911–1998)[12] founded the music department at Pueblo Junior College in southern Colorado in 1937 and was the only music faculty member until his departure in 1945. Kaplan stressed the socializing role of music in the postwar environment.

> The dramatic immediacy of the war and the crying need it has brought for scientifically and technically trained youth has crowded from the popular mind the abiding necessity for training our young people through the social sciences and the arts for crucial peace-building and peace-preserving years ahead, with the need they will bring for social understanding, economic wisdom, and the highest type of unselfish citizenship. (1943, 373)

Kaplan believed that the "immediate task and salvation" of the music program was to "become a vital part of community life" (1943, 374). Inspired by the previous sociological studies of Lynd and Lynd (1929) and van de Wall (1938), Kaplan collaborated with his music students to gain "an intimate knowledge of the music facilities and agencies in the community. The school men, the radio, the church choirs, the librarian, the music stores, the musician's union, the symphony orchestras, book stores—all of their musical activities, their aims, their contributions, their method of operation, their personnel, their problems" (1943, 372). He divided his study into four categories: (1) Agencies of Musical Education, including public and private K–12 schools, colleges, and community music programs; (2) Agencies of Musical Production, including bands, orchestras, vocal groups, and other music making activities; (3) Agencies of Musical Consumption, including live concerts, radio, recordings, and jukeboxes; and (4) Agencies of Musical Circulation, including libraries and music merchandisers.

Pueblo was an industrial city dominated by the Colorado Fuel and Iron Company's steel mill. Drawing from the Lynds' study of Middletown, Kaplan sought to take a snapshot of a southwestern city's musical culture. According to Kaplan, there were forty-one active private music teachers in Pueblo, although only thirteen of those responded to his survey. The thirteen teachers responding taught a total of 294 students (145 female and 94 male), with piano and organ being the most common instruments taught (185), followed by the accordion (31), violin (26), cornet (16), clarinet (10), and trombone (6). Kaplan also found an equal distribution of students coming from households where the primary occupations were professional, trades, office, unskilled, and farmers (Kaplan 1944, 20–27).

Kaplan lauded the two amateur band organizations active in Pueblo at the time for their role in providing a positive leisure time activity. The Phillips Crusaders Boys Military Band was founded in 1926 by D. Z. Phillips, the proprietor of a local music store. Originally comprising twelve boys, membership grew to 325 by 1944. The goal of the Crusaders Band was "character development," "substituting a supervised and constructive 'gang' for the lawless and destructive street gang" (Kaplan 1944, 32). The Stillman Lassies Band was established in 1930 and grew from its original number of twenty-five girls to a total of fifty-two in 1944. In 1939, a drum corps began to perform together with the band. Kaplan concluded, "We feel that this type of activity for girls of high school age is of great value. It offers a constructive substitute for much of the movie and romantic type of experience which girls frequently grasp as a source of vicarious experience and adventure" (34).

Kaplan painted a bleak picture of the musical culture of Pueblo. "An outstanding weakness of Pueblo musical life is the little opportunity in adult groups for creating music. Such opportunity can take place in the formal school-type activity, or informally in the home or club" (1944, 149). He suggested several initiatives to improve Pueblo's musical culture, including the expansion of evening adult education programs, municipal music programs in the parks and playgrounds, greater support and participation for the local orchestra and adult community chorus, greater cooperation between the city's private studio music teachers, encouragement of chamber music in the home and neighborhood, and the establishment of a community music organization similar to Flint's Community Music Association (167).

After leaving his teaching position at Pueblo Junior College in 1945, Max Kaplan continued to explore the relationship between music and leisure and worked on numerous projects to establish amateur music making as a community activity. In *Foundations and Frontiers of Music Education*, Kaplan concluded:

> [I]n itself leisure is neither a blessing or a curse; it is a phenomenon of our time and economic-social structure that reaches deeply into personal and group destiny and purpose ... only as creative, substantive directions are given to the leisure that is now an increasingly major part of our lives can we find our new sources of values. (1966, 16)

CONCLUSIONS

In a review of the historical currents of the community music movement,[13] community music scholar Lee Higgins attributed the gradual demise of the governmental and philanthropic support for amateur music making in the postwar era in the United States to the repressive policies of the Cold War and McCarthyism. Higgins concluded, "From an American perspective, community music as a strategy for human development, democracy and change was eluded [*sic*] to from the 1920s until around the 1950s but lost visibility and momentum soon after" (2012, 23).

Inspired by European community music projects and research, the early years of the twenty-first century have witnessed a resurgence of interest in community music and music making as a lifelong leisure time activity in the United States. As in the early initiatives discussed in this chapter, government and nongovernmental organizations, trade groups, professional societies, music businesses, and educational institutions continue to impact policies affecting the development of American musical culture and the role of music making as a leisure activity. According to Higgins, "historical perspectives are to be understood as a key component to the future providing pathways, counterpaths, flight lines, and openings towards events to come" (2012, 175). With an eye on the past, several questions come to mind. Are our current goals different from the goals of the American educators and administrators who promoted music making as a worthwhile leisure activity in the first half of the twentieth century? What are the best practices of programs aimed at promoting active music making in the community? What types of music should receive institutional support? Have certain musical cultures and minority groups been marginalized by the patronage of art music? Viewing the past with a fresh perspective, we can begin to assess current and future institutional initiatives to support music making as a rewarding leisure activity, while ensuring that the results are demo-cratic and beneficial to the greater society.

Notes

1. The chapter title is taken from an editorial that appeared in the magazine *Etude* 50 (November 1932), 763.
2. Lowell Mason (1792–1872), an American hymn composer and music educator, cofounded the Boston Academy of Music in 1833. He is also credited with the beginning of formal music education in the American public school system, introducing music education to the public school system of Boston in 1838.
3. The Progressive Era refers to a period in the history of the United States when a variety of social and political movements were formed to address social problems resulting from rapid industrialization, immigration, and urbanization.
4. Music memory contests were popular in the United States from around 1920 to 1932. Contestants were ranked on their ability to aurally identify compositions from the classi-cal music repertoire; see Keene (2009, 280–286).
5. "Industrial music" refers to musical organizations and activities sponsored by local com-panies for their employees; see Clark (1929).
6. See Levine (1988).
7. For a contemporary perspective on the relationship between the American community-music movement beginning in the early twentieth century and the international community-music movement of the late twentieth century and into the twenty-first cen-tury, see Yerichuk (2014).
8. The Jazz Age was also known as the "Roaring Twenties," a period in the United States char-acterized by prosperous growth of industry and wealth and a relaxation of cultural taboos. A new African American musical style, jazz, was exported from New Orleans and became a symbol at the time of youthful rebellion and hedonism.
9. Sunderman cites R. C. Rolfing, president of the National Piano Manufacturers Association, as the source for this information.
10. The "upper level of the secondary school" to which Stong is referring was equivalent to the first two years of higher education in the Pasadena school system.
11. For more about the community music work of Willem van de Wall and Max Kaplan, see Krikun (2010).
12. For a detailed overview of the career of Max Kaplan and his seminal work on music and leisure studies, see McCarthy, this volume, chapter 2.

13. For an overview of the historical foundations of community music in North America, see Bush and Krikun (2013). Two recent books provide an excellent introduction to community music research: Higgins (2012) and Veblen et al. (2013). *The International Journal of Community Music* is devoted to current research and practice in community music. Higgins also explores the different approaches and ideologies separating the early community music movement in the United States and the more recent community arts movement in Europe.

REFERENCES CITED

Bush, Jeffrey E., and Andrew Krikun. 2013. "North America: Historical Foundations." In *Community Music Today*, edited by Kari K. Veblen, Stephen J. Messenger, Marissa Silverman, and David J. Elliott, 13–24. Lanham, MD: Rowman and Littlefield.

Clark, Kenneth S. 1925. *Municipal Aids to Music in America*. New York: National Bureau for the Advancement of Music.

Clark, Kenneth S. 1929. *Music in Industry*. New York: National Bureau for the Advancement of Music.

Clarke, Eric Thatcher. 1935. *Music in Everyday Life*. New York: W. W. Norton.

Crawford, Richard. 1993. *The American Musical Landscape: The Business of Musicianship from Billings to Gershwin*. Berkeley: University of California Press.

Crawford, Richard. 2001. *America's Musical Life: A History*. New York: W. W. Norton.

Croly, Jennie Cunningham. 1898. *The History of the Woman's Club Movement in America*. New York: Henry G. Allen.

Disharoon, Richard A. 1980. "A History of Municipal Music in Baltimore, 1914–1947." PhD dissertation, University of Maryland.

Dykema, Peter W. 1916. "The Spread of the Community Music Idea." *Annals of the American Academy of Political and Social Science* 67: 218–223.

Dykema, Peter, Will Earhart, Osbourne McConathy, and Hollis Dann. 1917. *I Hear America Singing: 55 Songs and Choruses for Community Singing*. Boston: C. C. Birchard.

Dykema, Peter, Will Earhart, Osbourne McConathy, and Hollis Dann. 1923. *No. 2 Twice 55 Community Songs: The Green Book*. Boston: C. C. Birchard.

Gere, Anne Ruggles. 1997. *Intimate Practices: Literacy and Cultural Work in U.S. Women's Clubs, 1880–1920*. Champaign: University of Illinois Press.

Hazen, Margaret Hindle, and Robert M. Hazen. 1987. *The Music Men: An Illustrated History of Brass Bands in America, 1800–1920*. Washington, DC: Smithsonian Institution Press.

Higgins, Lee. 2012. *Community Music: In Theory and in Practice*. New York: Oxford University Press.

Human, Alfred. 1917. "How Mayor Preston Brought Municipal Music to Baltimore." *Musical America* 26: 29.

Jasen, David A., and Gene Jones. 2000. *That American Rag: The Story of Ragtime from Coast to Coast*. New York: Schirmer.

Jasen, David A., and Trebor Jay Tichenor. 1978. *Rags and Ragtime: A Musical History*. New York: Seabury.

Kaplan, Max. 1943. "Beethoven or a Bottle of Beer?" *Junior College Journal*, 373–375.

Kaplan, Max. 1944. *Music in the City: A Sociological Survey of Musical Facilities and Activities in Pueblo, Colorado*. Pueblo, CO: Self-published.

Kaplan, Max. 1966. *Foundations and Frontiers of Music Education*. New York: Holt, Rinehart, and Winston.

Keene, James A. 2009. *A History of Music Education in the United States.* 2nd ed. Centennial, CO: Glenbridge.

Koch, Franklin W. 1990. "Cooperative Promotional Efforts of the Music Supervisors National Conference and the National Bureau for the Advancement of Music." *Journal of Research in Music Education* 38: 269–281.

Krikun, Andrew. 2010. "Community Music during the New Deal: The Contributions of Willem Van de Wall and Max Kaplan." *International Journal of Community Music* 3: 165–174.

Krikun, Andrew. 2014. "Teaching the 'People's Music' at the 'People's College': A Historical Study of American Popular Music in the Junior/Community College Curriculum, 1924–1955." PhD dissertation, New York University.

Levine, Lawrence W. 1988. *Highbrow/Lowbrow: The Emergence of Cultural Hierarchy in America.* Cambridge, MA: Harvard University Press.

Lies, Eugene T. 1933. *The New Leisure Challenges the Schools.* Chicago: National Recreation Association.

Litterst, George, and Dean Malambri. 1999. "The Social Instrument." *Piano and Keyboard* 201: 9–26.

Lynd, Robert Staughton, and Helen Merrell Lynd. 1929. *Middletown: A Study in Modern American Culture.* New York: Harcourt, Brace and World.

Mark, Michael L., and Charles L. Gary. 2007. *A History of American Music Education.* 3rd ed. Lanham, MD: Rowman and Littlefield.

Mason, Daniel Gregory. 1932. Foreword. In *Music in American Life Present and Future*, edited by Augustus Delafield Zanzig, v–vi. New York: National Recreation Association.

Ottaway, Ruth Haller. 1935. "Historical Highlights of the Federation, 1898–1935." In *Book of Proceedings of the National Federation of Music Clubs.* Vol. 1, *Nineteenth Biennial Meeting, Philadelphia, April 23–30, 1935*, edited by Helen G. Weaver, 221–226. Ithaca, NY: National Federation of Music Clubs.

Rosenstein, David. 1917. "The National Federation of Settlements." *School and Society* 6(134): 72–78.

Schenck, Janet D. 1926. *Music, Youth and Opportunity: A Survey of Settlement and Community Music Schools.* Boston: National Federation of Settlements.

Snyder, Dean Atley. 1993. "From the Inside: A Descriptive View of SPEBSQSA." In *Barbershopping: Musical and Social Harmony*, edited by Max Kaplan, 13–32. Cranbury, NJ: Associated University Presses..

Sokoloff, Nikolai. 1937. *The Federal Music Project: The Second Preliminary Report Covering Its Scope and Activities during Its First Nine Months.* Washington, DC: Division of Women's and Professional Projects.

Sousa, John Philip. 1906. "The Menace of Mechanical Music." *Appleton's Magazine* 8 (September): 278–284.

Spurgeon, Alan L. 1994. "The Community Music Association in Flint, Michigan, 1917–1920." *Bulletin of Historical Research in Music Education* 16(1): 29–42.

Stebbins, Lucy Poate, and Richard Poate Stebbins. 1945. *Frank Damrosch: Let the People Sing.* Durham, NC: Duke University Press.

Stong, Audre Lewis. 1934. "The Relation of Music as Taught in Junior College to Certain Leisure-Time Activities of Students." Master's thesis, University of Southern California.

Sunderman, Lloyd Frederick. 1971. *Historical Foundations of Music Education in the United States.* Metuchen, NJ: Scarecrow.

Tawa, Nicholas E. 1984. *Serenading the Reluctant Eagle: American Musical Life, 1925–1945.* New York: Schirmer.

Tawa, Nicholas E. 2000. *High-Minded and Low-Down: Music in the Lives of Americans, 1800–1861.* Boston: Northeastern University Press.

Tremaine, Charles Milton. 1925. *History of National Music Week.* New York: National Bureau for the Advancement of Music.

Tremaine, Charles Milton. 1929. Foreword. In *Music in Industry*, edited by Kenneth S. Clark, v–vi. New York: National Bureau for the Advancement of Music.

Van de Wall, Willem. 1936. *Music in Institutions.* New York: Russell Sage Foundation.

Van de Wall, Willem. 1938. *Music of the People.* New York: American Association for Adult Education.

Veblen, Kari K., Stephen J. Messenger, Marissa Silverman, and David J. Elliott, eds. 2013. *Community Music Today.* Lanham, MD: Rowman and Littlefield.

Waldo, Terry. 1976. *This Is Ragtime.* New York: Hawthorn.

Ward, May Alden. 1906. "The Influence of Women's Clubs in New England and in the Middle-Eastern States." *Annals of the American Academy of Political and Social Science* 28: 7–28.

Willson, Meredith. 1950. *The Music Man: A Musical Comedy.* Vocal Score, edited by Abba Bogin. New York: Frank Music Corp. and Meredith Willson Music.

Wissler, Clark. 1929. Foreword. In *Middletown: A Study in Modern American Culture*, edited by Robert S. Lynd and Helen Merrell Lynd, v–vii. New York: Harcourt, Brace and World.

Yerichuk, Deanna. 2014. "'Socialized Music': Historical Formations of Community Music through Social Rationales." *Action, Criticism, and Theory for Music Education* 13(1): 126–154.

Zanzig, Augustus Delafield. 1930. "Richer Uses of Music as Recreation." *Music Supervisors' Journal* 16(4): 27–33.

Zanzig, Augustus Delafield. 1932. *Music in American Life Present and Future.* New York: National Recreation Association.

CHAPTER 15

A CONSUMER BEHAVIOR-INFLUENCED MULTIDISCIPLINARY TRANSCENDENT MODEL OF MOTIVATION FOR MUSIC MAKING

VALERIE L. VACCARO

Musical training is a more potent instrument than any other, because rhythm and harmony find their way into the inward places of the soul . . . making the soul of him who is rightly educated graceful.

(Plato, *Republic*, book 3)

INTRODUCTION

DURING a pivotal moment in the 1996 movie *Jerry Maguire*, Tom Cruise's character, Jerry tells the love of his life, Dorothy, "you . . . complete me" (the antithesis of another iconic quote from the same movie, "show me the money"). The premise of this study and proposed new theoretical model is that music making can be a creative means to self-expression that makes a person feel more complete, using the paradigm of *self-transcendence* (Koltko-Rivera 2006; Maslow 1971) and supported by the philosophical perspective of positive psychology (Seligman and Csikszentmihalyi 2000).

Jung's theory of *individuation* rests upon the core concept of the *transcendent function*, which is the "the realization, in all its aspects, of the personality originally hidden

away in the embryonic germ plasm; the production and unfolding of the original potential wholeness" (Hall and Nordby 1973, 84). Jung's perspective was that human beings
evolve toward wholeness via the *transcendent function* by reconciling between their
unconscious and conscious to develop a more complete identity that emerges from both
of those aspects of the self (Miller 2004). Smith (2013; this volume, chapter 9) refers to
the individuation process as *identity realization*, based upon his study of music making
in the lives of drummers, and discusses music makers living a "complete" life in accordance with the philosophy of eudaimonism (Norton 1976; Waterman 1993).

Contribution of Study

The purpose of this study is to provide a new Transcendent Model of Motivation for
Music Making (TMMMM) by way of a synthesized review of types of intrinsic rewards,
including the psychological, physiological, and spiritual motivations and benefits associated with music making participation for amateur and hobbyist musicians. It is highly
possible that intrinsic motivations for music making may be similar among different
populations ranging across the spectrum from amateur to professional. Therefore,
it is suggested that the TMMMM and related propositions developed in this chapter
may be applicable to all musicians, from amateurs to professionals, at different times
and stages in their lives, and, ultimately, may be universally applicable to individuals
pursuing important goals that help them to feel more "complete"—to achieve their full
potential and experience self-actualization and self-transcendence (Maslow 1943, 1954,
1968, 1969a, 1969b, 1971). The TMMMM framework is based upon the humanistic psychology of Maslow's "hierarchy of needs" and the more recent paradigm of positive psychology, which focuses on "how people's lives can be most worth living" (Seligman and
Csikszentmihalyi 2000, 5).

The new multidisciplinary TMMMM draws upon wide-ranging research from the
fields of consumer behavior, psychology, and music education. MacDonald, Hargreaves,
and Miell (2009, 468–469) asserted that "a more multidisciplinary and pluralistic position is in keeping with postmodern research priorities . . . [for] researchers . . . investigating musical identities including psychologists, music therapists, musicologists,
music educationalists and others." According to MacDonald, Hargreaves, and Miell,
"Musical identities are an important consideration for researchers interested in the
psychology of music, not least because we all have musical identities, but also because
identity "work" is a fundamental psychological process in which we all engage" (469).
Therefore, although this chapter is focused on music making, the new model proposed
here could have wider implications to enhance our understanding of other human goal-
directed motivation and behavior. The chapter provides a literature review and analysis of select theories and models of music making motivations to identify key common
elements. I draw upon relevant research from the already multidisciplinary field of
consumer behavior, including "extended self theory" (Belk 1988) and "self-completion
theory" (Wicklund and Gollwitzer 1981, 2013; Gollwitzer 1987). The chapter also reviews

Maslow's "theory of human motivation"—with a focus on Maslow's original hierarchy of needs (Maslow 1943, 1954), which is prominently found both in consumer behavior and music education research, and Maslow's more updated theoretical notion of transcendence (1968, 1969a, 1969b, 1971; Koltko-Rivera 2006). The TMMMM is based upon music education research related to higher-level needs and benefits derived from music making, such as flow and well-being research in the field of psychology, and from other relevant areas to provide a more holistic basis for the newly proposed model.

LITERATURE REVIEW

Identity Formation and Implementation for Music Makers

Forming a positive music identity is an important part antecedent to music making participation in adolescence (Pitts this volume, chapter 10), in middle adulthood (Rathunde and Isabella this volume, chapter 8) and later in life (e.g., Coffman 2009; Taylor 2011). Pitts noted that research shows early development of competent musical skills, external encouragement from others, and confidence (self-esteem) in one's musical abilities are important factors that contribute to a strong music maker identity.

Research by Smith (2013; this volume, chapter 9) provides some new perspectives on the meaning of a music maker's identity. The title of the book *I Drum, Therefore I Am* (Smith 2013) captures in a nutshell the notion that music making can be synonymous with one's self or identity. Smith proposed a new conceptual model of identity formation called the "snowball self," which is composed of meta-identities (e.g., being a musician, gender, ethnicity, etc.) and contextual identities, where an individual grows and learns via the symbiotic processes of identity realization and learning realization (2013, 29). According to Smith (this volume, chapter 9), the drummers' "identity 'realization' is meant in its passive and active senses—understanding who one is, and also acting upon that understanding: being, becoming, actively realizing an identity in the world, akin to what Hegel . . . describes as a person 'realizing his individuality.'" Smith likens the idea of identity realization to Maslow's concept of self-actualization, and (chapter 9) applies the philosophy of eudaimonism—when an individual lives life in harmony with his or her true self (Norton 1976). The philosophy of eudaimonsim follows the spirit of Shakespeare's words "To thine own self be true," which Polonius said to his son Laertes in *Hamlet*, act 1, scene 3.

Rathunde and Isabella's "tailoring model of identity development" (this volume, chapter 8) uses the analogy of the steps involved with tailoring a new suit to the process of creating an individual's own music-making identity during middle adulthood. Phase one: *self-differentiation* includes two steps: (1) a "measurement," where a person explores and discovers what attributes best suits them, and (2) a "design" step of commitment, where the individual uses his or her imagination and self-reflection to choose the most important attributes as part of a cohesive view of self. Phase two is *social integration*, which includes: (1) "pattern making" (exploration), where the individual engages in intrinsically motivated, freely chosen leisure activities which may result in "flow" experiences, and (2) "alteration" (i.e., commitment), which entails finding specific situations to connect with others to share one's true self.

There are relevant parallels in studies of identity in the consumer behavior literature that draw upon multidisciplinary research areas (e.g., psychology, sociology, anthropology, history). In particular, "extended self theory" (Belk 1988) seeks to explain consumers' relationship with possessions as a way of defining one's identity. "Self-completion theory" can also provide new, interesting, and relevant perspectives on music making motivations (Gollwitzer 1987; Wicklund and Gollwitzer 1981, 2013). Thus, there is a strong rationale for considering the application of some consumer behavior-related theories to develop a greater understanding of the motivations and benefits of music making.

Extended Self Theory and Music Making Identity

Who Are You?

(Pete Townshend, The Who)

According to Erikson (1968), the concept of *identity* represents who a person is (or thinks he or she is) and includes what other peoples' perspectives are of that person. Ball and Tasaki (1992) noted that there has been a resurgent interest in the concepts of self and identity which focus on earlier theories by Erickson (1959) in the field of psychology. A number of consumer behavior research studies have found that possessions play an important role in the development and maintenance of a consumer's self-concept and identity (e.g., Ball and Tasaki 1992; Belk 1988; Csikszentmihalyi and Rochberg-Halton 1981).

In a seminal article on consumer behavior, Belk (1988) presented a comprehensive, multidisciplinary synthesis of research into how individuals regard possessions as part of themselves. Belk defined the "extended self" concept to include self-perceptions, ideas, body parts, personal identifying characteristics (e.g., age, gender, occupation), objects, people, places, pets, money, collections, and the environment. I suggest that Belk's category of extended self personal characteristics also includes leisure (lifestyle) activities such as music making, which can be related to investment of "psychic energy," of our attention, time, and efforts in an object (e.g., a musical instrument) or in an activity such as singing. Belk's (1988) notion of extended self could also be inclusive of Hargreaves and Marshall's (2003) *music in identities* (MII) concept, which "refers to the ways in which music may form a part of other aspects of the individual's self-image, such as . . . gender, age, national identity, and disability and identity" (264). Further, "Individuals who are involved in music making (be that as a professional opera singer or an occasional singer in the bath tub) develop an identity that is crucially influenced by these activities" (MacDonald, Hargreaves, and Miell 2009, 463–464).

Belk (1988) asserted that objects could, by enabling a person to do things they could not normally do, symbolically empower and enhance the extended self with objects functioning as a way to "contribute to our capabilities for doing and being" (145). It is proposed in this chapter that playing an instrument is an important part of a music maker's identity—part of their extended self—which completes their identity through empowering them to do things such as making sounds that are extensions of the human voice and expressing human emotions in ways that a speaking voice cannot do. There is a bond between the musician and his or her instrument, which is most likely stronger if music making is central to an individual's identity and if that individual experiences a number of the personal, social, and health benefits associated with music making, as discussed in this chapter. Belk's (1988) perspective drew upon the philosophy of existential psychologist Jean-Paul Sartre, who proposed that people want things to enlarge their sense of self (self-image) and that people define who they are (their identities) by the possessions they have, and by their perceptions of what others think about them ("looking-glass self"). Further, Belk asserted that people also define themselves by what they do, based upon Karl Marx's view that doing and working play crucial roles in one's self-image.

The activities associated with music making are related to what Csikszentmihalyi and Rochberg-Halton (1981) described as an investment of "psychic energy" of attention, time, and efforts in an object (e.g., a musical instrument). There is also evidence that music making activities can generate peak experiences or "flow" (Csikszentmihalyi 1990) and may enable us to achieve self-actualization and self-transcendence, according to Maslow's theory of human motivation (1943, 1969a, 1969b). A study by Csikszentmihalyi and Rochberg-Halton (1981) of people aged eight to thirty showed that favorite possessions were objects related to the person's mastery of skills such as, for instance, musical instruments and athletic equipment. Belk asserted that in regard to objects such as tools, instruments, and weapons, "the greater the control we exercise, the more closely allied with self the object should become" (1988, 140). Also, Belk suggested that "apparently in claiming that something is mine, we also come to believe that the object is 'me'" (141).

Self-Completion Theory and Music Making

A natural complement to Belk's extended self theory view on the relationship of objects to one's extended self is self-completion theory (Wicklund and Gollwitzer 1981). "Self-completion theory" and "symbolic self-completion theory" are based, in part, on Lewin's (1926) theory of tension systems, which is associated with an intrinsically energized tension or motivation to reach one's goal (Wicklund and Gollwitzer 2013, 19). The premise of self-completion theory is that human beings define themselves by what they do and what they want to achieve (e.g., as "musicians"), the activities they participate in toward achieving salient goals—and they use symbols (e.g., representing training, status or titles, and performance) that must be acknowledged by society (e.g., social recognition).

According to Gollwitzer (1987, 350) "Self-Completion Theory provides . . . ideas on how people pursue the identity goals to which they feel committed." There are four key concepts in self-completion theory: (1) self-definition, (2) commitment to a self-definition, (3) symbols of completeness, and (4) social reality.

Self-definition refers to people's ideal conceptions of themselves as possessing a readiness or potential to enact certain content-specific classes of behavior. *Commitment to a self-definition* addresses an individual's motivation (intention) to reach the ideal condition. A self-defining goal needs to be important to the person, to be an activity that is of "central interest . . . such as participating in a sport, playing an instrument, or studying a subject. . . . [Individuals] continuously active in that area . . . [have] a sense of control and capability . . . to interact with others . . . [and] progress toward the goal requires social recognition" (Wickland and Gollwitzer 1981, 92). *Symbols of completeness* are the building blocks of self-definitions. For example, a musician acquires an educational background in music theory and a fine-quality instrument (Gollwitzer 1987, 350). There are three types of symbols of completeness: (1) background experience and training needed for the activity, which can be related to Maslow's need for self-actualization and achievement (Maslow 1943, 1954), and competence (Ryan and Deci 2000); (2) occupying a position or status that furthers the relevant activities, which can be related to Maslow's need for self-esteem; and (3) performance of the act itself (e.g., musical performance). The more that symbols of completeness are associated with the person and acknowledged by others, the more complete will be the person's self-definition.

Symbolic self-completion, according to Wicklund and Gollwitzer (2013), can sometimes be *independent* of actual development of competence or the time and effort required for mastery of skills—which makes it more dependent on social image than on an individual's capabilities. There may be a "destructive side of a person's self-symbolizing efforts. . . . [A]ctive and impatient self-symbolizing tends to interfere with the building up of behavioral competencies . . . (and can be) damaging to communication and interpersonal relations" (Wicklund and Gollwitzer 2013, 10). With regard to *social reality*, "the sense of progress towards a self-defining goal is dependent upon the acknowledgement of others" (Wicklund and Gollwitzer 1981, 93). A person's sense of completeness is enhanced when more people are informed about it. If music makers achieve mastery over their instruments, they will have some self-satisfaction. They also need to be appreciated by others (e.g., receiving confirmation of music making identity and positive feedback from fellow musicians, friends, family, music critics and journalists, receiving applause from enthusiastic concert-goers, selling out concert halls, having others want to buy their music, getting their music played on the radio, having their music reach the top of Billboard magazine's charts, winning awards, etc.).

Based upon the previous section's discussion of music making and consumer behavior related to an individual's identity, here is Proposition I:

Proposition I: Music making (as an amateur or professional) is part of one's "extended self" identity.

Maslow's Theory of Human Motivation

> Music, sweet music, you're the Queen of my Soul
>
> (Hamish Stuart, Average White Band)

In the fields of consumer behavior and marketing, Maslow's hierarchy of needs (originating in the discipline of psychology) is an important theory of motivation found in every textbook of consumer behavior and principles of marketing (i.e., with the theory applied to areas related to consumer product choice and lifestyle activities). Maslow's "theory of motivation" is also found in music education research and is highly relevant to music making participation by students, amateurs, and professional musicians. The theory, including the hierarchy of needs (1943, 1954), is well known to include the following set of human needs, from the bottom of the pyramid up to the highest level of needs: *physiological, safety, love and belonging, self-esteem*, and *self-actualization*. The original theory postulated that human beings need to satisfy their lower level needs first, and then depending on opportunity, motivation and culture, could focus on higher-level needs. However, Maslow and other researchers have acknowledged that human beings are more complex, and that this is not always the case; people focus on different levels at different times, and human behavior is not so linear. One does not always have to fulfill lower-lever needs except for basic physiological ones—we can focus on higher-level needs instead of or before middle-level needs such as love and belonging.

Social Motivations for Music Making

> I get by with a little help from my friends
>
> (John Lennon and Paul McCartney, the Beatles)

Maslow (1943) asserted that human beings are motivated to take actions that they believe will help satisfy their social needs related to love and belonging. In a research review of reasons for music making participation, Hallam, Creech, and Varvarigou (this volume, chapter 3) found several examples in the music/personal category. Social/cultural music making benefits included performing with others, meeting like-minded others, experiencing feelings of belonging, developing friendships, engaging in social interaction, and seeking affirmation of one's musical self as part of a community.

According to Coffman (2009, 276), "Making music is often a *social activity*, and there is a small body of research that documents the social and psychological benefits of making music—people want to express themselves musically and with others, not just by themselves." A number of studies with students as well as older amateur music makers showed that social reasons are important motivations which influence music making participation (e.g., Jutras 2006, 2011; Kokotsaki and Hallam 2007; Taylor 2011). Social reasons include encouragement from teachers, family interest in music, perceived value of music making, music skills of family members, opinions and interactions with friends and other peers, and participation in a band (e.g., Creech 2008; Creech and Hallam

2003). Research by Jutras rated the importance of potential benefits of playing piano with 711 adult piano students from twenty-four states in the U.S. (Jutras 2006) and 1800 New Horizons music group members from twenty-eight U.S. states and Canada (Jutras 2011). Both studies found a number of important social/cultural benefits of music making: making new friends, sharing common interests, belonging, cultural understanding, and community (Jutras 2006, 2011).

Coffman (2006) conducted a survey and interviews with ninety adult participants who were members (novice to advanced) of community wind bands in Tasmania and found the main motivation for playing music was social or belonging needs that were met during music training, rehearsals, and community concerts. Further, Coffman (2009) studied a large sample of over 1,600 older adult members of the New Horizons International Music Association (NHIMA) learning or relearning instruments who play in bands, orchestras, and choirs. About 18.2 percent of the participants in Coffman's (2009) study experienced socialization benefits, including a sense of belonging, camaraderie, and new friends.

Research by Kokotsaki and Hallam (2007) on the perceptions of college music majors toward the benefits of participative music making as a social act found that the students felt they were active contributors to a group outcome, developed a strong sense of belonging, gained popularity and made friends with "like-minded" people, and enhanced their social skills. Bugos (2014), who examined attitudes toward a music program with group piano instruction and group percussion ensemble for beginning-level musicians, sixty to eighty-six years of age, found they preferred having *group* music instruction rather than individual music instruction. Thus, social motivation is an important reason for music making participation.

Self-Esteem and Self-Actualization Motivations for Music Making

In Maslow's original theory of motivation, he defined self-actualization as "the tendency . . . to become actualized in what . . . (a person) is potentially . . . to become everything that one is capable of becoming" (1943, 382). Maslow asserted that education should be about "helping the person to become the best that he [*sic*] is able to become" (1968, 74), including music and arts education, "which are excellent ways of moving towards the discovery of identity" (169) and "are so close to our psychological and biological core" (171). An extensive research review on music making motivations by Hallam, Creech, and Varvarigou (this volume, chapter 3) found examples which could be part of a *music/personal* benefits category that included: having a love of music, the desire to develop skills or competence, feeling involved in a meaningful worthwhile activity with a sense of purpose and motivation, and providing structure to life.

Here is some research related to Maslow's motivational needs of self-esteem and self-actualization. Coffman (2009, 376) identified a number of key reasons for music making participation: *personal motivations* (e.g., self-expression, recreation, self-improvement

...) and *musical motivations* (e.g., love of music, performing for oneself and others, learning more about music). Studies by Jutras (2006, 2011) rating the importance of potential benefits of playing piano also found a number of important personal benefits of music making including accomplishment, fun/enjoyment (which is really more related to "flow") personal growth, escape from routine, self-esteem, dream fulfilled, and many others. These music making motivations can be related to Maslow's motivational needs of self-esteem and self-actualization.

Kokotsaki and Hallam (2007) conducted a study with seventy-eight undergraduate and graduate music students in ensembles and found *musical effects* and *personal effects* (similar to personal motivations in Coffman's study), which can be related to self-esteem (confidence) and musical skill development and achievement which are related to self-actualization. Weren et al. (this volume, chapter 18) studied college marching band participation with a sample of 205 band members and referred to a "self-determination motivational continuum," with motivation type, regulation styles, and specific reasons for music making (based upon Ryan and Deci's self-determination theory). Extrinsic motivation included desire for social recognition (or other rewards) that could be related to self-esteem needs in Maslow's (1943, 1954) hierarchy of needs theory of motivation. Intrinsic motivation included learning new things and achievement, which can be related to the self-actualization level in Maslow's hierarchy of needs (1943, 1954). Intrinsic motivational reasons included enjoyment (e.g., pleasure, fun, excitement of the activity which is hedonistic in nature—discussed next).Weren et al. (this volume, chapter 18) concluded that "higher levels of intrinsic motivation are also associated with well-being, self-esteem, supporting the autonomy of others, self-actualization, behavioral effectiveness, greater volitional persistence, and better assimilation of the individual within his or her social group." Based upon this section's discussion, the following Proposition II is suggested:

> Proposition II: Music making (as an amateur or professional) can result in various types of need satisfaction, including social (e.g. belonging), self-esteem, and self-actualization.

Maslow's Transcendence, Csikszentmihalyi's Theory of Flow, and Music Making

> I've got the magic power of the music in me
>
> (Gil Moore, Mike Levine, and Rik Emmett, Triumph)

Maslow further developed his "theory of human motivation" to include the concept of *transcendence*, where an individual experiences "a loss of self-consciousness, of self-awareness ... [and] self-forgetfulness which comes from getting absorbed, fascinated, concentrated" (1971, 269). Maslow defined transcendence as referring "to the very highest and most inclusive or holistic levels of human consciousness, behaving and relating, as ends rather than as means, to oneself, to significant others, to human beings in general, to other species, to nature, and to the cosmos" (279). These ideas were subsequently adopted by Csikszentmihalyi (1990) in his concept of "flow," which evolved into the larger realm of positive psychology (Seligman and Csikszentmihalyi 2000). According to Csikszentmihalyi (1990), *flow* is an optimal experience when we feel "in control of our actions, masters of our own fate . . . a sense of exhilaration, a deep sense of enjoyment that is long cherished and that becomes a landmark in memory for what life should be like . . . something that we *make* happen" (3; emphasis in original). It is "the feeling when things were going well as an almost automatic, effortless, yet highly focused state of consciousness" (Csikszentmihalyi 1996, 110). Seligman asserted that having an "engaged life" "is about flow: being one with the music, time stopping, and the loss of self-consciousness during an absorbing activity" (2011, 11).

Smith (this volume, chapter 9) notes that flow is about "obtaining and maintaining . . . optimal or peak experiences . . . , whereas eudaimonism is about being true to oneself, which may in turn lead to a frequent or even largely constant sense of flow." Csikszentmihalyi (1996) found nine main elements of an enjoyable "flow" experience: (1) clear step-by-step goals, (2) immediate feedback, (3) challenge-skill balance, (4) awareness and action merged together, (5) intense focus, (6) no concern about failure, (7) lack of self-consciousness—feeling at one with the universe, (8) distorted time perception, and (9) autotelic activity—worth doing for its own sake and for the feeling of the experience. Music making is one type of activity that can potentially lead to the experience of "flow."

Music Making, Flow, Transcendence, Spirituality, and Feedback

Music can also provide satisfaction through performance in terms of *positive feedback* and the way it provides opportunities for experiencing flow and exhibiting music making skills. Flow has been demonstrated in composition (Chirico et al. 2015; MacDonald, Hargreaves, and Miell 2009), performance (Chirico et al. 2015; Freer 2007; Fritz and Avsec 2007; Marin and Bhattacharya 2013; Wrigley and Emmerson 2011), and practice (Butkovic, Ullén, and Mosing 2015; O'Neill 1999). Studies have found an association between greater numbers of flow experiences and high achievement in adolescent musicians (Fritz and Avsec 2007; O'Neill 1999). Sloboda (1991) showed that adults who experienced flow while playing music when they were younger than ten had an increased likelihood of being involvement with music as adults. Further, greater flow and involvement with music provide more motivation and reinforcement for individuals to continue to participate in music performance (Sinnamon, Moran, and O'Connell 2012; Woody and McPherson 2010).

Bernard (2009) studied flow, transcendent music making experiences, transcendent religious experiences, and music education based upon graduate students' autobiographical accounts. Bernard found transcendent music making experiences include two key criteria: (1) that the performer is "at the height of his or her abilities and ([2]) that the performer has a sense of being a part of something larger than him or herself in some way" (2009, 1). The first transcendent music making experiences criterion is related to the *symbol of completeness* to the musician's background experience and training. The second criterion is in accordance with the *social reality* factor in self-completion theory (Wicklund and Gollwitzer 2013), as well as Maslow's definition of transcendence (1971), and the concept of *flow* (Csikszentmihalyi 1990).

Butkovic, Ullén, and Mosing (2015) conducted a study of music practice behavior with Swedish twin cohorts involving 10,500 individuals. They found that 25 percent of the variance in music practice was predicted by flow experience and the personality trait of *openness* (due to shared genetic influences). A study by Wrigley and Emmerson (2011) of 236 Australian students provided the first empirical evidence of flow in a live music performance, but found students did not experience flow because their skills were not high enough for the challenge. A survey by Fritz and Avsec (2007) with eighty-four Academy of Music students in Slovenia showed flow was related to positive affect and subjective well-being, clear goals, challenge-skill balance, task concentration, and autotelic experience. Sinnamon, Moran, and O'Connell (2012) studied the flow experiences at two European music conservatories of eighty elite music students aiming to become professional musicians (ages eighteen to twenty-two) and 125 amateur music students taking weekly lessons (ages nine to nineteen) and found that all nine flow dimensions were important for both groups. Marin and Bhattacharya (2013) studied flow in piano performance with seventy-six undergraduate university students from the U.S., the U.K., and Australia, and found that flow was predicated by individual differences in the amount of daily music practice and by emotional intelligence. Also, flow was related to the specific compositional features and related emotional expressions of certain music. The diversity of these research samples by culture and age indicate that experiencing flow is possible for music makers with the right preparation, and even perhaps the right genetic makeup, and that flow can provide a rewarding experience to encourage continued music making participation.

Music Making and Spirituality

Palmer (2006) proposed that spirituality be taught in music education based partly on teachers' own experiences with the music making process. Palmer's view is "that supreme levels of spiritual awareness involve a sense of transcendence and connectedness to all life and the cosmos ... that has nothing to do with religion and doctrine and ... can be attained through correct practice" (2006, 156). Clift and Hancox (2001) conducted a study of eighty-four subjects aged eighteen to sixty-nine (mostly young adults), and found perceived benefits from participation in a university choral society included spiritual benefits (49 percent) as well as social (87 percent), emotional (75 percent) and physical (58 percent) benefits. A study by Shansky (2012) of interviews with members of a synagogue musical ensemble found that music ensemble members experienced a spiritual connection and enjoyed playing music and being part of the community, and that their music enhanced the worship service for the congregation. A study by Hays and Minichiello (2005a) of thirty-eight older adults in Australia revealed that music provided the subjects with the means to understand their spirituality. Hays found "[m]any informants believed that music merged the intellect, emotions, life experiences and spiritual self together as one" (2005, 29). A survey by Rohwer and Coffman (2006) of 480 adults aged thirty to eighty-six unexpectedly found that wind band members reported having significantly lower scores on a spirituality scale than nonband members' friends (who were not music makers). Based upon the aforementioned sections on transcendence, flow, and spirituality, the following Proposition III is presented:

> Proposition III: Music making (as an amateur or professional) can generate flow and transcendent experiences that include physical, emotional, and spiritual dimensions.

Intrinsic Rewards of Music Making: Well-Being, Happiness and Quality of Life

> Music is a . . . language . . . for all to sing, dance and clap their hands
> (Stevie Wonder)

What Is Well-Being?

Dierendonck and Mohan (2006) identified two types of *well-being*: "hedonic well-being," experiencing pleasure, joy, and relaxation (and avoiding pain and discomfort), and "eudaimonic well-being," pursuing challenging activities for the achievement of one's best possible self. Seligman (2010, 2011) maintained that elements of well-being consist of "PERMA: positive emotion, engagement, relationships, meaning, and accomplishment." Ryff (1989) proposed that for adulthood and old age well-being includes: self-acceptance, positive relations with others, autonomy, environmental mastery, purpose in life, and personal growth. Seligman's and Ryff's views on well-being have similarities related to the levels in Maslow's hierarchy of needs: social needs (e.g., relationships), self-actualization (e.g., meaning or purpose in life, accomplishment, environmental mastery, personal growth), and self-esteem (positive emotion, self-acceptance, autonomy). Thus, a synergistic perspective can be gleaned about the relationship between well-being and the fulfillment of Maslow's hierarchy of needs.

Music Making and Well-Being (Including Health Benefits)

An extensive review by Hallam, Creech, and Varvarigou (this volume, chapter 3) found *health-related* benefits from music making consisted of: experiencing pleasure, relaxation, and relief from family and work pressures, emotional release, increased energy and arousal, cognitive stimulation of learning, experiencing self-expression, increased confidence and self-esteem, spiritual fulfillment, and emotional and physical well-being.

Here are some examples of research studies related to music making and well-being. Jutras (2006, 2011) conducted research about the importance of health benefits of playing piano, and respondents reported experiencing mental, emotional, and physical health benefits. Croom (2015) applied Seligman's (2011) PERMA framework to a review of music education research and found support for the relationship of music practice and participation to well-being. Interviews with adults sixty-five and older in Australia by Hays and Minichiello found that music "promotes quality of life by contributing to positive self-esteem, by helping people feel competent and independent, and by lessening feelings of isolation and loneliness" (2005b, 261). Further, Hays found that "Music provided ways for defining and redefining their self-identity, knowing and understanding emotions, and maintaining personal well-being" (2005, 29). For the older adults, well-being was defined as staying "physically, cognitively, and socially active for as long as possible" (31). The study showed that music contributed to a higher quality of life, helping people to relieve stress, maintain their physical and cognitive functioning, and to feel less isolated. Music-related activities included listening to music, singing or playing a musical instrument as amateurs or professional, or engaging in music-related activities such as community radio broadcasting, concert management, or teaching music. Creech et al. (2013) also found indications about the power of music related to well-being in the lives of older adults.

As previously discussed, a number of studies have shown relationships between music making and quality of life—especially for older adults (e.g., Coffman 2002, 2009; Coffman and Adamek 1999). A study by Rohwer and Coffman (2006) of 480 adults, aged thirty to eighty-six, from eleven states in the U.S. showed that wind band participants reported having significantly higher quality of life than nonband members. Coffman's (2009) survey of over 1,600 adult music makers (ages twenty-three to ninety-three years old, mean age of sixty-seven) reported four music making benefit categories: (1) emotional well-being, (2) physical well-being, (3) cognitive stimulation, and (4) socialization.

Drawing upon the previous discussion, the following propositions are suggested:

> Proposition IV: Music making that results in need satisfaction, flow, and transcendent experiences can lead to other benefits such as emotional and physical well-being, happiness, and a better quality of life.
>
> Proposition V: Music making benefits and intrinsic rewards are positive reinforcement that generate feedback to encourage continued music making (as long as participants are healthy enough and have time, other resources, and support to continue this pursuit).

Stebbins (1982) asserted that when musicians experience feelings of enjoyment, self-enhancement, and self-actualization during rehearsal or performance, this will motivate them to repeat the experience and to improve performances. The proposed model in Figure 15.1 includes a "feedback loop" to reinforce and return to music making.

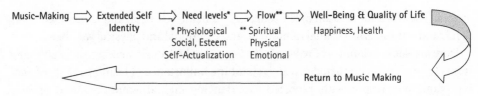

FIGURE 15.1 Transcendent model of motivation for music making

Based upon the research findings related to Propositions I to V, Figure 15.1 shown above presents the new Transcendent Model of Motivation for Music Making (TMMMM).

CONCLUSION

The new model proposed in this chapter was built upon multidisciplinary research from the fields of consumer behavior, music education, and psychology. The model begins with the development of one's music making identity, and then utilizes the paradigm of self-transcendence to represent and subsume the entire spectrum of human needs from Maslow's theory of human motivation (except for safety needs) (Maslow 1943, 1954, 1969a, 1969b, 1971). The purpose of the TMMMM is to represent the complete process of how an individual music maker can ideally experience all the main music making benefits, which include a strong extended self music identity; satisfaction of social, esteem, and self-actualization needs; flow dimensions including enjoyment, enhanced spirituality, and the physical or physiological benefits associated with mental, emotional, and physical well-being which contribute to a better quality of life. The TMMMM does not promise or guarantee that a music maker will experience all of the benefits; these may or may not occur at different times in one's lifespan, depending upon an individual's characteristics and situations. Future research can empirically and qualitatively test which individual characteristics (e.g., physical capabilities and limitations, brain functions—perhaps someday even genome testing—personality, demographics such as age, gender, ethnicity, income, occupation, marital status, family, life cycle stage, etc.), and environmental factors (e.g., social support, financial resources, time constraints) contribute to these various benefits, achievements, and outcomes.

Limitations and Future Research

One limitation of the proposed conceptual model is that it is based upon studies mainly from the U.S., the U.K., and Australia. Future research could test the TMMMM empirically with music maker samples from other countries (as well as by age and other demographic or lifestyle factors) to compare similarities or significant differences for each type of sample. There has been criticism (e.g., Hofstede 1980) that Maslow's hierarchy of needs is more reflective of an individualistic society rather than a collectivist one in regard to the importance of self-actualization versus belonging needs. This chapter asserts that the personal, social, and health benefits, and the importance of music making to one's identity, including the notion of experiencing flow and transcendence, are universal in nature, in alignment with Henry Wadsworth Longfellow's philosophical perspective that "Music is the universal language of mankind" (Longfellow 1835, 4).

Future research could extend the model in terms of what other personality characteristics contribute to an individual's extended self and musical identity to determine whether someone will be more likely to become an amateur or a professional musician (see e.g., Smith 2015). One interesting personality characteristic that could be tested would be from environmental psychology, to determine if more successful musicians are nonscreeners or screeners (Mehrabian 1977). Research by Mehrabian (1977) found that high achievers were more likely to be screeners, who are "persons who are most adept at screening the less relevant components of their everyday environments" (239). Vaccaro (2001) suggested that nonscreeners might be more inherently predisposed to be responsive to listening to music, but it may be that music makers who are screeners achieve more success in both practice and performance. Other personality traits that could be tested may be from the Kuntz (2012) self-reported personal traits of adult amateur musicians, and from the Coffman survey findings (2009).

Societal and Industry Implications

> Don't let the sun go down on me
> (Elton John and Bernie Taupin)

The research discussed in this chapter and the new TMMMM may have implications for music education and music making as a leisure activity due to industry issues and socio-cultural demographic trends of an aging population. A 2003 Gallup survey on attitudes toward playing music instruments found that "42% of those between the ages of 35 and 50 who learned to play an instrument still play, as well as 20% of people aged 50 and older. For some people, it's a lifelong pursuit" (Lyons 2003). Also, a 2009 Gallup survey commissioned by the National Association of Music Merchants (NAMM) on attitudes toward music making found that 9 of 10 Americans believe there are many benefits of playing musical instruments for children (e.g., creativity, making friends, building teamwork skills, intellectual development), but that time constraints and other commitments prevent many adults from participation in music-making (NAMM 2009). More recently, NAMM's website states that it "promotes the pleasures and benefits of making music . . . to people of all ages" (NAMM 2015). Fonarow (2012) noted that "the importance of amateur musicians can be seen in the changes in marketing campaigns for instrument manufacturers. . . . In a sense, we are in a golden age for amateurs who make music for pleasure." Fonarow explained that current promotional campaigns target amateurs by showing music making as a worthwhile, fun activity that is part of life (music instrument ad campaigns had previously focused on music as a career with the goal of stardom). These days, if more amateur musicians exist, there are more possibilities for them to experience aspects such as flow and well-being as described in the proposed Transcendent Model of Motivation for Music Making.

Mantie wrote about how individuals participate in music making for the sole objective of experiencing the joy of it, and how such engagement has been undervalued in music education:

> If you cannot do to the exacting standards of the professional there is apparently little point in trying. Many amateurs quickly realize they can never hope to "learn" enough to reach a professional level, and because participation for its own sake is insufficient there is little point in partaking in amateur music-making. (Mantie 2012, 228)

However, research with older adults by Coffman (2009) and others shows that more people do appreciate music making at the amateur or hobby level, although there are those who may get discouraged because they do not have enough time or the resources. Pitts (this volume, chapter 10) found key factors for continued adult music making participation depended on early development of competent music skills, encouragement from others, and past positive music making experiences.

A purpose of this *Handbook* is to enhance the understanding of how recreational music making brings meaning to people's lives. This chapter strives to achieve that objective by providing a new model of music making that draws upon wide-ranging research. The framework for the proposed TMMMM is based upon humanistic psychology (Maslow 1943, 1954, 1968, 1969a, 1969b, 1971) and the paradigm of positive psychology (Seligman and Csikszentmihalyi 2000). The foundation for positive psychology is the notion that people can strive to achieve their best selves by pursuing activities that can lead to flow, self-actualization and well-being, contentment and optimism by illuminating the path for "how people's lives can be most worth living" (5). I hope the research review in this chapter which supports the new TMMMM may shed new light on the challenges and benefits (physical, cognitive, emotional, spiritual) associated with music making for people at various life stages (in childhood, adolescence, middle adulthood, and retirement). The new model may also have wider implications for enhancing understanding of *any* human goal-directed motivation and behavior moving toward self-actualization and self-transcendence.

References Cited

Ball, A. Dwayne, and Lori H. Tasaki. 1992. "The Role and Measurement of Attachment in Consumer Behavior." *Journal of Consumer Psychology* 1(2): 155–172.

Belk, Russell W. 1988. "Possessions and Extended Self." *Journal of Consumer Research* 15: 139–168.

Bernard, Rhoda. 2009. "Music Making, Transcendence, Flow, and Music Education." *International Journal of Education and the Arts* 10(14). http://www.ijea.org/v10n14/.

Bugos, Jennifer A. 2014. "Adult Learner Perceptions: Perspectives from Beginning Musicians (Ages 60–86 Years)." *Update: Applications of Research in Music Education* 32: 26–34.

Butkovic, Ana, Fredrik Ullén, and Miriam A. Mosing. 2015. "Personality Related Traits as Predictors of Music Practice: Underlying Environmental and Genetic Influences." *Personality and Individual Differences* 74: 133–138.

Chirico, Alice, Silvia Serino, Pietro Cipresso, Andrea Gaggioli, and Giuseppe Riva. 2015. "When Music 'Flows.' State and Trait in Musical Performance, Composition and Listening: A Systematic Review." *Frontiers in Psychology* 6: 1–14, article 906.

Clift, Stephen M., and Grenville Hancox. 2001. "The Perceived Benefits of Singing: Findings from Preliminary Surveys of a University College Choral Society." *Journal of the Royal Society for the Promotion of Health* 121: 248–256.

Coffman, Don D. 2002. "Music and Quality of Life in Older Adults." *Psychomusicology: A Journal of Research in Music Cognition* 18: 76–88.

Coffman, Don D. 2006. "Voices of Experience: Interviews of Adult Community Band Members in Launceston, Tasmania, Australia." *International Journal of Community Music* 23(1): 37–47.

Coffman, Don D. 2009. "Survey of New Horizons International Music Association musicians." *International Journal of Community Music* 1(3): 375–390.

Coffman, Don D., and Mary S. Adamek. 1999 "The Contributions of Wind Band Participation to Quality of Life of Senior Adults." *Music Therapy Perspectives* 17(1): 27–31.

Coffman, Don D., and Mary S. Adamek. 2001. "Perceived Social Support of New Horizons Band Participants." *Contributions to Music Education* 28: 27–40.

Creech, Andrea. 2008. "The Role of the Family in Supporting Learning." In *The Oxford Handbook of Music Psychology*, edited by Susan Hallam, Ian Cross, and Michael Thaut, 295–306. Oxford: Oxford University Press.

Creech, Andrea, and Susan Hallam. 2003. "Parent–Teacher–Pupil Interactions in Instrumental Music Tuition: A Literature Review." *British Journal of Music Education* 20(1): 29–44.

Creech, Andrea, Susan Hallam, Hilary McQueen, and Maria Varvarigou. 2013. "The Power of Music in the Lives of Older Adults." *Research Studies in Music Education* 35: 87–102.

Croom, Adam M. 2015. "Music Practice and Participation for Psychological Well-Being: A Review of How Music Influences Positive Emotion, Engagement, Relationships, Meaning, and Accomplishment." *Musicae Scientiae* 19: 44–64.

Csikszentmihalyi, Mihaly, and Eugene Rochberg-Halton. 1981. *The Meaning of things: Domestic Symbols and the Self*. Cambridge: Cambridge University Press.

Csikszentmihalyi, Mihaly. 1990. *Flow: The Psychology of Optimal Experience*. New York: Harper and Row.

Csikszentmihalyi, Mihaly. 1996. *Creativity: Flow and the Psychology of Discovery and Invention*. New York: HarperCollins.

Deci, Edward L., and Richard M. Ryan. 1985. *Intrinsic Motivation and Self-Determination in Human Behavior*. New York: Plenum.

Dierendonck, Dirk van, and Krishna Mohan. 2006. "Some Thoughts on Spirituality and Eudaimonic Well-Being." *Mental Health, Religion and Culture* 9(3): 227–238.

Eccles, Jacquelynne S., Terry F. Adler, Robert Futterman, Susan B. Goff, Carol M. Kaczala, Judith L. Meece, and Carol Midgley.1983. "Expectancies, Values, and Academic Behaviours." In *Achievement and Achievement Motives: Psychological and Sociological Approaches*, edited by Janet Taylor Spence, 75–146. San Francisco: W. H. Freeman.

Erikson, Erik H. 1968. *Identity: Youth and Crisis.* New York: Norton.

Fonarow, Wendy. 2012. "Ask the Indie Professor: When Should Amateur Musicians Call it a Day?" *The Guardian*, January 24. http://www.theguardian.com/music/musicblog/2012/jan/24/indie-professor-amateur-musicians.

Freer, Patrick K. 2007. "The Conductor's Voice: Flow and the Choral Experience." *Choral Journal* 48(2): 9–19.

Fritz, Barbara Smolej, and Andreja Avsec. 2007. "The Experience of Flow and Subjective Well-Being of Music Students." *Psihološka Obzorja / Horizons of Psychology* 16(2): 5–17.

Gollwitzer, Peter M. 1987. "The Implementation of Identity Intentions: A Motivational-Volitional Perspective on Symbolic Self-Completion." In *Motivation, Intention, and Volition*, edited by Frank Halisch and Julius Kuhl, 349–369. Berlin and Heidelberg: Springer.

Hall, Calvin S., and Vernon J. Nordby. 1973. *A Primer of Jungian Psychology.* Oxford: Taplinger.

Hallam, Susan. 2002. "Musical Motivation: Towards a Model Synthesising the Research." *Music Education Research* 4(2): 225–244.

Hallam, Susan. 2009. "Motivation to Learn." In *The Oxford Handbook of Music Psychology*, edited by Susan Hallam, Ian Cross, and Michael Thaut, 285–294. Oxford: Oxford University Press.

Hallam, Susan. 2013. "What Predicts Level of Expertise Attained, Quality of Performance, and Future Musical Aspirations in Young Instrumental Players?" *Psychology of Music* 41(3): 267–291.

Hargreaves, David J., and Nigel A. Marshall. 2003. "Developing Identities in Music Education." *Music Education Research* 5(3): 263–273.

Hays, Terrence. 2005. "Well-Being in Later Life through Music." *Australasian Journal on Ageing* 24(1): 28–32.

Hays, Terrence, and Victor Minichiello. 2005a. "Older People's Experience of Spirituality through Music." *Journal of Religion, Spirituality and Aging* 18(1): 83–96.

Hays, Terrence, and Victor Minichiello. 2005b "The Contribution of Music to Quality of Life in Older People: An Australian Qualitative Study." *Ageing and Society* 25: 261–278.

Hofstede, Geert. 1980. "Motivation, Leadership, and Organization: Do American Theories Apply Abroad?" *Organizational Dynamics* 9(1): 42–63.

Jutras, Peter J. 2006. "The Benefits of Adult Piano Study as Self-Reported by Selected Adult Piano Students." *Journal of Research in Music Education* 54(2): 97–110.

Jutras, Peter J. 2011. "The Benefits of New Horizons Band Participation as Self-Reported by Selected New Horizons Band Members." *Bulletin of the Council for Research in Music Education* 187 (Winter): 65–84.

Koltko-Rivera, Mark E. 2006. "Rediscovering the Later Version of Maslow's Hierarchy of Needs: Self-Transcendence and Opportunities for Theory, Research, and Unification," *Review of General Psychology* 10(4): 302–317.

Kokotsaki, Dimitra, and Susan Hallam. 2007. "Higher Education Music Students' Perceptions of the Benefits of Participative Music Making." *Music Education Research* 9: 93–109.

Kuntz, Tammy L. 2012. "Self Reported Personal Traits of Adult Amateur Musicians." PhD dissertation, Case Western Reserve University, Cleveland, OH.

Longfellow, Henry Wadsworth. 1835. *Outre-Mer: A Pilgrimage Beyond the Sea, Volume 2 of 2, Chapter 1: Ancient Spanish Ballads.* New York: Harper & Brothers, 4.

Lyons, Linda. 2003. "Americans Want Music Students to Play On." Gallup.com, May 20, 2003. http://www.gallup.com/poll/8434/americans-want-music-students-play.aspx.

MacDonald, Raymond, David J. Hargreaves, and Dorothy Miell. 2009. "Musical Identities." In *The Oxford Handbook of Music Psychology*, in Susan Hallam, Ian Cross, and Michael Thaut, 462–470. Oxford: Oxford University Press.

Mantie, Roger. 2012. "Learners or Participants? The Pros and Cons of 'Lifelong Learning.'" *International Journal of Community Music* 5(3): 217–235.

Marin, Manuela M., and Joydeep Bhattacharya. 2013. "Getting into the Musical Zone: Trait Emotional Intelligence and Amount of Practice Predict Flow in Pianists." *Frontiers in Psychology* 4: 853. doi: 10.3389/fpsyg.2013.00853.

Maslow, Abraham H. 1943. "A Theory of Human Motivation." *Psychological Review* 50(4): 370–396.

Maslow, Abraham H. 1954. *Motivation and Personality*. New York: Harper and Row.

Maslow, Abraham H. 1968. "Music Education and Peak Experience." *Music Educators Journal* 54: 72–171.

Maslow, Abraham H. 1969a. "The Farther Reaches of Human Nature." *Journal of Transpersonal Psychology* 1(1): 1–9.

Maslow, Abraham H. 1969b. "Toward a Humanistic Biology." *American Psychologist* 24: 724–735.

Maslow, Abraham H. 1971. *The Farther Reaches of Human Nature*. New York: Viking.

McPherson, Gary E., and Susan A. O'Neill. 2010. "Students' Motivation to Study Music as Compared to Other School Subjects: A Comparison of Eight Countries." *Research Studies in Music Education* 32(2): 101–137.

Mehrabian, Albert. 1977. "Individual Differences in Stimulus Screening and Arousability." *Journal of Personality* 45(2): 237–250.

Miller, Jeffrey C. 2004. *The Transcendent Function: Jung's Model of Psychological Growth through Dialogue with the Unconscious*. New York: SUNY Press.

NAMM. 2009. "New Gallup Survey by NAMM Reflects Majority of Americans Agree with Many Benefits of Playing Musical Instruments." NAMM.org. https://www.namm.org/news/press-releases/new-gallup-survey-namm-reflects-majority-americans.

NAMM. 2015a. "NAMM Defined." NAMM.org. https://www.namm.org/about.

O'Neill, Susan A. 1999. "Flow Theory and the Development of Musical Performance Skills." *Bulletin of the Council for Research in Music Education* 141: 129–134.

O'Neill, Susan A. 2002. "The Self-Identity of Young Musicians." In *Musical Identities*, edited by Raymond A. R. MacDonald, David J. Hargreaves, and Dorothy Miell, 79–96. Oxford: Oxford University Press.

Palmer, Anthony J. 2006. "Music Education and Spirituality: Philosophical Exploration II." *Philosophy of Music Education Review* 14(2): 143–158.

Persson, Roland S. 2011. "The Multidimensional Model of Musical Giftedness (3MG): Breaking New Ground in Understanding Musical Talent and Musical Thinking." Paper given at the World Council for Gifted and Talented Children WCGTC Conference, Prague, August. https://www.diva-portal.org/smash/get/diva2:431753/FULLTEXT01.pdf.

Plato. 1970. *The Dialogues of Plato*. Translated by Benjamin Jowett. Vol. 4, *The Republic*, edited by R. M. Hare and D. A. Russell, 165–171 (book 3: 398–403). London: Sphere. https://theoryofmusic.wordpress.com/2008/08/04/music-in-platos-republic/.

Rohwer, Debbie, and Don Coffman. 2006. "Relationships between Wind Band Membership, Activity Level, Spirituality, and Quality of Life in Older Adults." *Research Perspectives in Music Education* 10(1): 21–27.

Ryan, Richard M., and Edward L. Deci. 2000. "Self-Determination Theory and the Facilitation of Intrinsic Motivation, Social Development, and Well-Being." *American Psychologist* 55(1): 68–78.

Ryff, Carol D. 1989. "Beyond Ponce de Leon and Life Satisfaction: New Directions in Quest of Successful Aging." *International Journal of Behavioral Development* 12: 35–55.

Seligman, Martin E. P., and Mihaly Csikszentmihalyi. 2000. "Positive Psychology: An Introduction." *American Psychologist* 55(1): 5–14. doi: 10.1037/0003-066X.55.1.5.

Seligman, Martin E. P. 2010. *Flourish: Positive Psychology and Positive Interventions*. The Tanner Lectures on Human Values. Ann Arbor: University of Michigan Press.

Seligman, Martin E. P. 2011. *Flourish: A Visionary New Understanding of Happiness and Well-Being*. New York: Free Press.

Shansky, Carol. 2012. "Spirituality and Synagogue Music: A Case Study of Two Synagogue Music Ensembles." *Research and Issues in Music Education* 10(1): 1–14.

Sinnamon, Sarah, Aldan Moran, and Michael O'Connell. 2012. "Flow among Musicians: Measuring Peak Experiences of Student Performers." *Journal of Research in Music Education* 60: 6–25.

Sloboda, John A., and Michael J. A. Howe. 1991. "Biographical Precursors of Musical Excellence: An Interview Study." *Psychology of Music* 19: 3–21.

Smith, Gareth Dylan. 2013. *I Drum, Therefore I Am: Being and Becoming a Drummer*. Farnham: Ashgate.

Smith, Gareth Dylan. 2015. "Seeking 'Success' in Popular Music." In *Music Education: Navigating the Future*, edited by Clint Randles, 183–200. New York: Routledge.

Stebbins, Robert A. 1982. "Serious Leisure: A Conceptual Statement." *Pacific Sociological Review* 25: 251–272.

Stebbins, Robert A. 1992. *Amateurs, Professionals, and Serious Leisure*. Montreal, QC: McGill-Queen's University Press.

Taylor, Angela. 2011. "Older Amateur Keyboard Players Learning for Self-Fulfilment." *Psychology of Music* 39: 345–363.

Vaccaro, Valerie L. 2001. "In-Store Music's Influence on Consumer Responses: The Development and Test of a Music-Retail Environment Model." PhD dissertation. Graduate Center of the City University of New York.

Waterman, Alan S. 1993. "Two Conceptions of Happiness: Contrasts of Personal Expressiveness (Eudaimonia) and Hedonic Enjoyment." *Journal of Personality and Social Psychology* 64: 678–691.

Weigelt, David. 2015 "50+ Facts and Fiction: Size, Wealth and Spending of 50+ Consumers." *Immersion Active*, March 9. http://www.immersionactive.com/resources/size-wealth-spending-50-consumers/.

Wicklund, Robert A., and Peter M. Gollwitzer. 1981. "Symbolic Self-Completion, Attempted Influence, and Self-Deprecation." *Basic and Applied Social Psychology* 2(2): 89–114.

Wicklund, Robert A., and Peter M. Gollwitzer. 2013. *Symbolic Self-Completion*. London: Routledge.

Woody, Robert H., and Gary E. McPherson. 2010. "Emotion and Motivation in the Lives of Performers." *Handbook of Music and Emotion: Theory, Research, Applications*, edited by Patrik N. Juslin, 401–424. Oxford: Oxford University Press.

Wrigley, William Joseph, and Stephen Bryan Emmerson. 2011. "The Experience of the Flow State in Live Music Performance." *Psychology of Music* 41: 292–305.

CHAPTER 16

....

DEVELOPING A CULTURAL THEORY OF MUSIC MAKING AND LEISURE

Baudrillard, the Simulacra, and Music Consumption

....

KARL SPRACKLEN

INTRODUCTION

....

POPULAR music and culture are sites of identity construction, where identity defines *belonging to* and *exclusion from* an imagined community delineated by symbolic boundaries. Extreme Heavy Metal, as a genre of popular music and a part of popular culture, is a site where such identity formation, myth making, and boundary maintenance can be seen (Kahn-Harris 2007). In this chapter, I explore how extreme metal bands originating from the north of England draw upon narratives of heritage and historical myths to construct exclusive, masculinizing metal identities. I am exploring their music making in its broadest sense to develop a new theory about the meaning and purpose of music in the lives of makers, listeners, and fans—as a key device in constructing alternative hyperrealities to the capitalist reality of late modernity. This research is based on a bigger project I have undertaken with colleagues, parts of which have been published elsewhere (see Lucas, Deeks, and Spracklen 2011; Spracklen 2013a; Spracklen, Lucas, and Deeks 2014). For the purposes of this chapter, I am presenting new data and analysis to develop a new cultural theory of music making and leisure. I draw in particular on Baudrillard's notion of the *simulacra* (Baudrillard 1988, 1994, 1995) to understand how the consumers and presenters (the musicians and the journalists) of black metal bands from the north of England construct ideas of warrior masculinities and Northern pride.

In this chapter, I employ a qualitative case-study research based on textual analyses of public interviews with three black metal bands[1]—Winterfylleth, Wodensthrone (previously discussed in Spracklen, Lucas, and Deeks 2014), and White Medal—to argue that these Northern English extreme "metallers" express a desire to tell histories that have been forgotten in a globalizing world: heritage narratives associated with the North. I have chosen these bands partly because they have formed a part of my earlier research, but mainly because they have made explicit attempts to situate their music making in narratives of pride, reclaiming hidden histories, and reclaiming a hegemonic masculinity. This action has allowed the first two bands a measure of commercial success and critical acclaim, with Winterfylleth in particular becoming so successful they have been featured artists on metal magazine covers. All three bands are using their agency to make communicatively rational decisions (Habermas 1984, 1987) about what music they construct: they are free within the limits of the simulation and the hyperreality to select certain ways of making music, as well as certain discourses and symbols about the music in its wider context. In turn, fans consume the music and write about it to legitimate their own desires to feel belonging and a sense of exclusive community in a modern world they wish to reject. That is, their use of heritage and myth is still circumscribed by the invented traditions (Hobsbawm and Ranger 1983) and symbolic boundaries of the wider extreme metal scene that are characterized by the legends of Germanic warriors and the defense of regional and national pride.

Theoretical Framework

This chapter draws heavily on the theoretical framework used in previous research (Lucas, Deeks, and Spracklen 2011; Spracklen, Lucas, and Deeks 2014). My own interest in leisure theory is in the tension between agency and constraint (Spracklen 2009, 2011, 2013a, 2013b) and the application of Habermasian rationalities to explain that tension. I am interested in understanding the meanings and purposes of leisure, as well as the meanings and purposes of music in contemporary culture. In the second half of the twentieth century, policy makers and academics became interested in the idea that leisure was an important part of people's everyday lives. Some academics predicted that the conditions of late modernity would lead to increasing leisure time and the rationalization of leisure, following the trends of the previous century (Kelly 1983; Roberts 1999). A second wave of leisure scholars argued that leisure choices in modern society were constrained by social structures such as class, gender, and "race" (Spracklen 2009). Others, such as Chris Rojek, believed that the period of time we were living in was so different from that which had gone before that leisure and society had become postmodern (Rojek 1995, 2000). In this view, leisure becomes the one space where people have the agency to make meaning and do identity work (Rojek 2010). At the same time, radical theorists such as Peter Bramham (2006) have shown that leisure is still an activity and a space that is limited by social, political, and cultural power.

Responding to the same shifts and fractures in Western society, researchers of popular music have theorized the development of neo-tribes as the effect of postmodernity on practices of consumption and identity formation (Bennett 2000, 2001, 2002; Maffesoli

1996). Neo-tribes, however, are too fluid and unbounded to be useful in understanding what is at work in extreme metal. In this cultural space, belonging is strongly determined by symbolic boundaries. Crucial to that belonging is boundary work—where myths and symbols are used to maintain the intersecting imaginary communities of northern European (northern English) black metal. In extreme metal (and perhaps in other music genres and spaces), what counts is the defense of the boundaries, and the negotiations and contestations over who has the power and will to determine the myths and symbols that make up the boundaries. Rather than seeing such community as being postmodern or liquid in a Baumanian sense (Bauman 2000), I suggest it is the case that existing inequalities of power and status have been mapped across from mainstream society to these communities. Extreme-metal culture in the north of England, then, becomes a space that on the one hand embraces an inner solidarity, and on the other hand reinforces and reproduces norms of masculinity, of whiteness, of Northern-ness, and of Englishness.

I am explicitly aligning my work to critical, post-Marxist leisure studies, which draw on Bauman (2000) and Habermas (1984, 1987; and see Spracklen 2009), and the post-Marxist subcultural tradition in popular music studies exemplified by researchers such as Hodkinson (2002) and Kahn-Harris (2007). Combined with this I am following a cultural anthropological approach that assumes all music spaces and leisure spaces are sites of contestation over boundaries, belonging, and identity (Cohen 1985). That is, making music, listening to music, and writing about it are all acts of communicative leisure: music making and music criticism are by definition communicative acts of leisure (Habermas 1984, 1987; Spracklen 2009, 2011, 2013a, 2013b). Communicative leisure is a form and a space where identity can be performed. Following Judith Butler (2006) and her work on the performance of gender, such performativity can be viewed as an expression of conformity or transgression. Just as people choose to perform certain identities to prove they are "true" heavy metal fans or musicians, others impose limits to the performativity: I am interested in the limits of the performances because they tell us something about the music industry today, the limits of agency, and the ways in which Butlerian heteronormativity is constructed (Butler 2006).

In this attempt to construct a cultural theory of music making and leisure, I am using the work of Jean Baudrillard to identity the subject of the performativity within these Northern English black metal bands. The performativity can be understood as a way of constructing an alternative England, and alternative north of England, a form of the real that is mediated by the black metal culture. This performativity creates a version of reality that is real to those who perform it, which is based on the material and social reality of the world, but which takes on a life of its own. That is, I am drawn to the notion of the *simulacra* as it helps us cut through the nationalist and masculine rhetoric layers of the imaginary community and its imagined equivalent to get to the heart of what is actually going on: the construction of a hyperreality (Baudrillard 1988, 1994, 1995). In the first page of *Simulacra and Simulation*, Baudrillard begins with a quote from Ecclesiastes: "The simulacrum is never what hides the truth—it is truth which hides the fact there is none. The simulacrum is true" (Baudrillard 1994, 1). He moves on to describing the "fable" by Borges of the cartographers who draw up a map that is so detailed that it maps the empire on a scale of 1:1 and covers the land completely, before claiming:

> Today abstraction is no longer that of the map, the double, the mirror, or the concept. Simulation is no longer that of a territory, a referential being, or a substance. It is the generation by models of a real without origin or reality: a hyperreal. The territory no longer precedes the map, nor does it survive it. It is nevertheless a map that precedes the territory—*precession of simulacra*—that engenders the territory, and if one must return to the fable, today it is the territory whose shreds slowly rot across the extent of the map. It is the real, and not the map, whose vestiges persist here and there in the deserts that are no longer those of the Empire, but ours. *The desert of the real itself.* (Baudrillard 1994, 1; emphasis in original)

The idea that the (post)modern state of society means that everything becomes a simulation (a simulacrum) of itself is a powerful one, and it has been critiqued by a number of scholars in cultural and political studies (Norris 1992). These attacks have been from two directions. Some critics have accused Baudrillard's theory of hyperreality of being a form of epistemological and ontological relativism, in which nothing is true or real, so everything becomes true or real (Sardar 1993). The title of the 1995 book *The Gulf War Did Not Take Place*, for example, has allowed Baudrillard to be mocked by realists who say this is nonsense. It may sound like Baudrillard is saying that the (first) Gulf War did not take place if all one does is read the title. And one might choose to read the book and find that Baudrillard uses unambiguous language to say that the Gulf War did not take place. But Baudrillard did not say he didn't think people were being killed in Kuwait and Iraq; he was concerned with showing how Western understanding of the War was mediated in such a way that it was impossible to know what was "actually" going on in the East. That is, what we know about becomes unknowable, and all we have are representations, simulations, and hyperrealities that stand as signifiers for the death going on somewhere out there in the real world. A more telling criticism of Baudrillard is the lack of a strong, critical theory in his work—that is, an apparent unwillingness by Baudrillard to pin his colors to the radical criticism of capitalism and the gender order. If everything is hyperreal then we are all equally making meaning for ourselves, and the power of white men becomes just another strategy for agency. But of course Baudrillard was a critic of capitalism and the gender order, and he was essentially a post-Marxist in orientation (Toffoletti 2014).

So while I accept there are limits to the Baudrillardian analysis, the notion that heavy metal musicians and fans might be engaged in the construction of simulacra of warriors, race, the North of England, of Englishness and Britishness and Saxon history, as a way of constructing subcultural legitimacy in the extreme metal scene is one that I pursue in the rest of this chapter. It seems to me that heavy metal music is precisely the kind of leisure form that lends itself to the abstraction of reality and its replacement by a hyperreality, in which hard certainties and narratives replace the complexities of the modern world (Kahn-Harris 2007). I will set out the ways in which the bands construct narratives in their communicative music making, myths and boundaries, and the ways in which they *simulate* place, race, identity, and history in a simulacrum constrained by the communicative agency of fans and critics. I then return to an engagement with Baudrillard and a wider analysis about hyperreality as a way of developing a new cultural theory of music making and leisure.

WINTERFYLLETH

Winterfylleth comes from Manchester, England. The band was founded in 2007, according to Winterfylleth (2014), "with the intention of honouring England's proud ancestral heritage and rich national culture . . . to bring awareness to England's historical stories, folklore, landscapes and ancestral past through their folk-influenced vitriolic black metal." They soon gained a reputation on the underground, and their debut album was released in 2008 by respected underground label Profound Lore. In an early interview on the Ravishing Grimness blog, the band's frontman, Chris Naughton (also the key songwriter and a guitarist), explained what he felt the band was trying to achieve:

> "Winterfylleth is also geared around raising the profile and awareness of our nations' history in a country where we seem to be losing our National Identity, and whose general populous is confused about their ancestry because of over Political Correctness and Cultural Pandering on the part of our government. While we don't feel we can directly influence political change or lobby against this level of political ridiculousness at a musical level, we can try to make people aware of what being 'English' has historically meant, and reinforce a sense of identity among a culturally confused populace," explains. Chris. . . .
>
> "We are obviously heavily influenced by the legends and folklore of our land, which not only convey a spirit that is very close to our hearts, but in the same way represent the spirit of our native people, and therefore that also of our land, in the same way folk music does. Folk music is after all, the music of 'the folk.' The people's music! The area that we come from is geographically ideal for wandering our beloved land. On our doorstep we have the awesome and mysterious Pennine 'Peak District,' the epic and beautiful Lake District, the West Pennine Moors, vast and bleak Yorkshire Dales. . . . Always strive to be informed about issues affecting your country or your culture and make sure that if you don't like something that is happening that you do something about it. . . . Don't fear the ignorance of the media if they call you a racist or try to sully your name, be true to what you believe and be intelligent with your truth. People will only 'know' if they are informed and it is up to individuals like us to bypass the apathy of our 'TV Generation' and get people back in touch with who and what they are. A country without a culture or an identity is like an accident waiting to happen. Bottom line, people need to feel needed and if their culture, or family—because of a cultural confusion—cannot provide them with a sense of 'self'

or 'community' then this is where problems will, and do, start to arise. Don't dwell in apathy . . . Hail Heritage! (Kelly 2008)

This construction of elitist politics, nationalism, loss of heritage, and local place (in this case, the hills of the north of England) put the band firmly in the sphere of other romantic, pagan, conservative nationalist bands such as Ukraine's Drudkh (Spracklen 2006, 2009). Interviews such as this one situated Naughton and Winterfylleth as defenders of a mythical, pure England where its people were not culturally confused. While this can be construed as meaning encouraging people to go for a walk on the moors or to listen to some folk music, the phrase "our nation . . . whose general populous is confused about their ancestry because of over Political Correctness" leaves no doubt that he is concerned with the majority white English, who he thinks need to learn to be proud again of their history—or, rather, the history of the Anglo-Saxons, which is presented in the lyrics of Winterfylleth as a pagan, rather than Christian, heritage, one associated with battles rather than the more mundane farmsteading and husbanding that also shaped the lives of the ancestors of today's white English.

The blog Ravishing Grimness is a fan-critic site that legitimates the ideologies associated with extreme metal. The band made these statements about their music making here so that the readers of the blog would be in no doubt that they were authentic in their conservative, romantic nationalism. Authenticity, of course, is constructed by those who would claim it (Wang 1999). What matters for the musicians of Winterfylleth, the blogger, and the readers of the blog, is that the band have shown they are a part of the global simulacra of "nationalist," "heathen" black metal, as well as the bigger contested simulacra of English nationalism and purity.

With this overt appeal to elitist ideology and English nationalism, the band started to attract attention from antifascists, with pressure being put on the bass player to answer to why he had made reference to the infamous neo-Nazi phrases "wpww" ("White Pride World Wide") and "14w" (fourteen words: "We must secure the existence of our people and a future for White children") on his MySpace page. He responded on the page by admitting they were taken from the White Pride movement. He attacked multiculturalism and Islam, and he confirmed he believed "In a world where the White man is now a minority, especially in his homeland. I feel it is totally acceptable and harmless to display my pride. If people want to assume that I am inciting hatred, then that is their own silly, ignorant misinterpretation" (Sovereign 2009). The row led Winterfylleth to be pulled from a festival in Manchester, and the bass player left the band. The controversy did not stop the band from gaining strong reviews for the live performances and album, or from signing a deal with big independent label Candlelight Records. Indeed, the controversy probably helped them gain the attention of fans, journalists, and labels seeking to find some authentic English "heritage" black metal with a controversial past. Black metal has reveled in nationalism, church burning, and murder, so it is important for musicians to position themselves in that "dark" light.[2] But with commercial progress the band needed to keep the controversy in full sight, while simultaneously denying it. With the backing of a bigger label and two new members they released their second album in 2010 (*The*

Mercian Sphere), and progressed into supporting well-known extreme metal bands on tours and playing festivals across Europe.

At the time of the release of its third album, *The Threnody of Triumph*, issued in 2013 by Candlelight, the band received an enormous amount of positive criticism from reviewers and fans on blogs. In doing the rounds of interviews, Naughton seemed keen to push the notion that the band was not racist or associated with National Socialist Black Metal (NSBM), but they were pushing an agenda to make people think about their histories and cultures. The following interview shows the paradoxes at the heart of the band's music making, and people's consumption of that music:

> Even a cursory look at Winterfylleth's website would reveal that making English black metal—or, more specifically English Heritage Black Metal—is of paramount importance to the band. Their album covers feature idyllic English countryside scenes, while their lyrics are based on ancient Anglo-Saxon poetry, telling of epic battles and legends. This got the band some unwanted publicity in the early days, leading to the cancellation of some early shows. Indeed, type Winterfylleth into Google and the first suggested search option—before even "Winterfylleth merch"—is "Winterfylleth racist." Naughton is clearly frustrated with the tag, which in the early days of the band's career came to define the band. "A lot of bands have had that. There have been bands that have been accused of it, and they've always tried to shy away from it and hide behind pseudonyms, not responding to those kinds of questions in interviews, but I think we were really overtly aware that mud sticks," explains Naughton. "We've always publicised the fact that that is not what we are. We've always tried to say if you think there is a problem, send us an email about it and we'll get back to you with details. I think it was a storm-in-a-tea-cup that for some reason defined who we are in the early years of the band's career. It has taken us until this point—where we have media coverage and the opportunity to articulate the fact that we're not the NSBM dickheads that everyone seemed to think we were."
>
> Winterfylleth may sing about the past, but their view is forward looking, Naughton says. "A lot of the stuff we talk about is socially and culturally relevant and there's always an underlying theme of change, political and social awareness. It's all about learning from the past, as humanity, otherwise we'll keep making the same mistakes and covering old ground. "The initial idea of the band was to sort of re-connect people with the failures and the great triumphs of history. We want to try and make people think a little bit more about things rather than living in, well, TV land," he says.
>
> So, a political black metal band? "I don't think we'd want to be seen as political," Naughton quickly replies. "I think it's more raising awareness of wider social and macro-political issues that sit behind that stuff. I've never really seen us as a political band, I've always thought of us as a band that would motivate people to research things and challenge ideas rather than tell people this is how you need to be."[3]

While it is true to say that the band are not part of the NSBM movement and they are not neo-Nazis, they do use the same discourses and symbols as neo-Nazis: the belief that the modern world is corrupt, that the medieval past is something that is glorious because nations were supposedly purer, and men supposedly more heroic and honorable. This myth making and use of symbols and signs constitutes the construction of the simula-crum, and the reception of the simulacrum, in one shared sense of identity and belong-ing. The band's music making and its consumption by fans makes the simulacra become the hyperreal normality of the scene. So it becomes possible for Naughton to deny being a political band while expressing strong political views, and to deny being a nationalist band while expressing a belief in the righteousness of England's Saxon heritage and the purity of England's countryside against the pollution of "TV Land."

WODENSTHRONE

Wodensthrone is a band from Sunderland in the northeast of England. It formed in 2005 as a more straightforward, "Satanic" black metal band, but the players soon became interested in exploring Anglo-Saxon narratives and imagery. They have used pseudonyms for members of the band, following the style of other black metal bands. The names they use are "Anglo-Saxon" in origin or in style: guitarist Chris Walsh, for example, is called Rædwalh, which seems to be an attempt to give a more authentic-sounding rendition of the East Anglian King Rædwald, the person almost certainly bur-ied in the famous mound at Sutton Hoo. This king is reviled by Bede for his rejection of Christianity and reversion to his previous paganism, so one can see why his name fits the band: anti-Christian, pagan or heathen, Anglian warrior-king buried in a mound with his treasures like a Beowulf, an archetype of warrior masculinity. In 2007, one member of the band (unnamed in the source) explained the development of the band and their aim:

> For a short while before we began to progress, naturally, towards a more atmo-spheric, epic sound, drawing influences from bands like Primordial, Drudkh and Enslaved among others. The lyrical focus also became more precise, dealing with Britain's forgotten, yet glorious, heathen past and the natural beauty of this ancient land. We ended up focusing the lyrics on "Woden" and everything that could tie into this Anglo-Saxon personification. The heathen way of life is very close to our hearts, so it gives us a large area to cover from a lyrical perspective. We weren't try-ing to prove anything, but we did feel that it [was] about time for British black/hea-then to metal unearth itself. We are trying to bring a little glory to Britain in this respect. . . . If you didn't know already, this country is full of pagan/heathen land-marks. It is strewn with castle ruins, stone circles, ancient forests, battlefields, and monuments that have endured centuries of affliction. Places of historical importance are places like Hastings, Avebury, Jorvik, Portchester Castle (which was once occu-pied by the Saxons), Cornwall, Wales, the Scottish highlands, Sherwood Forest; even Sunderland has its own share of history and folklore. On top of this areas such as the Pennines hold a special place in our hearts, as their stark natural beauty is a reminder of the Britain that once was. We shouldn't really need to point out the importance of the landmarks mentioned as it should be quite obvious by now. But an outsider

really shouldn't go to any of Britain's larger, congested, shameless, filth ridden cities. It makes us angry just thinking about it. (Smith 2007)

In this interview there is, as with Winterylleth, a concatenation of ideas, narratives, and ideologies at work. There is the strange claim, mirroring Winterfylleth, that there is a forgotten British history and a glorious natural landscape that the band wishes to celebrate. The band means of course an English history—the story of the rise of the English between the fall of Roman rule in Britannia and the coming of the Augustinian mission. The story of pagan Anglo-Saxons is surely not forgotten. It is a story of the hegemonic takeover of the British, a world of military prowess and unchecked power, but also a story—for most of the early English—of tending sheep and cattle, and plowing. Again, in confusing Britain with England, the member of the band talks about pagan or heathen landmarks that are important to the story of the Saxons, but also places that have no association with the Saxons, as they come before (such as stone circles) or after the dominance of the Saxons. The band member is moved by the beauty of the Pennines, linking his pagan, masculine, and northern identity to the wild hills that run through the spine of northern England—but the natural beauty of the hills is juxtaposed with the ugliness of the "congested, filth-ridden cities." This could be a simple nostalgic desire for a premodern world, a rejection of modernity, or it could be a concern about impurity and multiculturalism. And again, like Winterfylleth, Wodensthrone has chosen to promote itself to an underground blog that gives them status within extreme metal and black metal as "true."

The band issued a couple of split releases that gained excellent reviews in the underground scene, then secured a deal with Bindrune Recordings, a small independent label based in the U.S.A. specializing in pagan or heathen releases, for its first album, *Loss*. Released in 2009, the album drew heavily on Saxon martial history, laments for the slain, and sorrow and anger for the arrival of Christianity in Anglo-Saxon England. The album cover and imagery reflect a Germanic paganism that flirts with the runes and sunwheels used by openly neo-Nazi bands and organizations. Wodensthrone was accused, alongside Winterfylleth, of being neo-Nazi, and antifascists forced some shows to be cancelled (Lucas, Deeks, and Spracklen 2011; Spracklen, Lucas, and Deeks 2014). The controversy did not harm the band; like Winterfylleth, it was signed to Candlelight Records. Candlelight rereleased *Loss* and the band went into the studio to record its second album after some line-up changes. In 2012 it released the album *Curse*, which changed direction musically and lyrically, but was still recognizably a Wodensthrone album that used Saxon and other Germanic and Nordic mythology and history to reject modernity and Christianity. In an interview from 2012, a band spokesman is keen to explain why the band had been more opaque in its use of lyrics and themes:

I think that to the extent that these things can have on us, there have been misconceptions from listeners about what our intentions are musically, what our message is and the direction we want to take our music in, and we were conscious of quite deliberately challenging those notions. Sadly, the Internet being what it is, disinformation spreads incredibly easily, information filters through in all sorts of ways and ulti-mately these garbled approximations and conjectures form a corrupted "established truth" about the band which says we're a bunch of sentimental atavists with dubious political predilections. There seems to be an effort among both our audience and the press at large either to paint us into a nostalgic, romantic, rose-tinted black metal style that naively idealises a non-existent golden age (spiritual, nationalistic, cultural, you name it), and that has never been our intention. The lazy generalisations gain credence easily because people can digest them, slot them into their existing preju-dices, and not have to engage their brains, which says a lot for what is supposedly an enlightened subculture.

"Loss" was written to open a window on the Anglo-Saxon soul from the mod-ern world, NOT—and this is crucial to understanding the album—to describe one as better than the other, but to explore the contrasts, disjunctures, and ambiguities created by rupturing one world with the other. The point was to create a kind of cul-tural "chemical reaction" from which new ideas might emerge, from which the lis-tener could draw their own conclusions. It's designed to provoke thought rather than to spell out exactly what we want the listener to think, or even what WE think. In that context, the lyrics to a song like "Those That Crush The Roots Of Blood" could be read as a critique of the modern artists' romanticised approximation of lost cul-tures and ways of life, a staged naivety that is almost patronising. Lyrically, it paints in broad, crude strokes that have an immediacy and forcefulness that easily gains currency and thus is easily exploited by those with more sinister agendas. In short, it plays out the naivety we are often accused of, as a criticism of that backward-looking tendency. Granted, the subtext is quite hidden, but then why should the meanings be on surface level, spoon-fed to the listener? People value and encode knowledge more deeply by gaining it for themselves, by digging deeper, and we don't intend any of the explanation offered above to be taken as definitive; that would contradict everything I've just said, after all. It's up to the listener to draw their own conclusions, but if they jump to a silly conclusion, it's a reflection on their own judgement and something they will have to take responsibility for themselves.[4]

At this stage the band is keen to stress they are not "stupid neo-Nazis" pining for a golden age that never existed. The players say that the cultural essentialism and lan-guage of blood and roots is a metaphor, that they never intended to be romantic conservatives—and if people take their words to be literally true then it is the fault of the listeners for being too superficial. But this part of the interview reads like a confused and contradictory special pleading. They may not be racist, but they do want to provoke peo-ple to think in a certain way about the role of the past, masculinity, the role of religion, and the evils of the modern world. Again, we can see with Wodensthrone the construc-tion of the simulacrum, the concerns with Saxons, and the romantic conservativism, as well as the hegemonic masculinity and narrow reading of history, the concern with purity, and the belief that moderns have become less authentic, impure, or somehow "out of touch" with their roots. They are quick to condemn those on the Internet (the fans and reviewers and bloggers) who have taken all this to mean they are nationalist or racist, but they have deliberately constructed the simulacrum to be consumed by those fans in precisely such a way. The belief among fans that the members of the band actually believe the modern world is filled with impurities allows fans to think Wodensthrone understand their concerns about the eclipse of whiteness and hegemonic masculinity in Western nation-states.

White Medal

The final band is a one-man project from Gomersal, a small town in the suburban fringe of Leeds, Yorkshire, in the north of England: White Medal. The band was formed in 2008 as a way of exploring the history of Yorkshire, its pagan roots, and its landscapes, including the moors and fells of the Pennines and Dales. White Medal has released a string of EPs and tapes on its own label, or in collaboration with other small labels, and one full-length album, *Guthmers Hahl* (a supposed original Viking name for Gomersal) in 2013. The band has had good reviews in metal fanzines and the small-press produced *Iron Fist*, but it has not been signed up to a bigger label. The band is signed to its own label, which releases other black metal and extreme metal from around the world, and which also acts as a distributor of releases from similar DIY labels.

Many of the lyrics are in the Yorkshire dialect of English, which make the band's song titles look odd to non-English black metal fans, but funny to English people: "Alone as Owt", or "Afeeard Ut Setting Sun." This is a celebration of Yorkshire identity and landscape, Northern identity, but one that is masculine, drawing on white Viking, Saxon, and other male warrior narratives. The band is keen to stress it are not neo-Nazi, despite the choice for its name:

1. What does the White Medal name mean?
   White Medal is named after the White Rose of York, otherwise known as the Rose Alba, Rose Argent or simply, to most folk, known as the Yorkshire Rose. The symbol was created as a heraldic symbol for the royal house of York but has since been adopted as a symbol for Yorkshire as a whole and is featured on flags and Yorkshire based literature frequently. The symbol itself originated in a period of time which is of no interest to me or the basis of the project but as it is widely recognised as the paramount symbol of Yorkshire, it is used to get the regionalism aspect of the music across.

2. Is White Medal a Satanic project?
   No. Christianity and it's [*sic*] culture has displaced my own culture. Satanic projects only strengthen their "fight."

3. Is White Medal an NSBM project? After all, there is the word "White" in the band name!
   No White Medal is quite obviously not an NSBM project and to the many of you who have been so vehemently conditioned to fear the word "white"; get a fucking grip. (White Medal 2012)

The musician behind White Medal is using his communicative agency to create a particular celebration of Yorkshire and the north of England as an authentic, historically pagan space that has been taken over by Christianity, then the Normans. The musician claims ownership of a half-remembered pagan culture ("my own culture") that he supposes existed before the arrival of Christianity in the North. So far, this act of reclaiming and reproducing this pagan past is identical to the simulacra constructed by the other two bands. What is interesting about his defense of White Medal's name is that the white-rose symbol has no known connections to pagan Saxons or the early English kingdoms of Deira or Northumbria. The white rose of Yorkshire is a recently invented tradition, promoted by the Yorkshire Society and others, with its origins in the Christian-symbolic heraldry of the House of York (the elite family in the later Middle Ages that strove with its near-relations the House of Lancaster for control of England), and the wearing of white roses by Yorkshire-born soldiers at a battle in 1759. The House of York had little connection with Yorkshire's peasants, and in fact most of the land in Yorkshire at the time was controlled by the House of Lancaster—but still the white rose has become the symbol of the county. The musician behind White Medal has not chosen to call his band White Rose—it is named after the White Medal of the 1759 battle. So the band name allows the musician to draw upon myths and symbols of warrior masculinity—the medal and the civil wars of the Roses. And of course the band name has allowed him to sell music loaded with the potency of whiteness while simultaneously mocking those who say the band name is racist.

DISCUSSION

From Wittgenstein (1968) we know that people make meaning through the use of words in particular language games. That is, meaning is made by people in their conversations, their agency, their action, and their interactions. Geertz (1973) puts it much better, of course: we are, he says, caught in webs of significance that we have spun. The concept of the language game runs through the work of Baudrillard, and is the mechanism through which the simulacrum is constructed (Baudrillard 1994). In this brief exposition and analysis of the webs of significance around the music making of these three northern English black metal bands we can see the agency behind the myth making at work. For the musicians, there is a desire to situate their music making in a specific subgenre, with its own rules and symbols and histories. This in turn makes the musicians make music and write lyrics in a certain style that signifies their position within two related simulacra: one associated with the global space of "heathen" black metal, the other particular to England and narratives of Englishness and English/Saxon/warrior heritage (that these two contradict each other is not important). In turn, these musicians are fans of the music and have consumed music by similar bands so much that they already make their music according to the meaning of the language game in the "global" simulacrum. When they have made their music they have to keep making meaning about their music through finding fan-critics and journalists who are willing to interview them and review their records. They have to play the game of music making as myth making in the way they manage their reception of their music by fans. The fans in turn are active listeners, seeking legitimation and belonging through the words and symbols used by the bands. For the fans, they want to be given stories about Saxon warriors wrapped up in a simulacrum of protecting the soil and defeating invaders because they want to believe that there was a time when men were men and England was pure: they want their white English masculinity reaffirmed.

For cultural studies, Baudrillard's work has been rightfully influential, and the idea of simulacra and the notion of hyperreality can easily be adapted to critically discuss the processes of commodification at work in the hegemonic spread of Disney or other forms of global capitalism (Bryman 2004; Rojek 2010). For leisure studies, this chapter shows that music making is just another form of leisure. But music making for these musicians works for a purpose. In the music making of these black-metal musicians, there is a Habermasian communicative leisure at work. The music making they do is driven by their own choices and agency. The lyrics and symbols they adapt and adopt are chosen by them and given meaning by their agency. The simulacra they create are their own work. The fans in turn are part of this active, communicative agency. They make choices about what music they listen to, and what music to share. Music making in this particular leisure space, then, is more than just the performance of music. It is the performance of identity, the performance of boundary making, and the performance of music criticism. There is a large amount of agency going on in the maintenance of the simulacra, because they would collapse if the individuals were not collectively and actively legitimating them. From my personal knowledge of them, the musicians behind these bands, for example, are not actually neo-Nazis, but they want us to think they might be through their performances. And so fans and journalists persuade themselves there is something about the musicians and the bands; a suggestion—a sulfuric smell, perhaps—of evil and controversy. But the agency is nullified when one realizes that all this music making leisure is taking place within the bounds of the instrumental leisure of the popular music industry, and the instrumental leisure of global capitalism and late modernity (Spracklen 2009, 2011, 2013b).

CONCLUSION

In this chapter I have started to sketch out how Baudrillard's work might help us begin to unpack the work of music making in leisure. At stake are the tensions between the communicative agency of musicians and fans and the instrumental rationality of all popular culture and society in the global North. The idea of the simulacrum allows us to see that music making, leisure, and music making in leisure are all expressions of the same desire to make meaning and purpose in our everyday lives. Sometimes some people have enough agency and power to be the primary music makers, but everyone is able to take part in the construction of simulacra through their secondary music making meaning: by being active listeners, through writing about music, though sharing music, and through consuming music.

To construct a new cultural theory of music making in leisure, then, it is necessary to understand what the point of leisure is, and what the role of music is at this point in late modernity. In this postindustrial phase of society, social structures have been weakened but not dissipated. Elites have hegemonic control of significant parts of our lives. Work has become meaningless or casualized. People in the global North still have cultural and political power over the global South, but there are huge problems of alienation and marginalization associated with inequality. In this society, in this world we live in, leisure is our last refuge, and music is something that gives us some pleasure. It is no surprise that both are important sites of identity work, and the construction and contestation of meaning and belonging. Returning to Habermas, leisure and music-as-leisure are the last spaces of the lifeworld that have not been completely colonized by the systems of control and commerce.

NOTES

1. Black metal is a stylistic genre of extreme heavy metal that uses musical and lyrical themes to create a feeling of evil and extremity. The term does not refer to black performers.
2. The second wave of black metal in 1990s Norway was driven by Satanism and misanthropy. The turn to pagan or heathen forms of black metal developed out of the original anti-Christian ideologies.
3. http://orlandocrowcroft.com/music/the-rise-and-rise-of-winterfylleth/, accessed November 11, 2014.
4. http://www.mortemzine.net/show.php?id=3146, posted 2012, accessed 22 August 22, 2014.

REFERENCES CITED

Baudrillard, Jean. 1988. *Selected Writings*. Edited by Mark Poster. Cambridge: Polity.
Baudrillard, Jean. 1994. *Simulacra and Simulation*. Translated by Sheila Faria Glaser. Ann Arbor: University of Michigan Press.
Baudrillard, Jean. 1995. *The Gulf War Did Not Take Place*. Translated by Paul Patton. Bloomington: Indiana University Press.
Bauman, Zygmunt. 2000. *Liquid Modernity*. Cambridge: Polity.
Bennett, Andy. 2000 *Popular Music and Youth Culture: Music, Identity and Place*. Basingstoke: Macmillan.
Bennett, Andy. 2001. *Cultures of Popular Music*. Buckingham: Open University Press.
Bennett, Andy. 2002. "Researching Youth Culture and Popular Music: A Methodological Critique." *British Journal of Sociology* 53(3): 451–466.
Bramham, Peter. 2006. "Hard and Disappearing Work: Making Sense of the Leisure Project." *Leisure Studies* 25(4): 379–390.
Bryman, Alan. 2004. *The Disneyization of Society*. London: Sage.
Butler, Judith. 2006. *Gender Trouble: Feminism and the Subversion of Identity*. London: Routledge.
Cohen, Anthony P. 1985. *The Symbolic Construction of Community*. London: Tavistock.
Geertz, Clifford. 1973. *The Interpretation of Cultures*. New York: Basic.

Habermas, Jurgen. 1984. *The Theory of Communicative Action*. Vol. 1, *Reason and the Rationalization of Society*. Translated by Thomas A. McCarthy. Cambridge: Polity.

Habermas, Jurgen. 1987. *The Theory of Communicative Action*. Vol. 2, *The Critique of Functionalist Reason*. Translated by Thomas A. McCarthy. Cambridge: Polity.

Hobsbawm, Eric, and Terence Ranger. 1983. *The Invention of Tradition*. Cambridge: Cambridge University Press.

Hodkinson, Paul. 2002. *Goth: Identity, Style and Subculture*. Oxford: Berg.

Kahn-Harris, Keith. 2007. *Extreme Metal: Music and Culture on the Edge*. Oxford: Berg.

Kelly, John R. 1983. *Leisure Identities and Interactions*. London: George Allen and Unwin.

Kelly, Kim. 2008. "Voices of Blood: Winterfylleth." *Ravishing Grimness*, November 12. http://ravishinggrimness.blogspot.co.uk/2008/11/voices-of-blood-winterfylleth.html.

Lucas, Caroline, Mark Deeks, and Karl Spracklen. 2011. "Grim up North: Northern England, Northern Europe and Black Metal." *Journal for Cultural Research* 15(3): 279–295.

Maffesoli, Michel. 1996. *The Time of the Tribes: The Decline of Individualism in Mass Society*. London: Sage.

Norris, Christopher. 1992. *Uncritical Theory: Postmodernism, Intellectuals and the Gulf War*. London: Lawrence and Wishart.

Roberts, Ken. 1999. *Leisure in Contemporary Society*. Wallingford: CAB International.

Rojek, Chris. 1995. *Decentring Leisure: Rethinking Leisure Theory*. London: Sage.

Rojek, Chris. 2000. *Leisure and Culture*. London: Sage.

Rojek, Chris. 2010. *The Labour of Leisure*. London: Sage.

Sardar, Ziauddin. 1993. "Do Not Adjust Your Mind: Post-Modernism, Reality and the Other." *Futures* 25: 877–893.

Smith, Bradley. 2007. "Interview with Wodensthrone." *Nocturnal Cult*. http://www.nocturnal-cult.com/wodensthroneint.htm.

Sovereign. 2009. "Response to Discussion on Griffin Youth." *Cookdandbombd*, July 31. http://www.cookdandbombd.co.uk/forums/index.php/topic,20777.540.html.

Spracklen, Karl. 2009. *The Meaning and Purpose of Leisure: Habermas and Leisure at the End of Modernity*. Basingstoke: Palgrave Macmillan.

Spracklen, Karl. 2011. *Constructing Leisure: Historical and Philosophical Debates*. Basingstoke: Palgrave Macmillan.

Spracklen, Karl. 2013a. "Nazi Punks Folk Off: Leisure, Nationalism, Cultural Identity and the Consumption of Metal and Folk Music." *Leisure Studies* 32(4): 415–428.

Spracklen, Karl. 2013b. *Whiteness and Leisure*. Basingstoke: Palgrave Macmillan.

Spracklen, Karl, Caroline Lucas, and Mark Deeks. 2014. "The Construction of Heavy Metal Identity through Heritage Narratives: A Case Study of Extreme Metal Bands in the North of England." *Popular Music and Society* 37(1): 48–64.

Toffoletti, Kim. 2014. "Baudrillard, Postfeminism, and the Image Makeover." *Cultural Politics* 10: 105–119.

Wang, Ning. 1999. "Rethinking Authenticity in Tourism Experience." *Annals of Tourism Research* 26: 349–370.

White Medal. 2012. FAQ. *White Medal*. http://white-medal.blogspot.co.uk/p/writings.html.

Winterfylleth. 2014. Bio. http://www.winterfylleth.co.uk/biography/.

Wittgenstein, Ludwig. 1968. *Philosophical Investigations*. Translated by G. E. M. Anscombe. Oxford: Blackwell.

CHAPTER 17

....

FEELING PART OF THE SCENE

*Affective Experiences of Music Making Practices and
Performances within Leeds's Extreme Metal Scene*

....

GABBY RICHES

PLAY IT AGAIN, BUT THIS TIME
WITH FEELING: DISRUPTING THE EXTREME
METAL REFRAIN

EXTREME metal music, which encompasses a wide range of diverse subgenres, notably thrash, death metal, black metal, and grindcore, emerged in the United Kingdom
and United States during the late 1980s as a result of the increased fragmentation of
heavy metal (Weinstein 2000). It challenged the growing emphasis on technical virtuosity, vocal intelligibility, and conventional song structure. Extreme metal transcends
the conventional musical, discursive, and bodily boundaries of traditional heavy metal
through the use of guttural distorted vocals, down-tuned guitars, exceedingly complex
and fast drumming, unconventional and graphic lyrics, song titles, and album artwork,
and bodily engagements in moshpit practices (Kahn-Harris 2007). In this way, extreme
metal represents a shared musical radicalism which positions itself as different from
more traditional forms of heavy metal, exemplified by bands such as Black Sabbath,
Iron Maiden, and Judas Priest. Since extreme metal is more obscure and attracts less
"mainstream" attention, it is disseminated through small-scale, DIY (Do-It-Yourself)
systems and is usually performed in localized, underground music venues. As a leisure
practice, extreme metal plays an important role in constituting identities, creating affective spaces and experiences, and producing sites of resistance and constraint (Spracklen
2009). Yet, despite the increased scholarly interest in metal music studies, examinations
of metal experiences have not been significantly integrated into leisure studies discussions. Additionally, the affective and sensual aspects of music-making experiences,

performances, and spaces remain peripheral in most metal music accounts, with Berger (1999) and Overell (2014) being possible exceptions.

Popular music scholars, such as Driver (2011) and Hodkinson (2012), have suggested that greater attention needs to be paid to the entwinement of music, embodiment, sociality, gender, and affect. This has resulted in the incorporation and application of innovative theoretical frameworks and methodological approaches that move away from narrow discursive and symbolic understandings of music scenes and their subcultural leisure practices. Metal music scholars have looked at the pleasures derived from participating in metal scenes and its transgressive practices, the phenomenological aspects of extreme metal composition, practice and experience, and the ways in which fans ascribe meaning to metal's aesthetic and affective experiences (Berger 1999; Kahn-Harris 2004; Wallach, Berger, and Greene 2011). In her research on extreme metal scenes, Overell (2014) demonstrates that belonging to a metal scene is affective for both musicians and fans, as it is experienced through embodied processes that generate "a *feeling* of being *in* place" (12). Through ethnographic encounters with mostly male musicians, Overell highlights how extreme metal music and performances are nonrepresentational, as many of the musicians found it difficult to articulate the affective experiences of performing live. In other words, extreme metal sociality or "brutal belonging" was something that was embodied and felt rather than being an intentional, conscious, focused intensity.

Frith (1996) argues that music, like identity, is an experiential process that is constantly moving and fluctuating. He explains that musical experiences and performances are excessive—discursively out of reach as "something that *got away*"—and this is evident when fans and musicians struggle to articulate the affective and emotional qualities of particular musical experiences (116; emphasis in original). In relation to extreme metal, Kahn-Harris (2007) notes the difficulty scene members have when describing the attractive and pleasurable qualities of extreme metal, as they frequently refer to it as aggressive, brutal, and energetic. He suggests that the overuse of such descriptors exemplifies how "the scene offers only limited tools for talking about how music makes scene members feel" (53). The remarks put forth by Frith and Kahn-Harris demonstrate the "more-than-ness" of musical performances and experiences; because these ephemeral qualities are so important to music's "liveliness," music scholars have turned their attention to nonrepresentational theory (Thrift 2007).

Nonrepresentational theory draws attention to the embodied and affective dimensions of social practice, much of which exists prior to and exceeds reflexive or conscious thought. Thinking nonrepresentationally focuses on musical practices "at the moment of their doing" (Wood 2012, 201). Extreme metal music and its practices are taken-for-granted aspects of scenic life, always "done" but difficult to articulate. Therefore, a nonrepresentational approach highlights how musical meanings, subjectivities, and knowledges emerge out of *practical* contexts; placing a serious emphasis on "practices that cannot adequately be spoken of, that words cannot capture, that texts cannot convey," on forms of experience and movement that cannot be understood in the moment (Nash 2000, 655). Doing nonrepresentational research about extreme metal music making practices goes beyond ideological valuations of metal and, instead, seeks to explore how engagements in corporeal practices open up affective spaces that produce different ways of "doing," "becoming," "knowing," and "writing" (Smith 2000; Thrift 2007; Wood 2012).

Informed by a feminist poststructural framework, this chapter highlights how a performative approach to ethnographies of music leads to new ways of understanding music (sub)cultures, identities, and practices, and allows for different ways of writing about them (Butler 1990). Performativity denotes that our activities and practices are not merely expressions of an identity, but the very means by which we our constituted. In other words, heavy metal scenes and subcultural identities are produced and made culturally meaningful in the moment of being performed, in the act of their *doing*. This chapter examines how the fluctuating socio-spatial landscape of the Leeds extreme metal scene has impacted the lives of fourteen metal musicians with regard to their interpersonal band relationships, class and gendered identities, affective engagements in the scene, and commitments to their music making practices. Space is crucial to these discussions because spaces are produced through music making performances and embodied practices; hence, scenic spaces are also unstable, disruptive, and performative (Crouch 2003; Thrift 2007).

Sensing the Scene: A Performative Ethnography of Extreme Music Making Practices

This chapter draws upon eighteen months of ethnographic fieldwork conducted from February 2012 through August 2013 in Leeds, United Kingdom. My research primarily focused on the ways in which moshpit practices played a significant role in the lives of female metal fans. But because subcultural leisure practices and identities are constituted in particular contexts, I also examined the spatial and musical shifts that occurred within the extreme metal scene in Leeds and how these changes affected scene members. The socio-historical ethnographic component that this chapter focuses on involved interviewing and spending extensive time with six male and eight female metal musicians who were predominantly white and working class. Currently, there are few academic accounts of extreme metal bands and their practices in the north of England— with the exception of Spracklen, Lucas, and Deeks (2014)—and even less attention paid to the everyday lived experiences of female metal musicians.

My role as a researcher, being a white, heterosexual, non-British, female academic and avid extreme metal fan was advantageous in accessing participants and relevant information about localized scenic discourses and practices. My Canadian accent, scholarly interests, and lack of local scenic affiliations positioned me as an "outsider," which enabled me to interview and interact with a variety of people who operated in different, and often isolated, social circles within the scene. Without having any preexisting conceptions about or allegiances with the Leeds metal scene and its history, I took on a fluid role as "critical insider" as I continually took mental steps to observe, immerse, compare, contrast, and question as well as experience (Hodkinson 2002, 6). However, my presence was highly visible and at times disruptive because I was critically investigating people's everyday leisure practices and spaces. Focusing on the affective and nonrepresentational dimensions of musical performances and how my positionalities affected people's social relations and interactions illustrates how, similar to fans' relationships to metal music, ethnographers have the capacity to affect and be affected by others.

Bennett (2002) and Hodkinson (2012) assert that a great deal of contemporary subcultural accounts claiming to be ethnographic substantially lack sensory, embodied, and reflexive details with regard to obtaining access to the field, the role of insider knowledge, and everyday subcultural experiences. Yet, the influence of certain paradigmatic shifts, such as the "affective turn" and "sensorial revolution," has prompted scholars to acknowledge the multisensory and complex nature of lived experience. Subsequently, there has been a shift in focus from researching about bodies to researching *through* the body (Clough 2007). This new research emphasis has been taken up by popular music scholars like Driver (2011), who claims that considering the affective aspects of embodied experiences within subcultural settings opens up new ways of understanding how subcultural involvement *feels*. In order to capture the affective and immediate dimensions of extreme metal music making practices and identities, I used a body-centered method of inquiry—*performance ethnography*. This methodological approach has been useful for examining music making practices because it centralizes the sensory, nonverbal, and affective aspects of performance whilst attending to how musical spaces are constituted through the convergence of bodies, affect, music, and materialities of place (Morton 2005; Nash 2000; Smith 2000; Wood 2012). Performance ethnography, according to Conquergood (1991) and Hamera (2011), means that researchers are deeply committed to the research process by immersing themselves in the performative contexts of a (sub)culture. Hence, as ethnographers *do* and perform culture alongside their participants, knowledge is actively coproduced, and this forging of knowledge troubles dominant research narratives and inequities of power.

Despite the acknowledgment from music researchers about the affective and embodied qualities of music making, scholars within the fields of metal music, popular music, and leisure still distance themselves from the sensual and emotional experiences of music making performances, fandom, and researching these complex music worlds (Wood, Duffy, and Smith 2007). Widdowfield (2000) stresses the symbiotic relationship between researchers and their research processes: "not only does the researcher affect the research process but they are themselves affected by this process" (200). In response to the growing concerns around representation and the dis*place*ment of the researcher's body, scholars have incorporated performative and fictional writing techniques into their ethnographic texts. Performative writing, which developed within performance studies, is an evocative writing form that moves *with*, alongside, and sometimes through the fluid, contingent, improvised, sporadic currents of performed experience (Pollock

1998). The use of ethnographic fiction, another type of performative writing, addresses both the *being* and the *doing* of experience, and speaks to the lived body, which is usually rendered inarticulate in conventional ethnographic accounts (Inckle 2010). Fictional devices are considered more effective in conveying the raw, visceral experiences of everyday life as writers attempt to replicate the *sense* of the experience, so even if something did not necessarily happen the way it was reported, recollection made it feel as if it did (Rinehart 1998). The ethnographic accounts presented in this chapter are assemblages of ethnographic field notes, interview data, and fictional writing which when merged together aim to convey the messy, busy, ephemeral aspects of scenic life in situ. My own interpretations and deconstructions are already woven into the narratives, illustrated by my chosen writing genre. They are present in my descriptions, my positions within the narratives, and in my questions, responses, and silences (Diversi 1998). Performative, fictional ethnographic writing is important to music making research because it evokes a shared emotional, embodied experience between performer (author) and audience (reader). Bringing the reader into worlds that would otherwise be intangible and inaccessible opens up new possibilities for interdisciplinary scholars to feel and understand subcultural practices *differently* (Alexander 2005; Pollock 1998).

"It Doesn't Always Feel Friendly": Social Fractures within Leeds's Extreme Metal Scene

Stahl (2004) argues that the shift toward scenic perspectives of music making practices acknowledges that musical practices, and the socio-spatial contexts in which they operate, consist of multiple webs of connectivity and social affiliations. Scenes evoke a sense of socio-spatial heterogeneity in that they are always flexible, transient, temporal, and permeable (Kahn-Harris 2007; Stahl 2004). Glass (2012) observes that music scenes are highly spatialized and performative, whereby scene spaces are not just static locations where people "gather," but are emergent spaces that are continually shaped and made meaningful through the constitution of subcultural identities. However, it is important to emphasize that extreme metal scenes are generated by practices and performances from *particular* bodies. The extreme metal scene in Leeds is predominantly demarcated by white, heterosexual, working-class men. The vast majority of metal musicians and fans are men, and many of the well-known bands in Leeds are all-male. Leeds's scenic characteristics resonate with Cohen's (1997) research on the Liverpool indie rock scene. Cohen claims that the Liverpool rock scene is *actively* constructed as male, as the scene largely comprises male social circles and networks and is shaped by activities and norms that work to maintain and privilege male relationships. In the following sections, I highlight how the convergence of disappearing metal venues, subgenre popularity, and performativities of class and gender has led to a fragmented extreme metal scene.

For male musicians within Leeds's extreme metal scene, being involved in a band is an important pathway for establishing connections with influential scene members, such as promoters, venue staff, and other musicians, and helps to expand their social networks beyond the scene's geographical borders. Curtis,[1] a well-known musician and promoter within Leeds, commented on how a supportive scene is established and maintained through interactions that occur offstage: "I've got to know more and more people just from going out and going to see gigs, and speaking to people and talking to promoters and bar staff. And you're talking to *everyone* really 'cause, you know, you're getting to know people and it's just a really cool network of people in Leeds." For musicians such as Curtis, playing and performing are more than just being a musician, they are about making meaningful but imperative connections with people who occupy influential positions within the scene. Leeds's extreme metal scene is constantly in a state of flux; genres, conventions, musical spaces, and social circles crystallize as they are embraced by different fans and musicians (McClary 2002). Curtis's statement reflected these phenomena: "I mean, it's just kind of one of those things where bands come and go and they'll get a bit of a following for a while and then sort of dissolve into the background I guess, umm, or split up. And it's cool like that because different generations are coming through, starting bands and because of this, I guess, the genre changes a bit too."

Due to its fragmentation, Leeds's extreme metal scene is neither a coherent nor a singular community. It consists of multiple scenes that are constituted through intersecting gender, genre, spatial, and class distinctions. Curtis's experiences as a promoter illustrate these scenic fractures:

> "I kind of see Leeds as being two metal scenes," he explained. "There's like [chuckles] what I'd say is the Royal Park/The Well metal scene which is more like the dirty, death metal kind of stuff. And then there's the more sort of a bit older, you know, slightly higher income, proper jobs kind of Brudenell/Santiago scene, which is the sort of more refined, riffy, sludgy kind of stuff."
>
> "Oh I see," I replied, "because I've been to a variety of local gigs in Leeds, even at the same venue and it's rare that you see the same people at the gig."
>
> "Yeah totally that's it," Curtis agreed. "*But* again, there's like connections between the two but rarely do the bands sort of come together. Do you know what I mean? I guess it's 'cause those bands sort of circulate in different groups of friends, but my kind of . . . [chuckles], I know this is going to sound a bit weird, but my *mission* for the next few years is to try and start bringing them together," he replied looking off into the distance.
>
> "That's a great idea," I interjected, "because I noticed on Saturday there were a lot of people I did not recognize at the gig [Royal Park Cellars] compared to the night before, which was a completely different crowd as well."
>
> Curtis smiled as he shifted in his chair. He took a sip of his pint and responded. "Yeah, it's like where have all these extreme metallers come from! [laughs] I might know about twenty people who say they'll go to that gig, but then where has everyone else come from? They just come out of the woodwork completely, like, just hiding in the shadows. And that's cool because there's a wider scene outside of what we know, I guess."

Curtis's observations highlight how the disjointed nature of the Leeds extreme metal scene provides opportunities for bands to perform in front of multiple audiences, in a variety of spaces, and to connect with musicians who operate outside of their social circles. The scene's fluidity evokes a sense of excitement and anticipation. When bands dissolve and then rematerialize as new configurations and metal fans unexpectedly emerge "from the shadows," these flows of movement work to create and recreate multiple extreme metal scenes within Leeds.

Yet for other metal musicians, the scene's malleability contributes to a loss of community, feelings of isolation and exclusion, and decreased interest in scenic involvement. Jeremy has been involved in the metal scene for over a decade and is a well-established musician and promoter. He used to organize metal-themed club nights, festivals and extreme metal gigs, but due to poor attendance and ongoing frustrations amplified by the scene's unpredictability, he decided to refocus his attention on his band, Wizard's Beard.

> "It changes *all the time*," sighed Jeremy. "I mean it was practically dead a few years ago. It goes through spits and starts, spits and starts and it kind of dies down and then starts back up again. It's in a weird place at the moment—it's kind of up and down all the time, and there are some good gigs that come on but, uh, it doesn't feel like, uh [pauses, stares up at the wall]. The Leeds metal scene used to feel like everyone knew everyone; it was like a community. It doesn't feel like that too much anymore, I don't think." Jeremy hunched over, placed his elbows on the table and rested his chin gently on top of his intertwined fingers.
>
> "How do you think it feels now?" I inquired.
>
> "Umm, not [pauses] I don't know, it feels less like an actual scene as such, it just feels like a gig here and a gig there and stuff happening like independently of each other. Whereas before it all used to feel like it came together quite well, it's much more fragmented now."
>
> He cleared his throat and looked up at me, "I mean, that's got a lot to do with certain people moving up and moving on. Maybe their enthusiasm [for the scene] is not being replicated by other people and because of this the scene is thinning out a bit."

A common theme that emerged throughout most of the interviews with the musicians was how trends and genre popularity, all of which contribute to the scene's fragmentation, are heavily influenced by a small, exclusive group of male scene members. This means that bands struggle to get on bills and promoters end up losing interest in organizing gigs in the scene because of poor crowd attendance. Collin, a promoter and bassist of Proskynesis,[2] accounted for how the social exclusivity of the scene and the unpredictability of the next metal "trend" are real hindrances to death metal bands:

> "I think the disadvantage is the cliquishness. Like, you could have a gig where it's all packed and stuff and you're not really sure why. And then it sort of takes the next trend where your next gig's dead empty and then you realize, ah, that's why."

Tristen, the singer of Proskynesis, mentioned how he and Collin organized and spent a lot of time advertising a grindcore gig at the Royal Park Cellars and were expecting a great turnout due to the subgenre's popularity in the scene, but only a handful of fans were in attendance.

Collin elucidated on this discrepancy: "I think the whole thing working as a band in Leeds is it doesn't always feel like the friendliest place. Like [pauses] there are other bands in Leeds that are trying to get on the same gigs and you know that some people do shit to get you off that gig and stuff like that."

"It's not like they would try to get you off the gig if you were already on it," Tristen reiterated, "but, like, there's some bands that might sort of block other bands from playing it."

"Yeah they want their band first and stuff," Collin replied, looking irritated. "Which you can understand from their point of view, but when you're trying to build a scene it's not very helpful."

The frustration of playing to a poor audience, which is heightened by the existence of numerous promoters, spaces, social circles, and subgenres, is expressed by Jeremy as he spoke about why he began distancing himself from the scene and stopped promoting: "It makes it depressing going to gigs sometimes. When you go to see a band that you know is really good and there's hardly anyone there and sometimes it can be downstairs in here at the Royal Park Cellars. You know, there will be people who claim to want that kind of thing but are sat up here drinking, it's like 'oh why don't you go down?' 'I can't afford it.' 'Well if you can't afford it why are you in the pub?' You know, it doesn't make sense," shaking his head back and forth in annoyance. "If people like myself are losing money they're [promoters] not going to keep doing this because they can't *afford* to keep doing this. So I think that's why the scene's a little more disjointed than it used to be."

THIS IS *OUR PLACE*: EMOTION, AFFECT, AND THE DOINGS OF WORKING-CLASS IDENTITIES

In the same way that the characteristics of working-class music venues such as the Royal Park Cellars and The Well are that they are dingy, dirty, and "not really pleasant," being a working-class musician in a predominantly working-class, postindustrial city is also fraught with difficulty. Not all of the musicians I interviewed were full-time musicians. And even though they were aware that playing extreme metal was not about "making money," they continued to invest large amounts of energy, time, money, loyalty, and emotion into their bands. The musicians spoke about negotiating conflicting work schedules, tight budgets, and family responsibilities that required them to occupy multiple roles (musician, promoter, producer, and fan) in order to attain enough money to support their musical leisure practices. Proskynesis, formerly known as Revokation, have been the longest-running death metal band in Leeds. Tristen admitted that despite their longevity they still struggle to progress as a band:

> "It's difficult in this country to get a full length out quickly and get it released properly without having a bit of money behind you and, uh, we're like a *really* working-class band. We never really have enough money to really invest fully into developing and releasing albums and stuff like that."

I commented about how a lot of bands struggle to release full-length albums of good quality. I then turned to both of them who were sitting across the table from me at the Royal Park pub and asked, "Do you find being a working-class band difficult, seeing as though you all have full-time jobs? Is it hard to coordinate getting everyone together to jam or perform at a gig?"

Tristen replied, "umm it's not so . . . " He stopped mid-sentence and glanced over at Collin who was nodding his head.

"It is, though," Collin added, "'cause it's not the hours. If you wanna do it you're gonna make time for it. It's the fact that [Tristen] doesn't get his router 'till the week before and stuff like that," Collin said sarcastically as he turned toward Tristen. "'Cause of working shifts, you know, in a shop and stuff like that. He just doesn't *dare* ask his boss like . . . "

"Fuck off," Tristen interrupted.

". . . ahead of time."

Tristen replied impatiently, "It's got nothing to do with that."

Collin continued to talk over Tristen: "Anyway, but [shakes his head] we'll have a band practice and we'll ask [Tristen], 'When can you practice next week?' 'Well I don't know yet' [he crudely impersonates Tristen]."

"Look I don't want to talk about my job. This doesn't feel like an important thing," snapped Tristen.

I veered the conversation to issues around how they got involved in the scene but felt troubled by the way Collin continued to berate and undercut Tristen's comments throughout the interview.

Asking the "difficult questions" opens up avenues to explore the lived experiences of being a working-class musician, and because these questions expose the habitual aspects of scenic life, underlying emotional antagonisms surface and leave impressions that are quite disruptive and unpredictable. The emotional work that goes into performing and embodying a working-class, subcultural, masculine identity is part of the larger socio-cultural landscape of Leeds.

> I was walking with Jeremy down Royal Park Road; we're headed to the Royal Park Cellars to see a gig. As we passed an endless row of terrace houses and a dilapidated elementary school that was cordoned off by a wire fence I turned to him and inquired, "Do you consider the Leeds scene a working-class scene or has it changed over the years?" His gaze remained fixed on the road ahead.
>
> After a period of silence he commented, "Umm, I think it's always going to be a working-class community in Leeds. . . . I think for the most part it is. I mean, most

people I know in bands are struggling to, uh, find the money to do anything half the time, myself included [chuckles]. It's one of those things where, like, you're scraping by and then that usually gives you the inspiration to do something, uh, like play that kind of music."

"Right," I replied. "Would you consider yourselves a political band at all?"

"No we've never tried to be political, but because we're quite an angry doom band we seem to get lumped in with that whole 'working-class angry at the state of every-thing,' and obviously music comes from somewhere and it comes from not having any money, so it does have an impact."

Jeremy quietly pondered his thoughts as we continued walking toward the venue. "It comes from being pissed off at something," Jeremy continued, "which ultimately comes from those kinds of [economic] situations. And yeah, a lot of people seem to associate the whole 'dark and dreary up North' to doom bands in Leeds who all sound angry. That's why they must be angry, and it's kind of weird."

The conversations between Jeremy, Collin, and Tristen highlight the affective quali-ties of working-class identities and the emotional work involved in mobilizing working-class leisure music making practices. The everyday struggles of coordinating work schedules, making financial sacrifices in order for a band to progress, and the affective interrelationship between working-class musicians addresses the gaps in the literature where few considerations have been paid to the roles emotions and embodiment play in the formation and maintenance of class identities and practices.

"It's All about the Atmosphere": Affect, Space, and Extreme Music Making Practices

The Royal Park Cellars[3] is a central music space where local metal musicians perform because it is cheap to rent and located within a working-class, student-concentrated neighborhood where many of the musicians live. The opening band are tuning their gui-tars, positioning their amplifiers, and assembling their drum kit on the cramped stage at the Cellars. I headed upstairs to the main bar area as they set up. Out of the corner of my eye I spotted Hunter sitting at one of the tables. He is an established scene member, promoter, and plays in multiple metal bands which are all very well known in the scene. Having been involved in the scene for over ten years, he's become a household name within the Leeds extreme metal scene. I pulled up a rickety stool, took a sip of my beer, and Hunter began discussing about how much he enjoys playing at small venues, like the Royal Park Cellars.

"This is just a perfect sized gig because you've got bands that you really, really admire and yet it's still quite a small venue." He paused momentarily. He looked around the room while gently stroking his beard, "it's just something about big venues that I don't really like. The sound's a bit too clean and played 'cause the sound guys are all really sort of professional [chuckles], and, umm, it kind of sucks away a bit of the fun for me, I guess."

I nodded in agreement. "Yeah I definitely prefer smaller gigs as well. And within the past month there have been metal gigs three to four times a week—is this normal for Leeds?"

Hunter smiled. "I guess it's quite healthy at the moment, and for a scene to be healthy requires two main ingredients: decent bands and decent fans, basically [laughs]. If you got a good band people are going to turn out, and the more people turn out the healthier it gets."

I shifted the focus of the conversation. "And seeing as though you're playing tonight can you tell me some of the emotions or feelings you experience whilst performing live?"

"Umm, I guess before you start you feel excited and a little bit nervous, but while I'm playing I look forward to the next riff I'm playing and people's reactions to it." Hunter grips onto the bottom of his pint glass and mulls over the question: "I dunno, it's hard to say really, it's like you don't really think about much and if you do it's up here [waves his hands in a circular motion above his head]. It's definitely one of my favourite things to do—and just the big massive bass stack stood behind you just rattling away, it's unbelievable. The best thing *ever*," a radiant smile stretched across his face. He glanced at his watch, "speaking of which, I gotta set up downstairs."

He swiftly finished off the remainder of his pint. Before heading downstairs myself, I hastily rifled through my bag for a pair of items necessary for any Cellar's metal gig—earplugs.

During the gaps between band sets I bumped into Jeremy, who has come to the gig to support Hunter's band. We grab a table in the corner of the pub and discuss some of his most memorable gigs and favourite places to play.

"We love to play at just this one," he said, pointing toward the entrance of the Cellars signified by a black door covered in gig posters, "because we're good friends with Steve who runs it, and so that's why it's always quite good when we play down there. It's quite a good laugh and we know the place really well, we've been playing here through several bands for god knows how many years now. It's just a great place to play but it's horrible because it's dingy and dirty," Jeremy explained as he burst into laughter.

"Yeah I know," I exclaimed, "there's always pools of water on the floor."

"Yeah, well it floods regularly down there and stuff," Jeremy replied, "so that's kind of why we like it. I think it's definitely *our place*."

Hunter's and Jeremy's comments speak to the embodied-spatial dimensions of affects in that they actively constitute spaces through a range of embodied activities and practices (Duff 2010). For many metal musicians, the Royal Park Cellars is considered a "perfect metal venue" because of the affective engagements that are generated between bodies within that space. Grossberg explains that affects are probably the most difficult to articulate, yet provide the color, richness, texture, and tone to our everyday lived experiences. For him, affect defines and determines the "strength of our investment in particular experiences, practices, identities, meanings, and pleasures" (1992, 57). Performing live was described as a "different kind of feeling," and the sensations derived from these experiences were difficult to pin down. This is articulated by Jeremy as he recounted his experiences of playing live.

> "I just love being up there on stage and playing for people. Umm, I don't, I don't . . . " he stuttered momentarily while trying to find the words to explain the live experience. "I don't really know what it feels like. It's a very individual kind of feeling, and it's very different. I never play on the stage. I always play on the floor and I can get quite active to the point where I'm spinning around and my guitar head's whizzed past someone's face [laughs]. I totally lose myself in the moment and a lot of the time I don't realize that I'm being watched," he chuckled.

Jeremy's ability to lose himself in the moment during a performance highlights how affects are not only experienced in the body but emerge from other bodily encounters that are almost contagious. In other words, "one cannot help but feel moved by one's affects, in that one experiences affective responses even if one is not able to consciously describe or explain them" (Duff 2010, 884). Duffy (2005) argues that emotions elicited by music create and sustain various performative environments in which people interact. The difficulty in articulating the emotions experienced during a live performance is because such experiences are ephemeral and fleeting. "The emotions we experience in and through music are done so precisely because they cannot be expressed by any other medium" (Duffy 2005, 678). In this way, extreme metal music and its practices are non-representational and excessive, and the excessiveness of extreme metal music is what demarcates it as different from mainstream, popular music, which is why metal musicians invest so deeply (financially, emotionally, physically) into ensuring that they perform frequently in the scene. This is articulated by Grossberg in his discussion of rock music: "the fact that it matters makes it different; it gives rock an excess which can never be experienced or understood by those outside of the rock culture. And this excess in turn justifies the fan's investment in it" (1992, 61). In relation to Leeds's extreme metal scene, the "more-than-ness" that is produced through live extreme metal performances substantiates why musicians are so dedicated to the scene and to nurturing the artistic development of their bands. Expanding on Duffy's previous assertion, the musicians' inability to fully articulate the feelings produced through live performance illustrates the ways in which these practices are unconscious, taken-for-granted, embodied ways of becoming a musician and "doing" the metal scene (Duffy 2005; Glass 2012; Thrift 2007).

> After Proskynesis had finished their set I approached Collin and Tristen who were sat behind their merchandise table in a shadowy corner of the Cellars. I congratulated them on their excellent performance and was curious about the feelings and emotions they experienced whilst playing live.
>   "Once I block out the audience I can really get into the song even though I do screw up, but that's 'cause I'm just sort of throwing myself about to the song," Collin explicated, "but that's just part of life—if everyone just stood there making sure that

everything's perfect then it just wouldn't have the same atmosphere, you'd just be some boring thing to watch."

Tristen gestured in agreement, "For me I don't think it matters if, like, you know a note's missed or if something goes slightly out of time or if there's a mistake or anything like that, because if the performance is properly avid and ridiculous and you know the atmosphere is great and you can see everyone in the audience having a good time, that's more important." Tristen began getting excited as he talked about his affective experiences on stage.

"So are you thinking about or feeling anything when you're singing?" I asked as I moved closer to the table.

"It's all about conveying, like, sort of the emotion that I think the music should convey, if you know what I mean. So it's, like, if it's a big, heavy sort of massive riff then it's all about being big and sort of intense in front of people." Tristen quickly stood up to demonstrate the gestures he uses to emulate the musical intensity. He pushed his chest out, raised his shoulders, bent forward and grimaced in a menacing way. "And if it's a more sort of fluidly sort of like wishy-washy, you know—like a break, or a run, or something like that, then it's all about being a little bit more active and a bit more spazzy and running around like a flea sort of thing." He chortled as he playfully jogged in a circle and then finished by pacing heavily, almost in a stomping motion, back and forth in front of the table.

The vibrancy and energy of the extreme metal scene in Leeds emerge from the musicians' capacities to produce particular "affective atmospheres" in certain spaces (Anderson 2009). According to Anderson (2009) and Duff (2010), atmospheres are generated through a complicated "assemblage of social, material, and affective components, linked together in the sinews of practice, in the materiality of place, and finally in the emergent 'co-presencing' of bodies, place, and self" (Duff 2010, 891). The aforementioned accounts of the visceral characteristics of live metal performances also point toward the way in which extreme metal practices, and the spaces that are opened by these practices, are fundamentally interactive, risky, and unstable because something can always go wrong. Yet these performative "mistakes" or "missed notes" are actually embraced within the scene because these faults define the raw, unpredictable, sensuous facets of extreme metal musical performances as they generate positive, engaging, and affective atmospheres.

Later on in the evening I encountered Leslie, the drummer of Nu Pogodi!, outside whilst having a cigarette before the headlining band went on stage. As we huddled near the entrance to keep warm we discussed the Nu Pogodi! gig that happened last week and how she felt about that live performance.

"I wanted to throw up because I was so excited," Leslie laughed. "I don't know, I just feel, especially being behind Lynne and Vivian and I see them, like, going for it and I can see glimpses of the crowd; it's like that real special moment where everything just slots into place and everything makes sense." She began to blush as she recounted the performance. She slowly took a drag of her cigarette and continued, "And I think people find that with a lot of music moments, you know, you just have that perfect moment at a gig and you never forget it. And I just love the band, I love the girls, and it just works, like a hundred percent, you know!"

Leslie's rendering of the affective intensities experienced during a Nu Pogodi! gig illustrates how musical performances bring spaces, people, and places "into form" (Smith 2000, 618).

THE ETHNOGRAPHIC ENCOUNTER: TO AFFECT AND BE AFFECTED BY "OTHERS"

We Find It So Difficult: Severed Heaven

> Phoenix grips the bottom of the microphone, jumps down onto the floor in front of the stage, and crouches down to unleash a stomach-churning raucous growl. The contrast of the amber stage lights and the darkened venue creates a reverse silhouette that obscures her face. As she screams into the microphone her heavily tattooed arms are the only remaining feature visible to the audience. She angles her head up towards the ceiling and releases a primal scream that shatters the silence and is accompanied by a cacophony of female brutality that surges and penetrates every crevice of the room. Adrianna's head tilts forward. She rhythmically moves her upper body back and forth as she speedily strums her guitar. Beatrix strikes the thick metallic bass strings deeply with a pick and looks out into the audience. The vibrations are rattling my ribcage and the dissonance of the guitars propels me closer to the stage. Michelle's hands are a blur of movement as she batters the drums, and Wyla's bright blonde hair swirls around the neck of her guitar as she rapidly taps the strings. The feedback slowly fades out and a handful of hollers and applauds emerge from the back of the room. Phoenix looks up at the predominantly male audience and yells, "Good evening everyone, we're Severed Heaven and as you can see we're five women and we've got ten breasts between us!"

Formerly known as Blood Sundae, Severed Heaven established themselves in 2007 and are considered to be one of the only all-female extreme metal bands in Northern England.[4] Over the years they have opened for well-known extreme metal bands, performed at popular extreme metal festivals in the United Kingdom, and have accumulated national and international acclaim within particular underground metal circuits. Yet, they are discursively and physically marginalized from Leeds's metal scene because they are not affiliated with influential scene members, nor do they operate within dominant social circles, all of which are dominated by men. Consequently, many of their interactions and performances take place outside of Leeds.

We're at an all-day metal festival hosted in a community center in Nottingham, which is approximately 72 miles from Leeds. After they had collected their musical equipment and stored it in the "musicians' area" of the venue we decided to grab some drinks, go outside to the parking lot and cozy up in their rented touring van. Leading up to the interview I knew Severed Heaven were struggling with getting gigs, crowd attendance, and working on a full-length album. As an all-female working-class metal band, their experiences differed from those of the male musicians I interviewed because of the gendered norms and discourses that operate within the extreme metal scene. I decided to initiate the conversation by inquiring about the reasons why they lack a sizable female following. Overwhelmingly, the members of Severed Heaven agreed that most women are not really interested in metal and could potentially feel threatened when seeing and hearing female extreme metal musicians perform.

"Maybe we're a bit too harsh as well. A lot of women tend to go for the pretty metal. This is not pretty metal; it's dirty," joked Phoenix.

The entire van erupted in raucous laughter. Adrianna, who is also involved in another Yorkshire-based metal band, leaned forward so I could see her and in a serious tone commented, "The thing is . . . I deliberately avoid women in bands, not musicians, I mean vocalists. Just because vocally you'll be listening to some [metal] music on your headphones and I find that female vocals don't have enough depth, you know, it's not deep enough."

"Thank you, Adrianna," interposed Phoenix with an astonished look etched onto her face.

Beatrix, Wyla, and Michelle were motionless and slacked-jawed. Adrianna quickly attempted to ameliorate the situation, "No, no you're an exception, obviously. But do you remember me speaking about how any female vocalist is pissy and weak, and it's just not suitable for metal in my opinion. So I would rather listen to a male vocalist, you know; it actually has some balls to it."

Despite the evocative response from her band mates, Adrianna's remark, along with Phoenix's comment about "girls liking pretty metal," is not surprising considering the ways extreme metal discourses, within and outside the scene, work to normalize male fandom, which then positions female musicians and fans as inauthentic and unworthy of serious encouragement (Leonard 2007).

Attempting to break the silence I broached the topic again but framed it in a general way: "So are you saying that women's lack of involvement or interest in metal is just in Yorkshire or is that across the board?"

"I think we were talking about this earlier," Phoenix said as she looked at Wyla. "Like, women prioritize other things over than going to a gig, no matter what walk of life; from no matter what they're into there are different things that are more important."

"Yeah, I think women are more interested in personal affairs like family and stuff," Wyla clarified. She turned to face me: "You know, when you were saying about what issues or challenges we have encountered, well, we're all women and we struggle to move forward sometimes because we've got so many other priorities, whereas I think men are very—if they want to do it, they do it [her one hand vertically pounding into her horizontally positioned hand, like a chopping action]."

Beatrix chimed in, "Yeah, that is true. I think they have sort of [pause] I don't think this is how it should be, but I think a lot of women kind of have a sense of obligation in a lot of areas even though they may not want to have those feelings."

"I think men are just selfish; men are selfish," Michelle said flippantly.

Phoenix shook her head in a disapproving way and replied, "No, I think it's how they're brought up."

"So it's struggling not only as musicians but as female musicians who have to juggle other responsibilities that male musicians typically do not have to deal with," I clarified. "Why do you think that is?" I asked.

"Well, if you've got the passion it does get you further, I think," Phoenix claimed.

"But we have the passion," Wyla said with a quizzical look on her face.

"But do we though?" Phoenix doubtfully uttered as she looked around the van at the other band members.

"Yeah, I do!" Wyla shouted in an exclamatory fashion, revealing just how shocked and hurt she was by Phoenix's comment.

The tension was almost stifling as each of the band members anxiously made eye contact with one another, searching each other's facial expressions for a glimmer of reassurance. They then directed their attention toward me and I decided to liven up the conversation by focusing on something more positive. "So what have been some of the biggest achievements for Severed Heaven?"

"Not breaking up," Wyla laughed.

"Yeah it is quite an achievement. I thought it was going to happen this year," remarked Phoenix.

This caught me off guard—"Breaking up? Why is that?"

Phoenix exhaled heavily as she slowly circled the rim of her plastic cup with her index finger: "Just [pause] things don't progress. It's difficult to get everyone on the same page and you know it can't just be down to one person to do it all."

Wyla nodded her head, "I think for us . . . it's the same for any unsigned band, I mean where the scene is sort of dying. You don't really get any encouragement," she muttered disparagingly.

Beatrix folded her arms across her chest and attempted to articulate the reasons why they had difficulty progressing as a band: "I think, potentially, this may be totally wrong but, I think maybe some bloke bands, like one guy will maybe take the lead a bit more and he'll be quite happy to kind of boss people around a bit, which although it might not be great, it gets shit done."

"To be fair," interrupted Phoenix, "I've tried for *several* years but it's like hitting a brick wall, constantly, all the time."

From the back of the van Michelle piped up, "Yeah, but to be fair you're a bit, you know, [hesitates] not together sometimes."

"It's hard, I find it really difficult," admitted Phoenix guiltily with a downcast gesture.

Wyla leaned over and stroked Phoenix on the back to comfort her; "Yeah, like as a woman you consider other people's feelings more."

Beatrix added, "I think that's the thing, because we all prize on getting along, like, probably over everything else, which is why we've stayed together. But it's also why, you know, we don't want to piss anybody off, which means we don't really say 'right you're doing this today or you're out of the band.' "

"Right, so do you think that's different than men?" I probed.

"I think they can probably talk shit to each other and get over it more easily and then that sort of makes things happen," explained Beatrix.

"Women hold grudges," reaffirmed Phoenix as she wearily stared out the window.

The frustrated utterances from the members of Severed Heaven regarding the emotional and structural constraints they have to negotiate as musicians echo Bayton (1997) when she claims that, unlike men, women musicians constantly have to balance ongoing demands of family responsibility, career paths, personal relationships, and public performance. Furthermore, feelings of guilt, helplessness, and apprehension about "taking charge" and moving the band forward reflect the ways in which "femininity" is socially constructed as emotionally, physically, and technically helpless within heavy metal, whilst masculinity is associated with displays of technical competence and self-assured leadership (Bayton 1997).

I Didn't Mean It: Nu Pogodi!

I'm frantically grabbing onto the monitor, trying to maintain my position at the front of the stage as people repeatedly jostle into me from behind. I'm at the 1 in 12 Club, a DIY, not-for-profit music collective in Bradford, head-banging along to the Leeds-based d-beat, grind band Nu Pogodi![5] Vivian, the guitarist and lead singer, rapidly and aggressively spits out the lyrics at the top of her lungs into the swaying microphone, her discernible neck tattoos making her look intimidating. Lynne's dual raspy vocals echo throughout the room as she heavily strums her bass. Punchy and forceful rhythms are thundering out from behind the obscured drum kit, producing a wall of noise that feels like its tearing open my insides for all to see. And just as the first song comes to an abrupt finish Vivian seizes the mic and screams, "Being female is beautiful but sometimes having a womb sucks, fuck my woooooomb!"

The crowd applauded enthusiastically as the stage lights dimmed and Nu Pogodi! began disassembling their equipment. The building was absolutely freezing because the boiler was broken, so we headed upstairs to the café, grabbed seats at a long wooden table, and had a stimulating discussion, despite our jackets being fastened up to our necks and our hands shoved underneath our bottoms for warmth. At the time of the research, Vivian and Leslie were dating and open about their relationship with their close friends in the scene. It was nearing the end of the interview and I was curious as to how they negotiated their romantic relationship with their band responsibilities and engagements.

"Have there ever been issues with you being in a relationship, in a band and, like, living together? Has that ever created any tensions?" I asked looking first to Vivian and then to Leslie, who was perched on the windowsill above the table where Vivian was sitting.

Leslie remarked, "It actually brings us together."

"Yeah it does," Vivian repeated softly over Leslie.

"I mean if we're like saying 'fuck you' to each other and then go have a band practice, we'll be like, 'aww, I love you' [Leslie says in a high-pitched voice]. Do you know what I mean? It just takes out all the negative energy."

"It's like therapy," I responded good humoredly.

"To be honest," Vivian turned around to look at Leslie, "we have turned up at practice and I've been like, 'you're fucking doing my head in I can't even look at you,' and then we'll start screaming and I'll just be like 'rrggghhh' [growling voice] and I pretend that I'm screaming at your face and then I'll be like, 'I'm fine now.'"

Lynne began to laugh timidly.

"Sorry, that feels bad, but do you know what I mean? And then we'll play some music and we'll be like, 'oh fucking hell what are we like!' sort of thing," explained Vivian.

The atmosphere in the room gradually thickens as Leslie's facial expression turned sour. "No, I didn't know that but now I do." She forced a smile and began to impatiently collect her things.

"I didn't mean it," Vivian uttered apologetically.

"I'm going now anyways, so," Leslie said curtly.

"Fight! Fight! Fight!" Lynne yelled facetiously.

Without looking at Vivian, Leslie stormed out of the room and disappeared down the staircase. Vivian quickly grabbed her jacket off the back of the chair and trailed closely behind her. The rhythmic sounds of boots thudding on concrete and Vivian frantically shouting, "Leslie, I feel really bad, I'm sorry!" continued to ring in my ears. The room is uncomfortably quiet. I remained at the empty table, accompanied by gut-wrenching pangs of guilt, confusion, and embarrassment for generating such conflict.

These disruptive and conflictual interactions that emerged during my encounters with Severed Heaven and Nu Pogodi! were surreal and transformative instances for both myself and the musicians. They exemplify that "fieldwork is inherently confrontational in that it is the purposeful disruption of other people's lives" (England 1994, 85). In addition, these affective encounters also demonstrate how metal bands, comparable to the affective intensities produced by their performances and the scenes within which they operate, are fragile, risky, fleeting, and vulnerable to disruption.

Conclusions: More-Than-Music Making

This chapter has sought to illustrate how extreme metal music and its practices are affective, fragile, transitory, and "more-than-representational" forms of leisure. A performative ethnographic approach aligns with nonrepresentational ways of thinking as it emphasizes dialogical actions rather than texts, social relations and embodied practices rather than representations, and how emotional and affective processes of musical performance erupt in the heat of the moment (Morton 2005; Thrift 2007). Leeds's extreme metal scene is "more than representational" because its subcultural boundaries are always being challenged, constructed, and redefined through various music making practices and performances. Everyday encounters within the metal scene, such as performing live, are difficult to describe, but these unarticulated moments reveal how metal scenes are constructed out of a "spatial swirl of affects that are often difficult to tie down but are nevertheless crucial" (Thrift 2006, 143).

Experimenting with performative writing and ethnographic fiction enabled me to account for the ways in which subcultural identities emerge through leisure practices and how these practical unfoldings are unpredictable, diverse, and excessive. It was evident that being a metal musician exceeded the musical practices by which these identities are categorized. It is about establishing pathways for recognition, grappling with the tensions between musical progression and loyalty, fostering a sense of community, and dedicating oneself to producing a scene that offered the possibilities for bodily and social transformation. Yet, for bands like Severed Heaven and Nu Pogodi!, their music making pathways and leisure practices were far more complex and restricted than their male peers as they had to navigate intersecting extreme metal, class, and gendered discourses. Focusing on the lived experiences of working-class male and female metal musicians points to how Leeds's extreme metal scene is a gendered and classed leisure space that deeply affects those who perform within it.

NOTES

1. To protect the identities of all participants, all formal names have been anonymized. However, to avoid providing an ahistorical account, the names of bands and venues have not been altered.
2. At the time of the research, Proskynesis were an active metal group but disbanded in 2014.
3. At the time of the research, this was an active venue where most local and national extreme metal bands played. It closed down in August 2013.
4. At the time of the research, Severed Heaven were an all-female metal group, but they have now changed their line-up to include a male drummer and male rhythm guitarist.
5. At the time of the research, Nu Pogodi! were an all-female group. In 2013 they brought in a male drummer and then disbanded in December 2014 due to conflicting interests.

REFERENCES CITED

Alexander, Bryant K. 2005. "Performance Ethnography: The Reenacting and Inciting of Culture." In *The SAGE Handbook of Qualitative Research*, edited by Norman K. Denzin and Yvonne S. Lincoln, 411–441. 3rd ed. Thousand Oaks, CA: Sage.

Anderson, Ben. 2009. "Affective Atmospheres." *Emotion, Space and Society* 2(2): 77–81.

Bayton, Mavis. 1997. "Women and the Electric Guitar." In *Sexing the Groove: Popular Music and Gender*, edited by Sheila Whiteley, 37–49. London: Routledge.

Bennett, Andy. 2002. "Researching Youth Culture and Popular Music: A Methodological Critique." *British Journal of Sociology* 53(3): 451–466.

Berger, Harris M. 1999. *Metal, Rock, and Jazz: Perception and the Phenomenology of Musical Experience.* Hanover, NH: Wesleyan University Press.

Butler, Judith. 1990. *Gender Trouble: Feminism and the Subversion of Identity.* New York: Routledge.

Clough, Patricia T. 2007. "Introduction." In *The Affective Turn: Theorizing the Social,* edited by Patricia T. Clough with Jean Halley, 1–33. Durham, NC: Duke University Press.

Cohen, Sara. 1997. "Men Making a Scene: Rock Music and the Production of Gender." In *Sexing the Groove: Popular Music and Gender,* edited by Sheila Whiteley, 17–36. London: Routledge.

Conquergood, Dwight. 1991. "Rethinking Ethnography: Towards a Critical Cultural Politics." *Communication Monographs* 58(2): 179–194.

Crouch, David. 2003. "Spacing, Performing, and Becoming: Tangles in the Mundane." *Environment and Planning A* 35: 1945–1960.

Diversi, Marcelo. 1998. "Glimpses of Street Life: Representing Lived Experience through Short Stories." *Qualitative Inquiry* 4(2): 131–147.

Driver, Christopher. 2011. "Embodying Hardcore: Rethinking 'Subcultural' Authenticities." *Journal of Youth Studies* 14(8): 975–990.

Duff, Cameron. 2010. "On the Role of Affect and Practice in the Production of Place." *Environment and Planning D* 28: 881–895.

Duffy, Michelle. 2005. "Performing Identity within a Multicultural Framework." *Social and Cultural Geography* 6(5): 677–692.

England, Kim V. L. 1994. "Getting Personal: Reflexivity, Positionality, and Feminist Research." *Professional Geographer* 46(1): 80–89.

Frith, Simon. 1996. "Music and Identity." In *Questions of Cultural Identity,* edited by Stuart Hall and Paul du Gay, 108–127. London: Sage.

Glass, Pepper G. 2012. "Doing Scene: Identity, Space, and the Interactional Accomplishment of Youth Culture." *Journal of Contemporary Ethnography* 41(6): 695–716.

Grossberg, Lawrence. 1992. "Is There a Fan in the House? The Affective Sensibility of Fandom." In *The Adoring Audience: Fan Culture and Popular Media,* edited by Lisa A. Lewis, 50–65. London: Routledge.

Hamera, Judith. 2011. "Performance Ethnography." In *The SAGE Handbook of Qualitative Research,* edited by Norman K. Denzin and Yvonne S. Lincoln, 317–330. 4th ed. Los Angeles: Sage.

Hodkinson, Paul. 2002. *Goth: Identity, Style and Subculture.* Oxford: Berg.

Hodkinson, Paul. 2012. "Beyond Spectacular Specifics in the Study of Youth (Sub)Cultures." *Journal of Youth Studies* 15(5): 557–572.

Inckle, Kay. 2010. "Telling Tales? Using Ethnographic Fictions to Speak Embodied 'Truth.'" *Qualitative Research* 10(1): 27–47.

Kahn-Harris, Keith. 2004. "Unspectacular Subculture? Transgression and Mundanity in the Global Extreme Metal Scene." In *After Subculture: Critical Studies in Contemporary Youth Culture,* edited by Andy Bennett and Keith Kahn-Harris, 107–118. Basingstoke: Palgrave Macmillan.

Kahn-Harris, Keith. 2007. *Extreme Metal: Music and Culture on the Edge.* Oxford: Berg.

Leonard, Marion. 2007. *Gender in the Music Industry: Rock, Discourse and Girl Power.* Aldershot: Ashgate.

McClary, Susan. 2002. *Feminine Endings: Music, Gender, and Sexuality*. Minneapolis: University of Minnesota Press.

Morton, Frances. 2005. "Performing Ethnography: Irish Traditional Music Sessions and New Methodological Spaces." *Social and Cultural Geography* 6(5): 661–676.

Nash, Catherine. 2000. "Performativity in Practice: Some Recent Work in Cultural Geography." *Progress in Human Geography* 24(4): 653–664.

Overell, Rosemary. 2014. *Affective Intensities in Extreme Music Scenes: Cases from Australia and Japan*. Basingstoke: Palgrave Macmillan.

Pollock, Della. 1998. "Performing Writing." In *The Ends of Performance*, edited by Peggy Phelan and Jill Lane, 73–103. New York: New York University Press.

Rinehart, Robert. 1998. "Fictional Methods in Ethnography: Believability, Specks of Glass, and Chekhov." *Qualitative Inquiry* 4(2): 200–224.

Smith, Susan J. 2000. "Performing the (Sound)World." *Environment and Planning D* 18: 615–637.

Spracklen, Karl. 2009. *The Meaning and Purpose of Leisure: Habermas and Leisure at the End of Modernity*. Basingstoke: Palgrave Macmillan.

Spracklen, Karl, Caroline Lucas, and Mark Deeks. 2014. "The Construction of Heavy Metal Identity through Heritage Narratives: A Case Study of Extreme Metal Bands in the North of England." *Popular Music and Society* 37(1): 48–64.

Stahl, Geoff. 2004. "'It's Like Canada Reduced': Setting the Scene in Montreal." In *After Subculture: Critical Studies in Contemporary Youth Culture*, edited by Andy Bennett and Keith Kahn-Harris, 51–64. Basingstoke: Palgrave Macmillan.

Thrift, Nigel. 2006. "Space." *Theory, Culture and Society* 23(2–3): 139–146.

Thrift, Nigel. 2007. *Non-Representational Theory: Space, Politics, Affect*. London: Routledge.

Wallach, Jeremy, Harris M. Berger, and Paul D. Greene, eds. 2011. *Heavy Metal Rules the Globe: Heavy Metal Music Around the Globe*. Durham, NC: Duke University Press.

Weinstein, Deena. 2000. *Heavy Metal: The Music and Its Culture*. Rev. ed. New York: Da Capo.

Widdowfield, Rebekah. 2000. "The Place of Emotions in Academic Research." *Area* 32(2): 199–208.

Wood, Nichola. 2012. "Playing with 'Scottishness': Musical Performance, Non-Representational Thinking and the 'Doings' of National Identity." *Cultural Geographies* 19(2): 195–215.

Wood, Nichola, Michelle Duffy, and Susan J. Smith. 2007. "The Art of Doing (Geographies of) Music." *Environment and Planning D* 25: 867–889.

CHAPTER 18

MOTIVATIONAL AND SOCIAL NETWORK DYNAMICS OF ENSEMBLE MUSIC MAKING

A Longitudinal Investigation of a Collegiate Marching Band

SERENA WEREN, OLGA KORNIENKO, GARY W. HILL, AND CLAIRE YEE

INTRODUCTION

"HUMAN beings can be proactive and engaged or, alternatively, passive and alienated, largely as a function of the social conditions in which they develop and function" (Ryan and Deci 2000, 68). A person's perceptions of and attitudes toward an activity are affected by their feelings about themselves and others. The reasons a person is motivated to participate in musical leisure activities can be numerous. Music makers often focus on specific musical aspects of the experience as a central motivating force to participate in musical leisure activities, but other motivational components also need to be considered. Whereas a person may be driven by an intrinsic desire for musical growth, self-determination theory (SDT), a psychological theory of motivation, suggests that this drive must also be sustained and supported by the social environment (Ryan and Deci 2002). In other words, SDT proposes that the broader social context of the musical experience is important when investigating why people choose to participate and remain engaged in musical leisure activities.

Social network analysis (SNA) is an interdisciplinary theoretical framework and collection of analytical methods that enables the quantification of social relationships in groups of individuals (Valente 2010). More simply, it allows for a description of the social context of a musical ensemble. To the best of our knowledge, this study is the first to integrate SDT approaches to participatory motivation and SNA approaches in describing the structure of a social group to delineate and track over time the relationships between these two critical components of ensemble music making and leisure activities. After a brief review of the social dimensions of music making and the theoretical frameworks, we provide illustrations of the relationship between motivation and social networks in a musical ensemble, consider the implications of these findings for promoting self-determined motivation and well-being in musical ensembles, and identify directions for future research.

Music Making as a Social Experience

The communal activity of music making has been observed throughout human history. Some researchers, including neurobiologist Walter Freeman (2000), suggest that participation in social music making by early humans performed an important evolutionary role in the development and survival of societies. McNeill (2000) discusses how the communal experience of music making involves actively creating a sense of unity that facilitates cognitive coordination, shared emotional states, "boundary loss," and a development of trust in the community of music makers. Others have proposed that group music making modulates oxytocin and other neuromediators and hormones that facilitate social cohesion, bonding, and building trust and strength among members in communities (e.g., Dunbar 2004; Freeman 2000; Grape et al. 2003). This research underscores the biological and evolutionary mechanisms for understanding the innate desire to experience music with others. While social music making may no longer be integral to daily survival, humans may still have a primal predisposition to respond to group music making in a way that affects well-being and social integration.

Cross (2001) reviewed the nature of music from an evolutionary perspective. Cross concludes that music is a "product of both our biologies and our social interactions" (28). He elaborates on the role of music making in human cultures:

> [M]usic is uniquely fitted to have played a significant role in facilitating the acquisition and maintenance of the skill of being a member of a culture—of interacting socially with others—as well as providing a vehicle for integrating our domain-specific competences so as to endow us with the multipurpose and adaptive cognitive capacities that make us human. (Cross 2001, 38)

Although we do not directly address questions of the evolutionary role of music in this chapter, Cross's remarks underscore the integral relationship between present-day people's desire to participate in music making experiences and their social experiences. In the past few hundred years of human history, some cultures have begun to diminish and control the social experience of music making by delineating musical performers from musical consumers. Examples of this change include the concert tradition in Western societies, where high-level professional musicians perform a concert for an audience of passive listeners, and the potentially solitary consumption of recorded music (Small 1980). This decrease in active, everyday music making within a large part of our society and the subsequent creation of musical haves and have-nots, at least where participatory group music is concerned, seem to go against our natural human tendencies, at least as suggested by these evolutionary researchers.

Despite this cultural shift in communal music making and consuming, humans may not have lost their innate desire to connect with others through the medium of music. However, some in the music education profession have questioned the value of participating in large musical ensembles and suggest that this form of social music making is no longer relevant in an educational settings or even as a serious leisure activity like that of many recreational musical ensembles (Allsup 2012; Allsup and Benedict 2008; Kratus 2007; Williams 2011). *Serious leisure* (Stebbins 1992), which we suggest describes a person's participation in large recreational ensembles, can be defined as the "systematic pursuit of an amateur, hobbyist, or volunteer activity that is highly substantial, interesting, and fulfilling and where, in the typical case, participants find a career in acquiring and expressing a combination of its special skills, knowledge, and experience" (3). The discussions regarding the relevancy and social value of large ensemble participation has been centered primarily on anecdotal evidence or by a desire to uphold traditions, but rarely examined using quantitative methods. Nonetheless, research continues to demonstrate the emotional and psychological power of musical engagement (e.g., Csikszentmihalyi 1990; Lewis and Sullivan 2005; Persson 2001; Sloboda 1998; Welch and Adams 2003) and the importance of the broader context of that musical experience to its meaning (e.g., Bailey and Davidson 2005; Booth, Johnson, and Granger 1999; Fritz and Avsec 2007; O'Neill 1999). We seek to address this lacuna in the literature to understand the nature and purpose of social music making, especially in a serious leisure setting. Our goal is to empirically examine motivational and social network dynamics of a musical ensemble to gain a better understanding of why many people remain musically engaged with others.

Music making activities are intimately and inseparably connected to the social environment in which they are performed and experienced. We propose, therefore, that the social environment of a musical ensemble is related to a musician's motivation to participate and remain engaged in specific musical activities. Although research has been conducted on participatory motivation, specifically in student ensembles (e.g., Evans, McPherson, and Davidson 2012; Werpy 1996), adult ensembles (e.g., Carucci 2012; Cavitt 2005; Sichivitsa 2003), and marching band (e.g., Moder 2013; Zdzinski 2004), to the best of our knowledge no research to date uses rigorous quantitative methods, such as SNA approaches, to examine the relationship between participatory motivation and an ensemble's social dynamics. We seek to describe the associations between motivational profiles regarding music making and social network dynamics within a large musical ensemble.

MOTIVATIONAL AND SOCIAL NETWORK DYNAMICS: THEORETICAL FRAMEWORKS

Self-Determination Theory as Applied to Participatory Motivation

A number of theoretical frameworks are commonly used when investigating human motivation, but few exist for exploring specifically participatory motivation. SDT has become the most widely used and accepted theory for examining participatory motivation since it provides a more comprehensive framework than other approaches, such as self-efficacy or goals theory (Frederick-Recascino 2002). "SDT is an approach to human motivation and personality that combines traditional empirical methods and an organismic meta-theory that highlights the importance of humans' evolved inner resources for personality development and behavioral self-regulation" (Ryan and Deci 2000, 68). SDT assumes people are driven by a desire for personal growth that is necessary for fulfillment, developing a more cohesive sense of self, and satisfaction of innate psychological needs. When a person is self-determined they are more intrinsically motivated to pursue the things that interest them (Deci and Ryan 1985). Activities that hold intrinsic interest for a person have novelty, challenge, or a desired aesthetic value. SDT posits that there are three psychological needs: *autonomy* (de Charms 1968; Deci 1975), *competence* (Harter 1978; White 1963), and *relatedness* (Baumeister and Leary 1995; Reis 1994); all of these must be satisfied for an individual to become and sustain self-determined motivation (Deci and Ryan 1985, 1991; Ryan and Deci 2000). This organismic dialectic perspective suggests that humans have developed this motivation to guide them "toward more competent, vital, and socially integrated forms of behavior" (Deci and Ryan 2000, 252).

Autonomy refers to a person's desire to control his or her choices, behaviors, and effects on his or her environment. In other words, the locus of causality, or the perceived origin of a behavior (Deci and Ryan 2000) of an intrinsically motivated person is internal rather than external; essentially, the person believes they have the ability to effect change in their environment rather than the environment effecting change on them. *Competence* refers to an individual's self-perceived ability to master and be effective in an environment (Deci and Ryan 2002; White 1959); this feeling of competence proves significant when choosing activities that allow for the maintenance and growth of skills (e.g., Deci and Ryan 2002; Evans, McPherson, and Davidson 2012). Finally, *relatedness* refers to a person's desire to connect to others, which is supported by Baumeister and Leary's (1995) research on a human's need to belong. A desire to relate and belong to a group may be a powerful motivator for people to join musical ensembles. Unfortunately, most research to date has focused on aspects of autonomy and competence, so significant questions regarding the role of relatedness in participatory motivation still exist (Frederick-Recascino 2002; Vallerand, Pelletier, and Koestner 2008). The research on relatedness's relationship to motivation has been limited, in that it has focused on dyadic and didactic relationships, such as a parent-child (e.g., Frodi, Bridges, and Grolnick 1985) or teacher-student (e.g., McPherson and Davidson 2002). In this study, we extend this research by examining the broader social networks of an entire musical ensemble.

Another feature of SDT is that it is based on a multidimensional view of motivation, distinguishing between *intensity* and *type* as key dimensions of motivation. The types of motivation identified in SDT (Deci 1975; Vallerand 1997) create a self-determination continuum from highly intrinsic to amotivated (see Figure 18.1). Each type of motivation outlined in SDT suggests the underlying impulse for a person to regulate, or control, their behavior in a specific manner. For example, introjected regulation of behavior indicates a person is motivated to act based upon a feeling of guilt or anxiety (Deci and Ryan 2000). A brief explanation of each form of regulation along the SDT continuum is found in Figure 18.1.

In addition to identifying the types of motivation, the intensity of each type of motivation is posited to play a role. Together, the information about both the type and intensity of motivations allows for the creation of a more comprehensive motivational profile for an individual. Previous research has linked motivational profiles to a variety of behavioral outcomes, such as persistence at a task (Vallerand and Bissonnette 1992) and academic performance (Fortier, Vallerand, and Guay 1995). This research has shown that being self-determined is associated with positive psychological functioning (Deci 1980). The varying balance between types of motivation can be both additive and interactive, and *environmental factors* can either support or undermine the satisfaction of any of the three needs that must be satisfied to become self-determined. For people engaging in leisure activities, such as rehearsing and performing in music ensembles, it is reasonable to expect a motivational profile that is high in self-determined (intrinsic) motivation or high in both self-determined and nonself-determined (extrinsic) motivation (Vlachopoulos, Karageorghis, and Terry 2000), because they are most likely to support voluntary engagement in an activity. The first of these profiles, or one with more exclusively intrinsic motivation, would be associated with more positive psychological functioning in the environment.

According to Deci and Ryan (2000), a motivational profile that is primarily self-determined would facilitate more socially integrated forms of behavior, such as making friends. Integrating these ideas with social network analyses, we propose that individuals reporting higher levels of intrinsic or identified regulation would occupy different positions in the social network compared to individuals who have a more extrinsically regulated motivation. In other words, self-determination should support the formation of a more extensive number of social relationships (e.g., friendships) in a group. Additionally, the social ecology of a marching band, in the case at hand, should play a role in either supporting or undermining the satisfaction of the three areas of need proposed by SDT, especially relatedness, throughout the band season. Thus, by investigating individuals' self-reported motives to participate in an activity and relating them to the broader social context of a musical ensemble, we can move toward a greater

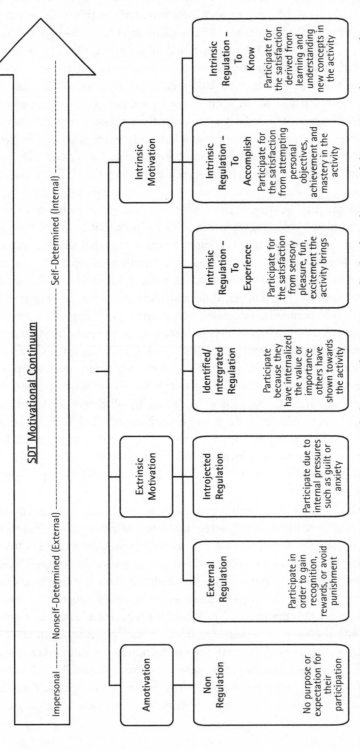

FIGURE 18.1 The Self-Determination Motivational Continuum, with the type of motivation and style of regulation and their associated reasons for participation; adapted from Ryan and Deci (2000), Vallerand and Ratelle (2002), Pelletier et al. (1995).

understanding of conditions that may support or undermine satisfaction in the three areas of need according to SDT.

Social Network Analysis and Social Structures of a Musical Ensemble

Social networks comprise individuals, or *actors*, and connections, or *relational ties*. An actor's position within the network provides information about the group dynamics and has implications for an individual's behavior and psychological well-being (e.g., Berkman et al. 2000; Berkman and Krishna 2014). Studying the structure of ties among actors in a network can elucidate the features of this social ecology that are important for understanding of the flow of information, resources, and support (Borgatti et al. 2009). At a broad level, networks emerge as a result of group members' pursuits of fundamental goals to belong and affiliate (Baumeister and Leary 1995; Heinrich and Gullone 2006), and to attain and maintain status (Hawley 1999). Individual differences in motivations, behaviors, and biology are associated with these factors, and lead to different patterns of ties around an individual. In networks, connections between individuals also depend on the nature of their ties with other members of a group. This is known as the *network self-organization* phenomenon (Robins and Lusher 2013). For instance, *reciprocity* is observed in human networks and describes the phenomenon "if you treat me as a friend, I will treat you the same way," whereas *transitivity* is the propensity to form friendships with friends of friends. Reciprocity and transitivity are referred to as *network structural processes* because these processes are self-organizing properties of a network itself, not characteristics of individuals.

In human social networks, measures of network position could be derived from nominations collected from individuals (i.e., *egos*) and their peers (i.e., *alters*) within a defined social group (Borgatti, Everett, and Johnson 2013), in this case a musical ensemble. Various indices of network position have been developed to quantify individuals' social ecologies by focusing on their position in a network (Robins 2013; Valente 2010). Complete network data, referring to multi-informant (egos and alters) assessment of network ties (Wasserman and Faust 1994) within a bounded social system (e.g., marching band), allows for consideration of directed and mutual ties. An individual's outgoing ties depict network activity or gregariousness; incoming ties describe network popularity and preferential attachment (Robins 2013; Valente 2010). Mutual friendship ties tend to depict social relationships that are characterized by greater levels of stability, intimacy, and social support (Cauce 1986). We can also observe these three types of network ties in different types of networks (i.e., friendship or advice networks; see Trobia and Lo Verde, this volume, chapter 26). By considering these indices of position in friendship and advice networks, we are able to describe the multiple dimensions of individual embeddedness in the social environment in which music making occurs. Importantly, we are able to relate measures of network position in friendship and advice networks to individual differences in participatory motivation.

The Present Study

Our goal was to describe the associations between motivational profiles regarding music making and an individuals' position in a social network structure within a large musical ensemble. To address this goal we sought a large recreational ensemble with regular and sustained engagement that would allow for the creation and development of complex social relationships. The collegiate marching band is a large musical ensemble, often with hundreds of individuals who engage in the activity as a serious leisure pursuit. Although a small minority of individuals will view their participation as a pre-professional requirement (e.g., music education students), the majority of collegiate marching band members have made the significant commitment to participate independent of a professional or educational requirement. While there are often additional external incentives for participation, such as college credit or access to athletic events, members choose to participate of their own volition rather than as a university requirement. Marching band activities naturally require significant time spent in both musical and nonmusical activities (e.g., traveling, supporting an athletic team), which offers a greater number of opportunities to develop relationships beyond those of many other concert ensembles where the primary interaction is musical rehearsal. Consequently, this type of musical activity is a model system for investigating the relationship of participatory motivation and the development of friendship and advice networks.

We anticipated that the choice to participate in musical ensembles for leisure purposes would be associated with higher levels of intrinsic motivation and result in greater integration into the ensemble's social network. Additionally, we expected that retention and positive outcomes in these leisure activities would be related to the features of the social network that enable supporting and enhancing a person's intrinsic motivation while participating in the activity. This study integrated SDT approaches to participatory motivation and SNA approaches in describing the structure of a social group to delineate the relationships between these critical components of group music making and leisure activities. More specifically, we addressed the following research questions:

1a. Is there a predominant motivational profile for members of a collegiate marching band?
1b. How do motivational profiles change over the course of the band season?
2. What is the relationship between a person's motivational profile and his or her position in the friendship and advice networks?

RESEARCH DESIGN AND METHODS

Participants

Participants were undergraduate students from a Division I collegiate marching band located in the southwestern United States. Each collegiate marching band is idiosyncratic to its home institution (e.g., traditions or style); however, more broadly, this marching band is representative of the most typically observed "corps-style" collegiate marching program in its purpose, basic organizational structure, and the activity that is fundamental to its appearance and sound. The overwhelming majority of members are nonmusic majors. Participation in this band involves eight to twelve hours of rehearsal per week (across three or four practice sessions) as well as six or more hours of performance per week. Most performances are associated with activities surrounding the university's football program, but also include local marching festivals and other university athletic events. Consent was obtained from 220 students (72 percent of the active marching band members), and 205 (68 percent of the active marching band members) completed network assessments on two occasions.

The sample of participants was 48 percent male and 52 percent female. Mean age was 19.43 years (SD = 1.51; range: 18–30 years). Ethnic/racial composition of the band reflected the ethnic composition of the university: 5.3 percent African American, 5.3 percent Asian American, 62.1 percent European American, 20.9 percent Hispanic/Latino, and 3.4 percent Native American. Participants had completed 1–14 semesters of college (M = 4.45; SD = 2.52) and had completed 1–6 seasons of marching band at the college level (M = 2.17; SD = 1.21). Approximately 27 percent of participants reported being in other ensembles at the university and 24 percent were members of Kappa Kappa Psi, a coeducational music service fraternity.[1] Participants in formal leadership positions constituted 13 percent of the sample population. Retention data were collected at the beginning of the following band season, which indicated that 64 percent of participants returned to the band, 18 percent graduated and therefore were not eligible to return, and 18 percent chose not to return to the band.

Procedure

At the end of September and end of November in 2013, all participants received an email with a unique username and password and were asked to complete an online survey focusing on demographic characteristics and activity-related motivations. At both timepoints, students completed the online survey during one week prior to a band rehearsal at which the in-person social network data collection took place. At the conclusion of the rehearsal, participants were asked to complete social network measures as described below. The choice of assessment timeframe was intended to observe the initial configuration of social relationships, which formed over the first six weeks of the season, and the end of the regular band season, in order to capture continuity and change in social ties.

Measures

Friendship and Advice Nominations and Network Data

For the friendship and advice network inventory, an alphabetized list was constructed that contained the ID codes and names of all students who agreed to participate in the study.

Participants began by writing their own ID on the first page of the questionnaire booklet. They were then asked to list the IDs of their band-mates who were their closest friends; they could name as many classmates as they wanted. The same procedure was used to ask them which band-mates they go to for advice. Students returned the alphabetized list with the ID codes and names of all participants to the study team. This list was subsequently destroyed, so that the questionnaires contained only ID numbers and no names.

Data based on friendship and advice nominations were arranged in two binary matrices, with each row and column representing an individual within the band.[2] Using the unilateral friendship matrix two measures of friendship network position were constructed: (1) the *number of incoming friendship nominations* depicted friendship network popularity, and (2) the *number of outgoing friendship* nominations described friendship network gregariousness. From the mutual tie matrix, a third measure of friendship network was created—*number of mutual friendship ties*. Using the unilateral advice matrix, two measures of advice network position were constructed: (1) the *number of incoming advice nominations* depicted network sources of advice, and (2) the *number of outgoing advice* nominations described network seekers of advice.

Participatory Motivation Scales

In the absence of existing measurement scales, we adapted two established scales (Pelletier et al. 1995; Ryan et al. 1997) intended to assess the motives for participation in physical activity. While both scales are grounded in SDT and measure types and intensity of motivation, their subscales allow for different conclusions to be drawn regarding the type of motivation or goal for participating. Researchers suggest that the use of these two scales simultaneously may be advantageous in this type of research (Frederick-Recascino 2002).

Participants completed a twenty-eight-item Sports Motivation Scale (SMS; Pelletier et al. 1995), adapted for marching band, which asked them to indicate the reasons they were presently participating in marching band. A sample item was: "Because it is one of the best ways to maintain good relationships with my friends." Summing the corresponding items created a total score for each type of motivation along the SDT continuum. A total motivation composite index score was calculated using a preestablished weighted formula (Fortier, Vallerand, and Guay 1995). This composite index score can be used to determine the predominate type of motivation—self-determined, nonself-determined, or amotivated. The SMS was shown to be internally consistent and reliable (Cronbach αs for the subscales ranged from .70 to .88 for collection 1 and .72 to .91 for collection 2).

Participants also completed a nineteen-item Motives for Physical Activities Measure–Revised (MPAM–R) (Ryan et al. 1997), adapted for marching band, that asked them to indicate the reasons they were presently participating in marching band. A sample item was: "Because I want to improve existing skills." Summing the corresponding items created a composite score for different categories of intrinsic motivation—enjoyment, competence, and social. The MPAM-R was shown to be internally consistent and reliable (Cronbach αs for the subscales range from .72 to .90 for collection 1 and .76 to .96 for collection 2).

Results

Is There a Predominant Motivational Profile for Members of a Collegiate Marching Band?

To address this question, we used descriptive analyses to examine the mean levels of motivational composite index and individual types of motivation (see Table 18.1). Means and standard deviations obtained from these analyses revealed that the motivation composite index score for all participants at the beginning of the season overwhelmingly indicated self-determined participation in marching band. Motivational data collected using both scales show that marching band members had high levels of intrinsic motivation to participate, suggesting that members felt a sense of satisfaction of the three psychological needs, allowing for self-determined participation. Participants reported moderate levels of extrinsic reasons for participating, but the

Table 18.1 Mean Levels and Their Change over Time for Participatory Motivation at Collections 1 and 2

	Collection 1		Collection 2				
	M	SD	M	SD	t	df	p (2-tailed)
SMS							
Motivation composite index	51.99	16.04	45.53	17.25	−5.34	126	.000***
Intrinsic: to know	4.24	1.56	4.01	1.54	−1.26	149	.208
Intrinsic: to accomplish	5.00	1.35	4.50	1.40	−5.01	148	.000***
Intrinsic: to experience	5.56	1.08	5.10	1.21	−5.56	148	.000***
Extrinsic: identified regulated	5.18	1.14	4.92	1.17	−3.17	148	.002**
Extrinsic: introjected regulated	3.59	1.47	3.36	1.41	−2.14	148	.034*
Extrinsic: externally regulated	3.97	1.39	3.77	1.31	−1.61	148	.110
Amotivation	1.66	0.95	1.95	1.15	3.25	148	.001**
MPAM–R							
Enjoyment	6.51	0.65	6.29	0.79	−4.13	146	.000***
Competence	5.89	1.09	5.70	1.23	−2.66	145	.009**
Social	5.84	0.99	5.87	0.98	0.23	145	.816

Note: All types of motivation except the composite index were measured on a seven-point Likert scale, where 1 indicated no motivation of that type and 7 indicated the highest intensity of motivation of that type. Composite index scores that are positive indicate a self-determined motivational profile; negative scores indicate a non-self-determined motivational profile. Extremely negative scores, which were not observed in the data, indicate an amotivational profile.

*** t-test is significant at $p < 0.001$ level (2-tailed).

** t-test is significant at $p < 0.01$ level (2-tailed).

* t-test is significant at $p < 0.05$ level (2-tailed).

intensity of those types of motivation was minimal compared to high levels of intrinsic motivation (see Table 18.1). The vast majority of participants reported almost no level of amotivation.

How Do Motivational Profiles Change Over the Course of the Band Season?

To examine the changes in the mean levels of motivational composites between collection 1 and collection 2, we conducted a paired-samples t-test, which is a statistical measure used to compare two groups in their mean differences for a variable of interest. Our analyses revealed that despite the high levels of reported intrinsic motivation at the beginning of the season, there was a statistically significant decrease in motivation along the motivational continuum over time (see Table 18.1). Despite this decrease, a majority of the band appears to have reported sufficiently high levels of intrinsic motivation to sustain self-determined participation in marching band at the end of the band season, as indicated by the composite index at collection 2.

These results show a statistically significant decrease in intrinsic motivation, but the composite scores for the subscales suggest this change was driven by decreases in feelings of autonomy and competence rather than relatedness. Levels of social motivation, an indicator of relatedness, increased during the season, although not significantly. More simply, participants remained highly motivated to connect to others in the band even though they were less motivated to master elements of the activity and to feel enjoyment.

What is the Relationship between a Person's Motivational Profile and His or Her Position in the Friendship and Advice Networks?

Structure of the Friendship Network

We start by considering the structure of friendship networks. Network-level descriptive statistics indicated that the network of 193 individuals had 1204 unilateral friendship ties at collection 1 and 1117 ties at collection 2. The friendship networks had a density (i.e., proportion of existing ties relative to the total possible ties) of .039 for collection 1 and .036 for collection 2, which is a level consistent with other research on human social networks (Wasserman and Faust 1994). We used *gplot* package in *R* (R Core Team 2015) to visualize the friendship network at collection 1.

To investigate this relationship, we computed Pearson's product-moment correlations to examine the relationship between a person's motivational profile and position in the friendship network. Our analyses revealed a positive relationship between social

Table 18.2 Bivariate Correlations of Motivational Responses and Social Network Indices at Collection 1

	Friendship Networks			Advice Networks	
	Indegree	Outdegree	Reciprocated	Indegree	Outdegree
SMS					
Motivation composite index	.15	.23**	.18*	.15	.10
Intrinsic: to know	.00	.04	−.01	−.02	.02
Intrinsic: to accomplish	−.03	.03	−.04	−.02	−.03
Intrinsic: to experience	.08	.17*	.15*	.04	.11
Extrinsic: identified regulated	.15	.29**	.20**	.11	.10
Extrinsic: introjected regulated	−.11	.11	−.03	−.16	.01
Extrinsic: externally regulated	−.03	.15*	.02	−.09	.01
Amotivation	−.10	−.13	−.12	−.14	−.04
MPAM–R					
Intrinsic: enjoyment	.00	.08	.03	.00	.11
Intrinsic: competence	.02	.08	−.01	.00	.03
Intrinsic: social	.24**	.25**	.20**	.09	.19*

** Correlation is significant at $p < 0.01$ level (2-tailed).

* Correlation is significant at $p < 0.05$ level (2-tailed).

motivation and the size of a given individual's friendship network within the marching band (see Tables 18.2 and 18.3). Those individuals who reported higher levels of social motivation tended to be more popular, gregarious, and more likely to have their friendships reciprocated. The relationship between social motivation and the size of the person's social network strengthened over the course of the season. There was no relationship between the change in social motivation and the change in network size from collection 1 to collection 2, but this is to be expected as there was no significant change observed in the self-reported levels of social motivation over the course of the season. These results suggest that individuals who are highly socially motivated at the start of the band season continue to build the size of their friendship networks throughout the season.

A positive relationship between the level of intrinsic motivation and the size of the individual's friendship network was observed. At collection 1, this positive relationship was true only for outgoing and reciprocal friendship ties (see Table 18.2). In other words, more highly motivated individuals tended to be more gregarious and develop stronger mutual relationships. An investigation of individual types of motivation along the continuum revealed that intrinsic motivation to experience (i.e., enjoyment of the activity) and identified regulation (i.e., others deem the activity valuable) correlated to higher levels of network size. Identified regulated individuals were motivated to

Table 18.3 Bivariate Correlations of Motivational Responses and Social
           Network Indices at Collection 2

	Friendship Networks			Advice Networks	
	Indegree	Outdegree	Reciprocated	Indegree	Outdegree
SMS					
Motivation composite index	.27**	.25**	.31**	.08	.21*
Intrinsic: to know	.00	.12	.08	−.06	.02
Intrinsic: to accomplish	.05	.14	.12	.01	.10
Intrinsic: to experience	.15	.18*	.21**	.00	.13
Extrinsic: identified regulated	.27**	.28**	.26**	.09	.14
Extrinsic: introjected regulated	.04	.21**	.15	−.09	.06
Extrinsic: externally regulated	.05	.14	.07	−.01	−.04
Amotivation	−.18*	−.14	−.22**	−.11	−.14
MPAM–R					
Intrinsic: enjoyment	.16	.13	.20*	.06	.13
Intrinsic: competence	.12	.17*	.16	.03	.07
Intrinsic: social	.32**	.34**	.34**	.03	.21*

** Correlation is significant at $p < 0.01$ level (2-tailed).
* Correlation is significant at $p < 0.05$ level (2-tailed).

participate because they had internalized the high value and importance others had for the activity. At collection 2, this positive relationship was observed between highly motivated individuals and all three friendship network indices, which indicates that self-determined regulation was becoming more aligned with the size of a person's friendship network (see Table 18.3). Again, identified regulation was correlated with friendship network size. A stronger relationship was observed between identified regulation and friendship network indices, suggesting that this connection to the values of others may be associated with continued engagement and positive outcomes. A positive correlation was observed between an increase in the number of friendships a person made over the season and an increase in the level of most types of motivation on the SDT continuum.

Structure of the Advice Network

Network-level descriptive statistics indicated that the network of 193 individuals had 680 unilateral advice ties at collection 1 and 683 ties at collection 2. The advice networks had a density (i.e., proportion of existing ties relative to the total possible ties) of .021 for collection 1 and .022 for collection 2.

We computed Pearson's product-moment correlations to examine the relationship between a person's motivational profile and position in the advice network. Our analyses revealed a positive relationship between the number of outgoing advice ties and the level of social motivation observed at collection 1 (see Table 18.2). At collection 2, a positive correlation between high levels of intrinsic motivation and outgoing advice ties was observed, which suggests highly intrinsically motivated people do end up increasing the size of their advice networks over the course of the marching band season (see Table 18.3).

Discussion

A Self-Determined Ensemble

Leisure activities can be defined as "those activities that people do in their free time, because they want to, for their own sake, for fun, for entertainment, for goals of their own choosing, but not for payment" (Argyle 1996, 3). This definition suggests that a person's motivation to participate in a leisure activity would be strongly intrinsic. Since we consider marching band a serious leisure activity with volitional engagement, we expect that motivation to participate would be strongly intrinsic. The results of this study support this assertion; the motivation composite index score for all participants at the beginning of the season overwhelmingly indicated self-determined participation in marching band.

A decrease in most types of motivation was observed during the season, but a majority of the band still reported levels of intrinsic motivation sufficient to sustain self-determined participation in marching band at the end of the band season. There are significant demands on time and energy for collegiate marching band members throughout the fall band season. Additionally, as students, the band members must balance this activity with their academic studies and with other aspects of their personal lives. We hypothesize that these demands and the fatigue of the season may, at least partially, contribute to a decrease in feelings of self-determination toward participation in the band. As the band season progresses, there are more deadlines and pressures to perform at a higher level; research has associated these extrinsic influences with a decrease in intrinsic motivation. Further investigations into the causes of this decrease would be useful in order to help better understand other environmental dynamics that affect specific types of motivation.

The mean levels of social motivation, an indicator of relatedness, increased during the season, although they failed to reach levels of statistical significance. These findings suggest that relatedness may be one of the most continuously met psychological needs maintaining self-determined motivation to continue participating in marching band, which is important for at least two reasons. First, social motivation remains high and statistically unchanged throughout the season, which suggests the social element of marching band participation may be an important predictor of a person's choice to maintain engagement in the activity. This type of motivation may also be an important mediator for changes in other types of motivation associated with decreased well-being, such as external rewards or negative evaluation (e.g., Ryan and Deci 2000; Vallerand and Ratelle 2002). For example, feeling related and integrated into a social network may help buffer against the effects of negative evaluation that have been shown to decrease intrinsic motivation. Second, most of the research on participatory motivation from an SDT approach has focused on measuring perceptions of autonomy and competence. The focus on these two needs has often meant that relatedness has been under-addressed in previous psychological literature on participatory motivation (Frederick-Recascino 2002; Vallerand, Pelletier, and Koestner 2008), as well as under-developed in the daily practice of the activity. Psychological research often focuses on helping members meet their autonomy and competence needs, while neglecting social needs. This can be observed in some informal band practices as well, when the primary focus is on skill development with minimal attention paid to social development as a method for improving motivation. These results suggest that the third psychological need—relatedness—may be just as influential in understanding the motivational dynamics of participation in social experiences and thus warrants in-depth investigation in future research. Moreover, investigating any possible mediating effects from other types of motivation, such as social motivation, on satisfaction of each the other psychological needs will be important. These results suggest that intrinsic and social motivation perform important roles in a person's choice to join and remain engaged in the marching band.

Associations between Participatory Motivation and Social Network Dynamics

Taking a closer look at the social environment of the marching band using SNA allows us to observe ways in which these social networks may support or hinder motivation. The following subsections explore how the friendship and advice networks of the marching band may support a person's participatory motivation and fulfillment of the three psychological needs according to SDT. We also discuss additional questions and areas of research that may be useful in clarifying the relationship between motivational and social network dynamics in music ensembles, especially, those for leisure purposes.

Participatory Motivation and the Friendship Network

Individuals who are highly socially motivated at the start of the marching band season continue to build the size of their friendship networks throughout the season, as suggested by the positive relationship observed between social motivation and the friendship network indices. These individuals become more integrated into the social network of the band as a whole. In general, it seems reasonable to expect that people who value social relationships would increase the number of friendship ties, at least to a point, in multiple directions (incoming and outgoing) over the course of the band season, rather than decrease the number (Ojanen et al. 2010).

The observed positive relationship between the level of intrinsic motivation and the social network indices may suggest that people seek out others who also find marching band important and have a similar set of values. This preference for similar others (also known as "homophily" in networks research) is commonly reported in research on a variety of social networks (McPherson et al. 2001). Furthermore, this type of motivation is associated with internalization and transmission of values (Ryan and Deci 2000, 2002), which may be important to the functioning of an ensemble where shared performance goals can aid in positive performance outcomes for the entire group. This concept of internalization, or *integrativeness* (Gardner and McIntyre 1993), has been theorized as part of a socio-educational model of music motivation (MacIntyre, Potter, and Burns 2012), but to our knowledge has never been quantified as in the current approach. The *social contagion* model (Wild and Enzle 2002) also suggests that the values and perceived motivation of others in our social networks can have an observable effect on a person's motivation. Self-determined regulation becomes more aligned with the size of a person's friendship network over the course of the season. As previously discussed, overall intrinsic motivation decreased, possibly due to stressors or burnout occurring over the course of the season. Previous research suggests that when the activity is inherently interesting to the person, intrinsic motivation is most relevant, but when the activity becomes less interesting or too challenging, higher forms of extrinsic motivation, in this case identified regulation, become most relevant to maintaining positive outcomes (Koestner and Losier 2002).

Friend-seeking behaviors can also be an indication of feeling autonomous, since network theories suggest that having more friends can provide a more stable and supportive system, allowing an individual to feel safer to engage more freely with the environment (Kadushin 2002). Moreover, higher levels of intrinsic motivation are also associated with well-being, self-esteem, supporting the autonomy of others, self-actualization, behavioral effectiveness, greater volitional persistence, and better assimilation of the individual within his or her social group (e.g., Ryan and Deci 2000). The positive correlation between an increase in the number of friendships over the season and an increase in the level of most types of motivation supports the notion that relatedness has a possible mediating effect on motivation; further investigation is necessary, however, to determine the nature of this effect and if it can be used as an intervention to improve motivation. Overall, people who are more self-determined to participate in marching band also have larger friendship networks. More research is warranted to determine the directionality and predictive nature of this relationship between motivation and social networks. Although a causal relationship is not established in this analysis, these relationships also indicate a need to conduct further research into how friendship networks might be important to supporting motivation, as feelings of autonomy or competence in our study decreased over the season.

Participatory Motivation and the Advice Network

A positive correlation between social motivation and advice-seeking behaviors may be related, in part, to a person's perception of the people from whom they are seeking advice. Research suggests that people view friends as being more available in a time of need (Siciliano 2015) and that advice ties are more likely to occur between friends (Lazega and Pattison 1999) or between people who have a similar status within an organization (Lee 1997; Siciliano 2015). These results have established that highly socially motivated people tend to have larger friendship networks. Therefore, those people who are socially motivated and have larger friendship networks would also be more likely to seek out advice from friends.

In an ensemble where realizing shared goals is directly related to performance outcomes, providing and seeking advice from others would be an important part of attaining these shared goals, but this connection was not easily observable in these results. There are numerous explanations for a lack of correlation. First, research has found that even when there is a formal leadership structure, people tend to seek advice from those in their friendship network (e.g., Lazega and Pattison 1999). Second, perceptions of incompetence or competition within the marching band may also contribute to a lack of advice seeking and giving behaviors (e.g., Lee 1997; Siciliano 2015). This possible connection between advice and friendship networks in the band supports our assertion that the social context (i.e., creation of friendships) may be integral to the overall musical performance of the group, especially, if it aids the development of advice ties essential to the flow of performance-related information. A more detailed investigation into the nature of relationships between the formal, and possibly informal, leadership structures and friendship networks may shed light on the role or roles of advice and friendship networks for participatory motivation. Finally, even if band members mainly develop advice ties with formal leaders in the band, the statistical power needed to observe the expected relationship with motivation may not be present.

Summary and Directions for Future Research

The results from our study suggest that marching band members are predominantly self-determined to participate in marching band and are particularly motivated for social reasons, regardless of their experience over the course of the band season. The members who were highly motivated were also more integrated into the band's social networks. While these findings are useful to highlight the central nature of the social experience of marching band, the present analysis does have some limitations. The results are correlational and would benefit from further analysis that could yield information about the direction of influence between motivational and social variables and their predictive value. This analysis could lead toward the development of interventions to provide an environment that is more supportive of intrinsic motivation and general psychological well-being. Furthermore, research regarding the possible mediating effects of relatedness on autonomy and competence would broaden our understanding of the interconnected nature of the three psychological needs. Deepening the investigation to include the participants' relationship with directors or other staff would also be valuable, as

research suggests those relationships are influential in cultivating an intrinsically motivated climate in musical settings (Creech and Hallam 2011; Evans, McPherson, and
Davidson 2012; Matthews and Kitsantas 2007).

Another useful direction may be to investigate representative motivational profiles for groups within the ensemble, which may yield a pattern of associations among
motivation, networks, and retention. The use of the motivational composite index
score was a first step toward this type of investigation; a cluster analysis would provide
more possibilities for complex statistical modeling and has been used with some success in educational settings (e.g., Vansteenkiste et al. 2009). Additionally, investigating motivational trends within band sections or formal leadership may yield further
information regarding how the social structures of formal and informal relationships
within the marching band may affect motivation. This avenue for exploration has
the potential for leading to interesting discoveries about leadership structures that
may support or inhibit motivation and the flow of information in ensembles such as
marching bands.

Replication of this study with other marching bands and recreational ensembles is
also vital. This study is a snapshot of one band's season. Different types of bands with
different goals, experiences, and leadership structures may yield different results.
Comparisons between different musical and social contexts will provide useful variance in order to draw broader conclusions about leisure music making and the development of possible interventions to support ensemble well-being and retention. Within
the same ensemble, increasing the number of data collection periods would also help
to better understand the changes occurring in the morphology of networks and their
context. As indicated by SDT, the social ecology of a marching band will play a role in
supporting or undermining the satisfaction of the three psychological needs. Detailed
longitudinal data could lead to specific interventions that may facilitate positive changes
in motivation.

Finally, investigating the role(s) played by biology in this system may also yield valuable results. Research has demonstrated that biology and behavior are interconnected
(e.g., Granger et al. 2012) and that biobehavioral processes may be influential in the
observed structure of social networks (e.g., Kornienko et al. 2014). Discovering relationships between biology and social network structure is another important area for
potential future research. Additionally, SDT researchers have discussed individual differences in a person's abilities to be motivated and to satisfy their psychological needs
(e.g., Deci and Ryan 2000); it is possible these biobehavioral processes affect motivation as well. This also leads back to an earlier discussion in this chapter in which we
speculated that social music making modulates certain hormones and neuromediators
that are found to facilitate social cohesion and bonding among members in a group
(e.g., Dunbar 2004; Freeman 2000; Grape et al.; McNeill 2000). Examining the associations and interactions between biology, social networks, and motivation may be an
important direction for continued investigation of music making as leisure in large
ensembles.

Conclusions

The results of this study suggest the social environment may be influential in the success and longevity of participation within leisure musical ensembles such as collegiate marching bands. Although the musical experience is certainly a reason to participate in leisure musical ensembles, the motivation to connect to other people through this medium appears critical, at least as demonstrated in this ensemble. Although connecting to others and experiencing social support have been documented as reasons for adult participation in leisure musical ensembles (e.g., Carucci 2012; Coleman and Iso-Ahola 1993) and marching band (e.g., Moder 2013; Zdzinski 2004), these reasons have never been empirically linked to the formation of social networks. Creating an environment that supports and fosters intrinsic motivation includes nurturing these social relationships. Ensembles that maintain high levels of self-determined motivation to participate may yield improved psychological well-being, positive perceptions of autonomy and competence, greater volitional persistence, and more social cohesion and support, in addition to positive performance outcomes. These patterns underscore the need to encourage further research in this area to inform music educators and other music leaders in how they can create and curate more intrinsically motivating music making experiences.

Notes

1. "Kappa Kappa Psi operates primarily as a student service and leadership recognition society whose chief aim is to assist the Director of Bands in developing the leadership and enthusiasm that is required of his/her band. Our goals are to provide the band not only with organized and concentrated service activities, but to give our membership valid and wholesome experiences in organization, leadership and social contacts" (http://www.kkpsi.org/about/who-is-kappa-kappa-psi/).
2. In the matrix, cell x_{ij} corresponds to i's relation to j, as reported by i. That is, if i nominated j as a friend, cell x_{ij} was coded as 1. If i did not nominate j as a friend, cell x_{ij} was coded as 0. This matrix represented unilateral or asymmetrical friendship ties. A matrix for advice network was constructed in the same manner. Based on the unilateral matrices, a mutual ties matrix in which cell x_{ij} was coded as 1 only if i nominated j as a friend and j nominated i as a friend (and a reciprocated friendship matrix) were created.

References Cited

Allsup, Randall Everett. 2012. "The Moral Ends of Band." *Theory into Practice* 51(3): 179–187.

Allsup, Randall Everett, and Cathy Benedict. 2008. "The Problems of Band: An Inquiry into the Future of Instrumental Music Education." *Philosophy of Music Education Review* 16(2): 156–173.

Argyle, Michael. 1996. *The Social Psychology of Leisure*. London: Penguin.

Bailey, Betty A., and Jane W. Davidson. 2005. "Effects of Group Singing and Performance for Marginalized and Middle-Class Singers." *Psychology of Music* 33: 269–303.

Baumeister, Roy, and Mark R. Leary. 1995. "The Need to Belong: Desire for Interpersonal Attachments as a Fundamental Human Motivation." *Psychological Bulletin* 117: 497–529.

Berkman, Lisa F., Thomas Glass, Ian Brissette, and Teresa E. Seeman. 2000. "From Social Integration to Health: Durkheim in the New Millennium." *Social Science and Medicine* 51: 843–857. doi: 10.1016/S0277-9536(00)00065-4.

Berkman, Lisa F., and Aditi Krishna. 2014."Social Network Epidemiology." In *Social Epidemiology*, edited by Lisa F. Berkman, Ichiro Kawachi, and M. Maria Glymour, 234–289. New York: Oxford University Press.

Booth, Alan, David Johnson, and Douglas A. Granger. 1999. "Testosterone and Men's Health." *Behavior and Medicine* 20: 1–20.

Borgatti, Stephen P., Ajay Mehra, Danial J. Brass, and Giuseppe Labianca. 2009. "Network Analysis in the Social Sciences." *Science* 323: 892–895.

Borgatti, Stephen P., Martin G. Everett, and Jeffrey C. Johnson. 2013. *Analyzing Social Networks.* Thousand Oaks, CA: Sage.

Carucci, Christine. 2012. "An Investigation of Social Support in Adult Recreational Music Ensembles." *International Journal of Community Music* 5(3). doi: 10.1386/ijcm.5.3.237_1.

Cauce, Ana M. 1986. "Social Networks and Social Competence: Exploring the Effects of Early Adolescent Friendships." *American Journal of Community Psychology* 14: 607–628. doi: 10.1007/BF00931339.

Cavitt, Mary Ellen. 2005. "Factors Influencing Participation in Community Bands." *Journal of Band Research* 41(1): 42.

Coleman, Denis, and Seppo E. Iso-Ahola. 1993. "Leisure and Health: The Role of Social Support and Self-Determination." *Journal of Leisure Research* 25(2): 111–128.

Creech, Andrea, and Susan Hallam. 2011. "Learning a Musical Instrument: The Influence of Interpersonal Interaction on Outcomes for School-Aged Pupils." *Society for Education, Music and Psychology Research* 39(1): 120–122. doi: 10.1177/0305735610370222.

Cross, Ian. 2001. "Music, Cognition, Culture, and Evolution." *Annals of the New York Academy of Sciences* 930: 28–42.

Csikszentmihalyi, Mihaly. 1990. *Flow: The Psychology of Optimal Experience.* New York: Harper and Row.

de Charms, Richard. 1968. *Personal Causation.* New York: Academic.

Deci, Edward L. 1975. *Intrinsic Motivation.* New York: Plenum.

Deci, Edward L. 1980. *The Psychology of Self-Determination.* Lexington, MA: D. C. Heath.

Deci, Edward L., and Richard M. Ryan. 1985. *Intrinsic Motivation and Self-Determination in Human Behavior.* New York: Plenum.

Deci, Edward L., and Richard M. Ryan. 1991. "A Motivational Approach to Self: Integration in Personality." In *Nebraska Symposium on Motivation, 1990.* Vol. 38, *Perspectives on Motivation*, edited by Richard A. Dienstbier, 237–288. Lincoln: University of Nebraska Press.

Deci, Edward L., and Richard M. Ryan. 2000. "The 'What' and 'Why' of Goal Pursuits: Human Needs and the Self-Determination of Behavior." *Psychological Inquiry* 11: 227–268.

Dunbar, Robin. 2004. *The Human Story: A New History of Mankind's Evolution.* London: Faber and Faber.

Evans, Paul, Gary E. McPherson, and Jane W. Davidson. 2012. "The Role of Psychological Needs in Ceasing Music and Music Learning Activities." *Psychology of Music* 41: 600–619.

Fortier, Michelle S., Robert J. Vallerand, and Frédéric Guay. 1995. "Academic Motivation and School Performance: Toward a Structural Model." *Contemporary Educational Psychology* 20(3): 257–274.

Frederick-Recascino, Christina M. 2002. "Self-Determination Theory and Participation Motivation Research in the Sport and Exercise Domain." In *Handbook of Self-Determination Research*, edited by Edward L. Deci and Richard M. Ryan, 277–296. Rochester, NY: University of Rochester Press.

Freeman, Walter J. 2000. "A Neurobiological Role of Music in Social Bonding." In *The Origins of Music*, edited by Nils L. Wallin, Björn Merkur, and Steven Brown, 411–424. Cambridge, MA: MIT Press.

Fritz, Barbara Smolej, and Andreja Avsec. 2007. "The Experience of Flow and Subjective Well-Being of Music Students." *Psihološka Obzorja / Horizons of Psychology* 16(2): 5–17.

Frodi, Ann, Lisa Bridges, and Wendy Grolnick. 1985. "Correlates of Mastery-Related Behavior: A Short-Term Longitudinal Study of Infants in their Second Year." *Child Development* 56: 1291–1298.

Gardner, Robert C., and Peter D. MacIntyre. 1993. "On the Measurement of Affective Variables in Second Language Learning." *Language Learning* 43: 157–194.

Granger, Douglas a., Christine K. Fortunato, Emilie K. Beltzer, Marta Virag, Melissa A. Bright, and Dorothée Out. 2012. "Focus on Methodology: Salivary Bioscience and Research on Adolescence: An Integrated Perspective." *Journal of Adolescence* 35(4): 1081–1095. doi:10.1016/j.adolescence.2012.01.005.

Grape, Christina, Maria Sandgren, Lars-Olof Hansson, Mats Ericson, and Töres Theorell. 2003. "Does Singing Promote Well-Being? An Empirical Study of Professional and Amateur Singers during a Singing Lesson." *Integrative Physiological and Behavioral Science : The Official Journal of the Pavlovian Society* 38(1): 65–74. doi:10.1007/BF02734261.

Harter, Susan. 1978. "Effectance Motivation Reconsidered: Toward a Developmental Model." *Human Development* 1: 34–64.

Hawley, Patricia H., 1999. "The Ontogenesis of Social Dominance: A Strategy-Based Evolutionary Perspective." *Developmental Review* 19: 97–132.

Heinrich, Liesl M. and Eleonora Gullone. 2006. "The Clinical Significance of Loneliness: A Literature Review." *Clinical Psychology Review* 26: 695–718.

Kadushin, Charles. 2002. "The Motivational Foundation of Social Networks." *Social Networks* 24: 77–91. doi: 10.1016/S0378-8733(01)00052-1.

Kappa Kappa Psi. "Who Is KKPsi?" http://www.kkpsi.org/about/who-is-kappa-kappa-psi/.

Koestner, Richard, and Gaëtan F. Losier. 2002. "Distinguishing Three Ways of Being Highly Motivated: A Closer Look at Introjection, Identification, and Intrinsic Motivation." In *Handbook of Self-Determination Research*, edited by Edward L. Deci and Richard M. Ryan, 101–122. Rochester, NY: University of Rochester Press.

Kornienko, Olga, Katherine H. Clemans, Dorothée Out, and Douglas A. Granger. 2014. "Hormones, Behavior, and Social Network Analysis: Exploring Associations between Cortisol, Testosterone, and Network Structure." *Hormones and Behavior* 66(3): 534–544. doi:10.1016/j.yhbeh.2014.07.009.

Kratus, John. 2007. "Music Education at the Tipping Point." *Music Educators Journal* 94(2): 42–48.

Lazega, Emmanuel, and Philippa E. Pattison. 1999. "Multiplexity, Generalized Exchange and Cooperation in Organizations: A Case Study." *Social Networks* 21(1): 67–90.

Lee, Fiona. 1997. "When the Going Gets Tough, Do the Tough Ask for Help? Help Seeking and Power Motivation in Organizations." *Organizational Behavior and Human Decision Processes* 72(3): 336–63. doi:10.1006/obhd.1997.2746.

Lewis, Michael, and Margaret Wolan Sullivan. 2005. "The Development of Self-Conscious Emotions." In *Handbook of Competence and Motivation* edited by Andrew J. Elliot and Carol S. Dweck, 185–201. New York: Guilford Press.

MacIntyre, Peter D., Gillian K. Potter, and Jillian N. Burns. 2012. "The Socio-Educational Model of Music Motivation." *Journal of Research in Music Education* 60(2): 129–44. doi:10.1177/0022429412444609.

Matthews, Wendy K., and Anastasia Kitsantas. 2007. "Group Cohesion, Collective Efficacy, and Motivational Climate as Predictors of Conductor Support in Music Ensembles." *Journal of Research in Music Education* 55(1): 6–17.

McNeill, David. 2000. *Language and Gesture*. Cambridge: Cambridge University Press.

McPherson, Gary E. 2001. "Commitment and Practice: Key Ingredients for Achievement During the Early Stages of Learning a Musical Instrument." *Bulletin of the Council for Research in Music Education* 122–127.

McPherson, Gary E., and Jane W. Davidson. 2002. "Musical Practice: Mother and Child Interactions during the First Year of Learning an Instrument." *Music Education Research* 4: 141–156.

McPherson, Miller, Lynn Smith-Lovin, and James M. Cook. 2001. "Birds of a Feather: Homophily in Social Networks." *Annual Review Sociology* 27: 415–444.

Moder, Jennifer Ann. 2013. "Factors Influencing Non-Music Majors' Decisions to Participate in Collegiate Bands." PhD Dissertation, University of Missouri, Kansas City.

Ojanen, Tiina, Jelle J. Sijtsema, Patricia H. Hawley, and Todd D. Little. 2010. "Intrinsic and Extrinsic Motivation in Early Adolescents' Friendship Development: Friendship Selection, Influence, and Prospective Friendship Quality." *Journal of Adolescence* 33: 837–851. doi:10.1016/j.adolescence.2010.08.004.

O'Neill, Susan A. 1999. "Flow Theory and the Development of Musical Performance Skills." *Bulletin of the Council for Research in Music Education* 141: 129–134.

Pelletier, Luc G., Kim M. Tuson, Michelle S. Fortier, Robert J. Vallerand, Nathalie M. Brière, and Marc R. Blais. 1995. "Toward a New Measure of Intrinsic Motivation, Extrinsic Motivation, and Amotivation in Sports: The Sport Motivation Scale (SMS)." *Journal of Sports and Exercise Psychology* 17: 35–53.

Persson, Roland. 2001. "The Subjective World of the Performer." In *Music and Emotion: Theory and Research*, edited by Patrik N. Juslin and John A. Sloboda, 275–289. Oxford: Oxford University Press.

R Core Team. 2015. "R: A Language and Environment for Statistical Computing." R Foundation for Statistical Computing, Vienna, Austria. http://www.r-project.org/.

Reis, Harry T. 1994. "Domains of Experience: Investigating Relationship Processes from Three Perspectives." In *Theoretical Frameworks for Personal Relationships*, edited by Ralph Erber and Robin Gilmour, 87–110. Hillsdale, NJ: Lawrence Erlbaum.

Robins, Garry. 2013. "A Tutorial on Methods for the Modeling and Analysis of Social Network Data." *Journal of Mathematical Psychology* 57: 261–274.

Robins, Garry, and Dean Lusher. 2013. "Simplified Account of Exponential Random Graph Model as a Statistical Model." In *Exponential Random Graph Models for Social Networks: Theory, Methods, and Application*, edited by Dean Lusher, Johan Koskinen, and Garry Robins, 29–48. New York: Cambridge University Press.

Ryan, Richard M., and Edward L. Deci. 2000. "Self-Determination Theory and the Facilitation of Intrinsic Motivation, Social Development, and Well-Being." *American Psychologist* 55(1): 68–78.

Ryan, Richard M. and Edward L. Deci. 2002. "Overview of Self-determination Theory: An Organismic Dialectical Perspective." In *Handbook of Self-Determination Research*, edited by Edward L. Deci and Richard M. Ryan, 3–36. Rochester, NY: University of Rochester Press.

Ryan, Richard M., Christina M. Frederick, Deborah Lepes, Noel Rubio, and Kennon M. Sheldon. 1997. "Intrinsic Motivation and Exercise Adherence." *International Journal of Sport Psychology* 28: 335–354.

Sichivitsa, Veronica O. 2003. "College Choir Members' Motivation to Persist in Music: Application of the Tinto Model." *Journal of Research in Music Education* 51(4): 330–341. doi: 10.2307/3345659.

Siciliano, Michael D. 2015. "Advice Networks in Public Organizations: The Role of Structure, Internal Competition, and Individual Attributes." *Public Administration Review* 75(4): 548–559. doi:10.1111/puar.12362.

Sloboda, John A. 1998. "Does Music Mean Anything?" *Musicae Scientae* 2: 21–31.

Small, Christopher. 1980. *Music, Society, Education*. Hanover, NH: Wesleyan University Press.

Stebbins, Robert A. 1992. *Amateurs, Professionals and Serious Leisure*. Montreal, QC: McGill-Queen's University Press.

Valente, Thomas W. 2010. *Social Networks and Health: Models, Methods, and Applications*. New York: Oxford University Press.

Vallerand, Robert J. 1997. "Toward a Hierarchical Model of Intrinsic and Extrinsic Motivation." *Advances in Experimental Social Psychology* 29: 271–360.

Vallerand, Robert J., and Robert Bissonnette. 1992. "Intrinsic, Extrinsic, and Amotivational Styles as Predictors of Behavior: A Prospective Study." *Journal of Personality* 60(3): 599–620.

Vallerand, Robert J., Luc G. Pelletier, and Richard Koestner. 2008. "Reflections on Self-Determination Theory." *Canadian Psychology* 49(3): 257–262. doi: 10.1037/a0012804.

Vallerand, Robert J., and Catherine F. Ratelle. 2002. "Intrinsic and Extrinsic Motivation: A Heirarchichical Model." In *Handbook of Self-Determination Research*, edited by Edward L. Deci and Richard M. Ryan, 37–64. Rochester, NY: University of Rochester Press.

Vansteenkiste, Maarten, Eline Sierens, Bart Soenens, Koen Luyckx, and Willy Lens. 2009. "Motivational Profiles from a Self-Determination Perspective: The Quality of Motivation Matters." *Journal of Educational Psychology* 101(3): 671–88. doi: 10.1037/a0015083.

Vlachopoulos, Symeon P., Costas I. Karageorghis, and Peter C. Terry. 2000. "Motivation Profiles in Sport: A Self-Determination Theory Perspective." *Research Quarterly for Exercise and Sport* 71(4): 387–397. doi: 10.1080/02701367.2000.10608921.

Wasserman, Stanley, and Katherine Faust. 1994. *Social Network Analysis: Methods and Applications*. Cambridge: Cambridge University Press.

Welch, Graham, and Pauline Adams. 2003. *How Is Music Learning Celebrated and Developed? A Professional User Review of UK and Related International Research Undertaken by the British Educational Research Association*. Southwell: British Educational Research Association.

Werpy, Steve Francis. 1996. "Relationships between Selected Factors of Motivation for Participation in High School Band and General Motivation for Musical Experience." PhD dissertation, Northwestern University, Evanston, IL.

White, Robert W. 1959. "Motivation Reconsidered: The Concept of Competence." *Psychological Review* 66: 297–333.

White, Robert W. 1963. *Ego and Reality in Psychoanalytic Theory*. New York: International Universities Press.

Wild, T. Cameron, and Michael E. Enzle. 2002. "Social Contagion of Motivational Orientations." In *Handbook of Self-Determination Research*, edited by Edward L. Deci and Richard M. Ryan, 141–160. Rochester, NY: University of Rochester Press.

Williams, David A. 2011. "The Elephant in the Room." *Music Educators Journal* 98(1): 51–57.

Zdzinski, Stephen F. 2004. "Contributions of Drum Corps Participation to the Quality of Life of Drum Corps Alumni." *Bulletin of the Council for Research in Music Education* 159: 46–57.

PART III

SCENES, SPACES, AND PLACES

···

LEISURE MUSIC PRODUCTION

Its Spaces and Places

···

ROBERT A. STEBBINS

WHEN casual dabbling in music is excluded from consideration, performing this art is of necessity a serious leisure activity. Furthermore, as with all serious leisure, the production of amateur and professional music is conducted in various physical spaces that are endowed with special meaning[s] for the participant. That meaning—which is discussed below as "place"—is associated with certain core activities pursued in this space. Stebbins (2013b) and Elkington (2014) have identified and explored seven types of spaces for serious leisure, of which six facilitate a deep commitment to making music. They are discussed in this chapter as: showcase, resource, sales, helping, virtual, and tourist spaces.

In particular, interest here centers on making, or performing, music as a serious pursuit (explained shortly) and the spaces that frame this set of activities. It should be noted that many musicians who regularly make music in public—some are full- or part-time professionals—also fill one or more related roles, including those of teacher, composer/arranger, booking agent, repair specialist, and volunteer for, or employee in, the local musicians' union. These roles are not covered in this chapter, there simply being insufficient space to also analyze this equally complex facet of the musician's lifestyle.

We start with an examination of the two closely related concepts of space and place. The two are then integrated with the serious pursuit of music. Next, space, place, and music are theoretically framed in the serious leisure perspective (SLP). The main part of the chapter revolves around the seven types of space and the sense of place they engender in those who occupy them; they are first described and then six of them are applied to the worlds of performance in jazz, rock, folk, and classical music.[1] The lifestyle that emerges from movement in and out of these spaces is examined in the conclusion.

SPACE AND PLACE

···

Leisure space conceived of in geographic terms has conventionally referred to the physical settings where leisure activities are pursued. These settings may be natural or artificial or a combination of both. And nowadays they may not be physical, but virtual. David Crouch summarizes the importance of understanding leisure in terms of geographic space thus conceived of:

> Leisure happens, is produced in spaces. These spaces may be material, and related to concrete locations. Yet the spaces, and therefore geographies, of leisure may be metaphorical, even imaginative. Imaginative spaces are not merely in the virtual space of contemporary nature but also in the imagination of [the] consumer and the representations of the agencies providing in producing leisure sites: visual culture and other narratives of communication. . . . Space, then, can be important in metaphorically "shaping," contextualizing leisure and commercial and public policy prefiguring of the meaning of leisure sites, and the leisure experience may be transformed by the way in which individuals encounter those spaces and activities. (Crouch 2006, 127)

In the language of this chapter, leisure activities also occur in geographic space as just described. This context helps shape those activities and give them meaning for the individual participant. As Crouch's words imply, geographic analysis usually focuses on leisure in general.

Such "leisured encounters" are encounters in different ways: with people, with material space, with one's imagination, ideas, and metaphors of place. Yet, space is not synonymous with place. Indeed, at the core of the various meanings of the terms is the dispute between that abstract spatial analysis, which tends to view places as nodes in space, simply reflective of the spatial imprint of universal physical, social, or economic processes, and that concrete environmental analysis, which conceives of places as milieus that exercise a mediating role on those processes and thus affect how they operate and exist (Agnew 2011). The first is a geometric conception of place as a mere part of space and the second is a phenomenological understanding of a place as a distinctive coming together in space. From this view point, if place in the former sense is definable entirely in relation to a singular spatial metric, place in the second sense is constituted by the impact that being somewhere has on the constitution of the processes in question (Agnew 2011; Cresswell 2013).

Places emerge in space, as well as have spaces between them. Yi Fu Tuan has likened space to movement and place to pauses—stops along the way:

> What begins as undifferentiated space becomes place as we get to know it better and endow it with value. . . . [T]he ideas "space" and "place" require each other's definition. From the security and stability of place we are aware of the openness and freedom and threat of space, and vice-versa. Furthermore, if we think of space as that which allows movement, then place is pause; each pause in movement makes it possible for location to be transformed into place. (Tuan 1977, 6)

Space, then, has been seen in distinction to place as a realm without meaning—as a "fact of life" which, together with time, produces the basic coordinates for human life

(Cresswell 2013). When humans invest meaning in a portion of space and then become attached to it in some way—naming or having memory of some space—it becomes place. As an example, note later the reaction of professional violinist César Avilés to playing in Carnegie Hall, which as a space is a famous venue for musical performances. Although this basic dualism of space and place runs through much of the traditional human geography literature, it is confused somewhat by the idea of social space—or socially produced space—which, in many ways, plays the same role as place (Lefebvre 1991).

SPACE, PLACE, AND THE PURSUIT OF MUSIC

Sam Elkington (2014) moved beyond general leisure to look more particularly at the spaces of serious leisure. He explored how and in what ways space is experienced by participants when pursuing an amateur, hobbyist, or career volunteer activity. The SLP, he observed, has failed to address the issue of space on the phenomenological level. In this respect we must note that space is not synonymous with place, in that the first also has an "aesthetic" meaning. Any given space "reveals a perceptual environment that joins a distinctive physical identity and coherence, a resonance, with a memorable character with which an individual actively engages through action." (Elkington 2014, 96). Furthermore, Elkington said it is evident that "place possesses a certain resonance and form as a repository of social, cultural or personal significance in the form of knowledge and memories." (101) Knowledge and memories are, in turn, part of a culture. They depend in various ways on the physical setting for how people remember events experienced there in the past.

Serious leisure participants also develop a strong attachment to and identification with the space in which they pursue their core activities. Elkington stated that the strength of attachment is substantially determined by the capacity of that space to facilitate expressions of skill and knowledge and to generate desired experiences, among them, that of flow. He applied his ideas about the spatial meanings of serious leisure to all the core activities pursued there. I wish to add here that those ideas can also be applied to devotee work (discussed shortly) and therefore to all the serious pursuits. Furthermore, it is possible to show how and where these meanings vary by category of core activity. The next section presents the SLP and the concepts of activity and core activity that animate the serious pursuits.

THE SERIOUS LEISURE PERSPECTIVE

The SLP is a theoretic framework that synthesizes three main forms of leisure, showing, at once, their distinctive features, similarities, and interrelationships. Those forms are the serious pursuits, casual leisure, and project-based leisure, briefly defined as follows (see Stebbins 2012 for a more complete explanation):

SERIOUS PURSUITS

Serious leisure is the systematic pursuit of an amateur, hobbyist, or volunteer activity sufficiently substantial, interesting, and fulfilling for the participant to find a (leisure) career there acquiring and expressing a combination of its special skills, knowledge and experience.

Devotee work is activity in which participants feel a powerful devotion, or strong, positive attachment, to a form of self-enhancing work. In such work the sense of achievement is high and the core activity endowed with such intense appeal that the line between this work and serious leisure is virtually erased.

CASUAL LEISURE

Casual leisure is immediately intrinsically rewarding, relatively short-lived pleasurable activity requiring little or no special training to enjoy it. It is fundamentally hedonic, pursued for its significant level of pure enjoyment, or pleasure. Some examples appear in the section on leisure activities.

PROJECT-BASED LEISURE

Project-based leisure is a short-term, reasonably complicated, one-off or occasional, though infrequent, innovative undertaking carried out in free time, or time free of disagreeable obligation. Such leisure requires considerable planning, effort and, sometimes, skill or knowledge, but is for all that neither serious leisure nor intended to develop into such.

In addition, the SLP explains how these three forms and their pursuit are shaped by various spatial, psychological, social, cultural, and historical conditions. That is, leisure always occurs within this larger multifaceted context (e.g., stand-up comedy, Stebbins 1990; amateur foodie leisure, de Solier 2013; outdoor pursuits, Davidson and Stebbins 2011).

Serious Leisure

Let us now add to the foregoing definition with the observation that amateurs are distinguished from hobbyists by the fact that the first, who are found in art, science, sport, and entertainment, have a professional counterpart (e.g., amateur and professional musicians), whereas the second do not. Hobbyists, some of whom do have commercial counterparts, fall into five types: collectors; makers of, or tinkerers with, things; participants in activities (in music they perform the folk arts and barbershop song, Stebbins 1996b); players of sports and games (they lack professional counterparts); and the liberal arts hobbies (self-education in an area of life or literature).[2] Serious leisure volunteers offer uncoerced, altruistic help either formally or informally with no or, at most, token pay and done for the benefit of both other people (beyond the volunteer's family) and the volunteer.

Serious leisure is further defined by six distinguishing qualities (Stebbins [2007] 2015, 11–13), qualities found among amateurs, hobbyists, and volunteers alike. One is the occasional need to *persevere*, such as in learning how to be an effective museum guide. Yet, it is clear that positive feelings about the activity come, to some extent, from sticking with it through thick and thin, from conquering adversity. A second quality is that of finding a *career* in the serious leisure role, shaped as it is by its own special contingencies, turning points, and stages of achievement or involvement. Careers in serious leisure commonly rest on a third quality: significant personal *effort* based on specially acquired *knowledge, training, experience,* or *skill,* and, indeed, all four at times. Fourth, several *durable benefits*, or broad outcomes, of serious leisure have so far been identified, mostly through research on amateurs. They are self-development, self-enrichment, self-expression, regeneration or renewal of self, feelings of accomplishment, enhancement of self-image, social interaction and belongingness, and lasting physical products of the activity (e.g., a painting, scientific paper, piece of furniture). Self-gratification, or the combination of superficial enjoyment and deep fulfillment, is a further benefit and also one of the main benefits of casual leisure, where however, the enjoyment part dominates. Of these benefits, self-fulfillment—realizing, or the fact of having realized, to the fullest one's gifts and character, one's potential—is the most powerful of all.

A fifth quality of serious leisure is the *unique ethos* that grows up around each instance of it, a central component of which is a special social world where participants can pursue their free-time interests. Unruh (1980, 277) developed the following definition:

> A *social world* must be seen as a unit of social organization which is diffuse and amorphous in character. Generally larger than groups or organizations, social worlds are not necessarily defined by formal boundaries, membership lists, or spatial territory.... A social world must be seen as an internally recognizable constellation of actors, organizations, events, and practices which have coalesced into a perceived sphere of interest and involvement for participants. Characteristically, a social world lacks a powerful centralized authority structure and is delimited by ... effective communication and not territory nor formal group membership.

The sixth quality revolves around the preceding five: participants in serious leisure tend to *identify* strongly with their chosen pursuits. In contrast, casual leisure, although hardly humiliating or despicable, is nonetheless too fleeting, mundane, and commonplace for most people to find a distinctive identity there.

Leisure Activities: General and Core

I have set out elsewhere a short definition of leisure (Stebbins 2012, 4): *uncoerced, contextually framed activity engaged in during free time, which people want to do and, using their abilities and resources, actually do in either a satisfying or a fulfilling way (or both).* An *activity* is a type of pursuit, wherein participants in it mentally or physically (often both) think or do something, motivated by the hope of achieving a desired end. Life is filled with activities, both pleasant and unpleasant: sleeping, attending a concert, mowing the lawn, taking the train to work, having a tooth filled, eating lunch, playing tennis matches, running a meeting, and on and on. Activities, as this list illustrates, may be categorized as work, leisure, or nonwork obligation. They are, furthermore, general. In some instances they refer to the behavioral side of recognizable roles, for example, member of the audience, tennis player, and chair of a meeting. In others we may recognize the activity but not conceive of it so formally as a role, exemplified in someone sleeping, mowing a lawn, eating lunch (not as patron in a restaurant), and browsing the Internet.

The concept of activity is an abstraction, and as such, one broader than that of role. In other words, roles are associated with particular statuses, or positions, in society, whereas with activities, some are status-based while others are not. For instance, sleeper is not a status, even if sleeping is an activity. It is likewise with lawn mower (person). Sociologists, anthropologists, and psychologists tend to see social relations in terms of roles, and, as a result, overlook activities whether aligned with a role or not. Meanwhile, certain important parts of life consist of engaging in activities not recognized as roles. Where would many of us be could we not routinely sleep, eat lunch, and browse the Internet?

This definition of activity gets elaborated further in the concept of *core activity*: a distinctive set of interrelated actions or steps that must be followed to achieve the outcome or product that the participant seeks. As with general activities, core activities are pursued in work, leisure, and nonwork obligation. Consider some examples in serious leisure: a core activity of alpine skiing is descending snow-covered slopes, in cabinet making it is shaping and finishing wood, and in volunteer fire fighting it is putting out blazes and rescuing people from them. In each case, the participant takes several interrelated steps to successfully ski downhill, make a cabinet, or rescue someone. In casual leisure, core activities, which are much less complex than in serious leisure, are exemplified in the actions required to hold sociable conversations with friends, savor beautiful scenery, and offer simple volunteer services (e.g., handing out leaflets, directing traffic in a theater parking lot, clearing snow off the neighborhood hockey rink). Work-related core activities are seen in, for instance, the actions of a surgeon during an operation or the improvisations on a melody by a jazz clarinetist. The core activity in mowing a lawn (usually a nonwork obligation) is pushing or riding the mower. Executing an attractive core activity and its component steps and actions is a main feature, drawing participants to the general activity of which it is a part. Why? Because this core directly enables them to reach a cherished goal. It is the opposite for disagreeable core activities. In short, the core activity has motivational value of its own, even if more strongly held for some activities than others and even if some activities are disagreeable but still have to be done. All general leisure activities revolve around one or more core activities.

THE SPATIAL MEANING OF CORE MUSICAL ACTIVITIES

In common with other leisure participants, those engaged in the serious pursuits interpret in light of the related core activities the space in which they are pursuing them. So far seven types of space for this kind of work and leisure have been identified. Each is defined and illustrated with some representative serious pursuits, which are then compared with the use of these spaces in performance music. The goal of this approach is to paint a broad picture of the space in question and then show where music fits in this canvas.

Conquered Space

A wide variety of serious activities have as part of their core the conquering of some sort of space. That is, the special meaning of that space is constructed according to how it bears on the core activity being undertaken. Here we find the sports, board games, nature challenge activities, some participation activities (defined in note 2), and possibly others. For example, football players know at any time during a match that, if they are to score, so many yards or meters must be covered. In the "nature challenge activities" (Davidson and Stebbins 2011), climbers for instance are aware of the height and other physical features of the mountain face they aim to ascend. Then there are the routes to be followed or spaces to be occupied in the various board games and in games like chess, checkers, and cribbage.

As an example of the role of space in the participation activities, consider how it is conquered when fishing. First, there is the space in which fish are caught: open sea, trout stream, backwater bayou, or local pond. Second, there is the question of the depth of water in, or on, which to fish: close to the bottom, just below the surface, on the surface (e.g., dry-fly fishing). The meaning of space is both complex and distinctive in such participant activities as caving, hunting, canoeing, and SCUBA diving, among numerous others.

Showcase Space

Conquering space is obviously central to a number of amateur and hobbyist pursuits. Not so, however, for many musicians.[3] For them, showcase space has the prominence that conquered space does for alpinists, football players, and so on. Showcasing creative works is the realm of the fine arts and entertainment fields. The theater, concert hall, and comedy club exemplify one genre of space for displaying these efforts. Another is the variety of exhibition venues for presenting paintings, sculptures, and ceramic pieces, which include, depending on the art, shops, streets, offices, pedestrian corridors, and these days even some transportation terminals. Nonetheless, they do share some of their space with busking street performers, who may also present their acts in pedestrian corridors as well as along certain streets. Additionally, subway stations are a main space for some of these artists. Showcase space is different for writers. For them (and the liberal arts hobbyists who read their works), the book shop (brick and mortar, online) and the book fair are central.

For musicians, such spaces become places according to how they are interpreted by the individual performer and by the larger music-based social world in which this person is involved. Thus, jazz musicians are aware of the more and less renowned local outlets for their music, as in the jazz clubs, restaurants, parks, and venues featuring an annual series of concerts. To be invited to play at the most prestigious of these spaces is an honor and a sign of high rank in local jazz circles. Additionally, jazz musicians hip to national and international scenes also know of equivalent showcases at these levels, among them Village Vanguard (New York), Ronnie Scott's (London), and Le Duc des Lombards (Paris). It is also, of course, a big honor to be invited to perform in spaces of this caliber.

Similar outlets exist in the world of classical music. At the top of the list for local professional orchestras is the concert hall in which the most renowned of them hold their main concert series. For example, the Boston Symphony Orchestra presents its main series at Symphony Hall, the Royal Concertgebouw Orchestra performs routinely at the Royal Concertgebouw in Amsterdam. The Teatro alla Scala in Milan serves a similar function for world famous opera stars who appear there off and on in operatic productions presented in six to eight performances stretching over approximately two weeks. It is likewise for musical theater in New York and London, where some plays may run for several years, however, and the number of commercial theaters showcasing this art is considerable: forty in New York (Broadway League 2009) and another forty in Theatreland in London's West End (Wikipedia 2014).

We must include as a significant part of showcase space that devoted to rehearsals of the group (classical, jazz, rock, folk, etc.), for here musicians showcase for each other. Such space becomes a place when the director and the other musicians interpret how they and the others are playing. For example, they feel the session is too long or tedious or by contrast highly exciting or interesting. That said, professional music groups vis-à-vis amateur groups rehearse less often than they perform. Among the reasons for this are that such sessions are costly and the musicians are expected to know the music (hence the importance of personal practice in the resource space considered next).

Famous rock groups publicly perform primarily by touring around the world, playing in different spaces for a session or two. Most of these sessions amount to one- or two-night stands in cities to which, for market reasons, they are unlikely to return for many years, if at all. Thus each showcasing space becomes a place imbued with all sorts of memories (e.g., size and enthusiasm of the audience, sight lines, green room facilities, ease of access to performance facilities, weather conditions). Typical showcase spaces for these groups are a city's large venues: sports stadia, hockey arenas, public parks, and big auditoria (primarily university and municipal).

Famous folk musicians in English-speaking countries from the mid-twentieth century to the present now get showcased in similar ways. Meanwhile, their local colleagues often operate as many local jazz musicians do, offering their art a couple of sessions a week in nightclubs or other settings. Here, too, there is a loose ranking of performers appearing in these spaces and a measure of prestige that flows from being asked to play there.

Top-rated jazz, classical, rock, and folk musicians get invited to another distinctive event: the international music festival, which is usually an annual affair. In general, these festivals unfold in several spaces around town selected for showcasing, as in nightclubs, hotel ballrooms, auditoria, parks, street corners (some may be buskers), and the like. The Tanglewood Music Center and Interlochen Center for the Arts are exceptions in this respect, since each occupies a single geographic area.

We have been discussing to this point the direct, live showcasing of music performance. Nevertheless, such performance is also available indirectly on long-playing records (they are still in significant demand; Hastad 2012), CDs, and DVDs. If the recording is of a live performance, the showcase space typically remains perceptively unchanged, though its meaning as a place may be elevated commensurate with the importance of the recording (e.g., major recording company vs. a local enterprise). But being herded into a studio to record, say, a CD's worth of jazz or folk music puts showcasing in a different light. Such spaces include recording equipment, special acoustical properties, and appropriate lighting for any video work that may occur. That a recording will result from these sessions leaving to posterity the musicians' performance helps transform these spaces into showcase places.

Resource Space

This is space used by amateurs, hobbyists, and occupational devotees to produce a good or perform a service; such space includes all the necessary equipment and supplies found within. The scientist's laboratory is arguably the archetypical example. Although often less clearly demarcated, scientific field stations constitute another set of spaces for scientific core activity. Here observations of birds or insects are conducted or, looking upward, astronomical phenomena are viewed. Then there is the atelier for making and tinkering. Included here are the kitchen and woodworking shop as well as the miscellaneous locations in which the skilled trades operate, among them the garage and back garden (for gardening, work on old cars, etc.). In devotee work, construction sites and locations where repairs and maintenance are conducted (as in plumbing, heating, and roofing) exemplify resource space.

Now, comparing all this with the arts, the study is the prized space for writers (when not showcasing their works). It is likewise for "committed readers," or those hobbyists who read extensively to acquire literary knowledge, a passion that necessarily takes time and requires concentration (Stebbins 2013a). And paralleling this use of space for core activities are the places where musicians, dancers, athletes, and others go to maintain and perfect their skills.

Musicians need a space to "practice," be it a separate room or a corner of a room that also has other uses. Practicing is a second major core activity in the musical life, with the most committed artists spending far more time at this part of their pursuit than at showcasing what they can do. Indeed anecdotal evidence suggests that the best classical musicians practice as much as four hours daily (Kageyama 2014), but this depends on the type and nature of practice. Counted as practicing is learning musical parts, working them up to perfection, interpreting the composer's directions, and acquiring background information about the work being perfected. And while practicing the performer may also be drawn to a nearby desk, library, and computer—other important accessories in the practice space. Last, but not least, are the metronome, printed music, music stand, and for some, a piano or keyboard, amplification equipment, valve oil, rosin, earphones, or a stereo (for educational listening—see below), and so on. Since many committed musicians want to hear how they are progressing with perfecting, for example, a piece of music, an audio recorder becomes another essential part of the resource scene.

In short, the musician's resource space is arguably the most complex of all the spaces this person encounters in the course of engaging in this serious pursuit. As a place it is "home base." Here surrounded by the aforementioned resources musical performers prepare to meet their public. They know that the search for fulfillment begins here, even while they also know that it is most fully realized in their performances. Thus, as a place, this space has a forward feel about it. Here one also anticipates and imagines showcasing the polished music in the spaces in which this will take place. Resource space joins with showcase space as two of the musician's most important geographic settings.

Sales Space

For the occupational devotees in small business, the shop from which they vend their product or service is a special space. Along similar lines we find the public outlets for hobbyist makers of, say, quilts, knit goods, and ceramic objects. They sporadically—and for some even regularly—set up stands at craft fairs, shopping centers, and flea markets, among other places.

Group-based amateur and professional musicians (e.g., rank-and-file members of orchestras) may be only marginally involved in selling their art, if they are so involved at all, but it is different with freelancing performers, who must necessarily become small business people. Thus, such performers in jazz, folk, and rock oftentimes assiduously contact nightclub and restaurant managers about getting booked as individuals or small groups for, say, a one- or two-night stand or somewhat longer series of appearances. Here, the quality of the performing space is crucial. Is it large enough? Are the sight lines decent? How are the acoustics and the lighting? Deficiencies on these and other performance-related dimensions can seriously adulterate the music making experience. With considerations like these, such spaces quickly become places.

When musicians hire booking agents to find work for them and online and brick-and-mortar CD outlets sell their recordings, the issue of sales space leaves the musician's hands. Nevertheless, when performers sell CDs at their concerts, nightclub acts, festival appearances, and similar gigs they are directly in charge of their sales spaces. In these circumstances they must somehow announce this commercial opportunity to their audiences and arrange for someone to sell the CDs in an easily accessible location.

Today, a website is an indispensable sales space for all musicians determined to promote their artistic products. It is simultaneously a virtual space (see below), albeit one very quickly transformed into a sales place for the musician or musical group that it markets. Whereas musicians may ask a friend, relative, or commercial service to construct their website, the musicians themselves determine the content of these promotional outlets. For them they are essentially sales spaces; pamphlets in cyberspace, as it were.

Helping Space

This is the space within which help is provided. The help may be that of either volunteers or professionals, with the latter being conceived of in the SLP as devotee workers. Among the second, the offices of counsellors and consultants serve as a main space within which they pursue their core activities. Other spaces for some of this group's core activities may include a home office, a public or institutional library, and a specialized bookstore.

Career volunteers also have their distinctive spaces. These are evident to some extent by where they serve, as in a zoo or museum, on a board of directors (board room or equivalent), at a primary school, or at a hospital. This core activity space for volunteers who work to preserve or maintain the natural environment is a river, forest, or a community park, as well as the air we breathe, the water we drink, and the earth we live on. Recreational volunteers serve in spaces like camps, sport centers, municipal recreational facilities, and sites for sporting competitions (e.g., gymnasia, swimming pools, ski hills, running courses).

As for professional musicians, some of them occasionally perform gratis, which they think of as a charitable contribution to a worthwhile cause. Not under consideration here are the amateur musicians who charge little or nothing for their performances. Since receiving a wage is not an issue, these people can gain little sense of performing volunteer work, for they perform out of self-interest not out of a sense of altruism. Additionally, some professional charitable work is conducted at schools, nursing homes, veteran's hospitals, community parks, shopping malls, among many other locations. In North America, at least, these pros, to the extent they are paid by a third party for their charitable performances (typically by the Music Performance Trust Fund, a joint effort of the American Federation of Musicians of the United States and Canada and the recording industry), also lack this sense altruism.

In the end it is only the occasional professional who alone or in a (usually small) group actually plays gratis and thereby altruistically provides a musical service. The helping spaces in these instances are, for example, schools, nursing homes, venues for private parties, and those for receptions. As with all volunteering, altruism is mixed with self-interest (Stebbins 1996a), in this instance in the opportunity the musician finds to play strictly for the love of it, to perform as a pure amateur while also helping out.

Virtual Space

Sam Elkington (personal communication, October 31, 2012) has suggested that "virtual space" should also be part of any leisure space analysis undertaken in the name of the SLP. It is the home of, among other activities, the Internet-based serious pursuits.

A main use of such space occurs during leisure-based surfing of the web, a serious leisure expression of which is seen in the reading undertaken in pursuit of a liberal arts hobby. Another facet of this space is evident in skilled, knowledgeable gaming done in interaction with other people in cyberspace. In these examples—and there are no doubt others—the space in question is our vague sense of what cyberspace actually is. It is impalpable, difficult to fathom, and yet, real enough to give its users a unique spatial sense. Above all it is vast. So much so that John Perry Barlow, an American poet and essayist, once joked that, "in Cyberspace, the 1st Amendment [in the American Constitution] is a local ordinance."

Musicians use the Internet in at least three ways. One is to entertain themselves, an activity that is hardly unique to musical space and hence not an appropriate subject for this chapter. Another use is for learning. These days there is on the web a substantial amount of, for instance, music history, theory, and biography. Also available there are announcements of festivals, music camps, instructional programs. Local clubs (e.g., jazz, rock, folk) and musicians' union periodicals inform members and the larger interested public by way of their newsletters and weekly bulletins about performances and other pertinent events. This has become a vibrant part of the social world of these musicians. A third way to use the Internet is to engage in discussions by way of blogs and Internet forums.

Considering these diverse Internet features leads us to a third key space in the everyday life of the musician, namely the listening space. It is covered here under the heading of virtual space primarily because so much music these days can be heard in it, as in that delivered through wi-fi, over cable, and via downloadable CDs and DVDs. They are not really virtual entities; I have nevertheless included in this space purchases of actual CDs, DVDs, and even long-playing records made at bricks-and-mortar or online stores.

Why is virtual listening space so important for musicians? The broadest answer is that every musician aspiring to competence in a particular genre of music must learn its *style*. What does good rock, folk, jazz, classical music sound like? Listen and learn. A narrower answer is that as a musician I must also know the *idiom*, which is to say that I must listen to how the best in my genre express that genre. The more creative and hence the more changeable (evolutionary) a genre, the longer such specialized, detailed listening needs to continue. The inveterate musician-listener in fields like jazz and classical music soon learns that composers, soloists, and ensembles are forever coming up with something new. This includes expressing standard musical ideas in new ways. Here listening is both educational *and* critical, for that which is new in an art is not necessarily acceptable to its established *art world* (Becker 1982, chap. 8). The importance of virtual space in music today is examined at length by Christopher Cayari (this volume, chapter 25).

Tourist Space

Much of modern tourism is centered on space of some kind, including scenic vistas, architectural wonders, and urban streetscapes. For most tourists, seeing such attractions is a type of casual leisure, namely sensory stimulation. More rarely, however, some tourists make a hobby of viewing and studying a particular type of space. Thus, conceivably, these enthusiasts might tour around the world to contemplate its tallest buildings, different old towns (where cities began), or ancient ruins. As an example, Bauckham (2013) has studied "groundhoppers," or people passionate about getting to know in detail through direct observation the many different (association) football grounds on which the world game is routinely played.

But what about tourism space for musicians qua musicians? Not of interest here is what musicians on tour do as tourists when not filling their musical responsibilities. The activities mentioned in the preceding paragraph indicate some possibilities they might consider. But conceivably, while on tour and as part of their learning space, they may want to patronize local venues offering their kind of music (e.g., those venues noted in discussion of showcase space). For instance, jazz musicians might look up or be invited to a local jam session. Jazz, classical, and rock musicians might visit, where available, the museums or homes of now-deceased famous performers of their art.

Conclusions

These seven types of space are perceivable by way of one or more of their basic properties: visual, olfactory, tactile, and auditory (including little or no sound, as in the grand pause). In other words, they are available to us through our senses. For musicians the olfactory sense would be the least prominent of these four, though anyone who has played in nightclubs and restaurants would be able to attest to it (e.g., smells of liquor, food, and, where tobacco use is still permitted, cigarette smoke). The visual side is arguably most prominent in the light show that is as much at the center of some rock concerts as the music and its performers.

Some serious pursuits have core activities that are spatially anchored in more than one of the seven types. Thus, athletes have space to be conquered and another space to use as a resource for training; the painter has an atelier (resource) and one or more exhibition venues (showcase). Music certainly is spatially highly diverse, perhaps as much as any serious pursuit. The spatial world of musicians as a category is composed of all types except, for some musicians, that which is conquered (see note 3). Nonetheless, some amateurs do not normally experience the sales and helping spaces.

In a fundamental sense, the music-based lifestyle of the most involved artists consists of participation in all of the six types of spaces. That lifestyle is anchored in continual movement between the resource and showcase spaces, with participation in both buttressed by the learning gained through listening in these two spaces, as well as in virtual space. Both amateurs and professionals share this central lifestyle. Many of the latter expand it, however, by entering from time to time certain sales spaces, with some of them going even farther to give (usually) sporadic gratis performances in the helping space.

Together, these spaces, and the places they become for the musicians who frequent them, add up to an exciting way of life. Most people outside the serious pursuit of music are unaware of music-based lifestyles and their geographic underpinning. In this regard some of them have earned the scorn of Frank Zappa: "The manner in which Americans consume music has a lot to do with leaving it on their coffee tables, or using it as wallpaper for their lifestyles, like the score of a movie—it's consumed that way without any regard for how and why it's made" (Quoteland.com/Frank Zappa). This chapter should serve as at least a partial correction to such misunderstanding.

NOTES

1. The term "rock" in this chapter refers to all its variations in style that have appeared since the music was born as rock 'n' roll in the 1950s (Frith 2014).
2. In activity participation the hobbyist steadfastly does a kind of leisure that requires systematic physical movement, has inherent appeal, and is pursued within a set of rules. Often the activity poses a challenge, though always a noncompetitive one.
3. I have argued that musicians and other performing artists do not conquer space. That is, conquering space is not a central goal of their core activities. But these artists do have occasionally to contend with certain environmental problems such as poor acoustics, lighting, and air conditioning. Such problems might be said to be conquered, or better yet "solved," so that the goal of presenting an acceptable show could be achieved.

REFERENCES CITED

Agnew, John. 2011. "Space and Place." In *Handbook of Geographical Knowledge*, edited by John Agnew and David N. Livingstone, 316–330. London: Sage.

Bauckham, David. 2013. "Serious Leisure: The Case of Groundhopping." In *Routledge Handbook of Leisure Studies*, edited by Tony Blackshaw, 443–455. London: Routledge.

Becker, Howard S. 1982. *Art Worlds*. Berkeley: University of California Press.

Broadway League. 2009. "Broadway Theatres in NYC." http://www.broadwayleague.com/index.php?url_identifier=broadway-theatres-in-nyc-1.

Cohen-Gewerc, Elie, and Robert A. Stebbins. 2013. *Serious Leisure and Individuality*. Montreal, QC: McGill-Queen's University Press.

Cresswell, Tim. 2013. *Place: A Short Introduction*. New York: Wiley.

Crouch, David. 2006. "Geographies of Leisure." In *A Handbook of Leisure Studies*, edited by Chris Rojek, Susan M. Shaw, and A. J. Veal, 125–139. Basingstoke: Palgrave Macmillan.

Davidson, Lee, and Robert A. Stebbins. 2011. *Serious Leisure and Nature: Sustainable Consumption in the Outdoors*. Basingstoke: Palgrave Macmillan.

de Solier, Isabelle. 2013. *Food and the Self: Consumption, Production and Material Culture*. London: Bloomsbury.

Elkington, Sam. 2014. "Sites of Serious Leisure: Acting in Space and Place." In *Leisure in Mind: Meaning, Motives, and Learning*, edited by Sam Elkington and Sean J. Gammon, 93–111. London: Routledge.

Frith, Simon. 2014. "Rock." *Encyclopedia Britannica Online*, accessed December 1. http://www.britannica.com/EBchecked/topic/506004/rock.

Hastad, Nick. 2012. "The Rapacity of the Record Revival." *The Independent*, August 11. http://www.independent.co.uk/arts-entertainment/music/features/the-rapacity-of-the-record-revival-8026756.html.

Kageyama, Noa. 2014. "How Many Hours Should You Practice?" *Bulletproof Musician*. http://www.bulletproofmusician.com/how-many-hours-a-day-should-you-practice.

Lefebvre, Henri. 1991. *The Production of Space*. Translated by Donald Nicholson-Smith. Oxford: Blackwell.

Stebbins, Robert A. 1990. *The Laugh-Makers: Stand-Up Comedy as Art, Business, and Life-Style*. Montreal, QC: McGill-Queen's University Press.

Stebbins, Robert A. 1996a. "Volunteering: A Serious Leisure Perspective." *Nonprofit and Voluntary Action Quarterly* 25: 211–224.

Stebbins, Robert A. 1996b. *The Barbershop Singer: Inside the Social World of a Musical Hobby*. Toronto: University of Toronto Press.

Stebbins, Robert A. 2006. "Discretionary Time Commitment: Effects on Leisure Choice and Lifestyle." *Leisure Studies Association Newsletter* 74 (July): 18–20. ("Leisure Reflections" No. 12: www.seriousleisure.net/uploads/8/3/3/8/8338986/reflections12.pdf).

Stebbins, Robert A. (2007) 2015. *Serious Leisure: A Perspective for Our Time*. Paperback ed. New Brunswick, NJ: Transaction.

Stebbins, Robert A. 2009. *Personal Decisions in the Public Square: Beyond Problem Solving into a Positive Sociology*. New Brunswick, NJ: Transaction.

Stebbins, Robert A. 2012. *The Idea of Leisure: First Principles*, New Brunswick, NJ: Transaction.

Stebbins, Robert A. 2013a. *The Committed Reader: Reading for Utility, Pleasure, and Fulfillment in the Twenty-first Century*. Lanham, MD: Scarecrow.

Stebbins, Robert A. 2013b. "The Spaces of the Serious Pursuits: A Typology." *Leisure Studies Association Newsletter* 95 (July): 21–24. ("Leisure Reflections" No. 33: www.seriousleisure.net/uploads/8/3/3/8/8338986/reflections_33_secure.pdf).

Tuan, Yi-Fu. 1977. *Space and Place: The Perspective of Experience*. Minneapolis: University of Minnesota Press.

Unruh, David R. 1980. "The Nature of Social Worlds." *Pacific Sociological Review* 23: 271–296.

Wikipedia. 2014. "West End Theatre." http://en.wikipedia.org/wiki/West_End_theatre.

....

CHAPTER 20

AMATEUR AND PROFESSIONAL MUSIC MAKING AT DARTINGTON INTERNATIONAL SUMMER SCHOOL

....

HERMIONE RUCK KEENE AND LUCY GREEN

THE extent of amateur musical activities is well documented (see e.g., Finnegan 1989; Pitts 2005a), spanning participation in choirs, orchestras, or other ensembles; folk, pop, or jazz bands and sessions in formal and informal contexts; solo performance; or just making music for its own sake, alone or with others. While amateur music making has a long and complex history, such activities are playing an increasingly significant part in the social and emotional lives of those who participate in them, forming what can today be called a "leisure identity."[1] This identity has been influenced in the last few decades by a shift in the definition of self in relation to career (Grint 1991; Salaman 1974), toward the fragmentation of working life, and the increased importance of nonwork activities.

Leisure has gained significance in the formation of an identity and the perception of self, as people seek to prioritize freedom over necessity and engage in "trying to find out what matters to them the most, and then to do it . . . whether or not this is a realistic aspiration" (Blackshaw 2010, xii). An individualized approach to leisure time (Putnam 2000) furthermore suggests the possibility of transcending various limitations of class, gender, culture, or other markers that are imposed in other contexts: "What the world seems to be saying to men and women today, who now imagine themselves as individuals first and foremost, is this: 'forget who you are and if you cannot be who you want to be, imagine that you can'" (Blackshaw 2010, 88). Most leisure pursuits however, must coexist with work, family, or other commitments, and the routines of everyday life. This means the identities they confer have a temporary aspect that may be suppressed, by choice or necessity, once the activity finishes (Roberts 2011).

One type of (usually) amateur musical leisure pursuit—which will be the focus of this chapter—is that of a residential music school, often taking place in the summer and often known, therefore, as a "summer school."[2] Such events allow amateur participants to privilege their leisure identities almost exclusively for a period of time, through an immersive experience of music making and involvement, at a physical and psychological distance from their everyday selves (Pitts 2005a). For the duration of their stay at summer school they can call themselves musicians, like the professional counterparts who, according to Stebbins (2007), define their amateur status; in Stebbins's conceptualization of amateurism, it is relational to an equivalent professional (paid) activity. Opportunities and spaces that enable such a transformation can therefore become very important to their participants. Residential summer schools in general are an underresearched area.[3] Yet they afford invaluable foci for research into musical identities and attitudes toward music making: they can shed light on both "big leisure"—broad attitudes toward leisure and work—and "little leisures"—the activities that groups and individuals engage in and relate to across their lifespans (Roberts 2011)—as well as affording insights into a range of other issues of potential interest to music education scholars, including those of identity, participation, inclusion, and status.

The performance of Western Art Music is often characterized by hierarchical relationships between amateur and professional musicians inhabiting discrete musical and social spheres, separated by physical and conceptual distance. For example, as described by Small (1998), a symphony orchestra in evening dress elevated upon a stage and performing to a paying audience is a very different scenario from a community choir sharing their term's work at the end of a rehearsal with an audience of friends and family. From some perspectives, though, the amateur-professional distinction can be considered a spectrum upon which individuals are placed according to their context, and between which they can move at different periods of their lives.[4] Amateur or professional status could be measured in terms of a continuum of success (Kirschner 1998), determined by culture, reach, and influence of musical production. This conception though is framed in a rock music context, where, according to Kirschner "every upwardly mobile rock band seeks to be more successful . . . but only a lucky few achieve mass popularity or influence" (254). However, for many "classical" amateur musicians—particularly, perhaps, those who only ever consider themselves amateurs—"success" in terms of recognition by others or monetary reward is not the primary goal; rather, music is made "for the love of it" (Booth 2000). Therefore, musical activities in the classical field are broadly speaking separable according to the status of their participants in relation to what can reasonably be seen as an amateur-professional divide (at the point at which the activity occurs and regardless of the status of participants in other situations). Not only performance, but also teaching, learning, rehearsing, or otherwise making music usually fulfil clearly delineated leisure or work functions for their participants. Such activities are normally undertaken, if not alone, then alongside other people who have similar levels of experience first and foremost, with less emphasis on age or membership of large-scale social groups such as class, ethnicity, or gender, than on the amateur or professional status of those involved. (Owing to the close connection between religion and music, the religious dimension may be of high significance in some cases; however, this is not our focus in this chapter.)

This chapter will present some findings from an ethnographic case study of a major British music summer school: Dartington International Summer School (DISS). DISS was the first summer school to take place in the United Kingdom. Inspired by the Tanglewood Music Festival and Boston Music Center, it was established in a new and quite radical move in 1948 at the suggestion of the internationally renowned pianist Artur Schnabel as a "holiday school where every sort of musician ... could go" (Warrack 1950, 377). On one side of the coin, over its first six or so decades it attracted many musicians, as both tutors and students, who either were at the time or went on to become internationally acclaimed. Their numbers included, as but a few very disparate examples, Igor Stravinsky, Jacqueline du Pré, Daniel Barenboim, and Ravi Shankar. On the other side of the coin, DISS has hosted thousands of amateur musicians, many of whom, as we shall discuss below, have been regular attendees often over an extended period. As such, DISS represents an atypical setting for Western Art Music: a forum for music making shared by participants of all ages and backgrounds, including those who, in their everyday lives, are recognized as amateur, semiprofessional, aspiring professional, fully professional, and internationally acclaimed musicians.

The summer school mounts a five-week program of teaching, along with performances primarily given by the professional tutors, but also often involving amateur and aspiring or semiprofessional participants. Courses in a range of what we will here call Western Art Music instruments and genres are delivered through master classes, workshops, orchestral, chamber, and choral rehearsals. There is some representation of jazz, folk, popular, and non-Western musics. Classes are indicated as suitable for particular levels, with a minority open only to "advanced" participants, or those who have been preselected on the basis of ability. Most courses are in practice open to all and encompass a wide range of musical levels, often involving some degree of collaborative music making between individuals from across the amateur-professional spectrum. In addition, there are numerous opportunities for informal music making: participants get together on an ad hoc basis to play chamber music, madrigals are sung in the gardens, and music is played in the bar on whatever instruments are to hand.

Many attendees have visited DISS regularly for years; in a very few cases, some have attended since the first summer school in 1948. According to the testimony of numerous participants, the summer school's consistent presence across their life span, the music made and heard there, and the friendships it enables grant it a unique status in their lives. Attending the summer school allows them to connect and reconnect with a way of being, which for the amateur participants is outside their professional and "normal" lives. It fosters the development of a "Dartington identity" that runs alongside the everyday self—intertwining with it to varying degrees, and revisited each year at DISS. The location, which enables this intensification and revisiting of an alternative self, becomes very significant; similar to the participants in a Gilbert and Sullivan festival studied by Pitts (2011), "music, place and identity [are] interwoven" (158).

The multilevel, multigenerational participant body at DISS, combined with the range of musical styles and activities on offer, creates a situation where differing aspirations coincide. In the majority of sites for musical leisure activities, participants of a similar age are united by "a sense of community with a common purpose" (Blackshaw 2010, 11).

Similarly, many such community or "nonformal" learning contexts are characterized by activities targeted at specific age groups (Silberman-Keller 2006). Although DISS represents a temporary community for the duration of the summer school, and beyond it in terms of social and musical connections maintained, it brings together a particularly diverse group. Each of the participants have their own purpose for attending, whether motivated by teaching and learning, performance, or leisure.

For some amateur attendees, the summer school's primary status is as a space where their leisure identity can take full sway; for professional musicians, whether established or aspiring, DISS fulfils a different role as an opportunity for performance, teaching, and learning. There are aspects of attending which fulfil a "holiday" function for the full-time professional musician—for example, the opportunity to stay in one location rather than moving around on tour—but distinctions between "work" and "leisure" are unclear for many professionals in the creative sector (Whiting and Hannam 2015). Social interactions often provide a forum for professional networking and the development of musical contacts which can lead to future engagements (Cottrell 2004; Dobson 2011).

This chapter focuses on the leisure experiences of amateur participants at DISS, and considers how these experiences are colored by the presence of professional and aspiring or semi-professional musicians. Using Borsay's (2006) conception of leisure as "symbol, play and the other" and Bakhtin's (1968) idea of the "carnivalesque,"[5] the impact of DISS upon musical and leisure identities and the relationships between diverse groups of musicians are explored. The chapter draws on data from a case study of DISS carried out by the first author as an insider researcher study over two years of fieldwork (2012–2013). During the five-week period of DISS in both years, data were gathered from a variety of sources: sixty-six interviews with participants across the musical spectrum, aged between sixteen and eighty; field notes; thirty-minute observations of classes, rehearsals, and performances; participant observation in classes, rehearsals, and performances; and seven participant diaries written by amateur and professional subjects. Interview participants were recruited using a combination of a questionnaire distributed during the 2012 summer school and purposive sampling of professional performers and tutors, who were contacted via email prior to the 2013 fieldwork. Data were analyzed inductively using thematic analysis (e.g., Boyatzis 1998; Gibson and Brown 2009; Saldaña 2009). Ethical procedures were in place including permissions, information about the right to withdraw, and anonymity. All names used here are pseudonyms.

The Otherness of DISS: A Site for Utopia?

It's hard to sum up in a single paragraph what Dartington is, does and gives. But essentially it's a manor house surrounded by a large, rolling estate so beautiful it hurts, and the location of what was historically an attempt to create a utopian community: an experiment in how to live responsibly, ethically and well, with arts and crafts as central to the plan.

(White 2012)

We will consider DISS first of all in its capacity as a location for the "other," before going on to examine the construction of an alternative symbolic identity which it can allow and the possibility of "play" through imitation of work and education activities. Originally founded at Bryanston School, DISS moved to Dartington Hall in 1952. Located in rural southwest England, the Dartington estate was purchased in 1925 by Leonard and Dorothy Elmhirst as the site for their utopian experiment in social justice through rural regeneration, education and the arts (MacCarthy 2014). Centered on a medieval Great Hall and courtyard, the estate provides surroundings of outstanding beauty, described by Leonard Elmhirst as "one endless garden" (cited in Ballenger 2012, 8). The Elmhirsts brought together a community of artists, musicians, dancers, and dramatists, including the composer and educator Imogen Holst, the potter Bernard Leach, and the actor Michael Chekhov, and sought to involve the estate's residents and the local community in their educational and artistic endeavors. "It is these two threads, the recourse to nature and the vision of a less oppressive society, that place Dartington within the tradition of utopia" (Nicholas 2007, 2).

According to Borsay (2006), the "other" in leisure can refer to both locations and experiences that differ from the "normal" and everyday. There is a freedom to take risks and indulge in different behaviors, engendered by the perception of leisure activities as "inconsequential" and separate from real life (Roberts 2011). Such behavior shares characteristics with Bakhtin's (1968) conception of the "carnivalesque." Originally describing medieval festivals, the carnivalesque has been used to analyze events, music, and dance cultures (Anderton 2008; Halnon 2004; Matheson and Tinsley 2014). It is a subversion of the natural order of society, a "second life" (Bakhtin 1968), where rules are suspended, mock figures of authority are paraded, hierarchies are overturned by equal participation, and inhibitions are lost amidst immorality and grotesque physical humor (Borsay 2006; Matheson and Tinsley 2014; Morris 1994). Importantly, though, these changes are confined to the "carnival" period, and the challenges that they present do not extend beyond it (Blackshaw 2010). According to Gardiner (1993), the carnivalesque can also be used to reconsider the notion of an idealized society presented by visions of Utopia. In his conception, Utopia becomes a "manifestation of pervasive social and ideological conflicts with respect to the desired trajectory of social change" (Gardiner 1993, 22).

Although conceived as a separate enterprise from the wider Dartington project described above, DISS and its participants feel the legacy of the idealistic artistic and political vision of the setting, describing both their own responses to Dartington as a "spiritual home," and their personal experience of the Elmhirsts and their influence:

Yesterday's talk about Imogen Holst was fascinating. Like her, when I walked down through the garden I thought about how beautiful the place is—it's a real spiritual home for me too. (Susan, amateur participant, diary extract)

. . . and there was a real sort of spirit that seemed to be to do with the Elmhirsts—
they were a very gracious couple, delightful couple they were, and I remember what
was always nice about Dartington, what does make it special is that everybody talks
to everybody else, even if they're professional and in a different class from participants, particularly ones who in those days like myself didn't even play an instrument.
(Rosie, amateur participant)

DISS presents a contrast to a more conventional situation where amateur and professional musicians occupy separate spaces:

It's different here because of the way everybody rubs shoulders with each other and
the fact that there are the professional artistes [Simon's term; professional performers are usually referred to as "artists" at DISS] , there are the music students and the
aspiring professionals, there are people like me who are essentially holidaymakers
and amateur musicians on the fringe of it all, but unlike other settings, Dartington
has a creative rubbing of shoulders between all of those groups, so I enjoy having drinks and friendly coffees with a number of the artistes that I've known for a
long time—and you get to know them a bit better as a participant in a creative field.
(Simon, amateur participant)

The inclusive atmosphere Simon describes is often referred to as the "Dartington
spirit," recognized here by participants from aspiring professional and professional
backgrounds:

I did some chamber music last year, and that kind of summed up what Dartington
was about—we played through some piano quintets with Huw Watkins [pianist and
professor of composition at the Royal College of Music] because he just had a spare
hour in his lunch hour, and the two violinists were, well, amateurs, you know, really
enthusiastic, and it was just great because you had this international guy who was
quite happy to play through some stuff with some people who weren't so great and
that was, that was for me what I took away as the Dartington spirit if you want. (Peter,
aspiring professional)

A spirit of absolute generosity and inclusion, inclusion of everybody who wants to
make music. And that really is what music is about, it's not about excluding people
from it because they're not of this standard or they haven't reached this grade, or they
haven't done that, it's actually drawing everyone in together and proving to those
people that it can be enjoyed by anybody at any level, perhaps not altogether at the
same time but sometimes it can. (Louise, tutor)

It was really nice to see how the two best musicians acted so patiently, and didn't
seem the least bit bothered that they were being held back. They were happy to show
what I consider to be the "true spirit of Dartington," where enjoyment of music making is far more important than standard. (Esther, tutor, diary entry)

This spirit has a utopian quality to it: like the Elmhirsts' original project involving a
range of artists along with rural workers and community members at Dartington Hall,

DISS seems to aspire to equality by breaking down hierarchies between, in this case, amateur and professional musicians. The utopian possibilities of music itself are also important; Levitas (2010) refers to the "capacity of music to transport the listener or performer into a better world" (216), while Barenboim (2006) argues that the act of making music with others enacts an "alternative social model, a practical Utopia, from which we might learn about expressing ourselves freely and hearing one another." Toby, a tutor, described DISS as "idealistic," going on to explain how it seems to offer an environment where status relationships are suspended by prioritizing "the music":

> It's the sort of openness of the attitude and the openness to everyone really, the music obviously being the unifying factor but everything else—there's sort of a much more eclectic mix of people and influences than a lot of other festivals. (Toby, tutor)

Alongside this utopian quality, the distant location and residential nature enable behaviors outside the usual professed moral code of the participants. A favorite phrase at DISS is "what happens on the hill stays on the hill," and there is a sense of freedom which underpins much of how participants view their social and musical experiences. This liberation ethos again echoes the excesses of the carnivalesque, where anything is possible and norms of social behavior may be challenged:

> I also loved it because it was this very relaxed space . . . like a personal, like a place to grow up safely, outside of—so quite a lot of it was like falling in love, or like fancying the pants off people, because music's really sexy, and it was in that, it has that really kind of, there's a real feeling of it being a hothouse, a bit of a kind of emotional and sexual hothouse basically, so without wanting to be too explicit about what I got up to, definitely the fact that there were people here I fancied definitely played a really big part in it—I just remember that sense of this is a place where I can, because music is the linchpin of it which has no demographic, this is a place where I can meet people of all genders, nationalities, sexualities, you know, ages, across the spread, and they all felt like really important friendships, which was lovely. (Susan, professional participant)

Partly because of this release from "normality," the time-bound nature of DISS is crucial. As Blackshaw (2010) states, the function of the carnivalesque may ultimately be merely to reinforce the status quo. Behaviors that challenge existing power structures too much are abandoned at the end of the carnival time and do not survive the return to "normality." Instead, they provide an alternative view, that "critical utopia" which Gardiner describes—but one which may not be able to translate into other areas of the participants' lives or extend beyond the duration of the summer school.

A further problem with conceptualizing DISS as a Utopia is the financial reality of its "holiday" status. For the amateur participants, DISS represents a significant financial outlay; one tutor described it as an "elitist academy," due to the high cost of attendance. The fee structure, based on different types of accommodation, is such that those paying maximum fees are essentially subsidizing the aspiring professional students, many of whom receive bursaries or pay the lowest rates. Staying in the more expensive accommodation grants access to the professional tutors and performers, since they share one dining room while those staying in the cheaper accommodation eat together in another. This also creates a division of ages, since the majority of the older participants stay in the more expensive (and more comfortable) accommodation, while those in the younger age group are either bursary students or not in a position to afford the higher costs. Not only is greater access to higher status musicians enabled by superior economic capital, but there is also an extent to which longevity of participation grants individuals a higher level of social capital within the society of DISS. While this does allow longstanding friendships between older amateur musicians and professional tutors to develop, economic and generational separation can undermine any utopian vision of a more equal musical society.

Tutors talked about how the financial aspect of DISS affected their teaching:

> I'm trying to understand where they're coming from and convey some of my experience in a way that is something they recognize, and tell some stories—and at the same time show them a bit of how the music works—so I'm very conscious that I'm stuck in the middle; I'm also offering an experience to people who've paid to have a cultural holiday. (Tom, tutor)

Sara expressed similar views, in addition perceiving a conflict between the mixed ability of the people that she teaches and her ability to do a good job:

HRK: And what's it like teaching on the summer school, how do you find that experience?

SARA: Interesting question—it's very challenging in a different way to the rest of the year. I love it, I always really have a great week—can I be completely frank? I find it very difficult as well. For me it's difficult because I have this kind of customer satisfaction thing that I have to uphold, and I guess that everyone you speak to who teaches here is going to say that, so it's just this thing that people pay a lot of money to be here, and I always teach to the best of my ability, but I'm always teaching a very mixed group. (Sara, tutor)

One very popular activity is the summer school choir, which is attended by the majority of the participants, some of whom sing regularly during the year, and some of whom participate in choral singing only at DISS. Each week finishes with a performance of a major choral work with solo roles taken by tutors and participants in advanced-level classes, accompanied by an orchestra of aspiring and professional musicians. Jack, conducting the choir in 2013, talked about the sense of responsibility that he felt to ensure that the participants had a good time, given that most people paying maximum fees sing in the choir. For him this presented a challenge in terms of balancing their enjoyment and his desire to produce a good performance at the end of the week.

DISS therefore shares many characteristics of a utopian site, where freedom from social and musical division enable an openness of communication; nonetheless, the temporary nature of the summer school and the differing financial status of the participants serve to some extent to undermine this potential for equality. Further altered status is granted by the adoption of an alternative identity, particularly for those participants who come from an amateur music making background, something considered in the following section.

LEISURE AS SYMBOL: AN ALTERNATIVE IDENTITY

In Borsay's conception, leisure can fulfil a symbolic function by providing a surrogate or alternative identity. As stated above, DISS gives amateur participants the opportunity to prioritize their musical identity for the duration of their stay. People can introduce themselves by talking about what instrument they play, and can enjoy the luxury of making music all day, knowing that they are surrounded by like-minded people, as described by Ted:

> You can talk to anybody, I can walk around with a big smile on my face and nobody's looking at me thinking "he's a bit odd," and of course I love singing, and that's it, I mean I can sing, and sing, and sing, I can sing again—of course, I get problems with my voice, unfortunately. I mean that's the thing, that's what takes me, I love singing, and it's nice to have a week away from the real world and you know have a singing holiday, oh, it's just heaven for me. (Ted, amateur participant)

For the aspiring professional, the immersion in music offered by DISS can be a turning point in realizing what they want their career to be and enabling them to make the alternative identity a reality. Data here show one participant who has just reached that turning point, and one who reflects retrospectively on the influence DISS has had on her professional career development:

> For me Dartington has been just the place to be right now, just to make me see what I really want to do. (Raquel, aspiring professional)

> HRK: And what was that like coming here as a seventeen year old?
> FIONA: Wow, it was amazing, I mean it was definitely sort of the first time for me to be so completely immersed in just, like, music for two weeks, only about singing and music, it was really wonderful. It was a bit scary, though, because there were so many amazing singers, like for example in the madrigal group there were a lot of people who could sight-read really well and I wasn't very good at that, because I was not very experienced, but it was really exciting, also to do—I did a vocal workshop with Evelyn Tubb [soprano and renowned early music specialist] and

she was so nice and everyone was really very encouraging and I think it really, it all played a big part in me wanting to be a professional singer. (Fiona, professional participant)

For some amateur participants, though, this immersion in an alternative musical life reminds them of opportunities that are lacking elsewhere, or that they no longer have due to having chosen another path in life. Emily had studied music at a conservatoire but had no access to classical music ensembles or performances due to the remoteness of her home location. She was delighted to be in an environment where she was surrounded by music, but to some extent it served as a harsh reminder of what was missing in her everyday life:

It's just mind blowing. I mean, for where I live to see something like this—you'll see it once a year, twice a year. To have the opportunity to see three concerts in a day some days is just, my mind cannot comprehend it, it's just amazing—such a privilege, you know, for me. I think for me it's very, the experience is very different from other people who have come because I'm so thirsty for this, I know that in a week I'll be home and I will not have any of this so all those concerts have been fantastic. (Emily, amateur participant)

Clare also talked about the contrast to regular music experiences, drawing attention to the difference in standard between those with whom she makes music regularly and her colleagues at DISS, and the subsequent contrast in performance outcome. She also discusses her administrative role in her regular choir, which differs from DISS, where her only responsibility is to sing:

The whole thing I really enjoy about Dartington is being able to come here and sing with people who sing well, in tune, and can sight-read so you can just get down to things, you can learn a huge amount in an hour and a half. Now in my own choir, when we get back to the next rehearsal half the choir have forgotten what we learned the previous week and have to learn it all over again, and I keep going because I'm the membership secretary, keep the registers—I've belonged to that choir since 1973 and I'm doing it as sort of like a voluntary job, helping to keep the choir together and keep it going—but I find those rehearsals so tedious because the music we're doing I could learn in half a dozen rehearsals, so to come to Dartington and do that, to learn something that I've never sung before, that I'm not likely to sing at home, and to sing it to a really good standard in a very short time… (Clare, amateur participant)

These differences in experience manifest themselves among tutors as well. Rebecca was teaching a course in beginner musicianship, having originally attended DISS as an amateur participant. In an observation of her class and in her interview she defined herself as a teacher and a chamber musician, rather than a professional performer. She described her experience of playing with the resident professional string quartet:

At the end of the week they very kindly let me play through the Schubert Quintet with them just for fun, and that was the most amazing musical experience of my life I have to say, because I do a lot of quartet playing anyway, back in [home town], I play in two string quartets regularly, but it's quite unusual to find even one or two musicians on exactly the same musical wavelength as oneself, I mean, and to find four, just mind-bogglingly unlikely. (Rebecca, tutor)

Although Rebecca's role at DISS was that of a tutor, she was not, as she herself stated, a professional performer. On this occasion, though, she was able to experience the "reality" of playing with those for whom music is a profession. This allowed her to find people "on the same musical wavelength," something she struggled to find in her everyday musical life; but her reference to how they "let her play through" the music shows her perception that there was still a perceived status relationship between her and the professional performers.

The alternative identity found at DISS creates a close correlation between the place and the surrogate self—the "music, place and identity" described by Pitts (2011)—which affords it great significance and engenders loyalty to the location. Silberman-Keller (2006) identifies how sites for nonformal learning often take on the characteristics of a "second home," a quality DISS has for many long-term participants. This can cause great happiness but also be a source of sadness and conflict as changes occur in the surroundings. Revisiting DISS over many years presents an unusual level of continuity—it is uncommon to be able to regularly reexperience an activity which has been a constant since youth. This may heighten the longstanding participants' sensitivity to changes in the environment which are beyond their control, as exemplified by Adam's reaction to a change in the walking route around the site:

Walk across to Aller Park [studios]—why can't we walk across the field any more? So many happy memories of doing so; feels as if they have all been cut off. Guess I don't like change. (Adam, amateur participant, diary data)

Returning to DISS also brings participants into a sharp contrast with their younger selves in ways that can conflate changes in their broader identity with how they feel about the summer school:

It does feel really different, and Dartington has gone in a different way, summer school, I know that the summer school has worked hard to try and maintain that same thing but for me the feeling of the place has changed a lot, there's a lot more rules here than there used to be, you can't, you know, it's just different, I don't want to sound bitter—it's just, I feel very sad about it actually. I think that the place has become a lot stiffer and the arty, slightly off-the-wall thing has disappeared and it disappeared long ago—so when I was a student, I had kind of long lunches sitting outside the White Hart with my bare feet like a hippy kid, playing whistle with a friend playing mandolin, and people were sitting all over the grass, and it was just this big loungey kind of mess of people, and there was this kind of slightly upper-class thing, kind of strand running through it, but there was room for everybody, and now it feels a little bit more, it just feels a bit more kind of stiff, you know, there were lots of love affairs that went on and it was kind of quite romantic—but it felt different. But it is different, I'm married with kids, so of course I don't expect to be still experiencing those things, but the vibe was different. (Sara, tutor)

It can be seen therefore that DISS allows for alternative identity exploration, which may be temporary (with attendant frustrations or challenges) or have more long-term implications; attendance at the summer school can also highlight broader changes in self-concept, altering across the life course. Alongside the potential for shifting identity, DISS offers opportunities for teaching and learning, which are experienced in diverse ways by the participants according to their expectations of attendance.

Teaching and Learning: Leisure as Play and Mimesis

According to Mantie (2012), the very fact of viewing a leisure activity as a learning experience alters its quality, as the shift from participant to learner changes the focus from communal to individual goals. This is interesting in the context of DISS because the diverse nature of those present implies a huge range of individual aspirations and expectations. This dichotomy between a focus on the learner and on the participant is highlighted by the range of musical abilities represented. An important aspect of leisure activities is their function as play—a type of activity that is seemingly inconsequential and insignificant (Borsay 2006; Roberts 2011). According to Blackshaw (2010), play becomes mimesis when it mimics activities carried out by others in an employment or education capacity. This would usually occur in a separate setting from one where the learning is "real," forming part of the goal of becoming a professional musician:

> Well, the people there [at conservatoires] have to achieve a result, there's a goal, and the goal is some kind of achievement, it's the BMus and for most of these undergraduates it's the beginning of a professional life in music—that's the big difference, because this is sometimes the beginning of a professional life in music for students who come here and sometimes it's absolutely not, and for a vast number of Dartington regulars it's their summer of growth and joy and wonderful music making and more depth of understanding. (Louise, tutor)

Learning may fulfil a different role for the amateur participants at DISS, who have space to explore new areas of knowledge for the sake of pleasure:

> It's experiential, it is not goal directed, whereas some of the time, you know, people want to learn something for a particular function—people here want to try to, they're doing it for their interest. (Tom, tutor)

For some of those who are "imitating" formal education, their personal goals may though be just as real as the goals of those for whom it is a part of their professional development. As Stebbins (2007) explains, the pursuit of a "serious leisure" career can entail attitudes that are as committed as those of the professional, although the goals may be different. An extract from researcher field notes exemplifies one possible goal—the cataloguing of works that have been played during the week, and the serious challenge of fitting in as many music making possibilities as possible each day:

> Another group come and sit next to me—they're talking about chamber music—one man says "I've played with 23 people off the list and I've played 11 works." "Every night before I go to bed I write a page of diary recollection about what I've done, who I've played with, what works I've played" reply—"I make a list every week of all the works I've played for the past 15 years." "I've been playing the Schubert A minor, in our way, that the quartet did the other night." They start talking about the late night concerts—"If you know you're playing at 9 am you've got to give that priority over everything else." (field notes, August 16, 2012)

Teaching and learning at DISS often bring the "make believe" and the "real" together, as less advanced students "mimic" the learning of the aspiring professionals. The early brass course is renowned for the professional development and networking opportunities that it provides—"as an early brass player, you look around the profession and find someone who has not been to Dartington; I just can't find anyone" (Elizabeth, tutor). For the amateur participants, some of whom are complete beginners, it offers a very different experience:

> There's a room of twelve people—some of them are really hungry twenty-one-year-olds who just want to be cornetto players in the future and just want to put in all the work, then you have partly deaf nice old German chaps that can't hear when you shout a bar number and then can't play the notes that are in front of them—I mean obviously the super advanced students, they're well aware that they're not being pushed in some pieces, but we've made sure they have the chance so when it comes to the *tutti* pieces with the mixed-ability ones, it's fantastic because they're just really supportive of the beginners, rather than thinking "you're holding me back." In the beginner lessons there's a couple of ladies who are in the later stage in life, total beginners with no background; they have an absolute love of the repertoire, but not burdened by absolute burning desire to become professionals. (Graeme, tutor)

This can be a positive and supportive experience, offering multiple learning opportunities, as described by one of the tutors:

> In our group it's kind of a microcosm of Dartington itself in that we've got an Academy [Royal Academy of Music] student, who's an extremely able player but he's taking his first steps as an early player, at the very high end of—he's going to go out into the profession in a few years, and then we've got a professional modern trombonist who, again, retraining kind of mid-career, kind of thinking I really want to specialize in this, and then we've got a man who's choosing to spend his holiday learning from scratch having never ever played a brass instrument before, all in the same room, and they're all equally deserving of my attention and the attention of the whole place, and that, you know, they're all learning so many things, and

the Academy student is learning about teaching and learning, about tolerance, and learning about how older people learn, at the same time as we're giving him, you know, advice from the coal face of being a professional about what we you do about tuning on a professional date, how you ornament, then turning round and saying by the way, to get a note out of this instrument you need to push the arm to that place. And it's in the same room, and of course that makes him less pressured, no one gets too arrogant, no one is arrogant, because we're all, you know, we all sit down to dinner together, it's unique for musicians. (Elizabeth, tutor)

Jane, an amateur participant on the early brass course described above, referred to how her experience at DISS was different from her everyday musical life, where she plays in an amateur early music consort:

It's quite a contrast to what we normally do. I like it because it's quite academic, the tuition is really good quality, and it's really nice to play with professionals, but I also find it quite challenging sometimes because it's a whole step up from the way we normally practice and play, which is much more relaxed, so I learn a lot but it's challenging.

HRK: So in what ways would you say it's a step up from what you normally do?
JANE: I think we don't ever—we consider ourselves lucky if we can get through a piece to the end, we tend not to focus on the musicality and the articulation and phrasing in the same kind of way as—I think you approach it from a much more amateur perspective, whereas here the expectation is that you approach it from a professional perspective and also that you've got the skills to go with that.

Jane went on to talk about how the challenges presented at DISS could be positive "when you can rise to it," but that "sometimes it's too much of a challenge and then you come away feeling that you've not achieved, or that you've achieved less, doing worse than you did when you started." This could be applied to any teaching and learning situation, but the presence of musicians of significantly different experience and background at DISS might suggest that the negative impact of such challenges could be increased. When the higher-level musician whom a learner aspires to equal is playing alongside them, the difference in expertise must be more noticeable and could potentially be disempowering to the less experienced amateur. This is also interesting in the light of Blackshaw's conception of leisure as mimesis (2010); the possibility of imagining that you can be who you want to be might be somewhat tarnished by the obvious differences in musical ability between who you are and the physical representation of who you want to be.

Mixed-level music making can also serve to reinforce existing hierarchies and differences in ability, however subtly. The string orchestra in 2012 exemplified this dichotomy. On one level it provided multigenerational, multilevel music making, free from hierarchies:

I took a photograph yesterday in an orchestra rehearsal—there was a kid, I mean he must be like eight, and there was this really elderly woman on the same desk, playing together—and I put it up on Facebook and I thought this is Dartington, this is Dartington, there's no, to a certain extent there are no levels or professionals or amateurs, everybody's together performing and getting on with it and I think that's the essence of music at the end of the day—breaks down all barriers. (Emily, amateur participant)

My own observation of the same concert captures this inclusive spirit, but also reveals some underlying tensions about the standard of the performance and its participants:

The string orchestra concert at 7.45 is great—very much what you might call "in the spirit of Dartington"—there are all ages and levels playing together, three different conductors who are all very renowned in their own field, there are stewards and houseparents [the terms used to describe helpers in DISS] mixed in the orchestra. During the Penderecki there are quite a lot of mystified looks between desk partners—Faith explains later that they only actually rehearsed it once! It sounds great though and it's good to see all these people playing and listening to this kind of music. [The conductor] is also clearly totally in command of what's going on, which makes a huge difference in such a complicated piece. It's interesting that the [artistic director of DISS at the time of the study] piece was cancelled—apparently there was a muddle with ordering the music and not enough time to rehearse it—I wonder if it's him that wants to program his own music and then isn't happy with it! At the end of the concert [the conductor] says "We have no encore. Usually for this piece we would have a week's rehearsal—with this group of artists (someone mutters 'artists') we've only had two one hour sessions—thanks to their constant (inaudible) we've managed to achieve it. I hope I haven't abused you too much (laughing from orchestra) and happy returns to Dartington!" (field notes, August 9, 2012)

Jane's view of the standards of teaching, learning, and performance at DISS was that they are "very high" compared to other amateur music making situations where she stated that "degrees of poor playing are often tolerated." This view was not shared by everyone; for some, the mixed levels could be a source of frustration. Jack, a tutor who had originally attended DISS as a composition student, described how he had found the experience disappointing because of the varied standard of the other students and the contrast between his desire to work hard and their lack of a serious attitude. Having progressed to tutoring the composition class, he had experienced similar challenges, referring to the group of students as a mixture of postgraduate students and those who just had a very "holiday" attitude. For Jack, there was a disconnect between the perfectionism that he applies in his professional life as a conductor and composer and the standards that are achievable at DISS given the mixed ability of the participants. David, a tutor in free improvisation, expressed similar views:

The difference in technical ability of people in the class actually provides some problems, because some people want to do things they can't, but then of course we don't want to not allow them to do those things, absolutely not—they should be free to do them, however it makes the piece suffer—so it's a constant, for me it's a lose-lose in that sense, musically—and for, in many senses the class participants, if the mind-frame is right it's a win-win, because anything goes—and then even if it's wrong it's not wrong.

HRK: So do you find it frustrating?

DAVID: No, I don't find it frustrating, it's just a fact—because the only way to get rid of this is only to work with people you've chosen and trust and who are the same professional level with you and that's impossible in any summer festival, it just wouldn't work.

If the participants do not experience the effects of the tutors' dissatisfaction with the musical product, it could be argued that it does not matter; if they are able to enjoy the music making and benefit from the expertise of the tutors, then from their perspectives they are getting what they want. There are times, however, when participants felt the tutors did not deal well with the mixed standards of the group:

One of the reasons I didn't do the piano this year was last year I came away just thinking that I was useless, I mean he was nice enough and he never actually said anything bad, but he never said anything good to anyone. Basically what you'd get was "that's better" and it just felt, it just felt as if I was, I wasn't playing because I thought I was great at it, and all I could think was all the things wrong, yes I know about that bit, I need to work on this, I need to do this and I need to that and actually I'm not very good at all, and I just came away thinking I don't need to be told that I'm brilliant, because I'm not, but I'd like to think that there's something good about what I'm playing—what are the bits that I don't like, and what are the bits that I can extract and it just made me realize more just how much that level of encouragement is important. (Jennifer, amateur participant)

CONCLUSIONS

It's like a microcosm of music in the wider world, so you have the performers, you have the arts administrators and the trogging team,[6] and you have the audience, you have the amateur performers as well.

(Susan, professional participant)

DISS represents an intense community comprising many kinds of participants in classical music making in the U.K., whose different roles would normally keep them in separate hierarchically defined spheres. DISS aspires to an inclusive vision of a musical universe where, like the utopian, unifying vision of music making embodied by Barenboim's West-Eastern Divan Orchestra (Barenboim 2006), the making of music matters more than status or difference. However, as Beckles Willson (2009) states, such a vision makes large assumptions about the possibility of classical music to act as a unifying force merely by making music together; as she identifies, the gap between musical and political discourse can be reinforced rather than challenged by making music with the "other." The microcosm of DISS is confined to the summer and to a specific location—and if its idealistic, democratic version of shared learning and music making is contained only in the environment of the summer school, it is worth considering its effects on the individual participant, its position in the wider musical community, and the potential to reenact or represent such musical democracy elsewhere.

When everything returns to the status quo at the end of the summer, how much influence does this shared space for music and leisure have upon the amateur and professional participants who attend? If the "second life" (Bakhtin 1968) offered to the amateur participants can exist only at Dartington, it could serve to highlight its absence as a permanent musical identity in their everyday lives. Of course, we are not implying that there is anything "wrong" with enjoying a DISS identity for a short time—but if it cannot be replicated elsewhere, and if this utopian vision of music for everyone does not exist in the "real world," then what does this escapism achieve and what can it tell music researchers, educators, community musicians, and others?

These are important questions that are relevant not only to the limited universe of DISS, but also to the wider context of Western Art Music. Opportunities are increasingly being sought for audiences and performers to integrate and interact socially as they do at DISS (Pitts et al. 2013), motivated by both the desire for audience development and retention, and, perhaps more cynically, by the funding possibilities which these relationships can offer. These interactions can serve, as they sometimes do at DISS, to reinforce rather than challenge hierarchical relationships between audience and performer, emphasizing the status of professional musicians as mysterious "other."

Musicians of widely different levels of experience and expertise are increasingly making music side by side in other contexts. Cuts in funding for the arts in the U.K. have led to many ensembles and venues seeking to reduce their budget for performances; this, combined with the burgeoning participation and outreach activities by professional organizations since the 1990s (Winterson 1996), has led to many collaborative music making opportunities and performances between amateurs and professionals.[7] Participants in these events bring different aspirations, expectations, and identities, which can be disrupted to either negative or positive effect by juxtaposition with musicians who are in some way "different" from them. Although it is impossible for leaders and participants in these situations to take into account the individual requirements of each person present, an awareness of the differing needs of those making music for leisure or work purposes can only add to the enjoyment, mutual understanding, and musical satisfaction of those involved.

NOTES

1. For studies of attitudes to amateur music in a range of contexts see, among others, Booth (2000), Durrant and Himonides (1998), Everitt (1997), Finnegan (1989), Peggie (2002), Pitts (2005a), Regelski (2007); for studies of the beneficial effect of music making and music

making in later life, see Ansdell (2010), Creech et al. (2013), DeNora (2000), Gaunt et al. (2012), Lamont (2011), Pitts (2009), Taylor and Hallam (2008, 2011), Taylor (2010, 2011), and Varvarigou and Creech (2011).

2. Music summer schools have grown up in the U.K. since 1948. They combine elements of summer schools that arose in North America to address educational inequalities, providing intensive remedial or acceleration programs (Cooper et al. 2000), North American summer camps (activity holidays, often themed around social, educational, or cultural development), and summer schools in universities across Europe, North America, and Australasia, which provide intensive learning or curriculum enhancement. Most U.K. music summer schools are targeted at a specific market: children, young musicians, adult amateurs, or aspiring professionals. Those encompassing a range of abilities are usually genre or instrument specific. Selective courses for aspiring professionals offer young musicians of an advanced musical level access to renowned professionals and opportunities professional networking. For the amateur, summer schools are a cultural holiday with like-minded others; learning forms a significant part of the experience, but is characterized by practices associated more with nonformal than formal education.

3. There is only one study of music summer schools in the U.K. (Pitts 2004; see also 2005b, 2011); studies of U.S.A. summer camps include Brandt (1988), Cooper et al. (2000), Diaz and Silveira (2013), Nemser (2014), Paul (2010), Zelensky (2014), Seeger and Seeger (2006), Joselit and Mittelman (1993), Sales and Saxe (2004).

4. See Drummond (1990) and Finnegan (1989) for discussion of the amateur-professional continuum; for discussion of the professional and aspiring professional musician, see Bennett (2008), Cottrell (2004), Coulson (2010, 2012), Kingsbury (2001), and Nettl (1995).

5. These conceptions can be used effectively to consider music making for leisure in this context, although they do not apply as well to other free-time and hobby activities, where there is less separation between the "other" and the "real"; for example, volunteering for a charitable organization or do-it-yourself in a domestic setting.

6. "Trogs" are volunteers who carry out administrative and concert management tasks at DISS, usually students and recent graduates hoping to make a career in arts administration.

7. Examples of such projects include the Ex Cathedra choirs (www.excathedra.co.uk) and Highbury Opera Theatre (highburyoperatheatre.com).

REFERENCES CITED

Anderton, Chris. 2008. "Commercialising the Carnivalesque: The V Festival and Image/Risk Management." *Event Management* 12: 39–51.

Ansdell, Gary. 2010. *Where Music Helps: Community Music Therapy in Action and Reflection.* Farnham: Gower.

Beckles Willson, Rachel.2009. "Whose Utopia? Perspectives on the West-Eastern Divan Orchestra." *Music and Politics* 3(2): 1–21.

Bakhtin, Mikhail. 1968. *Rabelais and His World.* Cambridge, MA: MIT Press.

Ballenger, Carol. 2012. *Dartington Hall: One Endless Garden.* Wellington: Halsgrove, 2012.

Barenboim, Daniel. 2006. "In the Beginning was Sound." Lecture 4, "Meeting in Music." Broadcast lecture, Reith Lectures. BBC Radio 4. http://downloads.bbc.co.uk/rmhttp/radio4/transcripts/20060428_reith.pdf.

Bennett, Dawn E. 2008. *Understanding the Classical Music Profession: The Past, the Present and Strategies for the Future*. Farnham: Ashgate.

Blackshaw, Tony. 2010. *Leisure*. New York: Routledge.

Booth, Wayne C. 2000. *For the Love of It: Amateuring and Its Rivals*. Chicago: University of Chicago Press.

Borsay, Peter. 2006. *A History of Leisure: The British Experience since 1500*. Basingstoke: Palgrave Macmillan.

Boyatzis, Richard E. 1998. *Transforming Qualitative Information: Thematic Analysis and Code Development*. Thousand Oaks, CA: Sage.

Brandt, Thompson A. 1988. "Summer Music Camps: A Historical Perspective." *Bulletin of Historical Research in Music Education* 9(2): 119–130.

Cooper, Harris, Kelly Charlton, Jeff C. Valentine, and Laura Muhlenbruck. 2000. "Making the Most of Summer School: A Meta-Analytic and Narrative Review." *Monographs of the Society for Research in Child Development* 65(1): i–vi, 1–127.

Cottrell, Stephen. 2004. *Professional Music-Making in London: Ethnography and Experience*. Farnham: Ashgate.

Coulson, Susan. 2010. "Getting 'Capital' in the Music World: Musicians' Learning Experiences and Working Lives." *British Journal of Music Education* 27(3): 255–270.

Coulson, Susan. 2012. "Collaborating in a Competitive World: Musicians' Working Lives and Understandings of Entrepreneurship." *Work, Employment and Society* 26: 246–261.

Creech, Andrea, Susan Hallam, Maria Varvarigou, and Hilary McQueen. 2013. "The Power of Music in the Lives of Older Adults." *Research Studies in Music Education*, 35 (1): 87–102.

DeNora, Tia. 2000. *Music in Everyday Life*. Cambridge: Cambridge University Press.

Diaz, Frank M., and Jason Silveira. 2013. "Dimensions of Flow in Academic and Social Activities among Summer Music Camp Participants." *International Journal of Music Education* 31(3): 310–320.

Dobson, Melissa C. 2011. "Insecurity, Professional Sociability, and Alcohol: Young Freelance Musicians' Perspectives on Work and Life in the Music Profession." *Psychology of Music* 39(2): 240–260.

Drummond, John D. 1990. "The Characteristics of Amateur and Professional." *International Journal of Music Education* 15: 3–8.

Durrant, Colin, and Evangelos Himonides. 1998. "What Makes People Sing Together?" *International Journal of Music Education* 1: 61–71.

Everitt, Anthony. 1997. *Joining In: An Investigation into Participatory Music*. London: Calouste Gulbenkian Foundation.

Finnegan, Ruth. 1989. *The Hidden Musicians: Music-Making in an English Town*. Cambridge: Cambridge University Press.

Gardiner, Michael. 1993. "Bakhtin's Carnival: Utopia as Critique." In *Bakhtin: Carnival and Other Subjects*, edited by David Shepherd, 20–47. Amsterdam: Rodopi.

Gaunt, Helena, Andrea Creech, Marion Long, and Susan Hallam. 2012. "Supporting Conservatoire Students towards Professional Integration: One- to-One Tuition and the Potential of Mentoring." *Music Education Research* 14: 37–41.

Gibson, William, and Andrew Brown. 2009. *Working with Qualitative Data*. Thousand Oaks, CA: Sage.

Grint, Keith. 1991. *The Sociology of Work: An Introduction*. Cambridge: Polity.

Halnon, Karen Bettez. 2004. "Inside Shock Music Carnival: Spectacle as Contested Terrain." *Critical Sociology* 30: 743–779.

Joselit, Jenna, and Karen Mittleman. 1993. *A Worthy Use of Summer: Jewish Summer Camping in America*. Philadelphia. PA: National Museum of American History.

Kingsbury, Henry. 2001. *Music, Talent, and Performance: A Conservatory Cultural System.* Philadelphia, PA: Temple University Press.

Kirschner, Tony. 1998. "Studying Rock: Towards a Materialist Ethnography". In *Mapping the Beat: Popular Music and Contemporary Theory*, edited by Thomas Swiss, John Sloop, and Andrew Herman, 247–268. Oxford: Blackwell.

Levitas, Ruth. 2010. "*In eine bess're Welt entrückt*: Reflections on Music and Utopia." *Utopian Studies* 21(2): 215–231.

Lamont, Alexandra. 2011. "The Beat Goes on: Music Education, Identity and Lifelong Learning." *Music Education Research* 13(4): 369–388.

MacCarthy, Fiona. 2014. *Anarchy and Beauty: William Morris and His Legacy, 1860–1960*. New Haven, CT: Yale University Press.

Mantie, Roger. 2012. "Learners or Participants? The Pros and Cons of 'Lifelong Learning.'" *International Journal of Community Music* 5(3): 217–235.

Matheson, Catherine M., and Ross Tinsley. 2014. "The Carnivalesque and Event Evolution: A Study of the Beltane Fire Festival." *Leisure Studies* 35(1): 1–27.

Morris, Pam. 1994. *The Bakhtin Reader: Selected Writings of Bakhtin, Medvedev and Voloshinov*. London: Arnold.

Nemser, Ari. 2014. "Overnight Summer Music Camp and the Impact on Its Youth: A Case Study." MA thesis, Florida International University.

Nettl, Bruno. 1995. *Heartland Excursions: Ethnomusicological Reflections on Schools of Music*. Chicago: University of Illinois Press.

Nicholas, Larraine. 2007. *Dancing in Utopia: Dartington Hall and Its Dancers.* Alton: Dance Books.

Paul, Timothy. 2010. "Factors Concerning Student Participation in Summer Band Camps." *Missouri Journal of Research in Music Education* 47: 13–22.

Peggie, Andrew. 2002. "Bloody Amateurs." In *Bloody Amateurs*, edited by John L. Walters, 29–31. Reading: Unknown Public.

Pitts, Stephanie. 2004. "Lessons in Learning: Learning, Teaching and Motivation at a Music Summer School." *Music Education Research* 6(1): 81–95.

Pitts, Stephanie. 2005a. *Valuing Musical Participation*. Aldershot: Ashgate.

Pitts, Stephanie. 2005b. "What Makes an Audience? Investigating the Roles and Experiences of Listeners at a Chamber Music Festival." *Music and Letters* 86(2): 257–69.

Pitts, Stephanie. 2009. "Roots and Routes in Adult Musical Participation: Investigating the Impact of Home and School on Lifelong Musical Interest and Involvement." *British Journal of Music Education* 26(3): 241–56.

Pitts, Stephanie. 2011. "'Everybody Wants to Be Pavarotti': The Experience of Music for Performers and Audience at a Gilbert and Sullivan Festival." *Journal of the Royal Musical Association* 129(1): 143–60.

Pitts, Stephanie, Melissa C. Dobson, Kate Gee, and Christopher P. Spencer. 2013. "Views of an Audience: Understanding the Orchestral Concert Experience from Player and Listener Perspectives." *Journal of Audience and Reception Studies* 10(2): 65–95.

Putnam, Robert. 2000. *Bowling Alone: The Collapse and Revival of American Community*. New York: Simon and Schuster.

Regelski, Thomas A. 2007, "Amateuring in Music and Its Rivals." *Action, Criticism, and Theory for Music Education* 6(3): 22–50. http://act.maydaygroup.org/articles/Regelski6_3.pdf.

Roberts, Ken. 2011. "Leisure: The Importance of Being Inconsequential." *Leisure Studies* 30(1): 5–20.

Salaman, Graeme. 1974. *Community and Occupation: An Exploration of Work/Leisure Relationships*. Cambridge: Cambridge University Press, 1974

Saldaña, Johnny. 2009. *The Coding Manual for Qualitative Researchers*. Thousand Oaks, CA: Sage.

Sales, Amy L., and Leonard Saxe. 2004. *"How Goodly Are Thy Tents": Summer Camp as Jewish Socializing Experiences*. Lebanon, NH: Brandeis University Press.

Seeger, Anthony, and Kate Seeger. 2006. "Beyond the Embers of the Campfire: The Ways of Music at a Residential Summer Children's Camp". *World of Music* 48(1): 33–65.

Silberman-Keller, Diana. 2006. "Images of Time and Place in the Narrative of Nonformal Pedagogy." In *Learning in Places: The Informal Education Reader*, edited by Zvi Bekerman, Nicholas C. Burbules, and Diana Silberman-Keller, 251–272. New York: Peter Lang.

Small, Christopher. 1998. *Musicking: The Meanings of Performing and Listening*. Middletown, CT: Wesleyan University Press.

Stebbins, Robert A. 2007. *Serious Leisure: A Perspective for Our Time*. New Brunswick, NJ: Transaction.

Taylor, Angela. 2010. "Participation in a Master Class: Experiences of Older Amateur Pianists." *Music Education Research* 12: 199–217.

Taylor, Angela. 2011. "Continuity, Change and Mature Musical Identity Construction: Using 'Rivers of Musical Experience' to Trace the Musical Lives of Six Mature-Age Keyboard Players." *British Journal of Music Education* 28(2): 195–212.

Taylor, Angela, and Susan Hallam. 2008. "Understanding What It Means for Older Students to Learn Basic Musical Skills on a Keyboard Instrument." *Music Education Research* 10: 285–306.

Taylor, Angela, and Susan Hallam. 2011. "From Leisure to Work: Amateur Musicians Taking up Instrumental or Vocal Teaching as a Second Career." *Music Education Research* 13(3): 307–325.

Varvarigou, Maria, and Andrea Creech. 2011. "Bringing Different Generations Together in Music-Making: An Intergenerational Music Project in East London." *International Journal of Community Music* 4(3): 207–220.

Warrack, John. 1950. "The Bryanston Summer School of Music." *Musical Times* 91(1292): 377–381.

White, Michael. 2012. "Why Dartington Is Still a Small Repository of Heaven." *Daily Telegraph*, August 13.

Whiting, James and Kevin Hannam. 2015. "Creativity, Self-Expression and Leisure." *Leisure Studies* 15(3): 372–384.

Winterson, Julia. 1996, "So What's New? A Survey of the Education Policies of Orchestras and Opera Companies." *British Journal of Music Education* 13(3): 259–270.

Zelensky, Nathalie K. 2014. "Sounding Diaspora through Music and Play in a Russian-American Summer Camp." *Ethnomusicology Forum* 23 (3): 306–330.

······························

CHAPTER 21

"WHAT'S YOUR NAME, WHERE ARE YOU FROM, AND WHAT HAVE YOU HAD?"

Utopian Memories of Leeds's Acid House Culture in Two Acts

······························

RONNIE RICHARDS

INTRODUCTION

······························

CRITCHER defines Acid House as "no more than music associated with LSD" (2000, 146). The discussion in this chapter will serve to expand on Crither's definition. Reynolds's (2008) historical account of the impact of Acid House and the drug Ecstasy on Western popular culture is a useful backdrop. Reynolds considers himself a participant observer attempting to examine dance music subcultures "in their natural environment" (2008, xvii), and proposes that his text is not purely academic (xviii); however, he utilizes structural concepts, including race and social class, to examine the significance and development of Acid House music and culture. Reynolds documents the original synthesis of the drug Ecstasy, the emergence of electronic dance music in the United States, and the advent of Acid House in the United Kingdom circa 1988, proposing the existence of a "utopian/dystopian dialect running through Ecstasy [Acid House music] culture" (xxvi). Aspects of Reynolds's analysis seek to question both the positive (aspirations for a better world) and negative (drug-related, illegal) contexts of Acid House.

This discussion utilizes a biographical and autoethnographic method to illustrate key signifiers of Acid House music culture. Aspects of this biographical/autoethnographical method include narrative in both fictional and nonfictional contexts. Regarding these approaches to biographical writing, Roberts suggests that the use of techniques such as fictionalized speech may provide a depth of sociological analysis that is "more revelatory of the self than other forms of writing" (2002, 69). He also emphasizes the benefits of autoethnographic method in relation to the incorporation of researcher reflexivity and as a challenge to traditional hegemonic presentations of academic studies. Denzin (1997) agrees with the importance of researcher reflexivity and proposes the need to utilize a contemporary ethnographic approach to research, "which embraces experimental, experiential and critical reading[s] that are always incomplete, personal, self-reflexive and resistant to totalizing theories" (246). Following on from this approach, a more traditional style will be adopted in the analysis of all the key signifiers and their association with utopia and Acid House.

ACT I: *LOCATION, LOCATION, IDENTIFICATION*

The purpose of this discussion is to identify some of the key signifying factors of Acid House culture.[1] To achieve this, a narrative method is used which incorporates the memories and experiences of the author. The fictional narratives contained in this writing are drawn from the author's autobiographical memories of events related to the development of Acid House music culture in Leeds at the end of the 1980s. This narrative method serves to both identify signifiers and allow for the reflective practice identified by Roberts (2002) and Denzin (1997).

> Lucas and Anna sat waiting for me on the stone steps of Corn Exchange.[2] The expression on Anna's face suggested she was not pleased that I was late again. Lucas shook his head in a disapproving manner, but the look on his face suggested that my habitual lateness was not an issue. I approached them both and attempted to sit on Lucas's knee. He moved quickly, which resulted in me landing unceremoniously between the two of them.
> "Ha ha ha. What are you wearing?" I asked.
> "I saw it in yesterday's newspaper" he began. "They printed a guide to what ravers should wear. Look I'm not lying—Anna has got it in her pocket."

Chakraborty, Neogi, and Basu (2011) define raves as "parties with loud, electronic techno-rock music, laser light shows, and all night dancing held in clandestine locations" (2011, 594). Critcher uses the term "rave culture" to describe "the late 1980s and early 1990s [where] there emerged in the U.K. a new youth cultural phenomenon" (2000, 145). According to Critcher, the concept of "rave culture" is used as a generic term to "emphasise the totality of the cultural form and its innovating nature" (145). For Critcher, the concept of rave is used to describe the actual party or event (the rave) and the culture (including drug consumption, dance, and music). Reynolds (2008) suggests that the word "rave" had become common by 1988, "but only as a verb, e.g. I'm going raving at this warehouse party. A year later 'rave' had become a noun, while 'raver' for many, was a derogatory stereotype, an insult" (64). Chakraborty, Neogi, and Basu use the concept of raver to describe an individual who attends a rave, suggesting, "[A] raver is a person who has an exciting and uninhibited social life" (2011, 594). The swift decline in the capital of the concept of "raver" is linked to the continued widespread appropriation of Acid House culture. The sense of belonging, notion of pride, and right to call oneself a raver become diminished as a greater number of people begin to lay claim to the term. Collin and Godfrey (1998) proposed that as the popularity of Acid House began to develop mainstream recognition, the concepts of rave and raver adopted a significance of disingenuousness.

For the purpose of this discussion, the concept of a *rave* is used to describe a party or event, while the term *raver* is used to describe a person who attends such events. Further, those who consider themselves adherents of Acid House music and culture will also fall into the category of raver. Though the concept of "rave culture" will not be used as an organizing concept here, it must be acknowledged that its generic use in the vernacular (as Critcher suggests) is still commonplace. Therefore, the operation of the precursor "Acid House" enables a specific consideration of a temporal and cultural phenomenon. The term "Acid House" will be used as an organizing concept throughout this chapter.

Anna reached into her inside jacket pocket and produced a neatly folded sheet of paper. She passed it to me and I unfolded it. The page had been removed from *The Sun* newspaper. The date at the top of the page read Wednesday the 14th of September 1988. The page presented an "Acid House fashion guide." The main picture featured a blonde female model dressed entirely in smiley-face attire and accessories. The feature also contained a "lingo" guide to assist its readers with the "correct things to say" when in attendance at an Acid House party. An offer for *The Sun*'s own version of an Acid House smiley T-shirt was also included on the page. I almost fell off the step with laughter—firstly in response to *The Sun*'s interpretation of Acid House, and secondly due to the fact that Lucas had taken *The Sun*'s guide almost literally. He had not copied the guide's fashion suggestions item for item, however his T-shirt, jacket, and baseball cap were emblazoned with the ubiquitous yellow smiley face. He, like many influenced by the media, seemed to easily buy into the symbols associated with rave culture.

"It is about being more subtle," I explained. I pointed to the small ten pence-sized smiley face badge which was attached to my denim jacket, just below the collar. "There are some people still wearing smiley face clothes, but not many!" I said.

"I have spent all my money on these clothes," Lucas proclaimed. "I am flat broke now and I definitely cannot afford to get new clothes—not until my dole comes through, and that's not for another two weeks!"

Anna began to giggle, "I told you not to buy those silly expensive clothes. Now you have nothing new to wear this weekend."

Lucas's mouth motioned to say something, but he knew Anna was right. He looked at me for some degree of support, but I simply smiled and shrugged my shoulders. Dejected, he averted his gaze to his shoes, his long bob hair style obscuring his face. Realizing her boyfriend was upset, Anna quickly changed the subject.

"Where is everyone else?" she asked.

I was unsure . . .

As a rule, my extended peer group would meet in the city center on a daily basis between Monday and Friday. Due to the fact that only a few of us were in full-time employment, the flow into the city center would commence at approximately midday. Our employment situation was symptomatic of conditions at the time. Charlesworth (2000) presents a bleak picture of both the leisure opportunities and job prospects for traditional working-class communities, linked to the decline in industrialization and the economic restructuring that resulted in widespread unemployment.

Roberts (1999) places this situation in a postmodern context. For him, the decline in traditional employment opportunities resulted in not only a decline in economic independence from the state but also a reduction in traditional determinates of identity. For Roberts, occupation and profession no longer influenced individual (or group) identity. Instead, the concept of lifestyle became more important. According to Roberts, leisure choice is a salient aspect of lifestyle and identity. It can be suggested, therefore, that our leisure activities and our allegiance to an Acid House culture had replaced the formation of a social class identity based on employment and career. Acid House culture became important in the provision of identity.

Hebdige's seminal 1979 study sought to ascertain the relationship between subcultural identity and style. Hebdige utilizes a structuralist framework to analyze "the expressive forms and rituals . . . of subordinate groups—the teddy boys and mods and rockers, the skin heads and the punks" (1979, 2). For Hebdige, style—and the subcultures each specific style represents—is a visual representation of "defiance and contempt" (3). Hebdige proposes that style is a calculated and premeditated form of visual resistance to existing hegemonic power structures, a symbolic representation of difference (from mainstream culture) and rebellion. Allegiance to Acid House in this context can be regarded as a direct reaction through clothes and bodily practice to the prevailing social conditions of isolation, poverty, and lack of opportunity.

"I bet they are at Top Mac's," I suggested. "I was with a few of the guys just before I came here—that's why I was late. I told them I was coming here, so I guess they will all be down here sooner rather than later."

"Who was there?" Anna enquired.

As I began to dictate a list of those who were in attendance at my previous location, our attention was drawn to a small group who had just alighted a bus at the collection of stops adjacent to the Corn Exchange.

"There is Louise," Anna indicated.

Placing two of her fingers into her mouth, Anna produced a loud whistle. One of the female members of the group, which consisted of three females and two males, acknowledged the whistle and waved in our direction. After a brief discussion amongst themselves, the group headed over towards us.

I did not know any of the group personally, but I did recognize a couple of them through attending the Warehouse on Saturdays. The three females were immaculately dressed: Kickers shoes, flared Joe Bloggs denim jeans, and multicolored Naf Naf jumpers. The two males were dressed just as exceptionally. One was dressed in Chipie chino pants and a blue Chipie pullover. The other male wore a pair of C17 denim dungarees and a pale Benetton shirt.

Brand-name clothing existed for many years prior to Acid House music. What made particular labels synonymous with Acid House was the style in which they were worn. However, as important as specific key clothing labels were in relation to Acid House culture, an inability to purchase these labels was not necessarily a barrier to participation. Designer clothes were desirable, but not compulsory. Instead, a specific style of dress emerged that allowed members of the "culture" to be as easily identified as those who were not. Charlesworth (2000) identifies the association of status and identity regarding "trendy clothes" as forms of symbolic capital (53). He argues that style extends beyond clothes to other aspects of style and fashion, such as hairstyles and knowledge of the music, thus potentially enabling poseurs and interlopers to "pass" for adherents of Acid House.

Why was style important to Acid House? It must be considered that there was a practical element to the manner in which the majority of the adherents dressed. Nightclubs could be hot and sweaty environments, so early styles of dress included casual wear such as t-shirts and jeans. Specific French (Naf Naf, Chipie) and British (The Duffer of St George) clothing manufacturers became popular labels favored by Acid House participants. Flared jeans also became a popular item, with Lancashire-based denim manufacturer Joe Bloggs launching a 30-inch flared jean in the late 1980s (Lynn 1991). Early Acid House style was androgynous, with dungarees, sweaters, and hooded tops held in esteem amongst male and female participants. The practical element also included the appropriation of traditional outdoor or adventure labels such as Berghaus and Karrimor. This aspect of style and practicality related closely to the environmental (sometimes open-air) element of raves. If an individual was leaving an event at 9 a.m. after several hours of dancing, warmth and comfort were priorities. Style served as a key marker of identification. During a conversation with a party promoter of the late 1980s, Garratt (1998, 130) indicates, "You'd meet someone on the street and you might not know who they were, but you'd be wearing exactly the same clothing. . . And you'd get talking. That sort of thing happened all the time."

> As the group approached, Louise, the young woman who had responded to Anna's whistle, chimed, "Are you guys out this weekend?"
>
> We knew that this was no general query. In effect this was a question of intent with regard to which rave we were planning to attend, as well as an opportunity to establish status within the group. As Louise and her friends stood in front of us, I began to feel Lucas moving slowly at the side of me. I looked in his direction and the baseball cap had already been removed. Slowly, ever so slowly, he placed his hands into his jacket pockets. He then inched his hands closer until they were linked together through his pockets and resting on his crotch. This brought his jacket together so that his smiley face T-shirt was less visible to the approaching group.
>
> "We are not sure where we are going," Anna replied. "Maybe the Astoria Friday? Not at all sure about Saturday. What about you guys?"
>
> "I've got my mum's car this weekend so will probably go to Monroes' in Blackburn on Friday. We all went last week and it was amazing!," Louise said in an increasingly enthusiastic tone.

Anna, Lucas, and I had heard of Monroes', but due to our lack of transport, getting there was near impossible. We had been trumped.

"It was the most amazing night," Louise continued. "Amazing music. Amazing environment. And the people, the people were so friendly! It was like having your most favorite family members in a club! It was our first time there but we felt like we knew everyone. We all got membership cards so it means we don't have to join the queue next time we go."

She paused and reached into her pocket and removed her purse. From the purse she produced a small credit-card-sized plastic item. The Monroes' membership card was passed to Anna, who subsequently passed the card on to me. I then passed the card to Lucas, who returned it to Louise.

"It's the best club I have ever been to," Louise continued. "Ever since last week all I have waited for is this weekend so that I could go again. It will be brilliant! If there is any space in my mum's car then you can come. I will give you my phone number. Ring me any time before seven as I will be going out and then you will not be able to contact me [mobile phones were expensive luxury items during this period]. If there is a space then you can definitely come."

Lucas and I sat in silence. The invitation was definitely only open to Anna.

"Have you got a pen? I will give you my home number," said Louise.

None of us had a pen. I proposed they try Storeys' arcade opposite. There was a nod of recognition from Louise and her group toward Lucas and myself. We both nodded back. As Anna, Louise, and the others headed toward the amusement arcade, Lucas relaxed and released an audible sigh of relief.

After approximately ten minutes, Anna came running back over, the smile on her face evident.

"Please, please, please," she gushed. "Please God allow them to have a space for me on Friday. Monroes'. I am going to Monroes!"

"What about me?" Lucas enquired in a concerned whisper.

It would be too simplistic to identify both Anna's sense of joy and Lucas's sense of disappointment based solely on their ability or inability to attend Monroes'. Lucas's nonattendance at Monroes' would result in another weekend in Leeds. This was not in itself a negative proposition, as for us, weekends in Leeds were (mostly) joyous times. Anna's elation and Lucas's disappointment were associated with the rare opportunity to affiliate with other members of Acid House culture beyond our geographical confines—the chance to become acquainted with members of the wider Acid House community (or family, as Louise had described) beyond the diminutive level of Leeds. We were all fully aware of Acid House events being held in cities such as Blackburn, Manchester, Liverpool, London, and abroad in locations such as Ibiza. These locations all served as "Meccas" of new experiences. Our social and economic situation served to highlight the limitations of possible leisure experiences. This shared experience too was conducive to group cohesion. Acid House provided us some understanding of who and what we thought we were and our position in society. The importance of locations such as Monroes' highlights the significance of space and place in the formation of Acid House culture.

Space and Place

For all the individuals referred to during this fictional autoethnography, geographical location presents a significant aspect for understanding Acid House culture. Location can be understood as a key site of social cohesion. For example, specific nightclubs served as catalysts not only for immediate peer association, but also as subsidiary to a wider culture and associations. This was augmented by the ability to access and experience locations beyond one's immediate geographical position. Nightclubs provide an obvious location for social cohesion (Chatterton and Hollands 2003). However, due to circumstances (which were predominately financial), the ability for any of us to extend our geographical confines were extremely limited. This resulted in the awareness that although we were part of "something," there was so much more we were excluded from. Meeting individuals like Louise perpetuated these feelings. Further consideration is required of the manner in which everyday locations such as shopping centers, fast food restaurants, and stone steps also become essential meeting points and key sites of social cohesion. For example, in locations such as shopping centers, the intended use of the area becomes subverted. The act of shopping in this context becomes irrelevant to the actors. Instead the need to congregate, to socialize, and to develop peer relationships/friendships becomes the primary concern. If the nightclub is regarded as the pinnacle site of interaction (Malbon 1999; Rill 2010), secondary locations, such as those mentioned, present intermediate opportunities for consistent inter-personal interaction.

Amsden, Steadman, and Kruger (2011) and Crouch (2000) suggest the significance of location in terms of the concepts of space and place. For both Amsden and colleagues and Crouch, the concept of place refers to a geographic area of human interaction. This interaction can be based on numerous activities, such as "recreation, home life, or work" (Amsden, Steadman, and Kruger 2011, 34). For the purpose of this discussion, human interaction is based primarily on the basis of leisure and the culture of Acid House music. Utilizing the theoretical framework of place attachment, the primary concern of Amsden, Steadman, and Kruger is a comprehension of the processes by which meaning is ascribed to specific places. Once an understanding of meaning is achieved, The authors seek to determine the relevance of place and its relationship to the development of community cohesion and identity. According to Crouch, the concept of space is instrumental if the complexity of the concept of place is to be fully understood: "Space comprises the geometric co-ordinates of interactions that are physical, economic, social and so on" (Crouch 2000, 66). If the concept of space, therefore, refers to the specific location, place symbolizes "human practice that activates at the local level of human life" (6). Stebbins (this volume, chapter 19) agrees with Amsden and colleagues that place becomes meaningful when a degree of attachment or memories is associated with a specific space.

Utilization of the concepts of space and place can be considered as initial tools in providing a greater understanding of specific locations, such as nightclubs and shopping centers, for example, and the subsequent significance these had on the development of an Acid House culture. I now consider how the concepts of space and place might be applied to Acid House culture. "Embodiment" provides a useful way in:

> Embodiment is a process of experiencing, making sense, knowing through practice as a sensual human subject in the world. The subject engages space and space becomes embodied in three ways. First, the person grasps the world multi-sensually. Second, the body is "surrounded" by space and encounters it multi-dimensionally. Third, through the body the individual express him / herself through the surrounding space and thereby changes its meaning. (Crouch 2000, 68)

The application of *embodiment* allows for space and place to be understood in terms of social relations—cultural relations and the manner in which identity is formed in the context of everyday life. Space and place exist everywhere. What is important is the manner in which individuals interpret space and place and the effect this interaction has. This can be considered as a two-way process. Space and place affect the individual, but the individual also affects space and place. I propose that these spaces and places therefore become instrumental in the development of identity for those concerned. They are key sites of socialization and are instrumental in the development of social relations and (sub)cultural development. The shopping center, therefore, was just as important as the nightclub in the development of identity, community and Acid House culture.

"When will you know?" Lucas asked.

"Not until late Friday," Anna replied. "I will have to stay in until I get confirmation, but if it is not too late, and I do not go, I can always meet you in the Astoria later?"

Anna sat back on the step next to Lucas and placed her arm around him. She pulled him close and gave him a reassuring kiss.

"Let's go." I suggested.

"Where?" Lucas replied.

"For a start, let's go and find you some decent clothes so you can take that God awful jacket off!"

I stood up and outstretched both arms in order to provide both Anna and Lucas an aid to rise up off the step. Before setting off, Lucas paused to dust off any residual dirt that had been collected on his jeans from the dirty stone steps. Together, we headed off with the hope of both new clothes and new experiences.

ACT II: *LOCATION, LOCATION, LOCATION*

> It was Tuesday, and for the first time that month Gary felt content. He removed his large rucksack from his back, placed it on the floor, and began to survey the old factory. Gary felt confident that this venue would be perfect. His anxiety had been escalating over the previous weeks, ever since his former venue had fallen through. He wasn't exactly sure how this had transpired, but the police had somehow found out that there was going

to be a rave and subsequently increased their presence and security at the factory. It was a frustrating aspect of the game Gary played, but this had happened to him before. He had lost a considerable amount of money preparing the original building, but with the police presence so intense he had to accept the financial loss and relocate to a new venue. How had the police found out this time? A leak of information from within his organization? This was possible but not likely. The majority of his team were close family members who all benefited directly (both financially and through increased social status) from the success of each rave. Had a rival found out about the location and informed the police, or was it simply luck on the part of law enforcement? Although this matter was a concern, it was not a situation he could solve immediately. Gary's primary concern was securing this new venue and ensuring that it would be ready for the event on Saturday. Four days was a tight schedule, but Gary felt confident that if he could organize the troops promptly and efficiently, the short preparation period could in fact work to his benefit, as by the time anyone else had realized he was here, it would be too late as the event would have commenced.

Once a successful rave was in full flow, "police would often turn up outnumbered and powerless" (Critcher 2000, 147). Early venues tended to be abandoned industrial premises such as warehouses and factories (Collin and Godfrey 1998; Critcher 2000), remnants and reminders of a once thriving manufacturing economy (Charlesworth 2000; Roberts 1999).

From the dilapidated state of the interior, Gary was sure that the factory had been unused for at least ten years. He bent down and removed a torch from his rucksack. With the illumination provided by the shaft of torch light, Gary could ascertain that the fabric of the building was still in very good condition. All the windows were intact and there was no sign of residue from water penetration. The factory existed over two levels with an extensive ground floor and a smaller mezzanine level. Gary's experience dictated that if he situated the DJ booth on the higher level he could easily fit two thousand revelers on the ground floor. More revelers meant more income. Gary smiled to himself; all the stress now seemed worth it. This new venue was actually better than the previous one in both size and accessibility for his potential clientele. The task now was to prepare the building.

Lashua (2013) describes the practice of transforming unused urban spaces into sites of temporary transgressive places of leisure as "DIY leisure." Kempson (2015) proposes the significance of DIY leisure spaces and the development of subcultural movements. Although some aspects were illegal, Acid House culture provided the opportunity for several of its adherents to display and develop their entrepreneurial skills. These skills ranged from the printing and design of flyers, rave promotion, musical performance, and production. These activities were all directly linked to the culture of Acid House and provided certain individuals the opportunity to live lifestyles not dictated by traditional work-nonwork balances. Acid House culture afforded some the means to provide a degree of economic stability at a time when traditional job roles were minimal.

As Gary continued to make mental notes of the tasks he had to prioritize, the large metal factory doors groaned loudly as they were pushed open from the outside.

"So Steve, what do you think?" Gary asked.

Gary had become aware of Steve through hearing him play on local pirate radio. Steve had gained a high level of popularity and a reputation as one of the best underground DJs in the north of England. Gary soon realized that the addition of Steve on his team would strengthen the profile of his events and that Steve's reputation could also increase attendance and any subsequent profit. Gary's intuition proved correct; with Steve as his DJ his events had seen an increase both in attendance and reputation.

"I can't see a thing," Steve replied. "I don't have a torch. Where are my decks going?"

Gary pointed his large industrial torch in the direction of the mezzanine level.

"Up there, I think. There should be more than enough space for you up there," Gary indicated.

"Can we go up and have a look?" asked Steve.

Gary pointed the bright torch beam in the direction of a collection of large boxes blocking the stairway that provided access the upper level.

"I don't think we will be able to get up there today, mate," Gary suggested. "Once Sean and the rest of the crew tidy this place up tomorrow then it should not be a problem."

Steve nodded his head as confirmation.

"I will ring Martin later tonight," Gary continued, "and ask him to come down with me and have a look at the electrics tomorrow day."

Gary was the epitome of the Acid House entrepreneur (Anthony 1998; Hook 2010). Unemployed since leaving school, he had started organizing small parties with a little group of friends but soon realized he could do it better (and more profitably) on his own. Subsequently, he had been organizing and promoting his own raves for just over a year. By now he had a tried and tested method for both locating and preparing his venues. Ordinarily, he would locate a disused factory or warehouse. The further away from the general population the better, as this would allow him the anonymity and freedom to plan and prepare his venue without fear of detection. Once the venue had been identified, the next step would be gaining entry. Usually a pair of bolt cutters would suffice. On some occasions access would be gained easily through broken windows or doors. The longer a building appeared disused, then the more appealing the venue was, as this suggested the lack of private ownership and therefore less possibility of being exposed. Gary felt no remorse with regard to the illegal entry and use of these buildings. As far as he was concerned, the buildings did not belong to anyone. They were unused, so who was he hurting having a rave there?

Upon entry, the most important aspect was to secure an electricity supply. Over the years Gary had formed a team; Martin, his brother-in-law, was his trusted electrician. If Martin could not revive a building's electric supply then he would use an elaborate system of cables to connect a building's existing supply to the nearest street light. If this were not possible then generators would have to be hired. For Gary, the street light method was the preferred option, as this would reduce his overhead.

Once power had been secured, the next step was the physical preparation of the venue. Again, Gary had a small team, led by his younger brother Sean, whom he would employ to ensure that the disused industrial space became the ideal space for dancing. This transformation included the use of speakers, lights, lasers, and smoke machines. To ensure anonymity, all these items would be hired from separate companies and payment would be made by cash. A makeshift bar (selling nonalcoholic beverages such as water and Lucozade (a glucose energy drink historically used as an aid to recovery from ill health) would also be erected at a vantage point close to the dance area. Alcohol tended not to be consumed by a large majority of early ravers, replaced instead by illegal drugs such as Ecstasy and amphetamines (Collin and Godfrey 1998).

"How many people do you think this place will hold?" Steve asked.

"Two thousand, I reckon. At £15 a head that should be a tidy profit," Gary indicated, rubbing his thumb and forefinger together.

"£15 entry? Don't you think that is a bit expensive? What if everyone can't afford it? They will miss the party." The tone of concern was evident in Steve's voice.

"Miss the party? If they can't afford it they won't get in. I've got overheads and I'm not a charity!" An agitated, high-pitched tone in Gary's voice became evident.

"But Gary, it's not about the money, is it? I know you pay me to play at your events, but to be honest I don't do it for the money; the people love us," proclaimed Steve.

"And I love them . . . and their money, just as much as they love us!!"

"Gary, surely all this must mean more to you than money? On Saturday I want you to look at the expressions on everyone's face. Pure happiness. I want you to speak to some of the ravers. They will tell you! We are a part of something, mate; this movement will change the world. There will never be a time when I am not part of this," declared Steve.

"Change the world? Mate, are you right in the head? I mean this whole rave thing is fine. I enjoy the party, the minor celebrity status, but changing the world? I don't know about that. This rave organizing game has changed my life, no doubt, but changing the world is just a bit too deep."

The term "utopia" was coined by Thomas More in 1516. In a literary, fictional context, the word has two suggested meanings based on its Greek and Latin origins—*Outpia*, which means "nowhere," and *eutopia*, which equates to somewhere good (Kumar 1991; Parker 2002). In his book *Utopia*, More presents the island of Utopia as a representation of an "ideal society." Levitas (2011, 186) suggests that when attempting to define the concept of utopia, the aspects of "content, form and function" (4) must be considered. A definition of utopia based on content relates to the (common) assumption that utopia is the presentation of a "good society" established by individual or group perception. For example, different social or ethnic groups may have conflicting opinions on the specific tenets of a good society. Form relates to the manner or context in which a utopia may exist. For example, More's utopia exists in a literary form. Kumar (1991) proposes that a utopia can be represented in the forms of architecture, social idealism, and political ideology. Instrumental to form is the significance of time, place, past, present and future. Key to these spatial / temporal considerations is the aspect of function. Function addressees the manner in which a utopia is characterized or the specific goals a utopia seeks to achieve. Levitas (2011) and Midgley (2000) both indicate that the concept of utopia can serve as a framework and structure for social, cultural, and political change.

Several authors have compared the experience of Acid House music to a utopian occurrence (Anthony 1998; Collin and Godfrey 1998; Keane 1997; Reynolds 2008; Thornton 1995). In his analysis of the cultural and social significance of Acid House music and the "Madchester" music scene, Haslam suggests that "the momentary diversion of Madchester gave us a little glimpse of utopia" (1999, 188). Haslam's justification for this claim is drawn from his analysis of the manner in which Acid House was able to build a perceived sense of community among its participants. Haslam proposes that a shared consciousness was demonstrated at a time when the concept of society was deemed devoid by the prevailing Conservative party ideology. For Haslam, the concept of utopia equates to a confirmation of identity and belonging. Key to the Acid House utopia appears to be the need to create distance from the "discontent, boredom and frustration" (Anthony 1998, 5) of life in Britain in the late 1980s. Collin and Godfrey (1998) go to great lengths to explain the prevailing political ideology of this time, which apparently served to foster the sense of alienation expressed by Anthony. For Collin and Godfrey, the elevation of political influence had a subsequent detrimental effect on both the economic and social fabric of the society. The neoliberal politics continued by successive Thatcher governments served to create a society "fragmented and individualized" (Collin and Godfrey 1998, 6). The significance of Thatcher's politics is also detailed by Haslam (1999) and Reynolds (2008). It is in this specific cultural, social, and political climate that the foundations for an apparent Acid House utopia began to develop, presenting members of Acid House culture with their version of an apparent ideal society, located in community and a chemically enhanced definition of the experience of love.

In opposition to this decline in both community and identity, Anthony gives an example of the apparent unity found within the Acid House cultural experience: "At any big dance party there was an across the board mixture of races holding hands and giving out total love and respect for one another. . . . The E generation became the We generation" (Anthony 1998, 42). Aspects of Anthony's discussion begin to provide some clarity regarding specific content of the Acid House utopian ideal. Here, the structural factor of "race" is placed at the center of a discussion of unity. Other structural concepts can be considered a feature of the Acid House experience. Collin and Godfrey (1998) propose narratives of social class, sex, and gender as being elements of the Acid House experience.

Acid House provided its adherents with an apparently new perception of life. For many it provided a release from a life of limited opportunities during a time of decline of community identity and provided a collective consciousness. Acid House provided a new world where previously perceived limitations (both interpersonal and social) were no longer relevant. They considered themselves at the vanguard of a new way of thought and action (Anthony 1998; Collin and Godfrey 1998; Keane 1997; Reynolds 1997; Thornton 1995).

If utopia is regarded as a framework for a proposed ideal society, Kumar (1991) proposes the existence of historical religious and spiritual concepts, which, to some degree, can be associated with utopian thought. These can be demonstrated in Acid House music. For example an early Acid House record proposes:

> Brothers
> Sisters
> One day we will be free,
> Of fighting
> Violence
> People crying in the streets
> When the angles from above
> Come down and spread their wings like doves
> As we walk
> Hand in hand
> Sisters, brothers
> We will make it to the promised land.
>
>   (Joe Smooth 1987)

There is evidence of spiritual themes present in these lyrics. Other popular Acid House/rave records that contain obvious spiritual themes include *Say a Little Prayer, Peace and Harmony, Your Love and Feel so Real* (see Discography, below). This link between the experience and culture of Acid House music and spirituality is also supported by Garratt, who states, "It was very spiritual. Some of those moments in the club were unbelievable. People literally went into trance states . . . not from the use of drugs but through the music and the human energy that was going around" (1998, 117).

This conversation of global change annoyed Gary. His motivation was not connected to this goal. He was keen to bring the conversation back to the logistics of this weekend's event.

"Have you got any flyers left?" Gary asked.

"Not many. I will need a few more if you want me to flyer people as they leave the city center clubs on Friday," Steve replied.

Gary was lucky. The details of the original flyer did not need to be changed, as the location of the rave was never disclosed on the flyer. Instead a premium rate number was indicated. An initial meeting place would be disclosed and then various other smaller meeting places would be provided, with members of Gary's team in each location. The final location would be revealed only once the convoy had passed through at least four check points. This process was primarily done to ensure that if the police had become aware of the event, then their presence could be monitored at each check point by Gary and his team. Emerging mobile phone technology ensured communication was maintained.

"I will come and pick you up early on Saturday," Gary indicated. "All the sound equipment will be arriving then and you can come down and ensure that your decks are set up correctly. I reckon Saturday's party will kick off at around one o'clock, so whatever you get up to early Saturday night, make sure you are here by at least eleven so we can get things rolling."

Steve nodded again in agreement. He was looking forward to Saturday. If everything went according to Gary's plan, then Saturday would be the biggest event he had played at. There was no way he was going to miss that experience.

"Right, then," said Gary, "let's lock this place up and get moving. We've got a rave to organize," he said jubilantly.

Gary shone his torch in the direction of the large factory doors and both men began to make their way to the exit. As they did so, the large metal factory doors again groaned loudly as they were pushed open from the outside. For a split second both Steve and Gary thought that their location had been compromised. However, as the approaching figure stepped into the illuminated shaft of light provided by the torch, their fears quickly subsided.

"Hi chaps. Sorry I'm late."

"Lindley, you idiot. I almost had a heart attack!," proclaimed Gary.

"Like I said, mate, I'm sorry. I had to see a man about a dog. And it was a big dog, if you know what I mean?"

Both Gary and Lindley began to laugh. As Lindley approached the two men he stretched out his right arm and gave Gary a strong, firm handshake. He motioned to shake Steve's hand, but at the last moment removed his hand and instead gave Steve a number of patronizing taps on the top of his head.

"How is the superstar DJ?" Lindley asked sarcastically.

If Steve represents the idealistic Acid House adherent, then Lindley represents the alternative end of the spectrum. For him, the appeal of Acid House lay in the hedonistic elements of the culture. Lindley also represents the organized criminal element which became associated with the continued development of Acid House culture over time (Anthony 1998; Collin and Godfrey 1998; Haslam 1999).

Steve looked in Lindley's direction but did not give him a direct, immediate answer; instead he mouthed the almost inaudible word "wanker" under his breath.

"What did you just say?" Lindley asked, threateningly.

Before Steve could answer, Gary quickly interjected in an attempt to diffuse the situation.

"What do you think of the venue?" Gary asked Lindley.

Lindley held his gaze on Steve for a few seconds and then turned in the direction of Gary.

"It's a big place. I had a good look around outside before I came in," declared Lindley. "From a security perspective I can't see many problems. I will place four of my men on the main doors and maybe two or three round the back just in case any naughty kids try and sneak in. From what I saw, the front door is the only real accessible entrance from the outside. As long as we place someone on all the internal fire exits then it's a simple job."

Gary had met Lindley during the third rave he had organized. Lindley was a few years older than Gary and was quite a well-known individual in their local community, primarily through his association with the local football team's hooligan "firm" (Bussmann 1998). There did not appear to be many local people that Lindley did not know. Lindley had heard of the success of Gary's raves and had decided to attend one of his events. He did not care for the music that much, but he immediately realized how his specific skill set could result in a profitable situation, primarily for him but for Gary also. Lindley had approached Gary and offered to provide security for all his events. Although Gary was at first uncomfortable with the idea, he considered in the long term it would probably be beneficial to have a character like Lindley on his side rather that against him to any degree. Gary eventually agreed, and Lindley had provided security for all his subsequent events.

As well as providing security, Lindley had recognized that as long as he had control over the flow of people entering an event, he could also affect the flow of illegal drugs entering the venue. Drug dealers working for Lindley were given *carte blanche* to sell in and around the venue. Known local dealers not working for Lindley would be barred entry or "persuaded" to work for him. Any unauthorized dealers caught selling drugs in or around a venue would have their supply taken off them and given a "gentle" reminder not to return.

In their study of Ecstasy use among fourteen to sixteen year olds in Northern Ireland, McCrystal and Percy suggest that the "dealer" was the primary source of Ecstasy (2010, 512).

The reputation of Lindley and his security team also meant that local criminals would be discouraged from attempting to steal any onsite proceeds generated by the admission fee and bar. This situation also suited Gary. Lindley's presence offered a degree of personal safety during the rave. Gary also felt that access to Ecstasy at his events was just as important as having the correct music. Knowing Lindley could provide both, was a huge bonus to the increasing reputation of his parties. Gary had decided to stay away from the actual drug-dealing aspect of the Acid House culture. He considered himself an event organizer and promoter. Selling drugs presented itself as being too fraught with risk. The illegal position of organizing raves and the possible judicial ramifications were enough for him. The situation also made sense financially. He would pay Lindley a flat rate to provide security, and Lindley would keep all the money he made from selling Ecstasy. This meant the admission and bar takings were all Gary's. Lindley also supplied him with cheap or free drugs, which for Gary was another added bonus. To date, having Lindley as part of his team had resulted in generally trouble-free events.

It is necessary to understand the significance and position of Ecstasy (MDMA) in relation to Acid House culture. Critcher (2000) suggests the importance of the drug Ecstasy in the emergence of dance music culture. Pilcher (2008) provides a historical account relating to the drug's original synthesis in Germany in 1912. The widespread use of the drug is linked to the actions of Dr. Alexander Shulgin (Pilcher 2008; Saunders 1997; Thomas 2002). Between 1975 and 1978, Shulgin was the first academic to test the drug on humans (himself), to present on the effects of the drug at academic conferences, and to publish articles regarding the drug in academic literature (Benzenhofer and Passie 2010). In regard to the drug's legal status in the U.K., both Saunders (1997) and Critcher (2000) indicate that the drug was classified as a Class A illegal substance in 1977. The rise in popularity of Ecstasy and the drug's association with dance music developed in the gay (disco) clubs of Chicago and New York in the early 1980s (Pilcher 2008). Collin and Godfrey (1998) chart the origins of Ecstasy in the U.K. from the emergence of the drug on the Spanish island of Ibiza. British holidaygoers experiencing the drug there in the mid-1980s sought to replicate the experience on their return to the U.K. Ecstasy use at that time was undertaken by a small clique of U.K. individuals; wider Ecstasy use began with the rise in popularity of Acid House music and culture in the period of late 1988 and early 1989.

> Steve despised Lindley. He considered him and his security team to be violent thugs who were only on the scene for financial reasons. For Steve, Lindley represented the opposite of the real ethos of Acid House adherents like himself. Steve tried to have as little contact with Lindley as possible. The animosity between the two was mutual. As far as Lindley was concerned, there were dozens of DJs who could undertake Steve's role. Lindley failed to understand Gary's sense of loyalty to Steve. Gary fully appreciated the need to provide high-quality music at his events.
> "So what's the plan?" questioned Lindley.
> Gary repeated the key points of the preparation phase. Over the next few days the factory would be transformed almost beyond recognition. Confirming the eleven o'clock meeting time for Saturday, the three men exited the venue. Upon leaving, Gary reached into his rucksack, removed a large chain and padlock, and secured the factory door.
> The three men began the walk back to their cars, which had been strategically parked approximately a mile away. Their hopes for Saturday were big. The anticipation was incredible.

Conclusion

Overall, these two acts illustrate the significance of individual and group identities, the importance of embodiment, and the changing intersection of social constructs such as social class. The Acts highlight the possible utopian connotations of Acid House culture in the context of the developing Leeds scene of the late 1980s. As suggested previously, Critcher (2000, 146) defines Acid House as "no more than music associated with LSD." This chapter serves to highlight the richly textured sense of emotion and social relations that demonstrate Acid House was something much more than that. Instrumental to understanding the significance of Acid House culture for its followers is the manner in which the embodiment of space and place served to create geographical locations with significance beyond the expectation of mainstream society. What is salient with regard to the content of a possible Acid House utopia was its possibility to be an actual lived reality linked to lived experiences in these specific spaces and places. Thousands of people across the United Kingdom were able to undergo intense personal and interpersonal experiences linked to Acid House music. This lived reality therefore presents a situation that appears contrary to the assumption that utopias do not exist. It is proposed that in order to draw a greater understanding of these specific sites of social interaction and their possible link to utopia, an application of the concept of liminality might be considered in future research (Jaimangal-Jones, Pritchard, and Morgan 2010).

DISCOGRAPHY

Bomb the Bass. 1988. *Say a Little Prayer*. Rhythm King Records, UK. https://www.youtube.com/watch?v=LF559UnQ7zM.

Brothers in Rhythm. 1990. *Peace and Harmony*. 4th and Broadway, UK. http://www.youtube.com/watch?v=HGcjsmtsiQs.

Dream Frequency, 1991, Feel so Real, City Beat, UK [Digital audio file] Available from: http://www.youtube.com/watch?v=7cMMxH_oyUo [Accessed 16 January 2015]

Joe Smooth, 1987, Promised Land, DJ International Records, USA [Digital audio file] Available from: http://www.youtube.com/watch?v=Vo9x2y9MHbA [Accessed 16 January 2015]

The Prodigy, 1991, Your Love, XL Recordings, UK [Digital audio file] Available from: http://www.youtube.com/watch?v=zHPU2i9KPDk [Accessed 16 January]

Together, 1990, Hardcore Uproar, FFRR, UK [Digital audio file] Available from: http://www.youtube.com/watch?v=dYZiTQoSF9A [Accessed 16 January 2015]

NOTES

1. The title of this section is a reference to the Channel 4 television show *Location, Location, Location*, airing in the United Kingdom since 2000; the heading returns, altered, later in the chapter.

2. The Corn Exchange is a Grade One listed building (listed buildings are identified by English Heritage as having architectural and historical significance. A building classed as Grade One indicates a building has exceptional cultural and historic importance), originally constructed between 1861 and 1863 (www.victorianweb.org). It can be regarded as a remnant of the agricultural significance of Leeds. Located in the Kirkgate region of Leeds city center, situated on the junction of Call Lane and Duncan Street.

   Historically, the Call Lane area was associated with soliciting and prostitution (www.secretleeds.com) and was void of extensive commercial investment. In recent years, however, the area has been transformed through gentrification (Hollands and Chatterton 2003), with the development of fashionable wine bars, restaurants, and city-center residential accommodation.

REFERENCES CITED

Amsden, Benoni L., Richard C. Stedman, and Linda E. Kruger. 2011. "The Creation and Maintenance of Sense of Place in a Tourism-Dependent Community Leisure Studies." *Leisure Sciences* 33: 32–51.

Anthony, Wayne. 1998. *Class of 88: The True Acid House Experience*. London: Virgin.

Banerjee, Jacqueline. 2011. "The Corn Exchange, Leeds, by Cuthbert Brodrick (1821–1905)." *The Victorian Web*. http://www.victorianweb.org/art/architecture/brodrick/2.html.

Benzenhofer, Udo, and Torsten Passie. 2010. "Rediscovering MDMA (Ecstasy): The Role of the American Chemist Alexander T. Shulgin." *Addiction* 105: 1355–1361.

Bussmann, Jane. 1998. *Once in a Lifetime: The Crazy Days of Acid House and Afterwards*. London: Virgin.

Chakraborty, Kaustav, Rajarshi Neogi, and Debasish Basu. 2011. "Club Drugs: Review of the Rave with a Note for the Indian Scenario." *Indian Journal of Medical Research* 113: 594–604.

Charlesworth, Simon. 2000. "Bourdieu, Social Suffering and Working-Class Life." In *Reading Bourdieu on Society and Culture*, edited by Bridget Fowler, 49–64. Oxford: Blackwell.

Chatterton, Paul, and Robert Hollands. 2003. *Urban Nightscapes: Youth Cultures, Pleasure and Corporate Power*. London: Routledge.

Collin, Matthew, and John Godfrey. 1998. *Altered State: The Story of Ecstasy Culture and Acid House*. 2nd ed. London: Serpents Tail.

Critcher, Chas. 2000. "Still Raving: Social Reaction to Ecstasy." *Leisure Studies* 19(3): 145–162.

Crouch, David. 2000. "Places around Us: Embodied Lay Geographies in Leisure and Tourism." *Leisure Studies* 19(2): 63–76.

Denzin, Norman K. 1997. *Interpretive Ethnography: Ethnographic Practice for the 21st Century*. London: Sage.

Garratt, Sheryl. 1998. *Adventure in Wonderland: A Decade of Club Culture*. London: Headline.

Haslam, Dave. 1999. *Manchester, England: The Story of the Pop Cult City*. London: Fourth Estate.

Hebdige, Dick. 1979. *Subculture: The Meaning of Style*. London: Methuen.

Hook, Peter. 2010. *The Hacieda: How Not to Run a Club*. London: Pocket Books.

Jaimangal-Jones, Dewi, Annette Pritchard, and Nigel Morgan. 2010. "Going the Distance: Locating Journey, Liminality and Rites of Passage in Dance Music Experiences." *Leisure Studies* 29(3): 253–268.

Jansen, Karl. 1997. "Adverse Psychological Effects Associated with the Use of Ecstasy (MDMA) and Their Treatment." In *Ecstasy Reconsidered*, edited by Nicholas Saunders, 112–128. London: Nicholas Saunders.

Keane, Johnathan. 1997. "Ecstasy in the Unhappy Society." *Soundings* 6: 127–139.

Kempson, Michelle. 2015. "'I Sometimes Wonder Whether I'm an Outsider': Negotiating Belonging in Zine Subculture" *Sociology* 49: 1081–1095.

Kumar, Krishan. 1991. *Utopianism*. Milton Keynes: Open University Press.

Lashua, Brett. 2013. "Pop-up Cinema and Place Shaping: Urban Cultural Heritage at Marshall's Mill." *Journal of Policy Research in Tourism, Leisure and Events* 5(2): 123–138.

Levitas, Ruth. 2011. *The Concept of Utopia*. Oxford: Peter Lang.

Lynn, Matthew. 1991. "UK: Profile—Shami Ahmed, Managing Director of The Legendary Joe Bloggs Incorporated Company." *Management Today*, October 1. http://www.management-today.co.uk/news/408953/UK-Profile---Shami-Ahmed-managing-director-Legendary-Joe-BloggsIncorporated-Company/.

Malbon, Ben, 1999. *Clubbing: Dancing, Ecstasy and Vitality*. London: Routledge

McCrystal, Patrick, and Andrew Percy. 2010. "Factors Associated with Teenage Ecstasy Use." *Drugs: Education, Prevention and Policy* 17(5): 507–527.

Midgley, Mary. 2000. *Utopias, Dolphins and Computers Problems of Philosophical Plumbing*. London: Routledge.

Parker, Martin, ed. 2002. *Utopia and Organization*. Oxford: Blackwell.

Pilcher, Tim. 2008. *The Incredibly Strange History of Ecstasy*. London: Running Press.

Reynolds, Simon. 1997. "Rave Culture: Living Dream of Living Death?" In *The Subcultures Reader: Reading in Popular Cultural Studies*, edited by Steve Redhead, Derek Wynne, and Justin O'Connor, 84–93. Oxford: Blackwell.

Reynolds, Simon. 2008. *Energy Flash: A Journey through Rave Music and Dance Culture*. London: Picador.

Rill, Bryan. 2010. "Identity Discourses on the Dancefloor." *Anthropology of Consciousness* 21(2): 139–162.

Roberts, Brian. 2002. *Biographical Research*. Buckingham: Open University Press.

Roberts, Ken. 1999. *Leisure in Contemporary Society*. Oxford: CABI.

Saunders, Nicholas. 1997. *Ecstasy Reconsidered*. Exeter: Nicholas Saunders.

Thomas, Gareth. 2002. *This is Ecstasy*. London: Sanctuary.

Thornton, Sarah. 1995. *Club Cultures Music, Media and Subcultural Capital*. Oxford: Polity.

CHAPTER 22

....

RED LIGHT JAMS

A Place Outside of All Others

....

JOSEPH MICHAEL PIGNATO

INTRODUCTION

....

ALTHOUGH I have been making music for as long as I can remember, I didn't start taking playing seriously—that is to say, start thinking about myself as a musician or of music as a lifelong pursuit—until the 1980s, when I was in my early teens. A multitude of factors informed my pursuit of music and subsequent life as a musician. Few of those factors have been as influential as a series of jam sessions that I shared with one of my closest friends, Douglas Fried.

Doug and I were hardly unique for the times. Throughout the 1980s, American teens gathered in garages, basements, and bedrooms to play their favorite riffs, bang out beats, and preen rock star poses pilfered from music videos in heavy rotation on MTV. Donna Gaines (1998) explains the importance of rock music in the lives of New Jersey teenagers of the period: "The kids could learn most everything they needed to know about the meaning of life from their friends, their scene, and most important, their bands" (195).

In the intervening decades, much has been written about teen music making and about how amateur rock musicians learn to play (Bennett 1980; Campbell 1995; Green 2002). This chapter is not about how rock musicians learn to play music. For the most part I have omitted references to music learning or to repertoire, genre, or influential rock musicians. Although Doug and I certainly had our musical preferences, the focus here is a personal and collective consideration of why young people might gather in garages, basements, and bedrooms in the first place. I offer ways to understand what young people do in those contexts beyond music making; to honor, if you will, the importance of those activities too often overlooked as play, as teenage rebellion, or simplistically as kids being kids (Gaines 1998).

Roger Mantie (2013) commented that "if we wish to enhance people's potential for well-being and quality of life . . . , it behooves us to better understand music and/as leisure" (135).

For Doug and me, the Red Light Jams represented just that, an instance of music making as leisure that supported our well-being, improved the quality of our lives, and provided us with a space of our own. This chapter incorporates structured reminiscence (Bornat 2004; Webster and Haight 2002) and elements of narrative inquiry (Bochner 2012) to explain ways in which Doug and I attached meaning to and drew meaning from those sessions, and to consider our jam sessions as a constructed place that lingers in our memories to this day—one that Doug and I curated, ritualized, and demarcated as a place apart from, in opposition to, and unfettered by the constraints of our daily lives.

RED LIGHTS AND REMINISCENCE

I first met Doug in 1979, around the age of twelve, when we were enrolled in middle school. We attended the same suburban New Jersey secondary school where we grew closer—so much so that friends and family often joked that we were like twins. At the time of this writing, Doug and I have been friends, on and off, in and out of touch, for some thirty-six years. Our jam sessions took place early in that friendship, during a four-year span between 1981 and 1985. Although some of the sessions included other musicians, the jam sessions typically included just the two of us. Doug played electric guitar, and occasionally sang. I played drums.

During those four years, Doug and I jammed roughly one or two, sometimes three times a month. We have estimated that we shared roughly fifty to seventy-five total jam sessions. These jam sessions remain recurring points of reference in our lives. They serve as a kind of touchstone in our friendship, something about which Doug and I have reminisced and have come to understand as foundational to our lives as musicians, as people, and most certainly as friends. As Doug recently surmised during one of our many conversations, "Really, the Red Light Jams, they're probably the thing that most connects us to this day. It's like, that was our thing; still is, really."

Although Doug and I were inseparable throughout secondary school and even into college, separate lives, silly squabbles, and the demands of adult life led us apart. Between 1990 and 2002 we were, except for a few chance encounters, out of touch. During those years, Doug and I established our adult lives, our families, and our careers. Throughout, I often found myself thinking about the Red Light Jams, viewing them as one of the primary reasons I had become a musician, and as impetus to my maturation and eventually to my careers as a composer, player, record company executive, and, eventually, professor of music. As it turned out, Doug had come to understand the Red Light Jams in similar ways.

In 2002, Doug and I reconnected at a reunion of old school mates. Although one or two of them had participated in a few Red Light Jams, Doug spoke to me privately about the jams, referring to them as "our thing." In that conversation he shared a similar sense that the jams had been "something [he] returned to again and again" throughout his adult life. Since that reunion Doug has often shared with me ways in which he felt the

Red Light Jams helped him mature into the musician, music instructor, and "adult person" that he has become. According to Doug, the lessons learned during those experiences "guided him" as he formed and managed the business of several gigging bands. He recalled how the Red Light Jams informed his "improvising, general musicianship, and maybe most important, personal confidence." Despite living separate lives for more than a decade, Doug and I remained tethered by the shared experiences of the jams. Doug observed, "I know there were a couple of years where, you know, we didn't keep in touch, but there was still . . . there was still that connection that was always there, and a lot of that, I think was from the Red Light Jams."

About seven years ago, after Doug and I jammed with some friends at a party, I started thinking about exploring the themes in this chapter. After the party, Doug enthused that the impromptu jam session had been "almost like the Red Light Jams," full of freewheeling energy and uninhibited spirit. It dawned on me then that those jam sessions came up nearly every time Doug and I got together. Some of it was the nostalgia one might expect in the course of a lifelong friendship. Much of our adult friendship, however, focuses on our contemporary lives—our work, our families, our aging, how we wish we had more time to get together. Further, Doug and I shared many other experiences as youth, some that lasted longer than the Red Light Jams, including playing in bands with other friends, participating in school music programs, and maintaining a close-knit circle of friends. Neither of us has been particularly prone to "remember when" stories. In other words, in the course of our contemporary friendship, we do not generally reminisce. We do, however, reminisce about the Red Light Jams.

In addition to reminiscing about them when together, Doug and I each think about the jams frequently in our "everyday inner life" (Bornat 2004, 35). That the experiences of those jam sessions should recur in our inner thoughts suggests to me that they have enduring meaning in our lives. I reach these conclusions after much consideration, first through informal reminiscing and later through the more formalized methods described in this next section of the chapter.

REMINISCENCE AS METHOD

Structured reminiscence, often used in therapeutic contexts and in geriatric care (Bornat 2004; Gibson 2011; Haight and Haight 2007; Webster and Haight 2002), provided a method for making sense of our Red Light Jams. Structured reminiscence requires careful, directed considerations of remembered experience (Bornat 2004; Haight and Haight 2007; Webster and Haight 2002). Those facilitating such reminiscence usually seek a particular outcome, changes in behavior, improved mental health, or deeper understanding of meaningful experiences (Bornat 2004). I sought the latter—deeper understanding of the Red Light Jams as meaningful experiences.

With structured reminiscence in mind, I contacted Doug to organize the sessions that informed this study. I asked if he would be willing to consider thinking about the Red

Light Jams in a more systematic manner—systematic enough that we could formalize our understanding of the jams but flexible enough to allow the dynamics of our friendship to inform that understanding. Doug enthusiastically agreed. To start, I emailed Doug a list of general thoughts regarding the ways in which we collectively remembered, discussed, and expressed our views about the Red Light Jams. I arrived at that initial list based on the following: my own thoughts, recollections of things Doug had said over the years, and a review of some of our email exchanges from the past decade. After sending those initial thoughts, I asked Doug if they seemed on the mark, if they represented a fair, albeit preliminary, assessment of our feelings and experiences. I then invited Doug to contribute his own thoughts. After several months of trading email messages, a surprising degree of agreement became evident in our words, expressions, and clarifications.

After reviewing those exchanges, I organized discussion prompts for us to share electronically, first via email and then eventually in a series of voicemail messages, informal conversations, and a structured reminiscence session. I entered the prompts into my computer, randomly sorted them, and let them sit for a while so that I could return to them with a fresh mind, unencumbered by the process of preparing the text. After a few weeks, I reviewed the random prompts and spoke my responses into a recorder. Shortly after recording my responses, Doug shared his during a long telephone call. That call, which started as a kind of structured interview, finished as a collective reminiscence, structured by the prompts I had prepared earlier. Throughout the course of that conversation and in subsequent exchanges, we refined our reminiscences, compared our thoughts, and engaged in careful consideration of our own understandings, those of the other, and of various possible interpretations of our experiences—historically, contextually, and as personal narrative.

The results of those structured reminiscences are presented here, drawing on techniques commonly employed in an approach to qualitative research known as narrative inquiry (Bochner 2012; Clandinin 2006). In the past decade, many music education scholars have championed narrative inquiry as a means to "seek places and moments of intersection and reflection that help us understand ourselves and each other" (Barrett and Stauffer 2009, 2). Arthur Bochner (2012) identified five essential elements of narrative inquiry that distinguish it from traditional social science reporting. I relied heavily on each of those elements, paraphrased in the list below, throughout the preparation and writing of this chapter:

1. The chapter depends heavily on first person. Using first person provided me with "a way of telling about the social world" and the intertwined personal worlds that produced the Red Light Jams (Bochner 2012, 155).
2. The chapter chronicles the implications of a single case, The Red Light Jams, as they influenced our lives over the course of decades.
3. The chapter incorporates elements of my personal narrative, Doug's personal narrative, and our collective narrative.
4. At the core of this chapter are things deeply personal such as my youth, my love of music, and my enduring friendship with Doug.

5. Finally, the chapter details the "relationship experience" of that friendship as Doug and I lived "connected lives across the curve of time" (Bochner 2012, 158)

Although reliant on each of these elements, this chapter does not represent a strict formulation of narrative inquiry in the sense that I do not narrate the story of the Red Light Jams as much as report on them and my experiences as a participant. Similarly, I neither tell Doug's story nor share his complete narrative, but rather, I share those thoughts and expressions most germane to the purpose of understanding what, beyond music making, young people do in jam session contexts. I have identified Doug's words throughout the text. For some of the analysis, I have used shorthand in the form of initials, (D) for Doug and (J) for Joe, to distinguish our words from one another.

From Space to Place

Morton (2005) observes that "practice actively shapes the times and spaces of our world" (664). The thoughts, recollections, and expressions shared throughout this section reveal the degree to which Doug and I endowed a particular space with value, meaning, and experience (Tuan 1977). Through our actions, the utilitarian space of a basement took on new meanings and became something greater, a place of our own.

The Red Light Jams took place in a basement room of the suburban New Jersey home where I lived during my adolescence. The room, some 25 feet by 12 feet in area, occupied about a third of the total basement space. That area had been finished to provide additional recreational living space. The decor was relatively simple: low pile carpet laid directly over a cement floor; olive-colored wall paneling; an old dart board with no darts; a few crooked pictures; a dingy hopper window; a single light fixture; and mismatched furniture taken from each of my family's previous residences. The other two-thirds of the basement—storage, workshop, and utility space—played little role in setting the ambience for the Red Light Jams save for providing steady streams of dust and dank air.

In addition to the furnishings, the basement housed my first set of drums. There, I played, practiced, and listened to music, mostly by myself. To support those activities, I had a stereo turntable, speakers, and some portable cassette recorders to make primitive tapes of practice sessions and to experiment with multitrack recordings, sound effects recordings, and the occasional radio demo reel. Prior to meeting Doug, the basement was a somewhat solitary space; not lonely, just a place reserved for me to listen to music, think about music as well as life in general, and to practice drumming.

When we first started jamming, Doug, still reliant on rides from his parents, would bring an amplifier, a guitar, and eventually a microphone and speaker. We would carry the equipment from the trunk of his parents' automobile to the basement with determined grit. We always had great fun, but the space remained uninspiring. It was a musty old basement, a workaround to the fact that we had nowhere else to play. The *space* hadn't yet become a *place* unto itself.

One day, while listening to "Heart of the Sunrise," a particularly challenging tune from the progressive rock band Yes, I decided to shut the lights in the basement hoping to focus more deeply on the recording—not as a musical study but as a kind of transcendence. I wanted the music to transport and transform me away from suburban New Jersey and into the person I hoped to be. The lone window, a narrow rectangular hopper, peaked out just above ground level, yet it let in just enough daylight to prevent me from my lofty intensions. In a desperate attempt to realize my vision, I plugged the window frame with a cushion from the old sofa along the back wall. The room went dark, completely dark, which of course made it impossible for me to find my way to the stereo or to operate the turntable or to navigate the basement safely. The complete absence of light, although transformative, was wholly impractical.

About a week later, I was at one of the many malls that populated northern New Jersey. During a chance stop in the local head shop[1] to sift through psychedelic posters, I came upon a set of colored lightbulbs, red, green, and blue. I bought the set and took them home with the intent of listening to "Heart of the Sunrise" bathed in colored light; less distracting than white light and much safer than the inky darkness of my earlier attempt. After returning home, I switched the bulb out of the lighting fixture in the basement, turned the light on, and plugged the hopper window to shut out the daylight. At first I tried the blue bulb but it was too dark. Green light was hard on the eyes, almost as distracting as the sun's glare. The red bulb, my last hope, changed everything. The crimson glow impressed me deeply. I recall sitting there for a long while, on my drum throne, thinking, "Doug needs to experience this."

The next time Doug came over I told him about the red light, about how listening in that hued environment changed the way I felt about the music, about the basement itself, about everything. Doug and I switched the standard light bulb out for the red and began to jam. That session differed from earlier jams in scope, nature, and effect. We played much longer than we had in previous sessions. Doug recalled, "I remember our first Red Light Jam. You were so excited. At first I didn't really get it but then, it was like we just got lost in it. It drew me in." We began to play in a "liberated" (D) manner. Rather than rooting around for what to play or engaging in chatter about our gear, about school, or about anything outside that space, we began to make sounds. We just played. We listened, and more importantly, we began to hear in new ways. It was like "a completely new world had opened up" (J), one delineated from the world we had inherited. In order to appreciate the necessity of that "completely new world" in our lives, one must consider the time, the place, and the ethos of the world Doug and I inhabited.

PROUDER, STRONGER, BETTER

Wood, Duffy, and Smith (2007) note that "([p]erforming) places are material spaces with specific histories, locations, and fabrications. They provide acoustical contexts that are irretrievably entangled into particular social, cultural, economic, and political frames" (873). In the course of our reminiscing, Doug and I repeatedly referenced the time, place, and ethos of 1980s suburban New Jersey. Central to our experiences in that particular epoch were fears for the future. We recalled feeling pressured to grow up in ways reflective of our suburban surroundings, concerns about the threats posed by nuclear disaster, and tensions and crises within our families, at school, and among our social networks.

Doug described feeling a great deal of pressure: "well there was a lot of pressure, whether it was at school, or just kind of the messages we got at home, especially at that time, like about what we needed to become, as men, or whatever." Doug recalled conflicts between familial expectations for academic success and his burgeoning love of playing guitar:

> I had a tough time concentrating on school because I was falling in love with playing guitar and singing. Learning a new instrument through the Red Light Jams opened up a whole world to me and it was unexplored. There was so much music out there that I wanted to learn . . . I had more interest in music than school; however, my parents wanted me to concentrate on my school work to prepare me for college.

Pressure also figured into my understanding of the period:

> I remember always feeling a lot of pressure to grow up, which is something I guess a lot of teenagers feel, but it was like grow up to become a certain something or maybe someone. I remember feeling somewhat alienated by the suburban competition thing. Like you didn't count if you didn't buy in to the materialism or social status.

In the 1960s and '70s, Bergen County, the bucolic suburban area where Doug and I lived, transitioned from a rural, working-class enclave to tony hamlet, in large part due to segregative zoning laws that encouraged middle-class housing development (Kirp, Dwyer, and Rosenthal 1997), easily marketed in light of the area's proximity to New York City and the availability of commuter trains and express buses. Owing to a ban on sales tax for apparel and in response to the booming housing market, Bergen County became, at least during the 1980s, the shopping mall capital of the United States, with some half-dozen shopping malls clustered in the County's 25 square miles (Satterthwaite 2001). That rapid growth fueled an obsessive, even obscene, materialism manifest in unprecedented suburban sprawl, the proliferation of automobiles, and the development of shopping mall culture (Schulman 2009).

By the 1980s, Bergen County ranked among the most suburbanized areas in the United States (Kirp, Dwyer, and Rosenthal 1997). The local culture reflected a kind of nouveau riche mentality. Although Doug and I came from middle-class families, the enveloping affluence was rapidly leaving us, and many of our peers, behind. We felt alienated by the "plastic world of the mall" (J) and the "superficial values that seemed important to a lot of other kids" (D). Donna Gaines (1998) explored similar feelings of alienation in *Teenage Wasteland: Suburbia's Dead End Kids*, an ethnography of working-class teens living in 1980s Bergenfield, New Jersey, researched and written in the wake of

412   JOSEPH MICHAEL PIGNATO

the Bergenfield Suicide Pact, an incidence of group suicide that occurred just a few short miles from where Doug and I grew up.

U.S. president Ronald Regan's 1984 reelection campaign, encapsulated in the "morning in America" television advertisement, heralded the midpoint of the 1980s. The campaign, officially called "Prouder, Stronger, Better," hailed a decade of renewed economic vitality, social and cultural optimism, and unbounded promise for the United States (Living Room Candidate [1984] 2012). Like many official narratives, the America of Reagan's "Prouder, Stronger, Better" campaign stood in stark contrast to the lived experiences of many Americans (Gaines 1998; Kirp, Dwyer, and Rosenthal 1997; Troy and Cannato 2009). White suburban teens, such as Doug and me, had things relatively easy, for sure, and yet the dissonance of the official messaging reverberated through our lives, perhaps because we were expected to follow course, to follow the narrative, to make it real in our adult lives, to "buy in," literally and figuratively.

Those expectations and the discord they roused informed much of the popular culture of the day. In fact, some of the popular cultural products produced during those years engendered dual readings—one that questioned, challenged, or even undermined the "Prouder, Stronger, Better" narrative and another that affirmed and celebrated it (Troy and Cannato 2009). Notable examples include the following: (1) Grandmaster Flash's "Close to the Edge" (1982), an explicit entreaty to address the impacts of racializing legislation, white flight, and urban decay, which was received by suburban white teens as a kind of new rap chic after weeks of relentless exploitation of the song's vanguard video on MTV (Sullivan 2013); (2) New Jersey native Bruce Springsteen's song "Born in the USA" (1984), originally a sharp critique of postwar life as lived by a Vietnam veteran, that came to be confused, even to this day, by some American fans, as an ode to patriotism (Greenberg 2009); and (3) the film *Wall Street* (1987), Oliver Stone's rebuke of the era's materialism, which was widely received as a celebration of conspicuous wealth, avarice, and unscrupulous competition (Arango 2009).

The Red Light Jams provided Doug and me with a space in which we could set ourselves apart from the official narrative of "Prouder, Stronger, Better," from the blind patriotism of the era, and from the alienating materialism of 1980s Bergen County. Doug explained:

> We'd descend into this other word. Our world. We could just be ourselves during the Red Light Jams. I think it definitely had a huge impact on me, feeling different than some of the other kids, not feeling like you're lumped in with everybody else.

I concurred, adding, "yeah, feeling like something else, something somehow different from the way others viewed us, kids at school, our parents, our siblings, even other friends." In one reminiscence, Doug described the Red Light Jams in clearly oppositional terms to the political messaging of the day:

> I think the Red Light Jams were the antithesis of what the Reagan era represented. I was not a fan of a lot of the music during the Reagan era. I don't recall much

improvisation from popular music during this era and the popular music at the time seemed to focus on marketing towards specific consumer segments. To me, Reaganism discouraged creativity and going against the norm. The Red Light Jams were all about taking chances and spontaneity. Reaganism didn't want citizens to think for themselves and question authority. The jams were all about doing what we wanted to do, constantly creating.

A sense of impending doom informed our lives, fanned by the fallout from the Three Mile Island nuclear disaster, which occurred less than 200 miles away from our homes. There was also the very real threat of thermonuclear war with the Soviet Union, a threat we heard about in the news, in television programming, and at the movie theatre. Motion pictures like *War Games* (1983) and the made-for-television movie *The Day After* (1983), reflected the degree of anxiety that permeated the popular consciousness (Troy and Cannato 2009).

Jamming in the obscuring shade of the red light helped us feel "like we could be safe for a minute by forgetting about all of that stuff, which you heard every day on the news or in school" (J). Doug aptly explained the safe haven of the Red Light Jams:

> They enabled us to be in our own world and forget about any negativity that was going on in the outside world like the whole Red Scare period or Three Mile Island and fear of nuclear war. During the Red Light Jams, I was having so much fun and was so busy creating that I didn't think about anything that was going on above that basement. The music and our friendship were all that mattered. Nothing else entered my mind.

In addition to suspending our fears, the creative fervor and social bonding of those sessions generated hopefulness hard to come by in those days. I recalled that "I could step out of my fears and feel a kind of optimism that I couldn't find anywhere else."

Tuan (1997) suggests "people respond to space and place in complicated ways" (chap. 1, loc. 91). Fearful of our impending adulthood, troubled by a world that wasn't real but was sold to us regularly and relentlessly in our schooling, via the media, and in the culture at large, Doug and I responded. The Red Light Jams were our response, our action, our community of two, our world, and our alternative to the world beyond. They were our way to be us in defiance of, and yet wholly dependent on, the ethos of "Prouder, Stronger, Better."

CATHARSIS

György Lukács's assertion that artistic activity is essentially cathartic activity moves us toward deeper understanding of the Red Light Jams. Lukács argues that "every artistic effect evokes man's vital essence" and is "closely attached to a critique of life" (as cited in Baldacchino 2009, 122). Lukács describes artistic endeavors as being dependent on "the central content of that 'world' which the work of art evidently reveals to its recipient" (Baldacchino 2009, 122). Jamming in the altered space established by the red light allowed us to evoke our vital essence as it existed in the early '80s and as we hoped it would develop in our futures. Just the same, Doug and I established the virtual space of the Red Light Jams as a kind of critique of our lives and of those we were expected to live. In setting ourselves apart from the expectations of the world in which we lived, we revealed new worlds of musical, emotional, and maturational possibilities as well as possibilities for our friendship.

Bela Kiralyfalvi (1990) expands on Lukács's notion of catharsis, describing it as "a moving and shaking effect that purges our passions and readies our souls" (23). The Red Light Jams represented *our* world, revealed to us, by us, through the act of uninhibited music making. In the process, session by session, the Red Light Jams provided Doug and me with a means to purge the expectations of our impending adulthood, to redefine ourselves; to paraphrase Kiralyfalvi, to make our souls ready for a life we wanted but couldn't wholly envision.

The refuge the Red Light Jams provided for us was more than figurative. In a personal reminiscence session, I described the Red Light Jams as alternatives to more troubling possibilities readily available to two teenagers in varying degrees of crisis:

> Doug and I had some serious strife at home, stuff that I'd rather not go into for this project but . . . let's just say we had reason to look for release and we could have, and both of us flirted with getting into some serious trouble; drinking, drugs, even potential violence. The Red Light Jams were somehow a better alternative, a way to say, "all's not right in the world, but we'll make it alright, at least right now, here, and in this space." We didn't think of the Red Light Jams as an alternative to other vices, if you will, but I think our own trepidation about more pernicious pursuits made the Red Light Jams more desirable, a place to release, safe for *purgative* expression. It's like we held our ground against so many external forces. Doug had his. I had mine. Some things we didn't even discuss for years until we were well into adulthood. But we knew, in a certain way. We sensed struggle, but also an overcoming, a—hmmm—maybe victory's not the best word, maybe small, and even sometimes grand triumphs of our spirits. The jams enabled those triumphs, even if what we were triumphing over remained unspoken.

Doug noted similar thoughts regarding the cathartic function of the Red Light Jams in his own reminiscences. On numerous occasions he recalled ways in which the jam sessions helped him cope with pressure in his adolescent life. To this day, Doug still models that purging catharsis in his adult life as he approaches fifty years of age:

> Well, you know, then and now, and every time I sit down to play guitar, and I know you have this too [chuckling], you forget about—well you know, at first, you're trying to get lost with it and eventually you do. It's a process. You forget about all the tension and things that are going on in your life; things that are negative. Whatever was going on back then—kids you didn't like, stuff at home, if the parents were, you know,

driving you crazy over something or getting on you. Especially, when you're in high school as you're approaching graduation, you're thinking about college, careers, and that's some scary stuff. Doing those Red Light Jams, playing music helped me. Even now, you know, just as an adult, thinking about the stresses of things going on with my kids, with their lives, things that are just, whether it's school for them, bills, any family stresses, in-laws and things like that, you know playing music now, and referring back to the Red Light Jams, I'll get lost within the music and forget about current day stresses as a 47-year-old person [chuckling], almost 50! [laughing loudly]

The Red Light Jams afforded us a mode of purgative catharsis that protected us, nurtured our developing identities, and expedited our maturation—as musicians, as friends, as human beings.

A PLACE OUTSIDE OF ALL OTHERS

Tuan (1977) notes that " 'space' is more abstract than 'place.' What begins as undifferentiated space becomes place as we get to know it better and endow it with value" (chap. 1, loc. 115). Collectively, Doug and I transformed that musty basement into what David Cleaver (2009, 40) calls a "lived musical space." The physical space of the basement was anchored in one world; that of Bergen County, New Jersey, of my family home, and of the existential contradictions of suburban life. The symbolic shift ushered in by the aura of a single red bulb was seismic. The new space encouraged musical doing, living, interacting, and bonding that removed us from the world to which we were otherwise bound, and allowed us to create what Foucault (1986, 24) calls, "a place outside of all places."

Symbolic "acts of meaning" (Bruner 1990) helped further delineate the Red Light Jams as a kind of virtual place, each of us acting for the other as much as for ourselves. I explained:

> I could be someone there, who I couldn't be elsewhere, at least early on. So during the Red Light Jams, I could try on personae, largely by mimicking my idols at the time, but in mimicking them, sort of trying them on for size but also for Doug's ears, to see how he responded, I was finding my own thing but also trying to figure out what our thing was exactly.

Doug recalled prodding me in similar ways: "I think I tried things there as much because I wanted to get better on guitar as I wanted to see if they'd fly there, like 'this is more than jamming in the red, we're building something' or maybe going somewhere, whatever. If you responded, I knew it was worth pursuing."

By trying on things for size, provoking the other, following the other's lead, Doug and I grew as musicians and as friends. Those actions, reactions, and the growth they encouraged allowed us to establish a space reflective of our aspirations as musicians, of our deepening friendship, and of the people we hoped to become. The basement transformed from the bowels of my home into a kind of self-contained, self-generating sphere of experience. By jamming in the red light and playing in ways more experimental, more representative of our desired personae, and more interactive, we established our "place outside all other places" (Foucault 1986, 24).

In the past, I have written about intentionality as "the nexus of inner mental processes and outward engagement of the world" (Pignato 2013, 9). In establishing the practice of and the virtual place that became the Red Light Jams, Doug and I engaged one another as well as the social worlds that surrounded us in determined and declarative ways. Tuan (1977) observes that "space and place are basic components of the lived world; we take them for granted. When we think about them, however, they may assume unexpected meanings and raise questions we have not thought to ask" (chap. 1, loc. 69). The Red Light Jams were our way of thinking about space and place—about the world we inherited and an idealized world we desired, one where we could be free from the pressures, fears, and constraints of our everyday lives.

Liberation emerged as another recurring theme in our reminiscences and exchanges. Doug and I referred to the Red Light Jams using words, phrases, and descriptors such as: "it was just like a feeling of freedom" (D); "no inhibitions" (J); "a place where you could just, you know not be afraid" (D); "completely liberating" (J). Doug expounded on the liberating nature of the sessions: "It was like it's an escape. I would go down your basement and it was just me and you, you know, we didn't have to think about college, or careers, or money, or issues with our families, or friends, or anything like that. In the Red Light Jams, we were free to be."

It was a symbiotic sense of liberation; we were free but we were in that freedom together and depended on one another to create that haven. The ways in which we felt connected permeated our personal reminiscences and our shared conversations. For example, in my personal reminiscence session I commented that "Doug and I were like brothers, we looked alike, hung together, and fiercely protected one another from turmoil at home, at school, in the day-to-day of being a teenager."

This inclination to look out for one another motivated us to create an enclave, a shelter from a world that otherwise scared the heck out of us. My comments during a personal reminiscence revealed a kind of survival mentality that often bubbled under the surface of our forays into the Red Light Jams and of our contemporary recollections of those experiences. I remarked, "I think without music, without the Red Light Jams, I could have gone in a really different direction, and I sensed that at the time; Doug too, I imagine . . . so there was this whole existential element to what we were doing. It's like, we need this to survive."

That basement awash in red light became our personal version of what Foucault calls a "crisis heterotopia" (1986, 24). Although speaking about the social function of heterotopias, Foucault described crisis heterotopias in terms apropos to our experience:

> There is a certain form of heterotopia that I would call crisis heterotopias, i.e., there are privileged or sacred or forbidden places, reserved for individuals who are, in relation to society and to the human environment in which they live, in a state of

crisis: adolescents, menstruating women, pregnant women, the elderly, etc. In our society, these crisis heterotopias are persistently disappearing, though a few remnants can still be found. (Foucault 1986, 24)

Doug and I, two adolescents in the midst of family, life, and existential crises, created a privileged, sacred, and forbidden place to take control of our relationship to society and to the human environment in which we lived. Red Light Jamming represented a kind of ritualized affirmation of the ways in which Doug and I protected, supported, and loved one another. The basement site transcended its utilitarian purpose and became a space to which we could retreat to express ourselves in ways that we could not with others such as our parents or siblings, our peers, people at school, or anyone else, for that matter, who comprised our teenaged social contacts.

Inherent to the leisure music making of the Red Light Jams were what Bruner (1990) calls "acts of meaning," ways for Doug and I to mark our territory, to set boundaries around *our* identities, *our* music, *our* place. Joyful acts of music making, playing, exploring, and friendship transformed the physical structure of the basement into an amorphous sea of meaning upon which we could drift free from the restrictions of our lives. Those same acts transformed the way we came to understand ourselves. Bruner (1990) notes that young people have "the ability to mark not only what is culturally canonical but to account for deviations that can be incorporated into narrative" (68). The Red Light Jams have endured as important parts of our individual and collective narratives. They allowed us to defy various forces not merely in an act of youthful rebellion but as ritualized, oppositional, and purgative catharsis.

GROWING UP

Tuan (1977) describes certain experience as "the overcoming of perils" (chap. 1, loc. 162). Doug and I created a space in which we could confront the perils, real or perceived, of our adolescence. In so doing, we developed coping skills that we have carried into our adult lives. The refuge provided by the Red Light Jams allowed us to mature in ways we would not have done otherwise. Throughout our reminiscence sessions, themes of maturation recurred. Doug and I used words like "grew" (D) and "matured" (J), or phrases like "we really developed," (D) and "we became adults" (J) to make sense of the impact of the Red Light Jams on our lives. Teasing out our maturation as individuals, the growth of our identities, and the improvement of our musicianship was difficult. Our reminiscences often intertwined those elements, so much so that they really appeared as a single recurring theme, one with multiple layers.

Doug and I came from musical families. My mother was a piano teacher, and many of my uncles, cousins, and family friends performed music regularly. My grandparents often hosted jam sessions of their own, parties that featured musicians from the Neapolitan diaspora, playing the music of southern Italy for hours on end. Those parties provided an audience for me, a measure against which I could make sense of my growth as a musician. The Red Light Jams helped me earn musical currency that had value beyond feeling like a better musician. I recalled:

> The more I could be me, my musical self, the perceived musician, or the musician I perceived that I wanted others to perceive in me; the more I could port that identity beyond the glow of the red light, first into interactions with the other musicians in my family, uncles, cousins, all of whom played music in some way, some quite well. I could hang with them, so to speak. Sure, I played a different kind of music, but I had a knowledge, or currency, I could share with them that I wouldn't have had otherwise. Hours of Red Light Jams helped me earn that currency.

Doug reported similar experiences. His mother was an organist and his family regularly gathered around a huge Wurlitzer electric organ for sing-alongs. Doug, to this day one of the best musicians I know, played multiple instruments. Although he was primarily a guitarist, he was a heck of a drummer, could dabble on keyboards, and sang. Today, he teaches private guitar lessons, private drum lessons, performs at senior centers around northern New Jersey, and works in a regularly gigging band, The Harmony Brothers, performing rock music from the 1960s, '70s, '80s, and '90s. Doug reminisced about ways in which the Red Light Jams prepared him for a life in music:

> It led to my feeling comfortable improvising. I guess, for example, most of the time when I play a guitar solo I, you know, I just make it up. I usually don't create the solo ahead of time, you know, I don't take the solo directly from the record. Just tell me the key and I'll go with it, and I think the Red Light Jams gave me the confidence; well I didn't know it at the time, that it was confidence, and I just kind of did it but as we did it, and we enjoyed it and it was fun, and I knew it was fun; it felt good. It felt right and as time went on, the better I got as a musician, the more experience I had as a musician over time; the Red Light Jams were something I could draw back and know that it was kind of the birthplace. . . . I think a lot of that stuff is derivative of the Red Light Jams.

The ways in which the Red Light Jams played an important role in our development as musicians and as people did not go unnoticed. For example, for every successive achievement in my career as a composer, drummer, or professor of music, my father likes to joke, "I guess you and Doug were doing more than just playing around in the basement."

Doug believes we were doing something more in that basement: concentrating, learning, and acting in a particularized manner. Doug used language to describe our efforts that were remarkably consistent with scholarly literature on how rock musicians develop (e.g., Bennett 1980; Campbell 1995; Green 2002). The Red Light Jams "took such concentration, but *free* concentration; not stressful concentration, but *fun* concentration," Doug explained. In discussing how the Red Light Jams informed our musicianship, Doug and I referred back to the fact that we were "absolute beginners, rank amateurs"

(J), when we started. Doug identified our amateur status as part of the appeal, as well as a defining feature of the Red Light Jams: "It's weird, because we didn't know what we were doing but yet it didn't matter anyway because we young and naïve. We . . . I guess, I don't know, there was some sort of confidence that we had too that we were like, 'well, what the heck?' You know, if we made a mistake, 'big deal.'" I expressed a similar sentiment: "Well, we wanted to be musicians but that wasn't really what motivated us. It was like, we just kind of did it [the Red Light Jams] to do it. No other reason other than it was fun, and, you know, our friendship."

Mantie (2012) has written on the ways in which music making for no particular purpose other than the "joy of participation" has been undervalued in music teaching and learning. Mantie explains, "[I]f you cannot *do* to the exacting standards of the professional there is apparently little point in trying. Many amateurs quickly realize they can never hope to 'learn' enough to reach a professional level, and because participation for its own sake is insufficient there is little point in partaking in amateur music-making" (228). Although Doug and I developed careers in music, I think that participating in amateur music making would have been just as important in our lives had we ended up pursuing other endeavors. Doug has worked in other fields, sometimes for years on end, and yet "a relationship with music or finding people to play with, or just jamming for the joy of it remained a constant" (D).

The Red Light Jams provided all the practical challenges of a bandstand minus the risks of an audience. We were bound to learn something from the sessions. However, learning was less an aim of the Red Light Jams than it was an inevitable consequence. Gareth Dylan Smith (2013) describes learning and identity in adolescent music making as entangled entities, two forces parrying, embracing, and ultimately melding in the contextualized spheres of practice. In a personal reminiscence session, I described learning as a byproduct of the Red Light Jams, dependent on the personal growth, maturation, and bonding the sessions engendered:

> Sure, we were developing our abilities to play music, to improvise, to negotiate creative differences, to write songs, but we were also becoming us, I, me, we. We were becoming rock musicians, but, in a way, that was kind of a byproduct, there was a more global sense, we supported one another on the path to becoming musicians, but more so to becoming adult human beings, individuals with a clear sense of identity. Yeah, so I think those things, our friendship, the way we matured individually but always in response to one another, were most important.

The notion that we responded to one another, considered the reactions of the other to all we did during the Red Light Jams, underscores the interdependency of the relationship. We needed the other to feel like ourselves, to construct meaning in and for the Red Light Jams, and to distance ourselves from the world that surrounded us.

Doug and I carried those selves with us as we interacted with our musical families, with other musicians in our community, and on into and throughout our adult lives. During a personal reminiscence session, I recalled being asked to play a gig in high school. I attributed my willingness to accept the gig to the experiences of the Red Light Jams:

> We had an acquaintance at school, really talented, but not someone we played with. Vinny eventually went on to a wildly successful career as a producer, musical director, and DJ. At any rate, his musical director skills were evident as early as the tenth grade. Vinny "hired" all of us to play a formal gig at a school function. Real public, like a lot of our peers, teachers, everyone. I don't think he wanted my drumming skills as much as he wanted me because I had electronic drums, which were all the rage in the 80s. Still, if it weren't for the Red Light Jams, I would not have believed I could play that gig, which required reading, playing tunes I was unfamiliar with, and improvising. That he wanted us to play with him was an affirmation that the work done during the Red Light Jams had repercussions in our local musician community

Doug reported similar feelings, not just during our high school years, but also in the present, as he pursues his music teaching, gigging, and related activities:

> Those experiences made me feel probably different than the other kids in the high school . . . and even like other musicians . . . I guess almost unique, you know, like an individual. I guess as a teen, that's always a big thing too. You always want that feeling of just being different or your own stamp of identity so that was definitely something that was a big impact. As a teen and as you're growing and trying to find yourself and who you are. . . . I don't know if you ever really know who you are (laughs) but, you know, during that time, I think it had a huge impact on me. That's what it means to me today too. I think also just the idea of knowing that we were young then but not afraid to try things. I think just for myself now, you know, I have some students that I teach and I try to encourage them to take the same approach.

In addition to viewing ourselves as musicians, learning how to play, and expressing our identities, Doug and I coalesced as friends in a way and to a degree that we might not have done otherwise. Doug explained, "I think also the connection, you know, with you, not just musically but, you know, our friendship. I think it got us closer as friends. It really connected us and connects us to this day."

CONCLUSIONS

In a recent email exchange, Doug summed up his feelings about the Red Light Jams: "everything was so new and exciting. I recall how inspired I was, yet I barely knew anything about the guitar. Everything was uncharted territory." The thoughts, expressions, and analyses provided in this chapter reflect an unraveling of experiences that, although distant in time and place, remain vital, constant, and informative in our current lives. I hope that this chapter, and the processes that led to its inclusion in this volume, have charted some of that territory—for Doug, for me, and for a better general understanding of the transformative power of understanding music as leisure. The following summative statements reflect the conclusions Doug and I reached during our personal and structured reminiscence sessions. The Red Light Jams:

1. had meaning that transcended the actual experiences;
2. provided refuge for catharsis and purgative expression;
3. informed our developing identities;
4. facilitated our developing musicianship;
5. solidified and provided a foundation for a lifelong friendship;
6. continue to inform our identities, our musicianship, and our friendship;
7. serve as a touchstone reference in our individual and collective narratives.

Although this chapter has been presented in a personal tone, I hope the recollections, reminiscing, and storytelling offer insights that extend beyond Doug's life and mine. Substituting the words "music as leisure," the titular focus of this volume, for the words "Red Light Jams" in the list provided above, reveals that the conclusions have some transferability beyond our personal experiences. Our conclusions illustrate the potential of jamming, a kind of recreational music making, as personal and social meaning making. There are many ways one might develop an identity, improve one's musicianship, seek cathartic release, negotiate complex personal and social worlds, and develop lifelong relationships. Music as leisure, at least in our lives but perhaps in a more general sense, brought all of these things together.

NOTE

1. A specialized retail shop that sells smoking paraphernalia and related ephemera.

REFERENCES CITED

Arango, Tim. 2009. "Greed Is Bad, Gekko. So Is a Meltdown." *New York Times*, September 7. www.nytimes.com/2009/09/08/movies/08stone.html?pagewanted=all&_r=0.

Baldacchino, John. 2009. *Education beyond Education: Self and the Imaginary in Maxine Greene's Philosophy*. New York: Peter Lang.

Barrett, Margaret S., and Sandra L. Stauffer, eds. 2009. *Narrative Inquiry in Music Education: Troubling Certainty*. New York: Springer.

Bennett, H. Stith. 1980. *On Becoming a Rock Musician*. Amherst: University of Massachusetts Press.

Bochner, Arthur, P. 2012. "On First-Person Narrative Scholarship: Autoethnography as Acts of Meaning." *Narrative Inquiry* 22:155–164.

Bornat, Joanna. 2004. "Oral History." In *Qualitative Research Practice*, edited by Clive Seale, Giampietro Gobo, Jaber F. Gubrium, and David Silverman, 34–47. New York: Sage Publications.

Bruner, Jerome. 1990. *Acts of Meaning*. Cambridge, MA: Harvard University Press.

Campbell, Patricia Shehan. 1995. "Of Garage Bands and Song-Getting: The Musical Development of Young Rock Musicians." *Research Studies in Music Education* 4(1): 12–20.

Cleaver, David. 2009. "Storying the Musical Lifeworld: Illumination Through Narrative Case Study." In *Narrative Inquiry in Music Education: Troubling Certainty*, edited by Margaret S. Barrett and Sandra L. Stauffer, 35–56. New York: Springer.

Clandinin, Jean D. 2006. "Narrative Inquiry: A Methodology for Studying Lived Experience." *Research Studies in Music Education* 27: 44–54.

Foucault, Michel. 1986. "Of Other Spaces." Translated by Jay Miskowiec. *Diacritics* 16(1): 22–27.

Gaines, Donna. 1998. *Teenage Wasteland: Suburbia's Dead End Kids*. Chicago: University of Chicago Press.

Gibson, Faith. 2011. *Reminiscence and Life Story Work: A Practice Guide*. 4th ed. Philadelphia, PA: Jessica Kingsley.

Grandmaster Flash. 1982. "The Message." On *The Message*. Sugar Hill Records SH-584. LP.

Green, Lucy. 2002. *How Popular Musicians Learn: A Way Ahead for Music Education*. Aldershot: Ashgate.

Greenberg, Steve. 2009. "Where is Graceland? 1980s Pop Culture through Music." In *Living in the Eighties (Viewpoints on American Culture)*, edited by Gil Troy and Vincent J. Cannato, 152–166. New York: Oxford University Press.

Haight, Barbara K., and Barrett S. Haight. 2007. *The Handbook of Structured Life Review*. Baltimore, MD: Health Care Professions Press.

Kiralyfalvi, Bela. 1990. "The Aesthetic Effect: A Search for Common Grounds between Brecht and Lukács." *Journal of Dramatic Theory and Criticism* 4(2):19–30.

Kirp, David L., John P. Dwyer, and Larry A. Rosenthal. *Our Town: Race, Housing, and the Soul of Suburbia*. New Brunswick, NJ: Rutgers University Press.

Living Room Candidate. (1984) 2012. "Prouder, Stronger, Better." *Museum of the Moving Image*. http://www.livingroomcandidate.org/commercials/1984/prouder-stronger-better.

Mantie, Roger. 2012. "Learners or Participants? The Pros and Cons of 'Lifelong Learning.'" *International Journal of Community Music* 5(3): 217–235.

Mantie, Roger. 2013. "Music and/as Leisure: Old Wine in New Bottles?" *International Journal of Community Music* 6:135–139.

Morton, Frances. 2005. "Performing Ethnography: Irish Traditional Music Sessions and New Methodological Spaces." *Social and Cultural Geography* 6: 661–676.

Pignato, Joseph. 2013. "Angelica Gets the Spirit Out: Improvisation, Epiphany and Transformation." *Research Studies in Music Education* 35: 25–38.

Satterthwaite, Ann. 2001. *Going Shopping: Consumer Choices and Community Consequence*. New Haven, CT: Yale University Press.

Schulman, Bruce J. 2009. "The Privatization of Everyday Life: Public Policy, Public Services, and Public Space in the 1980s." In *Living in the Eighties (Viewpoints on American Culture)*, edited by Gil Troy and Vincent J. Cannato, 167–180. New York: Oxford University Press.

Smith, Gareth Dylan. 2013. *I Drum, Therefore I Am: Being and Becoming a Drummer*. Farnham: Ashgate.

Springsteen, Bruce. 1984. "Born in the USA." On *Born in the USA*. Columbia Records CCK 38653. LP.

Sullivan, Caroline. 2013. "How We Made: Jiggs Chase and Ed Fletcher on The Message." *The Guardian*, February 27. http://www.theguardian.com/music/2013/may/27/how-we-made-the-message.

The Day After. 1983. Directed by Nicholas Meyer. Burbank, CA: ABC Circle Films.

Troy, Gil, and Vincent J. Cannato, eds. 2009. *Living in the Eighties (Viewpoints on American Culture)*. New York: Oxford University Press.

Tuan, Yi-Fu. 1977. *Space and Place: The Perspective of Experience*. Minneapolis: University of Minnesota Press.

Wall Street. 1987. Directed by Oliver Stone. New York: American Film Partners.

War Games. 1983. Directed by John Badham. Santa Monica, CA: Metro Goldwyn Mayer.

Webster, Jeffrey D., and Barbara K. Haight, eds. 2002. *Critical Advances in Reminiscence Work: From Theory to Application*. New York: Springer.

Wood, Nichola, Michelle Duffy, and Sandra J. Smith. 2007. "The Art of Doing (Geographies of) Music." *Environmental Planning D* 25: 867–889.

Yes. 1971. "Heart of the Sunrise," written by Jon Anderson, Chris Squire, Bill Bruford, and Rick Wakeman. On *Fragile*. Atlantic Records 2401019. LP.

CHAPTER 23

....

THE BEAT OF A DIFFERENT DRUMMER

Music Making as Leisure Research

....

BRETT LASHUA

IN this chapter I report on joining different groups of popular musicians as a drummer and a researcher. From my drummer-researcher's perspective in those groups, I conducted ethnographic fieldwork. This approach adopts Veal's (2006, 202) advice to leisure researchers that "becoming part of the group is the obvious way of studying the group." Such an approach starts from the supposition that music making allows unique perspectives on leisure spaces, communities, and people's everyday lives. Although scholarship has addressed the relations between music and leisure (Bennett 2005; Lashua 2013; Spracklen 2014; Stebbins 1996), I argue that researching and writing from within the group (of musicians) affords unique views that resonate with the shift toward local, fine-grained explorations of popular music making (Baker, Bennett, and Homan 2009). For example, Forsyth and Cloonan (2008, 58) argued that popular music studies have "moved in recent years away from concentration on big artists . . . to looking at the work of the vast majority of musicians who never make the big time but are vital components of popular music at a local level." That is, such views show how important and meaningful music making is in people's everyday leisure lives, identities, and communities (DeNora 2000). Exploring the everyday spatial relations of music making as leisure also spotlights the changing city.

This chapter draws from four years (2007–2011) of ethnographic fieldwork on music making in Liverpool.[1] I am originally from the United States, and when I moved to Liverpool in 2007 I was immediately caught up in the "contagious magic" (Roberts 2014) of its musical character. Liverpool has a rich musical heritage and thriving contemporary scenes (Barna 2011; Cohen 2007; Inglis 2009; Leonard and Strachan 2010). People and places in these scenes are mutually constituent; as people shape places, so too do places shape the possibilities for people's identities and everyday leisure experiences. Taking the nexus of music making, place, and identity as its central frame, I illustrate these "places and faces" through an EP-style[2] track listing (see Lashua 2007), offering a sampler of music projects in which I participated.

After two introductory "tracks" that describe Liverpool and the ethnographic approaches employed in the research, the third track showcases a song I recorded with a folk singer-songwriter. A paean to Liverpool Football Club's heritage, the song mourns the loss of the club's local, working-class roots and celebrates an alternative, fan-owned version of the team. The song exemplifies Liverpool's quintessential leisure character, combining music, football, and working-class political activism. The fourth track highlights another Liverpool legacy, relating music making and leisure to the politics of youth, place, and "race" (Lashua 2013; Lashua and Owusu 2013). I use this track to trace the exclusion of "urban music" (e.g., rap, soul, R'n'B, hip-hip, grime, dubstep) from Liverpool's city-center venues by focusing on an annual urban youth and street culture event called HUB Festival, at which I performed with a hip-hop group in 2009. The fifth track explores music making and leisure through rehearsal spaces in one cluster of the city's indie rock scene. Here I argue—in addition to the neglected experiences of drummers as foci in popular music and leisure studies—rehearsal spaces also offer fantastic, if undervalued, opportunities to explore the relations of music making, leisure, cities, and social identities (see also Bell, this volume, chapter 5). I conclude the EP by making further conceptual and summary links between leisure research and becoming a member of "the group" in terms of meaningful places of practice and play.

TRACK 1: LIVERPOOL: "WONDROUS PLACE"?

Liverpool is widely renowned as a musical city (Cohen 1991, 2007) and a creative city (Grunenberg and Knifton 2007). The music journalist Paul Du Noyer (2007) characterized Liverpool as a "wondrous place" of unique musicality. For Leonard and Strachan (2010, 1), "Liverpool both imagines and projects itself as a creative city. Within this imagining there is an underlying assumption that there is something special about Liverpool as a place which gives rise to this creativity and has an immutable effect upon the shape it takes." Higginson and Wailey (2006) argue this musical creativity stems from the city's geographic and cultural "edginess" as a port. Situated on the River Mersey in the northwest of England, the city has long musical traditions, fuelled by waves of immigration and the ebb and flow of people through its port (Brown 2005; Du Noyer 2007). In the early 1960s, the city became internationally famous as the home of the Beatles; other well-known Liverpool artists from around this time include Cilla Black, Billy Fury, Gerry and the Pacemakers, and numerous groups that soon fell under the "Merseybeat" moniker. Later waves of popular groups have burst from the city's lively scenes, including post-punk groups in the late 1970s and early 1980s, and dance music in the 1990s (Leonard and Strachan 2010).

Cities such as Liverpool are not static but are constantly changing, and music can be very much a part of these changes (Cohen 2007); Liverpool's urban character is both a product of its unique musical heritage and productive of new scenes and sounds. The music geographer Chris Gibson (Connell and Gibson 2003) quipped that people cannot move to Liverpool without joining a band; being a musician there is like a civic membership card. Cohen (1991, 1) commented that Liverpool was a city where "many people seemed either to be in a band themselves or to know someone who was in a band, and where many of those not in bands spent much of their time talking of forming or joining one." Roberts (2014) described this impulse to join in as a kind of "contagious magic" where, by virtue of coming into contact with the city (e.g., visiting sites where Lennon and McCartney once performed) its musicality "rubs off" or transfers to others. That is, simply being in Liverpool compels people to make music. When I arrived in 2007, I too found a frenetic energy; there was not only a rich geographical terrain for music making (e.g., a variety of pubs, clubs, and other venues), but also it seemed that almost everyone I met was a musician of some sort, offering a range of opportunities to collaborate and create. I drew from my experience as a drummer[3] and also joined in, captured by Liverpool's magic.

Track 2: Drum Tracks: A Drummer-as-Ethnographer

Popular music drummers are often seen as trivial band members, merely supplying a backbeat from the backseat of the group: many drummers tend to be unseen, unheard, and unknown (Smith 2013). Even within popular music studies there has been a limited amount of research about drummers and drumming (Brennan 2013; Mowitt 2002; Smith 2013). Drummers are often stereotyped as nonmusicians, like Ringo Starr, widely perceived as the least musical of the Beatles (e.g., John Lennon once joked that Ringo was not even the best drummer in the Beatles). When drummers do receive wider recognition, it is often not for their musicality. Iconic rock drummers, such as Ringo, Keith Moon (The Who), Charlie Watts (the Rolling Stones), and John Bonham (Led Zeppelin) are seen as jesters, oddballs, or fools; jokes about "dumb drummers" are as legendary and derogatory as jokes about "dumb blondes." Other views essentialize drummers as primitive brute animals, behaving wildly behind and beyond their drums (like the character "Animal" of the Muppets). However, as Smith (2013) argues, drummers are worthy of serious scholarly attention, and drummers contribute to the "art worlds" (Becker 1982) of music making and creative leisure. This track spotlights my position as drummer and as a leisure researcher, where the perception of sitting in the "backseat" (see Figure 23.1) allowed me a fantastic position from which to practice ethnographic research.

Ethnographic methods were not commonly employed in popular music studies until the 1980s (Bennett 2002). Ruth Finnegan's (1989) study of the everyday "hidden" practices of musicians in Milton Keynes, and Sara Cohen's (1991) research in Liverpool are

FIGURE 23.1 My drummer's-eye view while performing with a Liverpool hip-hop artist during the 2009 HUB Festival on Liverpool's Wellington Dock. (Credit: Brett Lashua)

landmark ethnographic studies. For Cohen, ethnographic approaches to music making offer important views because ethnographers aim:

> to learn the culture or sub-culture they are studying and come to interpret or experience it in the same way that those involved in that culture do, that is, to discover the way in which their social world or reality is constructed, and how particular events acquire meaning for them in particular situations. (1993, 124)

This aim is important because, rather than trying to understand how a culture or society objectively views musicians, ethnographers seek to understand how musicians subjectively make sense of their own social worlds. As Cohen elaborates, this fieldwork approach requires that researchers spend "a lengthy period of intimate study and residence with a particular group of people," and need "knowledge of the spoken language," which includes musicians' technical jargon as well as slang. Fieldwork involves "the employment of a wide range of observational techniques, including prolonged face-to-face contacts with members of the local group, direct participation in some of that group's activities, and a greater emphasis on intensive work with informants" (Cohen 1993, 124). My experience as a drummer allowed me to consider the importance of the many mundane moments of "being in the group" that would be interesting and insightful to observe. These included regular and routine (and thus easily overlooked) practices such as rehearsals and the "sound check" before a live performance (Lashua and Cohen 2010). These were moments and places I knew were important to the daily social worlds of musicians, and where I knew I could join in too, as a participant observer.

Participant observation is difficult to define due to its range of practices (Becker 1958; Bryman 1984). Evans (1988, 197) argued it is not only "ill defined" but also "tainted with mysticism" (perhaps not unlike the creative processes of music making or the "contagious magic" of Liverpool itself) and needs to be made less enigmatic. For Long (2007), the researcher must negotiate levels of participation during data collection. Involvement ranges along a continuum from the (1) complete participant, (2) participant as observer, (3) observer as participant, to the (4) complete observer. My fieldwork adopted the second role—participant as observer—which "involves researcher and researched being aware that their relationship stems from research activity," and in which the "researcher is involved in the social situation but also detached" (Long 2007, 95). Long adds that this role differs from the third level, observer as participant, as in that role "there is no intense relationship with those researched" (95). My fieldwork certainly involved "intense relationships" centered upon making music, spending large amounts of time in rehearsal, and performing together on stage. Although I became intimately part of several groups as a drummer, I also took care to maintain a critical distance as a researcher, continually reminding myself (e.g., in my field notes) that I was *not only* a member of the group, *but also* a researcher.

What Cohen, Becker, Long, and others (Bennett 2002; Hodkinson 2005; Veal 2006) make clear to me is that a large part of what facilitated my fieldwork was my "insider" status as a musician. As Hodkinson (2005, 136) noted, "holding a degree of insider status clearly can have implications for the achievement of successful and productive interactions with participants." However, being a musician-insider did not afford me automatic access or make the fieldwork (sites, or "things" to observe) patently obvious; there was also the risk of assumed knowledge of "how things work" that needed to be kept open for critical questioning. Adding that the idea of researchers as absolute insiders or outsiders was "deceptively simple," Hodkinson argued:

> The role of insider researcher may offer significant potential benefits but that, far from being automatic, the realization of such advantages and the avoidance of a series of equally significant difficulties is dependent upon caution, awareness and on-going reflexivity. (2005, 132)

Ethnographies of musical contexts (like any cultural milieu) require reflexive consideration of conducting fieldwork from a point of "initial subjective proximity" (Hodkinson 2005, 132). My role as drummer-researcher required a critical balance of my insider-outsider status. As Veal (2006, 202) cautioned, participant observation in any social setting raises questions of "whether to pose as a 'typical' member of the group, whether to adopt a plausible 'disguise' (e.g., a journalist or 'writer') or whether to admit being a researcher." As an American newly arrived in Liverpool, I was clearly an outsider; I was also an outsider as a researcher who knew little of music making in the city. However, I was also a musician with insider knowledge of live music performance and recording. As I did not disguise the fact that I was a musician *and* researcher, perhaps the most difficult part was simply getting started—gaining access (Thompson and Lashua 2014)—by meeting musicians and getting to know something about them and the city.

Following online desktop research into local musicians and live music events (e.g., viewing local "gig guides," as well as social media sites such as Facebook), the fieldwork began, as Becker (1958) suggests, via initial conversations with participants; in this case, musicians in pubs, clubs, and other venues. During fieldwork conducted from 2007 to 2009, Sara Cohen and I attended dozens of gigs, ranging from intimately small venues in cafés, living rooms, or record stores, to more typical "local" live music venues (e.g., pubs and clubs) where bands performed regularly, to larger events, concerts, and festivals, such as the opening and closing celebrations for Liverpool's year as European Capital of Culture (ECoC; Cohen and Lashua 2010).

As I became increasingly involved in a handful of the city's music scenes, I kept several accounts of my participation, including notebooks for "scratch notes" made during the fieldwork (Emerson, Fretz, and Shaw 2011), a drumming journal that offered an auto-ethnographic record (Ellis 1999) of practicing, performing, and buying new equipment as I reentered the world of drumming (I had not owned a drum kit for several years as I moved between academic posts in North America and the U.K.), as well as "scrapbooks" of digital photos, scanned copies of flyers and ticket stubs, links to websites and audio files, and other ephemera encountered during the fieldwork. Sara and I also conducted interviews, during which we asked musicians to draw maps of their everyday routes and itineraries in and through the city (S. Cohen 2012; Lashua 2011; Lashua, Cohen, and Schofield 2010). The interviews (with approximately sixty musicians) included rap, hip-hop, grime, folk, indie, rock, pop, and hardcore artists, ranging from those who were just starting out in their musical careers to those who had been playing for many decades.

As I met more musicians at gigs and through interviews, I invited some to recording sessions at the University of Liverpool's studio facilities. With me acting as studio engineer (Thompson and Lashua 2014), these sessions provided opportunities for further interviews, plus additional time to hang out and observe a group or artist in the studio. These recording sessions were also an opportunity for research reciprocity, giving back to the musicians who had shared their stories and allowed me to "hang out" with them. Soon, in addition to acting as a studio engineer, I was also helping bands as a "roadie" (Lashua and Cohen 2010), and then as a drummer too. This chapter draws from across these research records but is focused on analysis of the interviews, field notes, and photos of sites and performances.

TRACK 3: DOCKERS, PUBS, AND FOLK MUSIC: FOLK MUSIC IN LIVERPOOL

This track is centered on leisure that is manifested through folk music and football as forms of working-class politics in Liverpool. I first met "John"[4] at the Casa (short for "Casablanca"), a pub located on Hope Street. Although not a landmark Liverpool venue such as the Cavern Club (made famous by the Beatles), the Casa arguably warrants a place on the list of historic pub venues in Liverpool. In 1991, the Casa was bought by Liverpool dockworkers with their redundancy payments following a long-running

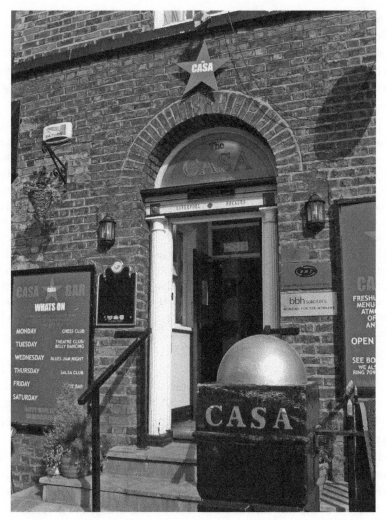

FIGURE 23.2 Hope Street entrance to the Casa. Note the words "Liverpool Dockers" above the door. (Credit: Brett Lashua)

union dispute over the use of casual labor. Inside, the Casa's walls are covered in memorabilia of trade unionism and historical photos of Liverpool's famous docks, while outside, the Casa's sign (see Figure 23.2) bears a simple red star (a global symbol of socialism). It is described by an online pub guide as a quintessential local venue "that has Liverpool written through it like a stick of rock [candy]" (Liverpool Underlined 2014). The pub memorializes the history of the working classes in Liverpool and also marks a moment in the decline of the city's once-famous port. Divided into several rooms, the Casa has a bar area with screens to watch football, a performance space, and meeting room. The performance space is relatively intimate, comfortably holding about seventy-five people, making it a great site for folk music performances.

John regularly hosts a folk music night at the Casa. Artists such as Woody Guthrie, Roy Bailey, Billy Bragg, and the Levellers have influenced him as a singer-songwriter. As host, he also performed, and I was struck by the overt historical and political references in his lyrics, chronicling miners' strikes, dockyard revolutions, and the oppression of the British working classes. Later, during an interview, he told me how he came to write protest music:

> I grew up, I suppose, when Thatcher was in power, so it was a very polarized time. Me dad was always interested in politics but not a political activist: he was a trade union representative. From the age of about twelve or thirteen I remember the miners' strike [of 1984–1985] with excitement. Also, Liverpool—from about 1981 onwards—was under huge industrial attack really. Just round the corner from the area I lived in there were lots and lots of factories, where all me mum and dad's friends used to work. I remember they all just went very, very quickly, almost from nowhere. I remember walking in to our front room and me mum's friend was in there crying because she had just lost her job: the factory had gone. And that happened to Liverpool very quickly in the '80s. So, both in terms what was happening in Liverpool and what was happening nationally, it almost seems like taking sides was a natural thing to do. The other thing is that many people don't see the fact that working people have a huge amount of social power.

This social power includes acts such as collectively buying pubs like the Casa, resisting privatization through cooperative (e.g., unionized) action, and striving to celebrate the history of the working classes. Consequently, John's songs tell stories of working-class heroes who built the city and the stories of other political activists and protestors working for a more just and equitable society.

In addition, John's songs fit within a kind of "trinity" of Liverpool cultural iconography: along with pop music and working-class politics, he also sings about football (soccer), specifically his love of the Anfield-based Liverpool FC (Football Club). Expressing his frustration with the way the culture of football had changed in his lifetime, with its international owners, expensive season tickets, and highly paid professionals, John had recently thrown his support into a newly formed nonleague "AFC Liverpool" team. Set up in 2008 by a group of 1,000 fans, this club aimed to provide a match-going experience for Liverpool FC fans who felt they had been priced out of Premier League matches. AFC Liverpool—AFC stands for "Affordable Football Club"—has adopted the same team color (red), its fans sing the same terrace songs, and the club is based on the sense of "local" working-class community many people feel has been eroded at Liverpool FC (Millward 2012).

During AFC Liverpool's second season, as they approached their league's title match, John had written an unofficial team anthem. As a well-known performer in the city connected to (highly interwoven) networks of musicians and football fans, he had the opportunity to have a song included on a game-day playlist during a Liverpool FC match at Anfield stadium; as a political statement, he had chosen his (as yet unrecorded) AFC anthem. However, it needed to be ready for the next game in only forty-eight hours. John asked me to arrange an impromptu session at the University of Liverpool's music studios, where I also served as session engineer and drummer. John, on acoustic guitar and lead vocal, also drafted in "Derek" (a multi-instrumentalist who contributed on bass and lead guitar) and "Alice," who coproduced the track and contributed on keyboards. We all sang backing vocals, as the tune is an attempt to capture the feeling of singing in the terraces, with a repetitive chorus sung en masse by (ideally) thousands of supporters. We layered vocals upon vocals in overdubs to emulate the collective sound of a match-day crowd. The following afternoon the song was broadcast to a capacity crowd of approximately 45,000 assembled for a Liverpool FC match. In its verses and in the tradition of a terrace song's sing-along style, Liverpool's football heritage and iconic players are celebrated; however, in the chorus the lyrics taunt that this year the only cup final that Liverpool fans will have to celebrate will be with AFC Liverpool. This song was not written or recorded for any payment or profit; it was leisure, done for the love of Liverpool music, football, and working-class culture.

For Spracklen (2013), folk music remains a powerful expression of leisure-as-politics. The experience of working with John to record this song connected me to the politics of Liverpool's folk music, football, and working-class cultures (Brocken 2013). Although Spracklen offers that folk music cultures often reject injustice and oppression, such as fascism or capitalism, he cautions against reproducing (potentially oppressive) traditional (romanticized) notions of identity, such as folk "Englishness" as white, male, heterosexual, and working class at the expense of greater diversity and inclusivity. Nevertheless, as a folk song, the AFC Liverpool tune John wrote bears hallmarks of class-based protest music (Street, Hague, and Savigny 2008), offering a rallying cry to Liverpool FC fans to support a more localized, "authentic" working-class club (Millward 2012). For John, music making and football are important expressions of working-class leisure in pursuit of socialist aims. His music carried echoes of Stuart Hall's oft-quoted lines about popular culture:

> Popular culture is one of the sites where this struggle for and against a culture of the powerful is engaged: it is the stake to be won or lost in that struggle. It is the arena of consent and resistance.... It is not a sphere where socialism, a socialist culture—already fully formed—might be simply "expressed." But it is one of the places where socialism might be constituted. That is why "popular culture" matters. (1981, 239)

This quotation also explains, in part, why music and leisure matter, especially as inferred through John's songwriting. For him, folk music, football, and leisure are ongoing sites of class struggle and also the stakes to be won (or lost) in the struggle. Meeting and working with John was important as I began to understand the people, places, and politics of Liverpool, where music making, "social consciousness," and leisure were deeply interconnected.

TRACK 4: LIVERPOOL ORBITAL? YOUTH, "RACE," AND PLACE IN URBAN MUSIC

Despite numerous grand redevelopment initiatives, such as its "boldly modernist" 1965 City Centre Redevelopment Plan (Sykes et al. 2013, 10), Liverpool does not have a ring road, and while parts of major motorways and broad thoroughfares cut into and through various parts of the city, there is no Liverpool loop, beltway, or orbital as around other major cities. However, during interviews, many musicians drew maps of their activities in the city that featured geometrical shapes, patterns, and lines—what Sara Cohen (2012) refers to as "tracks, bubbles, and borders"—that defined areas and sketched out different kinds of loops or orbital rings around Liverpool (Lashua 2011). This was especially the case with "urban" music makers (e.g., hip-hop, rap, R'n'B, soul, grime music).

Urban music makers' descriptions of where their music took place skirted around the edges of the city center, via recording sessions at friends' home studios, gigging at smaller venues outside the main entertainment districts or quarters of the city center, and through performances at festivals on the fringes of the city. During interviews with me, most of these musicians made mention of leisure activities in the city center, but only as a place for consumption (shopping, restaurants, etc.). If music making was mentioned there, it was only for rock or pop music (especially "heritage rock"; Bennett 2009), and not as sites for urban music. In the aggregate, these musicians mapped urban music in Liverpool without an "urban" geographic core (Lashua 2011). Urban music orbited the city center, but was not in it. In this track of the chapter, I trace the movements of young urban musicians around the orbital margins of the city via my participation in a hip-hop group's performance at the 2009 HUB Festival.

HUB Festival is billed as the largest free urban youth festival in the U.K. (Bowie 2009). The event was well attended in the years that I was present, with about 23,000 people in attendance in 2008, and 27,000 reported for 2009 (Yaqoob 2009). It occurs annually in May, and its 2002 inaugural event was held in Liverpool's city center, during the campaign to attract ECoC status. HUB Festival was initiated to illustrate the city's engagement with diverse groups of young people through urban music and youth "street" culture (e.g., skateboarding, graffiti arts, BMX). In years following the successful ECoC award, HUB Festival was relocated outside the city center. This was partly due to the ongoing redevelopment of the city center and central pier. Yet, according to several research respondents this move was also because the influx of thousands of young people, graffiti artists, and skateboarders was deemed both too disruptive in popular, central tourist areas, and too destructive to the urban environment (e.g., graffiti "vandalism" and skateboard "grinding"). During my first two years in Liverpool (2007 and 2008), HUB Festival was held in Otterspool Park, a green space along the banks of the River Mersey in the leafier southern suburb of Aigburth. When Sara and I attended in 2008, our photographs captured the almost pastoral feel of the Otterspool location (see Figure 23.3).

FIGURE 23.3 2008 HUB Festival along the Otterspool Promenade. (Credit: Brett Lashua)

In 2009, I performed at HUB Festival with a local hip-hop group. That year the festival site was the chronically unregenerated area around Wellington Dock on the city's north side, a bleak expanse of warehouses and mostly empty docks awaiting redevelopment (see Figure 23.1).

The musician seen performing center stage in Figure 23.3 is the same artist with whom I would play HUB Festival the following year (Figure 23.1). Thus, there were two significant spatial differences between these events. One difference was the sprawling parkland along Otterspool Promenade, to the south of the city center, compared to the gritty quayside festival site on Wellington Dock. The second difference was my position as a researcher: in 2008 I stood with the crowd on the grass; in 2009 I was with the group on the stage, looking out across the crowd and docklands. These differences allowed me uniquely varying perspectives on the festival.

The locations of HUB Festival highlight how leisure activities are caught up in the tensions and contradictions of culture-led urban regeneration. Used at first to attract the prestigious Capital of Culture award, the edgy "urban youth" and "street culture" vibe of HUB Festival was quickly removed from the city center and placed in safer, more manageable, and controlled environments—whether Otterspool's grassy parkland or Wellington Dock's waterfront wasteland. The city center itself thus becomes a site for a different kind of sanitized "urban" cultural renaissance. As Zukin (1989) and others (e.g., Cohen 2007; Florida 2002) have shown, the association of particular urban areas with music, culture, and creativity has made them a focus for physical regeneration. Yet, the subsequent gentrification and privatization of those areas have commonly resulted in the exclusion of artists, small businesses, and young people that had created a sense of cultural regeneration. HUB Festival may be read critically as reflecting both neoliberal and neoracist discourses (Giroux 2005) in urban regeneration that reproduce (and often exacerbate) socio-geographic exclusion for some people from certain areas and activities in the city (Silk and Andrews 2008). This, at least in part, helps to explain why HUB Festival has been held (with the exception of its first event) on the fringes of the city center. Ironically, the "hub" in "HUB Festival" implies the central part of a wheel, network, or other spatial organization. If cities are often symbolized as hubs, with arterial transportation links (highways, rail lines, communications, etc.) radiating outward from them, then the imagery of Liverpool's urban youth festival as a "hub" misses the mark.

Playing at the 2009 HUB Festival also helped me to see issues of youth culture in Liverpool. As the crowd became larger, livelier, and began to move with the music, event security appeared to become increasingly worried about its energy. The space, with the audience hemmed in along the length of the dock, was narrow and allowed little room to spread out. Soon, between songs the security team began to ask the singer to tell the audience to calm down. From my view on stage the crowd seemed energized, but no more so than at other events where we performed that summer (including a set at the 2009 Glastonbury Festival). The crowd was asked repeatedly to calm down; we also cut out an up-tempo song in favor of a slower tune, sung only with acoustic guitar accompaniment. Although the crowd was momentarily chilled, our next number was a mash-up of classic hip-hop songs that again had the crowd jumping. At this point we were forced to end our performance (we were told) due to risks to the crowd. While I had been forced to stop playing a few times in my life when performing with indie or rock bands, this was almost always for playing too loud and/or too late at night. The performance at HUB Festival with a hip-hop group was the only time I had ever been asked to stop playing because the music was "overstimulating" a crowd.

Certainly there is a need for crowd safety; however, the worries about an excited young audience jumping around to urban music seemed unwarranted and excessively controlling. In this example, music making as leisure spilled over into musical leisure more broadly. As I moved through the festival site before and after our set, the crowd was orderly (during a rock band prior to our set; for a soul group after us), and I could not help but wonder if the event organizers were actually more concerned with the stereotypical "dangers" of youth and hip-hop music. Such concerns rehearse well-worn fears about urban youth (Dimitriadis 2001; Forman and Neal 2004; Rose 2013) as racialized, classed, and out-of-place "others" (Lashua 2006). Relocating "urban" youth culture to the peripheral space of Wellington Dock illustrated that space (i.e., where young people are) was not the only concern; another factor was the perception of young people themselves (Rogers and Coaffee 2005). Urban music was too edgy even when not in the urban center, although it appeared easier to maintain order in an open, sprawling space (e.g., Otterspool) than in the confines of the docklands. HUB Festival spotlights the politics of urban youth and music making on the city's margins, and my drummer-researcher's perspective allowed me to see this marginality too.

TRACK 5: THE "PRACTICE" OF EVERYDAY LIFE: MUSIC MAKING, LEISURE, AND REHEARSAL SPACES

This penultimate track is focused on rehearsal spaces as significant "nodes" (Finnegan 1989) in the everyday routes and routines of musicians. For those not directly involved in it, pop music rehearsal, or "practice," is perhaps viewed with a sense of tedium and uninterest. Private and often intimate, rehearsals and where they happen are underappreciated; the onstage performance or recording studio event is presumed the measure of things (see Bell, this volume, chapter 5). Scholarly references to popular music rehearsals are few (Bennett 2000; Cohen 1991, 2007; Finnegan 1989; Frith 1993; Harrison 2011; Johnson 2003; Kahn-Harris 2007; Smith 2013), with mention of rehearsal spaces fewer and often only in passing (Hudson 1995; Lashua and Cohen 2010; Walser 1993).[5] For example, Leyshon (2001, 62) wrote that musical scenes flourish where "they produce a set of stabilizing institutions, such as performance venues, specialized record shops, rehearsal and recording studios, specialized music press, and record labels." However, focused primarily on the networks between nodes of musical creativity, Leyshon gave only nominal attention to rehearsal studios. Similarly, Bennett (2001, 5) described rehearsals as important "microorganizational practices which bond members of a group together," but left the wider spatial aspects of rehearsals unaddressed. Kahn-Harris (2007, 85) offered only that extreme metal bands "almost always hire properly-equipped rehearsal rooms," and in some countries (e.g., Sweden) rehearsal rooms are subsidized, with bands often sharing rehearsal spaces. He then moved swiftly along to describe recording demos. While researchers have met with musicians to conduct interviews in rehearsal rooms (Overell 2010), too often the space itself only serves as a static backcloth against which the action of the interview takes place. Although the works cited here make use, to greater or lesser degrees, of rehearsals, the rehearsal space is usually not a significant part of the research frame.

Rehearsals might be part of musicians' everyday mobilities (Lashua and Cohen 2010), but beyond a few cases (e.g., Björck 2011) rehearsal spaces appear to warrant scant further research attention. Walser offers another exception, beginning his book *Running with the Devil* "wandering" through a rehearsal space:

> In the catacombs of a nineteenth-century warehouse, hulking in a run down riverfront district, passageways wind through rough stonework to connect small rooms, each fronted by a sturdy iron door. Behind these doors musicians compose and rehearse through all hours of the day and night. Wandering the crooked hallways, I hear waves of sound clashing and coalescing: powerful drums and bass, menacing and ecstatic vocals, the heavy crunch of distorted electric guitars. In some rooms, lone guitarists practice scales, arpeggios, heavy metal riffs, and Bach transcriptions. Occasionally, I pass an open door, and musicians who are taking a break consider my presence with cool curiosity. (1993, ix)

In another exception, Cohen's fieldwork centralized two Liverpool rehearsal rooms, The Ministry and Vulcan Studios:

> The Ministry was situated in a rather deserted area of the city, whilst Vulcan Studios was situated further out in the docklands, surrounded by scrap yards, empty warehouses, and factories. Each was an old warehouse several stories high with rooms converted in a slapdash manner for rehearsing in. Both, particularly Vulcan, were grim and dilapidated in appearance, very cold, and badly in need of repair. Yet within each existed a hubbub of activity and creativity. (1991, 47)

Beyond these few examples, there is little attention paid to the spaces where musicians practice and perfect their performances (for a further exception, see Bell, this volume, chapter 5).

During preparations for a set at the aforementioned 2009 Glastonbury Festival, I spent weeks preparing with a hip-hop group, marking time in a half-dozen rehearsal rooms around the city, going over and over a short set. For me, although the brief performance at Glastonbury was exciting and memorable, the rehearsal time and spaces where the band socialized in the weeks before the festival were far more significant. It was a time that the six members of the group were able to enjoy, bond, joke around, and converse about more serious matters (such as racism in popular music). In some respects, the festival performance was merely icing on the cake, a brief celebration of all the practice put into being part of a group. While rehearsal studios can be vibrant, exciting, and creative spaces, they are also spaces for tedious, routine "drill" of preparing for live performances (Smith 2013). My rehearsals in Liverpool brought me into contact with many musicians, and as I moved in and through rehearsal spaces they also brought me into contact with parts of the city I would not otherwise have known.

Most rehearsal rooms in Liverpool are located centrally. Examples include Elevator Studios (on Cheapside, Dale Street, and also Upper Parliament Street), Crash Studios (also on Dale Street), Vulcan Studios on the Dock Road, Performance Studios (Victoria Street), Crosstown Studios (Oriel Street), Pacific Studios (Birchall Street), and Highfield Street Studios. Most of these are official "rooms for rent" rehearsal spaces. According to the musicians I spoke with, rates varied, although in most cases rents were approximately £300 ($430 [2016]) per month. A rehearsal space shared by two or three bands significantly reduced costs, if a suitably shared schedule could be negotiated between the them. For example, I rehearsed for several months with a hardcore group at Highfield Street studios in a dank cellar room shared between three bands. The £300 per month rent was divided equally between three bands, and further divided between members of the band (about £25 [$38] per month per person). Some rooms were more expensive, others less so; when the hip-hop group of six (including me) arranged to rehearse at Vulcan Studios ahead of our Glastonbury set we paid just £20 [$29] per hour (just over £3 each). The ground-floor room we used was not much more than a windowless rectangular box, but at least it was dry, and there were no stairs up or down which we had to haul heavy equipment.

While the cellar rooms at Highfield Street were cold, damp, and stale, and Vulcan was windowless, other rehearsal spaces were somewhat more salubrious. Rehearsal rooms in the Prince's Building occupy the upper floors of an office building in the city center. My field notes describe attending a rehearsal of an indie-pop group in the Prince's Building:

I am sitting on a surprisingly clean red sofa in a rehearsal room high above Dale Street in Liverpool's city center. I have just interviewed "Greg," a bassist/singer (he's now preparing for rehearsal). Located above an electronics shop and a health food store [see Figure 23.4], these rehearsal rooms are practically invisible from the street below. Prince's Building is a run-down Victorian-era red brick 5-storey structure constructed in the 1880s (it is also currently for sale). Greg's group rehearses on the fourth floor and he explained that this reflects the growing status of the band. The strata of the building mirror the success and standing of the bands within it. Topping the charts means topping this structure as well [at the time the Zutons had the top floor]. There is a lift [elevator], else the stratification would be reversed, with the ease of loading bulky musical equipment in and out of the building from the ground floor (and avoiding stairs) reserved for the most successful groups. Upon arriving, Greg punched in a security code and we entered a cold, musty foyer, closed and unaired. The lift barely accommodated the two [of] us, let alone any equipment.

FIGURE 23.4 Prince's Building, 81 Dale Street, Liverpool. (Credit: Brett Lashua)

FIGURE 23.5 Sunny rehearsal room, fourth floor, Prince's Building, Dale Street, Liverpool. (Credit: Brett Lashua)

Once on the 4th floor, he struggled with several locks on a battered wooden door and we stepped into a surprisingly light and spacious yellow room, currently shared by two bands [see Figure 23.5]. It was quite cold, and after he turned on several small electric heaters we chatted for an hour or so in the silence of the frosty room, sunk into the red sofa. Across the room, piles of numerous speaker cabinets, amplifiers, and road cases are arranged around the perimeter of the space. Components for many drum kits are stacked in this and that corner, piles of broken drumsticks and cracked cymbals litter the base of the walls. A keyboard is here, another is there, also propped against the walls. A lattice of cords and cables crisscross the floor, running from microphones to amplifiers, keyboards to monitors, and guitars to effects pedals. There is more gear than 5 bands would use, let alone the two who currently use the space, but Greg says it has accrued over the years, a tideline of instrument sediment, and he's been in the building for close to five years now, working his way up through the scene.

In his interview, Greg told me: "People are always really impressed with our room. We share it with another band . . . Yeah, this is pretty nice I suppose, for what you can come to expect from rehearsal space" and he commented on the daylight streaming through the windows as "novel" for practice rooms normally found deep within windowless warehouses or underground cellars. Being high up kept some of the noise of rehearsal

away from the city below. There was also an internal logic to the organization of rehearsals on each floor, and alternating rooms:

> I think they put the signed bands on the top floor so they can rehearse 24 hours a day.
> Other than that I think they'll like stagger rooms, like that's a daytime room, that's
> an evening room. So there are not always loads of bands playing, because if there's a
> band playing downstairs to us, they're really loud and it's just ridiculous. . . . They just
> turn everything up to 11—it's so loud, and it just comes right through the floor and
> we're trying to play over the top, it's just doesn't really happen.

Spaces such as this, although lacking in certain amenities, were more expensive than
less comfortable rooms in other areas of the city, such as Highfield Street. Greg's space
at Elevator was £420 ($600) per month, shared among two bands: "we end up paying
between the 7 of us—4 of them, 3 of us—£60 [$86] a month each." This is consider-
ably more than the £300 per month at Highfield Street; however, there were benefits to
rehearsing in the Prince's Building.

    During my later interview with the singer and keyboard player in Greg's band,
"Debra" spoke about the fruitful relations that developed through rehearsing in the
same building as other bands:

> Well, you know the band Hot Club de Paris? We obviously knew who they were, and
> a lot of friends know them, but we didn't know them ourselves. I remember we were
> coming out of practice one day, out of Elevator, and they were outside and they just
> stopped us and said "we think your band is awesome, we've heard you practicing"
> and—because they're on Moshi Moshi [record label]—they said "we've given your
> CD to Moshi Moshi and they absolutely love it"—and we were just like, we've never
> met them before and they came and told us all this, and they said "come for a pint
> with us," so we did. We met them, and it was amazing to meet them, because they're
> one of the biggest bands at the moment that have come out of Liverpool. And, then,
> just from there, you just realize how many other bands there are in Elevator. There's
> the Hot Melts directly above us. Then there's the Rascals underneath us, the Zutons
> above us as well, and it's really weird just as you walk around, you can hear everyone
> just practicing—so we heard Hot Club's new album, months and months before the
> label did or anyone else did, which was quite strange really.

This interview extract evokes the rehearsal space as a hub of relations between musicians, which, in this case, even led to a small record contract for this band. It also
illustrates some aspects of the importance of routine, everyday movements of coming and going, or walking to a nearby pub for a pint. Such "leisurely" movements and
moments are significant in developing and defining musicians' status and relations
within a local scene, and rehearsal spaces are thus important sites for developing local
networks.

    Rehearsal rooms might also be read as a barometer of urban regeneration. Members
of one band that had rehearsed in the "old" Elevator Studios (i.e., Prince's Building on
Dale Street) discussed their move to the "new" Elevator building (on Upper Parliament

Street) during an interview. We began with a discussion of the windows and daylight in their former rooms, on the third floor of the Dale Street building:

> That's a bit of a luxury in practice rooms these days. Like in the old Elevator Studios—we only moved, what was it, about two months ago?—in the height of summer you couldn't really open a window, it was so smelly anyway, above a smelly alleyway. The big windows all had Perspex screens to act as soundproofing, so it was just like a big greenhouse! Yeah, in the winter it is really cold and in summer it's really hot.
>
> Brett: Is that what inspired you guys to move?
>
> We got told it was closing down. They said it was but it hasn't. They tried to scare all the bands over into the new building, because they had this new building that was being funded by the council. They told everyone that the lease was up, but they'd actually signed another lease without telling the bands that were moving over. But my favorite thing is that [in the new building] there's a café there, you can buy beers and coffee. We probably would have moved over anyway, because you can go down, have a coffee and carry on like. It's slightly more expensive, ever so slightly, but not by much. You get more than you pay for though. We never had a good window or a café; I think it's worth an extra tenner [£10, $14] a month. And we share a space [with another four-piece band]; we pay £216 [$310] a month (per band),[6] which between four of us is like £54 [per person], which isn't too bad.

Although the "perks" of having operable windows and an onsite café increased the rates at Elevator, the musicians I spoke with were appreciative of such comforts and the opportunities for the wider socializing that they afforded. However, these perks, and the newly (re)developed buildings, were also viewed with some scorn and disdain, as part of wider patterns of urban regeneration and gentrification that pushed musicians out of one area and into another, whether they wanted to move or not. Overall, while rehearsal spaces may appear, at a glance, as liminal, peripheral, or inconsequential to musicians' more visible performances, they deserve more attention. As central sites of music making and musicians' leisure, rehearsal spaces matter a great deal.

Track 6: "Extended Play": Music Making and Leisure Research

The ethnographic research I've described and shared in this chapter illustrates my attempts to think through music making as leisure research: joining in as a drummer was an "obvious way to study the group" by "becoming a member of the group" (Veal 2006, 202). The "EP tracks" illustrate music making from a perspective that connects them to broader leisure contexts and relations (Rojek 1995). Viewed as leisure, a range of music making "matters" come into sharper focus, such as class politics (as described in Track 3: folk music making), youth spaces and identities (Track 4: HUB Festival and the exclusion of urban music and urban youth from the city center), and the "practices" of everyday life (Track 5: rehearsal spaces). Throughout, I also have shown how becoming a member of a music group can help to demystify ethnographic processes and music making practices, as well as the "magic" of Liverpool too.

Participating on stage, in studio, and at rehearsal brought me into closer contact and built better research relations with many musicians. My insider status as drummer-researcher also meant that I was present for the many interminable moments of waiting around that characterizes much of musical "activity" (e.g., the long hours after sound check before a gig, idle time during repeated "takes" during studio sessions, waiting for [always late] members to show up for rehearsals, etc.). Had I not been part of the group, I might not have been present for these moments. Had I not been part of the group, it would have been more difficult for me to make sense of them. Had I not been part of the group, it would have been difficult to see the significance of music making as leisure.

Music making matters as leisure: drumming in different bands allowed me to experience Liverpool in ways that I might not otherwise have known. Participating as a drummer meant that I had access to the quotidian leisure and easily overlooked practices and spaces of musicians' routes and routines. These stretched across the city and included not only venues, recording studios, and rehearsal spaces but also the best cafés and takeaways to refuel after practice or before a gig. Participation took me to places I would not otherwise have been, such as the "privileged" space of backstage, but also along different streets and neighborhoods. My mental map of Liverpool is plotted against the significant sites of music making and the places I associate with the musicians I met there. Music making opened up a different way to know the city; it afforded a different kind of wayfaring, through the beat of a drummer.

Notes

1. I am grateful to Sara Cohen at the University of Liverpool's School of Music. For two years (2007–2009) I worked as a researcher on Sara's (and John Schofield's) project "Popular Music, Cityscapes, and Characterization of the Urban Environment," funded by the Arts and Humanities Research Council. Sara generously supported several follow-up projects.
2. "EP" stands for "Extended Play," a format for releasing more recorded music than on a single, but less than on a full album, typically around five to six tracks.
3. This experience is fairly humble, and included playing and recording with a variety of bands in northeastern Ohio in the U.S.A., primarily during the 1990s.
4. All names in the chapter have been changed to protect anonymity.
5. The inattention to rehearsal in popular music studies differs from the attention to rehearsals in music education, and also in theater studies. Johnson (2003) argued that popular music rehearsals need to be "uncoupled" from music education and its "traditional associations with, broadly speaking, art music models" (155). See Campbell (1995), Cohen (2012), Davidson and Jordan (2007), Dickens and Lonie (2014), and Jaffurs (2004); for theater rehearsals, see Tompkins and Birch (2012).
6. One hip-hop group rented a smaller studio space in the new Elevator building and reported they paid £268 ($388 [2016]) per month for their space.

References Cited

Baker, Sarah, Andy Bennett, and Shane Homan. 2009. "Cultural Precincts, Creative Spaces Giving the Local a Musical Spin." *Space and Culture* 12(2): 148–165.

Barna, Emília. 2011. "The Scene as Online and Offline Music Network: A Case Study on Contemporary Liverpool Indie Rock Bands." In *Cultural Cyborgs: Life at the Interface*, edited by Wayne Rumbles, 105–114, Oxford: Inter-Disciplinary Press.

Becker, Howard S. 1958. "Problems of Inference and Proof in Participant Observation." *American Sociological Review* 23: 652–660.

Becker, Howard S. 1982. *Art Worlds*. Berkeley: University of California Press.

Bennett, Andy. 2000. *Popular Music and Youth Culture: Music, Identity and Place*. Basingstoke: Macmillan.

Bennett, Andy. 2001. *Cultures of Popular Music*. Buckingham: Open University Press.

Bennett, Andy. 2002. "Researching Youth Culture and Popular Music: A Methodological Critique." *British Journal of Sociology* 53(3): 451–466.

Bennett, Andy. 2005. "Editorial: Popular Music and Leisure." *Leisure Studies* 24(4): 333–342.

Bennett, Andy. 2009. "'Heritage Rock': Rock Music, Re-presentation and Heritage Discourse." *Poetics* 37: 474–489.

Björck, Cecilia. 2011. *Claiming Space: Discourses on Gender, Popular Music, and Social Change*. Gothenburg: ArtMonitor, University of Gothenburg Press. https://gupea.ub.gu.se/bit-stream/2077/24290/1/gupea_2077_24290_1.pdf.

Bowie, Jess. 2009. "Event Preview: Hub Festival, Liverpool." *The Guardian*, May 23. http://www.theguardian.com/culture/2009/may/23/hub-festival-wellington-dock-liverpool-b-boy.

Brennan, Matt. 2013. "'Instruments of a Lower Order': Historicizing the Double Status of the Drum Kit and Drummers." Paper presented at the International Association for the Study of Popular Music Conference, 17th Biennial Conference, June 25. Gijón, Spain.

Brocken, Michael. 2013. *The British Folk Revival, 1944–2002*. Aldershot: Ashgate.

Brown, Jacqueline Nassy. 2005. *Dropping Anchor, Setting Sail: Geographies of Race in Black Liverpool*. Princeton, NJ: Princeton University Press.

Bryman, Alan. 1984. "The Debate about Quantitative and Qualitative Research: A Question of Method or Epistemology?" *British Journal of Sociology* 35(1): 75–92.

Campbell, Patricia Shehan. 1995. "Of Garage Bands and Song-Getting: The Musical Development of Young Rock Musicians." *Research Studies in Music Education* 4(1): 12–20.

Cohen, Mary L. 2012. "Writing between Rehearsals: A Tool for Assessment and Building Camaraderie." *Music Educators Journal* 98(3): 43–48.

Cohen, Sara. 1991. *Rock Culture in Liverpool: Popular Music in the Making*. Oxford: Oxford University Press.

Cohen, Sara. 1993. "Ethnography and Popular Music Studies." *Popular Music* 12(2): 123–138.

Cohen, Sara. 2007. *Decline, Renewal and the City in Popular Music Culture: Beyond the Beatles*. Aldershot: Ashgate.

Cohen, Sara. 2012. "Bubbles, Tracks, Borders and Lines: Mapping Music and Urban Landscape." *Journal of the Royal Musical Association* 137(1): 135–170.

Cohen, Sara, and Brett D. Lashua. 2010. "Pubs in the Precinct: Music-making, Retail Developments and the Characterization of Urban Space." In *The Beat Goes On: Liverpool, Popular Music and the Changing City*, edited by Marion Leonard and Rob Strachan, 65–83. Liverpool: University of Liverpool Press.

Connell, John, and Chris Gibson. 2003. *Sound Tracks: Popular Music, Identity, and Place.* London: Routledge.

Davidson, Jane W., and Nicole Jordan. 2007. "'Private Teaching, Private Learning': An Exploration of Music Instrument Learning in the Private Studio, Junior and Senior Conservatories." In *International Handbook of Research in Arts Education*, edited by Liora Bresler, 729–754. New York: Springer.

DeNora, Tia. 2000. *Music in Everyday Life.* Cambridge: Cambridge University Press.

Dickens, Luke, and Douglas Lonie. 2014. "Rehearsal Spaces as Children's Spaces? Considering the Place of Non-Formal Music Education." In *Informal Education, Childhood and Youth: Geographies, Histories, Practices*, edited by Sarah Mills and Peter Kraftl, 165–183. Basingstoke: Palgrave Macmillan.

Dimitriadis, Greg. 2001. "'In the Clique': Popular Culture, Constructions of Place, and the Everyday Lives of Urban Youth." *Anthropology and Education Quarterly* 32(1): 29–51.

Du Noyer, Paul. 2007. *Liverpool: Wondrous Place from the Cavern to the Capital of Culture.* London: Random House.

Ellis, Carolyn. 1999. "Heartful Autoethnography." *Qualitative Health Research* 9(5): 669–683.

Emerson, Robert M., Rachel I. Fretz, and Linda L. Shaw. 2011. *Writing Ethnographic Fieldnotes.* Chicago: University of Chicago Press.

Evans, Mel. 1988. "Participant Observation: The Researcher as Research Tool." In *Qualitative Methods in Human Geography*, edited by John Eyles and David Marshall Smith, 197–218. Cambridge, MA: Polity.

Finnegan, Ruth. 1989. *The Hidden Musicians: Music-Making in an English Town.* Cambridge: Cambridge University Press.

Florida, Richard L. 2002. *The Rise of the Creative Class: And How It's Transforming Work, Leisure, Community and Everyday Life.* New York: Basic Books.

Forman, Murray, and Mark Anthony Neal, eds. 2004. *That's the Joint! The Hip-Hop Studies Reader.* New York: Psychology Press.

Forsyth, Alasdair, and Martin Cloonan. 2008. "Alco-pop? The Use of Popular Music in Glasgow Pubs." *Popular Music and Society* 31(1): 57–78.

Frith, Simon. 1993. "Popular Music and the Local State." In *Rock and Popular Music: Politics, Policies, Institutions*, edited by Tony Bennett, Simon Frith, Larry Grossberg, John Shepherd, and Graeme Turner, 14–24. London: Routledge.

Giroux, Henry A. 2005. "The Terror of Neoliberalism: Rethinking the Significance of Cultural Politics." *College Literature* 32(1): 1–19.

Grunenberg, Christoph, and Robert Knifton. 2007. *Centre of the Creative Universe: Liverpool and the Avant-Garde.* Liverpool: Liverpool University Press.

Hall, Stuart. 1981. "Notes on Deconstructing 'the Popular.'" In *People's History and Socialist Theory*, edited by Raphael Samuel, 227–239. London: Routledge.

Harrison, Anthony Kwame. 2011. "'We're Talking about Practice(-Based Research)': Serious Play and Serious Performance in the Practice of Popular Music Ethnography." *Journal of Popular Music Studies* 23(2): 221–228.

Higginson, Steve, and Tony Wailey. 2006. *Edgy Cities.* Liverpool: Northern Lights.

Hodkinson, Paul. 2005. "'Insider Research' in the Study of Youth Cultures." *Journal of Youth Studies* 8(2): 131–146.

Hudson, Ray. 1995. "Making Music Work? Alternative Regeneration Strategies in a Deindustrialized Locality: The Case of Derwentside." *Transactions of the Institute of British Geographers* 20: 460–473.

Inglis, Ian. 2009. "Historical Approaches to Merseybeat: Delivery, Affinity and Diversity." *Popular Music History* 4: 39–55.

Jaffurs, Sheri E. 2004. "The Impact of Informal Music Learning Practices in the Classroom, or How I Learned How to Teach from a Garage Band." *International Journal of Music Education* 22(3): 189–200.

Johnson, Bruce. 2003. "Performance Techniques: Rehearsal." In *Continuum Encyclopedia of Popular Music of the World*. Vol. 2, *Performance and Production*, edited by John Shepherd, David Horn, Dave Laing, Paul Oliver, and Peter Wicke, 154–157. London: Continuum.

Kahn-Harris, Keith. 2007. *Extreme Metal: Music and Culture on the Edge*. Oxford: Berg.

Lashua, Brett D. 2006. "'Just Another Native?' Soundscapes, Chorasters, and Borderlands in Edmonton, Alberta, Canada." *Cultural Studies ↔ Critical Methodologies* 6(3): 391–410.

Lashua, Brett D. 2007. "Making an Album: Rap Performance and a 'CD Track Listing' as Performance Writing in the Beat of Boyle Street Music Programme." *Leisure Studies* 26(4): 429–445.

Lashua, Brett D. 2011. "An Atlas of Musical Memories: Popular Music, Leisure and Urban Change in Liverpool." *Leisure/Loisir* 35(2): 133–152.

Lashua, Brett D. 2013. "Community Music and Urban Leisure: The Liverpool One Project." *International Journal of Community Music* 6(2): 235–251.

Lashua, Brett D., and Sara Cohen. 2010. "Liverpool Musicscapes: Music Performance, Movement, and the Built Urban Environment." In *Mobile Methodologies*, edited by Benjamin Fincham, Mark McGuiness, and Lesley Murray, 71–84. Basingstoke: Palgrave Macmillan.

Lashua, Brett D., and Yaw Owusu. 2013. "Merseybeatz: Hip-Hop in Liverpool." In *Hip-Hop in Europe*, edited by Sina A. Nitzsche, and Walter Grünzweig, 191–206. Münster: LIT.

Lashua, Brett, Sara Cohen, and John Schofield. 2010. "Popular Music, Mapping, and the Characterization of Liverpool." *Popular Music History* 4(2): 126–144.

Leonard, Marion, and Rob Strachan, eds. 2010. *The Beat Goes on: Liverpool, Popular Music and the Changing City*. Liverpool: Liverpool University Press.

Leyshon, Andrew. 2001. "Time-Space (and Digital) Compression: Software Formats, Musical Networks, and the Reorganisation of the Music Industry." *Environment and Planning A* 33: 49–77.

Liverpool Underlined. 2014. "The Casa." Accessed December 28, 2014. http://www.liverpool-underlined.com/georgianquarter/the-casa-pub/.

Long, Jonathan A. 2007. *Researching Leisure, Sport and Tourism: The Essential Guide*. London: Sage.

Millward, Peter. 2012. "Reclaiming the Kop? Analysing Liverpool Supporters' 21st century Mobilizations." *Sociology* 46(4): 633–648.

Mowitt, John. 2002. *Percussion: Drumming, Beating, Striking*. Durham, NC: Duke University Press.

Overell, Rosemary. 2010. "Brutal Belonging in Melbourne's Grindcore Scene." *Studies in Symbolic Interaction* 35: 79–99.

Roberts, Les. 2014. "Marketing Musicscapes, or the Political Economy of Contagious Magic." *Tourist Studies* 14(1): 10–29.

Rogers, Peter, and Jon Coaffee. 2005. "Moral Panics and Urban Renaissance." *City* 9(3): 321–340.

Rojek, Chris. 1995. *Decentring Leisure: Rethinking Leisure Theory*. London: Sage.

Rose, Tricia. 2013. *The Hip Hop Wars: What We Talk About When We Talk About Hip Hop—and Why It Matters*. New York: Basic Civitas.

Silk, Michael L., and David L. Andrews. 2008. "Managing Memphis: Governance and Regulation in Sterile Spaces of Play." *Social Identities* 14(3): 395–414.

Smith, Gareth Dylan. 2013. *I Drum, Therefore I Am: Being and Becoming a Drummer.* Farnham: Ashgate.

Spracklen, Karl. 2013. "Nazi Punks Folk Off: Leisure, Nationalism, Cultural Identity and the Consumption of Metal and Folk Music." *Leisure Studies* 32(4): 415–428.

Spracklen, Karl. 2014. "There is (almost) No Alternative: The Slow 'Heat Death' of Music Subcultures and the Instrumentalization of Contemporary Leisure." *Annals of Leisure Research* 17(3): 252–266.

Stebbins, Robert A. 1996. *The Barbershop Singer: Inside the Social World of a Musical Hobby.* Toronto: University of Toronto Press.

Street, John, Seth Hague, and Heather Savigny. 2008. "Playing to the Crowd: the Role of Music and Musicians in Political Participation." *British Journal of Politics and International Relations* 10(2): 269–285.

Sykes, Olivier, Jonathan Brown, Matthew Cocks, David Shaw, and Chris Couch. 2013. "A City Profile of Liverpool." *Cities* 35: 299–318.

Tompkins, Joanne, and Anna Birch, eds. 2012. *Performing Site-Specific Theatre: Politics, Place, Practice.* Basingstoke: Palgrave Macmillan.

Thompson, Paul, and Brett D. Lashua. 2014. "Getting It on Record: Issues and Strategies for Ethnographic Practice in Recording Studios." *Journal of Contemporary Ethnography* 43(6): 746–769.

Veal, Anthony James. 2006. *Research Methods for Leisure and Tourism: A Practical Guide.* 3rd ed. New York: Prentice Hall.

Walser, Robert. 1993. *Running with the Devil: Power, Gender, and Madness in Heavy Metal Music.* Middletown, CT: Wesleyan University Press.

Yaqoob, Janine. 2009. "Crows Flock to City Urban Youth Festival; Extreme Sports Enthusiasts Show off Their Skills." *Liverpool Daily Post*, May 25. www.thefreelibrary.com/Crowds+flock+to+city+urban+youth+festival%3B+Extreme+sports+enthusiasts...-a0200470065.

Zukin, Sharon. 1989. *Loft Living: Culture and Capital in Urban Change.* New Brunswick, NJ: Rutgers University Press.

CHAPTER 24

"FX, DRUGS, AND ROCK 'N' ROLL"

Engineering the Emotional Space of the Recording Studio

JENNA WARD AND ALLAN WATSON

INTRODUCTION

THE cultural and creative industries are seen as privileged sites for exploring the roles, functions, and impacts of innovation, imagination, and changing work practices and conditions (Hesmondhalgh and Baker 2008). Drawing on Rojek's (2010) construction of "leisure" from a cultural and social theory perspective, it becomes apparent that in many ways the ideas, or ideals, of the cultural and creative industries, and the avant-garde cultural policies that enshrine their status in the developed West, are not too dissimilar to theoretical appreciations of "leisure." Rojek (2010, 1), for example, states that leisure is "considered and culturally represented, to exist in a state of voluntarism." Rojek challenges and critiques the extent to which freedom and autonomy ever really exist, even in contexts of leisure and pleasure. For Rojek, the most significant questions for leisure studies are "freedom from what?" and "freedom from whom?" Following Baudrillard (1970), he explores the extent to which consumer capitalism dictates our appreciations of what might constitute pleasure and fun, that is to say the extent to which we are "bedazzled into enthusiastically colluding in our [sic] own disenfranchise-ment" (Linstead, Marechal, and Griffin 2014, 172). Such an argument has strong parallels with debates regarding autonomy in the cultural and creative industries. Ross (2003), for example, suggests that such industries often promise their workers "oodles of auton-omy" and "warm collegiality." Yet, Ross (2003, 2009) and others (Banks 2007; Holt and Lapenta 2010) have questioned the true autonomy of workers who are subject to "pun-ishing regimes of self-regulation, self-exploitation, flexibility and precarity" (Bennett,

Strange, and Medrado 2014, 140). Such debates have pointed to a situation that is more complex than workers simply being "duped" by the glamour of the creative industries.

Drawing upon these two parallel strands of thinking, this chapter seeks to reanalyze our own data set of interviews with those who work in the cultural and creative industries as music producers and sound engineers. The music industry is defined by stereotypical images and media representations of excess, pleasure, intensity, and play, which have given rise to folklore of "sex, drugs, and rock 'n' roll." By applying the "leisure lens" to our qualitative study of sound engineers, we seek to challenge and explore two main questions: (1) To what extent is the lived reality of working in studio contexts with creative artists reflected in the stereotypical representations of "rock 'n' roll"? and (2) To what extent is the "rock 'n' roll vibe" either an organic, voluntary state of creativity or a facilitated "emotional FX" elicited by studio staff to enhance particular musical performances? Pursuit of these research questions allows us, to address the "surprising lack of qualitative studies of working conditions in the cultural industries" and the general neglect of the labor process and individual subjectivity in the cultural workplace (Banks 2007).

We start our exploration of this normally closed and hidden world with a brief review of the contextually relevant literature on emotional labor, followed by a discussion of the contemporary recording studio sector, specifically the changing employment relationships of sound engineers and music producers with studio infrastructures. Next, we provide a brief methodological explanation before moving on to present the voices of those working in studio environments, paying particular attention to three key themes: emotional FX, drugs, and rock 'n' roll.

MUSIC PRODUCTION

The global music industry is, and in many ways always has been, in a state of flux. Watson (2013), however, marks the last half a decade as being characterized by an intensification of instability and technological change. In particular, through the late 1990s and early 2000s, issues around intellectual property rights and the illegal distribution of music coded in new digital file formats (see Leyshon 2001, 2003; Leyshon et al. 2005) have caused a full-blown "crisis of reproduction" (Leyshon 2009) within the music industry. The recording studio sector has been hit particularly hard, as the resulting crisis in funding across the musical economy has impacted negatively upon the recording budgets of record companies. Further, the increased availability and usability of high-quality digital software for home recording, and the means for distributing and promoting this music online, such as through social media, mean it is now possible to circumvent traditional music-production processes and facilities. Consequently, the recording industry is experiencing significant challenges in terms of its ability to control both production and distribution, which have become far more amorphous and complex.

Andrew Leyshon (2009), in his compelling account of the decline of the studio sector, argues that the reduction of demand for studio time is resulting in "a spate of studio closures, redundancies, and underemployment within musical agglomerations" (Leyshon 2009, 1309). Paul Théberge (2012), however, argues that the evidence to support claims regarding large-scale studio closures is largely anecdotal. Based on census data from the United States over the last decade, Théberge suggests that the number of commercial studios has actually grown over that period, and the number of people involved in sound recording also grew, along with studio income and employee pay.

Yet, debates over the rate and scale of studios aside, there is much qualitative evidence that suggests that the changes occurring in the sector have led to often negative transformational shifts in the nature of employment relations in the music industry, and particularly for those engaged in recording work. Watson (2013) explores these changes in detail. For those studios that have survived, and for new studios opening, the industry is markedly more precarious, to which the response has been the emergence of a culture of entrepreneurialism that is reshaping employment and work in the recording studio sector in a variety of ways. Perhaps most significant is that, given falling recording budgets, professional recording studios can now rarely afford to employ engineers and producers on permanent contracts. Contracted salaried positions are now rare in the recording studio sector, even in the largest of studios. Rather, we are seeing an increased shift toward more flexible and freelance models of employment, in which engineers and producers are brought in to work on recording projects as and when their particular expertise is required.

While, for studios, having the ability to recruit staff in this manner has allowed for an increased level of flexibility, control, and reduced overheads, it has also marked the beginning of a new employment relationship that is transactional, contractual, and short-term. This, combined with the emergence of increasing numbers of self-employed engineers and producers working from home studios or small project studios requiring much less investment and maintenance and thus much cheaper rates, has meant that competition for work between these freelance, project-based workers is often tough. The result is a precarious labor market marked by insecurity and anxiety as to where the next piece of work is going to come from (Entwistle and Wissenger 2006), and in which bulimic patterns of working (Gill and Pratt 2008, 17) are common; as Leyshon (2009) describes, periods that are light on work—resulting in little or no pay for freelance engineers—are mirrored by periods of punishing overwork when studios are busy.

Against this backdrop of *precarity* concerning changes in the employment relations of recording studio work there have been significant changes to the nature of the work itself. Yet, while in recent years a body of literature has emerged that considers issues of freelance work and employment insecurity across the creative and media industries (see e.g., Arvidsson, Malossi, and Naro 2010; Blair 2001, 2009; Blair, Culkin, and Randle 2003; Blair, Grey, and Randle 2001; Christopherson 2002, 2004; Dex et al. 2000; Gill 2002; Henninger and Gottschall 2007; Hesmondhalgh and Baker 2010, 2011; Lee 2011), as Hesmondhalgh and Baker (2010, 5) note, there has been a "surprising lack of qualitative studies of working conditions in the cultural industries." For Banks, corresponding with the general neglect of the labor process has been a "lack of attention paid to the issue of individual subjectivity in the cultural workplace" (2007, 27). It is the subjective issues around work and employment, namely the impact of changing employment relations on the workers and resulting changes in the nature of the work they perform, that is the focus of our research interest. In this chapter, we explore some of these changes, with a particular interest in the nature of the emotional labor in recording work.

Emotional Labor

Emotional labor (Hochschild 1983) is the term used to describe the process by which emotions and feelings become organizational commodities with an exchange value. "This labour requires one to induce or suppress feeling in order to sustain the outward countenance that produces the proper state of mind in others" (Hochschild 1983, 7). Importantly, this type of labor not only requires workers to manage their own feelings but also those of the customers, patients, or other employees they encounter, often in very difficult and challenging circumstances (see Ward and McMurray 2016). There is no surprise then that over thirty years of emotional labor studies have tended to focus on customer service roles. However, a growing interest in the established body of literature from across disciplines has seen a diversification in sites of study—including the cultural and creative industries (Hesmondhalgh and Baker 2008) and the recording studio (Watson and Ward 2013).

In the cultural and creative industries, having the ability to "produce the proper state of mind in others" (Hochschild 1983, 7) is key, in elicitating an appropriate emotional responses from others that enhance the performance, persona, or participation of those involved in the project (Hesmondhalgh and Baker 2008). However, what is often overlooked is the extent to which such emotional special effects are achieved through the management of personal emotions, reactions, and behaviors by employees in exchange for a wage. Emotional FX are produced through skilled performances of emotional labor wherein the worker manages the emotions of both self and other to create, control, and engineer particular vibes, or atmospheres, that help the artists and musicians achieve their desired performance.

While there has been substantial academic interest in the relationships between music and emotion (see Wood, Duffy, and Smith 2007; Wood and Smith 2004), and in particular the emotional and bodily performances of musicians and audiences (see e.g., Holman Jones 1999 on women's music; Morton 2005 on Irish traditional music; Duffy et al. 2011 on festival spaces), little has been written on the emotional labor of others working in the music industry. In particular, while there are numerous studies of the recording studio as a technological and creative sound-space of music production (see in particular: Horning 2004; Théberge 1997; Warner 2003; Zak 2001), few studies have considered the social and emotional aspects of studio work (exceptions include Watson 2014; Watson and Ward 2013). Revisiting this idea in this chapter, we focus on music producers and recording engineers, working in recording studios, as one such group of people performing emotional labor to elicit appropriate and desired emotive musical performances. Recording studios, then, are interesting sonic and cultural spaces in which emotions are "routinely heightened" (Anderson and Smith 2001) and where "the emotional content of human relations is deliberately laid bare" (Wood and Smith 2004, 535).

In this chapter, we explore the ways in which engineers and producers in recording studios deliberately manage their own emotions in order to influence, support, and elicit desired performances from artists. Emotional labor performances in these settings often aim to recast the technological, and often stark, physical space of the recording studio as a site of autonomy and play (referred to by Watson and Ward as "creating the right vibe")—characteristics more akin to leisure contexts than work contexts. These emotional labor performances, then, that are designed to turn the producers' and engineers' work spaces into sites of pleasure and excess, are performed against a backdrop of intense, unsociable, and sometimes uncomfortable working conditions for the producers and engineers. It is the intersection of "work" and "play" in this one physical space that makes the recording studio such a rich site for exploring the complexity and multifaceted nature of emotional labor.

METHODS

An empirical data set of twenty semistructured interviews forms the basis of the discussions presented in this chapter. Interviews were conducted between June 2010 and May 2013 with U.K.-based recording studio producers and engineers, all but one of whom were based in London. Interviewees were from a range of employment categories (freelance, contracted to a recording studio, or owner-operator of a studio) and worked in studios that ranged from very small project studios to large, internationally renowned recording facilities. Aside from two interviews that took place in cafés, all interviews were conducted at the recording studios in which the interviewees worked. Interviewing within the "context" allowed us a window into what is otherwise a closed and protected environment—one we all know exists and can all imagine, but one few of us have the opportunity to experience. From the interviewer's perspective, interviewing in these spaces allowed a deeper emotional and aesthetic appreciation of the work being spoken about by the research participants, as it allowed them to envisage the stories and accounts regaled upon them with some contextual resonance.

The identities of all participants have been protected with the use of pseudonyms; however, ages and genders remain unchanged. It is important to note and acknowledge that all twenty interviewees were men aged between twenty and sixty-five years of age. Rather than seeing this as a gendered bias, we argue that, given the relatively small sample size, this is representative of the occupation, the world of music production; recording and engineering continue to be dominated by men (see Leonard 2014). Some of the participants had university qualifications in sound engineering and/or music while others had no formal sound engineering qualifications, but rather had learnt their skills "on the job," having begun their careers as "runners" and tape operatives, working their way up to become engineers and/or producers.

All interviews followed a preestablished schedule of questions. There was, however, a high degree of flexibility to explore interesting ideas and issues that emerged from the discussions. The purpose of the interviews was to establish an appreciation of the nature of creative work in the studio, including the role of technology in the creative process, social capital building, and the political and economic landscape of music production. The emotional labor of music production was not, then, a preidentified focus of the study—instead, the emotional nature of the work was a theme that emerged strongly from discussions with interviewees. Interviews were transcribed verbatim and thematically coded. From these, a number of key themes emerged and have been the focus of specific publications (Watson 2013, 2014; Watson and Ward 2013).

Emotional FX

Recording studios are unique and particular sites of musical production. They are most often small, dark, insulated spaces, within which music is produced under conditions of intense collaboration. Brian, an experienced male engineer and studio owner in his fifties, describes how working in a recording studio is

> quite an intense process. . . . [Y]ou are all basically in a small room together for 18 to 20 hours, doing this thing and living it. You basically live with these people for a really intense period of time, sleeping very little, working in a really focused kind of environment.

In such an environment, it is essential that studio engineers and producers are able to build friendly, collaborative, and constructive working relations with their clients. Central to this is the ability of an engineer or producer to manage their own emotions in such a way as to facilitate the building and maintenance of relationships of affinity and trust. This type of relational work, termed as "emotional labor" (Hochschild 1983), was, to the producers and engineers interviewed, understood to involve "people skills." In many instances, these people skills were considered equally important to, and sometimes even more important than, the ability to perform competently a technical role and operate complex studio equipment. As John, an experienced producer-engineer in his forties from a major London recording studio, described, "It's probably more people based than it is technical. . . . [Y]ou've obviously got to deliver on the technical but it's not really the essence of the job." The importance of personal skills is also emphasized by Terry, a male studio engineer in his thirties:

> It is a very personal thing for some people. . . . I would say the social aspect of it is probably about 50 percent of the whole side of making records. . . . I think a lot of the artists that I work with are really looking to build a relationship massively with a studio and an engineer. So I would say that's a massive, massive factor in it.

Ashforth and Humphrey (1993) argue that in the performance of emotional labor there are interactive effects between the *work context* and *work content*, and the emotional state of an individual. In the case of studio work, "work content" refers to the particular music recording project and the genre of music being recorded, while the "work context" refers to the studio space and the relationships between studio workers (producers and engineers) and musicians and artists. Following this line of argument, we would expect that the manner in which a studio worker displays feelings to musicians recording in the studio will have a strong impact on the attractiveness of the interpersonal climate within the studio. Put simply, the better the ability of a producer to manage his or her own emotions, the more likely personal relationships of trust will be developed. This was alluded to by James, a male engineer-producer and studio owner in his forties, who described his own difficulties in this regard: "Having a good way with people is vital. But the thing is, I don't really have such a good way with people, which is a major problem for me. It's harder for me to win people's trust than a lot of producers."

However, this is not to assume that effective emotion management strategies have to be positive and empathetic. Indeed, some producers and artists may prefer a very different studio vibe—one imbued with tension, expectation, and even aggression (examples include Phil Spector and Steve Albini, with infamous reputations for berating and belittling artists in their studios), created through performances of antipathetic emotional labor (Korczynski 2002; Ward and McMurray 2016). Yet, in order to fully understand the necessity for this kind of emotional labor, it is necessary to consider recording studios not only as technical and social spaces, but also as spaces of musical performance. As we have seen above, the recording studio is not only a physical setting, but also a social setting, and it is the social setting that acts to determine the meanings being generated by a given performance. Musical performance is a setting in which the emotional is routinely heightened (Anderson and Smith 2001), but, as Small (1998) notes, performing generates emotions and meanings that differ from context to context. Recording studios are unique spaces of music performance, in the sense that the emotions of performances and relations are experienced in a very insulated space, often under conditions of intense collaboration. In this sense, the atmosphere and ambience that producers and engineers work to create through their emotional labor are crucially important. Nervousness, tension, and a lack of confidence in artists when faced with recording in a formal studio space, for example, can often (but not always) be prohibitive to artists producing a desired performance or a "good take." Getting a performance from a musician is often not about "forcing" a performance by putting people under pressure; rather, it is about creating a relaxed atmosphere and teasing out a performance, often by being relaxed and easy-going, and putting tense and nervous musicians at ease. As Ben, an experienced producer in his forties described, "Sometimes, once that red light goes on people do tend to tense up a bit, so getting the best performance isn't about going out there and throwing tea cups at the wall like Alex Ferguson. . . . You've really got to get the atmosphere right and get everybody relaxed." An open, relaxed atmosphere that encourages emotional expression through performance will come from projecting a relaxed and friendly disposition, which might often contradict the personal feelings of a producer or engineer. In other words, the recording studio staff work hard to engineer an ambience and vibe in the studio in which music making is more a relaxed and enjoyable leisure activity than one that is fraught with the tensions and stresses of a time-constrained project within a formal work environment. Emotional labor is, then, a key part in creating a particular atmosphere of leisure in the recording studio.

Unlike in truly live performance settings, studio performances occur without an audience present. In the studio, the producer or engineer becomes the audience. The emotional labor performed by producers and engineers is also important in this respect. In giving feedback on a performance, as Hennion (1990) describes, producers will draw not only upon a set of technical criteria, but, more importantly, upon their feelings about the music and the physical sensations they experience because of it. They must also feed energy to performers, in the absence of an audience, in an attempt to reproduce the dynamic and emotional nature of live performance within the studio. Being able to capture the dynamic and emotional nature of a live performance on record is crucial, as listeners who buy a recording will not be part of a live performance; rather, because they will use the recordings to create their own event, it becomes necessary for musicians and producers or engineers to create performances on record that will serve the purposes of these contexts. As producer Frank Filipetti describes, "In the end the performance is the thing. There are very few people who will buy a record because of the sound of it . . . Ninety-nine percent of the public buys a record because it does something to them, it moves them, there's an emotional impact, it moves their mind, it moves their body, it does something to them" (quoted in Massey 2000, 198)

For Jarrett (2012, 129), producers work hard to enable and to record sounds that, when listeners hear them, convey the impression of having "escaped the clutches of production and the constraints of recording technologies." Thus producers work to elicit a performance from a musician that is full of "authentic" emotion (Meier 2011) and which will therefore have an emotive impact on the listener in their everyday lives (see e.g., Juslin and Laukka 2004). Eliciting emotions in performance is, then, a key aspect of the emotional labor of producers and engineers. As Wood, Duffy, and Smith (2007) note, musical performances are about intimate encounters and the sharing of an emotional experience with other people involved in the performance. In many instances, songs—lyrics in particular—will be loaded with feeling and emotion drawn from particular emotional experiences of musicians and recording artists. For producers and engineers, displaying sensitivity and empathy toward these emotional performances is imperative. This "empathetic" emotional labor (Korczynski 2003) involves efforts "to understand others, to have empathy with their situation, to feel their feelings as part of one's own" (England and Farkas 1986, 91). Terry, a resident engineer at a medium-sized studio in northwest London, noted the need to be very sensitive, saying, "It is a very exposing experience for a lot of artists to come into the studio and say 'here's a song I've written' because they trust you to not turn around and say 'it's crap, your voice sounds terrible, your lyrics are awful, and you've just told me the whole story about your failed love life and I'm going to rip the piss out of you about it.' "

On the other hand, often studio producers and engineers must attempt to elicit strong emotions from the musician or recording artists to capture an emotive performance. With vocalists it is often necessary to get a recording artist into a particular emotional state in order to achieve a "believable" performance. Getting this performance may involve creating the type of relaxed atmosphere described in the previous section; however, at times it might also require a producer or engineer to make a musician uncomfortable, or even to upset them. Parallels can be drawn here with Grindstaff's (2002) and Hesmondhalgh and Baker's (2008) accounts of television workers being required to elicit the strongest possible version of the emotions felt by contestants on confessional talk shows and talent shows, respectively.

As Watson (2014) outlines, in response to the significant challenges that professional studios are now facing from home studios, professional producers and engineers often seek to defend the "value added" that comes from recording in a professional recording studio. It is common to point to the limited technical abilities of home recordists (see Cole 2011) when compared to the "experienced technique" (Zak 2001) of professionals. Further, the importance of having the experienced ear of a producer on a record is often emphasized as a key benefit of recording in a professional studio, one which is considered essential to producing commercially successful music. But, based on the above discussion, the "value added" of the professional studio, we would argue, is not limited to technical prowess or musical taste. It also includes the emotional support, encouragement, and critique that are so crucial to musical performance within a studio context. As Jack emphasized, "A lot of people record alone in bedrooms these days; they just stick a mic or a guitar into their computer and that's it, they don't have anyone to bounce ideas off, so they get a lot out of working with somebody else. . . . [A] lot of it is to do with getting the performance out of them as well." As well as mentioning performance, this interviewee touched on another important issue, namely the way in which the more social aspects of music making are also an important part of engineer's job. The emotional aspects of work that we have described above impact not only on the emotionality of the performance, but also on the ways in which an engineer fosters an artist's trust and respect (see Watson 2014). To achieve this, producers and engineers often have to tolerate, and in some of the more extreme cases participate in, behaviors that include the use and abuse of both drugs and alcohol. In the following section, we examine how this acts to further blur the boundaries between practices of work and leisure within the recording studio space.

DRUGS

I don't know whether I'm allowed to say this or not. . . . [I]t's just amazing that you can do that many drugs and actually come out of it with something at the end . . . I've seen that table covered in coke . . . and . . . you do a three-day session and everyone's on E.

(Anthony, male producer, forties)

Anthony's confessional exposé on the use and abuse of drugs and alcohol upholds the stereotypical images of excess synonymous with the music industry (for examples of substance abuse by artists across a range of genres see Miller and Quigley 2011; Raeburn et al. 2003; Shapiro 2003). Not only can the (ab)use of these substances be something of a status symbol in popular musical culture, but these substances are often considered to enhance the musical creativity of artists, performers, and musicians. Elsewhere we have briefly alluded to the way in which drug and alcohol use often played a significant role in creating the "right vibe" in the studio (Watson and Ward 2013), and it was therefore required of those working within these musical settings to be tolerant of, or even to partake in, their consumption. Paul, a male engineer in his thirties, explained just how tolerant he had to be, and why he felt this to be an important part of the creative and social process of creating music:

> I suppose they need to be comfortable. So if they need a couple of beers to be comfortable then that's fine. I suppose it is a bit weird because . . . you're working with people who you've never met before or only met a few times so if you need a couple of beers to relax then that's fine, but then you also get late night sessions where there's more people around here than need to be here. . . . We've had 20–30 people out there and they start having a party and you're in here and they'll come in one at a time to do their bit of recording.

This account of studio work epitomizes the connections and disconnects between music making, or "musicking" (Small 1998), and leisure. While the artists and performers have clearly redefined the physical space of the recording studio as a party venue, it continues to be James's workspace. For James, this is where he comes on a day-to-day basis to develop his craft and toils to produce the best possible results, while the artists to whom he refers see it as a space of leisure and enjoyment.

However, for some of the sound engineers and producers we interviewed, separating "work" and "play" became virtually impossible. Anthony, an experienced pop music producer in his forties, told us that, despite initially resisting, he had "succumbed" to taking drugs as part of the social act of music making, leading to an addiction that would last seven years. Anthony could no longer separate his work from play, as his own role in recasting the rules and norms of acceptability within the space of the recording studio became a lived reality for him beyond the boundaries of the studio sessions. Accounts of the social pressure to use drugs in recording sessions abound the biographies of well-known producers and engineers. Engineer Phill Brown, for example, describes his own use of drugs while working with the Small Faces in the late 1960s:

> Drugs in the form of speed and dope were in abundance on Small Faces sessions. . . . When we worked late into the night, the roadies occasionally offered me a toke or a blue [speed]. . . . It had been a long day and it was now around 2 a.m. I was particularly tired and had been fighting off sleep since midnight. One of the roadies saw me nodding off at the 8-track machine, came over and handed me a black pill. I felt a bit doubtful, but the roadie said, "Don't worry, it's fine. It will just help you to stay

awake." This allayed my fears and I swallowed the pill . . . by 2 or 3 a.m. [the next day] most of the bad side effects of the speed had hit me. . . . It was difficult to work. . . . The roadies thought this was very amusing; as I left for home they informed me they had given me a black bomber—a particularly strong form of speed. . . . Although I later took speed in the form of the milder blue pills, this experience made me avoid anything stronger. (Brown 2010, 20–21)

Those who resist temptation perhaps have a more complex and subtle relational challenge, as they have to continue to build relationships, trust, credibility, and authenticity within the music industry and yet distance themselves from such a culturally dominant practice. Paul made it clear that there was a fine line to be trodden in this regard, and that his approach was one of tolerance rather than totalitarianism: "I don't tend to go round saying 'Well don't have any more drinks!'" Anthony's take on the use of drugs and alcohol was similar in many ways to that of Paul's with regard to his tolerating the practice; however, his comments also present an interesting interplay of the emotional, practical, and technical justifications for his approach to managing the use of certain types of drug use:

There's no "No Smoking" signs in the studio. Generally, people just smoke outside but every now and then someone will turn around and say, "Is it alright to smoke?" and generally what I say is, "You can't smoke cigarettes in here because cigarettes just make so much smoke." Although I have got £2000 extractor fans that can clean the air in here . . . but some clients I still allow them to smoke joints . . . but it's a pain because when they do you have to Hoover the studio every night. . . . but I do think if a client feels happy and comfortable they are more likely to be creative, aren't they?

For Anthony, artists smoking cigarettes and marijuana is not difficult or problematic from a moral standpoint but from a purely practical one, in that their use required him to vacuum the carpet after sessions. And yet, this had to be weighed against his view that artists partaking in these activities in some way improved their creativity. Yet, despite this common-held belief, there appear to be limits to which their use is helpful to the creative process. A recent case in point is that of British rock band Kasabian, who in two high-profile interviews with British press admitted to high levels of drug use while recording, but stated that in future they would ban drugs from the recording studio because of the negative effects on the quality of their music. The interplay of these practical and creative issues problematizes stereotypical rock 'n' roll images of pure excess. It is to this issue that we now turn in our analysis.

Rock 'n' Roll

As Beer (2014) notes, little is actually known about the work of recording engineers by those outside of the music production community. In this section we extend our exploration of the "unknown" to the nature of the work undertaken in studio contexts. While a number of music producers have become as famous as the recording artists they work with (for example, Mark Ronson, Pharell Williams, and Timbaland), the actual practices of recording work very rarely make headline news. The tacit artistic, creative, and technological abilities of sound engineers are purposefully hidden and unspoken, in that the work they undertake is designed to enhance that of the artists, not to be seen or heard "center-stage." Beer (2014, 191) eloquently makes the point that studio music producers are "concealed agents making often unknown contributions to the sonic properties of culture." In contrast, artists, musicians, and performers of various kinds—as well as music producers in genres such as hip-hop and dance music—often make headline news and invite the public into their private and professional lives in pursuit of fame and fortune. What these often highly orchestrated sneak peeks present us with are images of wealth, excess, and glamour stereotypically associated with rock 'n' roll mythologies.

Despite the growing celebrity status of a relatively small number of music producers and the importance of recording studios within the overall value chain of the recorded music industry, recording studios and the working lives of producers and engineers continue to be marginalized in much academic research on the economics of the music industry, which has tended to focus on the effect of changes in the industry upon record companies (exceptions include Gibson 2005 and Leyshon 2009). Building on Watson's (2013) study of work and employment in the studio sector, we present a somewhat subversive image of rock 'n' roll through the voices of those who work in the industry and how they feel about what they do. As Andrew, an experienced male engineer in his sixties noted, "Some people see it as a very glamorous job, but in fact it isn't really." Further, as Ben describes, music recording is often not as "exciting" or as "rock 'n' roll" as one might think: "You see, it's kind of easy for bands because they do one record and then they go on tour. Then they're excited to come back in, but you're in the studio all the time." Producers and engineers work day in day out, often for long, grueling hours in that same space but with different artists. To them it is their place of work, routines, and repetition, and yet they respect and acknowledge the importance of helping artists experience that same space in new and creative ways.

Undertaking qualitative interviews with engineers and producers within their work settings has given us an invaluable insight into the working conditions of producers. Aside from the major recording facilities (what are informally termed within the sector as "pot-plant" studios because they have a formal reception area, adorned with indoor plants, for welcoming clients and guests), studios are most often dark, small, insulated spaces. Many of the studios in which the interviews were undertaken were in converted outbuildings of residential properties, or within a small industrial or storage unit. Aside from recording equipment, these studios are generally relatively sparse, with little in the way of creature comforts (other than a couch and a fridge), natural light, or fresh air. It is within these spaces that engineers undertake often repetitive and time-consuming tasks, over very long hours of work. As Jack, a young engineer in his twenties at a major London recording studio describes, "Most studio days are twelve hours in a session . . . so let's say you can start recording at 10 a.m. and record until 9 p.m., but you have to be in early at 8 a.m. the next day and finish at 10 p.m. and then you've got to set up for the next day . . . so it is pretty rough." As with any other sector of the cultural economy, the intensity and precarious nature of the work means that it needs to be done when it is there (see Watson 2013), and thus there is little tolerance for turning down work or over-running with work, as this has a detrimental effect on the day's schedule. This can result in periods of "punishing overwork" when studios are busy (Leyshon 2009).

Within these small, insulated spaces, recording studio workers are often subject to the "brutal power relations" (Leyshon 2009, 1316) that frequently play out in recording studios. Ben described his experience of these power relations in recording studios in the 1980s: "Work in a studio was equivalent to now working in a kitchen with Gordon Ramsay. It was that type of environment, where you'd have an engineer-producer who was just a complete bastard and get upset about the smallest things that didn't matter." As Richard, a young engineer in his twenties noted, "I think one of the most important things for people that are coming into the business and want to be engineers and want to work in studios, there's a very distinct hierarchy." The hierarchy consists of, at the top end, studio managers, producers, and chief engineers, down through senior engineers, engineers, and assistant engineers. At the very bottom of the hierarchies sit "tea boys" or runners, who do a range of jobs from setting up microphones and looking after the phones to making tea and cleaning the toilets. As Richard went on to explain, "As a new assistant working in studios you've got to be very . . . you've got to be there when you're needed. You might go and set up a mike or make a cup of tea, so it's quite hierarchical."

For many junior engineers, whether they have any formal training or education in sound engineering or not, their "formal" career in the recording studio sector begins right at the bottom of this hierarchy as a runner, with high demands being placed on them to perform both technical and menial tasks and work exhausting hours. As Jack went on to explain of his own experience:

> So I started here, and as you do when you're twenty-one fresh faced and got no ties . . . you have a social life but you don't after you start working here, and eventually I was doing 90 hours a week for probably about the first six, seven years of work-ing here. . . . I was very enthusiastic. It was averaging 90 hours; some weeks would be 150, 120 hours. Some weeks would be a bit quieter, like kind of 40.

Ben suggested that these long hours were "almost kinds of rites of passage to burn" for young studio workers. Such quotes emphasize that the nature of studio work is most often unglamorous and hard. Further, as the following quote from James highlights, it is also very often physically and emotionally demanding: "I was freelancing at [a studio] for a couple of years and then I didn't exactly have a nervous breakdown; I had a physical breakdown, which is like . . . I overdid it and it completely destroyed me. Long hours, a lot of stress and it was very, very difficult." James's deeply personal testimony of the emo-tional burnout he suffered as a consequence of the demanding and precarious nature of recording studio work presents an antithetical image of the rock 'n' roll lifestyle of the recording studio.

Conclusion

It is evident from the above discussion that recording studio work is demanding, unspoken, unglamorous, often repetitive and unexciting, and most certainly precarious. It is also emotionally charged. On the one hand, workers must manage their own emotions in such ways as to build relationships and elicit emotional performances from artists; on the other, workers can be subject to physical and emotional stresses from the job, including long hours and exposure to alcohol and substance abuse. These accounts of the "dark side" of organizational life (see Linstead, Marechal, and Griffin 2014; Ward and McMurray 2016) within the music industry stand in stark contrast to the aspirational stereotypical images of the rock 'n' roll lifestyle of excess enjoyed by those working in the music industry.

In closing this chapter, we argue that the application of the "leisure lens" to our qualitative study of sound engineers, our data, and analysis supports the arguments posited by a number of theorists concerned with exploring the lived reality of the creative industries (Banks 2007; Holt and Lapenta 2010; Ross 2003, 2009), in that the perceived autonomy, funds, and friendships associated with the cultural industries (Hesmondhalgh and Baker 2011) and leisure itself, are largely emotional FX; special effects created through emotional labor performances to maintain the illusions and folklore of voluntarism. Perhaps more importantly, though, these effects also serve to create, enhance, or maintain a creative "vibe" within the studio space that helps to elicit a desired emotional performance from artists. Such a "vibe," then, is not always voluntary, organic, or emergent, but is often the result of carefully engineering the emotional states of self (sound engineers) and other (artists).

References Cited

Anderson, Kay, and Susan J. Smith. 2001. "Editorial: Emotional Geographies." *Transactions of the Institute of British Geographers* 26: 7–10.

Arvidsson, Adam, Giannino Malossi, and Serpica Naro. 2010. "Passionate Work? Labour Conditions in the Milan Fashion Industry." *Journal for Cultural Research* 14: 295–309.

Ashforth, Blake E., and Ronald Humphrey. 1993. "Emotional Labour in Service Roles: The Influence of Identity." *Academy of Management Review* 18(1): 88–115.

Banks, Mark. 2007. *The Politics of Cultural Work.* Basingstoke: Palgrave Macmillan.

Baudrillard, Jean. 1970. *La Société de consommation: Ses mythes, ses structures.* Paris: Editions Denoël. Translated by Chris Turner as *The Consumer Society: Myths and Structures.* London: Sage, 1998.

Beer, David. 2014. "The Precarious Double Life of the Recording Engineer." *Journal for Cultural Research* 18: 189–202.

Bennett, James, Niki Strange, and Andrea Medrado. 2014. "A Moral Economy of Independent Work? Creative Freedom and Public Service in UK Digital Agencies." In *Media Independence: Working with Freedom or Working for Free?*, edited by James Bennett and Niki Strange, 139–158. New York: Routledge.

Blair, Helen. 2001. "'You're only as Good as Your Last Job': The Labour Process and Labour Market in the British Film Industry." *Work, Employment and Society* 15: 149–169.

Blair, Helen. 2009. "Active Networking: Action, Social Structure and the Process of Networking." In *Creative Labour: Working in the Creative Industries*, edited by Alan McKinlay and Chris Smith, 116–134. Basingstoke: Palgrave Macmillan.

Blair, Helen, Nigel Culkin, and Keith Randle. 2003. "From London to Los Angeles: A Comparison of Local Labour Market Processes in the US and UK Film Industries." *International Journal of Human Resource Management* 14: 619–633.

Blair, Helen, Susan Grey, and Keith Randle. 2001. "Working in Film: Employment in a Project Based Industry." *Personnel Review* 30: 170–185.

Brown, Phill. 2010. *Are We Still Rolling? Studios, Drugs and Rock 'n' Roll: One Man's Journey Recording Classic Albums*. Portland Oregan: Tape Op Books.

Christopherson, Susan. 2002. "Project Work in Context: Regulatory Change and the New Geography of Media." *Environment and Planning A* 34: 2003–2015.

Christopherson, Susan. 2004. "The Divergent Worlds of New Media: How Policy Shapes Work in the Creative Economy." *Review of Policy Research* 21: 543–558.

Cole, Steven J. 2011. "The Prosumer and the Project Studio: The Battle for Distinction in the Field of Music Recording." *Sociology* 45: 447–463.

Dex, Shirley, Janet Willis, Richard Peterson, and Elaine Sheppard. 2000. "Freelance Workers and Contract Uncertainty: The Effects of Contractual Changes in the Television Industry." *Work, Employment and Society* 14: 283–305.

Duffy, Michelle, Gordon Waitt, Andrew Gorman-Murray, and Chris Gibson. 2011. "Bodily Rhythms: Corporeal Capacities to Engage with Festival Spaces." *Emotion, Space and Society* 4(1): 17–24.

England, Paula, and George Farkas. 1986. *Households, Employment, and Gender: A Social, Economic, and Demographic View*. New York: Aldine Publishing.

Entwistle, Joanne, and Elizabeth Wissenger. 2006. "Keeping up Appearances: Aesthetic Labour in the Fashion Modelling Industries of London and New York." *Sociological Review* 54(4): 774–794.

Gibson, Chris. 2005. "Recording Studios: Relational Spaces of Creativity in the City." *Built Environment* 31: 192–207.

Gill, Rosalind. 2002. "Cool, Creative and Egalitarian? Exploring Gender in Project-Based New Media Work in Europe Information." *Communication and Society* 5: 70–89.

Gill, Rosalind, and Andy C. Pratt. 2008. "In the Social Factory? Immaterial Labour, Precariousness and Cultural Work." *Theory, Culture and Society* 25(7–8): 1–30.

Grindstaff, Laura. 2002. *The Money Shot: Trash, Class, and the Making of TV Talk Shows*. Chicago: University of Chicago Press.

Henninger, Annette, and Karin Gottschall. 2007. "Freelancers in Germany's Old and New Media Industry: Beyond Standard Patterns and Work and Life." *Critical Sociology* 33: 43–71.

Hennion, Antoine. 1990. "The Production of Success: An Antimusicology of the Pop Song." *On Record: Rock, Pop, and the Written Word*, edited by Simon Frith and Andrew Goodwin, 154–171. London: Routledge.

Hesmondhalgh, David, and Sarah Baker. 2008. "Creative Work and Emotional Labour in the Television Industry." *Theory, Culture and Society* 25(7–8): 97–118.

Hesmondhalgh, David and Sarah Baker. 2010. "'A Very Complicated Version of Freedom': Conditions and Experiences of Creative Labour in Three Cultural Industries." *Poetics* 38: 4–20

Hesmondhalgh, David, and Sarah Baker. 2011. *Creative Labour: Media Work in Three Cultural Industries*. London: Routledge.

Hochschild, Arlie R. 1983. *The Managed Heart: Commercialization of Human Feeling*. Berkeley: University of California Press.

Holman Jones, Stacy. 1999. "Women, Musics, Bodies, and Texts: The Gesture of Women's Music." *Text and Performance Quarterly* 19: 217–235.

Holt, Fabian, and Francesco Lapenta. 2010. "Introduction: Autonomy and Creative Labour." *Journal for Cultural Research* 14: 223–229.

Horning, Susan S. 2004. "Engineering the Performance: Recording Engineers, Tacit Knowledge and the Art of Controlling Sound." *Social Studies of Science* 34(5): 703–731.

Jarrett, Michael. 2012. "The Self-Effacing Producer: Absence Summons Presence." In *The Art of Record Production: An Introductory Reader for a New Academic Field*, edited by Simon Frith and Simon Zagorski-Thomas, 129–148. Farnham: Ashgate.

Korczynski, Marek. 2003. "Communities of Coping: Collective Emotional Labour in Service Work." *Organization* 10: 55–79.

Juslin, Patrik N., and Petri Laukka. 2004. "Expression, Perception and Induction of Musical Emotions: A Review and a Questionnaire Study of Everyday Listening." *Journal of New Music Research* 33: 217–238.

Lee, David. 2011. "Networks, Cultural Capital and Creative Labour in the British Independent Television Industry." *Media, Culture and Society* 33: 549–65.

Leonard, Marion. 2014. "Putting Gender in the Mix: Employment, Participation, and Role Expectations in the Music Industries." In *The Routledge Companion to Media and Gender*, edited by Cynthia Carter, Linda Steiner, and Lisa McLaughlin, 127–136. London: Routledge.

Leyshon, Andrew. 2001. "Time-Space (and Digital) Compression: Software Formats, Musical Networks, and the Reorganisation of the Music Industry." *Environment and Planning A* 33: 49–77.

Leyshon, Andrew. 2003. "Scary Monsters? Software Formats, Peer-to-Peer Networks, and the Spectre of the Gift." *Environment and Planning D* 21: 533–558.

Leyshon, Andrew 2009. "The Software Slump? Digital Music, the Democratization of Technology, and the Decline of the Recording Studio Sector within the Musical Economy." *Environment and Planning A* 41: 1309–1331.

Leyshon, Andrew, Peter Webb, Shaun French, Nigel Thrift, and Louise Crewe. 2005. "On the Reproduction of the Musical Economy after the Internet." *Media, Culture and Society* 27: 177–209.

Linstead, Stephen, Garance Marechal, and Rickey W. Griffin. 2014. "Theorizing and Researching the Dark Side of Organizations." *Organization Studies* 35(2): 165–188.

Massey, Howard. 2000. *Behind the Glass: Top Record Producers Tell How They Craft the Hits*. San Francisco: Backbeat.

Meier, L. M. 2011. "Promotional Ubiquitous Musics: Recording Artists, Brands and "Rendering Authenticity." *Popular Music and Society* 34: 399–415.

Miller, Kathleen E., and Brian M. Quigley 2011. "Sensation-Seeking, Performance Genres and Substance Use among Musicians." *Psychology of Music* 39(3): 1–22.

Morton, Frances. 2005. "Performing Ethnography: Irish Traditional Music Sessions and the New Methodological Spaces." *Social and Cultural Geography* 6: 661–676.

Raeburn, Susan D., John Hipple, William Delaney, and Kris Chesky. 2003. "Surveying Popular Musicians' Health Status Using Convenience Samples." *Medical Problems of Performing Artists* 18: 113–119.

Rojek, Chris. 2010. *The Labour of Leisure*. London: Sage.

Ross, Andrew. 2003. *No-Collar: The Humane Workplace and Its Hidden Costs*. New York: Basic Books.

Ross, Andrew. 2009. *Nice Work If You Can Get It: Life and Labor in Precarious Times*. New York: New York University Press.

Shapiro, Harry. 2003. *Waiting for the Man: The Story of Drugs and Popular Music*. London: Helter Skelter.

Small, Christopher. 1998. *Musicking: The Meanings of Performing and Listening*. Middletown, CT: Wesleyan University Press.

Théberge, Paul. 1997. *Any Sound You Can Imagine: Making Music/Consuming Technology*. Middletown, CT: Wesleyan University Press.

Théberge, Paul. 2012. "The End of the World as We Know It: The Changing Role of the Studio in the Age of the Internet." *The Art of Record Production: An Introductory Reader for a New Academic Field*, edited by Simon Frith and Simon Zagorski-Thomas, 77–90. Farnham: Ashgate

Ward, Jenna, and Robert McMurray. 2016. *The Dark Side of Emotional Labour*. Abingdon: Routledge.

Warner, Timothy. 2003. *Pop Music—Technology and Creativity: Trevor Horn and the Digital Revolution*. Aldershot: Ashgate.

Watson, Allan. 2013. "Running a Studio's a Silly Business: Work and Employment in the Contemporary Recording Studio Sector." *Area* 45(3): 330–336.

Watson, Allan. 2014. *Cultural Production in and Beyond the Recording Studio*. New York: Routledge.

Watson, Allan, and Jenna Ward. 2013. "Creating the Right 'Vibe': Transient Emotional Journeys in the Recording Studio." *Environment and Planning A* 45: 2904–2918.

Wood, Nichola, Michelle Duffy, and Susan J. Smith. 2007. "The Art of Doing (Geographies of) Music." *Environment and Planning D* 25: 867–889.

Wood, Nichola, and Susan. J. Smith 2004. "Instrumental Routes to Emotional Geographies." *Social and Cultural Geography* 5: 533–548.

Zak, Albin. 2001. *The Poetics of Rock: Cutting Tracks, Making Records*. London: University of California Press.

CHAPTER 25

....

MUSIC MAKING ON YOUTUBE

....

CHRISTOPHER CAYARI

IN 2005, Lim Jeong-hyun recorded and uploaded "Canon Rock," an electric guitar version of Pachelbel's Canon in D, to Mule.co.kr, a South Korean music website.[1] Recorded in his bedroom, Lim performed the solo to a background track arranged by professional Taiwanese guitarist Jerry Chang, known online as Jerry C (Burgess 2008). In the video, Lim wore a baseball cap covering his face as his fingers flew across his electric guitar, the sunlight from a window illuminating his room.[2] Lim recollected his experience of becoming an overnight sensation on YouTube in the description box of a video on *funtwo*, his YouTube channel:

> I was just an ordinary computer science student studying at Auckland University who liked to play the electric guitar. One fine day I woke up in the afternoon, [and I][3] wanted to get some feedback on my playing. So I uploaded a video clip onto a site called Mule. One day an anonymous person known as "guitar 90" uploaded my video onto YouTube. Millions of people around the world watched and commented on the clip, which to my surprise, led to me becoming a star.[4]

This neoclassical cover became one of the most popular videos on YouTube in the site's early years and inspired other musicians to create their own videos in a similar style (Burgess 2008). Viewers posted responses to the *guitar90* YouTube page of their own covers of "Canon Rock" or electric guitar arrangements of classical works. According to Burgess:

> In addition to the approximately 900 direct video responses to the 'Guitar' video, a keyword search for 'canon rock' in YouTube returns more than 13,000 videos, the majority of which appear to be versions of the original 'Canon Rock' track, performed not only on guitars but also on pianos, violins, and even a toy keyboard. These video responses frequently emulate the original mise-en-scene – with the performer seated on a bed, backlit by the light from a window, and looking down rather than at the camera. (2008, 106)

Seven years after Lim recorded "Canon Rock," he posted a second version titled "funtwo—Canon Rock 2012."[4] Lim capitalized on his Internet popularity, and in 2015 his YouTube channel had over seven million views and nearly 30,000 subscribers. He also monetized his videos and made MP3s of his virtual performances available for purchase on iTunes.

This chapter examines the way musicians like Lim have been making music online by exploring trends of multitrack audio and video recordings on YouTube. Amateur music making published on the Internet has become common since the turn of the twenty-first century, and websites like YouTube have provided a way for people to share their music making with a global audience. By thinking of YouTube as both a place as described by Stebbins (this volume, chapter 19) and a medium as described by Sterne (2003), we can better understand how the website and its users form a symbiotic relationship and how this relationship has shaped the way people make music through online video. I describe three trends of how people are making music for YouTube, including making music alone, becoming part of a collective, and collaborating with others. I then discuss potential drawbacks for musicians who post music videos on YouTube. The chapter ends with suggestions to researchers and theorists on how to explore music video creation on the Internet as a leisure activity.

THE PREVALENCE OF USER-GENERATED VIDEO CONTENT ON THE INTERNET

According to leading Internet provider Cisco (2014), in 2013 online video was responsible for 57 percent of Internet traffic and is projected to be as high as 75 percent in 2018. Duggan (2013) reported in a Pew Research Center study that 26 percent of Internet users have created and 36 percent of Internet users have curated videos by publishing online. This was up from 18 percent of Internet users who had created online videos in 2012.[5] Pew also reported that 48 percent of Internet users eighteen to twenty-nine years old had posted videos taken by themselves and were significantly more likely to have posted videos than any other age group; the 29 percent of Internet users aged thirty to forty-nine years old who created and posted videos were also significantly more likely to have posted videos than older age brackets. These statistics suggest a trend where user-generated video content is becoming more prominent on the Internet and younger age brackets are actively producing videos online.

Publishing user-generated performance videos on the Internet has become a popular activity for many amateur music makers, and websites like YouTube are inclusive of musics that transcend genre and performance style as anyone with an account can upload to the website regardless of their musical ability. In light of philosopher Walter Benjamin's (1968) claim that the popular use of media afforded "an increasing number of readers [to become] writers" (232), I have previously suggested that "YouTube is an art medium; a technology which allows listeners to become singers, watchers to become actors, and consumers to become producers creating new original works and supplementing existing ones" (Cayari 2011, 24). However, considering YouTube merely as an art medium falls short of capturing the complexity of the website's uses and potential. The affordances of video streaming on YouTube have allowed performances by amateur music makers to become accessible to the virtual masses—an instantaneous global audience. YouTube's users have developed ways to use the website that satisfy their needs, and in turn, YouTube has influenced the way people make and share music.

ESTABLISHING A FRAMEWORK OF YOUTUBE

To better understand how YouTube has shaped the way people make music, we can consider the website both a place and a medium. I suggest the music making of amateurs on YouTube and the resulting video projects are often credited with musical activities that can be categorized as *serious leisure*. Stebbins (2007) claims that serious leisure activities can be identified by six characteristics: the activities require perseverance and significant personal effort on the part of the participants. Serious leisure activities contribute to participants' identities and have their own unique ethos. Often, serious leisure activities produce durable benefits and sometimes participants can turn them into a career. Stebbins sums up serious leisure as "the systematic pursuit of an amateur, hobbyist, or volunteer activity sufficiently substantial, interesting, and fulfilling for the participant to find a (leisure) career there acquiring and expressing a combination of its special skills, knowledge, and experience" (347).

Stebbins (this volume, chapter 19) suggests that core musical activities can be performed in various spaces: conquered, showcase, resource, sales, helping, virtual, and tourist spaces. A space becomes a *place* when the participant or participants have a meaningful experience. As the practice of publishing music videos on YouTube has become more prevalent, the website has provided a space for a variety of core musical activities including but not limited to musical practice and performance, audio and video recording, sound mixing, and video editing. While the specific practices regarding how musicians create videos are outside the purview of this chapter, it is important to keep in mind the various activities required to publish videos online. YouTube can become a place where people find meaning while they practice and execute core musical activities. As these practices and activities occur frequently and are experienced by people, trends emerge.

YouTube, as a medium, has provided technology that affords musicians new ways to make music and share recordings with others. Media scholars often consider how a medium and its users influence each other; the users of technology adapt it to suit their needs and the technology also shapes the practices of the users and how they interact with media (Benjamin 1968; Jenkins 2006; Sterne 2003, 2012; Katz 2004). In her analysis of image and its effect on sound and social spaces, Berland (1993) suggested, "Each new medium finds different ways of moving images or sounds into the social spaces of its users, and so places and displaces its listeners differently" (27).

Sterne (2003) describes how a medium can be conceived as "a network—a whole set of relations, practices, people, and technologies" (225). He discusses the concept of mediated performance, suggesting a radio singer does not sing to the audience listening at home but actually sings to the medium: "The medium does not mediate a relation between singer and listener, original and copy. It [the medium] *is* the nature of their connection. Without the medium, there would be no connection, no copy, but also no original, or at least no original in the same form" (226). The radio performance requires the musician to sing differently than they would for a live audience in a concert hall. A medium emerges as people and technologies interact, resulting in a set of practices that change the way performers and their audiences experience sound, performance, and even identity. The "people, practices, institutions, and machines" (223) interact differently as the artist makes music with the medium forming a network of contingent recurring relations. Using this framework, I propose that YouTube can be thought of as a placeholder for the medium created as musicians make online video performances. Musicians on YouTube perform not to their future viewers but to the medium itself. YouTube, the medium, provides a place where video creators, musicians, and consumers make, share, and experience music.

This concept is well situated in the theory of Thibeault (2012), who claims we live in a post[live]performance world. By examining musical performance practices of the twentieth and twenty-first centuries from a media studies prospective, he argues:

> (1) that most of our experiences with music are through recordings rather than live performances; (2) that many pieces of music produced today that originate in a studio separate and estrange audience from performer, resulting in recordings that may be impossible to meaningfully perform live due to sampling or synthesis; and (3) that the prevalence of recordings radically changes the way we hear. (Thibeault 2012, 518)

YouTube, as a medium, has birthed a new way of music making that is distinct to a culture with ubiquitous online videos that appear in social media sites, emails, and mobile applications. YouTube, as place and medium, has inspired musicians to produce mediated musical performances that look and sound very different from live performances.

In the following sections I describe exemplars that represent three trends I have noticed about how music making as a leisure activity manifests itself through music video creation on the Internet: (1) amateurs show off their skills by creating individualized multitrack performances that emulate live performance practices and thus mediate musical ensembles; (2) musicians seek virtual ensembles that allow them to be part of a large collective of hundreds and sometimes thousands of musicians who are compiled by editors; and (3) performers collaborate with others, each contributing to various steps along the creation process, expanding the cadre of people with whom they can make music. These trends help us understand how YouTube, as a place and medium, has provided ways for people to perform and has shaped how music is produced for and experienced on the Internet.

THE BIRTH OF THE PRO-AM

There are many videos on YouTube that were recorded in one take, some that are live performances recorded in front of an audience and others that are recorded live specifically for a YouTube audience. Other videos, however, feature a process called multitracking, where musicians create video performances that are the result of multiple tracks being layered on top of each other with mastered audio, often accompanied by visual effects. These video performances are usually created specifically for display on the Internet and, as Sterne (2003) may suggest, would not exist in the same form if it were not for the aesthetic found within the medium.

Online performance styles like multitracking, stop-motion music videos, and virtual ensembles—each described later in this chapter—have emerged. These styles were and continue to be influenced by a YouTube amateur music video aesthetic that includes do-it-yourself recording practices and audio-visual equipment that ranges from built-in webcams and free editing software to professional cameras, microphones, lights, digital audio workstations, and video editing suites. The development of affordable recording technologies has contributed to the proliferation of recording at home and has led to new ways of amateur music production (Katz 2004). The line between professional and amateur on the Internet has become blurred due to the convergence of commercial and user-generated content (Jenkins 2006). As Burgess and Green (2009) claim, "YouTube *is* symptomatic of a changing media environment, but it is one where the practices and identities associated with cultural production and consumption, commercial and non-commercial enterprise, and professionalism and amateurism interact and converge in new ways" (90, emphasis in original). Indeed, amateurs and professionals not only coexist with each other on YouTube but, as Burgess and Green suggest, coevolve. This coexistence blurs the line between who is a professional and who is an amateur, and the convergence has resulted in the manifestation of *pro-ams*—those who exhibit the characteristics of both a professional and an amateur.

Strangelove (2010) suggests the bifurcation of professional-amateur and user-commercial is not the most rational way to categorize people and content on YouTube:

> The categories of amateur, professional, non-commercial, and commercial are not absolutely mutually exclusive – hybrid forms of online video productions are found that combine all four qualities. There are complex, contradictory, and fascinating interrelations between amateur video and the professional world of television and movie production. (177)

As the label of professional becomes blurred and users create content for YouTube, musicians have been able to harness the benefits of global audiences without the gate-keepers who used to hold rigorous auditions, own the rights to popular venues, and sell expensive tickets and recordings. Armed with a camera and computer, musicians are accessing a seemingly eternal and boundless audience online. Below, I share the story of two musicians who developed their own musical and technological skills through creating YouTube videos.

Uke Can Do Anything if You Put Your Mind to It

On YouTube, videos featuring professional ukulele players like Jake Shimabukuro and Israel Kamakawiwoʻole have been influential in the recent popularization of the small, fretted, string instrument. In a case study of teenage YouTube amateur musician Wade Johnston, I observed how he used his YouTube channel to create, consume, and share music (Cayari 2011).[6] The first four videos Johnston produced were raw, one-take per-formances filmed in his bedroom and kitchen. At the time of my study, his fandom included 5,000 subscribers and his view count before he deleted his videos in April 2015 had reached over 3.8 million. Johnston used his YouTube channel to share his music and advertise his albums and concerts in hopes of making it big.

As a high school songwriter, Johnston created a YouTube channel to post four of his original compositions. Shortly thereafter, he realized that publishing popular cover songs gained him followers more quickly than his original songs. In his quest for sub-scribers, he also realized that collaborating with others allowed him to connect his audience with his cohorts' viewers, exponentially expanding his reach on the Internet. Johnston's "wing it" (Cayari 2011, 15) editing style would often include multitracked vid-eos recorded in his bedroom or dorm room as the footage flashed from various takes of him playing his instruments and singing. Johnson played the ukulele, harmonica, shaker, and glockenspiel as he layered together songs featuring his baritone voice. He recorded his ukulele and vocal tracks and added to them on a whim; when he felt a video was done, he would stop recording additional parts.

Johnston not only created online music performances, but also interacted with his fans by speaking directly to them in his videos and responded to their questions through text comments. By doing these things, he shaped an online community, gained fans, and made music with others. His personable amateur performance style gained him thousands of subscribers. He would often reach out to other musicians on YouTube to collaborate; for instance, Johnston identified influential amateur ukulele players online and asked them to make music with him. One of his YouTube influences was ukulele player Julia Nunes, the winner of the Bushman World Ukulele Contest 2007, a contest in which Johnston received an honorable mention in 2008. Nunes offered him a spot in the *YouTube Live! 2008 Ukulele Orchestra* and the two performed at the live event. While at the gathering, Johnson was able to meet other amateur YouTube musicians, and planned a series of virtual collaborations in which the musicians sent audio-visual tracks and mixes back and forth to each other across the Internet, each taking turns contributing to the project. These videos further expanding Johnston's reach into the YouTube community by connecting his audiences to his collaborators and their audiences to him.

Performing with Me, Myself, and I

While most amateur musicians never have the opportunity to sign a contract with a professional recording label, pro-ams have found ways to harness the power of online video to turn their hobby into entrepreneurial opportunity. As Stebbins (1992) suggests, amateurs may try to cross into professional status after they have sufficient practice, experience, and skills. Joe Penna, more commonly known by his YouTube channel name MysteryGuitarMan, or MGM, is an example of this. At the time of writing this chapter, Penna had over 2.86 million subscribers and 351 million views on YouTube.[7] This expansive audience contributed to Penna's success as an entrepreneur. The Mystery Guitar Man persona Penna created on YouTube presented him as a quirky Brazilian musician living in the United States who was rarely seen without his sunglasses. His eccentric personality was similar to his video editing style, which usually included abrupt changes, bright colors, and silly asides. Lange (2014) found in a random sample of more than 168 MGM videos that 80 percent focused on special effects to edit and mediate musical performance. In 2010, Penna categorized his music videos into the following six groups: looping, animation, video tricks, storylines, music with random objects, and stop motion.[8] Most of his videos featured mediation more complex than the multitrack recordings that Johnston created. Looping videos used audio-recorded phrases that were turned into ostinati and layered onto each other. The visual part of those videos featured animation, storylines, and flashy visual effects. For Penna, no object was off-limits to create musical sounds. He created music out of wine glasses, PVC pipes, power tools, bubble wrap, and telephone books. He used unconventional instruments such as vuvuzelas, soda pop bottles, slide whistles, and kazoos. He also played traditional and popular instruments like guitar, piano, and ukulele. Classical music, popular music, and South American folk music often inspired his musical endeavors. Stop motion made his videos look "choppy," and contained pictures of Penna making faces at the camera, while the video and audio were pieced together to mediate a melody the way a piano roll would be played: one audio note and video frame produced at a time.

For Penna, YouTube allowed his amateur music making to turn from hobby into a professional endeavor as he dedicated his work time to making a living by creating videos and publishing them on the Internet. According to Lange (2014), as a nineteen-year-old, Penna was majoring in biology; however, when his YouTube channel became popular, he decided to cross the pro-am border. In his *MGM in 2010* video, Penna talked about how YouTube allowed him to support himself through the videos he created and published:

> I went from sleeping on the floor, not having enough money to even buy food some-times to being able to do YouTube full-time because of you (the fans). Thanks to the over 200 million of you guys who saw my videos. Thanks to everybody who bought T-shirts, everybody who bought stickers, everybody who helped out with charity by buying transparencies, everything like that.[9]

On September 13, 2011, Penna asked his viewers to join him to create the *Mystery Symphony*. The following is an excerpt from his call to action:

> Today, I'm making this extra bonus video as a challenge to you guys. So all the musi-cians out there, make sure you click on the first link in the description down below. That's going to take you to a page on my website where you can see all the music nota-tions if you play some kind of *music notatey instrument*, or if you play guitar, or bass, you can see the tabs too. Basically, I need as many people as possible to respond to this video with you playing what's in the music notation. We're going to cut all of the submissions into a huge song . . . and you're going to have to come back to find out which song it is.[10]

Penna held his audience in suspense for only nine days and on September 22, 2010, he published a stop-motion video of *In The Hall of the Mountain King* by Edvard Grieg, featuring 1400 video submissions and 1,560 minutes of footage consisting of 304.7 giga-bytes of data with over 2000 video and audio splices. In the video, Penna joked that there were 561 guitar videos but only 300 guitar notes in the arrangement, so he had to make choices on whom to include.[11]

On YouTube Becoming a Place for Individuals to Post their Music Making

Music making for YouTube provided Johnston and Penna a space to perform. By offer-ing musicians a virtual space to display their music making, YouTube allowed people to gather and partake in musical performance in ways previously unavailable. Tuan (1977) suggested, "Place is security, space is freedom" (3). He continued to posit that places are centers of value where needs are met. For virtual artists, the space YouTube provides can become a place as musical expression, artistic experimentation, and social interactions abound. When live performance was the only way for musicians to share their art with others, artist-audience interactions were limited to local spaces. However, on YouTube, mediated performances are shared immediately with global audiences. Feedback in the form of comments and ratings can guide musicians, suggestions can be offered for improvement, and requests can be made. Audiences can also show their loyalty to artists by subscribing. The statistics that go along with the aforementioned interactions often breed more attention online as YouTube algorithms suggest popular videos and relevance to its users, and they shape the way musicians create, share, listen to, and market music.

Joining a Virtual Collective

As the statistical trends reported by Duggan (2013) and Nielsen (2012) suggest, YouTube affords a space for musicians to self-publish their performances on the Internet. Whether it is to show off one's musical and technological skills, to perform with others, or both, musicians are beginning to participate in online culture through music video making. There are a variety of ways musicians engage with music in participatory culture, including covering, arranging, parodying, satirizing, multitracking, remixing, sample-based producing, creating mash-ups, creating tutorials, remediating, commenting, and discussing (Tobias 2013). The complexities of online music teaching, learning, and community were the subject of Waldron's (2013) work with Old-Time and Bluegrass musicians. While this literature has focused on individual user-generated content, not all amateur musicians have enough energy, time, skills, or resources to create their own video performances.

As the web became increasingly interactive, wikis became increasingly popular for Internet users to create collective intelligence (Reagle 2011). Forums and discussion boards evolved into sites where people could develop collective knowledge and set up venues for the sharing and evaluation of projects (Jenkins 2006). Regarding participatory culture and collective intelligence, Jenkins suggested, "None of us can know everything; each of us knows something; and we can put the pieces together if we pool our resources and combine our skills" (4). On the musical front, there are large collective ensemble projects where musicians send mini-performance videos to an editor like the participants in the *Mystery Symphony* compiled by Penna. These mini-performances feature individuals playing or singing one part of a musical work, which is then compiled to create an ensemble. In a collective virtual ensemble, submitted videos are compiled by an editor or a team of technicians to create a coherent product. Two such examples are Eric Whitacre's Virtual Choir and the Little Symphony's Virtual Orchestra Project.[12]

Singing in a Virtual Choir

No other virtual collective ensemble to date has received more press than Eric Whitacre's reoccurring virtual choir. Historical accounts of how the Eric Whitacre Virtual Choir began can be found in both Armstrong (2012) and Konewko (2013). Armstrong ethnographically explored how Whitacre recruited singers on his blog to create a virtual choir experiment that turned into a series of projects. In 2010, Eric Whitacre sent out a call for singers to record themselves performing individual parts of his choral composition,

Lux Aurumque;[13] he crowdsourced an ensemble of 185 singers who replied to his call. In his instructional video, Whitacre conducted the song in complete silence and then recorded himself playing piano so the singers had visual and auditory frames of reference. Whitacre offered the sheet music for free on his website so that singers could learn the parts. Participants recorded themselves performing one or more of the choral parts to the backdrops of their living rooms, recording studios, bedrooms, kitchens, rehearsal rooms, and practice rooms. The singers hailed from fourteen countries and sent in 243 tracks, which were compiled by a team of engineers. The first official virtual choir was published March 21, 2010. To create his fourth Virtual Choir in 2013, Whitacre moved off YouTube and used his own website, where singers could interact via forums and upload their videos directly. Whitacre's virtual music making endeavors also included a live-virtual hybrid choir combining a live choir and 30 singers via Skype[14] and his first Virtual Youth Choir, which included 2,292 singers under the age of nineteen from eighty countries.[15]

Armstrong (2012) found the reasons singers participated in Whitacre's virtual choir projects were varied and spanned social, musical, and technological goals. Some were excited to work with a famous composer. Others wanted to practice their singing abilities, reconnect with singing, or even sing in a choir for the first time. Another motivating factor was the excitement of joining a collective effort on the Internet that elicited new technologies. Whitacre took any and every person willing to record a video; one of Armstrong's informants commented, "Unlike most participants, [I am] not a singer and wouldn't do well at an audition. So, a virtual choir, where I could pick from many takes, is the only way I could sing with my favorite composer" (67). This large collective ensemble allowed for amateur musicians to find a community with which to perform.

Whitacre has been seen by some in the music profession as a classical rock star— perhaps a self-imposed moniker inspired by his 2011 TED talk[16]—and researchers have suggested his virtual choirs have infused new energy in the choral world (Konewko 2013). These collective ensembles displayed how people were interested in being a part of mass music making on the Internet; in fact, Whitacre's Virtual Choirs grew substantially in the first four collectives, with 185; 1,752; 2,945; and 5,905 singers, respectively. The concept, which started off as a conversation on Whitacre's blog, has grown to a string of international projects bringing together singers from over 100 countries.

An Orchestra Open to All

Besides the Eric Whitacre virtual choirs, other virtual collective musical groups have formed. The famous YouTube Symphony Orchestra was announced on December 1, 2008, at a live press conference in New York. Within the next two months, over 3,000 Internet hopefuls video-recorded themselves performing *Internet Symphony no. 1— Eroica* by composer Tan Dun. On April 15, 2009, this international collaborative effort culminated at Carnegie Hall where documentary videos were presented and ninety of the auditionees performed a live concert (Rudolph and Frankel 2009).[17] However, this highly competitive process ended with approximately 3 percent of participants winning a spot in the coveted performance. The YouTube Symphony Orchestra, while a magnificent feat that demonstrated the use of online video to recruit and audition on the Internet, overshadows the collective ensemble conceived by Cosarca, Craciun, and Corneanu from the University of Memphis in 2011 (Fenton 2012).

Similar to Whitacre's virtual choirs, the *Little Symphony Project* provided participants with videos that included music notation and a click track to guide their submissions. Users were encouraged to record one or more of the parts posted on the Little Symphony website. The collective virtual ensemble featured 106 participants from thirty countries and showcased the internationality of its performers.[18] For example, a quartet featuring a violinist from Japan, an ocarina player from the U.S.A., a soprano recorder player from Brazil, and a guitarist from Italy became the focus for a phrase while the large ensemble faded into the background. A brass quartet, a woodwind quartet accompanied by a keyboardist, a septet of violinists, a quintet of folk instruments, a scrolling group of twelve pianists, six vocalists, and a trio of flautists were all featured in the final mix.

The University of Memphis innovators' goal was similar to Whitacre's: bring classical music to the forefront of consumers' attention through social media, technology, and crowdsourcing a collective. Corneanu was quoted, "I have wanted to share music with people from different cultures and lifestyles, and with people who have experienced different levels and varieties of music education" (Fenton 2012, 6.). Virtual ensembles allow for people with varied experience and skill levels to perform together from across the world, unbound by space, time, or ability.

Being Part of a Collective Ensemble

The research regarding the results, benefits, and consequences of being in a collective ensemble is sparse and limited to Whitacre's ensembles. Yet in the few studies that have been conducted, researchers have noted benefits to participants. By creating mini-performances for a collective, Armstrong (2012) found some participants critically analyzed their performances, were inspired to rejoin the choral world by seeking out live performing groups in which to participate, and felt a sense of community with other virtual choir participants. Some of Armstrong's informants developed close relationships with other virtual choir singers and even met each other face to face. These outcomes were also common in a survey study of Whitacre's Virtual Choir participants. Paparo and Talbot (2014) suggested virtual choirs afforded participants musical engagement and learning beyond the rehearsal, opportunities for self-critique and self-reflection, an impetus for understanding vocal technique and musicianship, inspiration to continue to sing, opportunities to work with composers and conductors, a community of people with shared goals and purposes, and opportunities for choral music making.

These collective ensembles show how YouTube as a space became a place for thousands of musicians to make music and share with each other. A coordinator developed the idea to create a collective virtual ensemble and the public surrounding the medium to which that coordinator belonged participated in music making. In a collective virtual ensemble, musicians from across the world can record themselves performing a piece with an international online community. This music has traditionally been performed with a live ensemble, yet because of practices people have developed for making music on YouTube, a virtual ensemble is mediated into existence. Collectives allow performers who might not be confident creating a multitrack solo video to make music with other performers online, who give them support through the synergy of the virtual community. Similar to the way Mahler conceived a massive ensemble through a *Symphony of a Thousand*, virtual collective ensembles afford amateur musicians the opportunity to perform with thousands from across the world, albeit asynchronously.

INVITING OTHERS INTO MUSICAL COLLABORATION

So far this chapter has focused on individual and large collective videos. Another practice I have observed in music making on YouTube sits between the two. I conceive collaboration as including a give-and-take relationship, where two or more artists share the responsibility of creating videos through the planning, recording, editing, or any combination of the phases of a project. Collaboration on YouTube can be found in almost any category of video, from cooking and vlogging to education and music. In the case of Wade Johnston, I found that online collaboration on YouTube allowed for three things: (1) Johnston was able to perform with people he admired; (2) he shared ideas and techniques with other YouTube musicians; and (3) the audiences of his collaborators and his channel melded, allowing for new exposure for both him and his cohorts (Cayari 2011). In the following section, I present three examples of musicians reaching out to others by sharing their resources, talents, and unique YouTube video styles.

Reaching across International Borders

Johnston's multitrack music videos featured him as a one-person acoustic band that played popular music. However, multitrack music videos are made in a variety of genres and styles. French YouTube musician Julien Neel, also known by his handle as Trubdol,[19] has created over 140 videos. Most of Neel's videos, inspired by barbershop arrangements of popular, classical, Broadway, and video game genres, feature four "clones" singing, interacting, and performing as a one-person virtual barbershop quartet.

Neel attempted to publish a new virtual barbershop quartet performance every week as was evident from his Thursday video postings. While he published videos featuring his one-person quartet, he also performed one-man choirs and collaborations. Of Neel's 141 videos published prior to 2015, 49 were collaborations where he worked with

another person. He elicited the help of visual artists, instrumentalists, and other singers. His editing style usually featured stationary panels in a split screen allowing each
of the performers to have a prominent place in the video. Neel's efforts featured virtual
global connections in his playlist of international collaborations performing with others
from Belgium, Canada, France, Germany, Italy, Russia, South Africa, Sweden, United
Kingdom, and the U.S.A. Neel's attempt to reach across international borders was accentuated by his visual editing; At the beginning of most of his collaborations, he included
the flags of the countries from which his collaborators hailed.[20]

Stebbins (2007) suggests that serious leisure activities can often have financial benefits. Although creating a cappella video performances was something Neel started doing
for fun, he began, like Penna, to monetize his art while straddling the pro-am divide.
Neel used the Patreon website to solicit viewers to become patrons who pledged money
for each video he published, which would then be deducted from the patrons' financial accounts; viewers could put a cap on how much they would be willing to pay each
month. On Patreon, Neel wrote:

> I currently fund my productions on a string budget, with expenses for copyright &
> arranger fees, software, recording & lighting equipment, countless man hours edit-
> ing audio & video together. I lack financial back up & stability, I can't do many of the
> projects I'd like, or hire outside help. I'd love to build a small equipped studio, so that
> I could streamline my production, thereby enhancing the quality and regularity of
> my releases . . . for you![21]

At the time of writing this chapter, Neel's Patreon account had earned him $893.35 per
video. He wrote on his Patreon that if he was able to get $1,000 per video, he would
be able to "hire help for audio/video production from pros!" Not only did Neel's music
making on the Internet allow him to share a cappella music with a global audience who
would never have seen him perform if it were not for online videos on YouTube, but it
also allowed him to create music with people from all over the world who enjoyed performing barbershop and a cappella music.

Sharing the Resources

Another exemplar of individual virtual performance and international musical collaboration on YouTube is Lai Youttitham. The Lai[22] YouTube channel featured all three of
the themes I have noted in this chapter. Youttitham started posting videos in August
2007, showing off his electric guitar skills. His second video was the same "Canon Rock"
arrangement mentioned at the beginning of this chapter.[23] Yet, Youttitham included a
twist: collaborating with others. While the soundtrack of his video featured him performing over the Jerry C background track, the video footage featured a number of
other YouTube artists performing guitar. Youttitham soon began producing multitrack
videos by creating his own background tracks over which he would play solo electric

guitar. He also experimented with video collaboration, ripping videos from the Internet to remix with his own playing.

In a video entitled *About LaiYouttitham*, he told the story of his journey of travel and his love for music through dynamic text and personal pictures onscreen with a soundtrack of him performing "Drift Away" by Mentor Williams. The emotional story from the video is quoted below, in context with typos, emoticons and excessive punctuation (about which he apologized in an annotated note on the video):

> Hi! my name is Lai. I was born and raised in the beautiful city of Laos. At age of 19 I began to look for something new in life. Somewhere new. I made up my mind. . . . My destination? Canada! But first, I had to cross the Mekong River to get to Thailand. where the refuge camp was located. Long story short :) I made it to the other side and luckily didn't get shot. I got arrested & put in a temporary camp. I didn't know what was going to happen or why they put me in a temporary camp. Life in that camp was alright, there was always hope :) My brothers and sisters managed to send me some money to buy food. But instead I saved them up and guess what I bought. . . . A used guitar. The only refuge who had a guitar in that camp!
>
> Moving on to the second camp. Nicer bed room and one step closer to Canada. In the second camp, I was interviewed by a Canadian, to make sure I will become a good citizen before they accept me. It went well!! So I went on to the final refuge camp, where I learned English and other skills. I got hired as a volunteer worker forward slash as a band member. I got to take an electric guitar home to practice!! I still missed old friends from the first camp that i left behind. So some of them never got sponsored and got sent back home. I sent my guitar that I had bought to them in the first camp. The first song from the west that I fell in love with was . . . Drift Away!!!! Three years later, I became a Canadian citizen.[24]

Youttitham's story of benevolence accentuated his passion for sharing the gift of music to those around him. It was not long before Youttitham began to seek out other YouTube musicians with whom to make music. Some of Youttitham's *collab* videos featured multitrack recordings in a style that was a cross between Johnston and Neel. Youttitham explained how one collaboration came to fruition: "I was chatting with Rachael Stewart and this little project came up in our conversation and I told her to send her clips to me, boy did she nail it good, then I was just jamming to it and came up with this cover."[25] The video featured clips of Stewart singing a cappella and Youttitham playing guitar each by themselves. However, the video was mediated to create a cohesive performance of the two, as if they were making music together at the same time.

The Lai YouTube channel featured virtual choirs dedicated to a cause like "Sing for Japan" and "We Are the World 25 for Haiti," webcam jam sessions, and improvisatory video montages. However, most of Youttitham's *collab* videos had elements of both collectives and collaborations. As described above, a collective involves musicians creating videos to send to a video editor; a collaboration solicits performers to work together to develop an ensemble. His videos possessed elements of both. Youttitham's original song "iRoc" featured him playing electric guitar over his own background track, and in the middle of the video the call came, "Come and Jam with me / On the next YouTube

Collab / Check the description box for the info."[26] The description box provided a link to Youttitham's website where viewers could download the background track, and contributors were asked to upload their videos to YouTube. Videos began to surface in the next two months with titles including "iRoc" and "collab." The submissions varied in involvement: fully mastered performances with the background track and improvised solo as well as short clips of the musician playing with the background track barely audible or with the performer listening to the background track through headphones. Youttitham published a series of video compilations with people from all over the world soloing over his background tracks.

For Youttitham, these videos were not simply collectives, because he interacted with his fans throughout the process. He recorded himself playing bass, drums, and guitar to create a background track, asked his YouTube friends to create solos, and then combined elements from the cache of videos on YouTube with varying degrees of involvement from collaborators. Youttiham was the mastermind behind the projects, and provided resources, such as virtual meeting spots, background tracks, and editing services; however, it was because he invited his virtual friends to make music with him that the performances on his YouTube channel were mediated into existence. The results included not only international collaborations of virtual music making, but also a rise in awareness for Youttitham, who has gained over 75,000 subscribers and nine million views.

Performing with Your Hero

YouTube has been credited for kick-starting the career of commercially sponsored popular music artists like Austin Mahone, who was likened to a younger version of fellow pop star and YouTube native Justin Bieber (Halperin 2012). Mahone's YouTube channel prior to his record deal featured vlogs, live performances, a cappella covers, and professionally mastered music videos complete with an aesthetic one would see from professional commercial artists. In August of 2012, Mahone signed to Universal Republic Records and released his first single, "Say Somethin'," on iTunes. The concept elicited by Youttitham, where a well-known artist invites fans to virtually perform with them is exemplified in the video *"Say Somethin'" Sing! App fan video*.[27]

In November 2012, Mahone released the video, which featured him singing with fans from all over the world. The video was created using *Sing!*, a mobile phone application created by Smule, which allowed users to sing in a karaoke-style to a background track on their cell phones. Mahone requested that his fans create their own videos singing with the app. The video displayed Mahone singing the song into his cell phone while fans were superimposed on the screen giving the illusion that they were singing with their musical hero. The fans' videos were used for background singing, duet singing, and call and response singing with amateur singers appearing next to the famous pop music artist. The practices of mediated music making on YouTube inspired Mahone to be a bridge connecting commercial artistry and amateur performance.

POTENTIAL DRAWBACKS FOR MUSICIANS PRODUCING VIDEOS ON YOUTUBE

While this chapter has presented online music video creation in a positive light, I would be remiss if I did not discuss the downsides of creating music videos for YouTube. The reach of YouTube is ever expanding, and while the website is the third most visited website according to Alexa (2015), producing on YouTube can be daunting for amateur and hobbyist musicians who have to compete with commercial artists for viewers' attention, as suggested by Burgess and Green (2009). With over 300 hours of video uploaded to YouTube every minute (YouTube 2015), there is no guarantee that a musician posting on YouTube will find an audience, let alone subscribers. In live choral ensemble settings, musicians sometimes feel intimidated to sing because they cannot compete with professional, commercially produced content (Richards and Durrant 2003) and other more experienced performers (Bailey and Davidson 2005). Amateur video makers considering making music for YouTube may experience similar anxieties.

The permanence of digital content on the Internet can also be daunting for novice online musicians. For example, in Cayari (2011), I reported finding that Wade Johnston reluctantly posted his first four videos because he was afraid his friends might see his original compositions and not like them. While a YouTube channel owner has the ability to delete content from their website, all digital content leaves a footprint. This permanence can be intimidating to novice musicians, whether they are publishing videos as soloists or as part of a collective, as was found by Armstrong (2012). Furthermore, content creators cannot necessarily stop others from downloading and using their content in ways they did not originally intend. A complex power relationship between recorded performer and editor occurs when musicians are taken out of any step of the mediated music making process. Stanyek and Piekut (2010) discussed how Natalie Cole was able to perform a duet with her thirty-year-dead father, Nat "King" Cole, by using multitrack techniques similar to those discussed in this chapter. The performance created strife amongst the Cole family because Natalie's mother did not feel her husband consented to the virtual resurrection. Similarly, it takes trust for members of a collective ensemble to allow an editor to take their mini-performance and use it however they see fit. Armstrong also found that collectives have the potential to leave participants feeling like they were lost in the crowd, because they were unable to find their voice or image in the finished video.

Whether musicians are performing by themselves or with others, they may think twice before they publish a haphazard recording of themselves singing or playing an instrument. Participants in the Eric Whitacre Virtual Choir claimed that they spent a lot of time trying to make sure their video submission was good enough to put online (Armstrong 2012). In the case of Johnston, I found his perfectionism required him to spend inordinate amounts of time recording and editing an appropriate performance

(Cayari 2011), and this sentiment was reiterated in my classroom, when I facilitated music video creation projects for undergraduate music education majors (Cayari 2015). While they may divide the workload up amongst participants, collaborations are often more time-consuming than multitrack videos created by one person. Johnston found collaboration to be a time-consuming process, although it also had benefits like the enjoyment of working with others and an expanded audience.

Another potential pitfall comes into play when one considers how people interact with each other via YouTube. The face-to-face aspect of live ensemble preparation is something valued by many musicians; however, participating in an asynchronous virtual ensemble changes the ways in which musicians interact with their fellow musicians. While delving deep into this phenomenon is outside the scope of this chapter, musicians, researchers, and theorists should heed Turkle's (2012) warning that digital relationships can easily replace face-to-face social interactions, resulting in a *robotic love* in which machine interactions replace human interactions. However, as discussed in Armstrong (2012), Cayari (2011), and Konewko (2013), virtual music making is often the result of, or can lead to, live get-togethers where cooperating musicians have face-to-face interactions and make music together in person.

Finally, YouTube comments allow audiences to give a performer instant feedback on their art. Viewers have the opportunity to leave advice, opinions, accolades, *and* hate-filled comments at their whim for nearly any video they come across on YouTube. While most comments on YouTube across all types of videos are positive in nature, approximately 35 percent of comments contain negativity (Thelwall, Sud, and Vis 2012). Both positive and negative ramifications are possible as musicians read comments from viewers, and by posting on YouTube musicians put themselves in a situation where they may receive both good and bad critiques.

Space becoming Place and Medium

The practices that surround music video creation on YouTube are complex and bring with them a plethora of experiences and outcomes. I suggest that by providing a virtual space to produce videos, a medium emerges. Sterne's (2013) concept of medium as "a network—a whole set of relations, practices, people, and technologies" (225)—lends itself well to Stebbins's (this volume, chapter 19) description of how space becomes place. As people develop new practices and explore using technologies, ways of creating art emerge. YouTube conceived as a medium can become a place where musicians experience meaningful interactions and music making through solitary, collective, and collaborative endeavors. The downsides of these online video creation activities are often outweighed by the myriad benefits experienced by their creators and participants, which include but are not limited to social, musical, educational, and aesthetic outcomes. It is important for researchers and theorists to explore ways in which people are creating music through online video, both individually and with others. By doing so, we can begin to see how the medium and place of YouTube facilitate and restrict music making in the virtual age of streaming videos and collective intelligence.

Online music video creation has added one more color to the palette of available venues for musicians who want to perform. The trends discussed in this chapter are an attempt to generalize the complex and varied ways people are making music through video on the Internet. Whether one wants to create a video to show off musical skills, be part of a worldwide collective of musicians, work with a small group of others to produce video performances, or for any other reason, YouTube provides a space for that to happen. YouTube has become a virtual place for a complex web of relations, practices, people, and technologies that have afforded new ways of music making; as musicians continue to use YouTube and other online venues to perform, innovative ways to make music and experience core musical activities will continue to emerge.

Notes

1. Note about video references: To better facilitate readability and finding sources, links to videos available on YouTube can be found as footnotes. A YouTube playlist of all the videos in this chapter can be found at https://www.youtube.com/playlist?list=PLvYNNKSMpaM BUDtBu2RQFi7845WzuGiJz. Unfortunately, content on this playlist can disappear at the creator's or YouTube's discretion.
2. Lim Jeong-hyun [funtwo], "funtwo – Canon," YouTube video, 5:20, posted November 17, 2008, http://youtu.be/TF6cnLnEARo.
3. Text and speech on the Internet is reflective of the vernacular of the content creator. Unless otherwise noted, quotes throughout this chapter have been edited for grammar and punctuation.
4. Lim Jeong-hyun [funtwo], "funtwo – Canon Rock 2012," YouTube video, 5:26, posted October 2, 2012, http://youtu.be/ilOwXH5p1Ro.
5. No data for the curation of videos in 2013 is available.
6. The videos of Wade Johnston have been taken off YouTube. Wade Johnston, "Wadejohnston YouTube channel". Last accessed January 12, 2015, from http://www.youtube.com/user/wadejohnston. No information is available regarding why his channel's content was deleted.
7. Joe Penna. 2015. "MysteryGuitarMan," YouTube. Accessed May 30, 2015 from http://www.youtube.com/user/MysteryGuitarMan.
8. Joe Penna [MysteryGuitarMan], "MGM in 2010: Joe Penna," YouTube video, 2:41, posted December 30, 2010, http://youtu.be/lwLz1lBleG8.
9. Ibid.
10. Joe Penna [MysteryGuitarMan], "Your Symphony," YouTube video, 2:54, posted September 13, 2011, http://youtu.be/Vaol-RZO1mU.
11. Joe Penna [MysteryGuitarMan], "Mystery Symphony: Joe Penna," YouTube video, 2:27, posted September 22, 2011, http://youtu.be/Ul95hTnO3h4.
12. Eric Whitacre, *The Virtual Choir*, http://www.ericwhitacre.com/the-virtual-choir.
13. Eric Whitacre [Eric Whitacre's Virtual Choir], "Eric Whitacre's Virtual Choir: 'Lux Arumque,'" YouTube video, 6:20, posted March 21, 2010, http://youtu.be/D707BrlbaDs.

14. Eric Whitacre [TED], "Eric Whitacre: Virtual Choir Live," YouTube video, 12:32, posted March 22, 2013, http://youtu.be/cnQFvrWDYsU.

15. Eric Whitacre [Eric Whitacre's Virtual Choir], "Eric Whitacre's Virtual Youth Choir: What If," YouTube video, 5:27, posted August 14, 2014, http://youtu.be/DmJBJVoi928.

16. Eric Whitacre [TED], "A Virtual Choir 2,000 Voices Strong," YouTube video, 14:34, posted April 4, 2011, https://youtu.be/2NENlXsW4pM.

17. YouTube Symphony Orchestra 2011 [YouTube Symphony Orchestra 2011 Grand Finale], 2:22:11, posted March 20, 2011, https://youtu.be/LnKJpYGCLsg.

18. Little Symphony [Little Symphony], "Pachelbel Canon in D (106 Participants from 30 Countries): Virtual Symphony v 1.0," YouTube video, 6:57, posted January 16, 2012, http://youtu.be/PsHRaOdov7A.

19. Julien Neel, "A Cappella Trubdol" [YouTube channel] (2015), http://www.youtube.com/user/trudbol.

20. Julien Neel, "International Collaborations—Trudbol" [YouTube playlist] (2015), http://www.youtube.com/playlist?list=PL0B933243486B8EA1.

21. Julien Neel, "Julien Neel (Trubdol) Is Creating a Cappella / Barbershop Videos" (2015), http://www.patreon.com/trudbol.

22. Lai Youttitham, Lai [YouTube channel] (2015), http://www.youtube.com/user/LaiYouttitham.

23. Lai Youttitham [Lai], "We Are Canon Rock Lovers," YouTube video, 5:34, posted on September 22, 2007, http://youtu.be/yWF7jixAYvs.

24. Lai Youttitham [Lai], "About LaiYouttitham," YouTube video, 5:46, posted May 9, 2010, https://youtu.be/kM_-hgNxLik.

25. Lai Youttitham [Lai], "Katy Perry: Firework Cover!" YouTube video, 4:59, posted January 14, 2011, http://youtu.be/VXi5DcwRdAU.

26. Lai Youttitham [Lai], "iRoc (Original)," YouTube video, 3:10, posted April 1, 2009, http://youtu.be/8kzGKUd4LbM.

27. Austin Mahone [Austin Mahone], " 'Say Somethin' Sing! App Fan Video," YouTube video, 3:10, posted November 1, 2012, http://youtu.be/lSQYZFLTCyI.

REFERENCES CITED

Alexa. 2015. "Alexa's Top 500 Global Sites." *Alexa.com*. http://www.alexa.com/topsites.

Armstrong, Melanie. 2012. "Musicking in Cyberspace: Creating Music and Fostering Global Community through a Virtual Choir." Master's thesis, Tufts University.

Bailey, Betty A., and Jane W. Davidson. 2005. "Effects of Group Singing and Performance for Marginalized and Middle-Class Singers." *Psychology of Music* 33(3): 269–303.

Benjamin, Walter. 1968. "The Work of Art in the Age of Mechanical Reproduction." In *Illuminations: Essays and Reflections*, edited by Hannah Arendt, translated by Harry Zohn, 21–251. New York: Schocken.

Berland, Jody. 1993. "Sound, Image and Social Space: Music Video and Media Reconstruction." In *Sound and Vision: The Music Video Reader*, edited by Simon Frith, Andrew Goodwin, and Lawrence Grossberg, 25–43. London: Routledge.

Burgess, Jean. 2008. "All Your Chocolate Rain Are Belong to Us?" In *Video Vortex Reader: Responses to YouTube*, edited by Geert Lovink and Sabine Niederer, 101–109. Amsterdam: Institute for Network Cultures.

Burgess, Jean, and Joshua Green. 2009. "The Entrepreneurial Vlogger: Participatory Culture beyond the Professional-Amateur Divide." In *The YouTube Reader*, edited by Pelle Snickars and Patrick Vonderau, 89–107. Stockholm: National Library of Sweden.

Cayari, Christopher. 2011. "The YouTube Effect: How YouTube Has Provided New Ways to Consume, Create, and Share Music." *International Journal of Education and the Arts* 12(6): 1–28. http://ijea.org/v12n6/v12n6.pdf.

Cayari, Christopher. 2015. "Participatory Culture and Informal Music Learning through Video Creation in the Curriculum." *International Journal of Community Music* 8(1): 41–57.

Duggan, Maeve. 2013. "Photo and Video Sharing Grow Online." *Pew Research Center*. http://www.pewinternet.org/2013/10/28/photo-and-video-sharing-grow-online/.

Fenton, Laura. 2012. "Virtual Symphony a Reality for U of M Music Students." *University of Memphis Magazine*. https://issuu.com/univofmemphis/docs/spring2012magazine.

Halperin, Shirley. 2012. "'Baby Bieber' YouTube star Austin Mahone signs to Universal Republic." *Billboard*, August 28. http://www.billboard.com/articles/news/475366/baby-bieber-youtube-star-austin-mahone-signs-to-universal-republic/.

Jenkins, Henry. 2006. *Convergence Culture: Where Old and New Media Collide*. New York: New York University Press.

Katz, Mark. 2004. *Capturing Sound: How Technology Has Changed Music*. Berkeley: University of California Press.

Konewko, Mark. 2013. "The Phenomena of Eric Whitacre: Infusing New Energy in the Choral World?" PhD dissertation, Cardinal Stritch University. Madison, WI: ProQuest/UMI.

Lange, Patricia G. 2014. *Kids on YouTube: Technical Identities and Digital Literacies*. Walnut Creek, CA: Left Coast.

Nielsen. 2012. "Music Discovery Still Dominated by Radio, Says Nielson Music 360 Report." August 14. http://www.nielsen.com/us/en/press-room/2012/music-discovery-still-dominated-by-radio-- says-nielsen-music-360.html.

Paparo, Stephen A., and Brent C. Talbot. 2014. "Meanings of Participation in Virtual Choirs and Implications for Music Teacher Education." Paper presented at the National Association for Music Education Biennial National Conference, St. Louis, MO, March.

Reagle, Joseph. 2011. "The Argument Engine." In *Critical Point of View: A Wikipedia Reader*, edited by Geert Lovink and Nathaniel Tkacz, 14–33. Amsterdam: Institute of Network Cultures.

Richards, Helen, and Colin Durrant. 2003. "To Sing or Not to Sing: A Study on the Development of Non-Singers' in Choral Activity." *Research Studies in Music Education* 20(1): 78–89.

Rudolph, Thomas, and James Frankel. 2009. *YouTube in Music Education*. Milwaukee, WI: Hal Leonard.

Stanyek, Jason, and Benjamin Piekut. 2010. "Deadness: Technologies of the Intermundane." *TDR: The Drama Review* 54(1): 14–38.

Stebbins, Robert A. 1992. *Amateurs, Professionals, and Serious Leisure*. Montreal, QC: McGill-Queen's University Press.

Stebbins, Robert A. 2007. *Serious Leisure: A Perspective for Our Time*. New Brunswick, NJ: Transaction.

Sterne, Jonathan. 2003. *The Audible Past: Cultural Origins of Sound Reproduction*. Durham, NC: Duke University Press.

Sterne, Jonathan. 2012. *MP3: The Meaning of a Format*. Durham, NC: Duke University Press.

Strangelove, Michael. 2010. *Watching YouTube: Extraordinary Videos by Ordinary People*. Toronto: University of Toronto Press.

Thelwall, Mike, Pardeep Sud, and Farida Vis. 2012. "Commenting on YouTube Videos: From Guatemalan Rock to el Big Bang." *Journal of the American Society for Information Science and Technology* 63(3): 616–629.

Thibeault, Matthew D. 2012. "Music Education in the Postperformance World." In *The Oxford Handbook of Music Education*, vol. 2, edited by Gary E. McPherson and Graham F. Welch, 517–530. New York: Oxford University Press.

Tobias, Evan S. 2013. "Toward Convergence Adapting Music Education to Contemporary Society and Participatory Culture." *Music Educators Journal* 99(4): 29–36.

Tuan, Yi-Fu. 1977. *Space and Place: The Perspective of Experience*. Minneapolis: University of Minnesota Press.

Turkle, Sherry. 2012. *Alone Together: Why We Expect More from Technology and Less from Each Other*. New York: Basic Books.

Waldron, Janice. 2013. "User-Generated Content, YouTube and Participatory Culture on the Web: Music Learning and Teaching in Two Contrasting Online Communities." *Music Education Research* 15(3): 257–274.

YouTube. 2015. "Statistics." *YouTube*. http://www.youtube.com/yt/press/statistics.html.

CHAPTER 26

ITALIAN AMATEUR POP-ROCK MUSICIANS ON FACEBOOK

Mixed Methods and New Findings in Music Making Research

ALBERTO TROBIA AND FABIO M. LO VERDE

PREMISE

THE main subject of this chapter is the articulation of discourses on music within the Italian amateur music making world, as a result of specific networks of online interactions intertwining with the social division of leisure time, where "IKEAization" (Blackshaw 2010) and "Appleization" (Lo Verde 2013) processes seem to emerge. The social division of leisure time, here, as we'll discuss in the conclusion, is seen as the social background allowing and conditioning amateur activities.

The sporadic literature about the activities of amateur pop-rock musicians has emphasized the primary role of attitudes, values, and aesthetics over the simple sharing of skills and knowledge. Most authors argue that relationships and identity issues are also crucial in shaping the activities of these musicians, as well as the availability of free time and the amount of feasible commitment, often correlated to social and demographic variables (Bayton 1990; Bennett 1980; Finnegan 1989; Green 2002; Pitts 2005).

New technologies have dramatically changed the nature of amateur music making. In recent years, digital media and the Internet have changed the way pop-rock musicians learn and how they experience musical activities, alone and with others (Beer 2008; Miller 2012; Prior 2010; Rojek 2011). Networks of interaction have increasingly become more virtual than physical, moving to the Internet. The amateur nature of these practices, as well as their supposed private or provincial dimension, is less and less clear.

Italy has a strong tradition of musical production and consumption. The melodic song, a legacy both of the Italian *canzonetta* and the opera (Baldazzi 1989), has always had a preeminent position, as witnessed by the importance of the Festival di Sanremo[1] in the Italian music business (Agostini 2007). The Italian "sonic culture" (Magaudda and Santoro 2013) also has had a separate, eccentric history with respect to revolutionary Anglophone popular music. American and English pop-rock has been heavily imitated in instrumentation, form, lyrical content, and dress, and combined with Mediterranean traditions. In addition, a third main component includes a strongly politicized singer-songwriter tradition, the so-called *canzone d'autore* (Santoro 2010), inspired by the American folk revival of the mid-1960s and the French *chansonnier* (43). Mainstream Italian popular music, therefore, may be described as three-pronged. Italian amateur pop-rock musicians have been greatly influenced by this history, as well as by the advent of new technologies and cultural globalization.

In this chapter, we discuss our research regarding four communities of amateur musicians—drummers, bassists, guitarists, and keyboard players—found on Facebook, with the aim to understand their predominant topics of conversation, how they interact in a virtual landscape, and how they engage with globalization and the digital revolution. The methodological novelty of our approach is the combination of social network analysis (SNA) and textual analysis to study music making and leisure.

AMATEUR MUSIC MAKING: A BRIEF REVIEW

The distinction between amateur and professional musicians has become increasingly unclear. An amateur is "one who cultivates something as a pastime, as distinguished from one who prosecutes it professionally; hence, sometimes used disparagingly, as dabbler, or superficial student or worker" ("Amateur" [def. 2], *Compact Edition of the Oxford English Dictionary*, 1985, 67). On the other hand, a "professional musician" is often defined as someone who makes a living or part of a living from performing and in some cases also composing and/or arranging music (Green 2002, 9). In this sense, "being a professional musician is merely a question of figuring out what goods and services the market is willing to pay for" (Colletti 2013). Less clear is what the word "professional" means for musicians (e.g., Finnegan 1989). Such distinctions evade the specific contributions of amateur music making to a wide, dynamic economy (live music, local competitions, private teaching, trade in new and used instruments, etc.). Computers and new technologies have allowed amateur musicians both to produce professional-quality products and to reach huge audiences, diminishing the power of traditional gatekeepers (Hirsch 1972; Negus 1999; Rojek 2011). An intermediate, hybrid category of "semiprofessional" or "semipro" musician,[2] then, is rather widespread. This kind of musician forms the main musician population of social networking services (SNS), and it is to them that our attention is thus directed.

Semipro activities have the characteristics of "serious leisure" (Stebbins 1979, 2007). This arguably challenges Green's assertion that the music industry and the media have "dictated norms of performance and composition that result from such high levels of capital investment as to be virtually impossible for amateur musicians to attain" (Green 2002, 3). The recent success of TV programs such as the talent shows, and the "YouTubers" phenomenon demonstrates the opposite. Finnegan's (1989) "hidden musicians" today are more visible than ever. Nevertheless, they continue to remain almost hidden in the academic literature, where they are hardly considered—despite the assertions of Forsyth and Cloonan (2008) to the contrary (see also this volume, Lashua, chapter 23, and Smith, chapter 9).

Seminal contributions on amateur music making (e.g., Bayton 1990; Bennett 1980; Cohen 1991; Finnegan 1989; MacKinnon 1993) have emphasized the key roles of attitudes, value judgments, and aesthetic decisions in the performing experience of local, recreational musicians as well as of professional musicians. Indeed, an agreement on values and aesthetics seems to be more important to musicians than the sharing of skills and knowledge, such as instrumental techniques or musical patterns (Bennett 1980). In other words, amateur musicians are driven more by a desire to interact in a community with similar others than by a desire to learn more about the music. According to Green (2002, 124), musicians' values fall into two main categories: (1) performance and creativity, and (2) the musicians' individual qualities. Some of these values are discipline (in spite of what is commonly believed in the case of amateur music making), confirmation and confidence, achievement, passion, enjoyment, spiritual fulfillment, the enhancing of everyday life or the escaping from everyday life, and friendship and respect. Values and aesthetics vary between male and female musicians (Bayton 1990), across ethnicity and geography, age and education, and along different degrees of musical competence (Finnegan 1989; Green 2002; Pitts 2005). Unfortunately, these issues have not been adequately investigated. Additionally, we know very little about what happens on the Internet. Our research aims at answering some of these questions with respect to the online dimension.

A second fundamental dimension of amateur music making is the *relation* (Finnegan 1989) between private and public activities. Overall, we can distinguish three different interactional forms (Bennett 1980): musician to recording; musician to musician; musician to audience. The musician-to-recording interaction exists along a *continuum* that goes from copying to composing (Green 2002, 41). The musician-to-musician relationship is characterized by both cooperation and competition. Cooperation is often experienced as lack of criticism, group equality, and democracy (a band is a "community of peers," according to Green [2002, 16]), particularly in women's bands (Bayton 1990). Cooperation also includes peer-directed or group learning experiences (Green 2002, 76). Today, a great deal of learning occurs via the Internet, including on YouTube and SNSs, rather than in traditional classrooms (Miller 2012). In this case, the musician-to-musician relationships are indirect, but not necessarily one-sided, following the Web 2.0 creed that emphasizes user-generated content and the "architecture of participation" (O'Reilly 2007). Academic reflections on this matter are almost absent (Miller 2012).

Finally, in the musician-to-audience interaction, the definition of a pertinent "general-ized other" (Mead 1934) is fundamentally at stake: repertoires, playlists, gigs, and some-times a proper look are chosen accordingly (Bennett 1980). Pitts (2005, 7) maintains that the audience plays a vital role in contributing to and sustaining regular musical events, receiving in turn a sense of belonging. Online experiences may significantly change these processes, too. For example, how does a web event, where people perform to a separated audience, alter the sense of belonging?

Deeper analysis of the relationship between popular musicians and their audiences has often highlighted a sort of social or collective authorship (Becker 1982; Finnegan 1989; Toynbee 2000) sustained by the so-called fan labor (Baym and Burnett 2009, 434), or the breakage of the dividing line between the artists and their fans (e.g., Hebdige 1979; Rojek 2011, 209–212). Again, online communities assist in building new links and opportunities (see, for instance, the concept of collaborative innovation network, or CoIN[3]), as witnessed in economics, politics, and culture (e.g., Bauwens 2006; Benkler 2006; Gloor 2006; Jenkins 2006a, 2006b; Niessen 2014; Sennett 2012), and have also been crucial in the field of music making (Burnard 2012, part 3; Miller 2012; Smith and Gillett 2015).

As DeNora (2000) argued, music is a technology of the self and an integral part of human agency and everyday life. It accompanies the identity construction process (46–74). Pitts (2005, 5–6) found that relationships are crucial in this process:

> [M]usical identity, behavior, and confidence vary according to context, with a sup-portive environment and ongoing feelings of achievement and success necessary to sustain a sense of musical self-worth.... To be a "musician" involves not just ability and experience, but must also incorporate a degree of recognition from oth-ers and a strong sense of self-identification with the values and skills attributed to this label.

Leisure studies have also investigated amateur musical activity (see Stebbins 1996, and the special issue of *Leisure Studies*, introduced by Bennett 2005).[4] It is worth not-ing that music, in general, tends to accompany "active leisure" and maintenance activi-ties more than deskwork or "passive leisure," and activities undertaken by choice rather than for duty (Sloboda, O'Neill, and Ivaldi 2001). The main topics emerging in the limited literature on leisure and amateur popular music making are the frequency of practice schedules, the degree of commitment to musical activities, and the impor-tance of values inspiring, motivating, and accompanying musical activities. Bennett (1980), for instance, reports that many groups are founded on the commitment that "nothing comes before music." Music requires a "total" dedication and the exclusion of anything else.

A clear gender difference emerges when analyzing female music making. First of all, women are much less involved in popular music than men (see Bayton 1997; Cohen 1991; Green 1997, 2002). The reasons for these gender differences are many and varied. In rock, for instance, aesthetics and ideology are characterized by a strong identification with masculinity (e.g., Frith and McRobbie 1990; Wise 1990), although much has changed since the second half of the 1980s. Second, women are much less likely to be able to play when they join a band (Bayton 1990). The rudiments of playing their instrument are directly learned within the band, even though they are often notationally literate: "Being able to read and understand written music is no clear advantage in rock. Some even argue that it is a disadvantage" (240). In some cases, "it can be argued that getting into rock or pop is a form of rebellion against the norms of academic music" (242). Third, women are more often inexperienced with amplification and electronics. They have to learn many technical skills (from microphone positioning to jack plug soldering, from guitar effects settings to multitrack recording) and, unlike men, they do this only when the experience in a band begins (242–243). Fourth, few women learn to play from records since they prefer to learn playing with other women, avoiding struggling alone (243).

Since Bayton's seminal study, rock and pop schools and tuition (including online) have proliferated, pointing to a more hybridized form of learning rock and other popular music genres. The crucial variables in female music making, with respect to leisure, however, are age and the availability of free time. As they leave their teens, other obligations become incumbent in their lives, when domestic arrangements of all sorts become more and more problematic (Smith 2013; Teague and Smith 2015). We know very little about female amateur music making in Italy, and we know even less concerning female Italian pop and rock musicians.

Today, as we have said, SNSs have become important channels for sharing ideas, experiences, and techniques among amateur musicians. First, they allow the spreading of information and symbolic productions (lyrics, songs, performances, video clips, etc.) worldwide, generating "virtual music scenes" (Peterson and Bennett, in Bennett 2005). Sometimes, this challenges the amateur status of some activities, thus helping to erode the boundaries between private and public spheres. Second, Facebook, Twitter, YouTube, and other SNSs are used as sources of identity construction (Papacharissi 2011; Zhao, Grasmuck, and Martin 2008). Musical tastes and performances effectively contribute to the users' online self-presentation. Finally, they serve as a marketplace for the exchange or barter of new and used instruments and equipment.

Most sociological research on amateur music making was conducted prior to the prevalence of SNSs. Moreover, such contributions were based on ethnographic accounts, qualitative interviews, and only occasionally on social surveys using probabilistic samples. The landscape of social research methods and techniques now has dramatically changed. A different methodological approach might help to refine or revise some early findings and conclusions, as well as to explore previously unexplored territories. It is important, for instance, to investigate whether values and aesthetics still have key roles in contemporary music making, and how they might have changed. An innovative methodological approach should also investigate social interactions (Crossley, McAndrew, and Widdop 2015) and latent meanings and values, using unobtrusive techniques based on concrete behaviors. In this case, data and web mining might represent a suitable choice.

AMATEUR MUSICIANS ON FACEBOOK

In this section, we discuss how and why Italian amateur musicians who play drums, bass, guitar, or keyboards use Facebook. We examined patterns of information diffusion, cohesiveness, subgroups, power, and social roles among musicians by analyzing relational data extracted from the web, utilizing SNA techniques.[5] We also aimed to identify and map both the main areas of discussion and the latent semantic dimensions that characterize Facebook users' activities through textual analysis techniques.

Research Design, Data Collection, Data Organization

There are several Italian Facebook pages dedicated to amateur music making. Facebook pages are divided into *personal, group,* and *fan pages.* We decided to collect group data because interaction within groups is more direct, frequent, and of higher quality than personal or fan pages. All Facebook users can request to join a group. The moderators of the group decide whether or not to accept them. For this study we requested and were granted access to all of the pages we studied. A positional, ad hoc criterion was chosen for the sampling strategy of the pages: the most populated group for each basic pop-rock instrument—drums, bass, guitar, and keyboard—was in fact selected (see Table 26.1).

All data were extracted on December 23, 2014, using a Facebook spigot provided by the software NodeXL (Hansen, Shneiderman, and Smith 2011).[10] This software allows the researcher to collect both relational and textual data from a specific page or group

Table 26.1 Sampled Facebook Pages (December 23, 2014)

Name of the group	Number of formal members	Number of active members	% of active members	% of female members	Comments and "Likes"	Avg. number of replies per post
Batteristi italiani[6] (*drummers*)	9,167	1,237	13.5	2.7	3,169	16.2
Bassisti italiani (e non)[7] (*bass players*)	3,662	282	7.7	2.1	835	4.2
Chitarristi italiani[8] (*guitarists*)	4,389	370	8.4	3.5	786	4.0
Tastieristi italiani[9] (*keyboard players*)	1,607	212	13.2	4.2	619	3.3
Total/Mean	18,825	2,101	11.2	3.1	5,409	6.9

on Facebook through an optional plugin called Social Network Importer.[11] At the time of the study, queries could be extended up to the latest 200 posts or limited to specific intervals of time. For this study, we extracted all data available from each group. Textual data contained all of the comments each user posted during the period examined (from January 9, 2012, to December 23, 2014). At the end of the process, textual data were cleaned of errors, copied, and organized into another matrix for textual analysis with different software.

Italian Pop-Rock Musician Networks: Analysis and Discussion

As evident in Table 26.1, active members (those who regularly post messages and replies) are a small percentage of the total membership on each page (only 11.2 percent). This may suggest a lack of continuity in amateur music making. Many people enter a group, but for various reasons do not participate in its activities. An alternative explanation is that many members participate as "lurkers" and "peekers." We can also suppose that amateur musicians prefer other specialized sites, forums, or "affinity spaces" (Gee 2004),[12] where much informal learning (Green 2008) takes place, rather than SNSs.

Women were scarce in our sample (approximately 3 percent). The community of drummers was the most populated of the four pages, constituting nearly 60 percent of the total sample, and also the most active as indicated by the number of posted replies. The frequency of "likes" and comments posted in a group, however, is not a good predictor of its internal structure, although it is a good indicator of its visibility.

In order to obtain a more detailed picture of the inner relational processes in each group, we utilized SNA. This approach has proven to be quite useful when studying social phenomena on the web, as well as in different music worlds (Crossley, McAndrew, and Widdop 2015). A network analysis approach generally requires several measures and investigations, including: visual representation of the network, density and connectedness, the study of centrality and power, search for clusters, components, bridges, and sensible structures, and the detection of social roles (Knoke and Yang 2008). We explain these concepts and measures while presenting the results of the analysis.

Connectedness and interactivity are mainly measured by density, which is the proportion of present ties to the total number of all possible ties that could exist in the network. Density may range from zero to 100 percent. All four density measures are rather low:[13] 6.4 percent, on average (see Table 26.2). Real-life human networks have similar values, between 3 percent and 10 percent (Valente 2010; Wasserman and Faust 1994). The network of keyboard players is the most dense, while the network of bass players is the least dense. The latter also has the highest percentage of isolated nodes (5.3 percent); that is, individuals without any link to the rest of the network.

Two important indicators of connectedness and information flow within a network are also the average shortest path (or average geodesic distance)[14] and the diameter. On average, 2.5 ties are required to go from one actor to another in the network. Values

Table 26.2 Descriptive Statistics of the Networks

Network	No. of nodes	No. of ties	Density %	Diameter	Avg. shortest path	Avg. clustering coefficient	% of isolated nodes
Drummers	1,237	53,098	6.9	5	2.2	0.82	0.7
Bass players	282	1,799	4.5	6	2.7	0.8	5.3
Guitarists	370	4,254	6.2	7	2.5	0.85	3.8
Keyboard players	212	1,816	8.1	6	2,5	0.84	0.5
Mean	525.25	15,241.75	6.4	6	2,5	0.83	2.6

are quite similar for all four networks. The diameter, that is the maximum geodesic distance, is also similar, ranging from five (drummers) to seven (guitarists) degrees of separation (six, on average). These figures are typical in the case of physical networks, recalling the famous six degrees of separation discovered in the classic literature on social networks (e.g., Milgram 1967). Contemporary research utilizing the Internet reports a lower degree of separation between actors (e.g., four for Facebook, as in Backstrom et al. 2012). Based on this recent research, our values would be considered high, indicating, in some cases, a difficult flow of information. Also, the average clustering coefficients, which measure how strongly the neighborhoods of the nodes are mutually connected, are high (see Table 26.2),[15] revealing the presence of many local compact subnets. We can conclude that the four networks have a structure that is locally more dense and globally less dense, although with some individual differences. At the end of the chapter, we explain why these structures can be considered quite interesting.

Measures of centrality are aimed at identifying prominent, influential, prestigious, and reachable actors or nodes within the network (Knoke and Yang 2008). Two main centrality (i.e., power) measures are commonly used in SNA: degree and betweenness (see Table 26.3). Degree centrality simply counts the number of connections arriving at or departing from a given node, which suggests that actors with a higher degree centrality are more prestigious and/or influential within the network. Betweenness centrality measures how often a node appears on the shortest path among all pairs of nodes within the network, which suggests that actors with higher values of betweenness centrality typically act as brokers, intermediaries, or moderators. Our networks exhibit a high average degree centrality (34.7 connections) and high betweenness centrality (311). The bass players' network has the lowest average degree (12.75 connections), while the keyboard players' network has the lowest average betweenness (132.1).

Centrality measures apply to individual nodes, while measures of "centralization" concern the global network. Centralization measures the "inequality" in the

Table 26.3 Centralization and Power

Network	Avg. degree	Degree centralization %	Avg. betweenness	Betweenness centralization %
Drummers	85.85	36.7	702	4.8
Bass players	12.75	16.6	188.1	7.2
Guitarists	23	27.2	222	9
Keyboard players	17.1	34.4	132.1	15.6
Mean	34.7	28.7	311	9.15

distribution of centrality, and can be used to summarize the distribution of power within a network. It ranges from zero (when the nodes have all the same value of centrality) to one (maximum inequality). A highly centralized network is dominated by one or few powerful node(s). Degree centralization is moderate in drummers (36.7 percent) and keyboard players (34.4 percent), and fairly low in guitarists (27.2 percent) and bass players (16.6 percent). The latter is the most "democratic" network in terms of prestige and influence. Betweenness centralization is very low (9.15) on average. In short, these networks are crowded with many intermediaries and moderators. As a consequence, we see evidence of collaboration and supportiveness among musicians and the absence of strong hierarchies (see Toynbee 2000, 37).

Networks may be characterized by the presence of denser regions, substructures, and subgroups. They may differ in size, density, and cohesion. Various techniques may be employed in order to detect and describe such groups. These can adopt a bottom-up or a top-down perspective (Hanneman and Riddle 2011, 348–356). Traditional measures and techniques belonging to the bottom-up approach, such as cliques, n-cliques, n-clans, and k-cores, have not proven to be adequate in investigating vast and complex networks or the Internet, and are also computationally demanding (Bogdanov et al. 2013). Top-down approaches (i.e., connected components) have yielded better results. In recent years a "community structures" approach has been successfully adopted (e.g., Girvan and Newman 2002) in order to delineate a more meaningful and clear representation of network subgroups. A community structure must have the following features: (1) mutual ties, (2) a high frequency of ties among members, (3) a relative frequency of ties among subgroup members compared to nonmembers, and (4) a high closeness or reachability of subgroup members. To analyze the networks for these features we utilized the Clauset–Newman–Moore algorithm (see Table 26.4).

All networks have many *connected components* (M = 17.75) and *communities* (M = 12.75). Some groups are rather populated, but most are very small, containing a single musician in the case of connected components, or having not more than two members in the case of communities (see parenthetical values in Table 26.4).

Table 26.4 Subgroups: Connected Components and
           Communities

Network	# of connected components*	# of communities (Clauset-Newman-Moore)
Drummers	12 (9)	11
Bass players	22 (15)	14
Guitarists	23 (14)	16
Keyboard players	14 (10)	10
Mean	**17.75 (12)**	**12.75**

* Single node components in parenthesis.

Figure 26.1 shows the sociograms originated from the data matrices. Sociograms are visual representations of the relationships among the actors, where nodes represent actors (in this case, musicians) and lines represent ties (in this case, interactions the musicians had on Facebook[16]). In the figures, the size of each node is proportional to its level of centrality (i.e., power), while the thickness of a tie is proportional to its strength. Nodes and ties are positioned according to an algorithm (Force Atlas 2)[17] that attempts to highlight subgroups in the network. Finally, musicians belonging to the same subgroup (i.e., community) have the same shade of grey.[18]

The presence of networks that are locally denser and globally looser is confirmed. The structure of information sharing is moderately differentiated, depending on the type of instrument. The networks of the guitarists (c) and keyboard players (d) appear similar. They exhibit a strong central nucleus, surrounded by many little clusters. The centrality of the musicians within the nucleus is high and uniformly distributed, while some more powerful nodes connect the nucleus to the peripheral clusters. Thus, it seems that a nucleus of experts (i.e., individuals with higher values of degree centrality) share information (e.g., skills and knowledge) with peripheral cliques through the activity of some brokers (i.e., individuals with higher values of betweenness centrality). The drummers' network (a), on the contrary, is more evenly divided in a multitude of medium subnets. The bass players' network (b) has fewer subgroups and many central nodes.

Italian Pop-Rock Musicians' Discourses: Analysis and Discussion

Textual data were analyzed in order to understand what musicians talk about (content analysis) and which latent semantic meanings (attitudes, values, aesthetics) characterized their discourses (lexical correspondence analysis). Network and textual data come from the same Facebook groups, and were collected simultaneously through the software NodeXL.

(a)

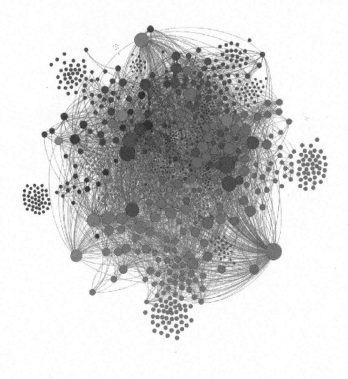

FIGURE 26.1 Social structure of the groups: four sociograms. (a) Drummers, (b) bass players, (c) guitarists, (d) keyboard players.

Textual analysis was carried out using a tool called the Thematic Analysis of Elementary Contexts provided by the software T-Lab (Lancia 2014). This tool is based on an unsupervised clustering technique called *bisecting k-mean*.[19] The Thematic Analysis of Elementary Contexts aims at detecting clusters of meaning which serve as isotopies (*iso* = same; *tópoi* = places), when people formulate their discourses. This analysis creates a map of themes characterized by the co-occurrences of certain semantic traits (Lancia 2014, 74–95). Six clusters emerged from the thematic analysis.[20] We labeled them as follows: (1) sound shaping, (2) studio recording, (3) marketplace, (4) musical references, (5) computer production, and (6) relations. The distribution of these themes in the corpus is illustrated in Figure 26.2.

(b)

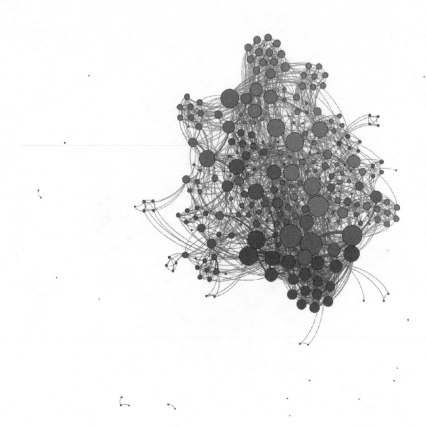

FIGURE 26.1 Continued

The themes are semantically oriented along some latent dimensions of meaning (factors) that emerge from *lexical correspondence analysis* (LCA) (see Figure 26.3). LCA is a factor exploratory technique for words (Lebart and Salem 1988). This approach assumes that words alone (the focus of classic content analysis) have no meaning. They make sense only in association with and/or in opposition to other words or groups of words, and are typical of certain kinds of individuals or groups of individuals. LCA is not interested in *similarities*, but in *differences*. Even words with a low occurrence, then, could be significant, provided that they are *typical* of a certain person or group of people (Barker, Mathijs, and Trobia 2008, 231). LCA has two main goals: (1) to find regularities in the data, and (2) to find only those few dimensions of meaning that explain these regularities, employing factor techniques (231).

(c)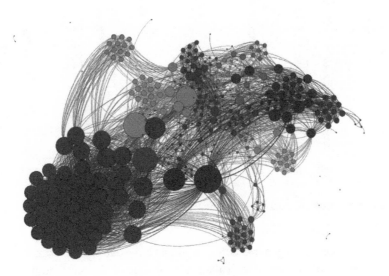

(d)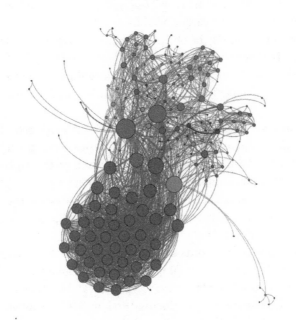

FIGURE 26.1 Continued

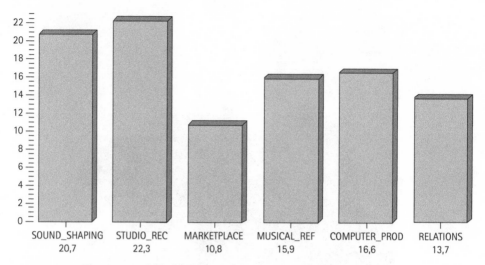

FIGURE 26.2 Thematic analysis (percentages)

Factor techniques, in general, aim at reducing large datasets in terms of a lower number of latent, synthetic variables, called factors. One of the main outputs is the factor space (basically a Cartesian coordinate system), whose axes are generally constituted by the first two factors extracted. The factor space shows the semantic orientation of significant words, modalities, or themes on opposite axes, thus contributing to their disambiguation. Words and meaningful groups of words (that is, isotopies) are considered significant if they are distant from the origin of axes (Benzecri, in Lancia 2012a, 18). Each axis allows the researcher to reconstruct an *ideal syntagm*—that is, *a theoretical model of a latent proposition* in the *corpus* (Barker, Mathijs, and Trobia 2008, 232).[21]

All geometric distances among the objects, on this space, are to be interpreted as distances of meaning. Therefore, two distant objects (e.g., words) on the factor space will be considered uncorrelated, and will have opposite meanings, with respect to a certain latent variable (i.e., axis); while two close objects will be correlated and have a similar meaning.

The two main extracted factors account for 51.3 percent of total inertia. In other words, 51.3 percent of the global latent meaning within the corpus is explained by the first two dimensions. The horizontal dimension (about 30 percent of the explained meaning) illustrates the semantic opposition of *theory* (on the right) versus *praxis* (on the left); while the second, vertical dimension (about 22 percent of the explained meaning) illustrates the opposition between *competence* (skills and knowledge, technique and culture) and *production* (see Figure 26.3).[22]

Studio recording (containing words such as *music, studio, band, recording, production, demo*) and sound shaping (containing words such as *sound, harmonic, frequency, brand, taste*) are the most discussed themes (22.3 percent and 20.7 percent, respectively). The musicians' conversations are mainly focused on how they can obtain certain sounds and record them effectively in the recording studio. Bassists and keyboard players are

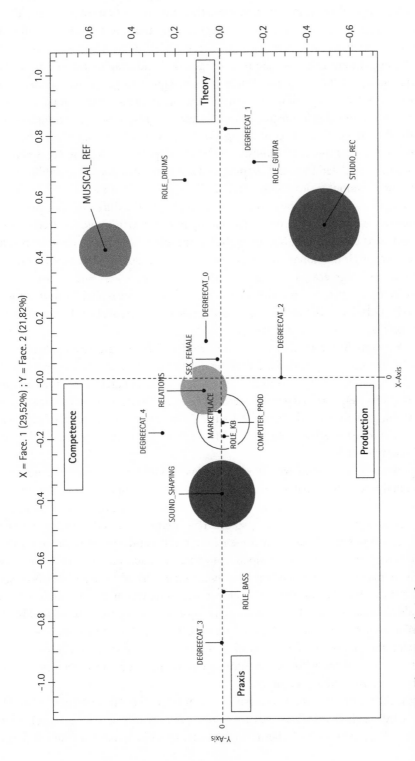

X = Face. 1 (29,52%) ; Y = Face. 2 (21,82%)

FIGURE 26.3 Thematic analysis: factor space

the musicians who are more concerned with sound shaping, that is, with the search for the right tone, sound, or atmosphere, through their instruments and equipment. Degree centrality is also correlated with this theme, meaning that prestigious and influential users (see the modality degreecat_4 on the factor space)[23] tend to be more interested in sound shaping. Interestingly, studio recording and sound shaping are semantically in opposition along the theory–praxis dimension (see Figure 26.3). It would seem that disappointment and dissatisfaction are common among these musicians, when they are in the studio, due to its rules, atmosphere, and the concrete results of a recording session.

The third theme extracted (containing words such as *sounds, interface, audio, PC, keyboard, synth, programming, Cubase, VST*)[24] is computer production (16.6 percent), which is strongly related to sound shaping and semantically opposed to studio recording. Although computer production and studio recording both allude to the recording process, this semantic opposition seems to highlight the difference between home and professional studio environments. Computer production is discussed, above all, by keyboard players, and, interestingly, by musicians who have either high values of degree (i.e., high relational power; see the geometric closeness between "computer production" and degreecat_4, in Figure 26.3) or by isolated nodes (see the low distance between "computer production" and degreecat_0). This theme is slightly shifted toward the "praxis" polarity of the factor space, and neutral with respect to the competence–production dimension (see Figure 26.3).

The same happens for another theme: marketplace. This theme contains words such as *value* (as synonym of price), *used, bidding, Mercatino Musicale,*[25] *check, euro,* and so on, and is related to buying or trading activities that often characterize amateur musicians groups. Its weight is 10.8 percent (see Figure 26.2). This is the least discussed theme among the musicians studied. From a statistical point of view, computer production and marketplace almost overlap (note that, in Figure 26.3, the circle representing this latter theme is completely hidden).

The presence of the theme we called "relations" (weight = 13.7 percent) confirms its fundamental role in the amateur music making world, as emphasized in the literature (e.g., Finnegan 1989). It contains words such as *thanks, congratulations, welcome, up, gentle, greetings, friend, cheating,* and so on. This theme is located at the origin of the axes, hence it is not reflective of any dimension. It transcends the semantic oppositions between theory and praxis, and competence versus production. "Female" is the closest modality to this theme. That is, women represent a majority of those people who discuss relation items, which is consistent with classic and more recent ethnographic accounts on female musicians (e.g., Bayton 1990, 1997; Björck 2011; Clawson 1999; Reddington 2012). Women are also the most isolated actors within the four networks (see the geometric closeness between "female" and "degreecat_0", in Figure 26.3). And indeed, isolated actors are those who require more attention to this subject (see the closeness between "relations" and degreecat_0).

The last theme of discussion concerns musical references (15.9 percent), characterized by words such as *metal, progressive, genre, Porcaro, King Crimson, Slayer, Banco,* and *PFM.*[26] The position of this theme on the factor space is peculiar, in that it is the only theme occupying the first quadrant at the intersection of theory and competence. We may interpret this cluster as referring to the culture that musicians share. No references can be found here to either Italian singer-songwriters (*cantautori*) or Italian melodic traditions. All of the musical references cited belong to both Italian and international rock music. These are essentially classic rock masters, which suggests a nostalgic tendency to recall earlier (more authentic?) epochs. It seems that drummers are quite interested in this theme. The high frequency of words alluding to progressive and metal also indicate a particular attention to musical virtuosity and technique, characteristic of these genres.

We also analyzed word co-occurrences in order to explore meaningful associations within the corpus (Table 26.5 and Figure 26.4). Co-occurrences may be interpreted as very basic sentences that characterize one's worldview. Sometimes they can reveal cognitive constructs, social representations, stereotypes, and prejudices (Krippendorff 2004).

First, we chose to analyze co-occurrences with the word *suonare* ("playing"),[27] which is the second most frequent word in the corpus (243 occurrences). "Playing" is associated most often with "I," the most frequent word in the corpus (*cosine* = 0.23; 349 occurrences). Therefore, the basic sentence this association suggests is "I play." Playing is mainly experienced (and reported in the musicians' discourses) on a personal level. Playing is also associated with the word "beautiful" (*cosine* = 0.17). Therefore, it is perceived as a very pleasant experience. This is confirmed by other associated words in the list, with a lesser cosine coefficient, we omitted here.

Interestingly, the prominent use of the word "video" (*cosine* = 0.128) may be reflective of the change in amateur music making resulting from the developments and diffusion of digital portable media and the Internet (e.g., YouTube) (Miller 2012). Additionally, the

Table 26.5 Word Associations: Suonare (*Playing*) (Cosine Coefficients, $p < 0.05$)

Word	Coeff.
Io (*I*)	0.236
Bello (*beautiful*)	0.170
Strumento (*instrument*)	0.144
Bastare (*to suffice*)	0.144
Sentire (*to feel*)	0.137
Insegnare (*to teach*)	0.133
Mancare (*to lack*)	0.133
Musica (*music*)	0.130
Alto (*loud*)	0.129
Video (*video*)	0.128

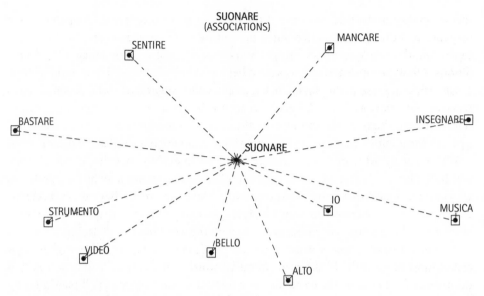

FIGURE 26.4 Word associations: suonare (*playing*)

presence of the verb "to teach" (*cosine* = 0.13) might refer to a basic need identified in the amateur world. Significant mentions of teaching (or self-teaching) suggest a sort of permanent, unavoidable barrier each musician, both professional and amateur, must work against, since there is no music without practice, skills, and knowledge (Green 2002).

We also tested the word "Italia,"[28] in order to elicit specific social representations of the Italian scene (Table 26.6 and Figure 26.5). Co-occurrences are quite enlightening here. A first group of words alludes to the Italian distinctive mix of musical influences and styles, introduced at the beginning of this chapter. This means, of course, to be "different" (*cosine* = 0.25), a hybridization of "styles" (*cosine* = 0.125), and a juxtaposition with the "abroad" scene (*cosine* = 0.224). Most significantly, it also implies "isolation" (*cosine* = 0.125). All posts analyzed here are written by Italians in Italian, and many threads are rather "provincial" in content. Performances, lessons and tutorials, virtual teachers, and online courses abound on the web. These can help amateur musicians enormously (this may also apply to female musicians, who—as said—tend to prefer learning in a band or through friends), although in many cases, including this one, linguistic differences seem to constitute a frustrating barrier.

Another group of words alludes to the Italian music tradition: classical ("conservatory," *cosine* = 0.158), traditional ("Neapolitan,"[29] *cosine* = 0.125), and popular ("autore," *cosine* = 0.112). The final group of words is related to practicing music locally: it requires an "entourage" (*cosine* = 0.15), "groups" are prevalent (*cosine* = 0.14), and it seems working in Italy is well accepted ("very well", *cosine* = 0.129). Musicians' conversations about Italy and music making in this country, therefore, are rather pronounced and contrasting.

Table 26.6 Word Associations: Italia (Cosine Coefficients, $p < 0.05$)	
Word	Coeff.
Differente (*different*)	0.250
Estero (*abroad*)	0.224
Conservatorio (*conservatory*)	0.158
Giro (*entourage*)	0.150
Gruppi (*groups*)	0.144
Molto_bene (*very_well*)	0.129
Lavorare (*to work*)	0.125
Campano (*Neapolitan*)	0.125
Insegnante (*teacher*)	0.125
Isolamento (*isolation*)	0.125
Stili (*styles*)	0.125
Autore (*author*)	0.112

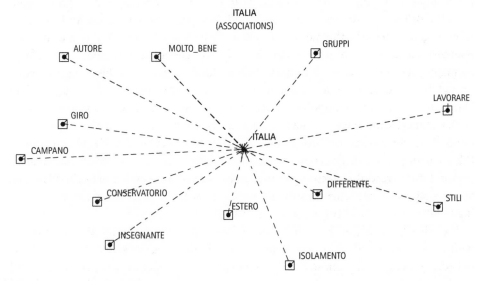

FIGURE 26.5 Word associations: Italia

CONCLUSIONS

The world of amateur pop-rock musicians in Italy appears as an "art world" à la Becker (1982), where—as we have seen in the topologies of the networks—online relations often serve as a substitute for physical sociability that was essential before the Internet. Collaboration and supportiveness among musicians and the absence of strong hierarchies characterize the networks analyzed. The structure of information sharing we observed is moderately differentiated, depending on the type of instrument. The models of online social interaction emerging from the analysis (see Figure 26.1) share some features with two typical social media structures that Smith et al. (2014) call the *Tight crowd* and the *Community clusters*. These structures are important because they "show how networked learning communities function and how sharing and mutual support can be facilitated by social media" (2). Besides, "some information sources and subjects ignite multiple conversations, each cultivating its own audience and community. These can illustrate diverse angles on a subject based on its relevance to different audiences, revealing a diversity of opinion and perspective on a social media topic" (3). Notably, however, this world is predominantly male. The presence of women is scarce. When women are present, their centrality is low. Their preferred topic of discussion focuses on the question of relationships.

The distinctive mix of influences and styles that characterizes Italian popular music (Santoro 2010) is evident from the analysis of word co-occurrences. Many contrasting elements seem to connote the representation of "Italy." The Italian classical music legacy, for example, is an important and meaningful reference. This reference is very distant from the British and American pop-rock tradition, yet it is unavoidable for those who want to gain success in the national popular music market. The pantheon of musical references, as emerges from the thematic analysis of elementary contexts, is populated by many heterogeneous "rock fathers." Intercultural conflicts and blending increased on a global scale with the Beat Generation, yuppies, and Generation X. Today's Italian "Millennials" who create popular music in their leisure time can draw from expressive cues, technical knowledge, languages, musical rules, and syntax from all over the world by accessing the Internet or through the increase in global cultural trade. The creation of this amateur pop music goes beyond simply imitation. The prevalence of "sound shaping" and studio recording techniques in their conversations is emblematic, in this sense. Sound shaping, in particular, is strongly associated with the presence of musicians having a high degree centrality (i.e., power) (see Figure 26.3).

The "visual," "sonic," and "textual" dimensions connoting the material that circulates within social media sites also represent a source for defining one's own "ethnomethod" in order to better equip oneself in the construction of one's own aesthetic circles and musical identity, as well as social identity *tout court*, within which music making may be a constitutive element (Magaudda and Santoro 2013; Torti 2000). The integration of the Internet into an amateur musician's daily life provides more visibility and connection with others as individuals, as well as musicians. As we have seen in this case, linguistic differences seem to represent an important barrier to effective communication.

Four thematic areas intertwine in the Italian amateur pop-rock musician's imagination. The first one recalls the meanings emerging from the relationship between competence and knowledge (see the first quadrant in Figure 26.3). This thematic area emphasizes the popular music traditions, and represents a sort of "theme of the origins," nostalgically recalling fathers and heroes within the "minor" world of pop and rock music. Interestingly, drummers are more concerned than other musicians with this semantic space.

The second quadrant combines practice and competence. It refers to praxis as oriented by competence and awareness. It might allude, for instance, to the world of live performance. In this sense, practices become legitimated by a difficult initiation process—not necessarily corresponding to formal music education (Gasperoni, Marconi, and Santoro 2004; Martinengo and Nuciari 1986)—now carried out mainly on the Internet, allowing pop-rock amateurs to feel like they are real musicians. The question here is which musicians can or want to be in the world of amateur music making, what is necessary to accomplish this task, and which competencies are still lacking. SNA suggests that Italian Facebook musicians are made up of self-made, apparently competent performers who represent points of reference for less skilled musicians through the moderating activity of influential brokers. Musicians who have a high degree centrality (i.e., power), in fact, characterize this quadrant.

The third thematic area addresses music production and amateur music praxis. It is a proactive dimension, imbalanced toward music as a practice, as described by Bourdieu (1972); that is, a coherent set of ways in which a specific social "style" is internalized and yields particular forms of expression of the emotions that are subsequently recognized as representative of a given social environment. Within a network of amateur musicians, this quadrant might relate to who they are, what they make, and what they identify with.

Finally, the fourth thematic area alludes to the semantic combination of theory and music production observed in the fourth quadrant. It refers to how theory and traditions affect individual and collective music making. It is the issue of the "tracks," to be understood in the double sense of "record" and "imprint." We recognize here the issue of musical values, indicating the ultimate aim of amateur music making activities. As we have seen, today this implies the definitive primacy of the visual over the aural and the textual. Guitarists are more numerous in this space.

In today's connected society, the amateur may overcome social and cultural barriers, while trying to reach the same wide audience as the professional musician, in spite of his or her relative lack of competence and knowledge. This is observed, for example, in amateur musicians who succeed in making their products "viral" (but not necessarily better) on the Internet, although this happens only occasionally. The online world allows for a global hybridization of musical elements, both cultural and technical, coming from a type of shared and collective *milieu* (Miller 2012). Recalling Blackshaw (2010), this may be described as the "IKEAization" of amateur music production—a do-it-yourself (DIY) musical product (Niessen 2014), an idea of music making as "following the instructions," having in mind the web-based art world as its main destination. The aim is that of intercepting the "emotive mediation" demand that comes from the social world itself. In order to succeed in this purpose, however, this emotive mediation must be deserved; it needs hard work, commitment, and the advice of more expert musicians who have a high reputation and centrality (Niessen 2014) within SNSs, for example. In this case, SNSs act as the user's manual for this DIY activity.

IKEAization concerns democracy, too. On one hand, in the online world social differences may not be as clearly delineated, as happens in the IKEA spaces, where working-class and middle-class comingle, yielding a sort of "democracy of taste" (Blackshaw 2010). This is the ethic of pop, which, as we have seen, may imply a nostalgic recall of past masters. On the other hand, other social differences may arise, in the form of a digital divide, where the problem is not necessarily economic, but is cognitive or aesthetic. The abundance of loops, plug-ins, and software (sometimes illegally) downloaded from the Internet does not guarantee the production of a decent musical product.

Together with IKEAization, we can also identify a simultaneous process of "Appleization" (Lo Verde 2013) of leisure amateur music making, heavily based upon a "life in the virtual." The diffusion of this process is characterized by:

(1) a high "coolness" factor, achieved—for example—by exploiting certain "fathers" of pop and rock;
(2) competence in mixing and synthesizing textual, sonic, and visual stimuli that are to be recomposed or recreated in one's own device, as Apple did in the first place ("studio recording," "computer production," and "sound shaping" are crucial here);
(3) amazing and being amazed;
(4) the feeling of being a big community, but not a "mass," as Apple consumers think.

This last aspect is clearly highlighted by the modular structure of the networks examined: they are, in fact, locally denser and globally looser.

Nevertheless, the process of Appleization may be also related to the "Second Enclosure Movement" (Rojek 2011), defined as "the attempt by the music business to dictate and police the unauthorized exchange of copyright material on the internet and to usurp and transform the structure of free exchange with subscription models" (214). Apple, in fact, has intentionally maintained control over what will and will not work with Apple devices and services. This may seriously threaten the online world as we know it and make use of it.

In conclusion, IKEAization and Appleization of leisure time seem to constitute the frame within which amateur musical activities are currently carried out. They represent the social background that allows and conditions such activities. Nevertheless, the structures of online networks represent a variable that plays a crucial role, modulating their impact. The online discourse itself, indeed, is significantly conditioned by the interactional structures we discovered through social network analysis. We have demonstrated that such interactional structures become an important intervening variable in the explanation of online amateur musical activities, and they should be taken into account when studying them.

NOTES

1. The Sanremo Festival is a very popular Italian song contest. All the songs proposed must be previously unreleased, and sung in Italian. It is transmitted live by the Italian public television (RAI1), and is considered a national event (http://en.wikipedia.org/wiki/Sanremo_Music_Festival). The festival has often been criticized for promoting the worst "conservative" tradition of Italian popular music.

2. The expression "semiprofessional" refers to a variety of work contexts and can mean that "sometimes you get paid and sometimes you don't, or that the musicians are paid, but not enough to live on even if they worked every night of the week" (Green 2002, 9).

3. According to Gloor (2006, 4), a Collaborative Innovation Network (CoIN) is "a cyberteam of self-motivated people with a collective vision, enabled by the Web to collaborate in achieving a common goal by sharing ideas, information, and work."

4. An attempt to integrate popular music literature and leisure studies in an explanatory model, from an analytical sociology perspective, is introduced and discussed in Trobia (2012).

5. For an introduction to SNA in the field of popular music studies, see Crossley, McAndrew, Widdop (2015), chapter 2. For a general basic introduction, see Knoke and Yang (2008). For a more comprehensive treatment, see Wasserman and Faust (1997), and Scott and Carrington (2011).

6. https://www.facebook.com/groups/143280199075382/.

7. https://www.facebook.com/groups/74196830706/.

8. https://www.facebook.com/groups/172668096139223/.

9. https://www.facebook.com/groups/tastieristitaliani/.

10. A "spigot" is an automatic data collector, exploiting social network sites' application programming interfaces (API), sometimes present in SNA software, such as NodeXL, Netvizz, or Gephi.

11. http://socialnetimporter.codeplex.com/.

12. According to Gee (2004, 67), "an affinity space is a place or set of places where people affiliate with others based primarily on shared activities, interests, and goals, not shared race, class culture, ethnicity, or gender."

13. SNA literature distinguishes among *loose-knit* (density < 40 percent), *medium-knit* (density ranges from 40 to 60 percent) and *close-knit* (density > 60 percent) networks (a classic reference is Bott 1971).

14. "Geodesic distance is the length of the shortest path between two actors" (Knoke and Yang 2008, 60).

15. The clustering coefficient ranges between 0 and 1.

16. A link was established between two nodes whenever they liked or commented the same post.

17. Force Atlas 2 is provided by the software Gephi (http://gephi.github.io/).

18. A legend is not necessary (and would complicate the effectiveness of the figures), since the different shades of grey simply indicate the sharing of a common feature, as happens in geographic maps.

19. Bisecting k-means is a combination of k-means and hierarchical clustering (Steinbach, Karypis, and Kumar 2000). See Lancia (2012b) for a more detailed explanation of the *Thematic Analysis of Elementary Contexts*.

20. The algorithm used by T-Lab produces several partitions of themes. The user can explore different solutions. We accepted the six themes partition as the best solution.

21. In linguistics and LCA, a *corpus* is a set of texts utilized in the analysis.
22. The labels characterizing each dimension originate from the words with the highest value tests (or v-tests), as emerged from LCA. The v-test is a statistical measure that is used in order to facilitate the interpretation of factor polarities (Lancia 2014, 229). The higher the v-test, the higher the importance of an object (modality, word, or cluster). Significant words are: "to use," "to try," "to find," "Euro," "price," "used," and many instrument brands, for the *praxis* polarity (negative values of x); "to listen," "to study," "to know," "to understand," "concept," "progressive," "metal," "album," for the *theory* polarity (positive values of x); "studio," "to record," "to produce," "production," "to work," "to obtain," "demo," "to invest," "advertising," "trend," for the *production* polarity (negative values of y); "metal," "progressive," "fusion," "genre," "Porcaro," "Gadd," "Banco," "PFM," "King Crimson," "Yes," "Dream Theatre," "Slayer," "Iron Maiden," "to discover," "to listen," "style," "virtuoso," "technique," "solo," "performance," "velocity," "maestro," "monster," "training," "to explain," for the *competence* polarity (positive values of y).
23. "Degreecat" is a recoded variable, corresponding to the level of normalized degree (i.e., relational power) each musician has. We grouped the values of the normalized degree distributions into five modalities: from degreecat_0 (null degree) to degreecat_4 (highest degree). Recoding was necessary, since correspondence analysis and the software T-Lab only accept categorical variables.
24. Cubase is a common software program for music production, while VST stands for Virtual Studio Technology, a software interface that integrates software audio synthesizers and effect plug-ins with audio editors and recording systems (http://en.wikipedia.org/wiki/Virtual_Studio_Technology).
25. Mercatino Musicale is a well-known Italian website for buying or trading new and used instruments and equipment (http://www.mercatinomusicale.com/).
26. Banco del Mutuo Soccorso (or Banco) and Premiata Forneria Marconi (PFM) are among the most successful Italian progressive bands of the 1970s.
27. We deleted from the list the following items: the names of the instruments (bass and guitar); words with $p < 0.05$ ("sound," and "to use"); and a stop-word ("via"). Co-occurrences are measured by the cosine coefficient (Salton and McGill 1984), which ranges from 0 (no association between two words) to 1 (perfect association).
28. "Italia" is actually a meta-entry, specifically created for the analysis, and added to the software dictionary, including the following terms: "Italia," "Italiano," "Italiana," "Italiane." This meta-word had thirty-seven occurrences.
29. Neapolitan music, particularly the Canzone Napoletana (e.g., "O Sole Mio"), usually accompanied by mandolins, represents one of the major components of traditional Italian popular music.

References Cited

Agostini, Roberto. 2007. "The Italian 'Canzone' and the Sanremo Festival. Change and Continuity in Italian Mainstream Pop of the Sixties." *Popular Music* 26(3): 389–408.

Backstrom, Lars, Paolo Boldi, Marco Rosa, Johan Ugander, and Sebastiano Vigna. 2012. "Four Degrees of Separation." *Arxiv.* http://arxiv.org/abs/1111.4570.

Baldazzi, Gianfranco. 1989. *La canzone italiana del Novecento.* Rome: Newton Compton.

Barker, Martin, Ernest Mathijs, and Alberto Trobia. 2008. "Our Methodological Challenges and Solutions." In *Watching "The Lord of the Rings": Tolkien's World Audiences*, edited by Martin Barker, and Ernest Mathijs, 213–239. New York: Peter Lang.

Bauwens, Michel. 2006. "The Political Economy of Peer Production." *Post-Autistic Economics Review* 37, article 3: 33–44. http://www.paecon.net/PAEReview/issue37/Bauwens37.htm.

Baym, Nancy K., and Robert Burnett. 2009. "Amateur Experts: International Fan Labour in Swedish Independent Music." *International Journal of Cultural Studies* 12(5): 433–450.

Bayton, Mavis. 1990. "How Women Become Musicians." In *On Record: Rock, Pop, and the Written Word*, edited by Simon Frith and Andrew Goodwin, 201–219. London: Routledge.

Bayton, Mavis. 1997. *Frock Rock: Women Performing Popular Music*. Oxford: Oxford University Press.

Becker, Howard S. 1982. *Art Worlds*. Berkeley: University of California Press.

Beer, David. 2008. "Making Friends with Jarvis Cocker: Music Culture in the Context of Web 2.0." *Cultural Sociology* 2(2): 222–241.

Benkler, Yochai. 2006. *The Wealth of Networks: How Social Production Transforms Markets and Freedom*. New Haven, CT: Yale University Press.

Bennett, Andy. 2005. "Popular Music and Leisure." *Leisure Studies* 24(4): 333–342.

Bennett, H. Stith. 1980. *On Becoming a Rock Musician*. Amherst: University of Massachusetts Press.

Björck, Cecilia. 2011. *Claiming Space: Discourses on Gender, Popular Music, and Social Change*. Gothenburg: ArtMonitor, University of Gothenburg Press. https://gupea.ub.gu.se/bitstream/2077/24290/1/gupea_2077_24290_1.pdf.

Blackshaw, Tony. 2010. *Leisure*. New York: Routledge.

Bogdanov, Petko, Ben Baumer, Prithwish Basu, Amotz Bar-Noy, and Ambuj K. Singh. 2013. "As Strong as the Weakest Link: Mining Diverse Cliques in Weighted Graphs." In *Machine Learning and Knowledge Discovery in Databases*, edited by Hendrik Blockeel, Kristian Kersting, Siegfried Nijssen, and Filip Železný, 525–540. Berlin and Heidelberg: Springer Verlag.

Bott, Elizabeth. 1971. *Family and Social Network*. 2nd edition. New York: Free Press.

Bourdieu, Pierre. 1972. *Esquisse d'une théorie de la pratique*. Genève: Droz.

Burnard, Pamela. 2012. *Musical Creativities in Practice*. Oxford: Oxford University Press.

Clawson, Mary A. 1999. "When Women Play the Bass: Instrumental Specialization and Gender Interpretation in Alternative Rock Music." *Gender and Society* 13(2): 193–210.

Cohen, Sara. 1991. *Rock Culture in Liverpool: Popular Music in the Making*. Oxford: Oxford University Press.

Colletti, Justin. 2013. "How to Tell If You're an Amateur Musician." *Trust Me I'm a Scientist*, November 4. http://www.trustmeimascientist.com/2013/11/04/op-ed-how-to-tell-if-youre-an-amateur-musician/.

Crossley, Nick, Siobhan McAndrew, and Paul Widdop, eds. 2015. *Social Networks and Music Worlds*. Abingdon: Routledge.

DeNora, Tia. 2000. *Music in Everyday Life*. Cambridge: Cambridge University Press.

Finnegan, Ruth. 1989. *The Hidden Musicians: Music-Making in an English Town*. Cambridge: Cambridge University Press.

Forsyth, Alasdair, and Martin Cloonan. 2008. "Alco-pop? The Use of Popular Music in Glasgow Pubs." *Popular Music and Society* 31(1): 57–78.

Frith, Simon, and Angela McRobbie. 1990. "Rock and Sexuality." In *On Record: Rock, Pop, and the Written Word*, edited by Simon Frith and Andrew Goodwin, 317–332. London: Routledge.

Gasperoni, Giancarlo, Luca Marconi, and Marco Santoro. 2004. *La musica e gli adolescenti: Pratiche, gusti, educazione*. Torino: EDT.

Gee, James P. 2004. *Situated Language and Learning: A Critique of Traditional Schooling*. New York: Routledge.

Girvan, Michelle, and Mark E. J. Newman. 2002. "Community Structure in Social and Biological Networks." *Proceedings of the National Academy of Sciences* 99: 7821–7826.

Gloor, Peter. 2006. *Swarm Creativity: Competitive Advantage through Collaborative Innovation Networks*. Oxford: Oxford University Press.

Green, Lucy. 1997. *Music, Gender, Education*. Cambridge: Cambridge University Press.

Green, Lucy. 2002. *How Popular Musicians Learn: A Way Ahead for Music Education*. Aldershot: Ashgate.

Green, Lucy. 2008. *Music, Informal Learning and the School: A New Classroom Pedagogy*. Aldershot: Ashgate.

Hanneman, R. A., and Mark Riddle. 2011. "Concepts and measures for basic network analysis." In *The SAGE Handbook of Social Network Analysis*, edited by John Scott and Peter J. Carrington, 331–339. London: Sage.

Hansen, Derek L., Ben Shneiderman, and Marc A. Smith. 2011. *Analyzing Social Media Networks with NodeXL: Insights from a Connected World*. Burlington, MA: Morgan Kaufmann.

Hebdige, Dick. 1979. *Subculture: The Meaning of Style*. London: Methuen.

Hirsch, Paul M. 1972. "Processing Fads and Fashions: An Organization-Set Analysis of Culture Industry System." *American Journal of Sociology* 77: 639–659.

Jenkins, Henry. 2006a. *Convergence Culture: Where Old and New Media Collide*. New York: New York University Press.

Jenkins, Henry. 2006b. *Fans, Bloggers, and Gamers: Exploring Participatory Culture*. New York: New York University Press.

Knoke, David, and Song Yang. 2008. *Social Network Analysis*. Thousand Oaks, CA: Sage.

Krippendorff, Klaus. 2004. *Content Analysis. An Introduction to Its Methodology*. 2nd edition. Thousand Oaks, CA: Sage.

Lancia, Franco. 2012a. *The Logic of the T-LAB Tools Explained*. http://www.mytlab.com/textscope.pdf.

Lancia, Franco. 2012b. *T-LAB Pathways to Thematic Analysis*. http://mytlab.com/tpathways.pdf.

Lancia, Franco. 2014. *T-Lab 9.1: Tools for Text Analysis. User's Manual*. http://www.mytlab.com/Manual_en.zip.

Lebart, Ludovic, and André Salem. 1988. *Analyse statistique des données textuelles*. Paris: Dunod.

Lo Verde, Fabio Massimo. 2013. "Introduction: McDonaldization, Ikeaization, Appleization of Leisure Time: Is It Cool Enough?" In *Mapping Leisure across Borders*, edited by Fabio Massimo Lo Verde, Ishwar Modi, and Gianna Cappello, xvi–liii. Cambridge: Cambridge Scholars.

MacKinnon, Niall. 1993. *The British Folk Scene: Musical Performance and Social Identity*. Buckingham: Open University Press.

Magaudda, Paolo, and Marco Santoro. 2013. "Dalla popular music ai sound studies: Lo studio delle culture sonore." *Studi Culturali* 10(1): 3–12.

Martinengo, Maria C., and Marina Nuciari. 1986. *I giovani della musica*. Milan: Franco Angeli.

Mead, George H. 1934. *Mind, Self, and Society from the Standpoint of a Social Behaviorist*. Edited and with an introduction by Charles W. Morris. Chicago: University of Chicago Press.

Milgram, Stanley. 1967. "The Small-World Problem." *Psychology Today* 1(1): 61–67.

Miller, Kiri. 2012. *Playing Along: Digital Games, YouTube, and Virtual Performance*. New York: Oxford University Press.

Negus, Keith. 1999. *Music Genres and Corporate Cultures*. London: Routledge.

Niessen, Bertram M. 2014. "Do It Yourself: From the Garage to the Construction of Reality." *Experimenta* 66: 93–108.

O'Reilly, Tim. 2007. "What is Web 2.0: Design Patterns and Business Models for the Next Generation of Software." *Communications and Strategies* 65(1): 17–37. http://papers.ssrn.com/sol3/Papers.cfm?abstract_id=1008839.

Papacharissi, Zizi, ed. 2011. *A Networked Self: Identity, Community, and Culture on Social Network Sites*. New York: Routledge.

Pitts, Stephanie. 2005. *Valuing Musical Participation*. Aldershot: Ashgate.

Prior, Nick. 2010. "The Rise of the New Amateurs: Popular Music, Digital Technology and the Fate of Cultural Production." In *Handbook of Cultural Sociology*, edited by John R. Hall, Laura Grindstaff, and Ming-Cheng Lo, 398–407. Abingdon: Routledge.

Reddington, Helen. 2012. *The Lost Women of Rock Music: Female Musicians of the Punk Era*. Sheffield: Equinox.

Rojek, Chris. 2011. *Pop Music, Pop Culture*. Cambridge: Polity.

Salton, Gerard, and Michael J. McGill. 1984. *Introduction to Modern Information Retrieval*. New York: McGraw-Hill.

Santoro, Marco. 2010. *Effetto Tenco: Genealogia della canzone d'autore*. Bologna: Il Mulino.

Scott, John, and Peter J. Carrington, eds. 2011. *The SAGE Handbook of Social Network Analysis*. London: Sage.

Sennett, Richard. 2012. *Together: The Rituals, Pleasures and Politics of Cooperation*. London: Allen Lane/Penguin.

Sloboda, John A., Susan A. O'Neill, and Antonia Ivaldi. 2001. "Functions of Music in Everyday Life: An Exploratory Study Using the Experience Sampling Method." *Musicae Scientiae* 5: 9–32.

Smith, Gareth D. 2013. "Seeking 'Success' in Popular Music." *Music Education Research International* 6: 26–37.

Smith, Gareth D., and Alex Gillett. 2015. "Creativities, Innovation, and Networks in Garage Punk Rock: A Case Study of The Eruptörs." *Artivate: A Journal of Entrepreneurship in the Arts* 4(1): 9–24. http://artivate.hida.asu.edu/index.php/artivate/article/view/82/36.

Smith, Marc A., Lee Rainie, Ben Shneiderman, and Itai Himelboim. 2014. "Mapping Twitter Topic Networks: From Polarized Crowds to Community Clusters." *Pew Research Internet Project*. February 20. http://www.pewinternet.org/2014/02/20/mapping-twitter-topic-networks-from-polarized-crowds-to-community-clusters/.

Stebbins, Robert A. 1979. *Amateurs: On the Margin between Work and Leisure*. Beverly Hills, CA: Sage.

Stebbins, Robert A. 1996. *The Barbershop Singer: Inside the Social World of a Musical Hobby*. Toronto: University of Toronto Press.

Stebbins, Robert A. 2007. *Serious Leisure: A Perspective for Our Time*. New Brunswick, NJ: Transaction.

Steinbach, Michael, George Karypis, and Vipin Kumar. 2000. "A Comparison of Document Clustering Techniques." In *Proceedings of the KDD-2000 Workshop on Text Mining*, 109–111. Boston, MA. http://glaros.dtc.umn.edu/gkhome/fetch/papers/docclusterKD-DTMW00.pdf.

Teague, Adele, and Gareth Dylan Smith. 2015. "Portfolio Careers and Work-Life Balance among Musicians: An Initial Study into Implications for Higher Music Education." *British Journal of Music Education* 32(2): 177–193.

Torti, Maria T. 2000. "Giovani e 'popular music' nella ricerca sociale italiana." *Rassegna Italiana di Sociologia* 41(2): 291–302.

Toynbee, Jason. 2000. *Making Popular Music: Musicians, Creativity and Institutions*. London: Arnold.

Trobia, Alberto. 2012. "Popular Music, Leisure e società: Tre meccanismi sociali." In *Consumare/Investire il tempo libero: Forme e pratiche del leisure time nella postmodernità*, edited by Fabio Massimo Lo Verde, 308–341. Milan: Bruno Mondadori.

Valente, Thomas W. 2010. *Social Networks and Health: Models, Methods, and Applications*. New York: Oxford University Press.

Wasserman, Stanley, and Katherine Faust. 1994. *Social Network Analysis: Methods and Applications*. Cambridge: Cambridge University Press.

Wise, Sue. 1990. "Sexing Elvis." In *On Record: Rock, Pop, and the Written Word*, edited by Simon Frith and Andrew Goodwin, 390–398. London: Routledge.

Zhao, Shanyang, Sherri Grasmuck, and Jason Martin. 2008. "Identity Construction on Facebook: Digital Empowerment in Anchored Relationships." *Computers in Human Behavior* 24(5): 1816–1836.

PART IV

ON THE DIVERSITY
OF MUSIC MAKING
AND LEISURE

CHAPTER 27

ENTERING INTO AN INDIGENOUS CYPHER

Indigenous Music-Dance Making Sings to Western Leisure

KAREN FOX

On my way home, waitin' for a bus at Churchill Square
Four Native men, women rappin' in air
Stories of pain, stories of the day
Encircled by baggy pants, ball caps sideways
Invitation to rap in a public space
Without rhythm or rhyming in my bones
Short phrases only—stepped into the unknown
"Bussing to my pad, avoiding work cads
Day's been long, tell me 'bout the shit"
Surprised—they rapped clear
Rush hour, busses, people disappeared
Until police accused us "disturbing the peace"
Who me?
An elderly woman being harassed
Transformed into havin' "street cred"!

THE emergence of a small cypher (i.e., two or more rappers informally freestyling) in a public place created music, a bit of b-dance, storytelling, political action, and embodied transgressive relationships (Fox and Riches 2014). The hip-hop cypher remixes cipher, spelled with an *i*, and its connections with the number zero, cryptography, and a person of no importance who fills space as improvising something from "nothing" or what is present, feeding off energy and the generosity of the group. The Native hip-hop cypher stretches back to Indigenous[1] creation stories, and resonates with Cree round dances and sacred hoops of the Plains Indians. Within fugitive moments, the urban Aboriginal hip-hop artists inserted their stories, bodies, and cultural practices into non-Native "productive" space-times. They folded me into their space-times, challenged where music-dance making[2] might root, and constituted a cypher, both secular and sacred, of young and old, Indigenous and non-Indigenous, personal and public. The response to this playfulness (or leisure?) was returned with surveillance and regulation.

Music-dance making triggers responses across mind-body-soul, inter-being, and spatio-temporal modalities. In this chapter, I articulate how non-Indigenous leisure practitioners and scholars, as responsive selves,[3] might listen to, and be with, Indigenous forms of music-dance making, from drumming to hip-hop, in ways that are transformative and generative for leisure.

Music, Hearing, Listening, Appreciating, and Understanding

Blacking (1974) posited that musicality is a vital part of human inheritance. I, and Indigenous peoples generally, suggest that musicality extends to other living entities and forces as well.[4] Trevarthan (2011) described the earliest interactions of infants and mothers as a call-and-response mimicry filled with rhythmic repetitions, dance-like body movements, and synchronized sounds. Powers and Trevarthen (2009) saw infants entering life as inherently poetic and musical beings "moving and hearing with pulse and rhythm, immediately sensitive to the harmonies and discords of human expression" (209). Erickson described the importance of musicality: "Our capacity to think with and feel with one another seems to be tied to our capacity to dance and sing in smooth, predictable rhythm with each other in our talk" (2009, 461).

I use the term *music* broadly, starting with Blacking's (1973) characterization of music as "humanly organized sound" and "sounds produced by other species that we can hear as organized sounds" (10). I include other-than-human sounds and Higgins's (2012) extension to include waterfalls, animals, trees, and forests. Since Indigenous life worlds are intimately connected to the urban, I build on Cage's musical experiments (Best and Kellner 1991)[5] inclusive of everyday city sounds and rhythms. Agreeing with Higgins (2012), I present music as phenomenal, existing not objectively, but for selves. Music moves entities (both at the macro and microscopic levels); entities vibrate with sound waves, pulsing toward and then through entities. For humans and many more: "When you are listening to music, the music is not just playing in you, it is rather, playing you, your body becoming a musical instrument, a resonating chamber" (Lipari 2014, 31).

To experience music, creating and receiving requires an intimate connection between making sounds and receiving them. It is not coincidental that one of the earliest musical instruments, the drum, is understood by Indigenous people as related to the heartbeat of Mother Earth that connects to all beings with heartbeats. Scottish percussionist Evelyn Glennie—who happens to be profoundly deaf—explained to musicians and listeners alike: we are *participants of sound* because we actually *touch* the sound (Glennie 1995,

2003; Riedelsheimer 2012). For people like Glennie—who, with her percussion teacher, learned to perceive the world despite the loss of one sense—touching sound suggests that listening is more than an auditory process. Listening is a multimodal process that involves (or can involve) all the senses, in a process called *polymodality*, and depends on paying attention.

The auditory system is conjoined with the vestibular system. Thus, hearing implicates a sense of balance crucial to being able to move through the world (Higgins 2012). Becker (2004, 27) claims:

> Bodies and brains synchronize gestures, muscle actions, breathing, and brain waves when enveloped in music. . . . This means that from the beginning of our lives, our physiology inclines us to mutual experience through sound. . . . The physiology of hearing discloses our connections to the larger environment, our sharing that world with other agents, and our capacity for attuning the dynamics of our behaviour with them.

In addition, recent neuroscientific research posits that auditory perception is based upon learned cultural patterns. People from one cultural system may hear other cultural-musical systems as out of tune or distort what is played so it conforms to known schema (Higgins 2012). Y. R. Chao, a musician and linguist, provided an example:

> [Chao] heard a piece of music and interpreted it as here in major and there in minor and its notes as being do, re, me, etc., only being slightly "off," but subsequently learned to his surprise that it was a scale of seven equal steps in the octave. The illusion persisted even after he was told. He had forced his own intervals into the new scale. (cited in Higgins 2012, 41)

Although music-dance making is universal and provides a physical interconnection, understanding the meanings of different practices requires more than just hearing. The diversity of music is more complicated even at the basic physiological level and requires skills of listening, apprehending, and understanding. Cultural values shape perceptual evaluations of music. Dominant and prevailing Western music-dance forms reflect specific structures, compositions, techniques, style, scales, and, in the case of voice, harmonics to highlight a singer above accompanying instruments. In addition, the trained expert performer is valued over the amateur or untrained participant.

Dominant Indigenous[6] music-dance making embedded in a relational life world is designed to nourish and sustain community relationships with its inhabitants and the place extending into the universe, as well as forces that protect or impinge upon all within. Therefore, a strong competence in music-dance making was and is a part of the community fabric, with particular individuals fulfilling roles (i.e., musicians, chanters, medicines elders or healers,[7] and dancers), when necessary, surrounded by a chorus of community dancers and singers. Performed in the outdoors, vocal music concentrates at lower energy levels, normal speaking pitches, with "densely overlapping textures, wide tunings, consistently loud volume and buzzy timbres" (Turino 2008, 188) to be inclusive of all voices. For dance, the music is repetitive, emphatically rhythmic, and regular.

Hearing and listening are often used interchangeably in colloquial English. Etymologically, hearing comes from the perception of sound by the ear—a physical and physiological process. Listening, however, is about receiving or accepting sounds, music, or language. That is, *to listen* in English is passive or intransitive. Transitive words, as in French, transfer some form of energy or action from the subject to the object; there is no transitive form of *listen* in English. *Listen* as a transitive verb conveys a sense of listening as *constitutive of* and *prior to* speaking. Listening becomes an invocation, a calling forth of speech, music, or dance. Radically, without a listener, the speaking or music-dance making simply may not occur. Conceptualizing listening as transitive supports Corradi Fiumara's (1990) concept of *maieutic listening*, where the listener is essential to the creation of knowledge. Maieutic listening *listens others* [and I would add *ourselves*] *to music and dance*.

Early settlers in North America acclimated to their own cultural practices and a passive form of listening placed the music of First Nations and American Indians within their own musical schemata. Like Chao cited earlier, they heard, according to their culturally constructed schemata, not music but high-pitched, harsh, and savage sounds (Peacock 1955; Troutman 2009). Since most settlers could not listen in the maieutic sense, they could not receive the full comportment of Indigenous music-dance making.

Corradi Fiumara (1990) argues that "maieutic listening involves the renunciation of predominately moulding and ordering activity; a giving up sustained by expectation of a new and different quality of relationship" (as cited in Higgins 2012, 8). As Chao discovered, this process is not straightforward, even for someone knowledgeable and seeking such experiences. On that day in Churchill Square, I became an elderly non-Aboriginal rapper (music-dance maker) disturbing the peace (attuned to a different social and political context) as part of a crew (alternative social and political relationship). Lefebvre (1991) considered such space-time moments rare and ephemeral, as daily patterns and dominant ideas of normality are enforced. Like maieutic listening, they become fleeting glimpses of "what might be or become."

Maieutic listening also leads us to gambol with what we understand as self and subjectivity.[8] Self, as understood in dominant Western scholarship, is a modernist concept as a human being freely constructed, stable, independent of the senses, autonomous, or a narrative center. Subjectivity in postmodern and poststructuralist scholarship is about the making of the subject and signifies how individuals situate and are situated in relation to power or "subjected" to or by forces of economics, societal convention, circumstances of history, and the physical world in general (Lalonde and Chandler 2004; Weedon 2004; Yvinec 2014). Guattari and Rolnik (2008) saw subjectivity produced at the "intersection of determinations of various kinds, not only social but economic, technologic, the media and so on" (48) rather than through language as the structuralists asserted. Guattari's sense of production focused on process and consequences of a biological body. Guattari's sense of subjectivity lends itself to MacDonald and Hamilton's (2014) aesthetic systems theory (AST), inclusion of more-than-human entities, and a focus on music-dance life worlds. Dominant North American leisure scholarship pre-dominantly relies on and naturalizes the individual, autonomous, coherent, stable self, with scholarship from the United Kingdom and Australia highlighting subjectivity.

However, none of these positions accounts for a self that is located within the life world of the earth or the cosmos—a self that communicates with and in communion with the natural world, a self that may be kin to plants and animals, a self within an enchanted, animate world, or a post-human self, a self with responsibilities toward these others (Descola 2013, 2014). Kohn (2013), building on Deacon (2012) and working with the Runa,[9] suggests that self is the:

> outcome of a process, unique to life, of maintaining and perpetuating an individual form, a form that, as it is iterated over the generations, grows to fit the world around it at the same time that it comes to exhibit a certain closure that allows it to maintain its self same identity, which is forged with respect to that which it is not. (Kohn 2013, 76)

Self and agency emerging from the matrices of life could be a person, anteater, or forest, and inter-subjectivities would be formed differently across space-time, such as Kanaka ʻŌiwi's relationship to *kalo* (i.e., taro) as younger siblings.

Other concepts of self and subjectivity that are fluid, impermanent, and insubstan-tial seem more relevant to an emergent and aesthetic world. Although these constructs begin as theories about humans, they leave openings for inclusion of more-than-humans. Manning (2013) sketched "self" as emergent form or moment instead of an object. Self is understood as an aspect of topology where subject and object lose their independence and space is a medium rather than a container. Living beings may not be separate beings, but "temporary configurations, aggregates of causes and effects, within an ever-changing flux" (Higgins 2012, 149) that provide the illusion of stability and coherence as subjectivity emerges in and out of relationships. Depending on how attention is focused on which of the zillions of sensations are affecting any entity at any moment, music and dance become vibrations, blending, changing, and creating new vibrations, interconnections, subjectivities, and possible inter-subjectivities.

In many creative, expressive endeavors, a fluid, less bounded and coherent subjectiv-ity enables collective and participatory realities and connections with a range of entities and consciousnesses. Indigenous peoples' music-dance making is an embodied physi-cality where and when purposeful and rhythmic physical movements are intimately placed within the cosmos. Lakota powwow singer, Severt Young Bear (1994), described his view: "Song and dance can't really be separated. Even though I'll talk about one or the other, they're always connected" (38). Chivarria (2015), of the Santa Clara Pueblo, clearly linked the music-dance with all creation:

> When one is dancing all the sound vibrates within you. Your body becomes one instrument among the others, a part of the whole. Through this do we become joined to creation, to those who have gone before and to those who are yet to be.... The chorus of voices blends with all these elements [including drums and rattles] to make a song to Heaven.

Singing the World into Existence

Indigenous creation and origin stories structured life worlds, encompassed myriad ecological, spiritual, communal, relational, historical, political, and ethical functions, and knitted together all living entities through everyday life, seasonal changes, and generational transitions. Through rhythms, physical movements, drumbeats, chants, and song, Indigenous people intersect and attune themselves with the world around them and ensure the continuation of life; the creation stories reverberate through space and time. Higgins (2012) suggests "that many of the world's peoples have strongly associated the continuity of music and a sense of the world continuing well" (65). Some Indigenous peoples of Australia speak of totemic beings who wandered through the continent in Dreamtime. The totemic beings sang the name of every entity that crossed their paths (i.e., animals, plants, rocks, water) and the world vibrated into existence. Songlines link sacred spirits that returned to the land and to beings on the land, and define intangible relationships between Indigenous lives, music, beliefs, practices, and the land.

An ocean away, the emergence of Diné people in the southwest United States came from music. Tapahonso (2015) in lyrical prose related the events:

> The beginning was mist.
> The first Holy Ones talked and sang as always
> They created light, night, and day
> They sang into place the mountains, the rivers, plants and animals.
> They sang us into life.

These myths, in Doniger's (1998) characterization, are about what is *believed* and is a "story that is sacred to and shared by a group of people who find their most important meanings in it" (2). The myth is about the past heard as meaning and relevance for the present—enfolding a space-time of the past always already in the present and future. Importantly, these myths are conveyed through music and its associated embodied form, dance, that ontologically places bodies in the universe and specific locations, as well as connects them to and across spatio-temporal dimensions. Unlike diachronic time (i.e., measured, linear time, whether straight or cyclical, which presumes atomism, and rationality), synchronous time "illustrates how every *now* is interleaved with every past and possibly future now . . . is dense, filled with memory . . . a concurrence of events" (Lipari 2014, 153). As Tapahonso (2015) states: "We must remember the worlds our ancestors traveled. Always wear the songs they gave us. Remember we are made of prayers." Music and dance (i.e., drums, rattles, flutes, prayers, chants, songs, and physical rhythmic movement) are modalities to be enmeshed in the world on its own terms. So, the shark-calling practices of Papua New Guinea or the sharks that appear when Kanaka Maoli rhythmically beat kapa (bark cloth) along a shore demonstrate an attention to and connection with the living entities that surround them, practices of previous generations, and ethics of how to interact with each other through rhythmic sounds.

Since concepts of space and time are inevitably and intimately intertwined in life worlds, Indigenous concepts of space and time sit uneasy alongside the Euclidean-Cartesian framework of Western ontologies and epistemologies. Using Cartesian coordinates and Euclidean geometry, location can be defined in terms of positions along intersecting axes, is topographical, and can be mapped, graphed, and measured. A map is placed upon or over a territory in order to explore, own, or exploit it. But there are other ways that space-time work. For example, wayfinders of Oceania (specifically Taumako) systematically observe and calibrate the relationship between the wind positions and the sunrise-sunset positions of the solstices. Within this system, the wayfinder's "mental tool" follows wind positions, behavior of animals and plants, and pairs asterisms (one above and the other below the horizon line), and patterns of swells. In addition, these phenomena are not separate from the wayfinder, who may with proper life awareness and skills influence the conditions grounded in a different understanding of space-time (George 2012). These navigators sailed, and continue to sail, long distances with great accuracy (Finney et al. 1994; George 2012). These space-time systems created different physical relationships with the "inside" of an individual wayfinder, spilling out and connecting with the "outside" world of air and water currents. Space-time is more like a constitutive lacuna holding the traces of the past while nourishing future occurrences and arenas for relationships and potentialities across space-time not conceived of in Euclidean-Cartesian space-time. Cultural topology, with its focus on relationality in space-time, is a Western tool for reimagining space-time as relational, constructed, transitive, and interactive that may bridge the differences between conceptualizations (Shields 2013).

Indigenous singing, chanting, drumming, and dancing are ontological and epistemological worldviews emphasizing space-time milieus, inter-subjectivities and relations within the posthuman or more-than-human life worlds (Braidotti 2012; Descola 2013, 2014; Kohn 2013). Even as there are some broad categories, the specifics emerge out of particular locations and genealogies for the Kanaka Maoli, Indigenous peoples of Australia, or Diné of the southwest United States of America. As music-dance entrains a complex of activities (e.g., oratory, dancing, distribution of resources, feasting, among other purposes), each manifestation will be intimately harmonized with the surrounding land, living entities, previous generations, and the universe. Second, Indigenous inter-subjectivities are located within matrices of human and other-than-human entities, natural forces, communal responsibilities to "all relations" and forces that make up their cosmologies. Music-dance making was and is a means to tune the matrices of sentience, energy, knowledge, inter-subjectivities, and wisdom for healing, order, celebration, and sustaining life.

The cypher at Churchill Square folded earlier creation stories of the earth's heartbeat into rush-hour traffic while reenvisioning a creation story for that moment. It sang the past into the present and embodied an alternative world and potentiality through music-dance making in a city where young Aboriginal people are made invisible. As I accepted the invitation, I too was enwrapped within an ontology that was both foreign and familiar to my heartbeat. Instead of discussing or debating the place of urban

Indigenous hip-hop artists, we enacted, embodied, and called into being the reality through b-box, rap, music, and b-dance. In that moment, we performed alternative selves, tuned ourselves and the world to a different rhythm, and tentatively opened a new potentiality, however small.

Traveling across Spatio-Temporal Registers

Historically, Indigenous peoples nourished and maintained their ways of knowing and being through rational and critical discourses *and* embodied and expressive practices. They contributed to the emerging government and legal structures in North America (Miller 1993). However, Aristotle's valuing of rationality above all else resounded in Western cultures through the centuries as Descartes's mind-body dualism combined with evaluative differences based on gender and race (Warren 2000). Higgins (2012) wonders: if Descartes had privileged humans as musical, would the mind-body dualism have emerged in exploration, economics, religion, or government?

Warner (2002) and Dueck (2007) suggest that Indigenous peoples valued, and value, embodied and expressive equal to, or more so than, rational and critical discourses. Indigenous cosmologies imagined, and imagine, life resonating with each other through rhythm, sound, movement, and music. Music-dance often houses their histories, knowledge, governance, and philosophical frameworks and sustains their spatio-temporal practices alongside, against, and within dominant Western cultural, economic, political, and militaristic forces. The aesthetic systems of Indigenous music-dance are, in MacDonald and Hamilton's (2014) terms, located in a life world of more-than-human selves. Higgins (2012) posits music connects a self to feeling emplaced in a larger world, a social membership, and oneself. Dueck argues that Indigenous public culture emerges when Indigenous peoples "move, feel, dance, make music, and imagine others doing so" (56).

These music-dance forms of corporeal activity and personal expression are essential and powerful in imagining forms of sociability that were open to settlers as they moved across North America and toward the Pacific. Of course, settlers did not equally value many forms, perspectives, or consciousnesses. They were misrecognized, misinterpreted, and overlooked even as they sustained American Indians, First Nations, Métis, Inuit, Alaskan Natives, and Kanaka Maoli. Although these music-dance forms were, and are, overlooked in Western scholarship, they haunt the history of Indigenous peoples' relationships with Euro–North American peoples and leisure practice and scholarship.

Cultural topology highlights the relationality of multiple elements. As the life worlds of Indigenous peoples and settlers came in contact, settlers were intent on changing Indigenous relationships. The complex and enmeshed cosmologies that framed daily lives were reduced to "primitive" and "early forms of civilized people." Explorers, colonialists, and settlers abstracted elements of Indigenous cultural practices (e.g., chanting, drumming, or dance) as degenerate or savage versions of their sophisticated leisure forms. With little mastery of specific Indigenous languages, they also framed the meanings and purposes of these practices within their ideological and militaristic perspectives (Silva 2004; Troutman 2009).

Furthermore, Indigenous music-dance making, like all creative and expressive practices, was, and is, a spatio-temporal stage open to adaptation, although it struggled with colonial and ontological controls. Imagine Euclidean-Cartesian space-time folding into Indigenous space-time with Indigenous relationships being distantiated, collapsed, and distorted by settlers. Both then and now, Indigenous peoples, through various strategies, including music-dance, create and envision anew, remix from past and present elements, wisely taking from what is being presented from other cultures to craft a path toward sovereignty. Therefore, like Troutman (2009), I avoid the adjective "traditional" for tribally derived musical practices, because the term is fraught with problems. It signals stasis rather than change, and reversion rather than innovation. I also avoid distinguishing between sacred and social, because holistic, synchronous spatio-temporal practices blur boundaries and incorporate many layers of meanings. Furthermore, such categories reinforce colonial and settler frameworks that disenfranchise Indigenous peoples' knowledge and wisdom.

MUSIC-DANCE, BELONGING TO THE UNIVERSE, AND NAVIGATING COLONIAL STRUCTURES

Indigenous music-dance is an existential practice that locates living entities, within the vibrating universe and entrains them in physiological patterns from muscle actions, breathing, heartbeat, and brain waves. The settler nations martialed power to dispossess Indigenous peoples of their culture, language, and lands. Indigenous peoples responded with multiple strategies from legal and military strategic moves to music-dance making in order to protect their lands and enforce treaties, nourish and sustain themselves, resist intrusion, and create new futures. Vizenor's (1999) use of *survivance* reverberates with all of these actions, including the role of music-dance making. Survivance is the active sense of presence, the continuance of native stories, not a mere reaction, and the renunciation of dominance, tragedy, and victimry. Although scholarship exists about Indigenous military and legal strategies after occupation or appropriation of lands, less attention has been focused on Indigenous music-dance making. There are myriad reasons for this oversight, including Indigenous peoples' need to hide their practices, given the persecution of or direct attempts to annihilate their cultures.

However, Indigenous music-dance making (as *poiesis* in the Ancient Greek sense and Warner's [2002] poetic world making) continued to sing into existence inter-subjectivities, resistance, creativity, and imaginaries, folded and distorted space-times as governments attempted, and attempt, to control meaning even as it may be impossible to achieve. Survivance through music-dance making created and creates excess, stretching boundaries and deforming leisure and Euclidean-Cartesian spatio-temporal practices of governmental control into Indigenous topologies paralleling Möbius strips (a surface with only one side and only one boundary), Klein Bottle (a bottle where its inside is its outside), or the sculptures of Diné artist Christine McHorse (especially the series entitled *Dark Light: The Micaceous Ceramics*).

Using non-Indigenous and Indigenous sources, I present several historical Indigenous music-dance legacies relevant to existing Indigenous music-dance making. There is substantial need for scholarship about Indigenous music-dance making, especially related to Western leisure, and the power of ritual as it continues to nourish and sustain Indigenous inter-subjectivities and communities while creating futures and resisting hostile colonial and settler forces. The tensions between Indigenous peoples in North America and Hawai'i and the governments of Canada and the United States were exemplified with the outlawing of cultural practices, such as specific ceremonies (e.g., the Sun Dance, hula, or potlaches), the imposition of non-Indigenous music instruction in residential schools, and the conversion to Christianity and its form of music (Bracken 1997; Kamae 1995; Troutman 2009). As early as the 1700s, missionaries to Hawai'i introduced choirs and religious hymns specifically to attract Kanaka Maoli (Kamae 1995), while outlawing hula and oli (chanting). Dewar's (1986, 27–32) analysis of the government policies and results of residential school practices could be summed up in the phrase "to pray and play white."

Across North America, the ceremonies and protocols of Indigenous peoples nourished relations, sustained governance and gift economies, and maintained life worlds. These ceremonies included a range of practices from sharing food and resources, music-dance making, games of chance and skill, and socializing. Many of these practices were foreign and judged "evil," "bad," or "primitive" by settlers who were unfamiliar with Indigenous cultures and languages or bounded by a Euro-North American Christian framework. Even when studied by ethnologists, these practices were often misrecognized through the lens of Western frameworks. So, the Sun Dance and Grass Dance of the Great Plains Indians were identified as war dances by the American government in the early 1800s and outlawed. Although the origins of the dances were, and are, disputed and much knowledge is still protected, the dances were, and are, vital for the continuity of communities and the peoples' relationship to the land and all beings of their life world. Great Plains Indians resituated their communal music-dance making from seasonal and relational matrices to American holidays such as the Fourth of July. The Office of Indian Affairs (OIA) (now the Bureau of Indian Affairs) was then willing to give permission, since they were "celebrating" the establishment of the "American Empire" (Troutman 2009; Van Alstyne 1974). For the Great Plains Indians, recognition of skilled dancing was redirected and connected to the demands of modern life, whether good health, righteous conduct, generosity, communal sharing, or strength (Troutman 2009). As American Indian tribes came together to stabilize and strengthen their cultural practices and tribal practices during the early twentieth century, individual forms of music-dance making merged and spread to preserve Indigenous unity through the pan-Indian movement (Browner 2004).

Midway across the Pacific Ocean, King Kalākaua orchestrated Poni Mōʻī (a coronation ceremony) in 1883 and the Jubilee three years afterwards as another example of survivance through stretching, deforming, and transforming political, economic, spiritual, and social spatio-temporalities. Kalākaua reestablished hula in public as a means to resist American desires, nourish Kanaka Maoli culture, and awaken national pride. The festivities included the first public hula performances in decades, a parade of canoes demonstrating moʻolelo kahiko (ancient history, story, myth, tradition, literature), and mele (song, chant, poem). The kumu hula (hula masters) and musicians created a new genre, hula kuʻi. In hula kuʻi, they sought to combine elements of Indigenous Hawaiian music-dance with those of Western music and dance (Silva 2004). Stillman (1989, 20) observed: "hula kuʻi was used as a vehicle for reinforcing pride in Hawaiʻi and being Hawaiian and also for validating Kalākauaʻs right to rule." For Kanaka Maoli, the performances and parade were a celebration of their moʻolelo (story, myth, tradition, history chronicle) and kinship attuned to the universe. Music-dance was, and is, an active force that contributes to and sustains the well-being of Kanaka Maoli and the ʻāina. ʻĀina translates into English as "land," but its nuances and overtones are rich and complex. ʻAi refers to eating and ʻāina more fully refers to "that which feeds" and encompasses the entire cosmos, including the land, sea, sky, and spiritual dimensions which were celebrated in place names, moʻolelo, mele, and other orature (Nāone 2008). Music-dance making are primordial vibrations that connect Kanaka Maoli to these entities and forces and directly nourish the ʻāina that feeds them. In these early decades, ceremonies were being topologically repositioned to: (1) maintain Indigenous space-time relations and attunement of life worlds, and (2) astutely respond and manipulate settler political and cultural systems.

Beginning in the early twentieth century, American Indians stretched their music-dance talents to accommodate and bend other non-Indigenous forms of music, such as jazz, blues, and country-western music, to vocalize living with the effects of oppression, neglect, and suppression of their culture. Even then, non-Indigenous people underestimated the ability of North American Native peoples' awareness of and engagement in current modern practices. In 1904, W. M. Thompson, an American entrepreneur, thought he was introducing the phonograph to a group of Aleut traders. To his surprise, they were not stunned nor induced to bargain differently. They not only recognized the tune of "In the Shade of the Old Apple Tree," but joined in on the chorus (Troutman 2009).

There were hundreds of American Indians who performed music and dance "derived originally from Euro-American and African American traditions from 1900 to 1940s for their local communities or on performance hall circuits that crisscrossed North America and Europe" (Troutman 2009, 201). Kanaka Maoli would adopt and make the ukulele "their own" emerging Hawaiian music as well maintaining traditional forms of music-dance making. Most of these Native artists have been relegated to the margins, with only a few receiving Western scholarly attention. These musicians adapted their musical talents and training from residential and missionary schools, despite arduous odds, to meet both non-Native performance standards and showcase Native music talents and elements such as rhythm, storytelling, and affective directions. Musicians such as Quapaw Fred Cardin, Blackfeet jazz musician Joe Morris, Creek-Cherokee vocalist Tsianinia Redfeather Blackstone, the originator of the steel guitar Joseph Kekuku, slack-key master Raymond Kaleoalohapoina'oleohelemanu Kāne, and entertainer and ukulele musician Alice Namakelua found spaces as individual artists through the twentieth century (Fox 2008; Ruymar 1996; Troutman 2009).

Jazz, the blues, and country-western music were genres that created space for American Indian musicians to articulate and embody their stories and future visions while singing back to settler-nations attempting to control music and dance (i.e., leisure space-time) in service of conquest, assimilation, and occupation of American Indian lands. Davis (1998) notes that the blues were first recorded by African American women and "sustained a feminist consciousness [in] the way they often construct seemingly antagonistic relationships as noncontradictory oppositions" (xv). Similarly, Indigenous women musicians have been overlooked. With current issues about missing Indigenous women and domestic violence (TRC 2015) in Canada, this unexamined early musical heritage connection with Indigenous women vocalists seems prescient. Because non-Indigenous audiences were unwilling to recognize Indigenous performances of popular music and their relevance to current life, American Indians used the training in the "arts of Indianness" learned at residential school to appeal to the imaginations of non-Indigenous audiences (Shorter 2009; Troutman 2009), even as they composed their own stories.

INDIGENOUS SPACE-TIME: THEN AND NOW

Most Indigenous rituals are concerned with physical and cosmological space, time, and relations. Cultural topology (Shields 2013)[10] may help us find a toehold in the power of these dynamics different from the Euclidean-Cartesian so common in dominant Western frameworks. Dominant Western frameworks presume a past that is over and in a distant time, individuals who are separate and autonomous and no longer present after death, and a material existence. Indigenous life worlds are constructed, experienced, and embodied differently. From a Euclidean-Cartesian point of view, the declining population, changes in "traditional" Indigenous practices, and the results of settler policies were clearly resulting in the extinction of Indigenous peoples and cultures early in the twentieth century. These conclusions fit with a linear, progression of space, time, and culture.

As mentioned earlier, Indigenous space-times adhere to different dynamics. Music-dance making played, and plays, different registers of energy, power, and forces that folded space-times upon themselves and navigated space-times as fluid and changing.

Like the art of Kanaka Maoli, Herb Kane, the spirits and wisdom of elders were, and are, always present and could be present through various embodied practices including music-dance. The Grass Dance, Sun Dance, and hula were and are calling into presence specific life forms or forces relevant to the rituals or ceremonies. After fifty years of absence, King Kalakaua, at his coronation in 1874, brought hula into the public arena to establish his claim on leadership, nourish his people and the 'aina, and breathe life into present and future imaginaries resonating with oli, moʻokūʻauhau (genealogy), and moʻolelo. Even as settlers misrecognized the events, Kanaka Maoli walked along the Möbius Strip using "arts of Indianness" to establish a presence and to survive in a world not of their making, even hostile to their well-being. Yet, the inside of the Möbius Strip that nurtured music-dance making and Kanaka Maoli life worlds, resounded through time: Kalākaua resituation of hula is now felt in the revitalization of the Hawaiian language, the voyage of the Hōkūleʻa to malama honua (i.e., care for the planet) and the "save Mauna Kea" movement.[11] On the North American continent, the Grass Dance and Sun Dance, among many, are openly performed today, Aboriginal hip-hop remixes ancestral stories, dance moves and current events, and ceremonies are often the basis for community decision-making, Idle No More, and other political strategies. Music-dance making remains the critical element for ontological security, which is not stable but requires tuning to the changing world and creating anew. From Indigenous worldviews, music-dance making nourishes through bringing past-present-future into people's lives with love (Snyder 2015).

Constructing "Indianness" for white audiences, remixing, and moving between space-times is not without costs (i.e., physical, psychological, spiritual, economic) for individual Indigenous musicians and dancers, who must inhabit space-times "betwixt and between" cultures, worldviews, and space-times within cultures. Whether they are musicians in the early twentieth or twenty-first century, Indigenous artists struggle to be recognized for their artistic creations, to be heard beyond "traditional" cultural scripts, and to embody possibilities through inventive compositions. King Kalakaua, who reigned from 1874 to 1891, may have been "the most reviled and ridiculed of the monarchs" (Silva 2004, 89), but the two celebrations displayed astute knowledge of Western and Kanaka Maoli traditions. Early Indigenous hip-hop artists struggled because they were "not traditional enough" or were "appropriating" Black hip-hop. Still, Indigenous artists continue in public spaces, underground and hidden from surveillance, or privately from one generation to the next, nourishing and sustaining a dynamic inter-being relationship with the universe. Indigenous peoples, understanding the power of music-dance for their well-being and survivance, consistently construct ways to protect, sustain, appropriate, and remix music-dance making relevant to their needs and desires. Indigenous music-dance (1) sustained an embedded relationship in the cosmos, (2) prioritized music making, (3) played between the differences in how music is constructed and valued, and (4) communicated in the open, but "hidden" from surveillance and violence by colonial settlers (Troutman 2009). Indigenous music-dance, as well as Indigenous adaptations and appropriations of Western music and dance, could and can be blatant and effective challenges to oppressive, colonial, and imperial forces.

Music-dance are part of Indigenous peoples' everyday life—individuals singing because of joy or feeling bad, asking permission to enter or begin, calling on the weather, nourishing and sustaining the earth, or surviving hardship and pain because a song emerged (Young Bear and Theisz 1996).

MUSIC-DANCE AND LEISURE(?) MAINTAINS WELL-BEING OF INDIGENOUS PEOPLE AND ʻAINA

Manu Meyer (2004), a Kanaka ʻŌiwi artist and scholar, remembers Kanaka Maoli lives and wisdom as living artistically in their speech, countenance, health, spirit, and everyday practices (i.e., art, physical activity, kapa-making, farming, fishing, planting, and eating). They lived with the intelligence of aloha—a sacred idea of compassion encompassing the importance of relationships, words as a life force, knowledge as multisensory and multidimensional, and life as a rich experience of continuity, change, and connection. Music-dance is an aesthetic system of waves, vibrations, intelligence, and movements that transmit beauty and resounds through, around, and in spatio-temporalities.

Contrary to early arguments about manawa nanea (Bean et al. 2002; Dahl et al. 2002; Fox 2001), leʻaleʻa may be the Hawaiian word—before American missionary orthography and dictionaries—most likely to correspond to the Euro–North American concept of "leisure." Leʻaleʻa reflects an "enjoyment of life" crucial to mental and emotional health as well as an overall and inter-subjective sense of well-being for Kanaka Maoli and ʻaina. Whether game- or sport-like activities such as konane (board game) and heʻe nalu (surfing), hula, oli, or mele, these cultural practices can be understood, and possibly apprehended, only by engaging with the larger contexts—cosmology, ontology and epistemology—that connect Kanaka ʻŌiwi with cultural practices, sustainability, and mālama ʻaina (hoʻomanawanui 2014).

However, music-dance making as a vital, significant, and valued component of leisure is not at all clear. The focus on productive, organized, diachronic time, and self-actualizing leisure forms obscures expressive synchronous time, aesthetic multimodal interactions, fluid and dynamic concepts of self, and dwelling in unpredictable and unknowable spatio-temporalities. Given postcolonial and decolonizing scholarship, the aptness of the leisure concept with Indigenous peoples is fraught with difficulty and colonial histories. In 2005, a leisure conference was held in Nanaimo, British Columbia. As part of the closing ceremonies, a group of children of the Indigenous peoples of the Pacific Northwest of Canada performed a dance replete with regalia and masks.

> In a longhouse situated in a local park, I sat near the door as the young performers came in with their black and red capes, carved masks of ravens, eagles, and fish. The children's countenance was serious and focused as they created and entered

into sacred space-time—inviting us to explore their histories, culture, presence, imaginaries and interbeing. Afterwards, as they walked out and quickly removed their masks and capes, heavy metal and sport t-shirts, purple hair, and mohawks appeared. I was amused, delighted, and reminded that Indigenous children inhabit multiple spaces and times, and this generation must dance to rhythms and melodies often unseen by others. (Fox 2005, research notes)

A senior leisure scholar would later remark that young Indigenous peoples do not need to learn to dance or drum but should learn math, computer technology, and economics. Seemingly, Indigenous music, dance, spirit, and beauty are still not highly valued in leisure or the modern world. The colonial capitalistic forces reverberated in Edmonton when a school temporarily suspended operating a recording studio painstakingly created by urban Aboriginal students. The reason? Music-dance would not lead to employment. Such rationales overlook the ontological needs for belonging, sustaining the earth and all life forms, as well as the entrepreneurial successes of urban Aboriginal hip-hop artists and their willingness to live in the artistic margins to sustain Indigenous music-dance making and practices. The challenge is to listen to (i.e., maieutic listening), if not nourish, music-dance making that invites beings to dwell within unpredictable, unknowable, and potential spatio-temporalities. Indigenous peoples have been and are living between, among, and within multiple times and spaces, folding, stretching, and deforming them to create paths, rhythms, and songs to nourish and create beauty in their lives. These movements span ancient practices made current, modern Indigenous daily practices, globalized and commodified forces, and ongoing relational connections with the cosmos.

On a clear, cool night with a bright moon, I was a "backstage hand" in the hula-drama of Kanu o ka 'Aina Charter School during the Ho'oku'ikahi Establishment Day Hawaiian Cultural Festival at the Pu'ukoholā National Historic Site for the uniting of the Hawaiian Kingdom by Kamehameha. Rhythmic swaying to the ipu, measured singsong chants, and the fluttering of the breezes embraced me. At the end of the hula-drama parents, kupuna (grandparents), kumus (teachers) and I joined the students in singing Aloha Pono'i[12]. "Chicken skin" erupted within and over us all as some deep presence engulfed us. The honoured guests from across the islands and Oceania joined us. Aloha Pono'i filled space and time. The Hawaiian national anthem was being sung at the birthplace of the Hawaiian kingdom. Knowledge, presence, aloha, and relationships were shared underneath the blessings of the sky and stars, connected to food and energy of the earth. Even as an outsider, the electric sense of mana (supernatural or divine power, power, variety of taro used in medicine) as well as a deep calm of belonging swept my very being. (Fox 2004, research notes)

Like the cypher in Churchill Square, this event also reimagined the world, reaching back and forth across time and space through music-dance. A chief loudly chanted a call after Aloha Pono'i; without hesitation, one of the male youths responded. Although I could barely apprehend the many-layered meanings of Ho'opāpā,[13] a young Kanaka Maoli stepped forth into an ancient but modern game that tested knowledge and skill that, for me, resonated with the cypher. The chief called again and soon female youths were responding—their voices and energy intermixing. I could feel a shift and hear a murmur within the mostly Indigenous crowd from Oceania. Moʻolelo, life, and mana were being shared, strengthened, and passed among the generations.

It is these multimodalities of music-dance enmeshed in a net of relations, forces, experiences, and vibrations that exceed the Euro–North American concepts of music, dance, and leisure. As scholarship begins to take seriously the knowledge, histories, and genealogies of Indigenous peoples, a different concept of the dynamic relationship about and between dichotomies such as leisure-work, sacred-secular, self-object, and aesthetics-rationality emerges.

MUSIC MAKING AND LEISURE: CYPHERS, HULA, CHANTING, AND GLOBALIZING FORCES

Stepping into the cypher is stepping into the unknown, the potentiality, the aboutness, the inbetweenness, and mystery of life. Fragile and ephemeral moments hold possibilities of transformation and the yet-to-be. Most importantly, they resonate, recall, and make anew all that has ever been relevant for this time, this place, and these people— embracing all beings in vibrations grounded in the heartbeat. Being in the cypher— crossing a threshold—opens to an experience beyond measurement and predictability. Although not replicable nor reduced to an essence, for they depend upon diverse selves and inter-beings, these moments and experiences have the potential to change lives and sustain movements devalued within a culture of measurement, control, and commodification.

Indigenous music-dance making were and are embodied practices that physically, metaphysically, and intellectually connect Indigenous peoples to the cosmos and make, unmake, and remake time, space, knowledge, meaning, and relationships. Diné and Kanaka ʻŌiwi embodied artistic and scholarly practices articulate beauty as essential for their well-being and for sustaining the cosmos. Ethical values, such as beauty, generosity, reciprocity, relationality, and music-dance making do not usually appear in leisure literature and scholarship. Music-dance making, as Eddie Kamae (1995) states for Kanaka Maoli—and I extrapolate to other Indigenous peoples—is an essential dynamic for ontological security, sustaining the cosmos, survivance, health, and well-being. Feld (1984) stated: "For any given society, everything that is socially salient will not necessarily be musically marked. But for all societies, anything that is musically salient will undoubtedly be socially marked, albeit in a great variety of ways." (406).

I have gestured to the ongoing, unbroken heritage of Indigenous music-dance using specific examples: the hula, oli, and mele through Hawaiian ukulele and slack-key guitar for Kanaka Maoli; the Great Plains Indian Sun Dances and Grass Dances, pan-Indian powwows, and individual Indigenous artists making their way in jazz, blues, and country-western. Modern-day variations can be seen as embodied in urban Aboriginal hip-hop, Inuit throat singing on popular music charts, and modern dance choreography with traditional Indigenous dance steps. They embody and sustain the power and presence of Indigenous music-dance making. They unsettle dominant Western leisure's sense of solidity and permanence with alternative rhythms related to embodiment, self, and relationality.

Indigenous music-dance making invites attuning leisure to the body, planet, and cosmos in songs, chants, and dance different from the drive for goals, flow, and control. Life lived relationally and in its ambiguity and uncertainty continually rearranges and reconfigures its components (Higgins 1992). Indigenous music-dance generates alternative spatio-temporal realities and reminds us that the Western concept of reality is only one among many and cannot demonstrate it "is the only reality." Indigenous music-dance values and renews sensuous and affective rationalities and aesthetics systems (MacDonald and Hamilton 2014). Music-dance resonates, embraces, affects, and reconfigures who we are and it can be the foundation for facilitating intercultural understanding. "Music affords a rich experience that addresses the entirety of the receptive auditor—body, mind, emotion, and spirituality" (Higgins 1992, 638–639).

The cypher, like Indigenous compositions over the generations, is an invitation to think about an ethics of attunement through forms of interconnection, congruence, and attention. It invites us to have an imaginative attunement of our own world with another without imposing our categories or power. Participating in music-dance energies tunes the entire being to the polyrhythmic, polyphonic, and polymodal movements of temporality (i.e., coordination, syncopation, repetition). Even as we fully enter the cypher, we always know there are aspects missed with a plurality of qualities we can "choose to ignore, dismiss as folly, relish with delight, or simply regret" (Lipari 2014, 173). Music-dance making demonstrates again and again that the idea of leisure is not reality; it is an expressive move of Western culture inhabiting time and space. Participating in an Indigenous cypher is maieutic listening—that is listening each other into an alternative space-time and music-dance making—resonating with, resisting, and enriching Western leisure while reverberating through the universe. In Indigenous words and traditions, may the written words of music-dance making bring forth change:

> We are children of Nokomis, protectors of the land
> We are learning our traditions, ancient knowledge in our hands
> This is a song of survival can you get with this Indigenous revival
> The movement of the people a revolution tribal
> Just another song of survival.
>
> (Red Eagle [Choctaw], *Song of Survival*)

> *'Uhola 'ia ka makaloa lā*
> *Pū 'ai i ke aloha ā*
> *Kū ka'i 'ia ka hā loa lā*
> *Pāwehi mai nā lehua*

Mai ka ho ʻoku ʻi a ka hāi āwai lā
Mahola e Nā Akua
Maholo e nā kūpuna lā ʻeā
Mahalo me ke aloha lā
Mahalo me ke aloha lā[14]

(Kēhua Camara, Kanaka Maoli)

NOTES

1. The word "Indigenous" is shorthand for innumerable peoples categorized under the United Nations political definition. There are no simple name strategies, given style manuals, political changes, and paradigmatic differences. I use multiple words to wander through colonial labels, words appropriated by Indigenous peoples, and the preferred choice of identifying specific locations, genealogies, tribes, and names within the language of the group.

2. I use "music-dance making" congruent with Indigenous artists and scholars who see both of these intimately connected and always already present.

3. I use "self" in line with Deacon (2012) and Kohn (2013) as an iterative form over generations that maintains a selfsame identity inclusive of more-than-human life forms.

4. The range of YouTube videos demonstrating the musicality of animals including parrots and Beluga whales indicates there is much to learn about cross-species musicality.

5. Cage's admonition that the emancipation of music required the use of all sounds opens music making to hip hop, human and nonhuman ensembles, and being present to society's sounds and rhythms. Unfortunately, such a move also supports the exploitation of "sound" as decontextualized commodity to being not be defined and manipulated in the service of the cultural codes of only one way of music making.

6. The modern understanding of Indigenous is based on a self-identification connected to historical continuity with precolonial and/or presettler societies; strong links to territories and surrounding natural resources; distinct social, economic, or political systems; distinct language, culture and beliefs; and resolve to maintain and reproduce ancestral environments and systems as distinctive peoples and communities.

7. There are no appropriate or exact words in English for the various roles and words in Indigenous culture associated with healing body, psyche and soul, promoting harmony between people and groups, or designating and leading ceremonial or ritual practices. I use the terms chanters, medicine elders, and healers as loose approximations.

8. This is a vast and complex area beyond the scope of this chapter, covering a multitude of disciplines and differences between Indigenous and non-Indigenous worldviews. All of them are problematic, given their singular focus on human beings for Indigenous life worlds. I have only gestured to these topics to support the examples within the discussion.

9. Runa are Indigenous people in Ecuador's Upper Amazon. Kohn's (2013) work with them forms the basis for his conceptual work about an anthropology beyond the human.

10. I leave space and time connected as implied by Lefebvre (1991) and connected with relations as constructed by Indigenous peoples.

11. Kanaka Maoli and others are currently contesting the Board of Land and Natural Resources decision to grant the University of Hawaii at Hilo a permit to construct the

world's second-largest telescope on ground sacred to Kanaka Maoli and undeveloped and pristine lands within the Mauna Kea conservation district.

12. "Aloha Pono'i" was the national anthem of the Kingdom of Hawai'i and the Republic of Hawai'i. The words were written by King David Kalākaua and the music composed by Henri Berger, the royal bandmaster, in 1874. It is now the state song of Hawaii.

13. Ho'opāpā is a contest of wit with poetic references, partial homonyms, and vocabulary knowledge to increase individual powers and decrease the powers of the opponent (Grassroot Institute of Hawaii).

14. English translation:

> The makaloa mat has been unfurled
> In love, [food is/was shared] we share;
> The great breath has been exchanged;
> Honored and adored is the Lehua;
> From zenith to horizon;
> Gratitude and thanks to our Akua;
> Gratitude and thanks to our beloved ancestors;
> Gratitude, admiration, thanks, and love;
> To all who are present, both seen and unseen.

References Cited

Bean, Rolinda, Keala Ching, Leianna Eads, Ku Kahakalau, Keala Kahuanui, Matthew Kakalia, Leimana Lindsey, He'enalu Luta, Auhea Puhi, Kina'u Puhi, Kaikealana Ruddle, and Karen Fox. 2002. "Native Hawaiian Ways of Knowing, Project-Approach Learning, and Leisure Education." In *Proceedings from the Pacific-Rim Leisure Education Conference*, edited by Norman McIntyre and Hitoshi Nishino, 249–253, Honolulu, HI: Tokai University Press.

Becker, Judith. 2004. *Deep Listeners: Music, Emotion, and Trancing*. Bloomington: Indiana University Press.

Best, Stephen, and Douglas Kellner. 1991. *Postmodern Theory: Critical Interrogations*. New York: Guilford Press.

Blacking, John. 1974. *How Musical is Man?* Seattle: University of Washington Press.

Bracken, Christopher. 1997. *The Potlach Papers: A Colonial Case History*. Chicago, IL: The University of Chicago Press.

Braidotti, Rosi. 2012. "Transposing Life." *Thamyris/Intersecting* 25: 61–78.

Browner, Tara. 2004. *Heartbeat of the People: Music and Dance of the Northern Pow-wow*. Urbana-Champaign, IL: University of Illinois Press.

Chivarria, Tony. 2015. Curatorial statement. *Here, Now & Always: Follow a Path of Stories into the Heart of the Native American Southwest* exhibit. Museum of Indian Arts and Culture, Santa Fe, NM.

Corradi Fiumara, Gemma. 1990. *The Other Side of Language: A Philosophy of Listening*. New York: Routledge.

Dahl, Rene, Rod Dieser, Karen Fox, Ku Kahakalau, Darlene Martin, and Maria Trillo. 2002. "The Cultural Encapsulation of Leisure Education Models." In *Proceedings from the Pacific-Rim Leisure Education Conference*, edited by Norman McIntyre and Hitoshi Nishino, 239–248, Honolulu, HI: Tokai University Press.

Davis, Angela Y. 1998. *Blues Legacies and Black Feminism: Gertrude "Ma" Rainey, Bessie Smith, and Billie Holiday*. New York: Pantheon.

Deacon, Terrence W. 2012. *Incomplete Nature: How Mind Emerged from Matter*. New York: Norton.

Descola, Philippe. 2013. *Beyond Nature and Culture*. Translated by Janet Lloyd. Chicago: University of Chicago Press.

Descola, Philippe. 2014. "All Too Human (Still): A Comment on Eduardo Kohn's *How Forests Think*." *Hau: Journal of Ethnographic Theory* 4(2): 267–273.

Dewar, John. 1986. "The Introduction of Western Sports to the Indian People of Canada's Prairie West." In *Sport, Culture, Society: International, Historical, and Sociological Perspectives*, edited by by James Mangan and Roy Small, 27–32. London: E. and F. N. Spon.

Doniger, Wendy. 1998. *The Implied Spider: Politics and Theology in Myth*. New York: Columbia University Press.

Dueck, Byron. 2007. "Public and Intimate Sociability in First Nations and Métis Fiddling." *Ethnomusicology* 51(1): 30–63.

Erickson, Frederick. 2009. "Musicality in Talk and Listening: A Key Element in Classroom Discourse as an Environment for Learning." In *Communicative Musicality: Exploring the Basis of Human Companionship*, edited by Stephen Malloch and Colwyn Trevarthen, 449–464. Oxford: Oxford University Press.

Feld, Steven. 1984. "Sound Structure as Social Structure." *Ethnomusicology* 28(3): 383–409.

Finney, Ben, with Marlen Among, Chad Baybayan, Tai Crouch, Paul Frost, Bernard Kilonsky, Richard Rhodes, Thomas Schroeder, Dixon Stroup, Nainoa Thompson, Robert Worthington, and Elisa Yadao. 1994. *Voyage of Rediscovery: A Cultural Odyssey through Polynesia*. Berkeley: University of California Press.

Fox, Karen Marston. 2001. "Manawa Nanea: Native Hawaiian Perspectives on Leisure." Paper presented at the 2000 Symposium on Leisure Research, Phoenix, AZ.

Fox, Karen Marston, and Gabrielle Riches. 2014. "Intersecting Rhythms: The Spatial Production of Local Canadian Heavy Metal and Urban Aboriginal Hip Hop in Edmonton, Alberta, Canada." In *Sounds and the City: Popular Music, Place and Globalization*, edited by Brett Lashua, Karl Spracklen, and Stephen Wagg, 225–240. London: Palgrave Macmillan.

Fox, Margalit. 2008. "Ray Kane, Master of Slack-Key Guitar, Dies at 82." *New York Times*, March 5. http://www.nytimes.com/2008/03/05/arts/music/05kane.html?_r=0.

Guattari, Felix, and Suely Rolnik. 2008. *Molecular Revolution in Brazil*. Los Angeles, CA: Simiotext(e).

George, Marianne. 2012. "Polynesian Navigation and Te Lapa—'The Flashing.'" *Time and Mind: The Journal of Archaeology, Consciousness and Culture* 5(2): 135–174.

Glennie, Evelyn. 1990. *Good Vibrations*. Long Preston: Magna Print.

Glennie, Evelyn. 2003. "How To Truly Listen" *TED Talks*, February. http://www.ted.com/talks/evelyn_glennie_shows_how_to_listen.

Higgins, Kathleen Marie. 1992. "Apollo, Music, and Cross-Cultural Rationality." *Philosophy East and West* 42: 623–641.

Higgins, Kathleen Marie. 2012. *The Music between Us: Is Music a Universal Language?* Chicago: University of Chicago Press.

ho'omanawanui, Ku'ualoha. 2014. *Voices of Fire: Reweaving the Literary Lei of Pele and Hi'iaka*. Minneapolis: University of Minnesota Press and First Peoples New Directions in Indigenous Studies.

Kamae, Eddie. 1995. *Words, Earth, and Aloha*. Documentary produced by Myrna Kamae and Rodney A. Ohtani. Hawaiian Legacy Foundation. DVD

Kohn, Eduardo. 2013. *How Forests Think: Toward an Anthropology beyond the Human*. Berkeley: University of California Press.

Lalonde, Chris, and Michael J. Chandler. 2004. "Culture, Selves, and Time: Theories of Personal Persistence in Native and Non-Native Youth." In *Changing Conceptions of Psychological Life*, ed. Cynthia Lightfoot, Chris Lalonde, and Michael Chandler, 207–229. Mahwah, NJ: Lawrence Erlbaum.

Lefebvre, Henri. 1991. *The Production of Space*. Translated by Donald Nicholson-Smith. Oxford: Blackwell.

Lipari, Lisbeth. 2014. *Listening, Thinking, Being: Toward an Ethics of Attunement*. University Park: Pennsylvania State University Press.

MacDonald, Michael B., with Andree Hamilton. 2014. "Aesthetic Systems Theory: Doing Hip Hop Kulture Research Together at Cipher5." *MUSICulture* 41(2): 34–53.

Malloch, Stephen, and Colwyn Trevarthen, eds. 2009. *Communicative Musicality: Exploring the Basis of Human Companionship*. Oxford: Oxford University Press.

Manning, Erin. 2013. *Always More than One: Individuation's Dance*. Durham, NC: Duke University Press.

Meyer, Manulani Aluli. 2004. *Ho'oulu, Our Time of Becoming: Hawaiian Epistemology and Early Writings*. Honolulu, HI: 'Ai Pōhaku Press, Native Books.

Miller, Robert J. 1993. "American Indian Influence on the United States Constitution and Its Framers." *American Indian Law Review* 18(1): 133–160.

Nāone, C. Kanoelani. 2008. "The Pilina of Kanaka and 'Āina: Place, Language and Community as Sites of Reclamation for Indigenous Education The Hawaiian Case." Unpublished Dissertation. Honolulu, HI: University of Hawaii.

Peacock, Ken. 1955. *Indian Music of the Canadian Plains*. Washington, DC: Smithsonian Institution, Folkways Records.

Powers, Nikki, and Colwyn Trevarthen. 2009. "Voices of Shared Emotion and Meaning: Young Infants and Their Mothers in Scotland and Japan." In *Communicative Musicality: Exploring the Basis of Human Companionship*, edited by Stephen Malloch and Colwyn Trevarthen, 209–240. Oxford: Oxford University Press.

Riedelsheimer, Thomas (Director). 2012. *Touch the Sound: A Sound Journey with Evelyn Glennie*. New York: New Video Group.

Ruymar, Lorene. 1996. *The Hawaiian Steel Guitar and Its Great Hawaiian Musicians*. Anaheim, CA: Centerstream.

Shields, Rob. 1999. *Lefebvre, Love, and Struggle: Spatial Dialectics*. Abingdon: Routledge.

Shields, Rob. 2013. *Spatial Questions: Cultural Topologies and Social Spatialisation*. Los Angeles, CA: Sage.

Shorter, David Delgado. 2009. *We Will Dance Our Truth: Yaqui History in Yoeme Performance*. Lincoln: University of Nebraska Press.

Silva, Noenoe K. 2004. *Aloha Betrayed: Native Hawaiian Resistance to American Colonialism*. Durham, NC: Duke University Press.

Snyder, Gail. 2015. "Native Pulse." *Local Flavor Magazine*, February 2. http://www.localflavor-magazine.com/native-pulse/.

Stillman, Amy Ku'uleialoha. 1989. "History Reinterpreted in Song: The Case of the Hawaiian Counterrevolution." *The Hawaiian Journal of History* 23: 1–30.

Tapahonso, Luci. 2015. Curatorial statement. *Here, Now & Always: Follow a Path of Stories into the Heart of the Native American Southwest* exhibit. Museum of Indian Arts and Culture, Santa Fe, NM.

Trevarthen, Colwyn. 2011. "The Infant's Voice Grows in Intimate Dialogue: How Musicality of Expression Inspires Shared Meaning." In *Dialogic Formations: Investigations into the Origins and Development of the Dialogical Self*, edited by Marie-Cécile Berteau, Miguel M. Gonçalves, and Peter T. F. Raggatt, 3–40. Charlote, NC: Information Age.

Troutman, John W. 2009. *Indian Blues: American Indians and the Politics of Music, 1879–1934.* Norman: University of Oklahoma Press.

Truth and Reconciliation Commission of Canada (TRC). 2015. *Honouring the Truth, Reconciling for the Future: Summary of the Final Report of the Trust and Reconciliation Commission of Canada.* Ottawa: ON: Government of Canada.

Turino, Thomas. 2008. *Music as Social Life: The Politics of Participation.* Chicago: University of Chicago Press.

Van Alstyne, Richard W. 1974. *The Rising American Empire.* New York: Norton.

Vizenor, Gerald. 1999. *Manifest Manners: Narratives on Postindian Survivance.* Lincoln: University of Nebraska Press.

Warner, Michael. 2002. *Publics and Counterpublics.* New York: Zone Books.

Warren, Karen J. 2000. *Ecofeminist Philosophy: A Western Perspective on What It Is and Why It Matters.* Lanham, MD: Rowman and Littlefield.

Weedon, Chris. 2004. *Identity and Culture: Narratives of Difference and Belonging.* Maidenhead: Open University Press.

Young Bear, Severt, and R. D. Theisz. 1996. *Standing in the Light: A Lakota Way of Seeking.* Lincoln: University of Nebraska Press.

Yvinec, Cédric. 2014. "Temporal Dimensions of Selfhood: Theories of Person Among the Suruí of Rondônia (Brazilian Amazon)." *Journal of the Royal Anthropological Institute* NS 20: 20–37.

CHAPTER 28

....

SONIC PARTICIPATORY CULTURES WITHIN, THROUGH, AND AROUND VIDEO GAMES

....

JARED O'LEARY AND EVAN S. TOBIAS

THIS chapter is concerned with the diverse ways that people engage with music or sound within, through, or around video games. We situate these forms of engagement in relation to what we term *sonic participatory cultures*, and discuss the specific ways that people engage with video games and sound or music as sonic participation. We refer to sonic participation as encompassing both music and sound, as some forms of participation involve music, others involve sound effects, and still others involve both. Our experiences and research inform the writing of this chapter: Jared identifies as a hardcore gamer, researcher, and music facilitator among many other identities, and Evan identifies as a music teacher educator interested in the ways people engage with video games and in the potential for video games and related engagement in music education. Jared would describe himself as being a member within the gaming community and engages in a majority of the forms of sonic participation described in this chapter through "project-based" leisure (Stebbins, this volume, chapter 19). Evan plays video games occasionally and studies participatory cultures in which music and media intersect in relation to music teaching and learning. The types of participatory culture and forms of participation we discuss in this chapter are situated in relation to Jared's personal experiences with video games and both authors' identification of examples in online media and related literature.

GAMES AS A LEISURE ACTIVITY
AND SONIC SPACE

For several decades, a significant segment of the population has engaged with video games. The Entertainment Software Association's 2015 report on computer and video game sales, demographic, and usage data indicates that over 150 million Americans play video games, with 42 percent playing at least three hours per week and the average age of gamers being thirty-five years old.[1] The ecosystem in which video games exist provides a context for deep engagement and enjoyment through a variety of personal and social rewards. Stebbins (2007) lists several types of "rewards" through serious leisure:

Personal Rewards
  1. Personal enrichment (cherished experiences);
  2. Self-actualization (developing skills, abilities, knowledge);
  3. Self-expression (expressing skills, abilities, knowledge already developed);
  4. Self-image (known to others as a particular kind of serious leisure participant);
  5. Self-gratification (combination of superficial enjoyment and deep fulfillment);
  6. Re-creation (regeneration) of oneself through serious leisure after a day's work;
  7. Financial return (from a serious leisure activity).

Social Rewards
  8. Social attraction (associating with other serious leisure participants, with clients, as a volunteer, participating in the social world of the activity);
  9. Group accomplishment (group effort in accomplishing a serious leisure project; senses of helping, being needed, being altruistic);
  10. Contribution to the maintenance and development of the group (including senses of helping, being needed, being an altruistic in making the contribution). (Stebbins 2007, 14)

These rewards may be applicable to serious leisure engagement with video games beyond a game's original design or intended engagements. Extended forms of engagement with video games exist within an open-source culture where hobbyists, amateurs, and volunteers modify games to test the limits of computer hardware or software development (Pasdzierny 2013; Sihvonen 2011); these practices are often encouraged by a variety of gaming companies and communities (Schäfer 2011).

The study of games is discussed in terms of game studies, gaming theory, ludology, and related scholarship located within larger contexts of media studies and participatory culture. An emerging subfield of ludomusicology currently encompasses "a study into the history of music and audio in video games; an engagement with the technological procedures and innovations in video game music; and analysis of video game music texts" (Hart 2014, 273). Though not all scholars self-identify as engaging in ludomusicology, this type of research includes ethnographic investigations into the music of games like *Grand Theft Auto: San Andreas* (Miller 2012), analysis of the performative nature of rhythm action games like *Guitar Hero* (Collins 2013), and analyses of music or sound and related engagement in video games such as *Team Fortress 2, Fallout 3, Silent Hill, Final Fantasy VI*, and *Lord of the Rings Online* (Cheng 2014). Several scholars have also focused on physiological and psychological aspects of engagement with music and sound in relation to video games (Grimshaw, Tan, and Lipscomb 2013; Zehnder and Lipscomb 2006).

A similar strand of research has also emerged in music education with a focus on the possibilities of musical engagement in relation to video games and its potential connections to music teaching and learning (Clements 2011; Clements, Cody, and Gibbs 2008; Tobias 2012; Tobias and O'Leary 2016). Studies attending to music learning and engagement in relation to rhythm action games in particular are at a beginning stage (Cassidy and Paisley 2013; Gower and McDowall 2012; Paney 2015; Peppler et al. 2011); however, few studies have focused on those who engage in the forms of sonic participation discussed in this chapter.

To establish a conceptual framework in relation to sonic participation within, through, and around video games, we first discuss existing frameworks of participatory culture, and then extend this work to address specific phenomena. We propose the notion of sonic participatory culture (or cultures) and sonic participation itself as ways of situating engagement with music or sound in relation to video games, participatory culture, and leisure. The remainder of the chapter focuses on three aspects of sonic participatory culture: (1) within video games, (2) through video games, and (3) around video games. The chapter demonstrates how video games mediate a wide range of sonic participation and leisure. We focus on each form of engagement separately for the purpose of clarity, as they often overlap and defy compartmentalized categorization.

PARTICIPATORY CULTURES

The rich and diverse ways that people engage with video games in relation to music and sound sit at a nexus of sonic and media cultures. This intersection of sound and media engagement gives life to a compelling array of leisure and participation, such as a music group that performs video game music, an individual who creates music within a video game world like *Minecraft*, or a person who remixes 8-bit[2] video game music and shares it through a dedicated online community. Each of these examples involves engagement related to video games, music, and sound, yet the forms of participation differ.

Notions of participatory culture emphasize the variety of ways that people engage with varied media as active participants (Delwiche and Henderson 2013; Jenkins 2006a; Jenkins et al. 2009; Williams and Zenger 2012). From a perspective of media studies,

Jenkins et al.'s (2009) framework of participatory culture—which addresses affiliations (informal or formal memberships), expressions (producing new creative forms), collaborative problem solving (working in informal and formal teams), and circulations (which shape the flow of media)—can explain aspects of how people engage with music or sound related to video games. However, given the multitude of ways people engage with video game music and sound, it would be inaccurate to deploy this framework in an all-encompassing manner.

Turino (2008) provides a helpful framework of participatory performance that addresses music-specific situations where "there are no artist-audience distinctions, only participants and potential participants performing in different roles, and the primary goal is to involve the maximum number of people in some performance role" (26). Turino's notion of studio audio art, in which music or sound is created electronically without necessarily being performed live in real time, addresses some of the ways that people create music and sound with, through, and around video games. Although Turino's participatory music framework might account for particular aspects of engaging with video game music or sound, it does not address the variegated ways that people engage with music or sound related to video games that do not involve live performance.

Miller's (2012) notion of "playing along," which addresses "intersections among gameplay, musical experience, and theatrical performance" (5), can be helpful in describing some of the ways that people interact with and embody music, sound, and video games. Miller positions "playing along" as a genre of participation, what Ito et al. (2010) describe as social and routinized ways that people engage with media. Playing along accounts for varied relationships between a person who plays video games and the game designers, other players, and the music or sound, highlighting the potential social nature of video game play. Miller foregrounds the players' experiences and how they engage with music, sound, and video games while also cautioning that playing along might involve conformity and trouble notions of agency. Miller's work provides a helpful way of understanding the connections between the media and musical aspects of one's engagement with video games, particularly when focusing on how one interacts with music that is part of a game environment. The notion of playing along addresses some types of sonic participation described in this chapter, yet broader frameworks of sonic participatory cultures are needed to address the multitudinous ways that people engage with video games and music or sound.

Schäfer (2011) provides a critical framework of *implicit* and *explicit* participation that is useful for understanding relationships between people and their engagement in sonic participatory cultures, media that enable participation, and the corporate sector. According to Schäfer, implicit participation is what occurs in relation to the affordances[3] and design of media or technology that people use to participate. Schäfer argues that, unlike explicit participation, implicit participation "does not necessarily require a conscious activity of cultural production, nor does it require users to choose from different methods in problem-solving, collaboration, and communication with others" (51). Common forms of implicit participation include uploading files to user-created content platforms such as Flicker, adding tags, using rating platforms, placing buttons on websites, or rating and watching videos on YouTube. Aspects of one's implicit participation, such as the use of a medium to engage with music or sound, impact explicit participation and occur in relation to larger contexts of music and media industries. Identifying and analyzing these relationships are important whether when one's sonic participation with video games is pursued as a form of leisure career (moving from hobby to career), through devotee work (devotion or positive attachment to self-enhancing work), or within casual (short-lived leisure pursuit) or project-based leisure (infrequent or one-off leisure pursuit) (Stebbins 2014).

Schäfer explains that explicit participation is driven by motivation and is heterogeneous in nature, often involving problem-solving, collaboration, one's conscious engagement with a cultural product, and communication with others. Common forms of explicit participation include sharing cultural products through P2P (peer-to-peer) file sharing, engaging in fan culture, cooperating in software development, contributing to a wiki or other collective intelligence resources, generating and sharing content online for or within a cultural product, or engaging in activism around a cultural product (Schäfer 2011). The types of engagement in sonic participatory cultures discussed throughout this chapter are primarily examples of explicit participation.

Situating the ways that people engage with video games in terms of participatory culture may assist in understanding how specific forms of leisure and participation exist in larger cultural contexts and connect with existing or emerging cultural phenomena. Frameworks that address expressions, affiliations, collaborative problem solving, and circulations (Jenkins et al. 2009); inclusive approaches to involving people in musical performance (Turino 2008); links between one's gameplay and sound or music (Miller 2012); or relationships between people, media, society, and the corporate sector (Schäfer 2011) are helpful for understanding certain aspects of the phenomena discussed throughout this chapter. However, much of the engagement or participation in relation to video games that we address necessitates an additional framework that accounts for both music or sound, and media.

As outlined below, it would be inaccurate to apply existing theories of participatory culture designed for particular aspects of media (Jenkins 2006a; Jenkins et al. 2009) or musical engagement (Turino 2008) as overarching frameworks to explain the breadth of ways that people engage with music and sound in relation to video games. Thus, we leverage aspects of existing theories of participatory culture when appropriate while simultaneously exploring a form of sonic participatory culture specific to and born out of the convergence of music, sound, and other media. We refer to larger cultural contexts and phenomena involving music, sound, and media as sonic participatory cultures and the more specific types of engagement as forms of sonic participation.

Sonic Participatory Cultures
within Video Games

Music and sound *within* video games often allow for an interaction between the game and a player, as the sonic aspects of video games can be used as a sonification of, or guide for, the player (Collins 2013). These interactions include direct (e.g., player actions) and indirect responses (e.g., game states) to actions within a game (Phillips 2014) that impact the sonic environment (Collins 2008a), or acoustic ecologies (Grimshaw 2012), along a continuum of interaction between gameplay and sound (Stevens and Raybould 2011). Some games move beyond interaction and provide active participation in music making. The key characteristic shared among the following forms of sonic participation cultures is that the music or sound occurs *within* the game environment itself.

Rhythm Games

Of the music games studied in academia, rhythm games like *Guitar Hero, Rock Band*, and *DJ Hero* have received the bulk of attention over the past decade (Cassidy and Paisley 2013; Gower and McDowall 2012; Peppler et al. 2011). This genre of music game often uses music-related peripherals for controllers that were born out of research at the Massachusetts Institute of Technology, which explored intuitive music interfaces (Phillips 2014), and often involve what Collins (2013) refers to as kinesonic congruity (kinesthetic + sonic)—a phenomenon that occurs when sound is integrated with body movements. Video games within this genre usually provide a simplified version of standardized music notation that matches buttons on the controller that are to be rhythmically triggered according to parameters present in onscreen indicators. Most games within this genre trigger music or sound when the correct button is pressed at the correct time, and will provide some kind of visual, audible, or haptic feedback when a button is incorrectly triggered. Playing the game in this manner might be seen as a form of playing along with or even performing the music (Miller 2012), or as a tool for learning a form of music literacy in leisurely settings (Peppler et al. 2011). Participation with rhythm games can occur in varied contexts ranging from individuals playing alone to groups of people playing together in leisurely or competitive contexts which include—and are not limited to—living rooms, video game stores, arcades, organizations, video game conferences, and expos.

Miller (2012) suggests that schizophonic performance, the linking of "physical gestures of live musical performance with reproduction of recorded songs" (85), is an important aspect of experiencing rhythm games. Tobias (2012) previously situated such gameplay as a form of engaged listening, highlighting how video games can provide an embodied way of experiencing music. For a segment of the population, digital media such as video games serve as a means of musical engagement and leisure. Sonic participation of this sort is both *explicit* through the way one plays the game and music, and *implicit* in engaging with a particular set of game mechanics and code (Schäfer 2011).

Games Supporting Music Creation

The ability for people to create, produce, and perform music within video games is a key factor in why gameplay might be considered in relation to sonic participatory cultures and in the context of leisure. For instance, a mode in the Super Nintendo Entertainment System (SNES) game *Mario Paint* enables people to create music by sequencing iconic characters and objects from the *Super Mario Bros.* series. Within this mode, players can create music by placing various gaming icons with different sounds on a standardized notation music staff, and stop, play, or loop their music. Although the game is no longer in production, emulators are still distributed online as a dedicated following of people continue to arrange music within this game in their leisure time and share them online in participatory settings. Examples can be found online by searching for "Mario Paint" with "composer" or "music."[4]

The game *FRACT OSC* by Phosfiend Systems is a music exploration game that uses musical puzzles to explore aspects of a digital audio workstation (DAW) such as sequencing, filters, instrument matrices, and panning. Each puzzle in the game is scattered throughout a world whose music changes in response to one's interaction with these musical puzzles. For instance, as the player is working on a MIDI matrix puzzle,[5] the music in the background responds according to the matrix the player is controlling. Once a puzzle is completed, a new music tool is unlocked in the game's music studio where the player is free to create and share original music.

Making music within video games is closely related to the game mechanics and code that enable this type of engagement. This type of sonic participation can be understood in relation to a player's explicit and implicit participation (Schäfer 2011) and the affordances or constraints of particular games. For instance, the game mechanics in games such as *Mario Paint* or *FRACT OSC* provide opportunities for people to make music in some ways but not others. This raises questions as to one's degree of agency or the relationships between a player making music, other players, and game designers (Miller 2012).

ABC Notation and Freestyle

Cheng (2014) uses a musicological approach to investigate the sonic performance practices of players in the massively multiplayer online role-playing game (often abbreviated as MMORPG or MMO for short)[6] *The Lord of the Rings Online* (*LotRO*). Within the game, players are able to create live (known as "freestyle") and preprogrammed music (known as "ABC") on a variety of instruments that can be heard by other players within the gameworld. Through the game's sonic affordances, players are able to put on impromptu and planned musical performances to either entertain or *grief* other players.[7] Using the freestyle approach to making music, players are able to improvise live music within the gameworld through keyboard strokes that correspond to notes for a virtual instrument. Using the ABC method, players are able to make music through precomposed works that are generated from a text file. To perform these prearranged songs within a gameworld that supports ABC songs, players write out text files with commands for time signature, key signature, and note names with corresponding durations, then recall the file within the game by typing "/play <filename>" with the corresponding filename. Players can create multipart pieces using multiple ABC text files, create an ensemble by triggering each part of the music at the same time in the gameworld, or combine aspects of ABC with freestyle performing to create improvised solos on top of preprogrammed music (Cheng 2014); several example videos can be found online by searching for terms such as "ABC" or "freestyle" with games like "LotRO"[8] or "Guild Wars 2"[9] and "performance," "music," "concert," or "song." An MMO becomes a form of participatory entertainment when the game and its players cocreate a fantasy world (Sihvonen 2011); having the ability to create live and preprogrammed music within a game grants even more depth to the level of participation a player experiences within the gameworld.

Note Blocks

The video game *Minecraft* has built-in mechanics for creating music within the gameworld using an in-game object, *note block*. The note block produces a pitch when struck or when powered by *redstone* (a material in the game that is used to simulate electrical circuits), which allows the player to create simple or complex musical expressions within a four-octave range ("Note Block" 2015). Players construct complex redstone circuits where each note in the song is represented by a single note block along a circuit that has switches and timers to trigger the blocks at precisely the desired moment, to create single or multipart music; several example videos can be found online by searching for terms like "Minecraft" or "note block" with "music" or "song."[10]

Leisure and Sonic Participatory Cultures within Video Games

It seems that, for many people interested in gaming, performing and making music within games is a worthwhile form of sonic participation. Perhaps rhythm games enable players to embody music through schizophonic performance (Miller 2012) or engaged listening (Campbell 2004; Tobias 2012) in ways that are fulfilling or recall *eudaimonia* in a manner similar to that which Smith (this volume, chapter 9) describes in relation to people composing and performing music in other contexts. While additional research is needed to better understand game players' perspectives on the systems they use to make music or the affordances and constraints therein, for some, any constraints are outweighed by the personal, social, or musical rewards resulting from their engagement. The time and effort that people invest in making music within games, as outlined throughout this chapter, suggest that people enjoy engaging in sonic participatory cultures as a form of leisure.

SONIC PARTICIPATORY CULTURES THROUGH VIDEO GAMES

While some people use music or sound to participate within video games, others treat video games as instruments for sonic participation. Dolphin (2014) outlines the concept of a sound toy as "interactive sonic-centric systems in which the end user may trigger, generate, modify, or transform sound" (45). When video games are treated as a sound toy, they become an interactive compositional system that allows access to musical experiences, sound worlds, and various compositional parameters with modern or 8-bit sound palettes. In these ways, video games mediate creative engagement that extends beyond game play itself.

Machinima, Vidding, and other Multimedia Appropriations

Vidding is a participatory filmmaking practice in which clips from movies and television shows are set to music in order to tell new stories or alter the perspectives of stories already told (Coppa 2008). This practice is occasionally used within the sonic participatory cultures of video games. *Machinima*, similar to but more common than vidding, is when gameplay is recorded with music or sounds dubbed over it (Collins 2013). Machinima has been used to create episodic online shows, movies, music videos, covers, and remixes that are extensions of the cultural industries they are appropriating. Vidding and machinima can use video game imagery; however, vidding involves participants appropriating existing media, whereas machinima involves recording new media through video gameplay.

Machinima, vidding, and other multimedia appropriations exemplify aspects of sonic participatory cultures through video games primarily in three ways: (1) people dub imagery from video games with new music or sounds, (2) people set video game music or sounds to new imagery, and (3) people use video game music or sounds as an instrument for new media. Those who dub images from video games with new music or sounds often do so in a way that recontextualizes the imagery, music, or sound with new meaning. One might reimagine what a video game such as *Battlefield 3* would have sounded like if the music and sounds had all been created within the 8-bit aes-thetic.[11] Similarly, one might try using vidding techniques to reimagine the meaning of music such as *Imagine Dragons*'s "Radioactive" by dubbing the song on top of video recordings from the video game series *Halo*.[12] Machinima techniques have also been used to reimagine movie[13] and game[14] trailers through the 8-bit aesthetic in the game *Minecraft*. These examples maintain the original music and sounds from the trailers while using new video game imagery to alter the meanings of the music and sound. Another example uses imagery from the *Super Mario Bros.* series to recreate the open-ing credits of the television show *Game of Thrones* with an 8-bit rendition of the show's opening music.[15]

Setting video game music or sounds to new imagery enables people to alter the meaning of the imagery, music, or sound. For example, people have: reimagined the imagery of two video game songs by using the software Photoshop and iMovie to pro-duce a fan-created music video;[16] combined video game music and imagery from the *Super Mario Bros.* series with Sir Mix-A-Lot's music video for "Baby Got Back" to cre-ate a music video mashup;[17] used sounds, graphics, and visual perspective through a drone to recreate *Grand Theft Auto 2* in real life;[18] and used sound effects, graphics, and cosplay[19] from the video game series *Super Mario Bros.* to enhance video recordings of parkour[20] demonstrations.[21] Other examples of this form of sonic participation involve reimagining movie and television clips with 8-bit music and sounds to create a form of 8-bit Foley.[22]

When video game music or sounds are sampled for new media creations, the sonic aspects of video games are often fragmented into short sonic elements used to create a collage of sounds; Pasdzierny (2013) refers to this as a *plunderphonic* approach to mak-ing music. To create music in this way, one can record isolated video game sounds to be used in sequences or layers to create new media or music. Examples include people isolating sounds from the campaign of *Battlefield 4* to create a "gun beat" out of gun and knife sounds, vocals, and in-game explosions,[23] isolating sounds from the game *Minecraft* to sequence a melody from in-game sounds,[24] using recordings of car horns from *Grand Theft Auto V* to create a multipart arrangement of the theme song from *Game of Thrones*,[25] and using games to play rhythmic and melodic gestures alongside other music.[26]

The desire for people to create and share "expressions" with others is a key aspect of participatory culture as discussed in media studies (Jenkins et al. 2009). As Jenkins (2006b) argues, "much of what the public creates models itself after, exists in dialogue with, reacts to or against, or otherwise repurposes materials from commercial culture" (137). Creating music and media through video games is indicative of sonic participa-tory cultures in which people express themselves or make meaning through appropriat-ing aspects of popular culture such as video games. These forms of sonic participation also invite engagement along a continuum of casual to serious leisure (Stebbins, this volume, chapter 19), through creative experimentation, artistic inquiry, or as activism, among other intentions with potential interconnections.

Modding and Coding

Modding refers to creating or altering a game's code or content to create modifications, known in gaming vernacular as "mods," from existing video games. Mods can include music or sound, graphical, character, or mechanical modifications (Sihvonen 2011) that range from hardware modifications (known as "hard mods") to software modifications (known as "soft mods") (Schäfer 2011). While modding is often done by individuals, mod culture is participatory, in that it encourages sharing mods, with the source code available to view and edit so that modders can learn from each other by exploring what and how something was altered. When collaboration occurs, it is often through asynchronous read-me text files that explain changes in code or through coding repositories like GitHub, which allow for open or team collaboration.

Music and sound mods occur when sound files in games are replaced or extracted by a player. For instance, the game series *Left for Dead* (*L4D*) implicitly made audio mods relatively easy to create, as the folders for all of the game sounds are clearly labeled; for example, shotgun sounds are located in a folder labeled "shotguns" under a parent folder labeled "weapons." This enables people to create soundpacks to modify the game's original sounds, such as replacing the game sounds for one of the zombies in the game with clips from "Scatman" by Scatman John. Instead of hearing the screams and growls of the zombie known as the Hunter, this soundpack mod results in the player hearing musical and vocal excerpts from "Scatman."[27] The ease of access to the audio files in *L4D* supports people who produce music, like Catalynx, who use these sound files in their music. Other modders have replaced sounds in games like *Super Mario Bros.*[28] and *Minecraft*[29] with recorded sounds and vocal effects, or used newly designed sounds.[30]

Aside from recording and swapping out sounds, other modders, like David Norgren, have created free mods for *Minecraft* that allow players to convert MIDI files into redstone circuits which contain note blocks that correspond with a selected MIDI file within the gameworld (Norgren 2013). Other modders have created entirely new games out of television shows in an 8-bit or 16-bit style that include new or covered music and sound.[31] Some have created 8-bit shorts from movies by creating a game world, sounds, and music as an 8-bit interpretation of the movie it is portraying.[32] Another example of a soft mod within sonic participation is a program called Audio Pad. Audio Pad is a separate program that assigns audio frequencies to keystrokes on a computer's keyboard. These assigned keystrokes can be used within a video game in place of a keyboard or controller. Instead of using a traditional controller to play a game with one or both hands, players can use Audio Pad to play a game with sound alone. In one case, this allowed a person to play the game *Super Mario World* by playing notes on a recorder—with his nose—to control the onscreen avatar, Mario (Ashcraft 2015).

Stand-alone games like *D-Pad Hero 1* and *D-Pad Hero 2*[33] are 8-bit appropriations that combine an 8-bit aesthetic with the mechanics of rhythm games such as *Guitar Hero* to imagine "what music games might have been like in the NES heyday"[34] (Hansen and Pedersen n.d.). The developers for these two games accept donations on their website from those who are willing to support their current and future development projects. These projects were developed through serious leisure and blur the line between leisurely and professional game development.

Beyond soft mods and coding, some modders have developed hard mods to recreate video game music through hardware, such as modified floppy drives.[35] Making such mods necessitates modifying a floppy drive and its software, enabling the drive to spin at frequencies that correspond with the notes programmed in the software to play video game music. Creators of mods afford themselves and others new ways of engaging with games that were not previously possible. In the context of sonic participatory cultures, those who create mods in a complex gameworld like *Minecraft*, for example, are effectively providing a service to the public that allows more people to make music or sounds that might not otherwise have been accessible to them. In these ways, those who create mods may lower the bar for entry into sonic participatory cultures and support others' participation. While some might independently create mods as a short-term project to accomplish a particular task as a form of project-based leisure, others create mods with collaborative problem solving through small team effort and community support.

01000011 01101000 01101001 01110000 01110100 01110101 01101110 01100101 01110011

As an aesthetic, or compositional form, a *chiptune* is a form of music that references or simulates sounds from around the 8-bit era.[36] Devotees often debate how chiptunes may have been created or what techniques might have been used—such as using a tracker for a console from the 8-bit era, circuit bending a Game Boy, or using virtual studio technology (VST) in a digital audio workstation (DAW)—as well as how "pure" or "impure" the resulting chiptune is (Paul 2014); however, the sonic aspects generally involve the use of sine, square, and triangle sound waves along with white noise to create music and sounds that hark back to the 8-bit era.[37] Paul (2014) and Pasdzierny (2013) both note that chiptunes are often considered by enthusiasts to be an instrument for composition as well as a compositional form. As instruments for composition, chiptunes are sometimes created through hardware or software hacks of consoles or handheld computer devices. For instance, Nintendo's Game Boy, partly due to its availability, has become an instrument for many chiptune artists who create live chiptunes, as the hardware can be easily modified to perform music as an electronic instrument.[38] To do this, some chiptune artists "circuit bend" their Game Boys to create music in ways that were originally unintended, while others use cartridges with custom software that allows the performer to play the handheld device as an instrument.[39] Although the majority of chiptune performers use Game Boys, some artists prefer sound chips from other game consoles, or combine multiple sound chips or gaming hardware together into instruments that often resemble guitar-like instruments,[40] piano-like instruments,[41] or are modeled after older handheld consoles and controllers.[42] Examples of chiptune artists and their instruments can be found online by searching for "chiptune" with "live" or "performance." Whether one plays "game music" with chiptunes or chiptune-related instruments, it is the 8-bit video game aesthetic that is important to such engagement.

Leisure and Sonic Participatory Cultures through Video Games

The engagement that occurs in sonic participatory cultures through video games extends gameplay into musical and sonic realms rich with creativity. Sonic participatory cultures through video games provide contexts that can combine enjoyment of video games and music or sound to express or explore creative possibilities. Engaging in the types of sonic participation discussed throughout this section requires skills ranging from coding to editing sound, some of which may serve as a barrier to one's participation. That being said, sonic participatory cultures through video games also account for ways that barriers might be lowered to increase the potential for people to engage. Veterans attempt to make it easier for those less experienced to engage with music and sound through video games by creating tutorials, developing mods, or otherwise sharing information online. These people might be seen to engage in sonic participatory cultures through video games as serious leisure volunteers by helping others for little or no pay for the benefit of both themselves and other people (Stebbins, this volume, chapter 19). The related informal mentorship and collaborative problem solving involved in sonic participatory cultures through video games is similar to other forms of participatory culture (Jenkins et al. 2009).

Sonic participatory cultures through video games include people engaging individually, collaboratively, or as part of collective efforts. Technology plays critical roles in mediating these cultures, particularly when those participating collaboratively or collectively are likely to be dispersed across space and time. Thus, one's sonic participation can oscillate between social and solitary engagement. The ability to engage with others online both synchronously and asynchronously complicates what some might view as a solitary form of participation, such as when an individual creates a music video through machinima physically alone at home. Furthermore, given that one could potentially earn income from advertising revenue on YouTube videos, selling mods, or performing chiptunes in live settings, sonic participatory cultures through video games also provide a context to explore how serious leisure can develop into a source of income or a career (Stebbins, this volume, chapter 19).

SONIC PARTICIPATORY CULTURES
AROUND VIDEO GAMES

In contrast with using video games *for* or *through* sonic participation, sonic participation *around* video games involves participatory engagement with music or sound of video games as its own entity. In the following subsections, we explore sonic participation *around* video games through discussing film scoring, sonic paratexts, performing, and affinity spaces and groups.

Film Scoring

Video game music production has similarities with film scoring in that music is often *diegetic* (within the gameworld; e.g. in-game radio) and *non-diegetic* (outside the gameworld; e.g. soundtrack). Unlike film scoring, however, video game music can interact with a player (Grimshaw, Tan, and Lipscomb 2013). The interactive nature of video games has led to people referring to this type of flexible and nonlinear music as "adaptive" or "dynamic." Such music encompasses varied techniques, including horizontal resequencing, vertical layering, or procedurally generated music.[43]

Unless an amateur, hobbyist, or volunteer video game music producer mods a game or performs live music, there are limited options for creating interactive music with video games. Instead, many write music to recordings of gameplay or game trailers in a manner that resembles film scoring. Music that represents the fantasy world of video games is known by practitioners as *filk*; the process of creating music for the fantasy world of a video game is known as *filking* (Collins 2013). Instances include composing original music for the game *Paper Mario*[44] or arranging popular music covers for video games within the 8-bit aesthetic.[45] A serious leisure participant,[46] Sam Joseph Delves, wanted to make a living scoring game music, so he created new music for the entire game *Ni No Kuni: Wrath of the White Witch* and recorded it with a live orchestra to create a digital portfolio for job applications.[47]

Sonic Paratexts

Paratexts are "independent cultural works that exist in relation to other texts" (Mittell 2013, 38). For the purposes of this chapter, a sonic paratext is an independent sonic creation that exists in relation to other music or sounds. Some examples of sonic paratexts include music arrangements, commentary, covers, mashups, multitracks, parodies, satires, and tutorials. Sonic paratexts often remediate other works by using functions and strategies from other examples of sonic paratexts (Potter 2013). Sonic paratexts often decontextualize video game music by presenting the music away from the games in which they originate. Sonic paratexts often act as a form of modern folk song by passing on information or lore to others in a way that can help develop a sense of community among players (Collins 2013). While sonic paratexts have been explored in relation to music education (Tobias 2013), we explore here some examples in relation to video games.

Covers often involve reimagining a popular song through the chiptune aesthetic in a variety of styles, such as alternative rock,[48] progressive rock,[49] classical,[50] jazz,[51] rap,[52] and electronic dance music.[53] One example covers the introduction of "Harlem Shake" by Baauer through computer software that replicates a variety of 8-bit era computer or console specifications to demonstrate what the song might have sounded like on each computer or console.[54] The specifications for each sound chip are displayed for each version of the song so that others can create their own covers in a similar manner. The video "8-bit Gangnam Style!"[55] not only covers the song with the chiptune sonic aesthetic, but recreates the music video within the 8-bit visual aesthetic. Other examples of covers often include multitrack a cappella versions of video game music. In these videos, some engage in another form of participatory culture known as *cosplay* where performers dress up in a manner that represents the game being sung. [56]

Mashups, like the multimedia appropriation "Baby Got Athletic," juxtapose video game music with other music. An example is a mashup of music from the video game series *Mario Kart* with the vocals from Taylor Swift's song "Shake It Off."[57] Sonic paratexts share similarities with machinima and vidding in that they reference or have direct connections to video games; however, sonic paratexts do not rely on using video games as part of the creative process.

Performing

While sonic paratexts can be created and shared digitally, some people perform them live. The group Video Games Live is a professional orchestra that performs video game–inspired arrangements and encourages concert attendees to compete in video game competitions, cosplay competitions, and even participate in the onstage performances by playing live video games that the orchestra accompanies,[58] or by singing along with familiar songs. Smaller performance groups, like Minibosses, perform video game music—often with a rock band setup—at various music venues (e.g., concerts, clubs, bars) and game venues (e.g., competitions, conferences, local gatherings) around the world.[59] Groups like the Minibosses will sometimes have video game imagery streaming in the background during performances to help contextualize the music being performed. Others perform alongside gameplay in a manner that is similar to pianists accompanying silent films.[60] In these ways, visual media and game play are important aspects of participants' musical engagement. Aside from these overt performance sessions, many people perform video game music in their leisure through formal or informal learning by ear or with some form of music notation, as suggested by descriptions in the "about" sections of YouTube videos that relate to video game music.

Most performances around video games might be seen as presentational music experiences (Turino 2009) as they are presented to live or virtual audiences in a manner that does not allow for audience participation in the music. However, these performances might also be understood as forms of participatory creative expressions that circulate media (video games or video game music) across time and space as they are shared with others. Furthermore, those who perform video game music might engage in collaborative problem solving when learning or teaching the music and leverage affiliations through their connections with others. These aspects of sonic participation reflect characteristics of participatory culture as outlined by Jenkins et al. (2009). In other words, considering the social and cultural contexts surrounding the performance of video game music can be helpful in understanding its connection to sonic participatory cultures around video games.

Affinity Spaces and Groups

Video game music affinity spaces and affinity groups are participatory spaces and groups in which forms of sonic participation are shared, occur, learned, or discussed (see Tobias and O'Leary 2016 for relations to music education contexts). While the terms "affinity spaces" and "affinity groups" are sometimes used interchangeably, *affinity spaces* tend to designate spaces or resources dedicated to a particular interest that people access, such as a wiki, whereas *affinity groups* often refers to the people engaging in and around a particular focus, such as creating sonic paratexts. In these spaces and groups the focus is on shared participation rather than personal identifiers such as gender, race, culture, sexuality, age, or even relationships between or among participants (Gee and Hayes 2010). Gee and Hayes stress how, in such spaces, both specialized and more general knowledge related to the group's focus circulates fluidly and in a manner in which people can work collectively to help one another. Affinity spaces provide everyone from beginners to experts with low-risk opportunities and multiple points of entry to share creative expressions, learn from, discuss, and converge around sonic participation within, through, and around video game music and sound.

At the time of writing, OverClocked ReMix[61] (OCR) is an affinity space with more than 12,000 remixes of video game music. These shared sonic paratexts can be uploaded or downloaded anonymously or by any registered member. When a downloaded sonic paratext is remixed by someone who visits OCR, these remixes can be uploaded on the website with attribution to the sonic paratext from which the remix derives. This is similar to what Swiss and Burgess (2013) describe as "collaborative poetry"; each of the creators of the original and remixed sonic paratexts have the opportunity to comment or ask questions to the creator and other visitors to OCR. In addition to sharing music, OCR hosts competitions, workshops, and forums that promote the participation and sharing of ideas and understandings with others who visit the affinity space or are members of the affinity group. While OCR is but one example of an affinity space with a focus on sonic participation around video games, several others like it exist. For instance, chiptune.com, chipmusic.org, micromusic.net, and other websites share and discuss the compositional form of chiptunes, the art of performing live chiptunes, and creating customized chiptune instruments.[62] The option to create and export music in *FRACT OSC* has created a following similar to *Mario Paint* as people create and distribute content such as songs,[63] tutorials, walkthroughs, and discussions in affinity spaces. Fans of *Minecraft* have created affinity spaces to assist with using redstone circuits and note blocks to make music. These redstone musical constructions are often shared via video and streaming services like YouTube or Twitch,[64] through podcasts, across multiplayer servers, or by copying and distributing a game's save file with the note block construction inside. Affinity spaces like abcnotation.com and LotRO-ABC.com contain hundreds of thousands of fan-created single and multipart ABC arrangements of music from the Renaissance to the present day, as well as original compositions using the ABC format that can be played in any game or program that uses the format. In some affinity spaces, aural skills are used to engage in collective analysis of sounds or music from older video games to imitate, through a VST, simulator, or emulator, the sounds of 8-bit games without having to use 8-bit hardware. A wiki can exist simultaneously as an affinity space and paratext that draws on collective intelligence to document fandom, history, lore, understandings, and so on (Mittell 2013) of video game music and sound.

The affinity spaces such as those discussed above have similarities with others that are focused on music but not games, such as the Finnish music site Mikserii (Partti and Karlsen 2010) and the Online Academy of Irish Music (Waldron 2011), and spaces not focused on music or sound, such as those around the game series *Civilization* (Squire 2011), *The Sims* (Gee and Hayes 2010), or similar affinity spaces (Hayes and Duncan 2012). The affiliations, informal mentorship, collaborative problem solving, and collective intelligence involved are common across many types of participatory cultures (Jenkins et al. 2009). The affordances of technology supporting affinity spaces, such as the integration of search and sort functions, also factor in one's explicit participation by providing or limiting opportunities for engagement and lowering the bar for involvement (Schäfer 2011).

Leisure and Sonic Participatory Cultures around Video Games

Sonic participatory cultures around video games reflect aspects of other participatory cultures where the appropriation of or interaction with existing content plays an important role. Some aspects of this engagement have their roots in fan culture, where people desire to interact with and participate with (rather than to solely consume) media they enjoy (Jenkins 2006a). This can be seen in the direct connection between video games and the content people create through sonic participatory cultures around video games. Sonic paratexts also involve skills and understanding specific to musical and technical domains. For instance, a person may draw on musical and technical skills and knowledge, ranging from performing particular pitches to identifying relation-ships between different music, when recording a multitracked vocal a cappella video or mashup of video game music. However, one might have in-depth knowledge of video games and technical skills with less developed musical skills or knowledge and still engage in the types of sonic participation outlined above. This might raise questions regarding: the role that quality plays in one's leisure, such as the time and effort that one exerts in sonic participation; the type of leisure in which one engages—whether it is casual, project-based, serious leisure, or devotee work (Stebbins, this volume, chapter 19); how people interact with each other and their expressions; or the roles that affinity spaces might play in one's leisure.

Affinity spaces serve as hubs for people to converge around shared interests in sonic participation, whether to share and circulate media (Jenkins et al. 2009), seek or provide assistance (Gee and Hayes 2010), or otherwise interact. The engagement that occurs in and through affinity spaces and groups not only supports leisure but can be seen as a form of leisure. Sonic participatory cultures around video games can be characterized by a unique ethos where a social world is constructed around participants' free-time interests that can support casual, project-based, or serious leisure (Stebbins, this volume, chapter 19), which may in turn foster a deep fulfillment akin to that which Smith (this volume, chapter 9) and Norton (1976) describe as eudaimonic.

Overlaps and Intersections of Sonic Participatory Cultures and Leisure

While this chapter organizes sonic participatory cultures into three separate sections (within, through, and around video games), the ways that people engage with video games, music, or sound can often flow across these multiple modes and contexts in overlapping and intersecting ways. One example substitutes the lyrics for Danny Elfman's song "This is Halloween," from *The Nightmare Before Christmas*, with lyr-ics that match the video game series *Portal*.[65] Not only is this video a sonic paratext posted on an affinity space (around), but the imagery from the game is dubbed with this new song to create a music video by using vidding techniques (through). The pre-viously discussed *Left 4 Dead* mod that uses clips from the song "Scatman" is a form of sonic participation *through* video games; however, it would fall into the category of sonic participation *around* video games if shared on an affinity space, and fall into the category of sonic participation *within* video games when played on a computer. Some forms of sonic participation might arise out of the high technical or musical barriers for engaging with music or sound through video games. For example, one might engage in film scoring for a recording of gameplay when creating new music for a video game, but lack the necessary skills to create new interactive music through modding.

LEISURE AS SONIC PARTICIPATION

Sihvonen (2011), in a discussion on the modding practices of the video game *The Sims*, suggests that "the malleability of the game thus functions as an incentive for the emergence of the multiplicity of gaming practices, each being negotiated in their own sociocultural setting and gaining meaning through individualist preferences" (166). Video games also act as incentives for the emergence of a multiplicity of sonic participation that occurs in a variety of social settings and affinity spaces that can blur the lines between leisurely and professional practices. More robust conceptual frameworks are needed along with additional work on the sonic participation addressed (and not addressed) in this chapter, and in-depth ethnographic studies of particular phenomena and those involved.

Additionally, this type of leisure, tied so closely to music and media industries, calls for critical analysis. For instance, the video game industry generally encourages modding as a form of explicit participation. The logic here is that modding is a "value-added" act; people might engage with a game longer if modding is possible. Because music and media industries can benefit financially from supporting participatory cultures and the forms of engagement that ensue by selling user-created content, or from when individuals' creations spur increases in game sales, this practice is sometimes described as a form of *playbour* (play + labour) (Kücklich 2005) from an unpaid co-worker (Schäfer 2011). In some cases, people creating mods and other user-generated content are compensated financially through agreements that may also benefit game developers. Additional research may be helpful in understanding relationships between implicit and explicit participation, sonic participatory cultures, economy, and power dynamics and their potential impact on leisure.

This chapter has outlined sonic participatory cultures within, through, and around video games as a productive site for better understanding how some people engage in leisure; however, additional research is needed to better understand who engages in sonic participation and why. At a minimum, acknowledging sonic participatory cultures at play within, through, and around video games sheds light on the richness and diversity of leisure in the context of video games, and potentially invites exploration of additional forms of interactive audio-visual media.

NOTES

1. Press Releases, *Entertainment Software Association*, April 14, 2015: http://www.theesa.com/article/150-million-americans-play-video-games/.
2. The 8-bit era is when gaming systems had relatively limited processing capabilities. These limitations led to a visual aesthetic that is characterized by pixelated imagery that lacks photo realism, and an audio aesthetic that is characterized by the use of sine, square, saw, and triangle waveforms along with white noise. Each type of soundwave is named after how the waveform

looks, and is accompanied by a distinct sound; white noise is equal harmonic distribution across the spectrum of the chip, and is commonly associated with the static ("snowy") sound on a TV. For more on 8-bit music, see writings by Collins (2006, 2008a, 2008b).

3. Schäfer, after Norman, describes affordances as the fundamental properties that determine how something is used. For our purposes, sonic affordances are the fundamental properties that determine how something can elicit sonic engagement.

4. http://youtu.be/Ico1Vhiyrb4.

5. A MIDI matrix is a grid where the x-axis represents a division of time within a phrase while the y-axis represents a pitch or sound (e.g., different drum sounds) that can be heard when a cell is turned on. A MIDI matrix puzzle is an aural dictation exercise where a player is matching the MIDI matrix to the game's music.

6. A game that supports large numbers of players (hundreds or thousands) who play with or against each other simultaneously.

7. "Griefing" is a practice where players intentionally cause grief to other players in a game. Sonic griefing occurs when a single player, or a group of players, spams songs in crowded areas, or interrupts other people's music performances, with the intention of griefing other players.

8. http://youtu.be/pnIpw_99b5c.

9. https://youtu.be/fU9woCZqemw.

10. http://youtu.be/9jX6qiwczcE.

11. http://youtu.be/vtbsje5dHtM.

12. http://youtu.be/_6SBTKmqakw.

13. http://youtu.be/yrkoM_CnoOo.

14. http://youtu.be/H8bqwwJaZwM.

15. http://youtu.be/a1KjPb_cViQ.

16. http://youtu.be/EIGGsZZWzZA.

17. http://youtu.be/GE3a7twiwTg.

18. https://youtu.be/B-UGixSMUUY.

19. Cosplay (costume + play) is a performance art common among fan cultures where cosplayers dress up as characters from, or styles within, a cultural product.

20. Parkour is a training discipline where participants move from point A to point B as quickly as possible; often while vaulting, climbing, running, and leaping over or between obstacles.

21. http://youtu.be/67qqEcGDCos.

22. http://youtu.be/NMpZrta2Cwc.

23. http://youtu.be/k3hZDwlcw3k.

24. http://youtu.be/MOnzz6321yk.

25. http://youtu.be/ZnZ5Mit2Q24.

26. http://youtu.be/rvBxQdaAk6c.

27. http://youtu.be/xgNo9P3Goig.

28. http://youtu.be/QoeCZCnVwSg.

29. http://youtu.be/MGPpMmXmxHo.

30. http://youtu.be/qukCulDOJzg.

31. http://youtu.be/X3E9gAL41Xc.

32. http://youtu.be/msK_YWowQ1U.

33. http://youtu.be/KpavJ5b32UY.

34. "NES" refers to the Nintendo Entertainment System. The "NES heyday" refers to the 8-bit era.

35. https://youtu.be/m5k1giMq1rM.

36. In binary code, the string of 0s and 1s in the heading of this section translates to "Chiptunes."
37. http://youtu.be/oipen5UN50Y.
38. http://youtu.be/-hisdP3sM9M.
39. http://youtu.be/hJjL7Hjwqfs.
40. http://youtu.be/kMh4YndbzHU.
41. http://youtu.be/m1pchpDD5EU.
42. http://youtu.be/S8e7g8kJIlo.
43. Horizontal resequencing, or branching, is a method where music segments are rearranged along a music timeline for continuous playing and variety. Vertical layering, or vertical reorchestration, is a method where multiple independent audio files can be stacked on top of each other to create variety. Procedural, or generative, music is based on indeterminacy (chance or randomization) through algorithmic variations within a game's code. For an in-depth discussion on these compositional method, see Collins (2008a, 2009), Paul (2013), Phillips (2014), Stevens and Raybould (2011).
44. http://youtu.be/y-7WQhYnKkw.
45. http://youtu.be/_Kd1Mzfp4_8.
46. See Stebbins, chapter 19, this volume.
47. http://www.samscoresninokuni.tumblr.com.
48. http://youtu.be/JjWXCbbSlIk.
49. http://youtu.be/SiGSrpZZFRg.
50. https://youtu.be/roHje14-K44.
51. http://youtu.be/hSCObIXDCJc.
52. http://youtu.be/FX6Yjsu6x40.
53. http://youtu.be/5DxQvWCn3aE.
54. http://youtu.be/1CO6ljU3vMs.
55. http://youtu.be/tWbKmS69PBM.
56. http://youtu.be/uyIHhI96Btk.
57. http://youtu.be/-TtWoXcc8PM.
58. https://youtu.be/spyc3WRimvc.
59. http://youtu.be/KswR1e-it-0.
60. http://youtu.be/VSBefGi7F-Y.
61. www.ocremix.org.
62. http://youtu.be/_kDhpFaf4EY.
63. http://youtu.be/BqBFTKLsgQ8.
64. Twitch is a social video service for gamers that allows live broadcasting of gameplay with commentary.
65. http://youtu.be/JZIVmKOdrBk.

References Cited

Ashcraft, Brian. 2015. "Man Plays *Super Mario World* with His Nose." *Kotaku*, January 28. www.kotaku.com/man-plays-super-mario-world-with-his-nose-1682088530.

Campbell, Patricia Shehan. 2004. *Teaching Music Globally: Experiencing Music, Expressing Culture*. New York: Oxford University Press.

Cassidy, Gianna G., and Anna M. J. M. Paisley. 2013. "Music-Games: A Case Study of Their Impact." *Research Studies in Music Education* 35(1): 119–138.

Cheng, William. 2014. *Sound Play: Video Games and the Musical Imagination*. Oxford: Oxford University Press.

Clements, Ann C. 2011. "Finding Your Groove with Popular Music through Video Game Technology." *Orff Echo* summer issue 44 (1).

Clements, Ann C., Tom Cody, and Beth Gibbs. 2008. "Interactive Gaming: Musical Communities in Virtual and Imagined Worlds." Paper presented at the conference "Cultural Diversity in Music Education Nine," Seattle, WA.

Collins, Karen. 2006. "'Loops and Bloops' Music of the Commodore 64 Games." *Soundscapes* 8. http://www.icce.rug.nl/~soundscapes/VOLUME08/Loops_and_bloops.shtml.

Collins, Karen. 2008a. *Game Sounds: An Introduction to the History, Theory, and Practice of Video Game Music and Sound Design*. Cambridge, MA: MIT Press.

Collins, Karen. 2008b. "In the Loop: Creativity and Constraint in 8-Bit Video Game Audio." *Twentieth-Century Music* 4(2): 209–227.

Collins, Karen. 2009. "An Introduction to Procedural Music in Video Games." *Contemporary Music Review* 28(1): 5–15.

Collins, Karen. 2013. *Playing with Sound: A Theory of Interacting with Sound and Music in Video Games*. Cambridge, MA: MIT Press.

Coppa, Francesca. 2008. "Women, Star Trek, and the Early Development of Fannish Vidding." *Transformative Works and Cultures* 1. http://journal.transformativeworks.org/index.php/twc/article/view/44/64.

Delwiche, Aaron, and Jennifer Jacobs Henderson. 2013. *The Participatory Cultures Handbook*. New York: Routledge.

Dolphin, Andrew. 2014. "Defining Sound Toys: Play as Composition." In *The Oxford Handbook of Interactive Audio*, edited by Karen Collins, Bill Kapralos, and Holly Tessler, 45–61. Oxford: Oxford University Press.

Gee, James Paul, and Elisabeth R. Hayes. 2010. "Passionate Affinity Groups: A New Form of Community That Works to Make People Smarter." In *Women and Gaming: The Sims and 21st Century Learning*, 105–123. New York: Palgrave Macmillan.

Gower, Lily, and Janet McDowall. 2012. "Interactive Music Video Games and Children's Musical Development." *British Journal of Music Education* 29(1): 91–105.

Grimshaw, Mark. 2012. "Sound and Player Immersion in Digital Games." In *The Oxford Handbook of Sound Studies*, edited by Trevor Pinch and Karin Bijsterveld, 347–366. New York: Oxford University Press.

Grimshaw, Mark, Siu-Lan Tan, and Scott D. Lipscomb. 2013. "Playing with Sound: The Role of Music and Sound Effects in Gaming." In *The Psychology of Music in Multimedia*, edited by Siu-Lan Tan, Annabel J. Cohen, Scott D. Lipscomb, and Roger A. Kendall, 289–314. Oxford: Oxford University Press.

Hansen, Kent, and Andreas Pedersen. n.d. "D-Pad Hero." http://dpadhero.com/Home.html.

Hart, Iain. 2014. "Meaningful Play: Performativity, Interactivity and Semiotics in Video Game Music." *Musicology Australia* 36: 273–290.

Hayes, Elisabeth R., and Sean C. Duncan. 2012. *Learning in Video Game Affinity Spaces*. New York: Peter Lang.

Ito, Mizuko, et al. 2010. *Hanging Out, Messing Around and Geeking Out: Kids Living and Learning with New Media*. Cambridge, MA: MIT Press.

Jenkins, Henry. 2006a. *Fans, Bloggers, and Gamers: Exploring Participatory Culture*. New York: New York University Press.

Jenkins, Henry. 2006b. *Convergence Culture: Where Old and New Media Collide*. New York: New York University Press.

Jenkins, Henry, Katie Clinton, Ravi Purushotma, Alice J. Robison, and Margaret Weigel. 2009. *Confronting the Challenges of Participatory Culture: Media Education for the 21st Century.* Chicago: John D. and Catherine T. MacArthur Foundation.

Kücklich, Julian. 2005. "Precarious Playbour: Modders and the Digital Games Industry." *Fibreculture Journal* .5: FCJ-025.

Miller, Kiri. 2012. *Playing Along: Digital Games, YouTube, and Virtual Performance.* New York: Oxford University Press.

Mittell, Jason. 2013. "Wikis and Participatory Fandom." In *The Participatory Cultures Handbook*, edited by Aaron Delwiche and Jennifer Jacobs Henderson, 35–42. New York: Routledge.

Norgren, David. 2013. "Minecraft Note Block Studio." http://www.stuffbydavid.com/mcnbs.

"Note Block." 2015. *Minecraft Wiki.* http://minecraft.gamepedia.com/Note_block.

Norton, David L. 1976. *Personal Destinies: A Philosophy of Ethical Individualism.* Princeton, NJ: Princeton University Press.

Paney, Andrew S. 2015. "Singing Video Games May Help Improve Pitch-Matching Accuracy." *Music Education Research* 17: 48–56.

Pasdzierny, Matthias. 2013. "Geeks on Stage? Investigations in the World of (Live) Chipmusic." In *Music and Game: Perspectives on a Popular Alliance*, edited by Peter Moormann, 171–190. Berlin: Springer VS.

Paul, Leonard J. 2013. "Droppin' Science: Video Game Audio Breakdown." In *Music and Game: Perspectives on a Popular Alliance*, 63–80. Berlin: Springer VS.

Paul, Leonard J. 2014. "For the Love of Chiptune." In *The Oxford Handbook of Interactive Audio*, edited by Karen Collins, Bill Kapralos, and Holly Tessler, 507–530. Oxford: Oxford University Press.

Partti, Heidi, and Sidsel Karlsen. 2010. "Reconceptualising Musical Learning: New Media, Identity and Community in Music Education." *Music Education Research* 12: 369–382.

Peppler, Kylie, Michael Downton, Eric Lindsay, and Kenneth Hay. 2011. "The Nirvana Effect: Tapping Video Games to Mediate Music Learning and Interest." *International Journal of Learning and Media* 3(1): 41–59.

Phillips, Winifred. 2014. *A Composer's Guide to Game Music.* Cambridge, MA: MIT Press.

Potter, James. 2013. "The Expanding Role for Media Literacy in the Age of Participatory Cultures." In *The Participatory Cultures Handbook*, edited by Aaron Delwiche and Jennifer Jacobs Henderson, 232–245. New York: Routledge.

Schäfer, Mirko Tobias. 2011. *Bastard Culture! How User Participation Transforms Cultural Production.* Amsterdam: Amsterdam University Press.

Sihvonen, Tanja. 2011. *Players Unleashed! Modding The Sims and the Culture of Gaming.* Amsterdam: Amsterdam University Press.

Squire, Kurt. 2011. *Video Games and Learning: Teaching and Participatory Culture in the Digital Age.* New York: Teachers College Press.

Stebbins, Robert A. 2007. *Serious Leisure: A Perspective for Our Time.* New Brunswick, NJ: Transaction.

Stebbins, Robert A. 2014. *Careers in Serious Leisure: From Dabbler to Devotee in Search of Fulfillment.* New York: Palgrave Macmillan.

Stevens, Richard, and Dave Raybould. 2011. *The Game Audio Tutorial: A Practical Guide to Sound and Music for Interactive Games.* Oxford: Focal Press.

Swiss, Thomas, and Helen Burgess. 2013. "Collaborative New Media Poetry: Mixed and Remixed." In *The Participatory Cultures Handbook*, edited by Aaron Delwiche and Jennifer Jacobs Henderson, 73–84. New York: Routledge.

Tobias, Evan S. 2012. "Let's Play! Learning Music through Video Games and Virtual Worlds." In *The Oxford Handbook of Music Education*, edited by Gary E. McPherson and Graham E. Welch, vol. 2, 531–548. Oxford: Oxford University Press.

Tobias, Evan S. 2013. "Toward Convergence: Adapting Music Education to Contemporary Society and Participatory Culture." *Music Educators Journal* 99(4): 29–36.

Tobias, Evan S., and Jared O'Leary. 2016. "Video Games." In *The Routledge Companion to Music, Technology and Education*, edited by Andrew King, Evangelos Himonides, and Stephen Alexander Ruthmann. New York: Routledge,

Turino, Thomas. 2008. *Music as Social Life: The Politics of Participation*. Chicago: University of Chicago Press.

Waldron, Janice. 2011. "Conceptual Frameworks, Theoretical Models, and the Role of YouTube: Investigating Informal Music Teaching and Learning in Online Music Community." *Journal of Music, Technology and Education*, 4(2–3): 189–200.

Williams, Bronwyn T., and Amy A. Zenger. 2012. *New Media Literacies and Participatory Popular Culture across Borders*. New York: Routledge.

Zehnder, Sean M., and Scott D. Lipscomb. 2006. "The Role of Music in Video Games." In *Playing Video Games: Motives, Responses, and Consequences*, edited by Peter Vorderer and Jennings Bryant, 241–258. Mahwah, NJ: Lawrence Erlbaum.

CHAPTER 29

"SINGER'S MUSIC"

Considering Sacred Harp Singing as Musical Leisure and Lived Harmony

THOMAS MALONE

AUTHOR'S PROLOGUE

IN this chapter I present a personally charged perspective informed by years of direct participation in the musical subculture known as Sacred Harp Singing. As a music educator and researcher I have traveled extensively within the Sacred Harp community, during which time I also completed my doctoral dissertation on the subject. I understand that, as a music and culture, Sacred Harp may be unfamiliar to many people and its norms and assumptions may differ from many other forms of choral music. Therefore, my goal in this chapter is to bring the reader closer to a less well-known view of music performance and participation, exploring how the values may vary in different contexts—especially those that operate outside of performance-based musical traditions. I do not intend to privilege Sacred Harp or any one type or tradition of musicking over another, but in some places my own voice, in identification with the Sacred Harp tradition, will serve to challenge the reader to consider things from an unaccustomed vantage point, and to potentially gain insights from the experience of dislocation from the familiar. My hope is that the occasional use of vignettes and narrative description, familiar to various qualitative research traditions, is helpful in creating the sense of a provocative encounter or conversation with a living point of view. Because participation in SH singing is open to all, readers of this chapter are encouraged to challenge my views by developing their own firsthand, and in no way to mistake this chapter for a definitive or exhaustive discussion of the topic.[1]

INTRODUCTION

Noted for its turbulent musical fabric of open and parallel fifths, high-decibel vocal production, and a grassroots DIY organizational structure, Sacred Harp singing has been described by the *New York Times* as "Gregorian Chant meets Bluegrass" (Greenfield 2007), and by San Francisco Public Radio as "The Punk Rock of Choral Music" (Aviram 2015). Yet, Sacred Harp singing (hereafter, SH) is older than either punk or bluegrass, and something far more than merely a niche genre or musical style (Nagoski 2006). SH is an enduring form of early American choral singing, "emphasizing participation, not performance, where people sing songs from a tunebook called *The Sacred Harp*, printed in music notation using four shaped notes" (Steel 2010, xi) (Figure 29.1).

While much of the core repertory, pedagogical roots, and compositional style of SH's four-syllable solmization system (known as "fasola") are rooted in America's colonial past, particularly the era of William Billings (Britton 1949; Grashel 1981; McKay and Crawford 1975), singing from *The Sacred Harp* tunebook remains a living, growing, and vital musical subculture that spans the continents of North America, Europe, Asia, and Australia, spreading and thriving without auditions, rehearsals, or performances (Miller 2008; Lueck 2014). Since most choral programs in education and in the professional sphere revolve around cycles of rehearsal and performance, SH offers a unique glimpse into a living choral practice that places value on neither. SH singers are unpaid volunteers and their participatory "singings" are free and open to the public, with daytime events held on weekends. Exploring SH through the lens of music as leisure therefore presents a promising means to help better understand this so-called "lost tonal tribe" (Jackson 1933. To that end, in this chapter I discuss participatory and social factors of music outside the presentational frame (Turino 2008), the ideas of serious leisure (Stebbins 1979, 1992), and philosophical notions of musicking and musical praxis (Elliott 1995; Small 1998) that help illuminate ways in which SH singing stands apart from the concertizing traditions of Western art music and choral performance.

SINGING WITHOUT PERFORMING

The website www.fasola.org states:

> Sacred Harp "singings" are not performances. There are no rehearsals and no separate seats for an audience. Every singing is a unique and self-sufficient event with

fa   sol   la   fa   sol   la   mi   fa

FIGURE 29.1 C major diatonic scale in four shaped notes with "fasola" syllables.

a different group of assembled participants. The singers sit in a hollow square for-mation with one voice part on each side, all facing inwards so we can see and hear each other.

For the SH tradition, singing in the hollow square does away with the dividing line between performer and audience, and, as indicated in the quotation above, eschews any notion of a separate audience at an SH singing. While there may be listeners near the back of the room, indicated by the circles on the far left of Figure 29.2, often these are family members of singers (living or deceased) who know the songs quite well and are present to help with other duties at the singing, so are not seen as separate or an audi-ence. The longstanding importance of the "hollow square" arrangement, in which sing-ers are arranged to face one another, is stressed by Hugh McGraw, editor of the 1991 edition of *The Sacred Harp*, who ties this seating arrangement to the lack of an audience, and to the philosophical ends of the singing itself in this passage excerpted from his 1984 teaching cassette "How to Sing Sacred Harp Music":

> Another tradition that goes with "fasola" singers is that they arrange themselves in a hollow square—the leader faces the tenor, bass is on the left, treble on the right, and the altos behind. The reason for the square is that "fasola" singers don't sing for an audience, they sing for their own enjoyment. (McGraw 1984)

While SH singers do sing for their own enjoyment, it is more than mere fun or enter-tainment, and yet a singing is not a church service, nor is it aligned with any single denomination. The texts are sacred, but the act of singing is a social one, and particulars of spiritual interpretation are left up to the individual. There is a particular reverence

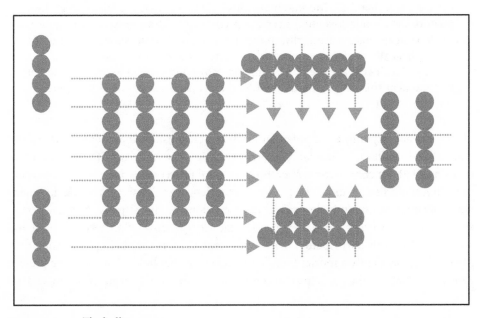

FIGURE 29.2 The hollow square

and joy described by singers, including those with no religious inclinations at all—a combination of exhilaration and exhaustion perhaps closer to Csikszentmihalyi's "flow" state than artistic, ideological, or aesthetic satisfaction or entertainment (Cskiszentmihaly 1990; Elliott 1995). Aristotle, whose work is foundational to contemporary views on music as leisure, asserted that such "eudaimonic" states of happiness or fulfillment (Smith, this volume, chapter 9) are inherently more available to the person of leisure who chooses to seek the enrichment of their personal spirit through musical activity than to the "vulgar" professional performer who works either to please an audience or to be compensated financially (Elliott and Silvermann 2014; Richter 2010). While this rather polarized distinction between paid and unpaid musicians is provocative, Aristotle's view does offer a compelling template for understanding the ways in which SH singing insists on placing itself outside of familiar commercial formats and presentational musical venues to maintain its essential characteristic as "singer's music."

"Singer's Music"

SH's deliberate and notable rejection of a performance orientation or professional ambitions is an essential component of its identity and aims, leading George Pullen Jackson to describe SH as "singer's music" (1944, 23), indicating that success and enjoyment in this music were centered among the interaction and interconnection of the participants with little or no concern for an assembled body of listeners or commercial enterprise:

> It would seem then that the Sacred Harp type of music is to be sung and not listened to, and that the critic who makes his judgments from the false observation point of the twentieth-century hearer is pretty sure to draw unhappy and impertinent conclusions.... And why, in the name of good sense, should she [the SH singer] bear the audience in mind when there is none. This is democratic music making. All singers are peers. And the moment selection and exclusion enter, at that moment this singing of, for, and by the people loses its chief characteristic. (Jackson 1933, 123)

Here we begin to glimpse the potential for SH to be considered as a living example of choral music without a familiar Western aesthetic or performance frame—a culture that sings without concertizing, a "culture of choral praxis" (Malone 2009). As a result, meaningful discussion about the lives and experiences of SH singers begins to depart from considerations routinely applied to discussions of choral presentational *performance* and/or *aesthetics*, since there is no acknowledged distinction between artist and audience. With this participatory orientation central to its very being (Clawson 2011), SH singing is evidently a music "founded on an ethos that holds that everyone present can, and in fact should, participate in the sound and motion" (Turino 2008, 29). As the mechanics of an SH singing may not be familiar to the general reader, in the following section I present the basic logistics of this musical culture and how it operates in practice.

The Leader and the Lesson

An important locus where the sounds, motions, and ideas of SH singing converge is in the shared musical directorship of the group that takes place in the center of the hollow square. In place of a single conductor, "leaders" are called from the body of singers and are free to direct the group in a song of their choosing. Their brief time in the center of the square, the song they select, and the manner in which they direct are called their "lesson." Clawson writes:

> Every attendee at a singing, from children too young to read to adults too old to stand unaided, is given an opportunity to lead by standing in the middle of the square, fac- ing the tenors, and beating time. The entire group sings the leader's song choice at his or her chosen tempo . . . no song is led more than once a day and no one leads twice until all have had an opportunity to lead once. (2010, 6)

This rotating sequence of leaders is arranged so that anyone who wishes to direct may have a turn to direct the group during the singing, and provides an element of impro- visational spontaneity, since no one knows which song will be next or when they will be called. Singers often choose their song to complement or contrast with the song that preceded theirs, making each singing a unique conversation of text and tones evolving in real time. By doing away with concepts of a fixed order (as one would find in a con- cert), and the roles of both audience and conductor, SH upends the authoritarian power dynamics and top-down leadership structures found in most forms of choral perfor- mance, prompting Alan Lomax to pen the following description in his liner notes for the highly influential recording of the 1959 United Sacred Harp Convention in Fyffe, Alabama. Lomax (1977) writes:

> All conducted [led] capably . . . there was no prettying up of the voice. The atmo- sphere was totally democratic, all participants displaying confidence in their natu- ral voice, each adding his embellishments and variations to the written part. This combination of musical skill and passionate individualism creates a thrilling choral texture, far from the classically admired blend, but a quite original and fascinating way to perform counterpoint. . . . Here, I thought, is a choral style ready made for a nation of individualists.

In the many decades since the early writings of Jackson and Lomax on the subject, scholarly interest in this "punk rock" choral music, and the people who keep it alive, has continued to grow, documenting the roots of SH as a social/sacred music among small Protestant communities in the southeastern U.S. (Cobb 1989: Jackson 1952, its expansion through folk festivals, workshops, and groups on college campuses (Bealle 1997), to its present status as an international musical subculture (Lueck 2014). Recent scholarship has emphasized ways in which cultural and vocational backgrounds of SH singers span a wide range of seemingly irreconcilable religious, political, and cultural spaces:

> You might find that of two women smiling next to each other, one is a devout Christian and the other an atheist Jew, or a row of people in matching "Camp Fasola" t-shirts may include a gay man, an Amish man, a Polish woman, and an Anglican from Canada. (Clawson 2011, 138)

Hospitality and Lived Harmony

Through their distinctive embrace of pluralism, SH singers foster deeply meaningful and lasting personal bonds with one another across demographic and ideological boundaries, through experiences of shared travel and intense music making (Miller 2008), all without top-down directives and large-scale funding from a single established religious, educational, or cultural arts organization. Eschewing such hierarchies, SH depends on an in-house culture of hospitality (see also Howell, Higgins, and Bartleet, this volume, chapter 31) and reciprocity that involves housing and feeding traveling singers at no charge, and mutual support across various geographic regions:

> Being a Sacred Harp singer brings great rewards of emotional energy, but also imposes sacrifices, especially of time and travel costs, and entails obligations. Members are expected to inquire after one another's well being across very wide geographic distances. Local hosts of annual conventions provide room and board for out-of-town singers they may not know. (Heider and Warner 2010, 19)

As a result, the accomplishments and commitments of an individual who has realized the identity of an established SH singer involves far more than musical talent or vocal ability; it requires a profound commitment of personal resources and time, and frequently becomes the prime organizing feature on the landscape of one's personal leisure. Such dedicated SH singers will organize vacations and travel plans, and structure family and even long-term employment decisions around SH singing calendar dates and places. In this way, it is more than a style of music—it is a *harmony that the singers live* with the very stuff, time, and resources of their social and professional lives. Being an SH singer is a lifestyle, a form of belonging, and, as Heider and Warner put it, "a salient identity cross-cutting other identities" (2010, 19)—or as the title of this chapter proposes, *a lived harmony*.

WHO BECOMES AN SH SINGER, AND WHY?

The social and demographic backgrounds of SH singers are varied, ranging from families in rural agricultural communities to the heads of departments in major universities

(Bealle 1997; Clawson 2011). While the material of SH music is religious in nature, there is no test or requirement for faith or belief to become an SH singer. The open-door nature of this musical tradition with its "come all ye" attitude and lack of auditions and rehearsals is a major appeal to persons who have been rejected from other forms of choral music making (Miller 2008, 128), or who have been told simply that they cannot sing (Knight 2010; Welch 2006). The fact that SH's musical fabric of abundant parallel fifths and octaves and full-voiced nonvibrato vocal production violates the musical norms of almost all other Western choral forms allows SH to serve, for some, as an "antichorus," a place to relish in a high-decibel form of dissent from standard sacred choral norms (Malone 2011, 14). SH music offers meaningful insights as a culture of choral praxis precisely because it exists for its own doers and not for the aesthetic needs of an audience or for evaluation by the familiar performance standards and traditions of more widely known concert-based choral practices. As a result, the music of SH singing is often beautiful but not always pretty.

A first-time hearer of SH singing may find it difficult to understand how this music, with its crashing maelstrom of pulsing chords, occasional tramping of enthusiastic feet, and strident *fortissimo* vocal barrage of syllables could be a relaxing escape from the stresses of daily life, or a form of spiritual enrichment. Yet, according to Turino (2008), musics with a dense and turbulent texture are ideally suited for participatory engagement because novices can join and find their place in the sound without drawing attention to themselves. He writes, "Dense textures and timbres are the most common traits of participatory music, and they have an important role in inspiring participation" (44). Furthermore, the various harmonic parts and musical actions that SH singers do (beating time, reading shaped notation, singing text underlaid with various musical lines) provide multiple points of entry for persons of various skill levels and experience, so that beginners can participate at their own level and still function as a genuine part of the musical fabric as it being created. For example, singers may ignore the shapes and syllables at first and learn the tunes by ear, or focus on keeping time and sight-reading rather than on the poetry of the lyrics.

As Heider and Warner (2010) describe, as one develops increased familiarity with the many interactive and ritual elements of SH singing, along with the tunes and poetry shared by the community, this swirling tempest of words and tones amidst the orderly square formation of chairs that defines the singing space, becomes a spiritual home or a second family to many of its dedicated participants. The rapidly executed patterns of the four fasola syllables and the shapes (see Figure 29.1) that singers use to sight-read the music are a type of ritual language that provides a challenge and learning opportunities for the novice, while conferring a feeling of ownership and belonging for those who have become fluent with their use (Heider and Warner 2010, 13; Miller 2008, 94). In the next section I discuss pathways to becoming a self-identified SH singer and a few of the challenges and moments of cultural disorientation that are inevitably presented to those who choose to make the journey.

"Oh, Who Will Come and Go with Me?"

Although SH, as a participatory music, is open to all, pathways to encountering it are far from obvious nor widely broadcast. SH singing has rarely been portrayed in film and television, with the exception of the 2004 film *Cold Mountain* and the 2006 documentary *Awake My Soul* (Hinton and Hinton 2006), and it cannot be heard with regularity on any commercial radio format. Thus, to pursue SH singing following an initial encounter requires willingness to risk personal discomfort and even transformation. As a lived harmony, it is a participatory music that cannot be learned at a distance. In some instances it takes its participants quite literally off the grid, into remote rural areas where cell phones do not work and modern conveniences may not be relied upon. As a result, its various cultural practices and musical norms often have to be learned by direct experience mixed with trial and error, a loose apprenticeship of self-initiation and voluntary induction, along with the help of more experienced SH singers.

Those who find value in their experience of early encounters with SH singing may choose to return and develop new understandings of and relationships to the music and the community of singers, while those who do not find value in the challenge are unlikely to return. An inevitable process of self-selection takes place through which certain profiles of SH singers and their common traits can be loosely sketched, even though there is no one single entry point or formalized pathway to finding and joining the SH community. I offer three vignettes that illustrate pathways by which one may begin to develop a personal identity as an SH singer. The general types presented here will be familiar and generalizable narrative tropes for those who have traveled within SH singing culture (Bealle 1997; Miller 2008).

Vignette #1: Born into It

Certain families and regional areas have deep historical roots with the SH songbook and its singing tradition (Steel 2010). These families or communities often include singing-school teachers, prominent local music leaders, and in some cases composers with songs in the book. For children who grow up in such families, the songs and texts may be intimately familiar through informal family singings, funeral services, and humorous parodies sung for recreation, even if their family rarely attends an SH singing school or convention.

While lifelong singers who excel in the SH community are held in particular esteem, not everyone who is born into such a family has the desire or opportunity to make important contributions. Many singers who do make such contributions may be culturally Southern, but have discovered the music recently (Miller 2008, 4, 34). Even within these singing families a large part of the family may have rejected SH singing as "old-fogey music" some generations ago, and it is in many cases a small outlying branch of the larger family that continues the passionate dedication, at times in defiance of their own church communities, who look on it as distraction from real worship, at best, and a semisecular "cult" at worst (Cobb 2014, xiii).

Vignette #2: Chance Encounter

For some SH singers, their introduction was a chance encounter, usually at a folk festival, college campus, or semipublic SH singing event. Often the sound of the voices and percussive feet strikes a resonant emotional accord with them before they even know what they are hearing. This type of singer is often "hooked" before they sing their first fasola syllables because of the visceral power of that first sonic impact. Since these encounters may take place apart from any religious context, and often appear to present SH as a folk tradition apart from any sacred or regional context, such participants may have less interest in the religious procedural traditions that come with organizing sing-ings or conventions, although these perspectives may shift once friendships are formed with more traditionally rooted singers (Bealle 1997).

Vignette #3: Media Encounter

This form of chance encounter is similar to the one above, but involves an audio record-ing, video, or piece of digital media that makes an impact on the individual, prompting them to want to understand more about SH culture, and what kind of people would gather to make this unusual sound. Before the advent of YouTube, the most common recordings serving this purpose were *Rivers of Delight* by the Word of Mouth Chorus and the 1959 *United Sacred Harp Convention* recorded by Alan Lomax (Bealle 1997; Miller 2008, 160). The rise of Facebook and YouTube in the past decade has led to a new form of archival and interpersonal sharing of SH in sound and image, including personal writings, videos, and contact information, which can link singers and newly interested individuals in ways never before possible. Today's young adult population—politically liberal, college-educated, religiously noncommittal, and musically omnivorous—forms a logical extension of the general demographic template of SH's northern tier over the past thirty years, people who, for the most part, likely discovered the music through college activities. For this population, assisted by the interconnectivity of the Internet age, the unprecedented spread of SH singing culture (at least their particular form of it) to Ireland, Germany, and Poland would seem to be a natural outgrowth of their own formation of an SH identity, whereas SH singers who are "born into it" may be faced with the prospect of belonging ipso facto to a global movement that may or may not resemble, in each particular, the SH singing culture of their parents and local region.

SH and the Musical Mainstream

While these three vignettes may describe in general only some common pathways to the lifestyle of an SH singer, perhaps they bring to light a larger trait shared more widely by many in the culture: the willingness to stand apart from the popular majority in terms of views and values, to risk being marginalized or ignored by mainstream culture and defiantly to find unity through that experience (Miller 2008, 160). Another aspect of their attraction may be the uncompromising vocal timbre and intensity of SH's musical fabric itself. The sound is charged, powerful, and captivating, with limited capacity for sudden or subtle or predictable changes in speed or direction that might help accom-modate the mainstream musical listener—nor is there any desire to do so. Attempts to popularize the sound of SH by merger or hybridization with pop or indie rock styles, for example 2010's "Tell Me Why" by M.I.A. or 2012's "Death to My Hometown" by Bruce

Springsteen, rarely succeed in pleasing either constituency beyond an initial and short-lived spark of recognition or novelty from either the pop or SH camp. Perhaps bringing the raw, untamed essence of SH into a more widely listened-to prerecorded musical idiom is problematic because a defining aspect of SH's nature, as with its participants, is to stand apart from more widely enjoyed commercial and popular forms. This is as true today is it was in the 1930s, when George Pullen Jackson observed that, "phonographic recordings of this strange choral music have not sold to any considerable extent" (1933, 126).

SH as Serious Leisure: "What Does One Get from It, Anyway?"

How does a musical subculture such as SH survive and grow without commercial commodification, a large governing or organizational body, or highly visible professionals or media figures to demonstrate and promote examples of excellence and right action in the music itself? Where does the motivation lie for thousands of singers to travel and sing across geographic, cultural, and ideological boundaries, weekend after weekend, month after month, year after year? Or put simply, "What does one get from it, anyway?" (Jackson 1944). One possible answer might be revealed best through the lens of leisure studies. What one *gets from it*, though experienced through music, is not musical in itself, but rather akin to what Aristotle called *eudaimonia*—an intrinsic benefit in the form of an enrichment of the mind and personhood through an active voluntary musical study or pursuit. Aristotle's idea and the nature of value found by participants in music-as-leisure were expanded upon in a provocative blog post by University of Sydney professor Goetz Richter (2010):

> In other words they have their *ends in themselves* and *not in the products* of their making. This, however, means that music is not driven by an intention to make a product with attributes that exist outside the activity of production. Music is thus not driven at all. It is *leisured*—it lets itself—and those who make it—be. [emphasis added]

Aristotle, in a manner quite like SH singers, placed a higher value on music making that is not product-based or commercial in nature (see also Smith, this volume, chapter 9). Aristotle viewed the *professional* musician as a potentially disreputable character, contrasted with the actively contemplative mind that chooses music as a form of leisure, a notion that harmonizes with my earlier assertion that SH cannot be properly understood in comparison to musics that are performance-based, and why the idea of a "professional" SH singer is anathema. Viewed from this philosophical perspective, the ends of SH are not musical per se, but exist in the enrichment of its participants through a shared experience of recreation, edification, and intellectual and artistic cocreation—"contemplation . . . music . . . and citizenship"—some of the characteristics that Aristotle saw as the means by which music-as-leisure provides a path to eudaimonic happiness (Owens 1981). Jackson described SH singers' particular form of happiness thusly:

> The group as a whole got its catharsis in songs and tears . . . a blessing that cannot descend on those ominously great masses of mere hearers of music. If these people were not happy, in the best and fullest meaning of the word, then I have never seen human happiness. (1933, 120)

There Are No Amateurs in Sacred Harp, and No Professionals Either

Stebbins and colleagues provide a useful lens for understanding SH singing as *serious leisure*, defined as:

> the systematic pursuit of an amateur, hobbyist, or volunteer core activity that is highly substantial, interesting, and fulfilling and where, in the typical case, participants find a career in acquiring and expressing a combination of its special skills, knowledge, and experience. (Stebbins 1992, 3)

An initial insight gleaned by directly applying Stebbins's Serious Leisure Perspective (SLP) to the phenomenon of the SH singing community is the realization that there are no "amateur" SH singers, simply because there is no such thing as a "professional" SH singer and no way to make a career in SH singing (notwithstanding Stebbins's 2014 notion of "careers in serious leisure"—see Smith, this volume, chapter 9). While the word "amateur" may be casually used to describe the untrained voices and grassroots organizations of SH singers and their activities, it is not appropriate when applied from the SLP. According to Stebbins, "Amateurs are people who engage part-time in activities that, for other people, constitute full-time work roles. One cannot be an amateur butterfly catcher or matchbook collector; no opportunity for full-time employment exists here" (1979, 14). Therefore, in the SLP model SH singers would better be viewed as hobbyists, activity participants, or more particularly as *folk-artists*, who "perform or produce strictly for their own enjoyment and perhaps that of others in the same community, while making their living in some other fashion" (Stebbins 1979, 35) (see Figure 29.3).

Attempting to place SH singing neatly on the SLP concept map shown in Figure 29.3 reveals that, while not in the same category as the amateur, the hobbyist is in no way less "serious." Stebbins indicates that the word "serious" in this context denotes not formality, but "the importance of these . . . types of activity in the everyday lives of participants," and the fact that they engender "deep self-fulfillment" (Stebbins 1992, 3). Other elements found in various hobbyist pursuits that may apply in the case of SH singing include travel for broadening awareness, the development of physical stamina and

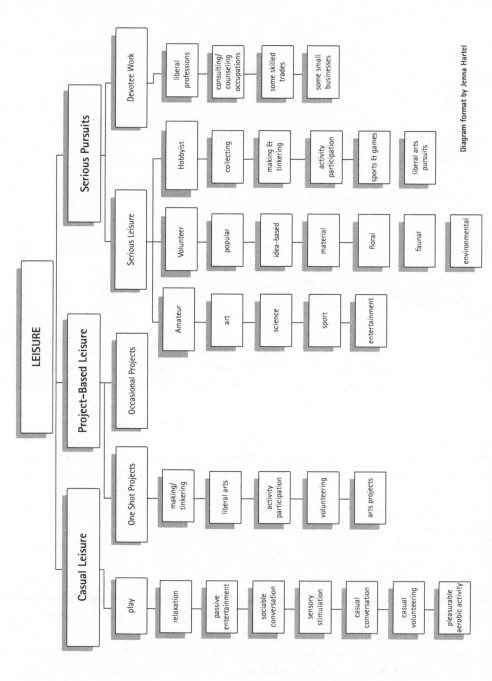

FIGURE 29.3 Serious Leisure Perspective Concept map (Hartel 2013).

Diagram format by Jenna Hartel

LEISURE

Casual Leisure
- play
- relaxation
- passive entertainment
- sociable conversation
- sensory stimulation
- casual conversation
- casual volunteering
- pleasurable aerobic activity

Project-Based Leisure

One Shot Projects
- making/ tinkering
- liberal arts
- activity participation
- volunteering
- arts projects

Occasional Projects

Serious Pursuits

Serious Leisure

Amateur
- art
- science
- sport
- entertainment

Volunteer
- popular
- idea-based
- material
- floral
- faunal
- environmental

Hobbyist
- collecting
- making & tinkering
- activity participation
- sports & games
- liberal arts pursuits

Devotee Work
- liberal professions
- consulting/ counseling occupations
- some skilled trades
- some small businesses

endurance through direct and continued experience of SH singing, and the existence of a spiritual dimension in aspects of the practice itself, not unlike, for instance, a martial art or meditation-based discipline. So, while SH singers view their pursuit as far more than a mere hobby, this deep fulfillment (*eudaimonia*) would ring true to their experience more than any cloaked aspirations to a possible career in musical performance embedded in understandings of the word "amateur."

"I Belong to this Band"

One of the most apparent benefits of being an SH singer is the feeling of belonging to a larger group with a sense of "authenticity and connection to tradition. Singers from the urban North who may move frequently and do not live near extended family can find in Sacred Harp a greater sense of rootedness" (Clawson 2011, 167). Yet, belonging for the SH singer is not like that of, say, a Civil War reenactor or cosplayer, because the SH singers do not imagine themselves in a different time or assume a borrowed or alternate identity. The website www.fasola.org states that "participants are not concerned with re-creating or re-enacting historical events. Our tradition is a living, breathing, ongoing practice passed directly to us by generations of singers, many gone on before and many still living." SH singers are not merely simulating an anachronistic activity that attracts their interest and admiration, in a form of personal homage or *fandom*. The new SH singer may feel he or she has discovered a musical outlet in contemporary life that music education programs and the wider culture appear to have overlooked or forgotten. A singer who feels they have no prospects for a musical life or active community can find exactly that—a choral group where "no one's singing is criticized or publicly corrected" (Heider and Warner 2010, 8). They find themselves in a singing movement that offers a very real model of lifelong music making and learning, since the participants regularly span the entire human lifespan with the very young and the very old each given the same respect and authority when directing the group of singers (Clawson 2011). Viewed in this light, for those who choose to become more deeply involved with it, SH offers all of the apparent interpersonal and social benefits of belonging to a "hobbyist" club, strengthened and catalyzed by the musical actions of keeping time, harmonizing, listening, vocalizing, and reading notation in a nonjudgmental group setting. Is it no wonder, then, that SH tends to "draw its adherents in deep—and hold them" (Cobb 2014, xiv).

Sacred Harp Addiction? Ritual, Flow, and Self-Knowledge

The ability to navigate one's own vocal part correctly in the complex and tangled texture of the SH's rapid-fire folk polyphony requires focus and concentration as well as aerobic, physical, and cognitive endurance. In a typical day of SH singing, participants regularly sing as much as four hours of music or more. That is as much as (or more than) is found in many Wagnerian operas! While all SH music may sound alike to the outside listener, there is in fact a variety of harmonic styles found in the songbook, and singers gradually discover the varying challenges and rewards of each (Steel 2010, 39). Thus, the skills and concentration required to read the notation, solmize the syllables correctly (Grashel 1981), follow the text and repeats, and pace one's energy and vocal resources for four hours of music making indicate a type of functional music literacy rivaling that required for larger, professionally oriented groups and styles (Jackson 1933, 116).

The profound dedication and bewildering vocal stamina of SH singers, along with their willingness to travel long distances at great personal expense to sing with one another, begs the question: could SH singing be a type of addiction? (Heider and Warner 2010, 15; Malone 2009, 220; Miller 2008, 75). The idea is not a new one, as the following quote from a revered SH teacher reveals.

> Tom Denson famously stated in one of his early-1900 singing schools, "If some of you don't like this music. . . . All I've got to say is you'd better get out. If you stay here it's going to get a-hold of you, and then you *can't* get away." (Cobb 2014, xiv)

In some cases, SH takes hold of certain individuals and becomes not just an activity among many that occupy the landscape of their leisure space, but the singing community becomes the space in which leisure is planned for and takes place. Travel plans, family vacations, and visits with old friends are adjusted to include singings in various parts of the country that may be held only at a certain time of the year. Vacations to Europe that may never otherwise have materialized are now budgeted for, since SH singing communities are developing in Poland, Ireland, and Germany (Leuck 2014).

In seeking to uncover more about the appeal that draws SH singers to, in the language of a popular SH song, "fly to unknown lands," I have posited in an earlier piece of writing (Malone 2009, 169) that one element is a structural aspect of the harmonies themselves, particularly the intonation of certain Pythagorean and "just" intervals in combination. These tunings and their effects cannot be heard in commercial music and cannot be felt the same way, even in recordings of SH singings—"Their effects are felt in the visceral impact of the singing itself and in emotional or spiritual peak moments. The bio-physical response to certain chords could explain why SH is something of an addiction to its participants" (Malone 2009, 220). Therefore, like the memory of a certain flavor that lingers in the mind, the *sensation* of being immersed in SH's unique, cocreated sonic structures compels the individual to seek out the people and places that can bring them back to that visceral experience.

Heider and Warner remind us in their discussion of SH as interactive ritual that "Doing patterned things together induces feelings of solidarity" (2010, 3), and that a chief characteristic of interactive rituals is their ability to engender feelings of intense solidarity "even in the absence of ideological consensus." They propose a theoretical model in which certain elements of collective consciousness such as shared mood, bodily copresence and focused attention "feed back on one another," yielding at times a potent release of social and emotional energy that Durkheim called *collective effervescence* (Heider and

Warner 2010, 15). Citing the work of Randall Collins (2004, 39), Heider and Warner note that this "feeling of emotional energy has a powerful motivating effect upon the individual; who ever has experienced this kind of moment wants to repeat it."

I'd Soar Away above the Sky

The intensive physical, emotional, and cognitive demands of SH singing lead to a phenomenon akin to the well-known "runner's high," which is understood to arise from the release of endorphins in response to prolonged physical and aerobic exertion. SH singers will often tell you that the peak of a singing is the session that follows the break or lunch, and this is where the most skillful and respected leaders of music are often seen in peak action. The effect of the skillful leader successfully taking the choir through a difficult piece is felt by the group, and can inspire novices to consider remaining in the SH community, and eventually attain similar command of the music. In such peak moments, while an inexperienced singer may feel they are being buffeted thrillingly on every side by fierce waves of sound in a tempest of crashing chords and angular harmony, a nearby experienced or fluent SH singer will be elevated by this same outpouring of energy. In such moments, the waves of "collective effervescence" (Heider and Warner 2010, 15) carry and uplift everyone in the room. The analogy of waves is an apt one, not only due to the preponderance of wave imagery in the texts and corresponding text painting in many of the popular rapid and contrapuntal "class songs" typically enjoyed after the midday meal, but because the act of riding or being carried by this tide of human voices and energy often leads one to the experience of flow and the widely described peak experiences in SH singing. As Heider and Warner (2010, 10) describe, "Eventually many singers reach a moment where the connection between the eye, the vocal folds, and the mouth bypasses the cerebral cortex, and [the syllables] fa, sol, la, and mi roll off the tongue correctly and easily without ratiocination."

While Csikszentmihalyi's theories of flow and optimal experience were originally derived from studying phenomena experienced by athletes, Elliott demonstrated their applicability to music in *Music Matters* (1995) as a cornerstone of his "praxial" philosophy of music. Elliott observed that within any musical moment there exists a balance between the challenge inherent in the task and the skill of the musician in relation to the task; when those are in balance the optimal experience or "flow" state is the result, with its accordant insight: "*I am the one doing this thing well.*" According to Elliott, repeatable experiences of this type, such as musical participation, have the effect of engendering moments of self-growth and self-knowledge for individuals as human beings, and not merely as musicians. As Turino (2008, 4) notes, "Because 'flow' experiences are pleasurable, people return to the activities that provide them again and again." This, argues Elliott, is a prime reason that human beings engage in music making at all—as a particular type of available and collectively generated "flow" experience, granting opportunities for increased self-authorship and knowledge.

In this way, any perception of SH singing as an addiction might be more correctly seen as a compulsion or desire to reengage with the ends of music making itself. The continuing urge to reengage with the challenge of SH singing as one's skills develop is simply the seeking out of the most potent flow experience available, to continue toward the goal of self-knowledge in the unique way that only music can offer. This perspective, taken with Heider and Warner's Durkheimian notions of interactive ritual and its ability to produce solidarity across demographic lines "where it had not previously existed," offers a rich theoretical framework with which to understand the deep personal commitments and peculiar joy or *eudaimonia* that flow from the peak experiences described by SH singers:

> Republicans and Democrats; devout Christians, Jews, Buddhists and atheists; farmers and college professors, all come together to sing a music in which individual voices are at once allowed to be themselves, not rendered smooth and featureless through classical training, but at the same time are subsumed in a mass of sound so that no one stands out. Sound rises and swells and bounces off the walls, physically tangible at times and catching the singers up in a consuming momentum. Sweat-stained clothes and speaking voices revealed by break time conversation to be hoarse show the physical effort of singing, but singer's expressions—their joy and their grief—as they sing, show the power this music and the experience of participating in it has over them. Through singing, they become a community. (Clawson 2011, 166)

"TRAVELING ON": THE GLOBAL FUTURE OF A REGIONAL PRACTICE

Were it not for the centuries-old value placed on reciprocal travel and hospitality among the singers, there might be no reason to think that SH singing would be more than a small, remote regional phenomenon today. The roots of this culture of mutual visitation can be seen among the eighteenth-century itinerant singing school teachers of the Billings era, who traveled and taught for weeks on end, paid only room and board, and bartered goods (Cooke 1986). There is reciprocity as well in the nineteenth-century Southern practice, where teachers, delegates, and representatives of the Southern Musical Convention and Chattahoochee Convention, among others, traveled between regional singings as emissaries from their local conventions (Cobb 1978, 60, 120).

In the twentieth century, the practice of travel and reciprocity was brought North by Hugh McGraw, who helped establish the first Conventions and All-Day Singings outside of the South (Bealle 1997, 200). McGraw was instrumental in founding and mentoring emergent university and folk-music-based groups in New England and the Midwest regions. As people began to show increased interest in the songbook and its traditions, he would travel to support and shape their practices to stand on the basic logistical and structural foundations of organized conventions and singings as practiced in the South. With him came a committed group of Southern singers who would travel to larger

Northern singings and, by doing so, formed the bonds that led to the Northern singers traveling south and visiting them in their home singings (Miller 2008, 77).

All of this reciprocity and growth took place apart from the professional and work lives of the participants. This process of uniting the social, spiritual, and musical lives of demographically and geographically disparate people around "the hollow square" was done on weekends, and was not conceived as a money-making enterprise. Thus, the space for SH singing might well be identified as belonging to personal leisure, exemplifying how, as Heider and Warner (2010, 2) proposed, SH does not merely "express solidarities, it creates them," and through interactive ritual actions it attains the capacity to supersede ideological and geographic boundaries. To this end, a SH teaching camp, called Camp Fasola, began in 2003 and has drawn numerous singers to travel to rural Alabama, thus extending the ties of friendship and reciprocity to an unprecedented transnational reach, including longitudes in Europe, Australia, and Asia (Williams 2015). While travel of such great distances entails risk and financial cost, many of today's traveling "teacher composers" make these journeys at their own expense, seeking only room and board (and transformative experience through music) in return. While dedicated and deeply invested in SH music and its continued growth and vitality, these SH community members have jobs and, like their antecedents in earlier centuries, do not (and can not) make SH their profession.

Conclusions

Consideration of SH singing through the Serious Leisure Perspective reveals that, whatever SH singers may be, they are neither amateurs nor professionals. SH's identity—and that of its singers—is entirely bound up in remaining a participatory form of musicking, operating outside of aesthetic considerations that arise from the separation of artist and audience. Just as Aristotle warned of the "dangers of introducing business, urgency and confusion into this art of leisure" (Richter 2010), SH singers can be genuinely affronted if their music is described as a performance or concert; for them it is something higher and nobler than that. In their pursuit of music they seek intrinsic, eudaimonic benefits, attained through musical interaction:

> Music is in the first instance a self-sufficient activity and hence a reflection of human freedom and autonomy. It is an activity of leisure, an activity which calls on our capacity for reflection, for listening, for calmness and relaxation and for the acceptance of the present in its presence. Music does not primarily crave public success. It invites human participation. It leads an autonomous existence of creative possibility and freedom. (Richter 2010)

This is a defining characteristic of participatory musics:

> What is important to understand is that for certain social groups throughout the world, participatory music, dance, sports, and festivals are not merely the informal

sidelines to the "real" event—professional athletics music and entertainment—but rather they are the center of social life. (Turino 2008, 35)

With the recent success of a new Camp Fasola in Poland (Perycz 2013) and the growth of other new singing communities worldwide, it appears SH singing will continue to offer its participants a vital and enriching form of serious leisure. In the unlikely event that professional aspirations were to emerge, they would irrevocably change the fabric of this music culture more than any changes of demographics or geographic reach. As George Pullen Jackson once observed, "the moment selection and exclusion enter," Sacred Harp singing is "at risk of losing its chief characteristic." By eschewing performance, and cultivating reciprocity hospitality and musical engagement for all, SH remains for its participants, not a genre or ensemble type, but a lived harmony.

NOTE

1. I wish to thank the editors for the opportunity to discuss this music through the framework of music making and leisure. The aims and scope of this volume offer an ideal setting for a reader's initial encounter, in print, with a form of musicking whose unique set of sonic and social characteristics are as complex and multivalent as the individuals who choose to participate in it.

REFERENCES CITED

Aviram, Shani. 2015. "Sacred Harp: The Punk Rock of Choral Music." *KALW*, May 28. http://kalw.org/post/sacred-harp-punk-rock-choral-music.

Britton, Allen Perdue. 1949. *Theoretical Introductions in American Tune-Books to 1800*. Ann Arbor: University of Michigan Press.

Bealle, John. 1997. *Public Worship, Private Faith: Sacred Harp and American Folksong*. Athens: University of Georgia Press

Clawson, Laura. 2011. *I Belong to this Band Hallelujah: Community, Spirituality and Tradition among Sacred Harp Singers*. Chicago: University of Chicago Press

Cobb, Buell. 1978. *The Sacred Harp: A Tradition and its Music*. Athens: University of Georgia Press

Cobb, Buell. 2014. *Like Cords Around my Heart: A Sacred Harp Memoir*. Denver: Outskirts Press

Collins, Randall. 1975. *Conflict Sociology: Toward and Explanatory Science*. New York: Academic Press.

Collins, Randall. 2004. *Interaction Ritual Chains*. Princeton: Princeton University Press.

Cooke, Nym. 1984. "Itinerant Yankee Singing Masters in the Eighteenth Century." In *Itinerancy in New England and New York*, edited by Peter Benes, 16–36. Boston: Boston University Press.

Csikszentmihalyi, Mihaly. 1990. *Flow: The Psychology of Optimal Experience*. New York: Harper and Row.

Elliott, David J. 1995. *Music Matters: A New Philosophy of Music Education*. New York: Oxford University Press.

Elliott, David J., and Marissa Silverman. 2014. "Music, Personhood and *Eudaimonia*: Implications for Educative and Ethical Music Education." *TD: The Journal for Transdisciplinary Research in Southern Africa* 10(2): 57–72.

Hartel, Jenna. 2013. "Diagrams of the Serious Leisure Perspective." *Serious Leisure Perspective (SLP)*, www.seriousleisure.net/slp-diagrams.html.

Heider, Anne, and R. Stephen Warner. 2010. "Bodies in Sync: Interaction Ritual Theory Applied to Sacred Harp Singing." *Sociology of Religion* 71(1): 76–97.

Hinton, Matt, and Hinton, Erica. 2006. *Awake My Soul: The Story of the Sacred Harp.* Videorecording. Directed by Matt and Erica Hinton. Atlanta: Awake Productions, 2007c. DVD.

Grashel, John W. 1981. "The Gamut and Solmization in Early American Texts." *Journal of Research in Music Education* 29(1): 63–70.

Greenfield, Beth. 2007. "Concerts by (and for) Singers." *New York Times*, April 20, Section E.

Jackson, George Pullen. 1933. *White Spirituals in the Southern Uplands.* Chapel Hill: University of North Carolina Press.

Jackson, George Pullen. 1944. *The Story of the Sacred Harp, 1844–1944.* Nashville, TN: Vanderbilt University Press.

Jackson, George Pullen. 1952. *Another Sheaf of White Spirituals.* Gainesville, FL: University of Florida Press.

Knight, Susan. 2010. *A Study of Adult "Non-singers" in Newfoundland.* Unpublished Ph.D. diss., Institute of Education, University of London.

Lueck, Ellen. 2014. "The Old World Seeks the Old Paths: Observing Our Transnationally Expanding Singing Community." *Sacred Harp Publishing Company Newsletter* 3(2), November 12. http://originalsacredharp.com/2014/11/12/the-old-world-seeks-the-old-paths-observing-our-transnationally-expanding-singing-community/.

Lomax, Alan. 1977. *White Spirituals from the Sacred Harp.* United Sacred Harp Convention. New World Records. NW 205. [Liner notes]

Malone, Thomas B. 2009. "The Rudiments as Right Action: Pedagogy and Praxis in the Traditional Sacred Harp Singing School." PhD dissertation, Boston University.

Malone, Thomas B. 2011. "Let us Sing! The Sacred Harp as a Culture of Choral Praxis." Paper presented at the MayDay Colloquium 23, Salt Lake City, June 16–19.

McKay, David, and Richard Crawford. 1975. *William Billings of Boston: Eighteenth-Century Composer.* Princeton, NJ: Princeton University Press.

Miller, Kiri. 2008. *Traveling Home: Sacred Harp and American Pluralism.* Urbana: University of Illinois Press.

McGraw, Hugh. 1984. *How to Sing Sacred Harp Music: Its History and Traditions.* Bremen, GA: Unique Musical Services.

McGraw, Hugh. 1991. *The Sacred Harp: The Best Collection of Sacred Songs, Hymns, Odes, and Anthems ever Offered the Singing Public for General Use.* Bremen, GA: Sacred Harp Publishing Company.

Nagoski, Amelia. 2006. "Mode and Method: A Choral Conductor's Guide to Concert Performance Practice of Sacred Harp." *Choral Journal* (October): 38–47

Owens, Joseph. 1981. "Aristotle on Leisure." *Canadian Journal of Philosophy* 11: 713–723

Perycz, Gosia. 2013. "A Hollow Square in My Homeland: Bringing Camp Fasola to Poland." *Sacred Harp Publishing Company Newsletter* 2(1), March 14. http://originalsacredharp.com/2013/03/14/a-hollow-square-in-my-homeland-bringing-camp-fasola-to-poland/.

Richter, Goetz. 2010. "Music and Leisure." *Thinking about Music: Sounding out Silence* [blog]. March 6. http://blogs.usyd.edu.au/thinkmusic/2010/03/music_and_leisure.html.

Small, Christopher. 1998. *Musicking: The Meanings of Performing and Listening*. Middletown, CT. Wesleyan University Press.

Steel, David Warren. 2010. *The Makers of the Sacred Harp*. Urbana: University of Illinois Press.

Stebbins, Robert A. 1979. *Amateurs: On the Margin between Work and Leisure*. Beverly Hills, CA. Sage.

Stebbins, Robert A. 1992. *Amateurs, Professionals and Serious Leisure*. Montreal, QC: McGill-Queen's University Press.

Stebbins, Robert A. 2014. *Careers in Serious Leisure: From Dabbler to Devotee in Search of Fulfilment*. New York: Palgrave Macmillan.

Turino, Thomas. 2008. *Music as Social Life: The Politics of Participation*. Chicago. University of Chicago Press.

Welch, G. F. 2006. "Singing and Vocal Development." In *The Child as Musician: A Handbook of Musical Development*, edited by G. McPherson, 311–329. New York: Oxford University Press.

Williams, Kathy. 2015. "A Long Time Traveling: A Sacred Harp Tour to the UK Convention, Camp Fasola Europe, and the Poland Convention." *Sacred Harp Publishing Company Newsletter* 4(1), May 15. http://originalsacredharp.com/2015/05/28/a-long-time-traveling-a-sacred-harp-tour-to-the-uk-convention-camp-fasola-europe-and-the-poland-convention/.

CHAPTER 30

....

"DJ HIT THAT BUTTON"

Amateur Laptop Musicians in Contemporary Music and Society

....

SHARA RAMBARRAN

INTRODUCTION

....

THE aim of this chapter[1] is to consider, from a socio-cultural perspective, the phenomenon of amateur laptop musicians in the contemporary digital age. It will highlight positive aspects of being a laptop musician, such as learning a new musical skill for leisure purposes and sharing music with peers. It will also highlight negative elements, such as the failures of audiences and some musicians to value developments in technology that, if appreciated, could result in creative works and experiences for both musicians and audiences. Finally, I discuss how the laptop can be appreciated *as* a musical instrument (or music machine, the term preferred by some musicians).

Digital technologies have motivated people to create music in a variety of ways (Bennett 2016; Duckworth 2005; Rambarran 2013; Théberge, 1997). Paul Théberge, in fact, makes the uncompromising claim, "Without electronic technology, popular music in the twenty-first century is unthinkable" (2001, 3). The use of technology has undeniably resulted in challenging and exciting ways of producing, performing, and consuming music, including providing those who create and perform music with opportunities to explore and experiment with an infinite number of sonics and structures.[2] Technology can be considered an *appliance* (the device or instrument to perform a sound) or *reliance* (the device or instrument to rely on the user for instruction or execution). Ranging from instruments to recording equipment, hardware to software music storage devices, technology assists many musical activities. This is encouraging for amateurs who wish to make and learn music at their own paces and in their own ways (see e.g., this volume, O'Leary and Tobias, chapter 28; Bell, chapter 5). Digital technologies have motivated individual users of technology to create music in a variety of ways (Bennett 2016; Duckworth 2005; Rambarran 2013; Théberge, 1997).

Bennett (2005, 233) tells us that "music is far from being merely a passive pleasure"—current forms of experiencing and making music may involve journeying the routes of folk (passing music through communities and across generations), education (learning to play an instrument, understanding the musical language, and building, for example, motor and social skills), or fast-tracking to the peak of the pop music industry for superstardom (via "reality" television competitions, for example). I argue, therefore, that music making is widely pursued and enjoyed as a leisure activity, individually and socially, as indeed it has been for centuries. Due to the developments and applications of digital technology, one could point to a shifting understanding of the term "musician," perhaps alongside a related debate around what is considered to be "music" (a discussion of which there is not sufficient room in this chapter). While digitally produced music practices have been adopted by countless thousands of musicians, some musicians and audiences may reject digitally produced music—or, to be more precise, music produced with what is perceived as "disruptive technology."

I use *disruptive technology* positively to describe the alternative and unexpected uses of technology, which can be achieved only by its manipulator, that is, the operator-user of the device. A common example would be the digital sampler, a device designed to store musical sounds (mainly simulations of musical instruments). Originally used mainly in professional recording situations, the digital sampler earned its reputation among amateurs who used the device to collect and store sounds from sound recordings, deploying these in the creation of music in genres such as hip-hop, electronica, and electronic dance music (EDM).[3] It took many years for those disrupting the use of technologies such as the sampler and turntable (as musical instrument)—e.g., hip-hop and EDM DJs—to be accepted as musicians, especially in academia and education (see e.g., Snell and Söderman 2014). At the time of writing, there appears to be another disruptive use of technology that has been developing for more than a decade—the laptop computer. Before exploring the laptop musician further, I turn to discussing the notion of the amateur.

The Concept of the Amateur

The "amateur" musician is not a new concept or phenomenon, but it is worth considering the socio-cultural context of his or her role in music briefly here. First, however, we need to consider the general concept of the amateur before we can understand the amateur musician. Defining the word "amateur" is complex, as noted by Wayne Booth who claims that amateurs are often regarded as "avocationists, connoisseurs, would-be or pre-professionals, leisure-timers, recreationists, hobbyists" (1999, 9). We can already see that this term is multidimensional, as Booth highlights various meanings attached to the word. He argues that the term can be negative if one thinks of its definition as someone who is inexperienced in an activity (9). Booth, however, insists that the word "amateur" is also positive, especially if one thinks of it as referring to people with a sense of passion when participating in an activity, and the eagerness to learn more of its skills and practices (9). With this in mind, the amateur should be considered as one who participates in an activity in an avocational and not in a vocational (i.e., professional) manner. While a professional (regardless of field) is usually seen as qualified (in terms of a high level of expertise, knowledge, training, and, if applicable, paid service), an amateur may have no desire to gain recognition or income in a particular domain. It is common, however, for the amateur and professional to have similar interests in a particular activity, as noted by Robert Stebbins, who argues that participants gain durable benefits of the same activity such as "self-actualization, self-expression . . . feelings of accomplishment, enhancement of self-image and enduring tangible products of the activity" (1980, 414). The potential emotional results of pursuing an activity, then, are similar for both the amateur and professional participants. Benefits include achievement of a fulfilled ambition and recognition of skills by their peers and the public, as these may motivate musicians to develop their abilities.

What divides the two "types" of participants is that the professional is likely to receive more opportunities for their work. The amateur (regardless of field) may not be considered as "serious" in their activity despite the dedication they may offer toward it. This is observed by Robert Drew when he states, "Amateurs share many professional attributes, if at less intensive levels: knowledge of technique . . . established institutions and traditions, and high standards. Yet, common parlance equates them with dabblers and dilettantes, and they are often stigmatized as inferior aspirants to professional status" (1997, 449). While Drew's observations regarding the position of amateurs—as "dabblers and dilettantes," or nonserious and superficial—may at first appear convincing, these terms may not be as applicable in the case of amateur musicians. The amateur musician may in some instances receive almost the same recognition and response as the professional, except perhaps in monetary terms. It is also likely that if amateurs wish to showcase their skills in a public environment, they may be semiprofessional (i.e., almost of professional standard but not quite) rather than professional, or amateur (see e.g., Smith, this volume, chapter 9).

When the term "amateur" is used, it is often in a leisure (and not paid work) context, meaning that it is an activity that takes place in a participant's free time. Therefore, to understand what constitutes an amateur, it is important to identify the ways that people participate in leisure activities. Stebbins convincingly identifies two types of engagement: those of the "amateur" and the "hobbyist" (1980, 414). The hobbyist participates in an activity purely for personal interests, comparable to the "dabbler" and "dilettante" identified by Drew; participation is on a largely individual basis and there are no intentions to transition the hobby into professional status (416). There is more to consider when identifying the amateur, however. While the amateur and hobbyist take part with similar intentions, that is, for leisure, pleasure, to gain knowledge, and/or, develop a skill, the amateur may desire to progress further by reaching out to the public and perhaps building networks with professionals. Stebbins refers to this as the Professional-Amateur-Public (PAP) (414) system, where an amateur's activity can draw the attention of either the professional, the public, or both. This can result in various outcomes for the amateur, such as personal achievement and a reputation. If an amateur, however, gains a positive reaction from the public, he or she may then be presented with an opportunity for turning their activity into a vocation (415). It is also worth noting that professionals frequently begin their leisure pursuits as a consumer (public), then an amateur, and then work their way into gaining professional status. Earning professional status "is governed by access to the different resources and opportunities available for making music" (Kirschner 1998; Shuker 2012, 53), as well, of course, as being a marker of expertise in the field.

The Amateur Musician

Anyone, regardless of musical ability, can participate in music, or "musicking," as famously suggested by Christopher Small, who said, "To music is to take part, in any capacity, in a musical performance, whether by performing, by listening, by rehearsing or practicing, by providing material for performance" (1998, 9). How can we apply this generous concept to the amateur musician? The academic material on amateur music making has been fairly limited. One notable exception is Ruth Finnegan's book *The Hidden Musicians*. Like Booth, Finnegan finds that defining the term "amateur" is complex (1989, 12).

There are many areas to consider with regard to the terms "amateur" and "professional" musician, but for the sake of this discussion it is appropriate to maintain that the musician is an amateur for avocational purposes. Relative to Stebbins's PAP system, musicians or nonmusicians who participate in musical activity for nonprofessional purposes would be identified as amateurs (Finnegan 1989, 15; Small 1998, 10). How an amateur musician emerges varies: whether it is through cultural practices (e.g., tradition, religion, education), social formations (e.g., friends forming groups or attending musical activity groups such as a choir), or through an individual's intention or desire to learn and master a musical skill by acquiring inspiration from established musicians and music (this could be influenced by attending concerts, watching performance video, or by listening to music).

It is likely, then, that a keen musician entering the field of music or, in this context, a particular music making community, would at first be considered a "local nonprofessional opportunist" (Finnegan 1989, 17). How they learn to play music will vary, as they may choose to pay for private tuition, learn in an educational establishment, join in extracurricular activities, or "teach themselves" (for example they may learn to play by ear; read books, guides, or magazines; learn from friends; or watch live and prerecorded instrumental lessons on digital online platforms such as YouTube). For the self-taught musician, Bennett argues that they will "not have the benefit of a more experienced musician as a guide . . . a beginner can therefore proceed at his or her own speed" (1990, 224). It is then up to the individual how they develop their musical skills, along with the decision to remain an amateur or aim to become a professional. Participants in music may learn through traditional methods of music making (e.g., established methods in classical, folk, or rock; see Green 2002; Veblen and Waldron 2012) or, as noted by Mark Katz, through technologically mediated means such as a player piano, phonograph, karaoke, hip-hop, music videogames, and smartphone apps (see e.g., Katz 2014, 476; Morris 2016; O'Leary and Tobias, this volume, chapter 28; Randles 2013; Snell and Söderman 2014). This of course, may lead to controversy as to whether technology should be regarded as musical instruments or a contribution in music. John Philip Sousa highlighted the threat of the demise of (professional) musicians and music teachers due to technology when he claimed that "[t]he child becomes indifferent to practice ... when music can be heard in the homes without the labor of study and close application, and without the slow process of acquiring a technique" (Sousa 2012, 116[4]). Although Sousa argued this more than a century ago, and he was referring to the growth of mechanical music at the time (the phonograph), this statement could also apply to subsequent music and communication technologies that may disrupt traditional music and music learning practices (such as composing music traditionally through instruction and tuition).

Nontraditional musicians, such as experimentalists, may be more likely to explore the instruments and machines when creating and performing music. Here, one may immediately think of John Cage's innovative work for "prepared piano" (e.g., "Amores, Solo for Prepared Piano," 1943) created by placing objects such as bolts and screws inside the piano (on its hammers and strings, for example), or the *musique concrète* of Pierre Schaeffer and his friend Pierre Henry, who both composed and performed works using "nonmusical" sounds. Today, hip-hop and electronica musicians similarly manipulate sounds. If new trends and techniques arise in creating music, the increasing ubiquity and affordability of technology should be considered as a constant assistance in the development of music making and performing. If there are concerns about or opposition to incorporating technology in music, it seems likely that in time (and depending on individuals' choices), musicians, whether they are professional or amateur, will continue to adapt to and adopt these changes. Returning to the concept of the amateur musician in a cultural tone, we do need to further understand why amateurs may wish to learn music.

The Cultural Context of the Amateur Musician

François Noudelmann (2012) explored the amateur music making of philosophers Jean-Paul Sartre, Friedrich Nietzsche, and Roland Barthes, focusing on a particular area of their lives: their passion for playing the piano. Noudelmann demonstrates how these famous thinkers blurred the distinctions between professional and amateur musicianship, and consumer behavior. Like Finnegan, Noudelmann finds that the word "amateur" is ambiguous because it depends on a musician's intention for playing. He questions the intention to learn to play music (2012, 95–96): is it to learn a skill, gain knowledge, or simply play for pleasure (or a combination of all)? In the cases of Sartre, Nietzsche, and Barthes, playing the piano enabled them each to elaborate their

understanding of the music and what was happening around them socially and culturally. For example, playing music encouraged them to play with emotion and temporal-
ities, which led Noudlemann to ask how "abstract thinkers experience emotions, the
body and touch? How do they find themselves implicated and disconcerted by these
feelings, these movements, and these durations of time?" (10). For Sartre, reading and
playing music were purely for leisure purposes. While playing musical scores, Sartre had
"fun with them, playing them half seriously, half sarcastically—as an actor caught up in
his own imagination" (11). Therefore, Sartre saw a way of playing for escapism, but yet at
the same time he could imagine that he was a serious performer.

Nietzsche, who lived immersed in music, took musical performance very seriously.
As his ability in piano playing was so advanced, it was hard to distinguish whether he
was a professional (i.e., expert, knowledgeable, trained) or an amateur (playing for pleasure and gaining a sense of self-actualization, accomplishment, and skill). As a musician, Nietzsche would study Chopin and Schumann deeply, as he wanted to feel their
emotions in their music (Noudelmann 2012, 64). Barthes, on the other hand, simply
played the piano for pleasure (107), in an innocent and disorderly way. He had a particular fondness for playing Schumann because his music was "*relational*, a reconciliatory
conjunction of subjectivity and objectivity, spirit and flesh" (Leppert 2012, 120). Barthes
argues, "There are two musics . . . : one you listen to, one you play . . . the same composer
can be minor when listened to, enormous when played (even poorly)—take Schumann"
(1977, 149). Therefore, when Barthes would attempt to play the music of Schumann, he
would offer a suggestion of the piece, such as changing the tempo or skipping musical passages, rather than mastering the musical works note by note (Noudelmann 2012,
104). Barthes admitted that it was his lack of technical skill that prevented him from
playing pieces perfectly, yet it was his way of playing the piano, and it was his best effort
in showing his appreciation and interpretation of Schumann's works.

Thus we may be able to make some general observations about amateur musicians: they may be viewed as non- or semi-skilled and possess motivations that differ
from professionals (e.g., a parody of original music or a drunken karaoke performance).
Amateurs can also display emotion in music (to be discussed below) but may not be
concerned about the reaction they may receive from the audience, but this will depend
on what they are hoping to achieve with their performance (such as a sense of accomplishment or an aim to reach professional status). The different approaches to playing
discussed here may apply to amateur musicians in any time period or genre—take for
example, an amateur musician in the current age of digital technology.

As noted earlier, Paul Théberge argues that popular music and technology are inseparable (1997, 2001). This is becoming increasingly true for many amateur musicians today,
since, as Katz observes, "[the] majority of amateur music making involves some sort
of technology mediation" (2014, 473). Digital technology in particular has offered various new opportunities in music making. The original creators and users of the sampler
and turntable, for example, were amateur musicians for the purpose of manipulating
preexisting music in genres, including hip-hop and electronica. Today, the "mash-up"[5]
is a thriving practice (see e.g., Rambarran 2013; Serazio 2008; Shiga 2007; Sinnreich

2010; Whiteley and Rambarran 2016). This manipulation could arguably have started only among amateurs because of their playfulness and experimentation with technology. Leading examples in hip-hop include DJ Kool Herc, Grandmaster Flash, and Grand Wizard Theodore, and their use of the Technics SL-1200 turntable, or the Acid House DJ team Phuture, and their use of the Roland TB303 synthesizer. The disruptive nature of such technologically mediated practices was perceived at the time as unprofessional by established musicians (Katz 2014, 471).

While it has been argued that we are witnessing "the rise of a new class of musicians, one directly tied to a technology long held to discourage, not promote, the musical amateur" (Katz 2014, 471), evidence from amateur musicians indicates that this discouragement is far from effective. Affordable software and computer programs have become accessible to many consumers, allowing them opportunities to create and perform music, almost regardless of ability (in terms of musical and computer knowledge). This is certainly evident, as we are now constantly surrounded with music produced by "amateurs," whether in a video game, an app for a smartphone or tablet, or, as I shall discuss, *laptop music*.

The Laptop Musician

Musicians have found countless ways of making music with technology. New technologies have enabled individuals to experiment in composing and performing. The laptop has been used as an instrument and music machine for over a decade and has enhanced (as well as to some extent perhaps begun to replace) other traditions of music making. The laptop computer is a significant example of a disruptive technology because "the computer removes the need to use anything other than itself" (Hugill 2008, 134). Common applications of this music machine exploit its potential as a mobile instrument, for example, for running VST (virtual studio technology) and DAW (digital audio workstation) software, which means the user can compose music without being constrained to (or building) a recording studio, thereby save money in recording equipment (see Bell, this volume, chapter 5).

Another factor to consider in using the laptop as an instrument or music machine is that the operator may need only to use a mouse or press buttons to play the music. This will depend on the skills that the operator (or indeed the musician) may possess and the software that they may use as the creation involved in the compositional (and operational) process will vary. For example, operating, playing, or performing is surely comparable, say, to a pianist who presses "keys" on a piano to create and produce sounds and compose music? There is also the ability of the user of the instrument to consider: how they discover and learn to play the instrument, which itself requires (and acquires) some form of creativity. These concepts are ideally convincing but can in fact be problematic, which furthers the question of how laptops can be regarded as an instrument. For example, scholar and journalist Erik Davis asks: "First software has turned the laptop into a musical instrument. Now who is in control: the machine or the musician?" (2002). Davis highlights that musicians are almost unlimited in how they create (or recreate) sounds on the laptop, and that opponents and exponents will have to learn to adapt to these technological changes. Davis suggests, however, that live "performances" may not be as interesting and spectacular to watch as traditionally performed musics, remarking, "Calling up audio files and filters with a QWERTY keyboard lacks the visual punch of a guitar solo and drumroll, and often there isn't a link between a keypunch and change in sound. Is it live or is it Memorex? . . . For all I know [she] . . . might have spent her time playing [virtual reality computer game] *The Sims*" (2002).

There are also issues of honesty in performance. Attias has cited cases of well-known, professional DJs who have been "caught in the act," where they have performed "live with disconnected equipment or faders in the wrong position" (2013, 23), which could only suggest that the music was being played by the computer, but not "performed" by the musician. In 2012, Canadian laptop musician Joel T. Zimmermann, also known as Deadmau5, infamously stated: "I don't have any shame in admitting that for 'unhooked sets' . . . I just roll up with a laptop and a MIDI controller and 'select' tracks and hit a spacebar" (Deadmau5 2012a, 2012b). Some professional musicians did not respond to this statement favorably. For example, Mr. C, real name Richard West (of 1990s U.K. electronica group The Shamen), responded to Zimmermann by saying, "FYI Deadmau5, there's a magic that happens when 2 tunes are mixed together properly by a real DJ & I don't mean by a software program . . . Now you run along & carry on button pushing to play your cheesy pre organized shit" (cited in Fish 2012). Although West was deeply irritated by Zimmermann's comment, he does acknowledge that laptop musicians can indeed be appreciated as musicians, but only through application of skill and technique: "If a DJ uses a laptop to be creative, have split second timing on various points that are marked in tracks, create loops, free up time to use samples and effects, then that's creative & OK" (cited in Small 2013). West's disdain recalls the famous critiques of John Phillip Sousa about the mindless execution of technology, lacking in "human skill, intelligence and soul" (Sousa 2012, 114).

Soloists, Collaborators, and Virtuosos

So why does the laptop appeal to the amateur music maker? I would like to propose three types of amateur laptop musician: the *soloist*, the *collaborator*, and the *virtuoso*. One facet of laptop music making that might attract the soloist is the aforementioned mobility of the instrument. The portability of the instrument has already been observed by musicologists such as Nick Prior, who remarked that, "[d]esigned to travel with the user, the laptop frees work from fixed working environments whilst inserting the user into . . . dispersed spaces" (2008, 916). For the soloist, applications could include remixing other people's works or constructing playlists in their various spaces, such as an office or bedroom. This could result in moments of escapism for the soloist, who just wants to learn about and explore making music. Just like the consumer who listens to music for private pleasure, the soloist laptop musician wants to indulge in their music making in private. Glenn Bach argues that "[l]aptop musicians spend so much time on their laptops, establishing such intimate relationships with their machines, that they appear to inhabit spaces implied by the words, images and sounds scrolling down and across the screen" (2003, 4). Amateur musicians may become heavily engaged in exploring the instrument, but for private purposes and leisure only. They may or may not intend to share their achievements and discoveries with peers, recalling the earlier description of Sartre, who preferred to play and perform piano in his own private space. The soloist may also feel sufficiently comfortable and confident to take their laptop to local places and spaces and play their music.

There are various ways in which musicians collaborate, whether it is to create (including mixing and remixing), exchange ideas, or perform. To facilitate this, they participate as collaborators in more traditional popular music ensembles, in laptop jams (Duckworth 2005, 162; Prior 2008, 913), laptop ensembles (O'Brien 2016), or a Scenius (a term coined by Brian Eno to describe a serious group improvising live; see Jeffries 2010). These collaborations can take place anywhere, such as in a café, living room, or in virtual/cyberspace (in real time or asynchronously over the Internet from various locations). Whether the musicians are a duo or a small group, their intention to collaborate will often transition from making music for purely leisure to making it for semiprofessional purposes (e.g., performing in larger and public spaces and places but not necessarily to generate income—see e.g., Smith, this volume, chapter 9). Share (formerly known as Share DJ), for example, is a laptop project formed in 2001, in which sessions take place in the Open Air Club in New York. Here, amateurs play and jam freely on their laptops, encouraged "to show and exchange ideas, giving each other feedback, catalyzing development of techniques and philosophies in new media" (Manalog interview cited in Duckworth 2005, 162). The Share project has since grown internationally (Amsterdam, London, Warsaw, Berlin).[6]

Other opportunities arise in virtual collaborations, where "each laptop musician virtually receive[s] and transmit[s] various combinations of audio, video, and control-message data over a shared network" (O'Brien 2016, 377). Collaboration in a laptop music session can be a time-saver because the participants do not have to carry vast amounts of equipment or physically move out of their space if they are having a long-distance or virtual collaboration, or a jam in a personal space (e.g., a living room). Music making in these ways can be accessible and cost-effective. The type of music making will vary, whether it is remixing, experimenting, improvising, or suchlike. Regardless of their musical ability, collaborator laptop musicians are attempting to show and share their musical passion by playing the laptop, for creating, performing, or both. If their intention is to perform live and demonstrate their skill in public places or spaces, then an ideal reward may be peer-recognition for their creativity.

The virtuoso can be seen as the amateur or professional who has learned and mastered the instrument in order to share music with peers and outsiders. Virtuosos are willing to perform live and hope to gain individual reputations as musicians, or at least recognition for their music. As with the soloist and collaborator, the choice of musical genre and type of composition varies, but it is likely that the virtuoso is leaning more toward experimentation—writing and producing her or his own music. In a live situation, virtuosos are likely to have a complex musical set-up (such as a controller, mixer, synthesizers) so that they can display their skills in public, and perhaps, put on a performance.

Flexibility and Options

For amateurs, the laptop serves as "the portable music making machine [of the new age], kind of like the guitar in the 1960s [and before]" (Rolnick, cited in Duckworth 2005, 164). The laptop as a mobile instrument or music machine means that it not only helps to produce and play the sounds that the musician has created, but the device (as a hardware and instrument) can also serve as a virtual recording studio and digital workstation, anytime and anywhere. It is, however, important to remember that the laptop cannot function as an instrument (or a virtual recording studio) without musical software (Prior 2008, 920).

Laptop musicians may use something simple such as GarageBand, eventually building their software set-up by investing in sound libraries, plug-ins, virtual instruments (such as Native Instruments), audio effects (e.g., Vengeance), and DAWs such as Logic or Pro Tools. More advanced musicians may opt for Max/MSP, where they can control, experiment, and create audio plug-ins, processors, and sounds. And then there is Ableton Live, which perhaps has contributed most to a rise in popularity of laptop music making. Ableton software was invented by German electronic group Monolake as a response to the nonavailability of software that specialized in live composition and recording (as opposed to previous software that was designed for recording, mixing, and playback).[7]

Performing as a Laptop Musician

John Richardson reminds us that there is a "corresponding visual component" (2012, 243) when music is performed. In this case, the music that is composed solely using digital technologies can liberate performance space and may shape the musician's performance. For instance, if we consider genres such as rock, jazz, pop, and classical, the musicians (and audience) may associate a particular place and space with the music that is likely to be performed (e.g., a rock band preforming in an arena) (Frith 1996; Warner 2003). For the machine users, unless it is some form of electronic dance music (where it is likely to be consumed in a club), the space is "mobile" and the use of such machines has "freed sounds from a performance context" (Frith 1996, 6–7), thus giving performers freedom as to how they perform. This then should challenge, if not encourage, our thinking on how we should view a performance. Take, for example, the laptop musician who performs live. The laptop musician, once set up and ready to perform, does not move his or her instrument, nor does the musician "move" (in some cases)—in the manner of most other musicians—in any demonstrable way. This, however, depends on the individual, and whether they wish to perform in private or public spaces. One obvious expectation is that due to the software used, the music that is spontaneously created on a laptop can be performed only from a laptop. Also, the performer cannot move the instrument, unlike a guitarist can move his guitar or control the sounds via bodily movement. Therefore, the immobility of laptops may restrict users from "performing" in performance, and may prevent them from being perceived as doing so. The concept of the laptop as a nonmovable instrument is not unusual, and can be traced back to synthesizers, or computers, that were played live, and indeed one may be reminded of electronic and synth pop groups such as Kraftwerk, Pet Shop Boys, and so on. As the late Andrew Goodwin observed:

> Playing analogue synthesizers is now a mark of authenticity, where it was once a sign of alienation—in pop iconography the image of musicians standing immobile behind synths signified coldness.... Now it is the image of a technician hunched over a computer terminal that is problematic—but that, like the image of the synth player, can and will change. (Goodwin 1990, 269)

Goodwin suggested that nonmovable digital instruments, such as the synthesizer, may make it difficult for the user to present their image as a musician in terms of displaying their musical competence, particularly in a live performance, but over time, the live audience will gradually accept the musicians (1990, 269). In a modern context, the laptop, like the synthesizer, stays in one position. Here, audiences might expect prerecorded tracks that are constructed as a playlist (like a club DJ). In addition to pressing the "play" button on the computer, there may be a lack of interaction between the musician and the audience as the laptop musician's concentration will likely be on the computer screen (at worst, checking their email messages!). As Mark Butler observes, "Introducing computers into performance has only increased anxieties around liveness: these devices are associated primarily with nonmusical pursuits, and their small and non specific control elements make it difficult to perceive connections between physical gestures and sonic results" (Butler 2014, 260).

So how can a laptop musician connect with the audience? Hugill claims that when operating an unmovable instrument, it is still necessary to communicate with the audience. He argues that "eye contact, visual cues, verbal and non-verbal communication during performance are all musically important.... Physical gestures do more than simply ensure synchronization between performers. They are part of the social exchange of performance" (Hugill 2008, 168). These gestures may include communicating with the audience with hand movements and facial expressions, emceeing (talking or toasting over the music),[8] or using musical cues (e.g., tempo changes or "bass drops") to grab the attention of the audience.

If the amateur musician is more advanced and can afford it, they may build their musical set-up by acquiring a MIDI controller, mixers, other circuit boards, and so on, which facilitate not only playing the music and improvising live, but also controlling lighting and projection shows. This additional set-up enables the musician to be liberated from the laptop screen (and mouse), and to interact with the audience through her or his display work, from improvising with the equipment to guiding the audience with gestures. Through this multitasking experience the performer may become more involved in their music by physically displaying their passion for utilizing the instrument and machines, and projecting that to the audience. This new level of activity breaks the boundaries between laptop music making and traditional music performance. As Hugill argues, "performance interaction can be between musician and technology, musician and other musician and even technology and technology" (2008, 124). It is the sounds utilized on and heard from the laptop that energize the performance. The performers, as argued by Stan Hawkins, are "inspired by the technologies that create relationships between body and machine, their sounds surfaces [are] inimitable" (2002, 153).

The Value of Performance

What constitutes a performance? Bob Ostertag argues that the use of technology in live music has altered performance and its reception by the audience, stating that the problem can be "dated to the moment when early tape pioneers first put a tape deck onstage and announced that their performance would consist of hitting the "play" button, and a confused audience scratched their heads and asked, was that really a performance?" (Ostertag 2002, 14). One may think of a musician who relies on backing tracks to play, or a singer who would simulate a live performance by miming (or "lip-syncing"). It is situations like these where more traditional professional musicians and audiences may not appreciate a laptop performance. Kim Cascone observes that the "cultural artifact produced by the laptop musician is ... misread as 'counterfeit,' leaving the audience unable to attach value to the experience" (Cascone 2004, 1; also see Cascone 2002). This may leave an audience confused, as one of the reasons for wishing to support a performer may be that audience members want to appreciate an artful performance that they may not be able to reproduce themselves due to their lack of musical ability; however, with the laptop, they may discover that they could themselves reproduce such a performance.

If we consider another situation, such as comparing laptop musicians to DJs in a performance setting, they are not generally recognized as the leading musician (unlike, say, a singer) in the show, as they are "not the center of attention, only the channeler of the dance floor's energy" (Ferreira 2008, 17). The responsibility of the DJ is to play music for the audience to dance to—therefore the "performance" is transitioned from the DJ's space (stage, booth, back of the room) onto the dance floor, and the music is expressed through the audience's bodily movements (dancing). This has also been observed in other genres that rely on technology, such as hip-hop, where audiences will try to glimpse the DJ's turntable's skills and records and at the same time translate the music through their bodily movement; therefore, the musical performance involves everyone and everything in a particular place and space.

CONCLUSION

Technology has enabled people, through choice and accessibility, to discover and teach themselves how to play and compose music. We have reached an historical moment where amateur and professional musicians can be almost indistinguishable because of the current methods of music making that are available. One prominent example today is the use of the laptop, which has reached the point of *appliance*, whereby professional and amateur users are largely able to "get past the technology and think only about the music" when engaging with it (Holmes 2002, 9). Not unlike many other emerging kinds of musicians throughout history, the reception of the laptop musician has been uneven. There may be hesitation from audiences and professional musicians to accept the laptop as a musical instrument. Part of the problem is that there are indeed "imposters" or "posers" who partake in laptop music making in the hope only of gaining an instant reputation (as opposed to those who genuinely want to learn, explore, and play the instrument). Such people arguably undermine amateur and professional musicians by giving the impression that music making equates to playing their digital record collection or prerecorded music. By giving this impression, the authenticity and seriousness of the music and performance are lost, highlighting a need for amateurs who are dedicated to learning the instrument to be taken seriously by the public. As Cascone argues, "Audiences need to reprogram their cultural apparatus for active reception in order to recuperate their ability to participate in the production of meaning" (2004, 2).

We are now in the age of digitalism, where the amateur can be either the public (consumer) or the professional—resulting in the blurring of the distinction—making the amateur musician more significant than ever. Amateur laptop musicians are gradually earning a place in musical culture and wider society, where they can produce and play music and invite audiences to become part of their performances and musical journeys. The laptop as a musical instrument allows amateurs the opportunity to explore, create, share, and experience music in their choice of time, place, and space. The success and appreciation of this enterprise will depend on how they will employ the machine. The user-friendliness, accessibility, portability, and the different musical means afforded by this machine may, in fact, make the "laptop the greatest single instrument ever!" (Ellison cited in Stubbins 2012).[9]

NOTES

1. The chapter title is from Dead or Alive, *DJ Hit that Button*, PWL Records, 1985.
2. In this chapter, the term "musician" applies to the person who is creative with sound and music. This person could also be the composer, producer, DJ, performer, etc. For similar views, please also see Hugill (2008).
3. For more on the sampler, its creative uses, and legal complications of sampling, see Butler (2006), McLeod (2007), Miller (2008), Oliver (2016), Sanjek (1992), Schloss (2004), Théberge (1997), and Vaidhyanathan (2003).
4. Originally published in *Appleton's Magazine* 8 (September 1906), 278–284, at 280.

5. A mash-up is when two (or more) identifiable works are remixed together. These works may consist of music, videos, or any other form of visuals and art.
6. See the website www.share.dj.
7. See www.roberthenke.com.
8. "Toasting" is a Jamaican and African musical style of chanting. It usually involves a DJ or musician chanting over a rhythm.
9. The author would like to thank the editors, peer reviewers, Professor Stephen Wagg, and Professor Derek B. Scott for their helpful comments on this chapter.

References Cited

Attias, Bernando Alexander. 2013. "Subjectivity in the Groove: Phonography, Digitality and Fidelity." In *DJ Culture in the Mix: Power, Technology and Social Change in Electronic Dance Music*, edited by Bernando Alexander Attias, Anna Gavanas, and Hillegonda C. Rietveld, 15–54. New York and London: Bloomsbury.

Bach, Glenn. 2003. "The Extra- Digital Axis Mandi: Myth, Magic and Metaphor in Laptop Music." *Contemporary Music Review* 22(4): 3–9.

Barthes, Roland. 1977. *Image, Music, Text*. London: Fontana.

Bennett, Andy, ed. 2005. "Editorial: Popular Music and Leisure." *Leisure Studies* 24(4): 333–342.

Bennett, H. Stith. 1990. "The Realities of Practice." In *On Record: Rock, Pop, and the Written Word*, edited by Simon Frith and Andrew Goodwin, 185–200. London and New York: Routledge.

Bennett, Samantha. 2016. "The Listener as Remixer: Mix Stems in Online Fan Community and Competition Contexts." In *The Oxford Handbook of Music and Virtuality*, edited by Sheila Whiteley and Shara Rambarran, 355–376. New York: Oxford University Press.

Booth, Wayne C. 1999. *For the Love of It: Amateuring and Its Rivals*. Chicago: University of Chicago Press.

Butler, Mark J. 2006. *Unlocking the Groove: Rhythm, Meter, and Musical Design in Electronic Dance Music*. Bloomington: Indiana University Press.

Butler, Mark J. 2014. "(In)visible Mediators: Urban Mobility, Interface Design, and the Disappearing Computer in Berlin-Based Laptop Performances." In *The Oxford Handbook of Mobile Music Studies*, vol. 2, edited by Sumanth Gopinath and Jason Stanyek, 259–291. New York: Oxford University Press.

Cascone, Kim. 2002. "Laptop Music—Counterfeiting Aura in the Age of Infinite Reproduction." *Parachute Contemporary Art* 107: 55–66.

Cascone, Kim. 2004. "'Grain, Sequence, System': Three Levels of Reception in the Performance of Laptop Music." *Intelligent Agent* 4(1): 1–2.

Davis, Erik. 2002. "Songs in the Key of F12." *Wired* 10(5). http://archive.wired.com/wired/archive/10.05/laptop.html?pg=1&topic=&topic_set.

Deadmau5 [Joel T. Zimmermann]. 2012a. "We All Hit Play," *Deadmau5 United We Fail*, blog post, June 25. http://deadmau5.tumblr.com/post/25690507284/we-all-hit-play.

Deadmau5 [Joel T. Zimmermann]. 2012b. "All DJs Are Glorified Button Pushers." *Gizmodo*, June 25. http://gizmodo.com/5921053/all-djs-are-glorified-button-pushers.

Drew, Robert S. 1997. "Embracing the Role of the Amateur: How Karaoke Bar Patrons Become Regular Performers." *Journal of Contemporary Ethnography* 25(4): 449–468.

Duckworth, William. 2005. *Virtual Music: How the Web Got Wired for Sound*. New York and London: Routledge.

Ferreira, Pedro Peixoto. 2008. "When Sound Meets Movement: Performance in Electronic Dance Music." *Leonardo Music Journal* 18: 17–20.

Finnegan, Ruth. 1989. *The Hidden Musicians: Music-Making in an English Town*. Cambridge: Cambridge University Press.

Fish, Alex. 2012. "Mr C. on Deadmau5: Complete Wanker." *Pulse*, June 28. http://pulseradio. net/articles/2012/06/mr-c-on-deadmau5-complete-wanker.

Frith, Simon. 1996. *Performing Rites: On the Value of Popular Music*. Oxford: Oxford University Press.

Goodwin, Andrew. 1990. "Sample and Hold: Pop Music in the Digital Age of Reproduction." In *On Record: Rock, Pop and the Written Word*, edited by Simon Frith and Andrew Goodwin, 254–273. London and New York: Routledge.

Green, Lucy. 2002. *How Popular Musicians Learn: A Way Ahead for Music Education*. Aldershot: Ashgate.

Hawkins, Stan. 2002. *Settling the Pop Score: Pop Texts and Identity Politics*. Aldershot: Ashgate.

Holmes, Thom. 2002. *Electronic and Experimental Music: Pioneers in Technology and Composition*. New York: Psychology Press.

Hugill, Andrew. 2008. *The Digital Musician*. New York: Routledge.

Jeffries, Stuart. 2010. "Surrender. It's Brian Eno." *The Guardian*, April 28. http://www.theguard- ian.com/music/2010/apr/28/brian-eno-brighton-festival.

Katz, Mark. 2014. "The Amateur in the Age of Mechanical Music." In *The Oxford Handbook of Sound Studies*, edited by Trevor Pinch and Karin Bijsterveld, 459–479. New York: Oxford University Press.

Kirschner, Tony. 1998. "Studying Rock: Towards a Materialist Ethnography." In *Mapping the Beat: Popular Music and Contemporary Theory*, edited by Thomas Swiss, John Sloop, and Andrew Herman, 247–268. Oxford: Blackwell.

McLeod, Kembrew. 2007. *Freedom of Expression: Resistance and Repression in the Age of Intellectual Property*. Minneapolis: University of Minnesota Press.

Leppert, Richard. 2012. "Material Culture and Decentred Selfhood (Socio-Visual Typologies of Musical Excess.)" In *Critical Musicological Reflections: Essays in Honour of Derek B. Scott*, edited by Stan Hawkins, 101–124. Farnham: Ashgate.

Miller, Paul D., ed. 2008. *Sound Unbound: Sampling Digital Music and Culture*. Cambridge, MA: MIT Press.

Morris, Jeremy Wade. 2016. "App Music" in *The Oxford Handbook of Music and Virtuality*, edited by Sheila Whiteley and Shara Rambarran, 477–494. New York: Oxford University Press.

Noudelmann, François. 2012. *The Philosopher's Touch: Sartre, Nietzsche, and Barthes at the Piano*. Translated by Brian J. Reilly. New York: Columbia University Press.

O'Brien, Benjamin. 2016. "Sample Sharing: Virtual Laptop Ensemble Communities." In *The Oxford Handbook of Music and Virtuality*, edited by Sheila Whiteley and Shara Rambarran, 377–391. New York: Oxford University Press.

Oliver, Rowan. 2016. "Bring That Beat Back: Sampling as Virtual Collaboration." In *The Oxford Handbook of Music and Virtuality*, edited by Sheila Whiteley and Shara Rambarran, 65–80. New York: Oxford University Press.

Ostertag, Bob. 2002. "Human Bodies, Computer Music." *Leonardo Music Journal* 12: 11–14.

Prior, Nick. 2008. "OK COMPUTER: Mobility, Software and the Laptop Musician." *Information, Communication and Society* 11(7): 912–932.

Rambarran, Shara. 2013. "99 Problems but Danger Mouse Ain't One: The Creative and Legal Difficulties of Brian Burton, 'Author' of The Grey Album." *Popular Musicology Online* 3. http://www.popular-musicology-online.com/issues/03/rambarran.html.

Randles, Clint. 2013. "Being an iPadist." *General Music Today* 27(1): 48–51.

Richardson, John. 2012. *An Eye for Music: Popular Music and the Audiovisual Surreal.* New York: Oxford University Press.

Sanjek, David. 1992. "'Don't Have to DJ No More': Sampling and the 'Autonomous' Creator." *Cardozo Arts and Entertainment Law Journal* 10: 607–624.

Schloss, Joseph G. 2004. *Making Beats: The Art of Sample-Based Hip-Hop.* Middletown, CT: Wesleyan University Press.

Serazio, Michael. 2008. "The Apolitical Irony of Generation Mash-Up: A Cultural Case Study in Popular Music." *Popular Music and Society* 31(1): 79–94.

Shiga, John. 2007. "Copy-and-Persist: The Logic of Mash-Up Culture." *Critical Studies in Media Communication* 24(2): 93–114.

Shuker, Roy. 2012. *Understanding Popular Music Culture.* 4th ed. New York and Abingdon: Routledge.

Sinnreich, Aram. 2010. *Mashed Up: Music, Technology, and the Rise of Configurable Culture.* Amhurst and Boston: University of Massachusettes Press.

Small, Charlie. 2013. "Mr C: Laptop DJs Are Not Real DJs." *DJ MAG*, January 27. http://djmag.com/content/mr-c-laptop-djs-not-real-djs.

Small, Christopher. 1998. *Musicking: The Meanings of Performing and Listening.* Middletown, CT: Wesleyan University Press.

Snell, Karen, and Johan Söderman. 2014. *Hip-Hop Within and Without the Academy.* Lanham, MD: Lexington.

Sousa, John Philip. 2012. "The Menace of Mechanical Music." In *Music, Sound and Technology in America: A Documentary History of Early Phonograph, Cinema and Radio*, edited by Timothy D. Taylor, Mark Katz, and Tony Grajeda, 113–122. Durham, NC, and London: Duke University Press.

Stebbins, Robert A. 1980. "'Amateur' and 'Hobbyist' as Concepts for the Study of Leisure Problems." *Social Problems* 27(4): 413–417.

Stubbins, Sinead. 2012. "Interview with Flying Lotus." *Lifelounge*, 2012. http://www.lifelounge.com.au/music/news/interview-with-flying-lotus.aspx (defunct).

Théberge, Paul. 1997. *Any Sound You Can Imagine: Making Music/Consuming Technology.* Middletown, CT: Wesleyan University Press.

Théberge, Paul. 2001. "'Plugged in': Technology and Popular Music." In *The Cambridge Companion to Pop and Rock*, edited by Simon Frith, Will Straw, and John Street, 3–25. Cambridge: Cambridge University Press.

Vaidhyanathan, Siva. 2003. *Copyrights and Copywrongs: The Rise of Intellectual Property and How It Threatens Creativity.* New York: New York University Press.

Veblen, Kari K., and Janice L. Waldron. 2012. "Fast Forward: Emerging Trends in Community Music." In *The Oxford Handbook of Music Education*, vol. 2, edited by Gary E. McPherson and Graham F. Welch, 203–220. New York: Oxford University Press.

Warner, Timothy. 2003. *Pop Music—Technology and Creativity: Trevor Horn and the Digital Revolution.* Aldershot: Ashgate.

Whiteley, Sheila, and Shara Rambarran, eds. 2016. *The Oxford Handbook of Music and Virtuality.* New York: Oxford University Press.

CHAPTER 31

....

COMMUNITY MUSIC PRACTICE

Intervention through Facilitation

....

GILLIAN HOWELL, LEE HIGGINS,
AND BRYDIE-LEIGH BARTLEET

INTRODUCTION: CONTEXTS FOR COMMUNITY MUSIC ACTIVITIES

....

IN many ways, community music and "music making in leisure time" may seem somewhat synonymous, given that both refer to music participation activities that may be considered distanced from music making as a professional endeavor, and music learning within the more formal structures and constraints of educational institutions. Both labels also imply an active rather than passive approach to music participation; community music projects are rarely concerned with music appreciation, for example (Veblen 2008). The prefix of "community" also suggests that these are music making experiences that are undertaken with others, and that they have a communal intention.

Drawing distinctions between community music and music making for leisure is a more contentious matter. While this volume will establish the breadth and depth of music making undertaken as leisure, "community music" as a set of common activities gathered under a single label continues to enjoy (or "be haunted by") a degree of "definitional uncertainty" (Brown, Higham, and Rimmer 2014, 13). Participants, nonparticipants, musicians, sponsors and supporters, community leaders, governments, schools, policy documents, and funding bodies may all have subtly different understandings of what comprises community music activity.

From a global perspective, the label "community music" may be applied to a wide range of music making practices, reflecting the political, economic, and socio-cultural environment, and how music and its social and aesthetic purpose are understood within that culture. Consider, for example, music making practices that identify or distinguish a particular ethno-cultural society, including contemporary practices that remain informed by ancestral understandings of music, as well as music making that forms an integral part of community life, that maintains connection with ancestral spirits, and that plays a part in remaining in balance with the natural world. These activities may look and sound very different from community music practices in societies where music making has been professionalized and commodified, so that "community music" comes to refer to amateur rather than professional music making, to organized approaches to music making that encourage community participation in one-off, short-term celebratory events, or to the use of music making to enhance community cohesion and shared identity in the face of increased individualism.

This short list represents the mere tip of the iceberg of what constitutes community music activity, and demonstrates the way that understandings of what community music is and does are culturally informed and constructed. In other words, determinations of which activities belong to the community music "bundle" can differ widely between cultural groups and across the globe. Furthermore, across this diversity some activities are strongly identified with leisure, while others have a more functional, productive, or developmental intention.

Understood with this breadth and as a global phenomenon, the definitional uncertainty of community music is no great surprise, and indeed suggests this is not a sign of weakness or lack of focus, but rather a strength and a reflection of the vibrancy and ubiquity of making and sharing music (Schippers and Bartleet 2013). Nevertheless, for the sake of clarity it is helpful to find some way of distinguishing between all of this activity. Higgins (2012) offers a conceptual framework with three broad groupings of community music activity: as the *music of a particular (cultural, ethnic) community*, emphasizing the musical content and the relationship between the music makers and the music; as *communal music making* (where the emphasis is on people and place, and the shared music making experience); and *community music as an active intervention* with a group of participants led by a skilled facilitator. This framework can be usefully applied across numerous cultural settings, although the prevalence and construction of each of these three groupings will greatly differ depending on where you are in the world.

It is to Higgins's third strand of community music activity that our attention now turns. While we acknowledge the concept of an "intervention" is highly complex, and sometimes contested, it does encapsulate an enduring approach to facilitation, which is useful to consider in the context of this volume. The interventionist approach is also very well established in the U.K., where a professional class of "community musician" enjoys a certain status and visibility, exemplified through: (1) the existence of Sound Sense, a professional representative association for community music leaders that advocates for community music practices and offers support and development to community music practitioners; (2) the availability of specialized, accredited training with industry relevance; and (3) a political and socio-cultural environment in which paid opportunities for music leaders exist and are generated through arts and social organizations' responses to government cultural policy. The interventionist approach can also be seen in other parts of the world, though perhaps without the same degree of cultural recognition of the practitioner's role as seen in the United Kingdom.

The purpose of this chapter is to drill down into those particular examples of community music activity where the music making takes place as an intervention under the guidance of a music facilitator, and to focus in particular on the role of the facilitators. That role is a distinctive one, requiring practitioners to engage deeply on both interpersonal and musical levels, and to work in a wide range of challenging settings, well beyond the confines of concert halls or education spaces.

This very distinctive "music leading" role has developed in response to cultural environments in which the ever-increasing commercialization and commodification of music practices has resulted in people's widespread disengagement from music making itself, where professionalization of musical skills is embedded within and supported by an eco-system of training institutions, qualifications and accredited attainment, and commercial and professional opportunities, all of which lead to a situation where society is often divided into "performers" and "audiences" (Small 1998). It is to the evolution of this cultural environment and eco-system that our attention now turns.

COMMUNITY MUSIC AS A VEHICLE FOR SOCIAL BENEFIT AND CHANGE

In the United Kingdom, the interventionist approach to community music is linked to the community arts scene that flourished during the counterculture era of the 1960s and 1970s. As a substrand of that movement, community music shared goals of activism, challenging repressive and hierarchical social norms, and commitment to personal growth and empowerment. There was a desire to address issues of access and inclusion in both social and musical-cultural contexts by asking questions such as: Who in society has access to music? Who makes and plays music? Who decides what is music and what is not? With community arts coming of age in an era of considerable social upheaval in the form of antigovernment and antiestablishment protest, social issues became the subject of art making, and the experiences of everyday people received greater prominence (Higgins 2008, 2012).

Community music activity also grew in response to shifts in government policy in relation to education curriculum, changes in expectations and delivery requirements of publicly funded arts organizations (Brown, Higham, and Rimmer 2014; Doeser 2014), and in response to the needs and agendas of formal service providers (government agencies and nongovernmental organizations, NGOs) in areas of health, education, and social services (Brown, Higham, and Rimmer 2014). It is this last set of relationships in particular that informs the contemporary activities of community musicians in the U.K. and elsewhere in the world (e.g., Australia; see Bartleet et al. 2009).

Some of this instrumentalization of music's potential to transform lives for the better can be traced back to several key historical antecedents. The Industrial Revolution saw not only the advent of large-scale changes to employment and an emphasis on small family units but the introduction of industry-sponsored workers' choirs and musical groups—precursors to many of today's community choirs and brass bands. These were understood as providing productive, pleasurable, and self-improving pastimes for workers (who might otherwise seek their pleasure in local ale houses and potentially get caught up in revolutionary action), and encouraging discipline and unity (ensuring a "docile" and "pliable" workforce). Furthermore, music was believed to improve the morals of both singers and listeners (McGuire 2009). This idea also informed the work of many religious missionaries, traveling into new territories as part of colonial expansion and using shared music making as a way to facilitate union with God and to inspire feelings of unity and community cohesion, and as a mechanism through which the colonized or proselytized could be "improved" and "civilized" (Beckles Willson 2011).

The contention that music making experiences have the potential to influence or bring about positive and beneficial change for participants on both individual and collective terms has its roots in antiquity. It is today widely supported by scholars working across multiple disciplines, including music therapy, music psychology, music education, medical ethnomusicology—each concerned with health and well-being outcomes, or the enhancement of individual capacities—in addition to fields of scholarly interest such as community development, international development, applied ethnomusicology, peace building, and conflict resolution (where interest in music is focused on social change outcomes and the relationship between a positive social environment and the maintenance of traditional cultures), to name some of the more prominent of these often interdisciplinary explorations (see, for example, Bergh 2010; DeQuadros and Dorstewitz 2011; MacDonald, Kreutz, and Mitchell 2012). This array of intentions and goals can also be observed in music programs initiated in places of the most extreme human needs, such as communities at war or in recovery from violent conflict (Howell 2015), and in the range of ways that many of the world's cultures employ music as a tool for healing (Gouk 2000).

Similarly, there are notable historical antecedents for the use of shared music making to create a sense of empowered communal spirit, social bonds, and cohesion. These include the employment of music as a vehicle for mobilizing large numbers of people to a common political cause or ideal. Turino (2008) cites the role of massed singing in the youth rallies of Nazi Germany and in the U.S. civil rights movement as two examples of music used for mobilization of the masses. While the ideologies underpinning those two particular movements were strongly contrasting, both effectively utilized the sense of unity, shared purpose, and courage that massed singing could generate (Stige 2012) toward their respective political aims.

Thus, this somewhat complex and contested instrumental understanding of music's role as a potential vehicle for social change and "improvement" is not new, and has contributed to community music's increasing visibility and prominence as part of a suite of responses to pressing social concerns and needs. Indeed, the ubiquity of music to the human experience has seen many community music projects in contemporary times initiated through government-funded agencies to address an expanded range of areas of social need and exclusion, with a corresponding tendency from community music organizations and practitioners to adjust their missions and purposes to match those of these agencies (Brown, Higham, and Rimmer 2014). This trend represents something of a shift away from the grass-roots social organization and community empowerment of community music's post-World War II roots toward the intervention model.

We can see, therefore, that contemporary community music practices are strongly informed by a history of social action, as well as by a set of beliefs and a growing evidence base about the potential of shared music making to bring about positive and beneficial individual and collective change. This history then collides with the contemporary needs of social service provision met by government and nongovernment bodies, and a project model of facilitator-led interventions has evolved.

The growth of the intervention model has driven the subsequent rise in importance and professionalization of the role of the community musician, or music facilitator. Furthermore, the multiplicity of sites where this work frequently takes place has necessitated a complex raft of musical and leadership skills, in order to enable musical and reflexive responses to the social or health needs of a particular target group, and through this musical action to cultivate some kind of change or transformation. Therefore, it is to the emerging and central role of the community music facilitator that we now turn, highlighting the wide variety of sites in which community music facilitators ply their craft and the unique "toolkit" of skills, values, and methods that they employ.

The Sites, Skills, and Attributes of the Community Music Facilitator

We contend that the critical contribution in realizing a wide array of extramusical goals is not only the music itself, but the ways in which it is employed in the hands of a skilled community musician or facilitator. It is the role of the facilitator that most clearly distinguishes an interventionist community music event from more general music-as-leisure. We use the term "community musician" to apply specifically to the skilled facilitator in the kinds of community music projects and activities that have a clear interventionist structure and intention.

Skilled facilitators who work in the "interventionist" mode consciously engage with people to find pathways through which music making opportunities might allow them to personally flourish with full and engaged participation. From this perspective, interventionist community musicians work strategically in order to generate music making environments that are accessible and inviting for those who wish to participate. In order to generate such opportunities, community musicians have relied on approaches to practice that are flexible and responsive rather than on a singular prescriptive methodology. There are, however, some well-used approaches that are useful to consider within the context of this chapter.

For example, community musicians usually consider their environments as "workshops"—learning settings that become sites for experimentation, creativity, and group work. With its emphasis on open-ended interactions, the workshop becomes a means of achieving a more democratic space favorable to creative music making. The structure of the workshop is contingent on and enables an open environment to foster active and collaborative conversation, dialogue, and music making. Through the reflexive, accepting, and unforced interactions between the facilitator and participants, the workshop can become a conduit through which diversity, freedom, and tolerance might flow. The following examples illustrate something of this diversity of setting and approach in action, and highlight the specific characteristics of the context in which the community music making takes place, as well as the musical communicative and leadership tools that the facilitator in each setting chose to employ. The examples demonstrate that to be successful in the role, community music facilitators must attend to multiple layers of relationship and interaction between themselves and participants, between the participants, and between each person and the musical material as it evolves.

Case 1: Story-Sharing through Music in an English-Language Learning Classroom

In the education system of the state of Victoria in Australia, a network of specialist English-language schools exists to support newly arrived refugee and migrant young people to learn English and adapt to Australian school culture before making the transition to a mainstream school. The learning environment in these intensive English-language schools is diverse in terms of its ethno-cultural linguistic mix, but also as a result of the varied prior schooling experiences of the students. Some arrive in Australia with age-consistent schooling experiences, while others, particular those from refugee backgrounds, have had severely interrupted prior schooling. Howell (2009, 2011) describes the way that a long-running music workshop program in one of these schools contributed to the students' educational goals (language acquisition and school culture adaptation) and well-being through composition projects that focused on their stories of journey and transition, and the musical knowledge and materials they brought with them from their country of origin.

Such a diverse cohort demonstrated different needs and responses in the music workshop program. Some students thrived, enjoying the opportunity to use skills and musical knowledge they had acquired in their countries of origin or through life in refugee camps, and the chance to assume leadership. Others, still dealing with culture shock and the stress of trying to learn a new language, intense insecurity and self-doubt, or even the debilitating symptoms of posttraumatic stress, needed to navigate their way more cautiously. These self-directed navigations confirm Osborne's observation that, when facilitated with skill and sensitivity to group and individual responses, music can be a "very secure and self-regulating" activity for vulnerable young people (Osborne 2009, 334), in the sense that participatory music activities can offer an individual a range of ways of participating, thus enabling her or him to regulate the intensity of their experience, to suit her or his own sense of safety and comfort. In the creative music making activities that Howell (2009, 2011) describes, the participation options range from very passive responding (where a child simply observes and follows activities without necessarily contributing) to gradually more active roles, such as mouthing words, then singing them, helping to distribute instruments, and then later playing and joining in, and so on. Thus, the facilitator needs to be attentive to the importance of these smaller, self-regulated interactions with the music activities, ensuring there are always opportunities to engage more deeply, or to retreat from active participation when desired.

In these workshops, improvisation processes promoted gentle and playful exploration of musical and narrative ideas, and song- and story-based projects built around names, languages, and countries of origin, personal attributes of courage, resilience, acknowledgment, exploration of emotions and responses, and celebration of self-identities (Howell 2009, 2011). While the workshops took place in a formal school environment, the music facilitation processes were not bound by a predetermined pedagogical approach or curriculum, but followed an open-ended, responsive process more akin to the community music leadership approaches and values described by Higgins and Campbell (2010), Leak (2003), and Moser and McKay (2005), among others. While the musical goals were the focus of all activities, the facilitator remained acutely aware of the diverse needs—educational, social, emotional, psychological—within the group, and worked to address these indirectly through the constantly evolving musical content, her communicative style, and the emotional safety of the music space.

Case 2: Music Creation toward High-Status Performance Platforms with the Amplified Elephants

In the example of the Amplified Elephants (Hullick 2013)—a sonic art ensemble for people with intellectual disabilities based in Melbourne, Australia—what began as a recreational program for participants in a broad-based arts learning program for people with intellectual disabilities has evolved to become a sonic arts ensemble with a growing professional profile and invitations to perform internationally. Mentored by established professional sound artist and composer James Hullick, the group has honed its craft and creative voice through processes of intense and critical listening, deliberate imposition of limitations and constraints on the music materials explored, experimentation with a variety of media, including "found" objects, and different approaches to embodied sound, alongside constant recording and facilitated reflection on these recordings and regular performances.

The Amplified Elephants occupy an unusual position as a community music group, given their increasing profile as professional performers. Hullick describes the group's

regular engagement with contemporary composers, conductors, and other music professionals as an "incredible opportunity for their career development" (2013, 230). The
consideration of their careers points toward a critical shift in the way that the group
positions itself in the musical landscape and on a career-focused, quasi-professional trajectory, even while they still work within a larger community music or social service
provider structure. The focus on career development is also a political stance, acknowledging that people with intellectual disabilities are often seen for what they *cannot* do,
rather than what they can, and this in turn often constrains opportunities to imagine or
develop a career path.

It is notable that Hullick describes himself as a mentor rather than a facilitator. This
choice of language positions the members of the group in the foreground and as the
group's primary creative agents. In assuming a role of mentor rather than facilitator,
Hullick asserts a more distanced stance that highlights the unique contributions the
members of the group make to its creations and their right to be acknowledged as
the owners and creators of the work. Nevertheless, Hullick's input is woven throughout
the narrative, and it is indeed *his* expertise in sonic art that has determined the musical focus and outputs of the group, given that "artists can only mentor the art that they
know" (2013, 223). He is constantly adjusting the level of input, which might range from
taking full compositional responsibility, to mentoring and facilitating a group-devised
composition through improvisation and repetition, to being an active member of
the group when they work in collaboration with outside artists. Hullick is also highly
attuned to the needs of individuals, in terms of their musical and ensemble strengths
and limitations, preferred ways of working and creating, and aptitudes for different
instruments and media.

Case 3: Health Promotion, Community Music, and Cultural Forms of Leadership

From Sierra Leone comes an example of community music activity that affirms and celebrates local music traditions yet also works as a community health intervention, as an
initiative of an international nongovernmental development organization working in
the area of public health that seeks to promote public health messages and encourage
changes in people's behavior (Bingley 2011). Bingley writes vividly about a gifted com-
municator and musician named Bambeh in rural Sierra Leone, who uses her intimate
knowledge of local music traditions and abilities as a facilitator and inspiring leader to
draw groups, mainly of women, together. While the sessions are ostensibly for the purpose of health care and promotion (for example, postnatal care for mothers and infants,
baby growth monitoring, nutrition advice), music is employed in overt and subtle ways
to first attract the group, to create a sense of safety and trust (by using local processes
and rituals of reciprocal sharing through music), to educate, to generate health-related
knowledge (through targeted song lyrics, composed to deliver a key message), and to
affirm and celebrate the community's achievements and development.

Bingley argues that Bambeh herself is central to the success of this model. She is a charismatic and dynamic leader, respected as an educated and literate woman and an employee of an international NGO, but also as a role model and trusted outsider, with the interpersonal skills to build trust and authority beyond the immediate participant group, and therefore to widen the reach of her health-focused intervention. The example of Bambeh shows again that, while the musical material (in this case local traditional music) is important and can be employed in powerful ways to connect with and inspire participants, it is the unique skill set of the facilitator that is the critical element in the success of an intervention.

Case 4: Music in Residential Homes for Those Living with Dementia

Community music in residential homes for the elderly often takes the form of communal singing of familiar songs from the past. Smilde, Page, and Alheit (2014), however, describe a U.K.-based community music project, Music for Life, that moves beyond reminiscence to directly connect the self within the person that the dementia has hidden. The project, which involves freelance musicians (often trained as orchestral players), sees participatory music as a powerful and essential element in building shared and individual identity. The goal of Music for Life is to enhance relationships between the residents, and between residents and their care-givers.

Over the course of eight weeks, the musicians work closely with a small group of residents and care staff, "using musical improvisation as a catalyst to bring about communication in the widest sense at various levels" (Smilde, Page, and Alheit 2014, 3). These are challenging workshops for the musicians, who must be highly alert to the smallest "verbal and non-verbal signals" (3) from the residents that suggest a desire to connect, influence, or lead. Everyone in the group is in an environment that is somewhat unpredictable, in which they are trying something new. It is the responsibility of the musicians to continue to inspire confidence among the group. At the end of each session they debrief with the care staff, strengthening those relationships as well, and facilitate the emergence of issues and insights. Everyone is engaged in learning and opening possibilities of change in themselves and others.

THE FACILITATOR'S TOOLKIT: SKILLS, ATTRIBUTES, AND COMMITMENT TO VALUES

These four examples demonstrate something of the wide range of settings, skills, and attributes that characterize the work of community music facilitators within the interventionist model, and the variety of goals and intentions that can underpin the work.

Across these four, we see that settings for workshops can encompass formal institutions (e.g., schools), community-based drop-in spaces, residential homes for the very frail and elderly, and fairly open, rural environments. This list is not exhaustive, but offered merely to demonstrate the considerable breadth of sites and settings where such projects can and do take place.

The case studies demonstrate that the skill set of the music facilitator or community musician includes a diverse combination of tools. Derivative from the French *faciliter* (to render easy) and the Latin *facilis* (easy), *facilitation* is concerned with encouraging open dialogue among different individuals with differing perspectives. Certainly there are music creation skills in improvising, composing, and arranging. There are also aural skills, for the ability to pick up musical materials by ear frequently plays a central part in facilitation, especially when participants are not familiar with music notation. The ability to read music and work with written notation is a further useful skill, but given that this knowledge may not be shared by members of the group, aural skills frequently come to the fore. Community music facilitators with notation and reading skills often use these to create their own documentation or written archive of musical materials to ensure they can be recalled and used at a later date, but unless this particular skill is already common knowledge across the group, it is less likely to occupy a central position in the workshop process.

Beyond musicianship, music facilitators also possess a raft of leadership, processual, and social skills in order to guide the group on a musical journey together. For example, the facilitator will constantly call upon her or his ability to "read" the responses of individuals and the group as a whole, constantly monitoring the nuances of interactions. The facilitator will need to be articulate, skilled in providing clear instruction and information to whatever extent the group requires it. The facilitator may at times need to challenge and provoke, and alternately reassure and encourage, responding to their knowledge of each individual. The facilitator also needs to be organized and plan their approach well, aware of imposed timeframes and restraints, and the intended musical goals that must fit within these. Facilitators need to be creative, able to improvise and think "on their feet," and ensure variety and appropriate pacing so that the group is carried along by its own momentum, energy, and sense of flow. Most critically, if each of these skills is understood as a kind of "tool," it is not the range of tools available but the facilitators' choice of the most appropriate tools for the task at hand that most distinguishes their work. As Higgins and Campbell (2010, 9) argue, facilitation "is an art," whether or not it takes place in an arts-based context.

The personal attributes of the music facilitator also play a role—for effective leadership benefits from a certain amount of charisma and likeability, the ability to remain positive and calm in less predictable environments, and a willingness to be open to one's own learning taking place alongside that of the participants. Finally, underpinning this range of skills and attributes is an understanding of musical excellence that is defined both through the quality of musical outcomes and the quality of the social bonds that are created through the process (Turino 2008, as cited in Baker 2014); in other words, facilitators understand that the personal and social growth of participants is as important as their musical growth (Higgins 2012).

Alongside skills and attributes, music facilitators working in interventionist ways around the world frequently share a number of characteristic traits in terms of values, beliefs, ethical commitments, and skill set. The values and beliefs held are concerned with rights, capacities, and capabilities. These include the idea that all people have a right to make, participate in, and enjoy their own music, and that they possess an innate capacity and lifelong potential for music participation and creativity. Music facilitators also share commitments to cultivate positive learning environments in which individuals of all ages and backgrounds feel welcome, included, and valued. They may challenge discriminatory social norms, working to overcome barriers that block access to participation for some people. Frequently we see a commitment to flexible approaches to teaching and learning, including the idea that a workshop will include expertise among participants, and that learning will take place in all directions (from leader to participants, from participants to leader, and between participants). Participation in shared learning has the potential to work toward emancipation and empowerment; open-ended community music making places ownership of the resultant musical outcomes in the hands of participants, at the same time as encouraging their continued musical growth. These ethical commitments imply a hospitable welcome that is central to the music workshop experience (Higgins 2012).

A Complex Role with Multiple Goals

As our discussion so far has described, interventionist community music projects may have multiple objectives that are focused upon beneficial outcomes for the participant group, and therefore will require a diverse set of facilitator skills, attributes, and values that extend well beyond mere musicianship. Community music project sites may have multiple project goals, both competing and complementing, and when these are considered alongside the multilayered social constructions of what music is, what it is for, who can participate in it and to what extent, then community music facilitation becomes a very demanding undertaking, with many inherent challenges.

Community music's values and intentions can certainly work in complementary ways, however, they may also exist within a hierarchy of priorities, explicit or otherwise. To consider just one example: around the world music is a highly gendered activity in the majority of social contexts, with gendered meanings between humans and instruments, gendered divisions of the "labor" of music (including who should participate and how), and the ways in which different (public and private) spaces may become gendered (Doubleday 2008). These norms can be challenging to override, even in a project with a strong and explicit commitment to the inclusion of both males and females.

Research into community-based music activities for young people in Australia, U.K., U.S.A., and Germany noted that boys dominated all of the "mixed gender" music activities on offer (predominantly focused on hip-hop, breakdancing, and DJing), despite some efforts from organizers to address the gender disparity in different ways (Baker and Cohen 2008). Pruitt (2013) found similar results in a community music project in

Australia that targeted young people from diverse cultural backgrounds, and provided opportunities for creating and performing their own hip-hop music and dance, with former participants encouraged to become leaders and facilitators of the workshops. Community choirs in postindustrial societies often find the opposite problem, with women comprising the majority of most mixed-voice choirs (Clift et al. 2010b, as cited in Clift 2012; Masso and Broad 2013).

Such gender divisions are not necessarily always exclusionary, and it is beyond the scope of this chapter to address the question of gender in community music in any greater detail. We raise it here to highlight some of the complexity of an undertaking with such a mix of social, musical, ethical, and political goals. Gender divisions also suggest something of the paradox of inclusion—that when a particular group is targeted for participation, another group may be subsequently (and often implicitly) excluded. If a community music activity is "open" to allcomers, a dominant group may evolve that "appropriates" the space. It demands a commitment to acts of hospitality and acceptance of what Higgins, after Derrida, calls *the impossible*, where the community within is bonded and yet must simultaneously remain open to newcomers. Thus the "community" never settles (Higgins 2007).

These examples also illustrate the competing priorities and interests that can arise in any community-based, collaborative project, and the fact that the facilitator can guide the group and the process, but not control every outcome. Tensions and divisions that exist within the community can be replicated or reinforced within the intervention (be it musical or otherwise).

Music facilitators are thus often charged with the task of developing the desired musical outcomes (noting that these ambitions may differ among participants, and between participants and sponsors or organizers), while at the same time remaining committed to the utmost social care for each individual and responding to complex cultural dynamics that pervade the context in which they are working. Rather than aiming to "strike a balance" between these goals, or to find a place of consensus that satisfies the needs of the majority, facilitation involves a constantly reflexive and responsive act, and a willingness to weight and counterweight contrasting and sometimes conflicting needs of a group in musical and social terms.

The skill set of a community music facilitator therefore often includes both musicianship and community development skills. Here, the community musician is a self-reflexive musician who puts an emphasis on the musical process working alongside participants in order to help them achieve their goals. Such musicians need to be able to support the group to realize their musical goals and potential, but they also need to work within an agreed framework of ethical values (such as inclusivity) and with a radar finely tuned to subtleties of communication that may inadvertently transmit messages that could contradict those values. Facilitation is a role that requires a combination of the attributes of a musician (able to perform, arrange, compose, improvise—to name but a few), a teacher (able to communicate information and support the development of new skills, with a highly flexible pedagogy), a community development worker (skilled in reading group dynamics and cultivating collective emancipatory action), a social or youth worker (sensitive to the practical and structural obstacles that members of the group may face, and factors that could reinforce marginalization), a health worker (attentive to the diverse physical and mental health needs of participants), and a leader (a personable individual with certain qualities of charisma and persuasiveness).

Facilitation as Improvisation

Improvisation as experience is often at the heart of community music practices. Thought of in this way, improvisation is not only a musical skill, but also a way of negotiating the world. Improvisation is born out of creative environments where opportunities are provided for people to release their musical imaginations in ways that are free and expansive, playful, personal, and interpersonal. Illustrated through the interplay of skills and open-ended processes and acceptances outlined above, there is a strong quality of improvisation inherent within community music facilitation.

In short, community music facilitators create a context that validates the experiments and explorations of all people—children, youth, and adults—who are potential makers of all styles of music (Higgins and Mantie 2013). To apply Small's (1998) term, improvisation evokes the human *musicking* potential, and the capacity to participate in the socially interactive process of making music. When thought of in this way, music making is embraced as "a trail of no mistakes," and a celebration of the many and varied musical pathways that musicians and facilitators can take (Higgins and Campbell 2010, 1). Furthermore, community music making that is improvisatory and collaborative echoes the organic and often complex natures of communities. The desire is not to bind or contain within predetermined rules or organizational boundaries—as is seen in organized sports, for example—but to allow the group's unique, time- and participant-specific response to emerge.

Potential Tensions and Dilemmas

The fact that such a comprehensive and diverse toolkit of skills is essential to the concurrent realization of musical, educational, and social goals points to the range of tensions and dilemmas that may exist within the community music context. We can see the existence of a tension between the historical antecedents of community music practice, as an act of defiance, disruption, or challenge to mainstream or commercial cultural controls, and a current reality that is more blurred. This sometimes prompts the question: to what extent is the community music workshop an act of activism? Different stakeholders (participants, practitioners, sponsors, and organizers) may hold divergent views on this, even while the project content may be intended to render more visible and audible a marginalized social group. Where the impetus for the work has come from an external funding source (such as a government agency), activism in the form of civil disobedience or strong agitation for change is less likely. However, the same kind of project model (for example, a songwriting workshop addressing social exclusion or injustice) could be driven from the grassroots and have an explicit activist agenda, intending to provoke community awareness, official response, and policy change (Mullen 2008).

With the historical roots of community music lying in grassroots activism and a "reclaiming" of musical space by everyday people, it can be challenging for some community musicians to strike the desired balance between what Higgins and Campbell (2010, 7) describe as the willingness to assume responsibility for the musical leadership and the desire to relinquish the control. Mullen observed reluctance among some community musicians to assume clear leadership roles, finding that they were so concerned with avoiding building hierarchies of authority that they preferred instead to engender more "laissez faire" and fairly unstructured approaches. These facilitators' concerns were well intentioned and informed by valid ethical choices, but inevitably resulted in what could be described as unfocused and unconvincing workshop environments (2008, 250). Issues concerning power, choice, and leadership can also arise in cross-cultural community music projects, particularly when the facilitator enters as an outsider to that community and must grapple with culturally different processes for assigning roles and making decisions (Howell 2012a, 2012b). Higgins and Campbell suggest that, rather than seeking to find a point of balance between these different outcomes, the critical ingredients are the facilitator's readiness to "move in and out of roles as the group dictates" (2010, 7) and being open to unpredictable and unexpected shifts in the musical journey's direction. In particular, outcomes and destinations are not predetermined, but emerge through the facilitation process and the group's shared experience.

The above discussion of skills and tools that the facilitator uses also touches on the question of goals of musical excellence, which is worth teasing out further as a potential tension for community music facilitators, given their equal concern for social care. Music learning is a discipline, one that has long histories in certain cultures of demanding obedience to rigid expectations of execution, submission to higher "expert" authority (e.g., in the Western tradition, to a conductor or to the "great works"), comparison and competition among participants, and suppression of individual expression in favor of the collective. Where "musical excellence" is defined in terms of an uncompromising set of performance norms, and when this is presented as the most important outcome, care for the needs and vulnerabilities of the individual will naturally become a lesser priority. In response, an interventionist approach to community music can be seen to adopt a more encompassing definition of musical excellence, one that Turino (2008) argues has more in common with non-Western musical traditions, where music making is understood as social and relational practice, and where its meaning lies within these relationships (Small 1998). As we have already noted, "musical excellence" in community music interventions can, therefore, refer to the quality of the social experience—the bonds formed, meaning and enjoyment derived, sense of agency that emerges for individuals and the group—considered alongside the musical outcomes created through the music making experience.

CONCLUSION

Throughout this chapter we have explored community music practice as an *intervention* under the guidance of a community musician operating as a music facilitator. Four examples were used to illustrate the central notions of the practice, revealing the types of sites, skills, and attributes displayed by those engaged in the work. We asserted that musical excellence manifests itself within community music interventions through the quality of the social experience—the bonds formed, meaning and enjoyment derived, and sense of agency that emerges for individuals and the group. Social impacts such as those listed are to be considered alongside the musical outcomes created through the participatory music making experience. Importantly, this chapter has attempted to articulate skill sets required by musicians who intentionally bring people together through music participation. It is this, the ability to recognize and name distinctive attributes associated with running, organizing, and evaluating community music activity that sets the "intervention" model apart from a more general music making experience. Clarifying pedagogic approaches is important for the future of community music if the field wishes to have an impact within the broader domains of music education and music as leisure. The four examples presented in this chapter—music in an English-language learning classroom, the Amplified Elephants, music and health promotion, and music in residential homes for those living with dementia—all serve to support our belief that community music opens up new pathways for reflecting on, enacting, and developing approaches to facilitation that respond to a wide range of social, cultural, health, economic, and political contexts. Community music practice as an intervention through facilitation will, we hope, resonate strongly with those in other areas of music making in leisure time, as musicians continually search for new ways to activate and respond to the ever-increasing changes in musical environments across the world.

REFERENCES CITED

Baker, Geoffrey. 2014. *El Sistema: Orchestrating Venezuela's Youth*. New York: Oxford University Press.

Baker, Sarah, and Bruce M. Z. Cohen. 2008. "From Snuggling and Snogging to Sampling and Scratching: Girls' Nonparticipation in Community-based Music Activities." *Youth and Society* 39(3): 316–339. doi: 10.1177/0044118X06296696.

Bartleet, Brydie-Leigh, Peter Dunbar-Hall, Richard Letts, and Huib Schippers. 2009. *Sound Links: Community Music in Australia*. Brisbane: Queensland Conservatorium Research Centre. 250-page report to the Australian Research Council.

Beckles Willson, Rachel. 2011. "Music Teachers as Missionaries: Understanding Europe's Recent Dispatches to Ramallah." *Ethnomusicology Forum* 20(3):301–325. doi: 10.1080/17411912.2011.641370.

Bergh, Arild. 2010. "I'd Like toTeach the World to Sing: Music and Conflict Transformation." PhD dissertation, University of Exeter.

Bingley, Kate. 2011. "Bambeh's Song: Music, Women and Health in a Rural Community in Post-Conflict Sierra Leone." *Music and Arts in Action* 3(2): 59–78.

Brown, Tony, Ben Higham, and Mark Rimmer. 2014. *Whatever Happened to Community Music?* London: Arts and Humanities Research Council.

Clift, Stephen. 2012. "Singing, Wellbeing, and Health." In *Music, Health and Wellbeing*, edited by Raymond A. R. MacDonald, Gunter Kreutz, and Laura Mitchell, 111–124. Oxford: Oxford University Press.

DeQuadros, Andre, and Philipp Dorstewitz. 2011. "Community, Communication, Social Change: Music in Dispossessed Indian Communities." *International Journal of Community Music* 4(1): 59–70.

Doeser, James. 2014. *Step by Step: Arts Policy and Young People, 1944–2014*. London: Culture at King's (King's College London).

Doubleday, Veronica. 2008. "Sounds of Power: An Overview of Musical Instruments and Gender." *Ethnomusicology Forum* 17 (1):3–39. doi: 10.1080/17411910801972909.

Gouk, Penelope. 2000. *Musical Healing in Cultural Contexts*. Aldershot: Ashgate.

Higgins, Lee. 2007. The Impossible Future. *Action, Criticism and Theory for Music Education* 6 (3): 74–92, http://act.maydaygroup.org/articles/Higgins6_3.pdf.

Higgins, Lee. 2008. "Growth, Pathways and Groundwork: Community Music in the United Kingdom." *International Journal of Community Music* 1(1): 23–37.

Higgins, Lee. 2012. *Community Music: In Theory and in Practice*. New York: Oxford University Press.

Higgins, Lee, and Patricia Shehan Campbell. 2010. *Free to be Musical: Group Improvisation in Music*. Lanham, MD: Rowman and Littlefield.

Higgins, Lee, and Roger Mantie. 2013. "Improvisation as Ability, Culture, and Experience." *Music Educators Journal* 38. doi: 10.1177/0027432113498097.

Howell, Gillian. 2009. "From Imitation to Invention: Issues and Strategies for the ESL Music Classroom." *Musicworks: Journal of the Australia Council of Orff Schulwerk* 14(1): 61–66.

Howell, Gillian. 2011. "Do They Know They're Composing? Music Making and Understanding among Newly Arrived Immigrant and Refugee Children." *International Journal of Community Music* 4(1): 47–58.

Howell, Gillian. 2012a. "The Practitioner as Foreigner: Challenges and Dilemmas in Cross-Cultural Music Projects." Paper presented at the 11th International Conference on Cultural Diversity in Music Education, Singapore.

Howell, Gillian. 2012b. "The Right to Play: A Children's Composition Project in Timor-Leste (East Timor)." Paper presented at the 30th International Society for Music Education, Thessaloniki.

Howell, Gillian. 2015. "Music Interventions: Shaping Music Participation in the Aftermath of Conflict." In *The Wisdom of the Many: Key Issues in Arts Education*, edited by Shifra Schonmann, 87–92. Munich: Waxmann.

Hullick, James. 2013. "The Rise of the Amplified Elephants." *International Journal of Community Music* 6(2): 219–233.

Leak, Graeme. 2003. *Performance Making: A Manual for Music Workshops*. Strawberry Hills: Currency Press.

MacDonald, Raymond A. R., Gunter Kreutz, and Laura Mitchell. 2012. "What is *Music, Health, and Wellbeing*, and Why Is It Important?" In *Music, Health and Wellbeing*, edited by Raymond A. R. MacDonald, Gunter Kreutz, and Laura Mitchell, 3–11. Oxford: Oxford University Press.

Masso, Alex, and Tina Broad. 2013. "Community Choirs in Australia." *Music in Australia Knowledge Base*. http://musicinaustralia.org.au/index.php?title=Community_Choirs_in_Australia.

McGuire, Charles E. 2009. *Music and Victorian Philanthropy: The Tonic Sol-fa Movement*. Cambridge: Cambridge University Press.

Moser, Pete, and George McKay. 2005. *Community Music: A Handbook*. Lyme Regis: Russell House.

Mullen, Phil. 2008. "Issues in Leadership for Community Music Workers." Paper presented at the 11th Seminar of the ISME Commission for Community Music Activity, Rome.

Osborne, Nigel. 2009. "Music for Children in Zones of Conflict and Post-conflict: A Psychobiological Approach." In *Communicative Musicality: Exploring the Basis of Human Companionship*, edited by Stephen Malloch and Colwyn Trevarthen, 331–356. Oxford: Oxford University Press.

Pruitt, Lesley J. 2013. *Youth Peacebuilding: Music, Gender and Change*. Albany: State University of New York Press.

Schippers, Huib, and Brydie-Leigh Bartleet. 2013. "The Nine Domains of Community Music: Exploring the Crossroads of Formal and Informal Music Education." *International Journal of Music Education (Practice)* 31(4): 454–471.

Small, Christopher. 1998. *Musicking: The Meanings of Performing and Listening*. Middletown, CT: Wesleyan University Press.

Smilde, Rineke, Kate Page, and Peter Alheit. 2014. *While the Music Lasts: On Music and Dementia*. Delft: Eburon Academic.

Stige, Brynjulf. 2012. "Health Musicking: A Perspective on Music and Health as Action and Performance." In *Music, Health and Wellbeing*, edited by Raymond A. R. MacDonald, Gunter Kreutz, and Laura Mitchell, 183–195. Oxford: Oxford University Press.

Turino, Thomas. 2008. *Music as Social Life: The Politics of Participation*. Chicago: University of Chicago Press.

Veblen, Kari K. 2008. "The Many Ways of Community Music." *International Journal of Community Music* 1(1): 5–22.

CHAPTER 32

....

LEISURE GROOVES

An Open Letter to Charles Keil

....

ROGER MANTIE

Can you write like you talk like you sing like you drum like you dance your life?

Charles Keil

DEAR Charlie,[1]

This letter is long overdue—both in terms of my commitment to you and your ideas, and in terms of my own editorial deadlines for this handbook. (Let the record show that I was one of the last to complete a chapter for this volume.) If you will permit the informality of this format, I wish to share with you some thoughts, observations, and comments on your work and the impact it has had on me, especially my thinking about music and leisure. Truth be told, I imagined this chapter as a letter ever since I decided to write about your work. However, having read through the issues of your self-published "journals," *Echology* and the *M.U.S.E. Letter*, it appears that this open letter form is somewhat old hat for you. (*So much for my attempt at originality.*) My hope is that, in discussing some of your ideas in this letter to you, readers of this volume might be motivated to dig in to your work and explore further.

Although we have not met face to face, our Skype interview and our email exchanges remain a highlight in my academic career.[2] To experience the vitality of your thought definitely gives credence to that "older and wiser" thing. *Sharp as a tack* certainly applies here. I have to come clean, though: I had not fully appreciated the extent to which your clarity of thought reflected a lifelong commitment to a core set of ideas and values. I had also failed to fully appreciate how integral your wife Angeliki has been throughout your career (despite your consistent mention of her in all of your book introductions, and her name appearing as a coauthor for both *Polka Happiness* and *Bright Balkan Morning*). I see now that she has been your life partner *and* intellectual partner. I say this not in any way to diminish the significance of your ideas. Quite the contrary, in fact. The consistency of your core ideas (and your attention to issues of gender, race, class, and sexuality) reflects, I think, the workings of a great and sensitive mind—one whose insatiable curiosity continues to deepen and enrich insights that have been purpose-driven from the start. Having spent a lot of time with your written work, and having spent many hours combing through sixty-plus boxes of your material at the Howard Gottlieb Archive Center at Boston University, it is abundantly clear to me that at no point have you ever been motivated by money, ego, or career aggrandizement (perhaps to your detriment at times?). You have been nothing if not principled throughout your life!

Some readers might be wondering what a letter to a retired professor of American Studies at State University of New York at Buffalo is doing in a handbook on music making and leisure. You might be wondering the same thing. After all, you are essentially an ethnomusicologist (among other things) with a special interest in music learning and teaching. To my knowledge, you haven't made leisure or recreation an overt object of your attention. I found only one explicit reference (and this not by you specifically), when Angeliki writes in your book *Polka Happiness*, "Contemporary discussions of recreation and music, even 'classical' and 'art' music, tend to center on a view of recreation as profane and 'art' as solely inhabiting the realm of aesthetics. . . . We [as a society] tend to lump together under 'recreation' both the market-imperialized leisure time spent in or around expensive gadgets and the kind of life-restoring sociability laced by poetry, myth, dance, music, and culinary alchemy, that occurs in what we [in this book] call 'polka happiness' " (*PH*,103).

Outside of this one rich reference (the themes of which I shall return to later), you don't really address music as leisure. In my reading of your work, however, I see leisure and recreation *everywhere*.[3] *Urban Blues* (1966), your first book, really set the tone. While the recreational aspects of *Urban Blues* could be read as perhaps more on the consumption side ("fans") than on the production side, your investigation makes clear that, while many of the blues musicians you studied made an occupation out of their music making, this was often ancillary to what the practice was about: the musical embodiment of particular values and a particular way of life. The blues—performer or nonperformer—are a way of being; they are leisure writ large. Your sensitive treatment of race here (and elsewhere!) also serves as a wonderful reminder that leisure practices are never innocent, but rather, as several authors in this volume have similarly pointed out, invariably embroiled in conflict and struggle. Leisure is laden with baggage.

To suggest that your study of the Tiv people of Africa, published as the award-winning book *Tiv Song* (1979), is a study of leisure practices may be to stretch the definition of leisure too far. And yet, to read your work through a leisure lens is to see music a little more like your friend Christopher Small did: as an eminently social practice rather than as an object or "thing"—*art*. By coining the word *musicking* to describe a practice that encompasses everyone, including even those who take concert tickets at the door, Small reminds us, as I believe you do, that music's value far exceeds the narrow boundaries drawn by the aestheticians—people whose interests seem driven, as Pierre Bourdieu has argued (present also in Nietzsche and Foucault among others), more by a desire to rationalize one group's taste as superior to another's than a desire to theorize the place of artistic activity in the lives of *all* people. As Small (1977) preciously said, "music is too important to be left to the musicians" (214). While it is true that in *Tiv Song* you study people who attempt to exist as full-time song composers (i.e., "musicians"), I would argue that the real story in *Tiv Song* is how music and music making are such an integral and important part of daily life for all Tiv, and how knowledge of Tiv society might contribute to the betterment of our own "localities."[4]

To explain further: I see leisure and recreation as what people do, outside of "work" and other obligations (e.g., family, personal maintenance) that gives joy and meaning to their lives. This is a little simplistic, of course, and paints perhaps too rosy a picture. (Scholars in Leisure Studies are no doubt having conniptions about now.) Leisure and recreation are not necessarily the same thing, for example, and neither is unequivocally good; whereas recreation implies activity, often nonserious activity, leisure can mean a variety of things, from time to activity to a state of mind (to name three). Thus, when we consider music making not as an occupational endeavor, but as part of a constellation of cultural-artistic practices bound up in the politics of everyday life, I think it becomes clearer that music making is leisure par excellence; your work helps us to see how and why people—*everyday* people—engage in music making.

A LIFE OF RESEARCH AND ACTIVISM

To be clear, this chapter is not about *you*, but about your ideas and how they might contribute to an understanding of music and leisure. I'm not sure how to discuss your ideas, however, without situating you and your career. First, I think we need to just get this out there: you are special, despite your best efforts to convince people otherwise. Attending Yale and the University of Chicago and studying with Leonard Meyer, Alan Merriam, David Schneider, and Clifford Geertz (among other "big" names) puts you in the distinguished pedigree category. To the list of notable teachers we add the (very partial— apologies for egregious omissions) list of close friends and colleagues: John Blacking, John Chernoff, Judith Cohen, R. Crumb, Stephen Feld, Ellen Koskoff, Lawrence Levine, Roswell Rudd, R. Murray Schafer, John Shepherd, Christopher Small, Chris Waterman, and so on.[5] I seriously doubt these people would give you the time of day if they did not respect you and your considerable intellectual acumen.

One does not need to read very far into your work to realize that, despite your often casual, if not colloquial prose, there is more than a bit of substance behind the pretense toward ordinariness. Exhibit one: you named your self-published journal *Echology*, based on the ancient Greek story of Echo and Narcissus (using it as a kind of heuristic, as you describe in "Echotastrophe"). Elsewhere you claim to thumb your nose at high theory as "a philistine and a troglodyte, [who sits] under a rock and snipe[s] at it" (*MG*, 177). *Hmmm* . . . I think you may be guilty of disingenuousness here, Charlie. *Urban Blues* and *Tiv Song*, for example, ooze theory.[6] You might chose to debate the difference between scholarship and theory, of course, but even there I doubt the sincerity; the theoretical rigor in your work is rather astonishing. I can, however, appreciate your humility. I have yet to encounter a pretentious sentence in anything of yours I have read.[7] I would not describe your work so much as rejecting high theory, but rather, as never relying on it or on impenetrable language as a shield, crutch, or substitute for cogent and insightful analysis based on questions that matter. Perhaps this is why I find myself so attracted to your work. While I take heed of Marshall McLuhan's perceptive insight that "the medium is the message," this too often seems to fuel academia's substitution of impenetrable style for meaningful substance (as epitomized in the Alan Sokal affair[8]). You never capitulate to the temptation to substitute a seven-syllable word where a one-syllable word will suffice.

I suspect your penchant for straightforward prose stems from your work as a cultural anthropologist focused primarily on what "average people" do. Although you spent considerable time in the circles of ethnomusicologists during your career, your efforts to popularize "applied sociomusicology" (as opposed to "applied ethnomusicology," the current trend)[9] seem to me reflective of your underlying concern with the everyday and the local rather than the special or exotic. This is not to undersell any of your investigations. *Bright Balkan Morning* (2002), for example, has become a staple in ethnomusicology. But whereas ethnomusicologists likely see the book as about the Romani musicians and their specific (exotic to the West) musical practices, I see the real story as about the culture of a town in northern Greece. It's about how people—regular, everyday people in various localities—participate in music as part of meaningful daily existence. Thus, I think your emphasis on "applied sociomusicology" conveys a stance or an attitude about why we should learn about various musics. Your work isn't so much an academic documentary and archival exercise, but one with profoundly practical intent. It is anthropology and sociology at the same time. As you wrote on several occasions, the goal in your work is to get "more participatory practices into our own lives and the lives of those around us."

I see this goal in all you have written. (I trust the connections between your work and my interest in leisure are becoming clearer by this point.) This goal of getting participatory musical practices into daily life is evident in the questions that animate your work. For example:

- "I am primarily interested in the relation between the blues and the people who are creating them today" (*UB*, 44)
- "Why do Tiv make songs? And why do they come out sounding so very Tiv?" (*TS*, 7)
- "I would like to find out what the polka stands for in the minds of Polish-Americans, and in turn, what the meaning of the Polka tradition for Poles might mean for the rest of us." (RP)
- "Why do some people want to stomp and spin together on weekends in an ethnic working-class idiom while most don't?" (*PH*, 3)
- "What part does music play in your life?" (*MM*)

In the books that flowed from these questions it is clear that these are not just fanciful curiosities, but rather, questions aimed at mobilizing a deeper, richer engagement with life in and through music and dance. While some might read these questions as an objectified "about them" investigation, I see the questions as about *us*. Your concerns seem, to me, focused on *doing something about* how we live, individually and collectively.

There is another side to your work, however, that transcends the straightforward promotion of music making. What *really* seems to motivate your life's work is a deep-seated conviction that Western society (*snivilization*, as you say) is going to hell in a handbasket. A few examples should suffice to illustrate your somewhat cynical view of "civilization" (and romanticization of the "primitive"?):

- "There may come a time ... when the screams of the dying drown out our best singers, when religion, the opiate of the masses, and art, the opiate of the elite, can no longer dull the pain. And I hope that time is coming soon" (*TS*, 186)
- "Instead of applying our ordering principles to [the Tiv's] energies, we should be tapping their energies to undermine our order, to criticize and revitalize, if possible, our existence" (*TS*, 183)
- [the mission of *MUSE*, Inc.] "is nothing less than the rebirth of satisfying communities and cultures in the midst of a growing, powerful, dominating but deeply discontented civilization" (*ML*, 2)
- "dance-rites-music will herald an end of patri-capitalist ideology" (*Echo* 1: 3)
- "What are the local rites that will make a global ideal of peace and justice into a reality?" (*Echo* 1: 3)

Participatory music making, you have consistently argued, is the cure-all to the ills of our corrupted Westernized lifestyles. If *we* (in the West) could only live more like *them* (the gentle peoples). In principle, I don't disagree. Like you, I share a commitment to social causes and to equality. I absolutely love the spirit of social justice that infuses all of your work, which consistently shows great sensitivity to all forms of oppression.[10] If I didn't similarly believe in the positive power of music I wouldn't have devoted my life to its learning and teaching!

I think what we can learn from your work is that leisure practices, such as participatory music making, are in fact forms of activism, even when situated within the seemingly benign context of "recreation." Not unlike Gunkel (2004), who argues, based in part on your work, that polka represents a form of resistance to mass culture, I see leisure as a site where freedom and resistance can be exercised. It is also a site ripe for abuse, of course. Some people do fall into passivity (*spectatoritis*, as it was called in the earlier part of the twentieth century) and Veblen's "conspicuous consumption," among other evils. Herbert Marcuse and others in the Critical Theory camp who regard leisure as an opiate designed to thwart the uprising of the proletariat make valid points of which we should take heed. But just because there are risks in leisure does not automatically discount its potential for good. Music and dance are two human capacities that cannot be extinguished by social inequality and oppression, and their engagement should not, in my opinion, be interpreted as any kind of opiate.

Being frank, while I respect and admire all of your work, I'm not completely convinced by some of your notions that pretechnological "tribal" societies were (are?) superior simply by virtue of their simplicity and "naturalness" (e.g., "If any society and culture reveals our species being, our human nature, primitive society is it"; *Echo* 1: 8). I don't disagree that there is much to be learned from such societies; many seem far more "civilized" (with apologies; I know you dislike that word) than our current Westernized global world of morally destitute, hypercompetitive, neoliberal market rationality, and many "primitive" societies do indeed embody music and dance in a way I find attractive. I am just not convinced we can turn back the clock. I admire your attempts to "[transform] this society locality by locality, and [learn] from the locals who were here before us" (*Echo* 1: 2). I too believe in hope and change and the possibility of making the world a better place, but I don't think we can return to a simpler era. Despise them if you must, but televisions and other *gadgets* are not going away. I'm not saying I endorse them (and in fact am one of those parents who tries, often in vain, to limit my children's "screen time")—but I accept them as unavoidable. Don't get me wrong: I sincerely appreciate those like yourself who bang the drum in the name of peace and harmony and simpler living. We desperately need more Charlie Keils in the world. I, however, must follow my own path—one where I try to promote the potential of leisure *qua* leisure to achieve (hopefully) similar ends.

Musicians in Everyday Life?

I trust by this point you can see how I view much of your work—with *Polka Happiness* being perhaps the most obvious example—as centered on music (and dance) as leisure practices. That is, while your socio-musicology work probes the meanings music holds for people in specialized, bounded contexts, so many of the musics that you have studied occur primarily (though not exclusively) in the context of what might be loosely described as *recreation*. Polka musicians and dancers gather in a hall on a Saturday night, the jazz and blues musicians and their audiences celebrate the music "after hours," the Tiv and the Romani engage song and dance apart from their "day jobs." That is, while music may, as Alan Merriam (1964) has ably demonstrated, have a panoply of functions (religious, ceremonial, etc.), most music and dance in the world is engaged with *for fun*, outside of or in addition to what people do to make a living. (To be clear, the "music in everyday life" in question here is not the commodified stuff we are constantly bombarded with, important though that may be in its own right, but the making and moving to music.)

Although you are retired, I know you are, at the time of this writing, still active. My hope is that you will take up the challenge of further exploring the messy intersection of vocation and avocation in music. You work doesn't avoid it completely, but you rarely look it square in the eye. You discuss, for example, how "even the best and most resourceful [Tiv] composers continue to do some farming" (*TS*, 102), essentially explaining that

(1) Tiv song composers cannot financially exist on song alone, and (2) Tiv composers *wish* they could exist financially without farming. You also point out how polka musicians almost always have day jobs, something that apparently affirms their membership in the working class and confers a kind of authenticity on the music—but you rarely interrogate the assumption that being a working musician should necessarily involve hardship and suffering in terms of having to maintain full-time employment in addition to one's musical pursuits.

In *Polka Happiness*, for example, Angeliki writes that musician Eddie Blazonczyk "is sweet and potent precisely because he is at the center of all that daily work, the everyday struggle to make a living and to steal time for play in a community vibrant with hard work, discipline, rivalries, fidelity, heartbreak, and humor" (*PH*, 117–118). While I appreciate the celebration of "ethnic-ness" (though perhaps not the implicit notion that ethnic struggle is to be endorsed), and I recognize that a good number of recreational musicians need to "steal time for play"[11] (or *make time for making music* as Gareth Smith and I might say), you seem to imply that people should not earn a living as musicians. While I suspect that your *real* message ("There shouldn't be a music industry"; *Echo* 1: 4) is that everyone should be so musically and "dansically" empowered that the occupational category of "musician" becomes nonsensical—I wonder where this leaves people who make, and desire to make, music as their primary occupation or vocation. When you write, "Music should exist live, for the moment, in present time and its makers should be rewarded with happiness and barter-like reciprocities" (*Echo* 1: 4), you seem to suggest that people who seek to make their living as full-time musicians have somehow "sold out" or that their motivations for making music are tainted. While I agree that participatory music making should not be for the privileged few and that our society would be better off if more people were musically (and dansically) active, I wonder if our world might be further impoverished if we were to lose the economy that supports (and, historically, has always supported) a class of full-time musicians and artists.

My point here is twofold. First, I think we must acknowledge that, despite historical variations in the exact nature of the music economy, there are people who have made, and continue to make a living working (vocationally) as musicians, earning money in a variety of ways (e.g., live performance, composing and arranging, recording, producing, etc.). I too dislike "ownership" and dislike thinking of music as an object to be bought and sold; I share your commitment to reduced commodification (which, thanks to the Internet, may already be happening). On the flip side, the people who cut my hair and fix my car don't work for free; if we want live entertainment, perhaps it is reasonable to expect the providers of the service to be paid with more than just "happiness and barter-like reciprocities." I cannot help pointing out also the hypocrisy when you claim to oppose all copyright laws when it comes to music, but then state, in the first issue of *Echology*, that all the contributions belong to the authors and shouldn't be reproduced without permission! I'm in no way advocating on behalf of copyright (a systems of laws I consider to have been co-opted by big industry), but I don't see how one can argue for "intellectual property" but not "creative property." The writing of words deserves protection but the writing of music does not?

Second, there are a good number of people who love making music but do not engage with it as their primary means of making a living. In the Leisure Studies field, Robert Stebbins has theorized depth of leisure involvement with the classification system of his Serious Leisure Perspective (http://www.seriousleisure.net), a perspective that is not without its own issues and limitations, but one that helps us, I think, make sense of those who treat their avocational interests with passion. Setting his classifications aside for a moment, allow me to describe three groups of people. First, there are those who *wish* they could pursue music vocationally. There are, I submit, some endeavors like music and other arts that many people find more agreeable than cutting hair, fixing cars, lawyering, doctoring, accounting, and so on, and these people would, *ceterbis paribus*, choose an occupation in the arts. Not everyone, of course, but many. By turning their backs on their passions due to what they consider, rightly or wrongly, more lucrative, stable, and secure financial occupations, some of these people likely endure frustrated lives, perhaps wondering what might have been if they had had the courage to "take a chance" on music as a vocation. A second group, perhaps like the Tiv composers and Polka musicians you studied, attempt to make the best of things by engaging in semi-professional careers, tolerating their nonmusical occupations in order to support what Robert Dubin (1956, 1979) terms their "central life interest." A third group—the ones I am mostly interested in—are content to treat their artistic interests strictly avocationally, engaging with music and dance in their "free" time, "for the love of it," as Wayne Booth (1999) has so eloquently put it.

Given the current breakdown in twentieth-century music commodification and restricted access or ownership models, the "pro-am" intersection in music in Western societies may be one of the twenty-first century's great revolutions. I hope you will take up the challenge to help us better understand the term "musician" in everyday life in the context of vocation/avocation vis-à-vis leisure and culture in various localities in the world. I know that if anyone can explore these tricky issues with the thoughtfulness and sensitivity they deserve, it is you.[12]

ON BECOMING A
(RECREATIONAL) MUSICIAN

[O]ne reason there were many more [polka] bands [in the 1960s and 1970s] was that young musicians were still being trained in the music-store schools . . . which specialized in turning out competent young musicians swiftly.

(*PH*, 162)

[M]any music educators armor themselves in the psychological statistics of nearly hard science. They study the statistical procedures appropriate to the measurement of the psychopedagogical techniques used to develop the appreciation skills of kids listening to written down music as recorded and then played on a record player in a classroom. How many layers of reification is that? Eight? Ten? "Hey Dr. Advanced Music Educator, could I beat this drum a coupla times?"

(*Echo* 2: 132; cf. *MG*, 227)

Don't wait for music education specialists to do this for you. You may find key allies in this field but most music teachers, in schools and school systems where they still exist, have very limited time, lots of curricular instructions, a struggle to develop specialists on instruments, a commitment to and skills built upon written music, and often a Western bias that says "don't tap your foot" rather than "let's dance!"[13]

One of the problems that concerns both of us is how one becomes a musician who sings, dances, and/or plays just *for the love of it*. Based on the things you have written above, it would seem (to my dismay) that you trust "teaching artists" rather than "arts educators" to get the job done. In part, I get it: the generalist nature of music education prevents most researchers and scholars from attaining the level of specialized rigor found in fields such as ethnomusicology, and yes, far too many school music teachers are in fact guilty of *miseducation* in music. I readily admit that the world of school music—at least as it exists in Canada and the United States—is still grounded in the kind of beliefs about music-as-art that position recreational music making as profane (Willis 1978), as you alluded to in *Polka Happiness*. Music, if it is to be taught in schools, must be "of the highest quality" goes the party line of most school music teachers. I often dream about how much more musical our society might be if music educators thought more like applied sociomusicologists. What if school music emulated what you tried to do with MUSE (Musicians United for Superior Education) in Buffalo in the early 1990s?[14] As one of your colleagues, John Blacking, famously put it: "Must the majority be made 'unmusical' so that a few may become more 'musical'?" (1974, 4).

On the other hand, it seems a little dismissive to completely ignore the work done by people who devote their lives to the study and practice of music learning and teaching, and who, because of their understanding of children, are far superior teachers than many "teaching artists" I've seen, who too often presume that personal artistic competency equates with an ability to teach effectively. "Good teaching" does not, in my view, reduce simply to personal experience or the way we were taught.[15] "Good teaching," moreover, recognizes its place within a larger framework. Teaching music in the context of a school is not the same as teaching it in a music store. The school music teacher is obligated (and motivated) to teach *all* the children who walk through the classroom door, not just those whose parents are willing to invest the time and resources to pay for private lessons. I find it just a little too facile to say, "Helping children to make music is easy. Just be there" (*Echo* 2: 132). *Seriously, Charlie?*

I mean no disrespect, of course. I recognize that you come from a very musical background and have an impressive pedigree, having learned percussion from no less than Sousa's long-time bass drum player, Gus Helmecke. Your studies with Alan Merriam and

Leonard Meyer provide you with more than ample academic music scholarship "cred." Your *oeuvre* leaves no doubt that you have thought long and hard about music learning and teaching and about larger issues of living. I just wish you might have offered up a more nuanced critique alongside your wonderful efforts to provide a "superior education" in music. Is it not unfair to place blame on individual school music teachers rather than the convoluted and unfortunate system of which they are products and in which they must operate?

It feels to me like you too often compare apples and oranges. My understanding sees the purposes of school music as connected to an egalitarian ethos of access and inclusion. The "music-store schools" you praise presumably weren't offering lessons for free, and while the teachers in such schools may have succeeded in turning out competent musicians, they also had the luxury of one-on-one instruction and a selection bias where parental support was a given. Most music educators tend to think, rightly or wrongly, beyond the ethnomusicological term *transmission*. At heart, I think you do too—despite your occasional use of phrases like "passing it on"[16] or "training." When you write, for example, that an aim of MUSE was to "help children incorporate (that is, incarnate or embody) the powers of playful creation so thoroughly via multicultural arts action so that they can not be pacified and alienated," it seems clear to me that you are ultimately concerned less with conceptions of learning that derive from what Anna Sfard (1998) describes as the "acquisition metaphor," and more with the kinds of *becoming* issues that are central to larger visions of what it means to be "educated." I'm not suggesting that all music educators share these larger visions of education, where learning is understood in terms of the kinds of people we become and the kind of society we desire to foster, but certainly many do (see e.g., Bowman 2002). My point is that the roles and responsibilities of "music teacher" and "music educator" should not be assumed as synonymous. During my time teaching music in schools I never regarded what I did as merely "teaching music." In my mind I was in the business of *educating*; music was what brought us together in the same room and provided the experiences for personal and interpersonal growth, but I never assumed that such growth was an automatic outcome of music.

Permit me to acknowledge that, despite my positionality as a former school music teacher, I too am critical of the music education profession—one that so often breaks my heart with its stubborn adherence to values and practices antithetical to my own conception of music education, one I view as fundamentally very closely aligned with your own. Music education as a discipline has not done a very good job of understanding music in its socio-cultural context, for example. Its origins in a "democratization of high culture" perspective have led to a situation (in Canada and the United States at least) where music—or more precisely, music of the received Western classical tradition—is taught not as a lifelong participatory practice, but as a universal art form where students become well-rounded, better people through their exposure to, and instruction in, large ensemble performance. My criticisms, however, recognize and appreciate the social reproductive forces (Bourdieu 1984) that create and sustain the failings and trappings you identify (see e.g., Mantie and Talbot 2015; Talbot and Mantie 2015). Even if and when school music teachers wish to teach in a manner more in line with the ideals you espouse, schooling shuts them down with its many layers of bureaucracy and unyield-ing demands for "standards" and "accountability." It is thus not that I disagree with your critique in principle, but that I think the conversation might be helped more by some sort of social-structuralist analysis which you are so well equipped to conduct. Is it that schools are truly incapable of teaching music properly and should get out of the business, or is it an issue of misrecognizing their *raisons d'être*? Perhaps the hope for recreational musicianship must indeed lie outside of public institutions in the form of organizations and agencies like MUSE, Inc.?

BORN TO GROOVE AND THE QUESTION OF (LIFE)STYLE

As you acknowledged in our interview, "Paideia con Salsa" best captures your schol-arly thoughts on music and education. As with all your work, your erudition shines through in spades. I love your idea of coupling pre-Platonic conceptions of *paideia* with New York Afro-Cuban dance musics. Your focus on resuscitating primary (what you like to call "primal") connections between music and dance seems in keeping with not only pre-Platonic conceptions of *paideia*, but also with later Aristotelian-inspired conceptions of *schole*, if we can look past Aristotle's proclivity to overemphasize "con-templation." Although Aristotle clearly falls a little more on the Apollonian side, and your "paideia con salsa" idea definitely leans Dionysian, together they seem to hold the potential to make life more worth living: the good life and the common good fused together in wonderful harmony. The meanings of both *paideia* (loosely: ideal socialized upbringing or education) and *schole* (leisure or school) are, of course, debated over by contemporary scholars, but, if we can agree to set subtle semantic differences aside for a moment, I think we might agree that we are more or less on the same page when it comes to the value of music and movement in idealistic visions of individual and collective liv-ing that is rewarding and life-affirming.[17] For me, this is education, not just "teaching music," because it is about a way of life, not just about musical competency.

This "way of life" educational approach seems to me a particularly significant obser-vation when placed in a leisure context. Leisure in the context of *paideia* and *schole* invariably involves the intersection of the Dionysian (what I want to do irrespective of others, consequences be damned) and Apollonian (what I know I should do and what others want me to do based on responsible and ethical behavior). Your own approach to this problem seems traceable to your educational background. Your research skills as a participant-observer have clearly been the secret to your career. *Tiv Song, Urban Blues, Polka Happiness, Bright Balkan Morning*—none of these would have been pos-sible without your brilliant powers of observation. As you told me in our interview, "The participant observation learned in an anthropology graduate school is a mode of being." What makes your work so much more interesting to me (as an educator) than the work of many others who ply the participant observation trade, is that you enact this "mode of being" in everything you do; it isn't just an academic exercise for you. Although we must acknowledge that your ability to transcend traditional Western work-leisure divides is an outgrowth of the privilege that all academics (among others) enjoy, I don't think this diminishes the significance of your chosen way of life. Many people who enjoy similar privilege fall prey to bifurcated existences that too often relegate leisure to scheduled Dionysian outings.

I am often left wondering, though, about your own Dionysian-Apollonian balance, especially in regard to what I perceive in much of your work as the privileging of the "natural" or "innate" over the "manufactured" or "developed." While I do appreciate your faith in the existence of some sort of essential vital drive or "muse within," as your acquaintance Jon-Roar Bjørkvold (1992) has put it, this sometimes seems a little simplistic. We do need to be wary of how our Westernized world threatens *homo ludens* and our primal impulse to move and dance. And yet, at times (too often?) you seem to pooh-pooh any sort of structured, accumulated, or formalized knowledge in music. I am reminded of how the jazz tradition has come to valorize the real life, "authentic" learning of "the street" over that of the supposed artificiality of the classroom. I can respect this to a point, but does this not seem a little inconsistent? The importance of *ethos* in ancient Greek education wasn't left to chance; it was very carefully and deliberately cultivated! You wrote your books and essays on the basis of a whole lot of *acquired* "classroom" knowledge. (Let us not forget those degrees from Yale and the University of Chicago.) You didn't have the advantage of Wikipedia, so I'm guessing you developed your knowledge of linguistics and Greek classics through a lot of dedicated study. When it comes to the learning and teaching of music and dance, however, you seem averse to any kind of developed or formalized knowledge. With apologies to Nike, "Just do it!" seems to be your *modus operandi* when it comes to music and dance. Is structured learning not implied when you talk about "saturating newborns, infants, toddlers, children of all ages, in local grooves/skills"? The words *saturating* and *skills* imply, to me, an act of intentionality, not something left to chance.

One could—and should—go further here and argue that, despite the presence of some inborn human capacity for and attraction to music and dance ("the muse"), we all end up socialized in one way or another into a preexisting sociocultural world: the Marx *history not of our making* kind of thing. Among the aspects of your work that attracts me is that I see the big picture of music and leisure inextricably linked to matters of class, style, and identity. As you write, style and identity are very much intertwined: "Style tells you who your home folks are. . . . Whatever the hell else is going on out there, I know I am a polka person, a blues person, or a jazz person" (*MG*, 291).

Perhaps your crowning achievement flowing out of the thoughts articulated in "Paideia con Salsa" is *Born to Groove* (borntogroove.org). I think the essays and exercises speak volumes about how you regard the place of music and dance in the world. As you write, "The underlying 'best guess' of *Born to Groove* is that saturating newborns, infants, toddlers, children of all ages, in local grooves/skills of all kinds will restore humanity to sanity over time, thru time, in time" (n.d., i). An admirable goal, to be sure.

I'm all for your "Afrocentric music-dance education." Again, though, I am not too sure how to reconcile what I see in *Born to Groove* (and the rest of your work) as a somewhat jarring juxtaposition between your towering intellectualism and your acritical endorsement of purity and/or innocence. What about those who aren't into Afrocentric music-dance education and just want to learn to play classical music on the cello?

What is unclear to me is where freedom and resistance factor into your theories of musical participation. On the one hand, you write in *Tiv Song* that, "[I]n the years since 1973 I find myself becoming more and more of a 'materialist,' a Marxist, someone who believes that cultural systems are organized, disorganized, and reorganized by socio-economic forces" (*TS*, 7). Style, as you say, "is a reflection of class forces" (*MG*, 202). No disagreement here. You also write: "Many of us have become so transfixed by the powerful high culture and mass culture Scylla and Charybdis[18] that we forget the vital currents of people's music and culture which still flow between them" (*Echo* 1: 11). Perhaps. But where does this leave us? What are we to make of people's choices to participate in and resist various cultural practices? You seem interested only in the grassroots simplicity of folk forms (e.g., salsa, polka, brass bands), as if these are more "honest" or real than developed, classical, or contemporary forms. Are you subscribing to the view that those who willingly engage in high culture and mass culture are dupes that lack agency due to their "false consciousness"? What of those who attempt to resist the forces that have resulted in their *class*, and hence style, membership? What if you don't like your "home folks"?

Although not all leisure consists of music, I think that, similar to other cultural practices, music involvement speaks not only to what one chooses to do with one's time, but to the kind of person one desires to be. True, some musical practices are more generic than others, but even those that escape "ethnic" connotations still carry socio-cultural identifications. Participating in a community orchestra or in Sacred Harp singing can both be considered leisure activities, but they carry very different markers of *distinction* (Bourdieu, *again*). In one I'm "cultured" (note the scare quotes), in the other I am involved in a "subculture." The rub here is that the freedom to choose who one wants to be isn't as simple as all that, right?

At a certain point one might be in a position to make choices about who one wants one's "home folks" to be, but this comes after a period of immersion over which we, as children, have little say. We are "stylized" by virtue of our birth into specific families, communities, and cultural value structures. Children born into the American Polish tradition in Buffalo may share certain affinities with children born into the southern Arizona polka heritage, but I don't think either would be confused about who their home folks were at a polka party! That said, accelerated processes of globalization (Appadurai 1996) have, for some time, been bringing into question the stability of what were once more clear-cut matters of cultural inheritance. We are still born into systems of value, of course. The Polish child of Buffalo and the Latino child of Tucson likely partake in different leisure activities—or perhaps not—but the Internet has forever altered the meanings of "tradition" and "change" as they relate to our received cultural inheritance. Bourdieu's concept of *habitus* seems apropos here. Our biographies are not necessarily deterministic, but undeniably exert a force. Both the Buffalo child and Tucson child might, at the insistence of their parents, learn something of the polka (which will stick with them throughout their lives), but they are probably more likely than their parents to be aware of the diversity of polka and more likely to incorporate this knowledge into their own practices. These children might also choose to do Sacred Harp singing, even if neither has a tradition of it in the family or the neighborhood, and might even figure out a way to create some kind of creolized polka–Sacred Harp music. (Okay, maybe I'm overreaching on this one, but you take the point.)

This brings me to two final issues related to (life)style: the question of loss and the influence of mediation. Two strikingly similar statements of yours, published over twenty-five years apart, help illustrate the former:

> If present trends continue, it may not be long before Negro music will be characterized by the interpenetration of two musical genres: a music of the people (soul styles), and a music for listeners only (advanced jazz styles). (*UB*, 32)
> If present trends continue, polka bands and dances in Buffalo will fade out completely early in the twenty-first century. (*PH*, 153)

I'm certainly not advocating the disappearance of socio-cultural practices such as the blues or polka, but you do seem rather attached to the notion of preservation. I find this somewhat paradoxical, because I know you aren't a preservationist; you are all about, as you said in our interview, zeroing in on "where the action is."[19] I do understand that practices cannot live without practitioners, and I understand the impulse to try to sustain those practices we consider valuable; identity is inextricably linked to continuity. It does feel, however, that at times you romanticize musics "of the people," especially working-class people, as if "people's music" is defined strictly in ethnic terms, and as if what *has been* is superior to what *might be*.

Perhaps you have never been able to shake Alan Lomax's warnings of "cultural greyout," but your apologia for "people's music" seems too often predicated upon villainizing mediated music and mass culture. You write, for example, about the dangers of "letting mediated music substitute for full environmental and social awareness in present time" (*MG*, 212), and of how pop culture comes at the expense of "specific ethnic traditions" (*PH*, 75). Like you, I celebrate the working classes (although I'm not sure it is fair or accurate to equate working class with ethnic these days), but I'm not prepared to suggest that mass culture equates to a loss of agency or that mediation is unconditionally evil.[20] There are simply too many exciting practices in the world (as evidenced in this volume) fostering and creating new communities that result from the potentialities of technology. You might argue that some of these are not "life-affirming," but maybe such an assessment is best left in the eye of the beholder? I recognize, of course, that many of your published thoughts on mediation in music pre-date the Internet and are focused on passive if not mindless consumption. Is it possible that, following Jenkins et al. (2009), the "participatory culture" made possible by the Internet might represent "people's music" today? After all, "beats" seems to be the operative word in young people's culture today. (So maybe you do have it right: we are *born to groove*.)

ON PARTICIPATION

I have many more thoughts and questions than available space, so in closing I'd like to focus on what is arguably at the center of all of your work: participation. As you write:

> I've been pushing versions of participation theory, groovology, a praxis-predominant, experiential approach to anthropology since the1960s (Keil 1966; Keil and Feld 1994; Keil 1995) but in recent green-minded decades it seems ever more urgent to work through and get past the language of the alienation theories . . . to simpler affirmations of life-groove-play-party-pleasure-joy in the here and now. . . . I think the beautiful truth of our human condition is participation: epitomized in music-dance-rites; always and all ways for pleasure; imagination-improvization-participation by every means possible in present time. Each of us is born to groove, born to be a prolific poetizer, musicker, dancer throughout life. Most children in the industrialized world, but now ever more globally, are being shut down, stopped, pushed off this path of creativity and full expression. . . . In the here and now, Participation gives us the best answers to the oldest questions about the meaning of life. (*TWP*, 40)

As I've hopefully made clear in this letter, I feel like your point about children being "shut down" actually weakens your argument. While I don't necessarily disagree, I don't agree either. Whether or not people are pushed off the path of creativity and full expression feels like a red herring to me, one that results in focusing attention on the alienation theories you oppose rather than on the potential to be found in groovology and participation.

If I ever get appointed Ruler of the Universe, I think one of my first acts will be to have every educator (*every* educator) read your essay "They Want the Music but They Don't Want the People" (Keil 2002). In addition to your usual perspicacity, I appreciate the concision. Your "groovology" model of participation, in my opinion, should be part of every curriculum involving music and dance:

> To create a groove, very small and mostly subliminal gaps or discrepancies in the timing/attacking-releasing/processes of performances, in the tuning/sounding/texturing of performances and in the sequencing/structuring of performances pull people into Participation, into creating processual and textural and structural PDs ["participatory discrepancies"] of their own. When the timing and tuning and sequencing are right and creating a groove, it is easy for the next participant to add a supplemental part and/or gesture into the groove. I usually have someone soloing into a jazz rhythm section in mind, but double dutch jump-roping is just as neat a model, and one can find PDs, grooves and CCs ["cohering consequences"] in sports, arts, rituals, performances, stylized interactions of all kinds. (*TWP*, 43)

While your description implies an emphasis on vernacular (and nonmediated) musics, I see no reason why your concept could not be applied to—and better inform—classical musics. While such musics often lack the iterative pulse aspect of groove-based musics, I often wonder if Western classical musicians might somehow reclaim the vitality I so often perceive as lacking if they focused more on *groove* as an ideal and less on "mistake avoidance." As you pointed out in our interview, there can be a groovology of almost anything (cartooning, humor—almost anything creative). I personally wonder if some sort of groovology of leisure might provide a wonderful pathway for people to imagine and experience richer, fuller lives, regardless of the nature of their pursuits.

Central to groovology seems your intriguing idea of participatory discrepancies. I love how you take subtle music and dance "discrepancies"—the minor "imperfections" that create feeling in music—and extend the idea to participatory consciousness:

> If you can participate once, in one song, dance, poem, rite, you can do it more times and in more ways until you are "at one" with the entire universe, or some very large chunks of it. The social moments where I get these "oneness" and "urge-to-merge" feelings most forcefully are when I'm dancing at polka parties, or salsa parties, or swept up in a black church service, or when making music. Trying to conceptualize or explain these euphoric feelings of "polka happiness" or "blues mellowness," a theory and rhetoric of participation helps keep the good feelings alive. Positivism and Marxism (with its language of negation, contradiction, alienation, commodification, reification, mediation, etc.) tend to reify our problems still further, as they name and describe them, whereas the language of participation offers hope. (*PD*, 276)

I completely agree that participation likely provides the best answers to the meaning of life: *I am because we are*, right?[21] While individualized leisure might still have a place in the world (I suspect we agree that reading isn't that bad), I think the "corrective" you seek is best found in what Stephen Tepper (2014) has called "bigger-than-me experiences." When we engage in music and dance, even soloistically, I think we achieve what evolutionary biologist Steven Mithen (2005) suggests is a sense of "we-ness" through music (215).

I trust it is clear that, despite a few quibbles here and there, I find immense value in your work, and feel it holds tremendous potential to help enrich understandings of music-dance in conceptions of the meaning of life. I trust it is also clear that, despite your self-proclaimed "applied sociomusicology" focus, I see what you do as getting to the heart of music and leisure. My own concerns focus more on the intersections between schooling and lifelong participation than the study of music and/in culture. In my utopian world, all education is leisure education. If we could get closer to such an ideal, I think some of your criticism of the shortcomings of music education might be assuaged, because school music instruction would become increasingly oriented toward a way of life than a subject to be learned. In the meantime, I hope that your work continues to inspire others the way it has inspired me.

I remain, Your Humble Devotee

Reference Abbreviations

Echo   *Echology* (Keil self-published four annual issues, 1987–1991)

MG   Keil and Feld (1994)

ML   *M.U.S.E. Letter* (Keil self-published two annual issues, 1992–1993)

MM   Crafts, Cavicchi, and Keil (1993)

PD   Keil (1987)

PH   Keil and Keil (1992)

RP   Keil (1973)

TS   Keil (1979)

TWP   Keil (2002)

UB   Keil (1966)

Notes

1. For the chapter title, see Keil and Feld (1994). Keil and Feld's title, with its double (triple?) entendre, is much hipper, of course. My attempt here is to allude, in part, to (1) the "grooves" of various "leisure lifestyles," (2) the celebration of leisure as "groovy" (with apologies to the Austin Powers franchise), and (3) the fact that those involved with recreational music making feel they have found a comfortable "groove."

   Having shared this manuscript with many people in advance of publication, I fully appreciate the polarizing response to the "epistolary" form of this chapter, which is intended to reflect and honor Keil's own style of straightforward, unpretentious prose. Subsequent to writing this chapter I came across Feld (2002). Feld, a frequent Keil interlocutor, provides insight into Keil beyond what I do here. Interestingly (for me), Feld similarly seizes upon Keil's vilification of commodification.

   I thank Karen Fox, Lucy Green, and Charles Keil for their insightful comments on this chapter, which have strengthened it immeasurably. The failure to adequately address their concerns and suggestions lies entirely with the author.

2. Our interview is in Mantie and Higgins (2015).

3. Keil has since informed me that the published version of *Born to Groove* (early 2016) contains two diagrams addressed specifically to issues of leisure and recreation.

4. "Localities" is the term Keil favors in much of his writing.

5. Readers less familiar with these names are encouraged to do a quick Internet query.

6. Granted, Keil might claim that these were based on his master's thesis and doctoral dissertation, where theory was a requirement and not a choice. Still, theory (but perhaps not "high theory"?) permeates all aspects of Keil's work.

7. The number of rejection letters from publishers in the archive center did not escape my notice, however. While Keil may be unpretentious, he was clearly not prepared to sacrifice his convictions!

8. Readers can do a quick Internet search. In brief, Sokal, annoyed at what he considered vacuous prose rampant in academia, submitted a paper of complete nonsense that was subsequently published by a peer-reviewed journal.

9. As Keil (1996) explains: "Not 'ethnomusicology' because the 'ethno-' means 'other' in the minds of most people and also fosters the misconception of a style or styles tied to one culture at a time, an equation no longer true if it ever was. 'Sociomusicology' because musicking only has definable feelings and meanings in social contexts. 'Applied' because grounding musicking in the coming years will require us to take our best understandings of what musicking and dancing can do for people in general and children in particular and then apply what we know in very specific situations." Jeff Todd Titon (1992) describes Keil's work as "public ethnomusicology."

10. Where I perhaps diverge from Keil is that I lack the fortitude to materially enact the commitment to simple living he proselytizes. Unlike Keil, I am not a Green Party activist. Unlike Keil, I do pay my federal taxes, I do own a TV (three, in fact), and I do play video games with my children on occasion (although I try to encourage "active" games like Rock Band and Just Dance). I don't necessarily agree with patricapitalist society, but it is the world in which I live and work. I try to problematize it and challenge it the best I can, especially through my teaching and my parenting, but I just don't have the strength and courage to commit to the simple, back-to-the-land tribal society lifestyle (that of the "classless societies") Keil promotes and enacts.

11. "[A]ll musicians hold jobs in addition to their polka work" (*PH*, 6).

12. Although just a minor "report"—one that just begins to scratch the surface—it bears mentioning that Keil (2007) does offer some preliminary thoughts on these issues.

13. "Dance Daily. Dance Early. Dance Now," December 12, 2015. (http://www.musekids.org/dancedaily.html).

14. For the record, MUSE Incorporated continues to operate, and continues to hire teaching artists.

15. Keil, on the other hand, writes: "After a number of years of teaching I finally figured out by intuition that there were some less coordinated students who would get *much* worse the minute I tried to help them" (*ML* 1: 24).

16. For example, Keil writes about "the importance of building a self-sustainable music-dance culture in each primary school where the older children are able to pass on an evolving 'tradition' to the younger ones" (*Echo* 3: 68).

17. See also: Smith, this volume, chapter 9, on *eudaimonia*.

18. Deriving from Greek mythology, meaning "having to choose between two evils."

19. Elsewhere Kiel writes: "[W]hy am I doing this [band]? Because this is where the action is. Musicians playing regularly for dancers have a hope of shaping a music that will change and grow strong" (*Echo* 3: 67).

20. Keil does, however, acknowledge playing drums and bass along with recordings! (*MG* 254).

21. For those less familiar, the phrase was popularized by Desmond Tutu, who was expounding on the African philosophy of *ubuntu*.

References Cited

Appadurai, Arjun. 1996. *Modernity at Large: Cultural Dimensions of Globalization*. Minneapolis: University of Minnesota Press.

Bjørkvold, Jon Roar. 1992. *The Muse Within: Creativity and Communication, Song and Play from Childhood through Maturity*. New York: Harper Collins.

Blacking, John. 1974. *How Musical is Man?* Seattle: University of Washington Press.

Booth, Wayne C. 1999. *For the Love of It: Amateuring and Its Rivals*. Chicago: University of Chicago Press.

Bourdieu, Pierre. 1984. *Distinction: A Social Critique of the Judgement of Taste*. Translated by Richard Nice. Cambridge, MA: Harvard University Press.

Bowman, Wayne. 2002. "Educating Musically." In *The New Handbook of Research on Music Teaching and Learning: A Project of the Music Educators National Conference*, edited by Richard Colwell and Carol Richardson, 63–84. New York: Oxford University Press.

Crafts, Susan D., Daniel Cavicchi, and Charles Keil. 1993. *My Music: Explorations of Music in Daily Life*. Hanover, NH: University Press of New England.

Dubin, Robert. 1956. "Industrial Workers' Worlds: A Study of the 'Central Life Interests' of Industrial Workers." *Social Problems* 3(3): 131–142.

Dubin, Robert. 1979. "Central Life Interests: Self-Integrity in a Complex World." *Pacific Sociological Review* 22: 405–426.

Feld, Steven. 2002 "Charlie Grooves." *City & Society* 14(1): 59–68.

Gunkel, Ann Hetzel. 2004. "The Polka Alternative: Polka as Counterhegemonic Ethnic Practice." *Popular Music and Society* 27(4): 407–427.

Jenkins, Henry, with Ravi Purushotma, Margaret Weigel, Katie Clinton, and Alice J. Robison. 2009. *Confronting the Challenges of Participatory Culture: Media Education for the 21st Century*. Cambridge, MA: MIT Press.

Keil, Charles. 1966. *Urban Blues*. Chicago: University of Chicago Press.

Keil, Charles. 1973. "Statement of Research Problem." Unpublished document, Howard Gottlieb Archive Center, Boston University.

Keil, Charles. 1979. *Tiv Song: The Sociology of Art in a Classless Society*. Chicago: University of Chicago Press.

Keil, Charles. 1987. "Participatory Discrepancies and the Power of Music." *Cultural Anthropology* 2(3): 275–283.

Keil, Charles. 1995. "Special Issue: Participatory Discrepancies." *Ethnomusicology* 39(1) (Winter): 21–54.

Keil, Charles. 1996. "Muse Incorporating and Applied Sociomusicology." Paper presented at a conference in Berlin. http://www.musekids.org/berlin.html.

Keil, Charles. 2002. "They Want the Music but They Don't Want the People." *City and Society* 14(1): 37–57.

Keil, Charles. 2007. "When Everyone Doubled Twice." *Allegro* 57(6). http://www.local802afm.org/2007/06/when-everyone-doubled-twice/.

Keil, Charles, and Steven Feld. 1994. *Music Grooves: Essays and Dialogues*. Chicago: University of Chicago Press.

Keil, Charles, and Angeliki V. Keil. 1992. *Polka Happiness*. Philadelphia, PA: Temple University Press.

Mantie, Roger, and Lee Higgins. 2015. "Paideia con Salsa: Charles Keil, Groovology, and the Undergraduate Music Curriculum." *College Music Symposium Forums* 55. http://symposium.music.org/index.php?option=com_k2&view=item&id=10885:paideia-con-salsa-charles-keil-groovology-and-the-undergraduate-music-curriculum&Itemid=126.

Mantie, Roger, and Brent Talbot. 2015. "How Can We Change Our Habits If We Don't Talk About Them?" *Action, Criticism and Theory for Music Education* 14(1): 128–153.

Merriam, Alan P. 1964. *The Anthropology of Music*. Evanston, IL: Northwestern University Press.

Mithen, Steven J. 2005. *The Singing Neanderthals: The Origins of Music, Language, Mind, and Body*. Cambridge, MA: Harvard University Press.

Sfard, Anna. 1998. "On Two Metaphors for Learning and the Dangers of Choosing Just One." *Educational Researcher* 27(2): 4–13.

Small, Christopher. 1977. *Music, Society, Education: A Radical Examination of the Prophetic Function of Music in Western, Eastern and African Cultures with Its Impact on Society and Its Use in Education.* London: Calder.

Talbot, Brent C., and Roger Mantie. 2015. "Vision and the Legitimate Order: Theorizing Today to Imagine Tomorrow." In *Envisioning Music Teacher Education,* edited by Susan Wharton Conkling, 155–180. Lanham, MD: Rowman and Littlefield.

Tepper, Steven J. 2014. "Thinking 'Bigger Than Me' in the Liberal Arts." *Chronicle of Higher Education,* September 15. http://chronicle.com/article/Thinking-Bigger-Than-Me-in/148739/?cid=at&utm_source=at&utm_medium=en.

Titon, Jeff Todd. 1992. "Music, the Public Interest, and the Practice of Ethnomusicology." *Ethnomusicology* 36: 315–322.

Willis, Paul E. 1978. *Profane Culture.* London and Boston: Routledge and Kegan Paul.

Index

Note: Page numbers followed by b, f, or t indicate a box, figure or table, respectively. Page numbers followed by n and another number indicate an endnote.

ABBA, 194
ABC notation and freestyle, 547–548
ABC's of Tape Recording (Crowhurst), 91
Ableton Live software, 594
Aboriginal hip-hop artists, 519, 531, 533, 535
About LaiYouttitham video, 480
Academy of Leisure, 14
Academy of Music, Slovenia, 271
Acid House (Leeds)
    allegiance to, via clothes, bodily practices, 388–389
    comparison of music at, to utopian occurrence, 396
    criminal element association with, 398–399
    Critcher's definition of, 385
    development of music culture in, 386
    Ecstasy use at, 385, 399–400
    embodiment and, 392
    entrepreneurial transformations of, 393–395
    Haslam on cultural, social significance of, 396
    identity development and, 386–390, 392
    opposing ideals of adherents, 397–398
    rave records, spiritual themes, 397
    raves at, 386–387, 389, 393–395, 398–399
    Reynolds's historical account of, 385
    role of location, space, place, in understanding, 391–392
    utopian ideal of, 396–397
    utopian memories of, 385–401
Adams, Bryan, 139
adolescence/adolescents. *See also* children; teenagers
    emerging musicians' influence on, 174
    functions of music for, 36, 39
    identity development of, 132, 139

long-term effects of music learning, 172, 175–176, 187
    music's benefits for, 35
    singing's benefits for, 41
    strong experiences of music in, 49
    use of music by, 37 b–38 b, 39
Adult and Community Music Special Research Interest Group, 5
adulthood. *See also* elderly people; identity development, in middle adulthood
    identity development in, 131–147
    learning ensembles, England, 205–207, 211–213, 215, 216
    motivation to continue, cease music participation in, 174, 175–178
    musical explorations in, 226–228
    musical opportunities in, 203–205
    nonmusician musical identities in, 208–210
    obstacles to music participation in, 173
    performing music in, 213–215
    socio-cultural benefits of music making, learning, 205–207
    strong experiences of music in, 49
    successful music learning in, 62
    transitioning skills from childhood, adolescence, 172
Aeolian Piano Company, 244
aesthetic judgment, 48
aesthetic systems theory (AST), 522–523, 526
affinity spaces and groups, 556–557
affirmation, compilations as celebration of, 108–110
"After the Ball" (Harris), 243
agency. *See* communicative agency; human agency; musical agency

Ahlers, Arvel W., 89
AKG412 microphones, 83
AKG D112 microphones, 83
Albini, Steve, 455
A-level Music qualification (England), 204
Alexa, 482
Alheit, Peter, 609
all-female metal bands, 310–313, 315 nn4–5
amateur, definition, 490, 586–587
amateur laptop musicians
    as collaborators, 593
    DJs as, 585–598
    flexibility and options of, 594
    performing by, 594–596
    Share Project, 594
    software used by, 594
    as soloists, 592–593
    as virtuosos, 593–594
amateur musicians. See also professional
        musicians; semiprofessional musicians
    advancing technology's impact on, 489
    community interactions of, 491
    cultural context of, 364, 589–591
    at Dartington International Summer
        School, 363–380
    description, 586–589
    DISS hosting of, 365, 368, 370
    entrepreneurial opportunities created
        by, 3475
    on Facebook, 494–507
    Fonarow on importance of, 275–276
    fundamental dimensions of, 491–492
    impact of digital technologies for, 490,
        590–591
    Kaplan on educating, 22, 24
    measures of status of, 364
    mimicking of professionals by, 234
    music as serious leisure for, 41, 235
    music engagement research on, 187
    music industry engagement by, 235
    participation in virtual collectives,
        475–476, 478
    personality traits of, 275
    pop-rock, from Italy, on Facebook, 489–512
    professional musicians comparison, 587
    self-description as, 209, 217
    self-education by, 588
        shared traits with professionals, 41
        social connotations in being, 210
        study of social, musical, personal goals
            in, 173
        types of music education by, 588–589
        Zanzig on quest for excellence by, 250
amateurs, at leisure (Stebbins), 33
America (pop music group), 120
American Federation of Musicians of the
        United States, 357
American Idol, 25
American Indians, 522, 526, 528–530
American Museum of Natural History, 248
American Musical Landscape (Crawford), 242
Amplified Elephants, sonic art ensemble
        for intellectually disabled people,
        607–608, 615
Amsden, Benoni L., 391
Anderson, Ben, 309
Anderson, Leon, 117
Anglophone popular music, 490
Ansdell, Gary, 379–380 n1
Anthony, Wayne, 396
Appleization, 489, 510
appropriation, compilations as celebration of,
        106–108
Aristotle
    on eudaimonia, 163, 568, 574–575
    on happiness, 32, 164
    on leisure, 32, 581
    opinion of professional musicians, 574
    overemphasis on contemplation, 629
    on use of music for purgation, 32, 36
    on value of music making, 574–575
    valuing of rationality by, 526
Armstrong, Melanie, 477, 483
artistic endeavors, Lukács's description of,
        413–414
The Arts: A Social Perspective (Kaplan), 14, 16
Ashforth, Blake E., 455
Asia
    music summer schools in, 380 n2
    Sacred Harp Singing in, 566, 581
Associated Board of the Royal Schools of
        Music (ABRSM), 31, 220 n2, 226
audio recorder, multitrack, 86
auditory system, 521

Aufegger, Lisa, 203, 204
Austin, Matthew, 117
Australia
    amateur choir survey, 181
    Amplified Elephants, sonic art ensemble for
        inttellectually disabled people, 607–608
    community-based music activities, 611–612
    Indigenous creation stories, 524
    Musical Futures program, 69
    music summer schools in, 380 n2
    research with elderly people, 38–39
    Sacred Harp Singing in, 566, 581
authenticity
    construction of, 286, 459
    in music classrooms, 70–71
    playing analogue synthesizers as, 595
    of polka music, 625
    sense of belonging and, 577
autoethnography
    defined, 117
    identity development, 138–139
    reflection and, 128
    space and place, 391
autonomy, 35
Avsec, Andreja, 271

Bach, Glenn, 593
Bachelard, Gaston, 101, 104–105, 107, 110.
        See also compilations
Bailey, Roy, 432
Baker, David, 62, 64
Baker, Sarah, 451–452
Bakhtin, Mikhail, 366
Ballantyne, Julie, 40–41, 181
Baltimore Symphony Orchestra, 248
Bamberger, Jeanne, 62–63
Bandcamp, 233
Barenboim, Daniel, 365, 369
Barlow, John Perry, 358
Barnes, Barry, 189, 190, 191
Barone, Tom, 171
Barrett, James, 87
Barthes, Roland, 589–590
Bartlett, Bruce, 93
Basic Psychological Needs Scale, 44 b
Basu, Debasish, 386–387
Battlefield 4, video game, 550

Batt-Rawden, Kari, 39. *See also*
        musical agency
Bauckham, David, 359
Baudrillard, Jean
    criticism of work of, 284
    The Gulf War Did Not Take Place, 284
    hyperreality theory of, 282, 283–285, 293
    influence on cultural studies, 293
    language game concept in works of, 292
    on role of consumer capitalism, 449
    Simulacra and Simulation, 283–284
    simulacra notion of, 281, 283–285, 286, 288,
        292–293
Bauman, Zygmunt, 153, 283
Bautista, Alfredo, 204–205, 218
Bayton, Mavis, 313
Beat Generation, 508
Beatlemania, 115
Beatles, 115, 120, 267, 426, 427, 430. *See also*
        specific Beatles
Becker, Howard S., 429, 430
Beer, David, 459, 460
Belgium, YouTube music making
        collaborations, 478–479
Belk, Russell W., 264, 265. *See also* extended
        self theory
Bell, Cindy, 181
Bennett, Andy, 115, 225, 300, 380 n4, 437, 586
Bennett, Dawn E., 156
Bergenfield (NJ) Suicide Pact, 412
Berland, Jody, 470
Berliner, Emile, 88
Bernard, Rhoda, 270–271
Berzonsky, Michael D., 135–136
Best Communities for Music Education, 26
Bhattacharya, Joydeep, 271
Bhatti, Mark, 106
Bieber, Justin, 481
Biesta, Gert, 125
Billings, William, 566
Bingley, Kate, 608–609
Birch, Anna, 443 n5
Birchard, C. C., 247
Bithell, Caroline, 181
Black, Cilla, 426
Blackfeet Indians, 530
Blacking, John, 520, 621

black metal music
    description, 294 n1
    White Medal, 281, 291–292
    Winterfylleth, 281–282, 285–288, 289
    Wodensthrone, 281, 288–291
Black Sabbath, 297
Blackshaw, Tony, 369, 374, 509
Blackstone, Tsianinia Redfeather, 530
Bloch, Ernst, 163
blogs
    musical engagement via, 233, 287, 289,
        298, 574
    Ravishing Grimness, 285–286
    virtual choir recruitment on, 475–476
Blood Sundae, 310
Bloom, David, 140
Bloom School of Jazz, 140
Bochner, Arthur, 408. See also narrative
    inquiry
bodily action coordination, use of music for,
    191, 193–194, 196–197
Body Consciousness (Foucault), 122
Boer, Diana, 36
Bonham, John, 427
Booth, Wayne C., 379 n1, 586–587, 588, 626
"Born in the USA" (Springsteen), 412
Born to Groove (C. Keil), 629–633, 635 n3
Borsay, Peter, 366, 371
Bosnian folk music, 195
Boston Academy of Music, 256 n2
Boston Music Center, 365
Boston Symphony Orchestra, 354
Bourdieu, Pierre, 69, 163–164, 199 n6, 620
Bowen, George Oscar, 249
Bowman, Wayne, 121
Bragg, Billy, 432
brain
    auditory system, 521
    impact of Indigenous music-dance on, 527
    music education's benefits for, 180
    music's impact on, 48
brain stem reflex, 48
Brandt, Thompson A., 380 n3
Brazil
    Musical Futures program, 70
    YouTube ensemble participation, 477
BRECVEMA framework, 48

Bright Balkan Morning (Keil and Keil), 619,
    622, 629
Brooks, Evan, 87
Brown, Allison, 73–74
Brown, Phil, 46–459
Bruford, Bill, 155–156
Bruner, Jerome, 417
Bull, Michael, 195
Bulldog Band, 251
Burgess, Jean, 471, 482
Bush, Jeffrey E., 257 n13
Bushman World Ukulele Contest (2007), 472
Butkovic, Ana, 271
Butler, Judith, 283

Cage, John, 520, 589
Campbell, Patricia Shehan, 443 n5, 607,
    610, 614
Canada
    Aboriginal hip-hop artists, 519, 531, 533, 535
    global collaborative performances, 479
    musical ensembles in, 173
    Musical Futures program, 69–70
    Music Performance Trust Fund
        partnership, 357
    New Horizons music group
        participation, 268
    state of music education in, 627
    tensions with Indigenous peoples, 528
    YouTube music making collaboration,
        478–479
"Canon Rock" (Lim Jeong-hyun), 467–468
canzone d'autore, Italian singer-songwriter
    tradition, 490
canzonetta, 490
Cardin, Fred, 530
carnivalesque concept (Bakhtin), 366, 367, 369
Casablanca pub (Liverpool, England),
    430–432, 431 f
Cascone, Kim, 596
CASP- 12, quality of life measure, 44 b
casual leisure. See also serious leisure
    benefits of, 351
    core activities, 352
    defined, 350
    identity and, 351
    informal classroom learning model and, 66

serious leisure comparison, 32–33, 210, 231
 tourist space and, 358–359
casual vs. serious leisure, 32–33
Cavern Club, 430
Cayari, Christopher, 358, 482, 483
CDs (compact discs), compilations on,
 99–100, 111 n3
Central Park, New York, 82, 246
Chakraborty, Kaustav, 386–387
Chanan, Michael, 84
Chang, Jerry (a.k.a. Jerry C), 467
Chao, Y. R., 521, 522
Charlesworth, Simon, 389
CHAT. See Cultural Historical
 Activity Theory
Chekhov, Michael, 367
Chernoff, John, 621
Chicago Jazz Ensemble, 140
children. See also adolescence/adolescents;
 teenagers
 benefits of El Sistema programs, 46,
  46 b–47 b
 emerging musicians' influence on, 174
 Green's research on, 226–227
 impact of learning an instrument, 172
 motivations for instrument choice, 173
 musical explorations by, 226–228
 need for support for lifelong engagement,
  177–178
 risk factors for music learning
  commitment, 173–174
 singing's benefits for, 41
 use of music by, 37 b–38 b
Chipmunks novelty singing, 91
chiptunes, 552–553
Chivarria, Tony, 523
choral performance. See also Sacred Harp
 (SH) Singing
 amateur choral society, 180
 competitions, 246
 concertizing tradition of, 566
 at DISS, 370
 global virtual collaboration, 475–476, 482
 musical identity and, 209
 participation in adulthood, 181
 People's Choral Union (NYC), 246
 spirituality and, 271

Christensen, Axel, 244
Christensen School of Popular Music
 (Chicago), 244
Cisco Systems, 468
Civilization, video game series, 557
Clark, Kenneth S., 247, 249–250
Clarke, Eric Thatcher, 251
classical musicians, 354–355
Cleveland Orchestra, 252
Clift, Stephen M., 41, 271
Cloonan, Martin, 425
"Close to the Edge" (Grandmaster Flash), 412
Cochrane, Graham, 94
coding, of video games, 551–553
Coffman, Don D., 269, 273, 275, 276
cognitive well-being
 El Sistema programs and, 46 b–47 b
 Music for Life Project findings, 45 b
 music's benefits for, 43
Cohen, Judith, 621
Cohen, Sarah, 301, 427–430, 434, 438, 443 n1
Cole, Natalie, 482
Cole, Nat "King," 482
Collaborative Innovation Network
 (CoIN), 511 n3
collective identity, use of music for affirming
 and exploring, 191
collegiate marching band study, of
 motivational profiles regarding music
 making, 326–336
 advice networks, 325–328, 330 t, 332–336
 changes in motivational profiles, 330
 friendship/advice nominations data, 328
 friendship networks, 328, 330–332, 334–336
 future research directions, 336–337
 goal, 326
 measures, 327–330
 participant profile, 326–327
 participatory motivation, 322–326, 328, 329
  t, 334–336
 procedure, 327
 results, 329–330
 SDT application in, 326, 328, 332–334, 337
 SNA application in, 326, 334
Collin, Matthew, 387, 396, 399–400
Collins, Randall, 579
Columbia College, 140

Commission on Music Education in the Community, 16

Commission on Music in the Community (MENC), 21

communicative agency, 285, 293. *See also* human agency; musical agency

communicative leisure, 283

Community clusters, 508

community music (communities of practice), 601–615. *See also* Acid House; collegiate marching band study; community music facilitators; Dartington International Summer School; ensemble music making; Indigenous music-dance making; Italian amateur pop-rock musicians on Facebook study; learning ensembles; Musical Futures; Sacred Harp (SH) Singing

  amateur musicians and, 41

  in Australia, 607–608, 611–612

  basis of attraction to, 49

  choirs, 364, 612

  Commission on Music in the Community, 16

  contemporary practices in, 605

  contexts for music activities, 601–603

  development as a profession, 24

  DIY recreational recording, 90, 93, 94

  dynamic nature of, 75

  enduring power of, 123

  in Europe, 255, 611

  fan communities, 40

  fluid objectives in, 217–219

  in gaming communities, 8, 541–543

  gender and, 611–612

  global perspective on, 601–602

  Higgins conceptual framework for, 602–603

  historical foundations of, 257 n13

  identity development in, 132, 195, 217–219

  intergenerational opera project, 41–42

  interventionist approach to, 601–615

  Kaplan's involvement with, 14, 16, 18, 20–27

  learning contexts characteristics, 366

  motivations to continue in adulthood, 175–178

  Music for Life Project, 44 b–45 b

  music recreation programs, 20

  in Nazi Germany, 604

  online, 25, 181, 472–473, 475, 492

  production community, 459–460

  in residential homes, for adults with dementia, 609

  scholarly studies of, 24–25

  seeking affirmation, verification in, 41

  in Sierra Leone, 608–609

  story-sharing, English-language learning classrooms, 606–607

  Tremaine's promotion of, 244–245

  in the U.K., 9, 203–205, 283–284, 303, 603, 609, 611

  in the U.S., 244–251, 253–256, 256 n7, 257 n13, 611

  as a vehicle for social benefits, change, 196, 267, 320, 603–605

  vocal singing, 194

  Wenger's definition of, 74–75

  workshops, 609

  WPA Music Program, 15

  on YouTube, 233, 467–484

community music facilitators

  improvisation by, 613

  multiple goals of, 611–613

  potential tensions, dilemmas, 613–614

  sites, skills, attributes of, 605–611

  toolkit of, 609–614

compilations, 99–112

  artistic aspect in creating, 100–104, 107

  on audiocassette tapes, 102, 111 n3

  Bhatti and, 106

  on CDs, 99–100, 111 n3

  as celebration of affirmation, 108–110

  as celebration of appropriation, 106–108

  hazards in creating, 108

  inner chords enlivened by, 101

  motivations for creating, 110–111

  as poetic spaces of connection, 100, 101, 104–106, 109

  repercussion phase, 100, 104–107, 109, 110

  resonation phase, 100, 104–108

  reverberations phase, 100, 104–107, 109–110

  scholarly work on, 102–104, 111 n4

  video, 481

completeness, symbols of, 266

computers. *See also* amateur laptop musicians
  advanced production capabilities, 490, 499,
    504, 510, 555
  computer-based music technology, 65
  creation of backing tracks on, 140–141
  in DIY recreational recording, 87, 457
  music availability on, 31
  online collaborations via, 472
  in pop-up studio, 83
  video gaming on, 542, 558
conquered spaces, 353, 469
Conquergood, Dwight, 300
contagion
  defined, 48
  social contagion model, of motivation, 335
continuing education programs, 204, 238 n1
Cook, Nicholas, 232
Coolidge, Calvin, 247–248
Cooper, Harris, 380 n3
cosmologies, of Indigenous cultures, 525, 526–
    527, 530, 532, 533
Cottrell, Stephen, 156, 380 n4
Coulson, Susan, 380 n4
covers (reimagining of a popular song), 555
Crawford, Richard, 242, 243
creation/origin stories, 524–526
creative analytic practices (CAP), 102
Creative Scotland's Youth Music
    Initiative, 238 n2
Creative Tape Recording recording guide, 91
creativity, Wallas's classic model of, 134
Creech, Andrea, 67, 68–69, 70, 72, 268, 272,
    273, 379–380 n1
Cree Indians, round dances, 519
"crisis heterotopia" (of Foucault), 416–417
Critcher, Chas, 385, 386, 399, 400
Croom, Adam M., 273
Cross, Ian, 320
Crouch, David, 391
Crowhurst, Norman H., 91
Crumb, R., 621
Csikszentmihalyi, Mihaly, 139, 265, 269–271,
    568, 578. *See also* flow state/flow theory
Cubase software program, 504, 512 n24
cultural determinants of amateur or
    professional success, 364
cultural globalization, 490

Cultural Historical Activity Theory (CHAT),
    206–207
cultural-musical systems, 521
cultural theory of music making and leisure,
    281–294
  Baudrillard's influence on, 293
  theoretical framework, 282–285
  White Medal, analysis of interview with,
    281, 291–292
  Winterfylleth, analysis of interview with,
    281–282, 285–288, 289
  Wodensthrone, analysis of interview with,
    281, 288–291
cyberspace, 357, 358, 593

Dabback, William M., 204
dabblers/dilettantes, 33
Dahlberg, Magnus, 198
daimon (true self), 152–154, 155–156. *See also*
    eudaimonism
Damrosch, Frank, 246
dance. *See* indigenous music-dance making
dance music, electric, 385
Dancing with the Stars, 25
Dartington International Summer School
    (DISS, U.K.), music making by amateurs
    and professionals, 7, 363–380
  alternative identity development at, 371–374
  aspirations of, 378–379
  Elmhirst's description of, 367
  establishment of, 365, 367
  financial realities at, 369–370
  inclusiveness of atmosphere at, 368
  opportunities at, 366
  otherness of, 366–371
  participants' reflections on time at, 371–378
  program description, 365–366
  school choir at, 370
  as a "spiritual home," 367–368
  teaching and learning at, 374–378
  time-bound nature of, 369
  utopian quality at, 368–371
  White's description of, 366–367
Davidson, Jane W., 443 n5
Davis, Angela Y., 530
Davis, Erik, 591–592
DAW. *See* digital audio workstation

Dawe, Kevin, 115

Dawson, Frank, 140

The Day After, made-for-tv movie, 413

Deacon, Terrence W., 523

Deadmau5 (Joel T. Zimmerman), 197, 592

death metal music, 297, 302, 303, 305

Deci, Edward L., 153, 162. *See also*
    self-determination theory

Deeks, Mark, 299

degreecat, 503 f, 504, 512 n23

Deleuze, Gilles, 112 n9

Della Fave, Antonella, 163

demonstration (demo) recordings, 93

DeNora, Tia, 39, 189, 191, 197, 225, 379–380 n1,
    492. *See also* musical agency

Denzin, Norman K., 386

Department of Music, National Education
    Association, 245

Derek and the Dominos, 112 n11

Developing Expertise theory (Hallam and
    Bautista), 204–205

devotee work
    defined, 161, 350
    helping space and, 357
    music making and, 165
    resource space and, 355
    sales space and, 356
    sense of achievement in, 161

Dewar, John, 528

Dewey, John, 65, 134

Diaz, Frank M., 380 n3

Dickens, Luke, 443 n5

Dierendonck, Dirk van, 153, 272

digital audio workstation (DAW), 86–87, 93,
    471, 547, 552, 591

digital sampling, 586

digital technologies. *See also* amateur laptop
    musicians
    benefits for amateur musicians, 590–591
    ease of production, dissemination with,
        235–236, 238 n10, 586
    impact on music motivation, 585
    music compilation proliferation
        from, 111 n5
    musicianship/musical practice and, 210
    teenager engagement with, 62
    Théberge on, 585

VST/virtual studio technology, 504, 512 n24,
    557, 591

Di Meola, Al, 142

Diné people, 524, 528. *See also* McHorse,
    Christine

Dire Straits, 120

disc-based gramophone, 88

Discipline and Punishment (Foucault), 123

disruptive technology, 586

DISS. *See* Dartington International
    Summer School

DIY (do-it-yourself) leisure, 393

DIY (do-it-yourself) recreational recording,
    81–95. *See also* home recording;
    recording music
    benefits of, 94–95
    editing, 91–92
    Hi-Fi vs. Lo-Fi, 92–94
    instructional resources, 93, 94
    multiple takes, 85–86
    music consumption vs., 188, 197
    pop-up studio, 82–84
    post-1945, tape mentality, 89–92
    pre-1945, recording as fun, 87–89
    starting with recording strategy, 84–85
    use of DAW in, 86–87

DIY (do-it-yourself) systems of
    dissemination, 297–298

DJ Hero, music game, 546

DJ Kool Herc, 591

DJs (deejays). *See also* Grandmaster Flash;
    Grand Wizard Theodore; Miller, Paul
    D'Shonne
    as amateur laptop musicians, 585–598
    appropriative art created by, 106–107

Doniger, Wendy, 524

double-diamond model, of identity
    development, 133, 134 f

downloaders, occasional, 34

D-Pad Hero 1 and 2, video games, 53

Dreamtime, creation myth, 524

Drew, Robert, 587

"Drift Away" (Williams), 480

Driver, Christopher, 298

Drudkh, 286, 288

drug use, in recording studios, 457–459, 462

drum kits, 71, 82–83, 152, 306, 313, 430, 440

drummer-researcher perspective, on music
    making, 425–443. *See also under*
    Liverpool, England
drummers/drumming. *See also* Smith,
    Gareth Dylan
  blurred life boundaries for, 9–10 n1
  eudaimonic lives of, 153, 155
  fulfillment from, 151–152, 154–155
  identity realization of, 151–152, 153
  indigenous music-dance making and, 520,
    523–527, 533
  in Italian amateur musicians Facebook
    study, 494–499, 503, 505, 509
  in the recording studio, 83–86
  Smith's study of, 62
  stereotyping as nonmusicians, 427
Drummond, John D., 380 n4
Dubbe, Richard F., 90–91
Dubin, Robert, 626
Le Duc des Lombards, jazz club
    (Paris), 354
Duff, Cameron, 309
Duffy, Michelle, 308, 410–411, 456
Duggan, Maeve, 475
du Pré, Jacqueline, 365
Durkheim, Émile, 578–579
Durrant, Colin, 65
Durrant, John D., 379 n1
Dykema, Peter, 246–247

ear, playing by. *See* playing by ear
East London Late Starters Orchestra (ELLSO,
    U.K.), 203
Eastman School of Music, 253
Echology journal (Keil), 619, 621
Ecstasy (MDMA), 385, 399–400
Edison, Thomas, 87
education. *See* music education
elderly people
  Australian research of, 38–39
  community music in residential homes,
    609–610
  music for reminiscing by, 36, 38
  music's benefits for, 35, 36, 38–39, 43, 173
electronic dance music (EDM), 385, 555,
    586, 594
Electronic Musician magazine, 93

Elfman, Danny, 558
Elkington, Sam, 210, 347, 349, 357–358. *See also*
    serious leisure
Elliott, David, 579
Elmhirst, Leonard, 367
El Sistema programs, 46, 46 b–47 b
Elvis impersonators, 3
embodiment, defined, 392
Emmerson, Stephen Bryan, 271
emotional FX
  elicitation by studio staff, 450
  emotional labor and, 452
  recording studios and, 454–457, 462
emotional labor
  defined, 452
  emotional work vs., 199 n3
  key role in recording studios, 456
emotional space of recording studios,
    449–462
emotional work vs. emotional labor, 199 n3
emotions/emotional well-being
  BRECVEMA framework impact on, 48
  from ensemble membership, 176
  music as an outlet for, 193–194
  Music for Life Project findings, 44 b–45 b
  music's benefit for, 31–32, 36, 37 b–38 b,
    42–43, 49, 191
  singing and, 41
Engeström, Yrjö, 206
England. *See also* extreme metal music, in
    England; Liverpool, England
  adult community-based groups, 203, 205
  ethnographic fieldwork on music making
    in, 425–443
  Every Child a Musician (ECaM)[3] program,
    209–210
  Leeds, Acid House culture, 385–401
  Leeds, Extreme Metal scene, 297–315
  Musical Futures program, 61–75
  music education in, 63, 64
  music qualifications in, 204
  Northern black metal bands, 281–294
  pop-rock music, 490
  study of adult learning ensembles, 205–207
  Taking Part survey, 178
  working-class music venues, 304
English Heritage Black Metal, 287

ensemble music making, 319–338, 363. *See also* choral performance; collegiate marching band study; learning ensembles
  adult preferences for, 268
  body as part of rhythmic movement in, 119
  changing goals in, 132
  community ensembles, 22
  in El Sistema programs, 46 b
  Kokotsaki/Hallam's study, 269
  by laptop musicians, 593
  learning ensemble, defined, 211
  motivational/social network dynamics, 176–177, 179, 205, 269, 271–272, 319–338
  in music education programs, 226
  by "nonmusician" adults, 203, 205–208, 211–216
  positive benefits of, 173
  questioning the value of participation in, 321
  SNA and social structures of, 325
  spiritual connections and, 271
  traits of people involved in, 189
  vocal ensembles, 250
Enslaved, 288
episodic memory, 48
EQ magazine, 93
Erickson, Frederick, 264, 520
Erikson, Erik H., 132, 264
ethnic identity, 39. *See also* Indigenous cultures
ethnographic fiction, 301, 315
ethnographic fieldwork on music making, in Liverpool, 427–443
Euclidean-Cartesian space-time, 525, 528
eudaimonia. *See also* happiness
  Aristotle on, 163, 568, 574–575
  drummers, drumming, and, 153–154, 155
  hedonic enjoyment vs., 153
  of Sacred Harp singers, 574–577, 580, 581
  video games and, 548, 557–558
eudaimonic well-being, 272
eudaimonism. *See also* daimon
  careers, flow, leisure play, and, 154–156
  ethical questions raised by, 162–163
  flow comparison with, 270
  Frankel on, 154
  identity realization and, 262

masculine stance promoted by, 163–164
  Norton on, 153
  problematizing, 162–164
  self-actualization and, 263
  serious leisure and, 161–162
  (un)popular music making and, 151–165
  Waterman on, 154
  Welton on, 164
Europe. *See also* specific countries
  community music advocacy in, 248, 255
  master-apprentice discourse in, 126
  metal bands/music in, 283, 287
  music conservatories in, 245, 271
  music making initiatives in, 242
  music summer schools in, 380 n2
  opinion of ragtime music in, 244
  Sacred Harp Singing in, 566, 578, 581
eutopia, 395
evaluative conditioning, 48
Everitt, Anthony, 379 n1
Every Child a Musician (ECaM)[3] program (England), 209–210
Ex Cathedra choirs, 380 n7
experiential learning framework (of Kolb), 134
experimentalist musicians, 589
extended self theory, 262, 264–266, 274, 275
extreme metal music, in England, 297–315. *See also* specific bands
  all-female bands, 310
  band fragmentation issues, 303–304
  dissemination via DIY systems, 297–298
  embodiment of sociality, "brutal belonging," 298
  emotion, affect, working-class identities, 304–306
  extreme music making practices, 306–310
  in Leeds, England, 297–315
  moshpit practices, 286, 299
  music making practices of, 300
  in Northern England, 285–294
  performative ethnography of music making practices, 299–301
  phenomenological aspects of, 298
  promotional challenges, 302–303
  range of subgenres in, 297
  Ravishing Grimness fan-critic site, 286

social fractures in Leeds metal scene, 301–304

spacial/musical shifts in, 299

subcultural literacy in, 284

Facebook. *See also* Italian amateur pop-rock musicians on Facebook study

impact on Musical Futures programs, 74

musical sharing on, 102, 233, 573

music industry and, 233

online desktop research via, 429

research on amateur musicians on, 489–510

role in identity formation, 493

self-expression on, 102

Fallout 3, video game, 543

Family Fun in Tape Recording (Ahlers), 89–90

fandom, 34, 300, 311, 472, 557, 577

Federal Music Project, Works Project Administration, 15, 252–253

Feld, Stephen, 621

Ferguson, Alex, 455

55 Songs and Choruses (Dykema), 247

Filipetti, Frank, 456

film scoring, 554

Final Fantasy VI, video game, 543

Find Your Voice process, 65, 76 n3

Finnegan, Ruth, 177, 188, 199 n7, 379 n1, 380 n4, 427, 588, 589

Fiumara, Corradi, 522

Fleetwood Mac, 120

Flicker, 545

Flint Community Music Association, 249

flow state/flow theory (Csikszentmihalyi)
  description, 154
  eudaimonism, play, careers, and, 154–156
  eudaimonism comparison, 270
  in identity tailoring process, 137–138, 137 f
  in music making, 265, 269–271
  Sacred Harp Singing and, 568

Folkestad, Göran, 227

folk musicians, 354–355

folk music revival, U.S. (mid-1960s), 490

folk-rock music, 195

Fonarow, Wendy, 275–276

Ford, Mary, 90–91, 92. *See also* Paul, Les

formative experiences of music learning, 173–175

Forrister, Donald, 171–172

Forsyth, Alasdair, 425

Foucault, Michel
  Body Consciousness, 122
  on care of/practices of the self, 122, 127
  "crisis heterotopia" of, 416–417
  critique of the "docile body," 127
  Discipline and Punishment, 123
  on establishing "a place outside of all places," 415–416
  music education and, 122–124, 128
  on relationship between agency and structure, 188

Foundations and Frontiers of Music Education (Kaplan), 14, 255

FRACT OSC, music exploration game, 547

France, YouTube music making collaboration, 478–479

Frankel, Viktor E., 153–154

Freeman, Walter, 320

French *chansonnier*, 490

Fried, Doug, 405–420. *See also* Red Light Jams

Frith, Simon, 223–224, 225, 236, 298

Fritz, Barbara Smolej, 271

"funtwo-Canon Rock 2012" (Lim Jeong-hyun), 468, 484 n2

Fury, Billy, 426

Gabrielsson, Alf, 48–49

Gadamer, Hans-Georg, 155

Gaines, Donna, 405, 411

GarageBand, software, 594

Garratt, Sheryl, 397

Gates, J. Terry, 33

Gaunt, Helena, 156, 379–380 n1

Gavin, Helen, 177

GCSE Music qualification (England), 204

Gee, James P., 511 n12

Geertz, Clifford, 292, 621

gender
  Acid House experience and, 396
  affinity spaces, groups, and, 556
  Baudrillard and, 284
  bias related to, 453
  Butler's work on performance and, 283
  children/adolescents' use of music, 37 b–38 b

gender (*Cont.*)
community music and, 611–612
differences, in music making, 492–493
entwinement of music and, 298
eudaimonism and, 163–164
identity formation and, 263, 264, 299
Leeds's extreme metal scene and, 302, 311, 315
leisure choices and, 282
leisure time and, 363
music, the body, and, 127–128
music education and, 122
music making and, 492–493
Generation X, 508
Germany
adolescent music listening research, 36
amateur choir survey, 181
community-based music activities, 611
Ecstasy study, 399
Sacred Harp Singing in, 573, 578
shared music making history, 604
World War II audiotape recordings, 89
YouTube music making collaboration, 478–479
Gerry and the Pacemakers, 426
Gibson, Chris, 427
Giddens, Anthony, 153, 188, 189, 190, 197
gig guides, 429
Gilbert and Sullivan festival, 365
Gill, Rosalind, 156
Gilmore, Patrick S., 243
Glass, Pepper G., 301
Glennie, Evelyn, 520–521
globalization, 490, 631
Gloor, Peter, 511 n3
Glyndebourne Opera Education Department (England), 42
Godfrey, John, 387, 396, 399–400
Gollwitzer, Peter M., 266
Goodall, H. Lloyd, 152
Goodwin, Andrew, 595
"Graceland" (Simon), 105
Grandmaster Flash, 412, 591
Grand Theft Auto, video game series, 543, 550
Grand Wizard Theodore, 591
Great Depression, U.S. (1930–1940), music and leisure during, 251–253

Great Plains Indians
communal music-dance making by, 528
sacred hoops, 519
Sun Dance, Grass Dance, 528, 531, 534
Green, Joshua, 471, 482
Green, Lucy, 62–63, 65, 68, 72, 74, 174, 226–227, 229. *See also* Musical Futures
Greenfield Community College (England), 73–74
Gregorian chant, 194, 566
Grolle, Johan, 246
Grossberg, Lawrence, 307–308
Guattari, Félix, 112 n9, 522–523
Guildhall Connect, 44 b, 65
Guildhall School of Music and Drama (London), 44 b, 65
guitar
autoethnographic meditations on, 117–121
Bennett/Dawe on cultural space of, 115–116
building an "imagined community" with, 119
creating a musical atmosphere with, 118
as "crossroads instrument" in music education, 116
cultivating curiosity with, 119–120
dimensions of leisure guitar culture, 121
emulating certain sounds with, 120
as extension of daily life, 121
gaining nearness to music with, 118–119
guitar events, 120–121
learning through listening with, 120
leisure culture of, 117–121, 123–124
place in leisure and schooling, 116–117
slack-key guitar, 530
guitar-based groups, 115–116
Guitar Hero, video game, 543, 546, 551–552
The Gulf War Did Not Take Place (Baudrillard), 284
Gunkel, Ann Hetzel, 623
Guthmers Hahl album, White Medal, 291
Guthrie, Woody, 432

Habermas, Jürgen, 188, 283
Hallam, Susan, 37 b–38 b, 67, 68–69, 70, 72, 156, 204–205, 207, 218, 268, 269, 272, 379–380 n1
Hamera, Judith, 300

Hamilton, Andree, 522–523

Hancox, Grenville, 41, 271

happiness. *See also* eudaimonia
    Aristotle on, 32, 164, 568
    El Sistema programs and, 47 b
    fulfillment, the daimon, and, 152–154
    leisure and, 250
    music engagement and, 38–39, 48, 64,
        272–273, 625
    Waterman's conceptions of, 153
    well-being and, 35, 41, 272–273

Hargreaves, Andrew J., 210

Hargreaves, David J., 262, 264

Harney, Ben, 243–244

Harris, Charles K., 243

Haslam, Dave, 396

Hawaii. *See* Kanaka Maoli (Native Hawaiian)
    culture

Hays, Terrence, 38, 272, 273

Hazen, Margaret Hindle, 243

Hazen, Robert M., 243

health/physical well-being
    Music for Life Project findings, 44 b–45 b
    music's benefits for, 35, 42–43
    singing and, 41

"Heart of the Sunrise" (Yes), 410

heavy metal music. *See also* black metal music;
    death metal music; extreme metal music,
    in England; specific bands
    all-female bands, 310–313, 315 nn4–5
    Baudrillardian analysis of, 284–285
    femininity and, 313
    in the U.K., 297
    in the U.S., 82, 297

Hebdige, Dick, 388

hedonic well-being, 153

Hegel, Georg W. F., 153

Heider, Anne, 570, 571, 578–581

Helmecke, Gus, 627

helping spaces, 357, 359, 469

Helson, Rake, 94

Hendry, Leo, 4, 62, 66

Hennion, Antoine, 198, 456

Henry, Pierre, 589

Hesmondhalgh, David, 451

Hewison, Robert, 156

The Hidden Musicians (Finnegan), 588

hierarchy of needs concept (Maslow), 35, 262,
    263, 267, 269, 272, 275

Hi-Fi vs. Lo-Fi, 92–94

Higgins, Lee, 255–256, 257 n13, 520, 524, 602–
    603, 607, 610, 612, 614

Higginson, Steve, 426

Highbury Opera Theatre, 380 n7

High Fidelity (Hornby), 102

High-Minded and Low-Down (Tawa), 242

Hill, Harold (character, *The Music Man*), 241

Himonides, Evangelos, 379 n1

hip-hop music. *See also* Indigenous
    music-dance making
    Aboriginal artists, 519–520, 531, 533, 535
    DIY recordings of, 93
    Glastonbury Festival performances, 438
    headline news related to, 460
    HUB Festival performances, 426, 428 f,
        435–436
    interviews with, 430, 434
    manipulation of sounds in, 589, 591
    Native hip-hop cypher, 519–520
    in New York City, 82

hobbyists, 33

Hodkinson, Paul, 283, 298, 300, 429

hollow square seating, in Sacred Harp Singing,
    567, 569, 581

Holst, Imogen, 367

homeless people, music's benefits for, 43, 173

home recording, 87–89, 92–94, 238 n10, 450

*Home Recording 101: Creating Your Own
    Affordable Home Recording Studio (D.I.Y.
    Music)* (Helson), 94

Home Recording and All About It (1932), 89

Home Recording for Musicians for Dummies
    (Strong), 94

The Home Recording Handbook (Everard), 93

Hornby, Nick, 102

Horning, Schmidt, 88, 89

how-to books, about DIY recording, 93

How We Gave a Phonograph Party, 88

HUB Festival (Liverpool, England), 426, 428 f,
    434–436, 442

Hugill, Andrew, 596

Huizinga, Johan, 19, 155

hula, 528–529, 531–533, 534–536

Hull House, 246

Hullick, James, 607–608. *See also* Amplified Elephants, sonic art ensemble
human agency. *See also* communicative agency; musical agency
  benefits in attending festivals, 41
  meaning making/identity work and, 282, 284
  practices of the self and, 127
  sociological viewpoint on, 188–189
  of students, benefits of MF program, 61
  use in making communicatively rational decisions, 282
human capital theory, 4
human-centered design (HCD) model, of identity development, 133
human motivation theory (Maslow), 263, 265, 267–270, 274
Humphrey, Ronald, 455
Hurtig, Brent, 93
Huta, Veronika, 153, 162
hyperreality theory (Baudrillard), 282, 283–285, 293

identity development. *See also* identity development, in middle adulthood; identity realization; identity tailoring process
  Acid House culture and, 386–390, 392
  in adolescence, 39, 62, 63–64, 139
  at DISS, 371–374
  from drumming, 151–152
  in early adulthood, 139
  early stages of, 140
  Erikson on, 132, 135–136
  extended self theory and, 262, 264–266, 274, 275
  and implementation for music makers, 263–264
  M-A-M-A cycles in, 145
  music's relationship to, 32
  "optimal" states/experiences, 138, 139
  persona creation on YouTube, 473–474
  psychological processes in, 262
  role of leisure in, 363
  role of social networking in, 493
  Schwartz on, 136
  self-definition and, 39, 225, 232, 266

Smith's "snowball self" model of, 263
  symbolic interaction theory and, 135, 136
  in young popular musicians, 232
identity development, in middle adulthood, 131–147
  autoethnographic account of, 138–139
  developmentalists on, 132
  Marcia's perspective on, 135–136
  stages, challenges, obstacles, 140–141, 143–144
  tailoring process (*See* identity tailoring process)
identity literature, 145
identity realization, 63, 152–153, 262–263
identity tailoring process, 133–138
  adjustments/alterations in, 144–145
  comparison of models, 135 t
  creative model, 134, 135
  design phase, 141–142
  double-diamond design model, 133, 134 f
  engaging leisure play activities in, 137–138
  experiential learning model, 134, 135
  flow in, 137–138, 137 f
  human-centered design (HCD) model, 133
  pattern making phase, 143–144
  Rathunde/Isabella's model, 263–264
  self-differentiation in, 136–137, 143, 146, 263–264
  self-reflection in, 137
  social integration in, 137, 137 f, 143
  tailoring model, 135 t, 137 f, 147 n2
I Drum, Therefore I Am (Smith), 263
Ihde, Don, 103, 111 n6
IKEAization, 489, 509–510
IMAGO community opera, 42 b
immune system, 41, 43
Indigenous, defined, 536 n1
Indigenous cultures
  American Indians, 522, 526, 528–530
  of Australia, 519, 524, 533
  cosmologies of, 525, 526–527, 530–533
  creation/origin stories, 524–526
  embodied/expressive practices of, 526
  of Hawaii, 524–526, 528–529, 531–534, 536
  of Pacific Northwest of Canada, 532–533
Indigenous music-dance making, 519–537
  aesthetic systems of, 522–523, 526

African American influence, 529
as an adaptable spatio-temporal stage, 526–527
blues and jazz influence, 530
chanting, 525, 527, 528, 534–536
creation/origin stories and, 524–526
drumming and, 520, 523–527, 533
as embodied physicality, 523, 534
existential aspects of, 527
globalizing forces, 534–536
historical background, 519–520
hula, 528–529, 531–536
legacies of, 528
navigating colonial structures, 527–530
as part of the community fabric, 521–522
self, subjectivity, and, 523
singing and, 524–526, 530, 532–533, 535
space-time, past and present, 530–532
space-time concepts and, 525
Sun Dance, Grass Dance, 528, 531, 534
survivance through, 527–528, 529, 531, 534
well-being and, 532–534
individuation theory, 152–154
    identity realization and, 262
    transcendent function in, 261–262
industrial music, 245, 256 n5
INSPIRE Music, 72, 76 n5
Instagram, 74, 238 n8
Institute for Studies of Leisure (University of South Florida), 14
instruments. *See* musical instruments
intellectual disabilities, music's benefits for, 43
Interlochen Center for the Arts, 355
The International Journal of Community Music, 24, 257 n13
Internet. *See also* Facebook; Instagram; Twitter; YouTube
    IMAGO and, 42 b
    Lim's popularity on, 468
    music in advertising on, 225
    music message boards, 49
    online video presentations data, 468
    spread of disinformation via, 289–290
    user-generated video content on, 468–469
    video cell technology, 157
    virtual space/serious pursuits, 357–358

Internet Symphony no. 1-Eroica (Tan Dun), 476–477
interventionist approach, to community music, 601–615
Iowa Band Law, 240
Ireland
    Ecstasy (MDMA) study, 399–400
    Sacred Harp Singing in, 573, 578
Iron Maiden, 297
Isabella, Russell, 263–264
Italian amateur pop-rock musicians on Facebook study, 489–512
    centralization and power, 497 t
    discourses, analysis and discussion, 498–507
    intertwining thematic areas, 509
    networks, analysis and discussion, 495–498, 496 t
    research design, data collection, data organization, 494–495
    sampled Facebook pages, 494 t
    social structures of musicians, 499 f–501 f
    subgroups: connected components, communities, 498 t
    thematic analysis: factor space, 503 f
    thematic analysis: percentages, 502 f
    Word associations: Italia, 507 f, 509 t
    Word associations: suonare (playing), 505 t, 506 f
Italian *canzonetta*, 490
Italian Millennials, 508
Ito, Mizuko, 544

Jackson, George Pullen, 568, 569–570, 575, 582
Jaffurs, Sheri E., 443 n5
jamming. *See also* Red Light Jams
    as group composition process, 229–230
    at guitar events, 121
Jarrett, Michael, 456
Jasen, David A., 244
Jazz Age, U.S. (1920–1929), music and leisure during, 247–251
jazz bands, 159, 205, 363
jazz blues, 529
jazz clubs, 354
jazz guitar, 116, 119

jazz musicians, 140, 352–354, 356, 359
jazz music schools, 116, 140
Jenkins, Henry, 544
Jeong-hyun, Lim, 467
Joel, Billy, 82
"Joe's Garage" (Zappa), 99
John, Elton, 275
Johnson, Bruce, 443 n5
Johnson, Corey W., 102
Johnston, Wade, 472, 478, 482
Joplin, Scott, 243
Jordan, Nicole, 443 n5
Jorgensen, Estelle R., 64
Joselit, Jenna, 380 n3
Judas Priest, 297
Julliard School of Music, 253
Jung, Carl, individuation theory, 152–154,
      261–262
Jurström, Ragnhild, 196
Jutras, Peter J., 273

Kahn, Otto, 247
Kahn-Harris, Keith, 283, 298, 437
Kalākaua (Hawaiian King), 529, 531
Kamakawiwoʻole, Israel, 472
Kanaka Maoli (Native Hawaiian) culture,
      524–526, 525, 528–529, 531–534, 536,
      538–537 n11
Kāne, Raymond,
      Kaleoalohapoinaʻoleohelemanu, 530
Kaplan, Max
   biographical background, 14, 23
   community music programs, 14, 20–21, 23
   "cultivated society" of, 15
   definition of leisure, 17, 32
   on functions of music in leisure, 24–25
   moving forward with vision of, 25–27
   music education role, 6, 14, 16, 18, 21–23,
      254–255
   on social function of music, 18, 23, 27, 254
   theory of recreational music, 18–20
   vision for music teachers, 22–23, 26, 27
   vision of societal function of music, 13–14
   written works of, 14, 16–17, 21, 255
Karlsen, Sidsel, 199 n2
Katz, Mark, 88, 589

Keil, Angeliki
   Bright Balkan Morning, 619, 622, 629
   Polka Happiness, 619–620, 624–625, 627, 629
Keil, Charles
   Born to Groove, 629–633, 635 n3
   Bright Balkan Morning, 619, 622, 629
   Echology journal, 619, 621
   journals of, 619
   Polka Happiness, 619–620, 624–625, 627, 629
   "They Want the Music but They Don't Want
      the People," 633
   Tiv Song, 620–621, 629
   Urban Blues, 620, 621, 629
Kekuku, Joseph, 530
Kenya, adolescent music listening research, 36
Keynes, Milton, 177
Kingsbury, Henry, 380 n4
Kiralyfalvi, Bela, 414
Kirschner, Tony, 152, 163, 364
Kohn, Eduardo, 523
Kokotsaki, Dimitra, 269
Kolb, David A., 134. See also experiential
      learning framework (of Kolb)
Konewko, Mark, 483
Koskoff, Ellen, 621
Kraftwerk, 595
Krauss, Allison/Union Station, 9–10 n1
Krikun, Andrew, 257 n13
Kruger, Linda E., 391
Kumar, Krishan, 395, 396–397
kumu hula (hula masters), 529
Kuntz, Tammy, 275

Lacher, Kathleen T., 34
Laing, Ronald D., 153
Lai YouTube channel, 479–481
Lakota Indians, 523
Lamb, Roberta, 128
Lamont, Alexandra, 39, 379–380 n1
Lange, Patricia G., 473
lapsed musical participation, 171–182
   motivations to continue/cease in
      adulthood, 175–178
   music learning, formative experiences,
      173–175
   music learning, lasting effects of, 178–180

laptop musicians. *See* amateur laptop musicians
Lashua, Brett, 393
Lave, Jean, 24, 212
Layla and Other Assorted Love Songs (Derek and the Dominos), 112 n11
Leach, Bernard, 367
Leak, Graeme, 607
learning ensembles. *See also* community music; ensemble music making
  being moved by music in, 216–217
  creating, interpreting, responding to music in, 211–213
  description, 205, 211
  feeling musical in, 215–216
  fluid objectives, shifting identities in, 217–219
  key factor to learning, 212
  performing music in, 213–215
  study of, in England, 205–207, 211–213
learning music. *See* music learning
"Learning to Live with Recording" (Tomes), 85
Lebler, Don, 181
Led Zeppelin, 427
Leeds, England
  Acid House culture, 385–401
  Extreme Metal scene, 297–315
Left for Dead (L4D), game series, 551
legitimate peripheral participation (of Lave and Wenger), 212
leisure. *See also* casual leisure; leisure and sonic participatory cultures; leisure music production; leisure play; leisure research, music making as; leisure space; leisure time; serious leisure
  amorphous boundaries of, 3
  Aristotle on, 32, 581
  casual vs. serious, 32–33, 231
  defined/described, 32–34, 333
  at DISS, 363–380
  Elkington on, 210
  enchantment as, 108–110
  Frith on, 223–224
  general and core activities, 351–352
  during the Great Depression, 251–252
  Green on, 63

guitar as, 115–128
Hendry on, 4, 62, 66
Kaplan on, 13–27, 32
Kleiber on, 146
Mantie on, 61
in midlife, 132
music education and, 66–69, 115–128, 226
music learning and, 178–180
Pieper on, 100, 109–110
as play and mimesis, 374–378
popular music as, 225–226
professionalization of, 230–233
project-based, 210, 350, 541, 545, 552, 558, 576 f
Rojek's construction of, 449
Shaw on, 4
space and place for, 347–349
as surrogate/alternative identity, 371–374
as "symbol, play, and the other" (Borsay), 366
through the lifespan, 31–50
undesirable connotations of, 4
leisure and sonic participatory cultures
  around video games, 557–558
  overlaps and intersections, 558
  through video games, 553
  within video games, 548–549
leisure career framework, 165 n4
Leisure in America: A Social Inquiry (Kaplan), 16–17
leisure music production, 347–360
Leisure: Perspectives on Education and Policy (Kaplan), 17
leisure play, 132–133, 138, 141, 146, 155
leisure research, music making as, 425–443
leisure space, 283, 293, 315, 347–349. *See also* serious leisure, spaces for
leisure time
  Aristotle on noble uses of, 32
  IKEAization and Appleization of, 489, 510
  individualized approaches to, 363
  music activities during, 187–198
  musical agency perspective on music activities, 187–199
  music creation by Italian Millennials, 508
  Stong's warning on dangers of, 252

leisure time (*Cont.*)
  teenagers engagement with music
    during, 62
  work time vs., 223
Lennon, John, 267, 427
Leonard, Marion, 426
Levellers, 432
Levine, Lawrence, 621
Levitas, Ruth, 369, 395
lexical correspondence analysis (LCA), 500,
  512 nn21–22
Leyshon, Andrew, 437, 450–451
Lies, Eugene, 251
Lindenberg, Siegwart, 34
Lindström, Siv, 48–49
listening. *See also* music listening
  as an invocation, 522
  auditory system mechanics, 521
  maieutic listening, 522, 533, 535
  passive, by Native Americans, 522
listening to music. *See* music listening
Little Symphony Project, on YouTube, 477
Liverpool, England, 425–443
  Casablanca pub, 430–432, 431 f
  characterizations of, 426–427, 430–433
  drummer-researcher perspective, on music
    making, 425–443
  as European Capital of Culture, 430
  folk music/football in, 430–433
  HUB Festival, 426, 428 f, 434–436, 442
  leisure research, 442–443
  music making, 437–443
  participant observation study method,
    428–429
  rehearsal spaces, 437–442, 439 f, 440
    f, 443 n5
  rock scene, 301
  unique musical heritage of, 426–427
  youth, race, place in urban music, 434–436
Lomax, Alan, 569–570, 632
Long, Jonathan, 429
Longfellow, Henry Wadsworth, 275
Lonie, Douglas, 443 n5
Lord of the Rings Online, video game, 543, 547
Loss album, Wodensthrone, 289, 290
*Love Is a Mix Tape: Life and Loss One Song at a
  Time* (Sheffield), 102

Lucas, Caroline, 299
Lukács, György, 413–414
Lynd, Helen, 248, 254
Lynd, Robert, 248, 254

MacDonald, David, 262, 522–523
MacDonald, Raymond, 210
machinima, 549–550, 553, 555
Madchester music scene, 396
Madison Square Garden, 82
Mahone, Austin, 481
maieutic listening, 522, 533, 535
Making the Ultimate Demo (Robair), 93
M-A-M-A cycles (in identity literature), 145
"Mamma Mia" (ABBA), 194
Manning, Nikki, 523
Mantie, Roger, 61, 75–76, 225, 276, 374, 405
  open letter to Charles Keil, 619–634
"Maple Leaf Rag" (Joplin), 243
Marcia, James E., 135–136
Marcuse, Herbert, 623
Marin, Manuela M., 271
Mario Paint, 547
Markus, Hazel, 207
Marshall, Nigel A., 264
Marx, Karl, 265
mash-ups, 436, 475, 590–591, 598 n5
Maslow, Abraham H.
  hierarchy of needs concept, 35, 262, 263, 267,
    269, 272, 275
  self-actualization concept, 152, 262, 263,
    266, 268
  self-transcendence concept, 261, 262, 263,
    269–270
  theory of human motivation, 263, 265,
    267–270, 274
  Toward a Psychology of Being, 139
Mason, Lowell, 242, 256 n2
Massingham, Ursula, 73–74
master-apprentice teaching style, 126, 172
MayDay Group, 27 n1
McCartney, Paul, 267, 427
McGraw, Hugh, 580
McHorse, Christine, 528
McIan, Peter, 93
McKay, George, 607
McLaughlin, John, 142

McNeill, David, 320
McQueen, Hilary, 67, 68–69, 70, 72
meaning of music, 6
mediating artifacts, 206, 217, 218
melancholy, shades of, 142
"The Menace of Mechanical Music"
    (Sousa), 243
MENC. *See* Music Educators National
    Conference
mental health
    Music for Life Project findings, 44 b–45 b
    music's benefits for, 43
Merriam, Alan, 621, 627–628
Merseybeat, 426
Mexico, adolescent music listening
    research, 36
Meyer, Leonard, 621, 628
MF. *See* Musical Futures
Middletown study (Lynd and Lynd), 248, 254
Midgley, Mary, 395
MIDI (Musical Instrument Digital Interface),
    86, 93, 140, 547, 592
Miell, Dorothy, 210, 262
Mikserii, Finnish music site, 557
Millard, André, 90
Millennials, 508
Miller, Kiri, 544
Miller, Paul D'Shonne (a.k.a. DJ Spooky, That
    Subliminal Kid), 107
Mills, Janet, 210
Minecraft, video game, 543, 548, 550, 551, 552, 557
Minichiello, Victor, 38, 272, 273
minor scales (Phrygian mode), 142
Mithen, Steven, 634
Mittelman, Karen, 380 n3
mixing console, 87
mix tapes, 6, 102
Mix trade magazine, 93
Mizerski, Richard, 34
modding, 551–553, 558, 559
Mohan, Krishna, 153, 272
moods, music's benefit for, 31–32, 36,
    37 b–38 b, 191
Moon, Keith, 427
Moran, Aldan, 271
Morris, Joe, 530
Morton, David L., 88, 409

Moser, Pete, 607
moshpit practices, 286, 299
Mosing, Miriam A., 271
motivation. *See also* collegiate marching band
    study, of motivational profiles regarding
    music making; participatory motivation;
    Transcendent Model of Motivation for
    Music Making
    to continue/cease music participation in
        adulthood, 175–178
    digital technologies' impact on, 585
    in ensemble music making, 319–338
    Hallam/Creech/Varvarigou's research, 268
    in identity tailoring process, 137, 138
    intrinsic, importance of, 141
    as long-term effect of music, 49
    Maslow's theory of, 263, 265, 267–270, 274
    in Musical Futures schools, 67, 71, 73
    Music for Life Project and, 45
    personal/musical, 268–269
    predictors, in purchasing particular
        recordings, 34
    for singing, 42
    social, 267–268
    social contagion model, 335
Motives for Physical Activities Measure-
    Revised (MPAM-R), 328, 329 t
MP3 players, 100, 108, 111 n3, 195, 468
MTV, 405, 412
Mullen, Phil, 614
multitrack audio recorder, 86
Multi-Track Recording for Musicians
    (Hurtig), 93
MUSE (Musicians United for Superior
    Education), 627
M.U.S.E. Letter (Keil), 619
musical agency, 7, 187–199. *See also*
    communicative agency; human agency
    bodily action coordination and, 191,
        193–194, 196–197
    collective dimension, 190
    collective identity and, 191, 195–196
    individual dimension, 190
    production, consumption, and, 188, 197–198
    self-identity and, 62, 192–193
    self-protection and, 190, 191, 194–195
    self-regulation and, 190–191, 193–194

Musical Futures (MF), 61–76
    classroom voice, choice, collaboration,
        66–67, 71
    Classroom Workshopping strand, 67
    community of practice, 74–75
    enabling of teachers as musicians, 68–69
    global spread of, 69–70
    at Greenfield Community College, 73–74
    impact on staff-student relationships,
        67–68, 74
    informal learning model of, 66–69
    mission of, 61, 64
    pedagogical practices of, 65–66, 70–71
    perceived risks to teachers, 72
    space/time/resource challenges, 70–71
    staffing challenges, 71–72
    student's opinion of, 67
    teachers in MF schools, 61–62, 65–75
musical instruments. *See also* drummers/
        drumming; guitar
    benefits of playing, 45–46
    children's motivations for choice of, 173
    children's self-fulfilling expectations, 174
    intimacy/closeness of playing, 121
    progressive era manufacturing of, 244
    YouTube instructional videos, 66–67,
        73, 227
musicality
    of animals, 536 n4
    Blacking/Erickson on, 520
    in Liverpool, 426
    musical identity and, 74, 208
    Roberts on, 427
musical life history study (Pitts), 174
musical participation, lapsed, 171–182
musical performances, live, benefits of
        attending, 40–41
music-dance making. *See* indigenous
        music-dance making
Music Division, National Federation of
        Settlements, 245
music education. *See also* Musical Futures;
        music learning; music teachers
    associated organizations, 5, 16, 21
    continuing education programs, 204, 238 n1
    dropout rate from teacher-directed
        American wind band system, 175

    Foucault and, 122–124
    gender and, 122
    guitar's place in, 116–117
    impact of politics of learning on, 124–126
    impact of teachers on, 172
    Kaplan's role in, 6, 14, 16, 18, 21–23, 24
    Keil's comment on, 626–627
    leisure/recreation and, 4
    limitations in the U.S., 64
    Mantie's opinion of, 628
    master-apprentice teaching style, 126, 172
    Music Foundation on, 64
    music learning's relation to, 121, 125, 126–127
    online communities, 25
    questioning of large ensemble
        participation, 321
    relation of the body to, 121–122, 127–128
    role of popular musicians in, 237
    role of teachers in, 126–127
    school-based, U.K. dissatisfaction with, 228
    sociological turn in, 24
    sociology of, 188
    as statutory in England, 63
    strategy for securing long-term positive
        impact for, 180–181
    Suzuki method, 206
Music Educators Journal, 21
Music Educators National Conference
        (MENC), 16, 21
Music for Life Project, 44 b–45 b, 609
"The Musician in America: A Study of His
        Social Roles. Introduction to a Sociology
        of Music" (Kaplan), 14
musicians. *See also* amateur laptop musicians;
        amateur musicians; nonmusicians;
        popular musicians; professional
        musicians; semiprofessional musicians;
        (un)popular musicians
    amateur vs. professional, 19–20, 25, 41
    Aristotle's opinion of, 574
    challenges of defining, 209–210
    developing self-identity as, 192–193
    experimentalists, 589
    helping space for, 357
    learning to play, playing to learn by,
        229–230
    motivations of, 33, 41

musical identity and, 208–210
music teachers' exemplification of being, 211
resource space for, 355–356
sales space for, 356–357
self-taught, 174, 175, 588
showcase spaces for, 353–354
TMMMM's applicability to, 262
tourism space for, 358
virtual spaces for, 357–358
work-life balance, 156
musician through activity, 210
musician through profession, 210
Music in American Life (Zanzig), 250–251
Music Industries Chamber of Commerce, 244
music industry, 234–236
    amateur musicians and, 234
    engagement with via social media, 233
    eudaimonism's shared ideology with, 163
    mentors working with young
        musicians, 224
    professional musicians and, 231
    young musicians and, 234–235
music in identities (MI) concept (Hargreaves
    and Marshall), 264
Music in Institutions (van de Wall), 253
musicking vs. music making, 458, 588
music learning. *See also* learning ensembles;
    Musical Futures; music education
    Biesta on, 126
    children's self-fulfilling expectations, 174
    classroom experiences in, 63
    communities, among Italian amateur rock
        musicians, 8
    curation of, in the classroom, 63
    ethnomusicology's interests in, 620
    formative experiences of, 173–175
    Foucault on, 123, 124
    history of, as a discipline, 614
    informal, 227
    lasting effects of, 178–180
    life history approach to, 172
    long-term effects of, 172–173, 175–176,
        178–180
    motivations to continue or cease in
        adulthood, 175–178
    Musical Futures program and, 64–66, 69,
        71–72, 75

music education's relation to, 121, 125,
    126–127
music making's connections with, 6–7
NHIMA programs, 203–204
in online communities, 25
politics of learning's impact on, 124, 126
technological disruptions in, 589
music listening. *See also* playing by ear
    to absent one's self from surroundings,
        194–195
    benefits of, 35, 36, 38–40
    online, 34
    self-regulation of, 193–194
    seven components of, 48
    "squirrel" listeners, 39
    by teenagers, 63
music making, 233, 467–484. *See also*
    ensemble music making; musicians;
    playing by ear; popular music;
    Transcendent Model of Motivation for
    Music Making
    advancing technology's impact on, 489
    aging adults and, 204
    Aristotle on the value of, 574
    benefits of, 41–49
    Bennett on, 586
    collegiate marching band study, 326–336
    communal, 321
    at Dartington International Summer
        School, 7, 363–380
    dependence on institutional structures,
        resources, 175
    differing reasons for, 6
    drummer-researcher perspective on,
        425–443
    in ensembles, 319–338
    extended self theory and, 262, 264–266,
        274, 275
    by extreme metal bands, 299–301
    flow theory and, 265, 269–271
    gender differences in, 492–493
    guitars and, 121
    happiness and, 272–273
    identity development and, 138–139
    increasing opportunities for, 31–32
    individual/collective manners of, 7–8
    in intergenerational community, 42 b

music making (*Cont.*)
  intrinsic rewards of, 272–274
  lapsed learners and, 171–182
  by laptop musicians, 585–598
  as leisure research, 425–443
  making time for, 4
  Mason's insight on, 242
  musicking vs., 458, 588
  neurobiological effects of, 204
  by Northern English extreme "metallers,"
    285–292
  plunderphonic approach to, 550
  and pursuit of the daimon, 155–156
  quality of life and, 272–273
  rehabilitative potential of, 204, 216–217
  self-completion theory and, 262, 264,
    265–266, 271
  as social experience, 320–321
  social motivations for, 267–268
  spirituality and, 31–32, 39, 270–272, 274
  sponsorship of, in the Jazz Age, 249
  study of (un)popular musicians, 156–162
  technology and, 31
  transcendence and, 270–271
  transcendent, 270–271
  well-being and, 35, 38, 40–47, 272–273
  by young people, 223–238
  on YouTube, 233, 467–484
music making practices, 8
The Music Man (Wilson, 1950), 241
Music Matters (Elliott), 579
music memory contests, 256 n4
Music of the People (van de Wall), 253
music participation
  benefits of, 172–173
  effects on self-growth, self-knowledge, 579
  interviews with "lapsed" musicians, 175
  lapsed, potential long-term value of, 171–182
  lifelong, laying foundations for, 180–181
  motivations for ceasing, continuing in
    adulthood, 175–178
  as potential source of confirmation,
    confidence, 41
  social aspects of, 176–177
  withdrawing from, as coping strategy, 176
Music Performance Trust Fund, 357

music production, 450–452. *See also* recording
    studios
  budget crisis in, 450–451
  changing employment relationships,
    451–452
  DIY recreational recording, 81–95
  leisure music production, 347–360
  Leyshon on decline of studio sector,
    450–451
  Théberge on growth of commercial
    studios, 451
Music Supervisors Journal, 246
Music Supervisors National Conference
    (MSNC), 245, 246–247
music teachers
  in El Sistema programs, 47 b
  exemplification of being a musician by, 211
  impact on students, 172, 174
  Jorgensen on, 64
  Kaplan's vision for, 22–23, 26, 27
  learning music without, 174
  master-apprentice teaching style, 126, 172
  in MF schools, 61–62, 65–75
  relation to public recreation agencies, 21
  Seeger's encouragement of, 27 n1
  Smith/Durrant on obligations of, 65
Music Teachers National Association, 245
music therapy, 253
musique concrète (of Schaeffer and Henry), 589
MySpace, 238 n7, 286

Namakelua, Alice, 530
NAMM. *See* National Association of Music
    Merchants
Nardi, Bonnie A., 218
narrative inquiry, 406, 408–409
National Association of Music Merchants
    (NAMM), 26, 245, 275
National Association of Piano Dealers of
    America, 245
National Bureau for the Advancement of
    Music, 244, 245, 247
National Education Association, Department
    of Music, 245
National Federation of Music Clubs (NFMC),
    245–246

National Institute for Music Education in
    Wartime, 27 n1
National Music Week (U.S.), 247–248
National Phonography Company, 88
National Piano Manufacturers Association,
    244, 256 n9
National Recreation and Park Association, 15
National Recreation Association, 15, 245, 251
National Socialist Black Metal (NSBM),
    287–288, 291
Native hip-hop cypher, 519–520
Native Instruments, virtual instruments, 594
Naughton, Chris, 285, 286, 287
Neel, Julien, 478–479
Nemser, Ari, 380 n3
Neogi, Rajarshi, 386–387
neo-Nazis, 286, 287, 289–291, 293
Nettl, Bruno, 380 n4
Neuman TLM103 microphones, 83
neurobiological effects, of music making, 204
neuroscientific research, 521
New Horizons International Musical
    Association (NHIMA, U.S.), 203–204
New Zealand, adolescent music listening
    research, 36
Nielsen, 475
Nietzche, Friedrich, 589–590
nineteenth century, music and leisure in the
    U.S., 242–243
NodeXL software, 498
nonmusicians. *See also* learning ensembles
    musical identities of, 208–210
    possible selves of, 7, 207–208
    self-confessed, musical lives of, 203–220
    stereotyping drummers as, 427
nonrepresentational theory, 298–299
Norman, Don, 133, 162
Northern English extreme "metallers."
    See White Medal; Winterfylleth;
    Wodensthrone
Norton, David, 152, 153, 154
Norwegian folk music, 195
notation program, 86–87
note blocks, 548
Noudelmann, François, 589–590
Nunes, Julia, 472

Nu Pogodi!, 309–310, 313–314, 315 n5
Nurius, Paula, 207

occasional downloaders, 34
Oceania, 525
O'Connell, Michael, 271
Olssen, Mark, 127
One Life: The Free Academic (Kaplan), 14
online communities, 25
online listeners, 34
ontological security (of Laing and
    Giddens), 153
"optimal" states/experiences, 138, 139
Orwell, George, 163
Ostertag, Bob, 596
otherness of Dartington International
    Summer School, 366–371
Outpia ("nowhere"), 395
Overell, Rosemary, 298

Packer, Jan, 40–41
Page, Kate, 609
paideia, defined, 629, 630
Palmer, Anthony J., 271
Pandora, self-expression on, 102
Papageorgi, Ioulia, 156
Papua New Guinea, shark-calling
    practices, 524
Park, Nansook, 35, 48
Parkinson, Tom, 70, 165
Parry, Diana C., 102
participant observation, 428–429
participatory motivation
    advice/friendship networks and, 326
    advice network and, 335–336
    friendship network and, 334–335
    measurement scales, 328, 329 t
    SDT approach to, 322–325, 334
Partti, Heidi, 156
Pasdzierny, Matthias, 550
Passeron, Jean-Claude, 69
passive identity realization, 153
Paul, Les, 90–91, 92, 95. *See also* Ford, Mary
Paul, Timothy, 380 n3
Peace and Harmony, 397
pedagogic authority, 69

Peggie, Andrew, 379 n1
Penna, Joe (a.k.a. Mystery Guitar Man), 473–474, 475
Pensado, Dave, 94
People's Choral Union, 246
People's Singing Classes (New York), 246
performance ethnography, 300
performative writing, 300–301, 315
performing places, defined, 410
Perkins, Rosie, 203, 204
persona creation, on YouTube, 473–474
Peters, Michael, 124
Peterson, Christopher, 35, 48
Pet Shop Boys, 595
Philippines, adolescent music listening research, 36
phonograph systems, 87–89
Phuture, Acid House DJ team, 591
physical disabilities, music's benefits for, 43
physical well-being. See health/physical well-being
Piekut, Benjamin, 482
Pieper, Josef, 100, 109
Pilcher, Tim, 399
Pink Floyd, 120
Pitts, Stephanie, 41, 209, 365, 373, 379–380 n1, 492
Plains Indians. See Great Plains Indians
Plato, 32, 261
play element of culture, theory (Huizinga), 19
Playground and Recreation Association of America, 15, 250
Playground Association of America, 15
"playing along" in video gaming, 544
playing by ear
    as challenge for teachers, 68
    in learning by beginners, 229
    musical curiosity cultivated by, 119–120
    by performing video game music, 555
    as tacit form of music making, 121
plunderphonic, approach to making music, 550
Poland, Sacred Harp Singing in, 573, 578, 582
Polka Happiness (Keil and Keil), 619–620, 624–625, 627, 629
polymodality, 521, 535
polyvocal phenomenology, 102–103

Poni Mōʻī (coronation ceremony), 529
popular music. See also (un)popular music
    Baker on, 64
    gender and, 122
    guitar-based groups, 115–116
    interrelated aspects of making, 231
    as leisure, 225–226
    Randles/Smith on, 65
    young people and, 233–238
"Popular Music, Cityscapes, and Characterization of the Urban Environment" project, 443 n1
popular musicians
    avoidance of motivation dependence by, 174
    copying/mimicking of, 234
    Green's research on, 62, 72, 227, 229
    Musical Futures and, 70, 72
    relation to audiences, 492
    role of, in formal education settings, 237
    work-life balance study on, 156
pop-up recording studio, 82
Portal, video game series, 558
possible self/selves
    description of, 207
    music as means of discovering, 45 b, 174
    performing music and, 213–215
    positive vs. feared, balancing, 207–208
    serious leisure and, 33
Powers, Nikki, 520
practicing music
    self-regulation of, 193–194
    solitary, 195
Pratt, Andy C., 156
Primordial, 288
Prior, Nick, 592
"productive consumption" notion (Barrett), 87
Professional-Amateur-Public (PAP), 33
professionalization of musical leisure activity, 230–233
professional musicians. See also amateur musicians; semiprofessional musicians
    amateur musicians comparison, 587
    cultural determinants of success, 364
    intertwinement with amateur musicians, 199 n7
    measures of status of, 364
    multifaceted identity of, 210

Music for Life Project and, 45
recreation programs networking with, 23
shared traits with amateur musicians, 41
Solmsen on, 32
work as leisure for, 33, 41, 230–233
young musicians' desire to become,
43–44, 193
Professional-Public (PAP) system (Stebbins),
587–588
Profound Lore (underground label), 285
Progressive Era, U.S. (1890–1920), music and
leisure during, 243–247
project-based leisure, 210, 350, 541, 545, 552,
558, 576 f
Proskynesis, 303–304, 308, 315 n2
Protestant work ethic, 4
Pro Tools, 87
Pruitt, Lesley, 611–612
psychological well-being, impact of
music on, 48
Pueblo Junior College, 254–255

quality of life, music making and, 272–273
Quapaw Indians, 530
Quintette du Hot Club de France, 9–10 n1

radio, availability of music on, 31
ragtime music, 243–244
The Ragtime Review (Christensen), 244
Ramones, 139
Randles, Clint, 65, 68
Rathunde, Kevin, 263–264
raves, 386–387, 389, 393–395, 398–399
Ravishing Grimness blog, 285, 286
Reagan, Ronald, 412
Recording Demo Tapes at Home (Bartlett), 93
recording music. See also DIY recreational
recording
bit-by-bit vs. perfect-take mentality, 84–85
historical background, 87–92
learning to live with vs. live to learn with, 85
Paul's "how to" guides, 90
software-enabled technology, 87
recording studios. See also DIY recreational
recording
conventional model, 84
drug use in, 457–459, 462
ecosystems of, 83
eliciting strong performances by
artists, 4459
emotional FX and, 454–457, 462
emotional labor in, 452–461
emotional space of, 449–462
home recording, 92–93
"live" ideal, 85
music performance's uniqueness in,
455–456
music production in, 450–452
Paul's "studio-as-instrument" approach, 91
pop-up, 82–83
power relations in, 461
rites of passage for young workers, 461
state-of-the-art, 139
unknown nature of the work in, 460–461
work content/work context in, 455
recreational music theory (Kaplan), 18–20
amateur vs. professional musicians,
19–20, 25
function of music, 18
implementation of programs, 20
leadership categories, 15
principles of, 19–20
recreationists, 33
recreation movement, development of, 15–16
Red Light Jams (of Fried and Pignato),
406–421
"acts of meaning" created in, 417
catharsis and, 413–415
connectedness created by, 406, 415–416
impact on musicianship, 406–407
musical currency created by, 418
"Prouder, Stronger, Better" narrative and,
410–413
role played in growing up, 417–420
space (location) of, 409
space transition to place, 410, 415–417
structured reminiscence about, 407–409,
411–415, 418–420
symbolic sense of liberation from, 416
Regelski, Thomas, 27 n1, 63, 74, 379 n1
rehabilitative potential, of music making, 204,
216–217
rehearsal spaces, in Liverpool, England,
437–442, 439 f, 440 f

Reinhardt, Django, 9–10 n1
"The Relation of Music as Taught in Junior
    College to Certain Leisure-Time
    Activities Students" (Strong), 252
religion. *See also* spirituality
    connections with music, 20, 39,
        271–272, 364
    leisure and, 146–147
    neo-Nazis and, 290
    transcendent music making and, 270–271
reminiscence (reminiscing), music and, 36
repercussion phase, of compilations, 100,
        104–107, 109, 110
residential homes, community music in, 609
resilience, music and, 39
resonation phase, of compilations, 100,
        104–108
resource spaces, 354, 355–356, 469
reverberations phase, of compilations, 100,
        104–107, 109–110
Revokation, 304
Reynolds, Simon, 385, 396
Rhythm for Life project (U.K.), 203,
        214–215, 219
rhythm games, 546–547
rhythmic entrainment, 48
Richter, Goetz, 574
Robair, Gino, 93
Roberts, Brian, 386
Roberts, Ken, 388
Roberts, Les, 427
Rochberg-Halton, Eugene, 265
rock guitar, 119
rock music (rock 'n' roll), 152, 450
rock musicians, 354–355
Rohwer, Debbie, 272, 273
Rojek, Chris, 449
Roland TB303 synthesizers, 591
Rolfing, R. C., 256 n9
Rolling Stones, 427
Rolnik, Suely, 522
Ronnie Scott's (London), 354
Ronson, Mark, 460
Roosevelt, Franklin D., 252–253
Ross, Andrew, 449–450
round dances, Cree Indians, 519
routinization, 189, 197

Royal College of Music, 368
Royal Concertgebouw Orchestra, 354
Royal Parks Cellars, 306–307
Rudd, Roswell, 621
Running with the Devil (Walser), 437
Russia, YouTube music making collaboration,
        478–479
Ryan, Richard M., 153, 162. *See also*
        self-determination theory
Ryff, Carol D., 272

Saarikallio, Suvi, 39
Sacred Harp (SH) Singing, 8, 565–582
    conventions, 580
    descriptions of, 566–570, 571
    eudaimonia of SH singers, 574–577, 580, 581
    "flow" state achieved during, 568
    global future of, 580–581
    hollow square seating in, 567, 569, 581
    Jackson's description of SH singers, 575
    leaders and lessons in, 569–570
    meaningful bonds of singers, 570
    musical mainstream and, 573–574
    New York Times article on, 566
    philosophical perspective on, 574–575
    San Francisco Public Radio on, 566
    as serious leisure, 574–581
    SH singers, pathways to becoming, 571–573
    singers' diverse backgrounds, 570–573
    as "singer's music," 568–569
    social aspect of, 567–568
    teaching camps, 581, 582
    uniqueness/self-sufficiency of, 566–567
The Sacred Harp tunebook (Billings), 566
sacred hoops, Plains Indians, 519
Sales, Amy L., 380 n3
sales space, 356–357, 359
Sanremo Festival (Italian song contest), 511 n1
Santa Clara Pueblo Indians, 523
Santana, Carlos, 142
Sartre, Jean-Paul, 265, 589–590
Satanic black metal, 288, 291. *See also*
        Wodensthrone
Saxe, Leonard, 380 n3
Say a Little Prayer, 397
Schaeffer, Pierre, 589
Schafer, R. Murray, 621

Schäfer, Thomas, 544–545, 560 n3

Schneider, David, 621

schole (leisure), 629

Schwartz, Seth J., 136

Scotland, Youth Music Initiative, 224, 238 n2

Scottish Opera, 42

SDT. *See* self-determination theory

Second Enclosure Movement, 510

Seeger, Charles, 27 n1, 380 n3

Seeger, Kate, 380 n3

self
    indigenous understanding of, 523
    Manning on, 523
    Western scholarship understanding of,
        522–523

self-actualization (Maslow), 152, 154, 262, 263,
    265, 266, 268

self-completion theory, 262, 264, 265–266, 271

self-concept
    differences in methods of acquiring, 175
    El Sistema programs and, 47 b
    identity tailoring and, 137
    as a motivation factor in learning an
        instrument, 207
    musical performance and, 45, 50

self-definition, 39, 225, 232, 266

self-determination theory (SDT)
    application in collegiate marching band
        study, 326, 328, 332, 334, 337
    as applied to participatory motivation,
        322–325
    described, 34, 319
    participatory motivation and, 322–325, 334

self-differentiation, in identity tailoring
    process, 136–137, 143, 146, 263–264

self-expression, in creating compilations, 101

self-identity
    leisure time, music, and, 62, 192–193
    as a musician, 174, 192–193
    using music for shaping, 190, 191

self-protection, use of music for, 190, 191,
    194–195

self-realization, 35

self-reflection, in listening to compilations, 101

self-regulation
    of practicing and listening, 193–194
    use of music for, 190–191

self-taught musicians, 174, 175, 588

self-transcendence concept (Maslow),
    261–263, 265, 269–270, 274, 276

self-worth, 43

Seligman, Martin, 35, 48, 270, 272, 273

semiprofessional musicians, 33, 157, 198,
    365, 490, 511 n2, 593. *See also* amateur
    musicians; professional musicians

Sennheiser 419 microphones, 83

serious leisure. *See also* casual leisure; devotee
    work; project-based leisure; serious
    leisure, spaces for; serious leisure
    hobbyists; serious leisure perspective
    (SLP), of Stebbins
    careers in, 351
    casual vs., 32–33, 210, 231
    collegiate marching band study, 326–336
    defined, 321, 350
    distinguishing qualities of, 32–33, 162,
        231, 351
    eudaimonism and, 161–162
    examples, 352
    in music making by amateur musicians, 41
    questioning of relevance of, 321
    Sacred Harp Singing as, 574–581
    semipro activities similarity to, 491
    types of participants in, 33, 321

serious leisure, spaces for
    conquered space, 353, 469
    helping space, 357, 359, 469
    resource space, 354, 355–356, 469
    sales space, 356–357, 359
    showcase space, 353–355, 356, 359
    tourist space, 358–359, 469
    virtual space, 348, 356, 357–358, 359, 414,
        469, 474, 483

serious leisure hobbyists, 350–351

serious leisure perspective (SLP), of Stebbins,
    7, 32–33, 157, 161, 210, 228, 234, 347,
    349–352, 357–358, 469, 575

serious leisure volunteers, 350–351

Sesquicentennial of Music in American
    Schools (1988), 23

Settlement Music School (Philadelphia), 246

sevdalinke, 196, 199 n3

Severed Heaven, 310–313, 315 n4

"sex, drugs, and rock' n' roll," 450

Sfard, Anna, 628
Shafighian, Atar, 68
The Shamen (UK electronica group), 592
Shankar, Ravi, 365
Shansky, Carol, 271–272
Share Project, 594
shark-calling practices, Papua New
    Guinea, 524
Shaw, George Bernard, 4
Shazzam, 102
Sheffield, Rob, 102
Shepherd, John, 621
Shimabukuro, Jake, 472
showcase spaces, 353–355, 356, 359
SH Singing. *See* Sacred Harp (SH) Singing
Shulgin, Alexander, 399
Shure SM57 microphones, 83
Silberman-Keller, Diana, 373
Silent Hill, video game, 543
Silveira, Jason, 380 n3
Simon, Paul, 105
The Sims, video games, 557
simulacra, 281, 283–285, 286, 288, 292–293
Simulacra and Simulation (Baudrillard),
    283–284
Singapore, Musical Futures program, 70
singing. *See also* Sacred Harp (SH) Singing
    benefits of, 41, 43
    Chipmunks novelty singing, 91
    choral singing, 181
    1890s societies, 248
    music-dance making and, 524–526, 530,
        532–533, 535
    People's Singing Classes (NY), 246
    virtual choirs, on YouTube, 475–476
    vocal ensembles, 250
Sinnamon, Sarah, 271
six degrees of separation, 496
Skånland, Marie S., 195
slack-key guitar, 530
Small, Christopher, 191, 364, 455, 588, 613,
    620–621. *See also* musical agency
Small Faces, 46–459
smart phones, 31, 194
Smilde, Rineke, 609
Smith, David, 204

Smith, Gareth Dylan, 164, 165, 227
    on authenticity in the music classroom, 70
    I Drum, Therefore I Am, 263
    on learners accepting instruction, 69
    on learning/identity in adolescent music
        making, 419
    on music teachers and producers, 68
    "snowball self" model of identity
        formation, 263
    study of drummers, 62–65
    study of work-life balance of
        musicians, 156
Smith, Marc A., 508
Smith, Sandra J., 410–411
Smith, Susan J., 456
SNA. *See* social network analysis
Snapchat, 238 n8
Snyder, Dean Atley, 251
social aspects of music making, 320–321
social contagion model of motivation, 335
social function of music, 18
social media
    band/musician identity development
        and, 233
    online music communities, 49, 74–75
    popular music, commerce, and, 237,
        238 n8, 450
social network analysis (SNA)
    in collegiate marching band study, 326, 334
    defined, 319–320
    integration of ideas with, 323
    resource for introduction to, 511 n5
    and social structures of musical
        ensembles, 325
Social Network Importer, Facebook
    plug-in, 495
social networks. *See also* ensemble music
        making; specific social networking sites
    benefits of, 50
    development of, 49, 50
    dynamics of, 319–338
    El Sistema programs and, 47 b
    in ensemble music making, 319–338
    in Leeds extreme metal scene, 302
    measures of network position, 325, 327–328
    music-related, 151

music-related well-being and, 42–43, 50
online musical engagement via, 233
participatory motivation and, 334–336
six degrees of separation and, 496
social motivation relationship to, 331
software
   Cubase, 504, 512 n24
   GarageBand, 594
   NodeXL, 498
   T-Lab, 499
   Vengeance, 594
Sokoloff, Nikolai, 252
sol-fa, cognitive tool, 206
Solmsen, Friedrich, 32
sonic culture, of Italy, 490
sonic now, defined, 151
sonic paratexts, 554–555
sonic participatory cultures
   and leisure, around video games, 557–558
   and leisure, overlaps and intersections, 558
   and leisure, through video games, 553
   and leisure, within video games, 546–549
sonic participatory cultures, around video
   games, 554–558
   affinity spaces and groups, 556–557
   film scoring, 554
   performing, 555–556
   sonic paratexts, 554–555
sonic participatory cultures, through video
   games, 549–553
   chiptunes, 552–553
   coding, 551–553
   machinima, 549–550, 553, 555
   modding, 551–553, 558, 559
   vidding, 549–550, 555, 558
sonic participatory cultures, within video
   games, 546–549
   ABC notation and freestyle, 547–548
   games supporting music creation, 547
   note blocks, 548
   rhythm games, 546–547
sound check, 151
SoundCloud, 233
Sound on Sound magazine, 93
source materials, 107
Sousa, John Philip, 243, 627

Sousa, John Sousa, 589
South Africa, YouTube music making
   collaboration, 478–479
spaces for serious leisure. *See* serious leisure,
   spaces for
Spector, Phil, 455
Spencer, Amy, 82
spirituality. *See also* religion
   Higgins on music and, 535
   music/music-making and, 31–32, 39,
     270–272, 274
Sports Motivation Scale (SMS), 328, 329 t
Spotify, 85, 102
Spracklen, Karl, 299, 433
Springsteen, Bruch, 412
Stahl, Geoff, 301
Stålhammar, Börje, 62, 74
Stanyek, Jason, 482
Starr, Ringo, 427
Stayed Up All Night website, 102, 111 n5
Stebbins, Robert A. *See also* casual leisure;
   devotee work; serious leisure
   amateurism concept of, 210, 364
   on amateurs gaining professional status,
     473, 588
   on amateur vs. hobbyist engagement, 587
   on financial benefits of serious leisure
     activities, 479
   leisure career framework of, 165 n4
   on musicians' motivation to improve, 273
   Professional-Public (PAP) system of,
     587–588
   on self-actualization, self-expression, 587
   serious leisure perspective of, 7, 32–33, 157,
     161, 210, 228, 234, 347, 349–352, 357–358,
     469, 575
Stedman, Richard C., 391
Steely Dan, 120
Sterne, Jonathan, 85, 470, 471, 483
Steverink, Nardi, 34
Stone, Oliver, 412
Stong, Audre, 251–252
Strachan, Rob, 426
Strangelove, Michael, 471
Stravinsky, Igor, 365
Strong, Jeff, 94

structured reminiscence, about Red Light
    Jams, 407–409, 411–415, 418–420
studio audio art, 544
subjectivity, in postmodern, poststructuralist
    scholarship, 522
Sun Dance, Grass Dance (war dances), 528,
    531, 534
Sunderman, Lloyd Frederick, 251, 256 n9
Super Mario Bros. series, 547, 550
Super Nintendo Entertainment System
    (SNES), 547
survivance, 527–528, 529, 531, 534
Survivor, 139
Suzuki method, 206
Sweden, YouTube music making
    collaboration, 478–479
symbolic interaction theory, 136
symbols of completeness, 266

tab (tablature), 238 n3
Taking Part survey (Arts Council
    England), 178
Tanglewood Music Center, 355
Tanglewood Music Festival, 365
Tanglewood Symposium (1967), 16
Tapahonso, Luci, 524
Tape Op magazine, 93
tape recorders
    Paul's recording innovations, 90–91, 92
    use in DIY recording, 89–90
Tape Recording for Hobbyists
    (Zuckerman), 89–90
Tape Recording (1953–1969) magazine, 89
TASCAM Portastudio, 93
Taupin, Bernie, 275
Tawa, Nicholas, 242–243, 253
Taylor, Angela, 41, 379–380 n1
teachers. *See* music teachers
Teague, Adele, 156, 164
Team Fortress 2, video game, 543
Teatro alla Scala (Milan), 354
Technics SL-1200 turntable, 591
technology. *See also* computers; digital
    technologies; Internet; software
    consumers and users of, 34
    digital audio workstation, 86–87, 93, 471,
        547, 552, 591

disc-based gramophone, 88
disruptive technology, 586
    impact of advances on amateur music
        making, 489
    Paul's sound-on-sound innovation, 91
    Pro Tools, 87
    recordings collectors and, 34
    shift to software-enabled, 87
    source materials and, 107
    synthesizers, 591
    TASCAM Portastudio, 93
    turntables, 591
    uploading set lists, photos, 40
teenagers. *See also* adolescence/adolescents;
    children
    Gaines's study of, 405, 411–412
    importance of music for, 62, 64
    intuitive musical knowing, 62–63
    listening to music by, 63, 179
    music-related identity of, 62, 63–64
    peer-pressure among, 174
    YouTube amateur musicians, 472
Teenage Wasteland: Suburbia's Dead End Kids
    (Gaines), 411–412
Tepper, Stephen, 634
Théberge, Paul, 451, 585, 590
Thematic Analysis of Elementary
    Contexts, 499
"They Want the Music but They Don't Want
    the People" (Keil), 633
Thibeault, Matthew D., 470
Thomas, Rose Fay, 245–246
Three Mile Island nuclear disaster, 413
The Threnody of Triumph album
    (Winterfylleth), 287
Tichenor, Trebor Jay, 244
Tight crowd, 508
Timbaland, 460
Tin Pan Alley, 243
Tiv Song (C. Keil), 620–621, 629
T-Lab software, 499
TMMMM. *See* Transcendent Model of
    Motivation for Music Making
toasting, 595, 598 n8
Tolfree, Elinor, 37 b–38 b
Tompkins, Joanne, 443 n5
tonic *sol-fa*, cognitive tool, 206

Tony Pastor's Café (New York), 243–244
Touching Eternity (Barone), 171. *See also* Forrister, Donald
Toward a Psychology of Being (Maslow), 139
Townshend, Peter, 264
transcendent function (in individuation theory), 261–262
Transcendent Model of Motivation for Music Making (TMMMM), 261–276
    applicability to all musicians, 262
    extended self theory and, 262, 264–266, 274, 275
    limitations/future research directions, 274–275
    music in identities (MI) concept and, 264
    roots of, 262–263
    self-completion theory and, 262, 264, 265–266, 271
    societal/industry implications, 275–276
transcendent music making, 270–271
Tremaine, Charles Milton, 244–245, 247
Tremaine Piano Co., 244
Trevarthen, Colwyn, 520
Troutman, John W., 527
Tuan, Yi-Fu, 413, 415, 417, 474
Turino, Thomas, 544, 604, 614
Turkey, adolescent music listening research, 36
Turkle, Sherry, 483
turntable technology, 591
Twitter
    impact on Musical Futures programs, 74
    music industry and, 233
    role in identity formation, 493

Ullén, Fredrik, 271
United Kingdom (U.K.). *See also* England; Ireland; Scotland
    ABRSM research on teaching, learning, playing musical instruments, 226
    adult learning opportunities in, 203–204
    amateur choir survey, 181
    community music in, 9, 203–205, 283–284, 303, 603, 609
    Dartington International Summer School, 7, 363–380
    developments in participatory arts in, 181
    dissatisfaction with school-based music education, 228
    extreme music festivals in, 310
    further education (FE) in, 238 n1
    graded examination system in, 204, 207, 220 n2
    higher education (HE) in, 238 n1
    IMAGO community opera, 42 b
    increased music-making participation, 31
    interventionist approach to community music, 603
    interview with "lapsed" musician, 175
    Musical Futures program, 61–76
    musical influences in adults' childhood lives, 204
    Music for Life Project, 44 b–45 b
    music summer schools in, 380 n2
    Rhythm for Life project, 203, 214–215, 219
    youth music project, 224, 227–228, 238 n6
    YouTube music making collaboration, 478–479
United Sacred Harp Convention (Alabama), 569
United States (U.S.)
    adult learning opportunities in, 203–204
    continuing education programs, 238 n1
    Diné people, creation stories, 524
    limited school music education in, 64
    mid-1960s folk music revival, 490
    Music Performance Trust Fund partnership, 357
    pop-rock music, 490
    Reagan's 1984 reelection campaign, 412
    Sacred Harp Singing tradition, 566
    state of music education in, 627
    summer music camps, 380 n3
    YouTube music making collaboration, 478–479
United States (U.S.), history of music and leisure, 241–257
    Great Depression (1930–1940), 251–253
    Jazz Age (1920–1929), 247–251
    nineteenth century, 242–243
    Progressive Era (1890–1920), 243–247
    World War II (1941–1945), 253–255

University College London Institute of
Education, 65
University of Liverpool School of
Music, 443 n1
unpopular musicians. *See* (un)popular
musicians
Unruh, David R., 351
(un)popular music, 151–165
(un)popular musicians, empirical study,
findings, 159–160
making time for music, 159–160
motivation for making music, 158
thoughts on making music, 159–162
(un)popular musicians, empirical study,
method, 156–157
findings, 158–162
method, 156–157
self-thoughts on music making, 159
Urban Blues (C. Keil), 620, 621, 629
Using Your Portable Studio (McIan), 93
U.S. Marine Band, 243
U.S. National Association for Music
Education, 5
utopia
characterizations, dual suggested
meanings, 395
DISS and, 366–371, 378–379
Leeds's Acid House ideal, 385–401
vision of education, leisure education
in, 634
Utopia (More), 395

Vaccaro, Valerie L., 275
van de Wall, William, 253, 254
Varvarigou, Maria, 268, 272, 379–380 n1
Veal, Anthony James, 429
Veblen, Karl K., 257 n13, 623
Vengeance, audio effect software, 594
vestibular system, 521
vidding, 549–550, 555, 558
video compilations, 481
video content, user-generated, on the Internet,
468–469
video games. *See also* sonic participatory
cultures; specific video games
explicit/implicit participation with, 544–545

leisure and sonic participatory cultures
around, 557–558
leisure and sonic participatory cultures
within, 553
ludomusicology's study, 542–543
music of, 543
participatory cultures, 543–545
rewards of, 542
sonic participatory cultures around,
554–557
sonic participatory cultures through,
549–553
sonic participatory cultures within, 546–549
2015 date on usage, 542
Village Vanguard (New York), 354
Virtual Choir, on YouTube, 475–476, 477, 482
virtual spaces, 348, 356, 357–358, 359, 414, 469,
474, 483
virtual studio technology (VST), 504, 512 n24,
557, 591
visual imagery, 48
Vizenor, Gerald, 527
Voegelin, Salomé, 151
volunteers, at leisure (Stebbins), 33
von Stade, Frederica, 193

Wailey, Tony, 426
Waldron, Janice, 475
Wallas, Graham, 134
Wall Street film, 412
Walser, Robert, 437
Walsh, Chris, 288
War Camp Community Service, 15
War Games film, 413
Warner, R. Stephen, 570, 571, 578–581
Waterman, Alan, 138, 141, 153, 154
Waterman, Chris, 621
Watkins, Huw, 368
Watson, Allan, 451, 457
Watts, Charlie, 427
Webb, Rebecca, 39
Weber, Max, 4
well-being, 31–50. *See also* emotions/
emotional well-being
community music and, 608–609
defined, 272

from ensemble membership, 173, 179
happiness and, 35
health/physical, 35, 41–43, 44 b–45 b
hedonic, 153
Indigenous music-dance making and,
    532–534
listening to music and, 36, 38–40
live music events and, 40–41
measuring, 35
music's promotion of, 35–49, 63,
    272–273
singing and, 41
subjective, 34–35
through the lifespan, 31–50
Wenger, Étienne, 24, 74–75, 212
Weren, Serena, 269
Wescott, Charles G., 90–91
West, Richard (a.k.a. Mr. C), 592
Western Art Music
    characterization of, 364
    concertizing tradition of, 566
    at DISS, 365
    relevance of, 379
"While My Guitar Gently Weeps"
    (Harrison), 115
Whitacre, Eric, 475–477, 482. See also
    Virtual Choir, on YouTube
White Album (Beatles), 115
White Medal, 281, 291–292
The Who, 427
Wicklund, Robert A., 266
Widdowfield, Rebekah, 300
Williamon, Aaron, 203, 204
Williams, Bronwyn T., 543
Williams, Mentor, 480
Williams, Pharell, 460
Wilson, Meredith, 241
Winterfylleth, 281–282, 285–288, 289
Wissler, Clark, 248
Wittgenstein, Ludwig, 292
Wizard's Beard, 303
Wodensthrone, 281, 288–291
women's club movement (Progressive Era,
    U.S.), 245
Wonder, Stevie, 272
Wood, Nichola, 410–411, 456

Works Project Administration (WPA), 252
Works Projects Administration (WPA), 15
World Leisure and Recreation
    Association, 14
World's Fair Congress of Musicians (Chicago
    World's Fair), 245
World War II, U.S. (1945–1941), music and
    leisure during, 253–255
WPA Music Program, 15
Wright, Ruth, 64
Wrigley, William Joseph, 271

The X Factor, TV show, 25

Yes, 410
You Love and Feel so Real, 397
Young Bear, Severt, 523
Youth Music Initiative (Scotland), 224, 238 n2
youth music making, 7
Youttitham, Lai, 479–481
YouTube
    being discovered on, 233
    birth of the pro-am on, 471–475
    "Canon Rock" video, 467–468
    collective ensembles, 477–478
    DIY-er recording instruction on, 94
    downsides of creating music videos for,
        482–483
    feedback/comments for musicians, 474
    framework for, 469–471
    "funtwo-Canon Rock 2012" video, 468
    guitar 90 pages, 467
    implicit participation, in watching
        videos, 545
    instrument instruction on, 66–67, 73, 227
    musical collaborations, 478–481
    music making on, 233, 467–484
    online performances, types of, 471–472
    performance space availability on,
        474–475
    performing with your hero on, 481
    persona creation, 473–474
    reaching across international borders,
        478–479
    resource sharing, 479–481
    role in identity formation, 493

YouTube (*Cont.*)
    ukulele performances, 472–473
    user-generated videos on, 468–469
    Virtual Choir, 475–476, 477, 482
    virtual collective musical
        groups, 476–477
YouTube Live! 2008 Ukulele Orchestra, 472
YouTube Symphony Orchestra, 476–477

Zanzig, Augustus Delafield, 250–251
Zappa, Frank, 99, 110
Zelensky, Nathalie K., 380 n3
Zenger, Amy A., 543
Zimmerman, Joel T. (a.k.a. Deadmau 5),
    197, 592
Zuckerman, Art, 89–90
Zukin, Sharon, 435